Chicago Mob Ultimatum

Pay, Quit, or Die

Chicago Mob Ultimatum

Pay, Quit, or Die

by Don Herion

Copyright © 2008 by Don Herion.

Library of Congress Control Number: 2008901423
ISBN: Hardcover   978-1-4257-7853-8
              Softcover   978-1-4257-7849-1

All rights reserved. No part of this book may be reproduced or transmitted in any form or by any means, electronic or mechanical, including photocopying, recording, or by any information storage and retrieval system, without permission in writing from the copyright owner.

This book was printed in the United States of America.

To order additional copies of this book, contact:
Xlibris Corporation
1-888-795-4274
www.Xlibris.com
Orders@Xlibris.com

40674

Contents

1. Touhy Mob vs. Capone Mob 13
2. Don Herion's Forty-five Years of Vaudeville 23
3. You Mean I'm Really a Cop Now? 28
4. First Assignment, Twenty-eighth District 34
5. My First Detail 38
6. The Full Moon and the Four Amigos 42
7. Squad Car: Working the Street 49
8. Dog Bites and Me 53
9. The Mob, the Captain, and Me 55
10. Hit and Run 62
11. The Flying Squad: Ryan's Raiders 65
12. The Puerto Rican Connection 71
13. Teens, Guns, and Murder 75
14. Willie Simpson and the Pink Ribbon 78
15. Midnights Are the Best 83
16. Hey, Guys, I'm One of You'se 86
17. Vice: How It All Began 92
18. You Are Now a Vice Detective 95
19. The Mob and the Numbers Racket 101
20. The Right Place at the Right Time 108
21. This Eldorado Was Not a Cadillac 113
22. The Blue Dahlia: Where Men Were Women 118
23. Car Chases 125
24. Bookmakers – The Mob – Who Cares? 130
25. Zagorski's Rathskeller: Was It Lottie or Louie? 134
26. 1968 Democratic Convention 139

27.	This Keg Is Not a Barrel	162
28.	What Are Friends For?	169
29.	The Best of the Best	175
30.	Armored Wire Room – Chicago Style	182
31.	Bears-BettorS-Bookies	189
32.	Racetrack Messenger Service Nightmare	204
33.	Harry "Hit Man" Aleman	211
34.	Hookers, Craps, and Augie	227
35.	Al Capone – Joe "Fifke" Corngold – Cicero, Illinois	233
36.	The Gold "N" Greek	241
37.	Nick, Sal, and Red	247
38.	Calvin Sirkin: Bookie with a Heart	254
39.	The Day We Busted Mob Boss, Joey "the Clown" Lombardo	258
40.	Butch, Harry, and Mama Sue's	267
41.	Felix "Milwaukee Phil" Alderisio – Mob Hit Man	272
42.	Life and Death of a Bookmaker – Hal C. Smith	282
43.	Dissolvo – Spies – The Mob – Bikinis	296
44.	Chicago's 42 Gang "A Farm Team for the Mafia"	302
45.	Manny and Zeke vs. the Mob	309
46.	Mob's Floating Crap Game	325
47.	President's Commission on Organized Crime	357
48.	Offshore Bookmaking Is Like Another Wall Street	376
49.	Organized Crime, Gambling, and the Movies	384
50.	Lenny Patrick: Jewish Hit Man	402
51.	The Fall of Mob Boss, Gus "Slim" Alex	416
52.	The Dinty Moore Episode	422
53.	Mob Boss Rocky Infelise Gets Wired	425
54.	James LaValley – Mob Enforcer	434
55.	James "the Schemer" Nicholas	446
56.	Bobby Johnson – Bookmaker – Suicide or Homicide	456
57.	John "Schavoni" Santucci – Burglar	460
58.	Cook County Sheriff – Vice Detection	464

59. Audie Murphy: War Hero vs the Chicago Mob 493
60. Chicago Streets and Two Cops 497
61. Just Another Gangland Hit "Las Vegas Style" 504
62. Gambling: The Great American Sport "Just Ask the Mob"......516
63. Lenny "I'm a Mob Guy" Palumbo 545

Dedication

To my wife Gen, our children, Patrick, Nancy, Don, Tom, Jayne, and Mary Ann, for I deputized them all on occasion. The girls made phone calls to suspect wire rooms, kept track of whoever answered the phone on how many rings. Gen accompanied me on numerous surveillances when I couldn't be seen. She had a bag of groceries in her arms and she could follow a suspect on an elevator or wherever he was going in a building. She should have been the cop. The boys also were great on surveillances. I just put them in the back of my station wagon where they would soon be fooling around. I had my walkie-talkie in the front seat and notified other crew members as to what was happening on our targets. I was not more that 100 feet away from the lookouts, but they never caught on. We nailed 10 vehicles and two hundred thousand football cards. Whenever I would attach a tracking device to a vehicle, I needed a lookout to warn me of impending danger, so they drew straws to see who won. The problem was that this had to be done after 3:00 AM. We never got caught, so they did a good job. Now all that's left is this book of memories of the good old days.

#1 Review:

Having been at Don Herion's side during much of his hot pursuit of the "Chicago Mob's Floating crap game and their other illegal activities, I stand in awe of his investigative talents. In short he was Chicago's top detective and deadly foe of mob gambling operations while on duty and sometimes as a vigilante, whatever it took to get the job done, he did it.

Bob Wiedrich
Reporter, Chicago Tribune "Retired"

#2 Review:

Don Herion's book is filled with true grit and vigilante wit like his mob busting style. They don't make cop's like him anymore, and now we all get to read his untold stories for the first time in their most intimate form. He's the real deal and leaves you hoping for more stories from the tough Chicago streets, alleys and bookie joints he once scoured.

Dave Savini,
National Edward R. Murrow Award winning investigative reporter,
CBS Chicago.

#3 Review:

There is one word for Herion, "relentless," being a bookmaker I must remain anonymous but this guy not only busted me four times but convinced me to move my operation to Australia and utilize toll free 800 numbers. I became an informant for him and pleaded that he wouldn't put me in his book. He didn't, but it turned out really good anyway.

Mr. X
The guy from down under.

Chapter 1

Touhy Mob vs. Capone Mob

When my partner Bob Peters and I reported to work on December 16, 1959, on the four-to-twelve watch, we had no idea that this would be a night that would remain in our memory for a long time. As usual the weather was miserable; it was about eight degrees, damp, and the wind was blowing, which made it seem a lot colder. It was a real nasty Chicago night.

We both were pretty good smokers; it seemed that whenever I would light up, Bob would light up and vice versa. That way, the interior of our squad car was always full of smoke. The windshield always had smoke scum on it, which made it hard to see at night; but that was all right, we would just wipe it off and keep lighting up.

We did have to crack our windows open slightly to keep from getting asphyxiated. At night, sounds would travel more clearly because of less traffic and because the windows were open; that's when we heard what sounded like a truck backfiring. We were traveling west on Washington Blvd. near Pine Avenue at the west end of our district, which usually was very quiet. I asked Bob if he thought what I thought those were not backfires; they were gunshots, and the hunting season was over. We decided to check out the area where the shots had come from and headed toward Pine Avenue. Just then, the squad operator gave out a message of shots fired at 125 North Pine Avenue and to check out two men running from the scene with what appeared to be rifles in their hands.

When we arrived at 125 North Pine Avenue, which was a two story brick building, we saw two white men lying on the front porch; there was blood everywhere. Both men had been shot in their lower extremities and were obviously in great pain. The front glass-door window had been blown out, and the bricks around the door showed signs of a lot of damage, probably from a shotgun. I asked both men, who were still conscious, what had happened and if they knew who had shot them. The older man just kept saying, "Those fucking dagos, they never forget."

We informed the squad operator that it was a bona fide shooting and requested a wagon or ambulance to transport the victims to the nearest hospital. Other squads on the scene were searching the neighborhood for the shooters and for any clues that they may have left behind. There was a bullet hole in the windshield of a car that was parked in front of the victims home. Apparently, that hole was made by one of the victims who had returned fire at the hit men. One of the officers that examined the hole said that there was blood on the hole so maybe one of the hit men had been wounded. A flash message was sent out to all the hospitals to be on the lookout for anyone who needed medical attention for a gunshot wound.

I asked the older man what had happened; he said that when he and his bodyguard walked up the front stairs and were about to enter his sister's apartment, they were both shot with shotguns by two guys who came out of nowhere. He said that they were both knocked down by the blast, and that's all he knew. At that point he began cursing the dagos again. I asked him his name; that's when he told us his name was Roger Touhy and the other man was his bodyguard, Walter Miller. It was then that I recalled reading about him in the newspapers recently; he had just been released from Statesville penitentiary after twenty-five years for a kidnapping that he didn't do.

We could see that Touhy had lost a lot of blood and looked pale; he didn't look as if he was going to make it.

The bodyguard said that he thought they had fired at least five shots at them but only hit them in the legs. The assassins had fired high enough, but both men were lucky that they weren't hit in the head, which probably would have been fatal, which, as things turned out, didn't matter. Touhy and Miller were transported to the hospital, where Touhy died but Miller survived his wounds.

I found out later that the bullet hole in the windshield of the car that was parked in front of the victim's home was made by one of the shots fired at the assassins by Walter Miller, Touhy's bodyguard. The bad news is that an inquisitive policeman had stuck a finger in the bullet hole and had cut his finger, which was the reason for the blood being in the bullet hole. So the odds are that the assassins were never wounded, and all the checking at the hospitals for a wounded killer was for nothing. My curiosity concerning Touhy got the best of me, so I started checking on what the hell he did to have the outfit kill him.

December 16, 1959
Roger Touhy told me that

The dagoe bastards never forget

Walter Miller "Bodyguard"

Roger "Terrible" Touhy, as he was called, was born in Chicago in 1898 and was the son of a Chicago policeman. There were seven kids – two girls and five boys. When he was a teenager, he got a job with Western Union, which gave him a chance to learn the Morse code; the job paid $12.00 a week. He met his wife, Clara, at the Western Union when she was sixteen years old, and eventually married her in 1922. Touhy had learned a great deal about unions and how they worked within Western Union. Every employer fought the unions then, and because he gave honest answers to a superintendent of the company and expressed his feelings about unions, he was fired. He then went west and got jobs as a telegrapher with a railroad in Denver and as an oil field engineer in Oklahoma. When World War I began, he enlisted in the navy where he taught telegraphy at Harvard to officers and enlisted men. When he was discharged, he needed to get back to work and got word that a New York geologist named Dick Raymond needed a helper. Touhy got the job, and traveled with Raymond all over southwest Oklahoma – that turned out to be very profitable for him. He invested in oil leases and sold them for a total of $25,000 within a year's time.

Being a city guy at heart, he returned to Chicago and married Clara; they moved into an apartment in Oak Park, Illinois. His next move was to buy a taxicab, which he drove nights; after a few months, he opened his own garage and auto sales place, with a capacity for ten cars. Business was very good, and he sold it and bought a bigger place on North Avenue. Up to this point, I couldn't find Touhy ever having been arrested or being in trouble with the law as most alleged mobsters usually are.

Touhy and his wife moved from Oak Park to another suburb in Des Plaines, Illinois where he bought a six-room bungalow and later had a swimming pool put in the backyard. The newspapers later called this house a "mansion" or a "gang fortress." Touhy claimed that the only gang that he ever had around his house was a guard with a shotgun after the Capone Mob tried to kidnap his kids.

Touhy got involved in the beer business by chance; he bought eight trucks at a bargain price, and then he sold six of them and wound up with the two trucks sitting around in his garage doing nothing. It happened that he knew most of the bootleggers and bar owners in his area so why not get involved. He called on a few of the saloon owners and then made a deal with two young fellas who would work hard to make a dollar. Also, he made a deal to buy beer from two breweries, which turned out legal one-half of 1 % prohibition beer, and sneaked the good beer out the back door. His trucks hauled the beer; the drivers made a profit of $20 a barrel, and they paid him a percentage on the purchase price of the trucks.

Touhy said that some police generally expected a payoff of $5 a barrel for beer being run into any given district. He also said that he didn't pay it and neither did his drivers because his operation was too small for the law to bother much with them.

One of Touhy's trucks carrying three barrels of beer was stopped by a police sergeant named Dan "Tubbo" Gilbert. He arrested the driver and took the beer to the station. It so happened that Touhy claimed he had met Gilbert when he was a labor organizer for the syndicate in a score of unions, and Gilbert did not like Touhy. The three barrels of beer turned out to be legal stuff ½ of 1% – and Gilbert had to release the beer, the driver, and the truck, which really pissed Gilbert off. Touhy said that he circulated that story around Chicago, which was quite embarrassing for Gilbert. It took Gilbert a long time to get even with Touhy, but he finally did, ninety-nine years of even.

Touhy really got his start big time in the bootleg business when a friend of his, Matt Kolb, a bootleg beer distributor made a proposition to Touhy that he couldn't refuse. Kolb had a falling-out with his partner who wanted to get out of the business, so he asked Touhy if he wanted to buy out his partner for $10,000. At one time Kolb had been tied up with the Capone mob, but the violence had scared him away from them. Touhy, who had been taking in about $50,000 a year from his automobile business, decided to be Kolb's partner and gave him the $10,000; he was the off and running.

Touhy found out that Kolb's beer was awful because it didn't taste good and was inconsistent in flavor So the first thing Touhy did was to consult with a chemist and ask him about how he could make good beer. He was told to find good pure water, which was the big thing in making good beer. After testing the water all over northern Illinois, it was decided that an artesian well near Roselle, Illinois, was the best. A wort plant was built there, and Touhy put his brother Eddie in charge of it. Wort is a liquid portion of mashed or malted grain produced during fermenting process before hops and yeast is added. Touhy wanted to make the best beer in America, and the saloonkeepers would come begging to buy it. Touhy used nothing but the best ingredients and did everything he could to make the best-tasting beer, which proved to be a success. Of course, this was an illegal operation and in violation of the federal laws; but everybody – from bankers, clergymen, mayors, U.S. senators, and the corner grocery clerk – drank his beer and enjoyed it.

Touhy had invested $50,000 in this business before he sold his first stein of beer. He even had union workers build barrels for him in a place in Schiller Park, Illinois, because barrels would spring leaks and release carbonation at times and could cause a lot of trouble. Touhy and Kolb had ten fermenting plants, each one a small brewery in itself. It was too much of a gamble to have the complete works in one place, which the federal prohibition agents might raid and chop up. Touhy's operation was well run and was a lot better than beer made in bathtubs in some basement.

Touhy was selling one thousand barrels a week at $55 a barrel to saloon owners. It cost $4.50 a barrel to produce beer using the finest ingredients; water was cheap, and there was a lot of it in beer. They sold beer to about two hundred locations outside the Chicago area to the west and northwest of Chicago. Because their business was scattered all over the suburbs, nobody realized that Kolb and Touhy were grossing about a million year from the beer alone. Federal agents stuck pretty much to the big cities like Chicago, so Touhy didn't catch too much heat from law enforcement.

It was still the late '20s when Touhy and Matt Kolb got involved with slot machines. They were against the law to possess, but they stood in the open in practically every roadhouse, drugstore, gas station, or saloon in Cook County. They had 225 of them in choice locations; they were clearing about $9,000 a week from the slots.

Touhy related how he had met Al Capone about a half dozen times back then, mostly in Florida on fishing trips. He said that he always refused to stay at his mansion or use his yacht on Palm Island in Biscayne Bay, near Miami. People around Capone always seemed to be getting killed, both friend and foe. He said that he or Kolb never carried a gun or did any of their employees. In 1927, Touhy had two business deals with Capone where he sold him beer for $37.50 a barrel; he ordered five hundred barrels. The beer must have sold well because Capone called him a few days later and ordered three hundred more barrels. Capone complained that fifty of the barrels were leaking. Touhy knew that the barrels were made by craftsmen and there was no way that they would leak, so he told Capone, "Don't try and chisel me, Al. I sold you eight hundred, and that's what I expect to get paid for." Capone paid the $30,000 in cash right on time. Capone tried to buy more barrels from Touhy a week later, but Touhy refused to sell him any because he had to take care of his regular customers; this was a lie.

Al Capone was resentful of Touhy and Kolb because he knew that they were making a lot of money. Touhy's partner, Matt Kolb, had the reputation for being the top man in running beer and slot machines in their part of Cook County. Kolb liked the notoriety and limelight, whereas Touhy was more of a family man and liked to stay out of the picture. When the mob murdered Matt Kolb in 1931, Touhy's name wasn't mentioned prominently in the papers. Capone envied his anonymity and begrudged him his income. Capone wanted to open up Touhy's territory with whorehouses and big-time gambling, so he sent two torpedoes out to see Touhy. Capone made an appointment by phone, and a meeting was set up in a roadhouse owned by Touhy in Schiller Park.

As the story goes, Touhy, being very resourceful, set up the meeting place like a grade B movie. He had hung rifles, shotguns, and pistols on the walls in the office. He had a friend on the county highway police who loaned him a couple of machine guns. He stashed them in an open closet for window dressing for the two mobsters to see. The roadhouse also had a gas station attached to it. Touhy made arrangements to have the attendant call him on the phone every time Touhy would scratch his head or blew his nose or stood up from his chair. He told the attendant not to pay any attention to what he would say to him on the phone, and that he was playing a joke on some friends. When the bad guys swaggered into the office, they became very meek after seeing the weapons on the walls and the machine guns in the closet. One of the guys named Frank Rio told Touhy what Capone wanted to do in the suburbs with whorehouses and gambling, even punchboards to get the school kids money. Touhy blew his nose, and in a minute the phone rang; he pretended to listen then began scowling and shouted into the phone that they were to send a few of the boys over there and take care of it. "Nobody can hijack our slots." Rio continued on about Al's feelings about opening up this virgin territory. Touhy laughed politely at this remark, but the mobsters didn't seem to think anything was very funny at this point. Touhy then coughed loudly, and on signal, a former county cop came striding into the office from the bar; he grabbed the two tommy guns and told Touhy that Louie and he were going over and take care of those bastards one way or the other. Touhy said, "Do whatever it takes, Joe." Joe left with the tommy guns and returned them back to the police arsenal where they had been borrowed.

The phone kept ringing, and Touhy acted like Edward G. Robinson on the phone, giving orders and directing his cohorts how to commit violence. The two mobsters seemed to get a little pale, and left the office before they probably thought they were going to be murdered themselves. This act seemed to work whenever Capone would send anybody out to see him; the phone would ring, and Touhy would act like Little Caesar. He kept telling the bad guys that the local people were dead against casinos or prostitutes. Touhy knew that he would have been put out of business soon after the Chicago mob got a foot in the door. He alerted the local police about the mob's plans and told them that if they got out in the suburbs, there would be shootings in the streets, and whorehouses and casinos all over there communities.

Now I understood why Capone wanted to get Touhy out of the picture. When the syndicate went out to the suburbs with their punchboards, all the merchants refused to handle them. Capone knew that he was throwing a monkey wrench into his plans for the suburbs, and would get his revenge.

The only thing that kept Touhy alive at the time was probably because of the charade he had been putting on with Capone's messengers. Some of them actually believed that the Touhy mob consisted of two hundred men who were all killers and that if they got into a war with the Touhy clan they would probably lose.

Actually, Roger "Terrible" Touhy was never on the roster of the Chicago Crime Commission as a public enemy. He had never been associated in any way with a capital offense. Al Capone was the only person who regarded Touhy as a terror and as the main stumbling block in his effort to take over the northwest suburbs. Touhy was pretty much a creation of sharp public relations, his own.

Even after Capone was sent to prison for income tax evasion, they still tried to get Touhy, and they did. Deciding violence was out, they resolved to use another method, helping the law get something on him. Touhy found himself in trouble with the Federal Bureau of Investigation. Touhy and several of his henchmen were arrested for the kidnapping of William Ham Jr. and that they had a strong case against them. A jury thought differently, finding him not guilty. Later the FBI switched the charge to the real culprits, the Barker-Karpis gang. By coincidence, Alvin "Creepy" Karpis had long been close to the Capone mob.

Next, the FBI arrested Touhy for the alleged 1933 kidnapping of Jake "the Barber" Factor, an international confidence man with ties to Al Capone. This was despite underworld grapevine information that the kidnapping was a fake, masterminded by Factor and the Capones. When FBI agent Melvin Purvis announced that his arrest of Touhy in the Factor kidnapping was a landmark in the art of detection Touhy's first trial ended in a hung jury, he was convicted the second time around and sentenced to ninety-nine years. Touhy kept yelling that he had been framed and that the Capone mob moved into northwest Cook County.

While Touhy was in Statesville prison, he and some others managed to escape for a time but were recaptured, and he was sentenced to another 199 years. There were many people, including several journalists, who considered him innocent of the Factor kidnapping and took up the fight to clear him. In the '50s, Touhy won a rehearing on his original conviction. Federal Judge John H. Barnes ruled that Factor had not been kidnapped at all but had disappeared on his own connivance. Judge Barnes severely criticized the FBI, Chicago Police, the state attorney, and the Capone gang. It took a few more years for legal jockeying before Touhy was released.

Just twenty-three days after Touhy won his freedom, I met him, lying in a pool of blood on the porch of his sister's home.

One noteworthy item that occurred after Touhy's death was the suicide of special agent Melvin Purvis of the FBI – who boasted about solving the alleged kidnapping of Jake Factor with the arrest of Roger Touhy – in 1960, a few months after Touhy was released.

The fact remains that after checking on Roger Touhy's background, he had enough nerve to take on Al Capone and his mob, and conned them into thinking that he had a bigger, tougher organization than they did. That's the only reason that they didn't assassinate him after they killed his partner Matt Kolb. Roger Touhy won a lot of the battles with Capone during prohibition, but Capone had to use the FBI, the police, and the state attorney's office to win the war.

I did a lot of thinking about just what the hell I was doing being a cop and how I got involved in getting on the job. In the short time I had been on the job, I handled a lot of gory things: people that got blown up, knifings, shotgun murders, little kids murdered, rapes, suicides, dogs heads being cut off, and so forth. I guess I have to blame my uncle Earl, who suggested that I apply for the job. Sometimes I wish that he had suggested the telephone company or maybe the post office I guess I better face the facts. I love this job.

St. Valentine's day Massacre

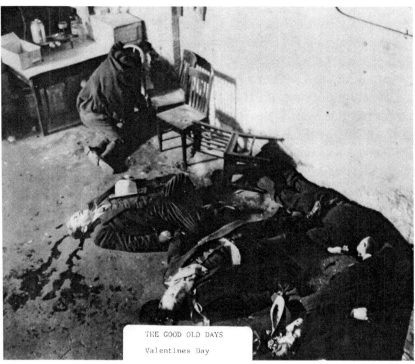

THE GOOD OLD DAYS
Valentines Day

Source: Chicago Daily News

Chapter 2

Don Herion's Forty-five Years of Vaudeville

Don Herion joined the Chicago Police Department on a lark.

He was bored working as a salesman for a bowling pin refinishing company. So when his uncle Earl told him that the police department was looking for applicants, he thought that he had nothing to lose, so he filled out the necessary forms, scored well on the written test, passed the physical examination, and joined the force on February 1, 1955. When he was sworn in as a police officer, he wasn't sure that he did the right thing.

It took him until August 27, 1992, to make up his mind about the job. That's the day he retired as a detective sergeant from the gambling unit of the organized crime division. He spent six years in the patrol division working at every job possible as a uniformed officer. He also spent thirty-two years working on organized crime gambling operations in Chicago and the suburbs. He was promoted to detective and then sergeant, and remained in the organized crime division.

He was the recognized expert on organized crime gambling operations, had conducted more than four thousand raids on mob-controlled gambling operations, and had arrested hundreds of mobsters and their associates, and still found the job a lark.

Along the way, he had seen his share of grisly underworld assassinations. Two of his informants had been murdered. One was beaten, tortured, and had his throat cut, and was found in the trunk of his own Cadillac in a western suburb parking lot. The other killed by seven .45 caliber slugs in the head in his own house in Chicago

But his zest for dealing often financially crippling blows to the Chicago Mafia remained undiminished.

He did such a good job that in 1979 he was transferred out of the organized crime division and sent to a district in uniform, watching the boats in Montrose Harbor. He stayed there for two months until a change in administration transferred the police official that dumped Herion. He was brought back to the organized crime division and proceeded to cause the mob numerous headaches.

He was no stranger to the ultimate victims of organized crime – the often tortured, disfigured, or murdered gambling or loan shark patrons who fell victim to the mob when they couldn't pay their debts.

Herion's career started off with more of a whimper than a bang The first two years, Herion walked a beat along a relatively quiet business area of a residential neighborhood on Chicago's Far West Side. He handled his share of school pedestrian crossings, domestic disputes, and parking violations. "Not exactly a thrill a minute," he recalled.

By 1957, however, things started looking up. Herion was assigned to a squad car with a partner, and his days became populated by burglars, armed robbers, arsonists, and murderers. At the same time, he started becoming aware of the behind-mob influence that permeated even that quiet neighborhood. Fellow officers pointed out the bookmakers and loan sharks that frequented some of the taverns and pool halls in the district. Some warned him to ignore any gambling violations that he might spot. "That's not your job," they cautioned.

In 1961, Herion was assigned to plainclothes vice control duties in the same district, an assignment that in the next five years would serve him well in developing that sixth sense that services detectives so well.

As the district changed gradually into the urban ghetto that it is today, Herion honed his skills investigating a variety of mob enterprises that often prey on the poor – bookmaking on horses and sporting events. The insidious nickel-and-dime policy or numbers racket, prostitution and mob hits, the inevitable harvest of organized crime.

The victims were stuffed into the trunks of cars, in sewers, even on their own front lawns. Others had been incinerated in the front seats of their automobiles.

In 1966 Herion was transferred to the gambling unit of the department's organized crime division. He was promoted to detective in 1968 and sergeant in 1970. Each time he was promoted, he remained in the organized crime division. In Jan 1993 he was asked by the Sheriff of Cook County, Illinois, to be a director of a vice detection unit to smash mob gambling operations in Cook County, a position he held for almost eight years.

Along the way, he employed the services of his wife and six children – three boys and three girls – often using them as "fronts" while conducting surveillances or making phone calls to the private phone numbers of mob bookmakers. They would then be distracted while their father and squad would crash through the barricaded doors of the gambling dens.

In the early 1970s, mob gambling bosses opened a campaign of death and terror in an attempt to extort monthly payments or "street taxes" from independent bookmakers not under the organized crime umbrella.

In one four-year period, twenty-eight bookies were murdered, beaten, and tortured as examples to others; scores of other bookmakers fled town. The victims were shotgunned, burned to death, garroted, overdosed with narcotics, or tortured with ice picks and electric cattle prods.

Even two of the mob's executioners during the campaign were themselves slain and their bodies stuffed in the trunk in one of their cars when they botched a hit on a mob gambling boss who didn't die after they shot him three times in the head. It was then that Herion began to fully understand the stranglehold the mobsters held over Chicago.

One of Herion's longest-running investigations was the mob's infamous floating crap game a multi-million-dollar-a-year racket that operates three nights a week and attracted hundreds of players from a fifty mile radius of the city. Due to circumstances beyond Herion's control, he had to work undercover on his off-duty hours to shut the game down on six different occasions, costing the gangsters millions of dollars in lost revenue.

Along the way, Herion had been the recipient of scores of threats from the mob.

In April of 1989, Herion put the game down for good. Mob boss Rock Infelise had a conversation taped between him and mob informant B.J. Jahoda of Infelise's efforts to get Herion out of the organized crime division. Infelise sent an unknown police official to the superintendent of police to get Herion sent to a subway detail. This tape was played in federal court in the trial of Infelise and nineteen other mobsters on racketeering and murder charges.

Herion had also been credited as the first law enforcement official to discover that the crime syndicate gangsters had started bankrolling huge cocaine deals with profits from illegal gambling enterprises to produce motion pictures.

Herion was selected as an expert witness to testify in June 24-26, 1985, in New York City, at the President's Commission on Organized Crime. At the conclusion of his testimony, the chairman, Judge Irving R. Kaufman, and other commission members congratulated him for his knowledge of organized crime and of the Chicago mob. Some of the witnesses included noted sports journalist Howard Cosell, chairman of the board of the Golden Nugget Casino Stephan Wynn, and Los Angeles Police chief Darryl Gates. Also NCAA basketball coaches, newspaper editors, U.S. attorneys from throughout the United States. And of course, organized crime members, some of which had to wear a hood to protect their identity

It seems that the government printed a book with the results of that hearing and the testimony of all the witnesses, as well as photographs of the evidence presented to members of the commission. A movie director by the name of John Irvin read the book during research on the Chicago mob and called Herion and asked him to be a technical advisor on a movie called *Raw Deal* that was going to be filmed in Chicago.

Herion accepted the job and also had a part in the movie, which starred Arnold Schwarzenegger. This was the beginning of a new hobby for Herion, who became a member of the Screen Actors Guild, which he is still a member. He has appeared in numerous other films with Patrick Swayze, Liam Neeson, Robert De Niro, Kurt Russell, Helen Hunt, Ken Olin, James Earl Jones, Wesley Snipes, Tommy Lee Jones, Darren McGavin, William Devane, Kyle Chandler, Sharon Stone, Katherine Harold, Robert Davi, Steven Segall, and Oprah Winfrey.

Chapter 3

You Mean I'm Really a Cop Now?

This story should probably start out with that famous cliché, "It was a dark and stormy night." Actually, it was a dark and stormy day when I started on the Chicago Police Department back on February 1, 1955, and I could add that it was colder than a well digger's ass as well. I had been notified to report to a police facility at 3900 South California Avenue on Chicago's South Side at 7:45 AM. with a pen and a notebook. Well, I wasn't nuts about the South Side in the first place, which is the home of the White Sox, whom I disliked immensely. Not to mention the smell of the Chicago stockyards and streets with numbers and no names. I had waived to accept a few months before when they notified me to report. At the time, I just couldn't face the fact that I was going to be a Chicago police officer. Hell, I wasn't that nuts about cops in the first place. I did think that I would have found another job that I liked before they would notify me again, but I didn't; so here I was on my way to begin training at the police academy for the next twelve weeks. I also disliked schools of any kind. Plus, I would have to wear a uniform. The more I thought about this, the more I noticed that I was driving a lot slower. It reminded me of going to the dentist's office. But what the hell, if I didn't like it, I could always quit and maybe reenlist in the army.

On my arrival at the police facility, I parked my 1951 Chevy and entered the building, thinking about my uncle Earl – who had talked me into applying for this job – and why in the hell I had listened to him. I can still recall the feeling I had when I entered the building. It was like going into a building made in hell; I followed an arrow pointing to the second floor saying Recruits. I walked into a large room containing about forty desks, the kind they use in high school. There was a podium at the front of the room; and standing behind the podium was the biggest police sergeant I had ever seen, and he was not smiling.

The room was filled with a bunch of guys who were filling out various forms, and they weren't smiling either. I noticed that there was a vacant desk at the rear of the room, which was always my favorite place to be in school anyway. I sat down, only to find out that I had forgotten my pen in the car. I started to think this might be an omen and that I ought to get the hell out of there. As I looked around, I must have had panic on my face because the guy sitting next to me smiled and handed me an extra pen he had. I noticed that he also was shaking his head. I glanced up at the sergeant and sure as hell he was shaking his head too, and he wasn't smiling. I began to wonder, if you screwed up on the police department, did they make you do fifty push-ups?

After all the paperwork was finished and turned into the sergeant, he introduced himself as Sgt Marston. He was not only big, he was mean looking; he reminded me of a drill sergeant that I had when I was in basic training at Ft Leonard Wood, Missouri. He appeared to be about forty-five years old and was probably on the job for twenty years or so. He informed us that from this point on, he was our class leader and would look after all forty of us for the next exciting twelve weeks. He explained that we would learn about the rules and regulations of the police department, state laws, city ordinances, how to handle any type of violation that we would run into in the patrol division – for example, crimes such as robbery, burglary, theft, murder, rape, arson and so on. We would also be trained on how to use a weapon, how to and when not to use it. At this point, I began wondering how the hell a cop was supposed to handle all these situations without getting screwed up.

At this time, the sergeant must have realized that he had all of us nervous, so he gave us a ten-minute break. I fired up a Lucky Strike in the hallway and began looking for the guy who had loaned me his pen. I found him and gave him the pen back, told him my name, and he said that name was Neil and that he had forgotten his smokes in his car and was about to have a nicotine fit. I gave him a couple and told him we were even.

Neil looked to be my age, five foot ten, 190 pounds, black hair, and, as I found out later, was Italian. Neil told me that he was here because he was sick of driving a truck and getting tickets because he had a heavy foot. So what the hell, if you can't beat 'em, join 'em.

Neil said that he didn't think he had a chance of getting hired, because he was a West Side dago, and all cops were Irish. I told Neil that I sure as hell wasn't Irish and that I was a kind of a mixed breed of French, Belgian, Norwegian, and Swede. I will say that some people have accused me of looking Irish.

After some more small talk, we found out that we lived fairly close to each other. He lived around Division Street and Pulaski Road, and I lived at North Avenue and Cicero, which was about 1 1/2 miles northwest of Neil's house. Neil suggested that maybe we should take turns driving to school and that way we would be sure that we would have enough smokes and pens, and also save on gas. I told Neil that his mother didn't raise any dummy; and it sounded good, and we shook hands on it.

When we returned to class – reluctantly, I might add – we were informed that we had to buy our own uniforms and weapon, which had to be a .38 special six-shot revolver. The instructor suggested we could buy these items at a couple of stores located on Roosevelt Road. All that the city supplied was a star, a shield for your hat, a call box key, and a baton "Club." The instructor also insisted that under no circumstances would we be permitted to carry our weapon until we received instructions about how a gun operates, how to use it, and when not to use it. We also had to pass the firing range test.

We were informed that now that we were in recruit school and had been accepted to be Chicago police officers, we should be proud of our new profession and obey all the rules and regulations, study hard, pass all the tests that we would be given, and just maybe after twelve weeks we would graduate from recruit school. At that time, we would be assigned to a police district in the patrol division and would be on probation for six months.

At that time, the sergeant said that probably at least 10 percent of our class would be flunked for one reason or another. The instructor warned us that anyone who came on this job because of the power he would have or had any thoughts of making money on the street better leave now, because the only place that the recruit would be going was to the joint, where he had better learn how to fight or dance real fast.

Our job was to serve and protect the citizens of Chicago, preserve the peace, and put the bad guys in jail. And make no mistake, there would be situations that would come up in our careers where our nerves and temptation would be tested. The best thing that a cop could have was common sense and the ability to think of the consequences should you cross over to the other side. You had better be able to do the time if you did the crime.

All in all, recruit school wasn't that bad. The work in the classroom was kind of like high school all over again. The differences were the subjects, of course. Instead of math, history, and English, we were lectured on law, city ordinances, first aid, and how to handle a weapon. Judo classes were OK. As well as the range, where we were instructed on how to fire our weapon from four positions – shoulder high, waist high, kneeling, and prone position.

I became an expert marksman pretty fast, but Neil had a hard time firing his .38 Smith & Wesson and rarely hit the target. Neil, of course, blamed the .38 as being defective as the reason that he was having a hard time. He asked me to try it, which I did and found that it was as accurate as mine. Neil told me that I just got lucky and was going to trade it in for a .38 Colt. Of course, he still had the bad luck of missing the target. He couldn't believe how unlucky he was to buy two new .38s that didn't shoot straight.

We all learned an important lesson one day when the instructor arbitrarily selected several of us to enact a stop and frisk in class. We were given a situation; first one and then the other played the officer and the suspect. Almost everyone flunked. The officer spoke in muffled tones and asked politely for some identification and muttered softly as to why the he was loitering in the alley at such a late hour. The instructor yelled out, "You just gonna stand there and ask him to put his hand in his pocket? Remember, rookie, your up in an alley, its dark, and we ain't here." Everyone, including a few policemen back for a refresher course, failed badly and knew it. The instructor concealed a couple of guns and knives on a student collaborator and arranged to demonstrate a search of a suspect. In real life, half of you guys would be on your ass by now, and this guy would be using your head for a soccer ball. The collaborator and another recruit were called to the front of the room. Two others were called up to frisk them. The recruits mumbled their orders, and without using their hands or getting too close to the men, they positioned the "suspects" on the wall. They both used their feet to kick at the subject's legs, spreading them to keep the men off balance. The instructor was now yelling about why all this kicking, why all the rough stuff. Two other recruits were called up; throughout the hour nobody found any of the weapons, and each man started his search by kicking or roughing up his classmate. The instructor was not a happy camper, and he showed it. He did say that rarely does any student ever find any weapons the first time. Those made us feel a little better anyway. He then demonstrated a proper frisk. He told us that when you frisk someone, it is for your own protection. "You have to put him under your control and frisk him systematically." The instructor used his entire body, placing the man in the position he wanted him, feet back and spread wide, every muscle tensed to keep his head far forward.

He then explained that you have to stand right in there. "Don't be afraid of him. You ought to be afraid if he isn't in this position. Now you got him. Put your leg inside his, and if he moves you can trip him up. Don't use your fingertips. Use your palms; start with the palms on his head and work one side of his body and then the other. Look at his hair, and don't be afraid to put your hands on his crotch; sometimes, bad guys conceal a small handgun there. If he gives you any shit, you can give him a little shot to remember you while you're there."

The instructor then showed us the concealed guns and knives. "These things were hardly hidden, fellas. But don't worry, before you get out of here, you will be able to find a needle in a haystack. After several weeks of practicing and discovering the many places a weapon can be concealed, we felt a lot better, had more confidence, and all the more anxious to get out in the street. Our respect for our instructors grew quite a bit, and most everybody's attention span increased in class because all the things that they have been teaching us might save our life someday.

Recruit school was fast coming to an end, to everyone's delight. Everybody in our class passed except one guy who seemed to have a small drinking problem and came to class a couple of times half whacked and fell asleep at his desk. We were all anxiously waiting graduation day on April 23, 1955, to find out where we would be assigned.

It was at this time that I began hearing the word *clout* being used as well as *Chinaman,* and that if you had either, you would probably get to be assigned somewhere close to your home. Some of the guys said that you had better make a phone call to your Chinaman or clout before the list came out. Well, seeing that I had neither, all I could do was let the chips fall where they may. When the assignments came out, I was informed that I was being transferred to the Twenty-Eighth District, which was located at 5327 West Chicago Avenue, only about two miles from where I lived. I think this was where I panicked a little, realizing that all the bullshit was over and the moment of truth was fast approaching.

Sgt. Marston told us that we were going to have a graduation ceremony, that there would be a group photo taken, and that we would be congratulated by the commissioner of police, Timothy J. O'Conner, and that just maybe the mayor, Martin Kennelly, might show up. We would also be given a diploma. Then we would have to listen to a few speeches about how lucky we were to be a member of the Chicago Police Department.

I was never fond of graduation ceremonies, even if it were my own. *But what the hell,* I thought, *here goes nothing.* Of course, it was a typical Chicago day, overcast with a chilly wind blowing. Then it started to drizzle off and on – wonderful spring day. We were all in full uniform and lined up in formation at a proper interval. Naturally, we couldn't talk or smoke during the proceedings, but I recall looking up and seeing flocks of pigeons flying over us and bombarding us with the white stuff. I thought that this could be an omen, being shit on before we hit the streets.

The festivities ended, and there were handshakes all around with everybody wishing everybody good luck, and bets were made about who would make the most pinches. I kind of just faded out of there and went home so I could take the uniform off and think about all the bad guys I was gonna put in jail when I hit the street on Monday.

Chapter 4

First Assignment, Twenty-eighth District

I called the district to find out what watch I was on and when to report for work. A desk sergeant told me that I was to report at 2300 hours Sunday night – as I was going on the midnight shift, otherwise called the dogwatch – and to be sure to bring a flashlight.

I told my wife to be, Genevieve, that we couldn't go out Sunday because I had to get some sleep before reporting for work. Gen had typed all my reports while I was in the academy; and she learned quite a bit about police procedures, laws, and ordinances, and how the police department operated. She probably knew more than I did.

I reported as ordered at 2300 hours at the Twenty-eighth District, all decked out in my blue uniform, ready to beat the world. I introduced myself to the desk sergeant, and he told me that he didn't have any orders about my transfer and to sit on a bench and relax. The next thing I heard was somebody calling my name. It was a lieutenant, who seemed to be aggravated about the mix-up. He asked me if I had a call box key and bullets in my gun. I thought, *Oh boy, this is a fun guy*, and the moment of truth has come. He told me to report to the rear room for roll call and to get my assignment, which was going to be a walking post.

The patrol sergeant, whose name was Bart Hines, told me that my post was on Division Street from Cicero Avenue to Kedzie Avenue.

Don't worry about making all my pulls on Division Street. Some of the call boxes have had a malfunction. I was also told to report back to the station at 0745 hours for check-off roll call.

I was driven in squad car number 121 by two policemen named O'Conner and O'Connell, and they told me to take it easy and that if I needed anything out in the Jaws of Death, I'd call the station and they would meet me. Beat men did not have any radios or any means of communication in those days, so you were on your own.

I made my first pull at 0100. The box was OK, and I gave the operator my star number. He said, "OK, kid, take it easy out there," and hung up. I made my second pull an hour later and again gave the operator my star number. The next thing I heard was, "What the hell are you bothering me for? I told you to take it easy, didn't I? Do you know what good night means, lad?" He hung up, swearing at me. I thought, *So this is the real world*. A couple hours later, I saw car number 121 and told them about my experience with the operator. They laughed and told me not to worry about it and that I should find an open gas station or restaurant and relax.

I was really confused. Here I was walking up and down the streets looking for bad guys and got my ass chewed out. O'Conner and O'Connell explained to me that everybody who walked a post could donate $2 a month to the operator if they wanted to and that the operator would take care of the call sheet. I explained that I was still on probation and didn't want to blow the job just yet; needless to say, it was a long night watching stray dogs and cats and occasional rats running around. When I checked into the district for check-off roll call, a couple of other guys who had been walking a beat told me not to worry about not making a pull during the night. They told me to just make my first pull at night and last pull in the morning and forget about it.

I saw a notice on the bulletin board when I reported for roll call the next night that the police were having tryouts for the police baseball team the coming week and to report to McKinley Park at 3900 South Western Avenue. I thought, *What the hell, I didn't have anything to lose*, so I gave it a shot, and I made the team as a pitcher and outfielder.

The coach told me that my district would be informed that they would have to carry me on a walking beat on the day watch for four hours a day and the other four hours I would be assigned to the police baseball team until the season was over. Needless to say, when I informed my lieutenant "Dan Healy" of this news, he was a little upset and let me know so. He told me, "You are now a policeman, not a fucking clown in a costume chasing little balls around. You're supposed to be chasing bad guys, not guys stealing second base."

We played for about ten weeks and ended the season playing the U.S. Navy combined baseball team in Wrigley Field and Comiskey Park with the proceeds going to the widows and orphans' fund. Our new mayor, Daley, was in attendance, as well as a pretty good crowd. We did win the rubber game when we beat a pitcher by the name of Johnny Podres, who was in the navy at that time and was a pitcher for the Brooklyn Dodgers; they had flown Podres in from Pensacola, Florida, just to pitch the final game. We beat the navy that day, and I was lucky enough to score the winning run. It was a good way to end our season. But the honeymoon was over, and I had to report back to my district full time the next day.

ONE OF MY FIRST ARRESTS

POLICE SHARPSHOOTERS WIN TROPHIES

Winners in recent police pistol tournament and turkey shoot receive awards at polic headquarters. Holding trophies are (l. to r.) Oren Matthews, first place; John R. Roel second; Don Herion, third; James Holzman, fourth; John Miklos, fifth, and Mae Stricl land, first in women's division. (Sun-Times Photo)

Chapter 5

My First Detail

I wondered how I would be greeted on my return to the district to work a full tour of duty. I found out in a hurry when my lieutenant told me that I was detailed to the South Side of Chicago at 106th and Bensley, "Trumbull Park," on the midnight shift. It seems that a few black families had moved into this residential neighborhood and a group of white rabble-rousers were breaking some of their windows and slashing the tires on their cars. The district police weren't able to handle this racial issue, which had turned to acts of violence. Mayor Daley was concerned about a race riot breaking out and ordered Police Commissioner O'Connor to send extra police to the area. Of course, my lieutenant decided that if I was in good enough shape to play ball all summer, I would be just right for the job.

After driving through the entire city (195 blocks to be exact), I got a good look at the South Side of Chicago, which didn't impress me at all. I reported, as ordered, to a small building that was set up as a command post for cops detailed to the district. I wondered if being a baseball player was such a good idea after all. Trumbull Park, as it was called, was located about twenty-five miles from my house, and there weren't any expressways to get there at that time. After roll call – which was conducted by a fat cigar-chomping sergeant who had also been detailed from the North Side of the city to this charade and didn't look to happy about it – I was assigned to the intersection of 106th and Torrance with another cop by the name of John and was told to sit in a squad car on the corner and take proper action for any violations of the law.

John wasn't really a bad guy as far as bad guys go, I guess. Let's just say he was different. He went on to explain to me that he had caught this detail before and had spent two weeks on the dogwatch, and nothing really ever happened on that shift. It all seemed to happen on the four-to-twelve watch, when all the wackos were out. He also told me that his six months probation period was over and that he could relax now and take it easy. I told John that I was almost over with mine and would be glad when it was done.

MYSELF AND JOHN MCKINLEY
1954 FORD –

Around 1:00 AM, John told me that he had to go to his car, which was parked about a block away, to get something and that he would be back in a few minutes. Our squad car, which at that time was all black with a red mars light on the roof, was parked behind a billboard on the corner of 106th and Torrance Avenue, and was not in full view to traffic in the area. As things turned out, this was a very good thing because it was then I found out what John had meant when he said that he could relax now that his probation was over. John had returned to the squad with a brown bag and proceeded to get in the backseat. It was then that he proudly showed me what he had in the bag – a pair of blue and white pajamas, which were brand-new. John explained that he couldn't sleep very well with his uniform on so he thought that he would try out his pajamas so that he could get his proper rest. John went on to tell me that the last time he caught this detail he didn't get any rest at all and he was concerned about getting caught sleeping while he was still on probation.

Needless to say, all I could do was stare at this wacko while he was putting on his jammies. John didn't say another word except wish me good night, and in a couple of minutes, old John was snoring so loud I had to close the windows on the car 'cause he sounded like a donkey in heat. At this point, all I could do was be on the lookout for any sergeant who might be by to check on us. I planned to get out of the squad and say hello to anyone checking up on my partner, who was lying on the backseat. I hoped that they couldn't see him. I looked up at the sky to see if there was a full moon, 'cause all the nuts come out when there is. There wasn't.

I hoped that John was right about nothing happening on the dogwatch and that there wouldn't be any racial disturbances around our location while we were protecting life and property. I was lucky, I guess, because the only disturbance around 106th and Torrance that night was John's snoring.

At this point, I figured that all these different situations that I had run into on my short time on the job were educational. But I couldn't help wondering if we were needed in an emergency how John would look, running around the street with his gun belt on over his blue and white pajamas.

I started to think about how I had gotten in this situation in the first place. It had to be because the lieutenant wasn't too happy about my participation on the police baseball team all summer, and of course, me being Joe the New Guy didn't help either. I just hoped I wouldn't be buried out in Goat Shit Heights for too much longer, but then shit goes down hill, doesn't it?

It must have been about 5:00 in the morning when I was starting to doze off myself and all of a sudden I got the shock of my life when an alarm went off. I almost fell out of the squad car because it sounded like a burglar alarm. It seems that John had neglected to tell me that he had an alarm clock with him, and it was very loud. At that point, I guess I lost it for a minute and called John a few choice names and told him he had better get himself a new partner tomorrow or rent a motel room. He just stared at me as if I was nuts but agreed that maybe it would be better if we dissolved our partnership under the circumstances and he would ask to work at another location the next night.

The good news was that nobody checked on us during our shift and we were relieved at 8:00 AM; and on the way home, my thoughts traveled to about six months ago when I was a civilian and had no idea about Chicago's finest or what they did, except maybe write tickets. Up to now, things were a little different than I thought they would be. But what the hell, I thought I had better make the best of it.

I did get a different partner – a guy named Jimmy – and we got along fine for the next two weeks of my punishment tour. Nobody tried to steal our intersection at 106th and Torrance. And I was sent back to my district to resume my career somewhat wiser than I had been.

Chapter 6

The Full Moon and the Four Amigos

    Walking a beat on the midnight shift was a new experience for me, as I had been working days for the past couple of months, which was really boring with handling school crossings and writing parking tickets. I was looking forward to getting out in the street at night and being on my own; it was me against the bad guys. Hell, I had been on the job for six months now, and I was ready for anything. It was July, and it was hot and humid, and it was very dark; but then I was working the dogwatch, and at night it is always dark, isn't it? I was assigned a walking post on Division Street between Pulaski Road and Cicero Avenue, which is one mile long. The area is mostly factories sprinkled with a couple of bars and greasy spoon restaurants, which are usually closed after 2:00 AM.
    I was given a lift to my assignment by a couple of cops who were assigned to the uniformed car in that area, O'Connor and O'Connell. They had been partners for a few years and were pretty good cops, from what I had been told. When they dropped me off at Division and Cicero, all they said to me was, "Stay out of trouble, kid, nothing ever happens around this area so don't worry about it." When they drove away, I heard O'Connor tell O'Connell that it sure was dark out, but that was probably because some of the streetlights were out on Division Street. I think they were trying to make me nervous.

Back then the police shirts all had long sleeves, and of course we had to wear a tie and a hat as well; it wasn't until years later that they came out with short sleeve shirts and no tie. I lit a cigarette, and the smoke just seemed to linger in the same place because there wasn't any breeze, just good old Chicago humidity. But no matter how hot it was, it was sure as hell a lot cooler where I was than the foundry that I passed by. There were some guys shoveling coal into a blast furnace, which had flames and smoke coming out of it; it looked as if they were in hell itself. I thought, *What the hell am I bitching about? At least I'm out taking a walk down the street*; the heat and humidity seemed to be a little better after I saw that scene. I made a pull on the call box, giving the operator my star number which was 4919 at that time. His reply was, "Take it easy, kid." Now that I was a member of the call box club, I wasn't worried about missing any pulls.

There were a couple of grills on my beat, but only one of them was open, so I decided to get a cup of coffee and the ever-popular donut before they closed. When I walked in the place, I discovered that they didn't have any air-conditioning, just a big old ceiling fan, which was circulating the smoke from the grill along with the fumes from the counterman's cigar. When the guy saw me walk in, he seemed surprised to see a cop in uniform; in fact, he was shocked. No one else was in the place, and I could see why. The counterman told me that he had been working the grill for two years on the night shift, and he never saw a cop come in the place. He said that his name was Bobby Joe Meeks and was from Hardburly, Kentucky, and had been in Chicago for about three years. I asked him if he could turn down the radio that was blaring out some hillbilly music about somebody's wife running off with the mailman and even took the dog. I got a cup of coffee but decided to forget about the donut because they were lying uncovered on the counter, attracting a few flies. Bobby Joe just kept raving on about how homesick he was and was going back home as soon as he got enough money. He told me he was twenty-eight years old, but I thought he was at least forty; maybe it was because of the two front teeth he was missing. After about three cups of coffee and Bobby Joe's cigar smoke, I decided to get out in the street where it was cooler. He was closing up anyway, so I told him good luck, and he told me, "Be careful out their, Officer, there's a full moon tonight."

About an hour later, car number 121 with O'Conner and O'Connell came down. O'Conner – who was about thirty-five years old, married, and had three kids – had been on the job for nine years; he and O'Connell teamed up about four years ago. O'Connell was about twenty-eight, single, and liked to play the horses. Both of them were known as great kidders and liked to play games on rookies. But the main thing was, they were both streetwise cops and if you ever got in a jam, they would be right there to help you. So my only communication with my fellow officers was the OC boys. Back then, we didn't have radios with us, so the best I could do was use a pay phone to call the station if I got in any trouble. I continued walking my assigned beat and started counting how many rats I saw as well as stray dogs and cats. The rats won hands down. I saw a real goofy thing when I crossed one alley; I saw this cat eyeing a rat that was eating some garbage near the mouth of the alley, only the cat didn't see this mangy dog that was eyeing him. All of a sudden, the rat must have seen the cat, and he scampered down the alley with the cat in hot pursuit; and the dog chased after the cat. The last I saw of them was all three of them disappearing in a yard down the street. I thought, *Maybe there is some truth to this full moon bullshit.* As I learned later, it's not bullshit; something weird always happens when the moon is full.

I kept walking east on Division Street, and every time a car would pass me by, the driver would seem to slow up and stare at me as if I was some kind of freak or something. I started to wonder just what the hell was I doing walking around in a blue suit, as if I was the sheriff of Dodge City. A couple of cars were drag racing, going west on Division Street; and when they saw me, they both hit their brakes and slowed up, as if I was going to chase them on foot or something. They both drove around the block, and when they made sure that I was on foot, they gave me the finger and said some things about my mother. At that point, I really didn't like this foot patrol bullshit and made up my mind that I would do whatever it took to get on a squad car. After another block or so, I had to relieve myself because of all that coffee I drank in the grill with Bobby Joe Meeks. There wasn't any washroom around so I had to visit the nearest alley. When I got back to the alley and was relieving myself, I thought I heard some glass breaking somewhere down the alley. When I looked down the alley, I was able to see a car parked against a wall, and somebody was in it, smoking a cigarette. I thought maybe it was some guy and his girlfriend making out, but you don't make out by breaking glass unless you're some kind of weirdo. But then again, there was a full moon, which was good for me because I could at least see the car. Back then, there weren't any lights in the alleys like there are today, so things were very dark. After a few minutes, the driver got out of the car and walked into the building he was parked behind. I decided to get a closer look and found that there wasn't anyone else in the car, but the rear door to a lamp store was half open and I could see a dim light inside and could hear voices. The voices sounded Spanish or some other foreign language; there were at least two or three of them. From force of habit, I got a terrible urge to smoke a cigarette. Boy, that would really be a brilliant move, wouldn't it? It's funny in these situations; sometimes a guy will do a stupid thing and screw up where you can get hurt or worse. An old-timer once told me that if you ever get in a spot where things can get a little touchy, use your common sense and things would probably work out. He also said that you can stick all that police academy bullshit up your ass, because you've got to get them before they get you.

One thing for sure was that I was on my own. We didn't have radios walking a beat; all we had was the call box, and that was about four blocks away. I think that I would rather face these guys than wake up that crabby bastard answering the call box. My only other option was to just get the hell out of there before anyone saw me; the store was probably insured anyway. *Face it*, I thought. I was on my own. God hates a coward, anyway.

I decided it would be better for me to try and surprise them inside the place before they came out; if they were spread out, I didn't know if I could cover them all. All of a sudden, I had the urge to urinate again. *That would be nice*, I thought, *a cop pissing in his pants*. I managed to get to the rear door, which had been about 1/4 inch open. I pushed it open just enough for me to get inside; thank God that it didn't squeak. So far so good. After checking my .38 for the third time in the last five minutes, I got behind some boxes and waited until I could determine how many bad guys were in the place. I could see four guys, and they were busy trying to move a safe out of the front office on a dolly. A couple of them were talking and giving orders to the other two guys. It sure sounded like Spanish to me; I had no idea what the hell they were saying at all. I noticed that the door to the office had a sign that said the premises were protected by ADT alarm system. I guess the crooks circumvented the alarm system, so I wasn't going to get any help there either. I also noticed that the phone lines to the phones on the desk had been cut as well. I decided to make my move when they were moving the safe out of the office, when they were all together. I thought that the louder I yelled "police" at them, the more shocked they would be, and they wouldn't know how many cops were with me, I hoped. When I did yell "police," all four of them kind of screamed out something in Spanish and were shocked out of their shoes; they raised their hands, and one of them pleaded with me not to shoot him. To tell the truth, at this point I really felt exhilarated and in charge of the situation. I kept yelling and waving my gun around and told them to turn around and put their hands on the wall. They didn't know what the hell I was talking about until I made a circling motion with my hand and every other word out of my mouth was a cuss word. Finally, I got them to turn around and put their hands on the wall. At that point, I began a conversation with other cops that were behind me; hopefully, the crooks would think that I wasn't alone and start some bad shit with me.

Now my problem was how the hell was I going to search all these sons of bitches for any weapons. I again yelled at my partners to cover me while I searched them for any weapons. I changed my voice once and said, "OK, Don, we'll cover you." I managed to search all of them the best I could, yelling at them while I was doing it. I couldn't find a gun but did find that they all had a switchblade knife; when I found one, I would yell back and tell my invisible partners what I had recovered. One of the bastards I found out had pissed in his pants; I found that out the hard way. I could sympathize with the poor bastard because I was almost pissing in my pants.

So far so good, but now what? Here I was with four Spanish bandits captured in the act of burglary and I didn't know what the hell I was going to do next. No radio, no communication, no way to get assistance. Who the hell was the prisoner, them or me? After about five minutes standing there, covering these guys – which really seemed like five hours – I lit up a cigarette, which was the best-tasting smoke I ever had. I started to get nervous and started to wonder if I had bullshitted them enough into thinking that I had other cops backing me up. If they thought that I was alone, they might get brave and try and jump me. Sure as hell, they started to talk to each other in Spanish, and every now and then one of them would turn his head around and try and see what or who was behind them. All I could do was holler at them and told them to shut the fuck up or they would get their ass kicked. I had no idea if they knew what I was saying.

This situation was not working out at all. I started to feel as if I was the prisoner and not the four amigos I had holding up the wall. The inside of the building was filled with boxes of lamps stacked up to the ceiling; there were some workbenches with different types of lamps on one side of the room and an entrance to an adjoining building. This was probably where the lamps were assembled and put into boxes. The two desks outside of the office were next to a washroom. The phones on the desks both had the lines cut; the phone inside the office had been pulled from the wall. I figured my only chance to get any help was to try and splice the phone lines together so I could call the station. People were right when they say, "Where are the cops when you need them?" At this point, the guy who had wet his pants called me senor and motioned toward the washroom as if he had to go again. That gave me an idea; I thought if I could get all four of the amigos in the washroom at the same time, maybe I could barricade the door with a chair or something. At least it was worth a try. I had looked in the washroom and there wasn't any window in it so I knew that they couldn't escape that way, and that would give me enough time to try and splice the phone wires together.

I yelled as loud as I could and said, "Amigos," and raised four fingers in the air and pointed at the washroom with my .38. They seemed to get the message, but while they were going in the washroom, they were all looking around as if they were expecting to see some other cops in the room. They started chattering again; thank God, the washroom door opened out so I could barricade it shut with a chair and anything else I could find. I started talking to my invisible partners again and answered myself a couple of times in strange voices as I was trying to splice the phone wires together. I used one of the switchblade knives I confiscated from one of the crooks to strip the wires. Of course, when you hurry, things get screwed up, but finally I got the wires in the right order and tried the phone. Of course it didn't work, so I had to start all over again. This game had been going on now for over two hours, and I had smoked a half a pack of cigarettes already. I noticed my hands were shaking a little while I was trying to reconnect the wires, and all the while, the four amigos were getting louder and louder in the washroom and started to pound on the door. I thought if things started to get out of hand, I would fire a shot in the ceiling; maybe that would slow them up a little. Finally, I got the wires together again, and I got it right; but wouldn't you know it, I forgot the phone number to the station. So I just called the operator and told her I was a police officer and where I was at and needed some help. After about a minute, I heard sirens getting louder and closer to me; and the closer they got, the braver I got. That was the best sound I had ever heard. Of course, I fired up another cigarette, and when I looked at the floor I counted eleven butts. I thought that if this job was going to be like this all the time, I would probably die of lung cancer when I hit forty.

Every car in the district showed up; at the time there were only four and a wagon, but when a call of a policeman needing help goes out, they drop whatever they're doing and answer the call. God help anybody who gets in their way because they will get rolled over. That sure made me feel good when I heard those tires screeching to a stop; it was a lesson that I would remember as long as I was on the job: you have to take care of your own, because if you don't, no one else will.

The four amigos were taken to the station where the detectives charged them with burglary, and they told me they also charged them with failure to learn English so they could communicate with the police. They were kidding, of course. O'Conner and O'Connell on car 121 asked me how the hell I caught these guys inside when they had broken into the rear of the building. I was going to tell them that I checked all the alleys on my beat as well as the street, but I knew I couldn't bullshit them, so I explained about drinking to much coffee in that grill and so on. A couple of the guys gave me a few attaboys and told me "good job." When I left the station, the first thing I did was stop and pick up a few packs of cigarettes and a Coke; no more coffee for me for a while. One thing was for sure, Bobby Joe Meeks was right about that full moon stuff; that's for sure.

Chapter 7

Squad Car: Working the Street

    The first time I relieved on a squad car, I worked with a guy named Bill O'Conner, who had been on the job for about eight years and was a World War II vet. His regular partner, Jack O'Connell had the day off; they were assigned to car 121 permanently. I learned a lot that first night on the four-to-twelve watch; thanks to Bill, who really knew his job. Bill let me drive that first night, and it sure was good, feeling like the real police for once. Squad 121 was a 1954 Ford and could really move. It was black with a white top and red mars light on the roof. We covered an area 3 ½ miles long and 1 mile wide, which was quite a large area for one car to handle. The first thing that Bill told me was to learn the boundaries of our sector, get to know the streets and the trouble spots. He gave me a map of our area and suggested that I become aware of where we were at all times.

    Our first job of the night was a domestic disturbance on the east end of the district, which was about three miles away. I began to speed up to get to the job as fast a possible when Bill told me to take it easy. He went on to explain that a domestic disturbance was not really an emergency call for help. When the police walk into a job like that too early, the emotional level is usually high, and the participants seem to forget what the hell they were fighting about, and they make you the enemy. He told me to stay alert and let him do all the talking, which was all right with me.

It seems that a neighbor had called the police when he heard his neighbor come home drunk and started abusing his common law wife, who was yelling at him for being drunk. She had slapped him in the face, and he retaliated by hitting her over the head with a bag of french fries that were soaked in catsup. The neighbor probably thought the catsup all over the woman's head was blood and that the husband was killing her. It really looked as if she had been hit in the head with an axe or something; but then with french fries all over the floor and some stuck in her hair, it looked kind of comical to me.

My partner explained to them that they were disturbing the peace and that their yelling and fighting was disturbing the neighborhood. He then explained to them that if they wanted to, they could sign cross complaints against each other, and they would both be arrested and have to appear in the court the next day. The alternative was that they could apologize to each other and clean up the floor. Needless to say, they were hugging and kissing each other when we left, but they did tell us that we should be out in the street catching criminals instead of bothering the likes of them.

I can tell you that was a great learning experience for me, because I would have gotten right in the middle of that mess, and who knows how things would have turned out? The next job we got was a call of a man down at the opposite end of the district. Bill told me to proceed over to the scene at a normal rate of speed, because that kind of a call is usually about some drunk passing out in somebody's doorway. Sure as hell, Bill was right. This guy lived across the boundary line of our district in Oak Park, Illinois, and was kind of a known alcoholic in the area and always passed out when he had more than a pint of vodka. Bill explained that we could lock him up, but then again he had been arrested numerous times in the past and would go to court the next day where the judge would release all the drunks with a stern warning about the evils of alcohol. If we did arrest him, he said that I would have to appear in court as the arresting officer tomorrow morning and explain to the judge as too why we arrested him. The whole thing would be a waste of time because the guy would get blasted again before we even got to work, unless his wife didn't kill him first.

The alternative would be to give him a ride a block away and tell him to go home and sober up. Bill then made a bet with me, that if we did the latter, our drunk would show up again on our side of the street later in the night. The Oak Park Police would dump him back in our district so they wouldn't have to be bothered to make an arrest. I said, "OK, let's take him into Oak Park and put him on a bench, and we won't see him the rest of the night." Needless to say, I lost the bet – which was a cup of coffee. An hour later, our drunk appeared back in our area, only this time he was four blocks further in to our district, lying on a park bench courtesy of the Oak Park Police. This time we gave the drunk a ride home and turned him over to his wife. We could see why the guy got drunk; she was about six foot tall, weighed 200 pounds, and looked as if she had been in a horror movie somewhere.

During the night, we took a break and stopped at a restaurant at the west end of the district to get something to eat. This also turned into another learning experience. I noticed that when we entered the restaurant, the people in it stared at us; some smiled and some didn't. Because we both went in the restaurant, my partner called the district and gave the desk sergeant the phone number where we could be reached. During those days, the only radio we had was in the squad car. We didn't carry any portables at that time.

Bill knew the owner and introduced me to him. His name was Gus; he was Greek and looked as if he enjoyed eating the food in his restaurant, as he weighed about 300 pounds. After we sat in a booth, Gus came over to us and informed us that there was a drunk sitting in the rear booth who was giving the waitress a bad time. He also said that the guy liked to fight. Could we do something about it, maybe just talk to the guy? Bill told Gus that we would take care of the problem. When Gus walked away, Bill said, "See, that's one of the drawbacks of being a cop, get used to it. If we were a couple of plumbers, we wouldn't have to worry about this bullshit."

My partner told me to just sit tight and go ahead and order something and he would be right back. I watched him sit next to the drunk and just kept smiling at him while he talked to him. After a few minutes, Bill returned and sat down and smiled at me and said, "No problem, let's eat." One minute later, the drunk got up, apologized to the waitress, paid his bill, smiled at Bill, and almost ran out the front door. I asked him how he had gotten that drunk to leave so fast. Bill explained that he could smile at the same time he talked about bad things that could happen to a drunk. Bill had told the drunk that he had already called for a wagon and that it would park in the back and that the drunk would be taken outside and stripped naked, transported to jail, and put in a cell with two female impersonators who liked other guys, especially drunks. Bill told him that if he left the restaurant before the wagon arrived, he might escape. He told me that sometimes when you smile at someone and tell them bad things that could happen to them, they believe you're serious. It doesn't work all the time, but it is always worth a try; instead of getting hostile with someone, you could wind up in a battle. I thought to myself, *They sure can't teach you this stuff in the academy. I sure have a lot to learn about this job.*

Nothing else happened the rest of the night except I did write my first parking ticket for being too close to a fire hydrant. The watch sure went a lot faster working in a squad than walking a beat; the only place to be was in a squad car, that's for sure. Beats should be for older guys who are probably worn out anyway from handling hundreds of goofy jobs over the years. For the first time since I got on the job, I felt as if I did the right thing. I really could get to like this stuff.

Chapter 8

Dog Bites and Me

The next day, I was back on a beat again. *Oh well*, I thought, *my time will come.* The next shift was the day watch, from 8:00 AM to 4:00 PM. This watch was the least active, and of course, there were school crossings that had to be covered. I was assigned to a different school crossing in the district at 8:00 AM, at noon, and at 3:00 PM. Talk about being bored. This was it. Until one day, an eight-year-old boy who had been teasing a stray dog got bit on the hand and was bleeding pretty well. I knew that the boy would have to go through a series of rabies shots if the dog got away, and that they were extremely painful. I tried to get the dog into a yard by enticing him with a sandwich that one of the other kids had, but that didn't work because the stupid dog ran out in the street and tried to bite a tire on a passing car. The car won.

I called the district for a squad car to meet me, and I told them what had happened. They made out a dog bite report and told the boy's mother to take the boy to a doctor and that the police would take care of the dog's examination at the health department and get back to her. I found a box and put the dog in it, and the squad took me to the district along with the dog. He explained that the dog's head would have to be taken to the health department by me to be examined for rabies.

Then he said that was my job and that I could find a saw in the garage to cut off the dog's head. He said he was sorry that he couldn't have a squad car take me downtown so I would have to take a bus. I went to the garage to find the saw for the unpleasant task of decapitating the dog. I was getting nauseous just thinking about it. One of the guys who was upstairs overheard the desk sergeant telling me how to handle this case. He introduced himself as John Beck and proceeded to tell me that I had better make friends with a local veterinarian and maybe he would cut the dog's head off for me and even dispose of the rest of the body.

I guess he felt sorry for me, because he put me and the dog in his squad car and drove down the street to his friendly vet and said that he owed him a favor. John took the box with the dog and went into the vet's clinic. After five minutes, he came out with the dog's head wrapped in a plastic in a different box. We drove back to the station, and he gave me directions to the health department and told me which bus to take. I thanked him and told him I owed him one.

Here I was in full uniform, carrying a box with a dog's head in it on a hot July day. Probably the other people on the bus thought I was out shopping on city time. I just started thinking how this job involved something every day and nothing was ever the same. I made my delivery to the health department and gave them a copy of the dog bite report. They told me that they would get in touch with the victim's parents about the results of the rabies examination and that my job was over and that I need to go back to the district.

It was a nicer bus ride returning to work, and I kind of felt as if I had helped the little boy who had been bitten, and I hoped that the dog did not have rabies. I got back to the station, and it was time for check off roll call, which was OK by me.

The desk sergeant told me that I was assigned to a different beat tomorrow, then asked me how I liked the job so far. I told him, "So far, it's not too bad, Sarge, but it sure is different." Then he said, "You ain't seen nothin' yet, lad." This seems to be a popular expression used around here.

Chapter 9

The Mob, the Captain, and Me

The next day when I reported for roll call, I was informed that I had been assigned to a beat at the east end of the district. I would be on Chicago Avenue between Pulaski Road and Kedzie Avenue. I thought, *OK, that's no surprise; I hadn't been on that beat before so at least I would be looking at something different.* Little did I realize how different it would be. The sergeant told me that I had also been given an added assignment on my beat. He explained that the captain of the district wanted me to sit in a poolroom that was located on Chicago Avenue in the 3500 block, and to make sure that there wasn't any gambling going on in the place. If there was, I should arrest the offenders immediately. Needless to say, I thought that this was an odd assignment for me to get; I thought that this was a job for the detectives. I asked the sergeant if this was the proper way to investigate gambling, and he said, "Let me explain the facts of this situation."

The sergeant, Jim Fahey, said that the two owners of the poolroom, Phil and Tony Guzaldo, had been raided by a downtown organized crime gambling unit for booking horses and sports. They were taking bets on the phone as well as from people in the area who walked in and placed bets with them. He explained that when something like that happened, it was an embarrassment to the captain of the district, Tom

Kelly, and that the captain had to take whatever means necessary to stop this type of activity.

Sergeant Fahey also explained that the two station detectives who had been working the east end of the district that day had been dumped and put back in uniform because they didn't uncover this bookmaking operation before the boys from downtown did. He then explained that somebody had to take the rap for this, and it sure as hell wasn't going to be the captain. That was why I had been assigned to the poolroom to prevent this type of operation from ever happening again. I told him that I was still on probation and that this wasn't a good position for me to be in. I also told him that I didn't just fall off a turnip truck and that I was going to do my job if I observed any gambling going on there and let the chips fall where they may. He told me that the dagoes were running that poolroom and that it belonged to a gambling boss by the name of Joe Gagliano and his assistant, Willie Messino, and that they ran all the gambling in the district. "So do what you gotta do," he said.

When I was leaving the station, a veteran detective, whom I will call Frank, said that he would like to talk to me for a minute and to meet him outside. He told me that he had overheard the sergeant giving me my assignment and wanted to explain a few things to me before I left. Frank told me that he knew some people that I knew and that he just didn't want to see me get screwed up, and that this conversation was off the record. I told him no problem. He told me that there was probably gambling going on in the district and that another agency coming in and making a raid was an embarrassment to the captain of the district. I told him that had been explained to me by the sergeant, but I couldn't understand why it was necessary to put a uniformed officer in the place.

At this point, he said that Captain Kelly was taking care of his position by putting an officer inside the place to prevent any further violations taking place. He said that it was also very possible for the downtown unit that made the raid to come back to see if the gambling had ceased after the raid. Frank explained that if the poolroom was raided again, the captain would be dumped and transferred out of the district, so he detailed an officer in the poolroom to prevent this.

I began to get a little nervous because I didn't like being made a fall guy, and I was a little pissed off, to say the least. Frank then told me that there probably wouldn't be anything going on in the poolroom anyway, especially after they found out that I was going to be sitting in front of them. But if I did happen to see anything, "think about it before you do anything." Then he told me that a situation like this had happened once before and the officer in question had gotten detailed to Trumbull Park at 106th and Bensley for a few months because he made the wrong decision. I asked him what the hell that meant. Frank said he would give me a lift to the poolroom and not to worry, everything would work out fine. I got to the poolroom and walked in and met one of the owners; he introduced himself as Phil Guzaldo. Phil was one of the brothers who were busted for bookmaking by the downtown gambling unit. If ever I saw a guy who looked like an outfit wannabe, it was Phil. He was wearing a sports shirt with a monogramed pocket, black slacks, and alligator shoes. He also had a gold necklace around his neck and a very large diamond ring. He looked as if he didn't refuse too many meals in his time either; he was about fifty years old and balding. He was extremely friendly and didn't act surprised when I walked into the poolroom. Obviously, he knew that I was going to show up to babysit the place. He told me to have a seat and shoot some pool if I wanted to.

It was only 10:00 AM so there wasn't anyone else around, so I thought, *So far so good.* Another guy walked in and introduced himself as Tony Guzaldo and offered me some coffee and told me to make myself at home. Tony wasn't surprised that a uniformed policeman was sitting in his poolroom; it was like an everyday occurrence, and this was really a joke. Tony also dressed as if he was a leftover from a mob movie. He wore a sports shirt, dark slacks, and brown alligator loafers also; they must have made a score in a shoe store somewhere. Tony wore a gold chain around his neck that was bigger than Phil's, and sure as hell he had a very large diamond on his pinkie. He was about five foot six, 145 pounds, and bald. When he walked in, I noticed that he had a newspaper under his arm, and I thought I saw a scratch sheet inside the paper. I thought that I was going to have a very interesting day, that's for sure

I noticed that there was a mirror in each corner of the front window, which had been positioned so that anyone who approached the poolroom could be seen. I thought that was interesting. There was also a shoeshine stand at the front of the room, which was next to a telephone booth. There were about six card tables set up as well as two pool tables. Pictures of Italian sports stars were hanging all over the walls as well and a two-by-three-feet by framed picture of Al Capone sitting in a box seat at Wrigley Field, talking to a Chicago Cub player. Capone was surrounded by his other goombahs and looked as if he was having a good time. At the rear of the room were pool cues on a rack on the wall, and below that was a table with a coffeepot, cups, and old donuts, some of which had been half eaten. I also noticed numerous decks of playing cards, chips, pads of paper, and a racing form. I glanced in the phone booth, and above the seat under the pay phone was a ledge with a pad of paper. I thought, *Herion, you got yourself in a world of shit*, and I wondered how I was going to handle things. I began to examine the position that I had been put in and couldn't make up my mind as to whom to dislike more, the bad guys or the captain that detailed me to this job.

Around noon, a few locals came in the poolroom and kind of looked at me and didn't know whether to shit or go blind. I just said hello and told them no, I wasn't the doorman, and that I was a police impersonator. Believe it or not, some of these dopes believed it. A very large black fella came in and said hello and asked if I was waiting for a shoeshine? I figured what the hell, I might as well look neat. The black guy said his name was Sam and asked how long I had been waiting to get a shoeshine. Obviously, he wasn't aware of the situation I was in. While I was getting the shine, I noticed the way the mirrors were set up each side of the front windows. I was able to see anyone who was walking toward the poolroom. I guess Sam sat in this seat and was probably the lookout for the Guzaldo brothers, to warn them of impending police activity in the area. About 12:10 PM, I heard the phone ring in the phone booth, and Tony Guzaldo walked in the booth and sat down, closed the door so that his back was blocking the door and so no one could see inside or what he was doing. I would assume the son of a bitch was writing down horse bets, even when he knew that a cop was sitting only ten feet away from him.

These guys are a real piece of work; they don't give a shit about anybody or anything. I will admit that I had an urge to pull open the door of the phone booth and grab the pad he was writing on and arrest the bastard. Then I could vision myself driving to the South Side of Chicago every day for who knows how long – not a good idea. But on the other hand, if I grabbed him with all the bets and arrested him, the captain would probably thank me for doing my job. "Are you kidding me?" Tony stayed in the booth until about 1:00 PM and kept answering the phone and writing on that pad; at least he wasn't walking around the place with a scratch sheet and talking about how much action he took in. I've got to admit that every time I saw anything like an unmarked squad car drive by, I did get a little nervous thinking that they were the dicks from downtown and were going to raid the joint again.

Within a short time, some other shady-looking guys wandered in the place; and before you knew it, some gin games were going, and some guys started shooting pool. But there wasn't any money on the table at least; they just kept score and were playing for fun, of course. I did overhear a couple of wise guys talking about the raid the day before; apparently, they were in the poolroom when the raid took place. They said that it was a good thing that Sam had spotted them coming so Tony and Phil had time to hide the whole week's action in the hollow part of a table that had been made for just such an occasion.

All the cops found was a marked scratch sheet and a few old horse bets that they found in the garbage can. It was enough to lock up Tony and Phil, and that's all they cared about.

Just listening to the conversation of the guys in the poolroom was very amusing, to say the least. It seemed that everybody talked the same. To say hello, they always seemed to put a "yo" in front of a name like 'Yo Paulie, how you doin? How's the family?' Or maybe, 'Vito, how's it going?' Then mixed in with the greetings, there would be some hugging and sometimes a kiss on the cheek.

All you had to do was change the names and substitute Rocky, or Angelo, or maybe Mario, because that was the way they all said hello. Sometimes they would playfully slap each other in the face. The majority of the boys would be wearing sports shirts, no ties of course, but a lot of gold chains and fancy gold bracelets. There also seemed to be a lot of guys wearing pinkie rings; and to top it off, a few of them were wearing sunglasses. Parodi cigars were also very popular, as were Cuban cigars. Everyone else smoked cigarettes; no one smoked a pipe. The ceiling, which at one time appeared to have been painted white, was now almost brown from all the smoking going on in the place. They didn't open the front door to get some air in the place either; they had to keep it locked in case some unwanted visitors tried to enter.

I thought it was a little strange how much some of these guys talked openly when I was only a few feet away from them. I guess they thought that I was an OK guy because I was in the place and I must be a friend of Tony and Phil, or maybe they just didn't give a shit what I overheard. Like one goof was asking about the poolroom down the street and wondered if they had been raided too.

I found out later that a guy by the name of Cosmo ran the other poolroom located two blocks east; he also booked horses and sports, and was related to the Guzaldo brothers. That was something to remember in the future, if the opportunity ever presented itself.

Then my new friend Sam, the shoeshine man and lookout for the Guzaldos, told one of the boys that he heard that a guy by the name of Joe Gags and Willie were pretty upset because of the raid. Willie's last name was Messino, and both these guys were the outfit bosses in the area. They also controlled all the jukeboxes, vending machines, and any other type of gambling, like punchboards, jar games, and a crap game every now and then. Their boss was another mob guy by the name of Jackie "the Lackey" Cerone, a reputed killer.

As things turned out, I had to sweat out a week in that dam poolroom, wondering if the downtown detectives were going to double back and bust the room again. Every day was the same in there – Phil answering the phone, Phil playing gin rummy, and all the other goofs trying to act like Murder Inc. At the end of the week, Captain Kelly saw it fit to parole me and assign me to another detail. While I was in that poolroom, I started out smoking one pack of Luckies a day; but at the end of the week, I was up to 2 1/2 packs.

I knew one thing for sure that I will not forget why or who put me in the poolroom. And for what reason – in my opinion – the blame has to be both on the police and the outfit; and who knows someday I might be in a position to get even. As the saying goes, "What goes around comes around." As things turned out later, I was in a position to lock up Tony, Phil, and Cosmo more than once. I even offered to sit in the poolroom again, but for some reason they turned me down.

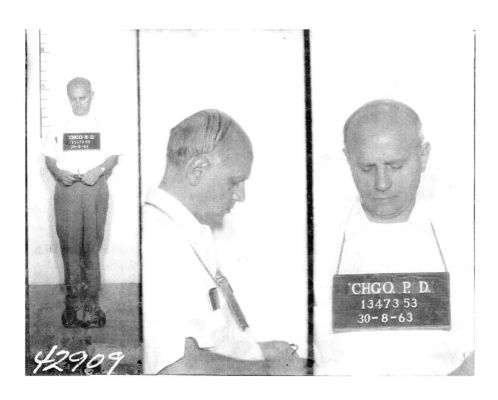

42909-8|30|63 Herion Co
Anthony Guzaldo MW 50 Gamb.
(Joseph Rini)

Anthony doesn't look to happy does he?
When I busted him in the pool hall I
told him that I was going to relieve him
of his favorite phone booth because it
was part of his bookmaking operation.
This made Anthony very sad.

Chapter 10

Hit and Run

I remember the day I bought my first new car. It was a 1955 Ford Fairlane Hardtop. I traded my 1951 Chevy Impala on it, and my uncle Earl paid the difference. It was tan and white, and the price was $1,900 with tax. A new car can really make you feel good. Everything else even looks better for some reason. I came home one night after working the four-to-twelve shift and parked my car in front of our apartment at 5455 West Augusta Boulevard. I recall it was the end of June 1957, a warm summer night. About 1:45 AM, we were awakened by a very loud crash; and my wife, Genevieve, told me that she heard a baby screaming. I told her to take it easy. I would call the Park District police because they handle all accidents on the boulevards. She rushed to get downstairs while I was taking my sweet time, never thinking that my car was involved in the accident. When we got outside, I got the shock of my life. There was my 1955 Ford, demolished and knocked up on the parkway against a tree.

There wasn't any other car around. All there was were pieces of a grill, headlight, chrome, and a green fender. The son of a bitch had taken off after he hit my car. Just another hit-and-run case. When the police finally showed up, I made the necessary reports, but I knew that this case was not going to be the top priority in their life, and they would probably just file it away. Well, it was a top priority to me, so who says I can't look for the bastards?

That afternoon, I went to work and told my partner, Bob, what had happened, and I told him that I was going to snoop around and see if I could find the car that hit mine. He was raring to get in on the hunt with me. We drove east on Augusta Boulevard, hoping to find a green car somewhere along the way or on a side street; it couldn't have gotten very far after he hit my car. We got lucky about ten blocks east on a side street; there was a green 1949 Ford with a missing grill and a right front fender gone. It was really screwed up. Naturally, the license plates had been removed, but we could check the VIN number to track down the owner. There happened to be a saloon on the southwest corner, so we talked to the bartender, who as it turned out would be on duty until 2:00 AM that morning. He was shown the 1949 Ford down the street, but he said he had never seen the car before in the neighborhood. He added that just before closing time, two guys and a woman carrying a baby had come in the tavern and used a pay phone to call a cab. He remembered that the cab was an American United because when the cab parked in front, the cab driver blew his horn, and that's when he saw it. We contacted the American United cab company dispatcher and asked him about a pickup one of his cabs made at the saloon the previous night. We told him that it was a police investigation, but he told us that we would have to come into their office on Western Avenue and speak to his supervisor before that information could be given out.

The next day, my partner picked me up in his own car, and we went to the cab company office. We identified ourselves to the supervisor and told him that the people that got in his cab were running from the law because they were suspected of being involved in a robbery and a hit-and-run. I kind of exaggerated a little. The supervisor let me talk to the cab driver on the phone, and he told us that he had picked up two guys and a woman carrying an infant from the tavern where the 1949 Ford had been abandoned. The two men were about twenty to twenty-five years old and spoke with Southern accents and appeared to be drunk. Luckily, he remembered the address where he dropped them off. Next stop was 879 North Paulina Avenue where we knocked on the door of the first-floor apartment. A guy opened the door, and we identified ourselves as police officers. He told us his name was Jimmy Hendrix and asked us why we were pointing guns at him. We told him that it was better to have guns pointed at him than hearing them make a loud noise. We also congratulated him for being very observant, and then asked him about the green 1949 Ford and why he left the scene of an accident. When he quit shaking, he told us that he did own a green 1949 Ford and that he bought it in Jasper, Alabama, at a used car lot in his father's name, Clayton Hendrix. He said that he paid $120 for it around May 1, 1957, and he drove it to Chicago, but he didn't own it anymore. He said that he traded it to a guy named Billy Gilbert for a 1946 Chevy coupe and that Gilbert lived at 522 Lake Street, Maywood, Illinois, first-floor rear apartment. About two or three weeks earlier, Billy Gilbert and a guy named Earl Ivey had told Hendrix that Gilbert had given the Ford to Ivey for work that Ivey did on a Willys owned by Gilbert. I asked Hendrix when was the last time he saw Gilbert or Ivey. He told us that Ivy and Gilbert had shown up at his apartment about 2:30 AM the day before, and had a woman and a child with them. He said that he knew her as Alma and thought she was Gilbert's girlfriend. They stayed the night and then left about 9:00 AM. They told him that they were going home in a cab. He also added that he had seen Ivy driving the Ford about a week ago. We took our guns out of Hendrix's face and told him that we would be back if he lied to us or warned Gilbert or Ivy.

We found 522 Lake Street in Maywood to be a run-down building just like the one on Paulina Street in Chicago. We knocked on the rear-door apartment; a white guy with a hillbilly accent answered it. We showed our identification as Smith & Wesson .38s. At that point he was asked his name; he replied Earl Ivey and thought that we were the FBI and he was on the most wanted list because he hit a car and left the scene. He thought that he had better get away because he didn't have a driver's license. He went on to say that he had a few beers during the night also. I asked who was with him, and he said he was with Billy Gilbert and a girl named Alma and her kid. We noticed that there were four mattresses on the floor and about forty empty beer cans as well, also pizza boxes – what a way to live. It takes all kinds, I guess. Ivey was placed under arrest and brought into the Twenty-eighth District where he was charged with a variety of traffic offenses. Ivey couldn't make bail for two days so he sat in the lockup. He gave me his insurance company's name, but that turned out to be bogus, of course; and when his court date came up, Mr. Earl Ivey was no where to be found. As far as I know, he's back in Alabama laughing. The main thing was that I got self-satisfaction from this whole ordeal, with help from my partner, Bob Peters. I've got to admit it was kind of fun being sort of a vigilante cop; as it turned out, it wouldn't be the last time.

Chapter II

The Flying Squad: Ryan's Raiders

Well, I guess it was my turn in the barrel again because after I was back a couple of weeks, my lieutenant notified me to report to 1121 South State Street, tenth floor the next day at 4:00 PM. I was to report to a Captain Robert Ryan. I asked the lieutenant what this was all about, and his reply was "Just do it, Herion, and make sure you're there on time." I couldn't figure out what the hell was going on at police headquarters, or what they needed me for, but I didn't have a choice anyway.

I reported as ordered and found myself in a large room that was used for racket court during the day. I was with about fifty other guys in uniform; some were detectives, and I didn't know any of them. I spoke to a couple of guys and asked them if they knew what was going on. Some of them thought that we were going to be used for a presidential detail or as an honor guard for some foreign dignitary. At 4:00 PM sharp, a door opened from behind the bench where the judge's chambers usually are and a captain of police introduced himself as Captain Robert Ryan. He told us that we were going to be part of a new unit called the Flying Squad and be a task force that would be sent to troubled areas throughout the city. Also, we wouldn't know which district we would work in until we reported to work that day. Any arrests that we would make would be handled by detectives assigned to the Flying

Squad. We would supply our own typewriters, the necessary forms, and do our own paperwork. Our job was to work the district where we were assigned that day and to help them in anyway possible. After a while, this unit would be known as "Ryan's Raiders" throughout the city. Captain Ryan appeared to be in his fifties and had been on the job at least twenty years. He seemed as if he knew what he was doing and gave us the impression that this "Flying Squad" was his brainstorm and wanted it to be successful.

We were formed into ten-man squads, nine men walking a beat and one man would be on a three-wheeler. We would be supervised by a sergeant who was in a squad car; if there was anything that we needed, we would have to notify the sergeant, and he would help us anyway he could.

It was a good idea to flood a district with a lot of police and make arrests for any and all violations of the law. At first, the local district cops were a little offended by our presence, but that changed when we rescued a few of them from some hostile situations.

We sure didn't waste any time getting out in the street. That first day, we were transported by wagons to the Second District, also known as the "Deuce," which was located on the South Side of Chicago in the Black Belt. We were told that the crime rate had gotten worse over the past year and that we would be a welcome sight to the guys in the district. Our sergeant's last words to us were, "Get out and get them before they get you." I thought that sounded interesting.

I was teamed up with a fella by the name of Bill, who had been on the job about ten years and was a pretty sharp guy. He was from the Thirtieth District and said that he had been a detective, but he had gotten dumped because he pinched some politician's son and didn't show him any favoritism because of his old man. "Oh well, shit happens," he said.

We were assigned to an area around Forty-eighth and Langley on the South Side of the city, which was entirely populated by blacks. The neighborhood looked like a war zone – boarded-up buildings, vacant lots, trash all over the place. Broken bottles were everywhere, and the ever-popular bunch of stray dogs wandered the streets and alleys. A lot of bars, liquor stores, barber and beauty shops, as well as storefront churches, a decent-looking restaurant was on the corner, so we decided to take a chance and get some coffee and figure out a plan of attack.

The guy behind the counter was a male, white, about fifty-five years old, six foot two, and 220 pounds. He had a blackjack in his left rear pocket and a .45 cal. automatic in a holster on his right side and obviously didn't much care who saw it. When he saw us come in, he had a big smile on his face and was real glad to see us. He told us his name was Sid and that he owned the place. I noticed that Sid was also selling packaged-goods liquor, which was on a shelf on the back wall. He had his liquor license displayed next to the cash register where everyone could see it. The goofy part was that this was just a grill, not a liquor store. As time went on, I learned that most stores in the Black Belt sold liquor, such as beauty shops, barbershops, and drugstores. I guess they were all making money, or they wouldn't bother with it, would they?

   I just had to ask Sid if it was necessary to carry a blackjack and a .45 while he was working, which was a dumb question, I guess. Sid just stared at me and said, "Officer, if you were robbed and shot at seven times in the past two years, what would you carry?" Besides that, since he had been packing his stuff for the last three months, he hadn't had a problem. I guess there was a method to his madness.

   I said, "If it's that bad around her, why stay in the neighborhood?"

   "'Cause business is good, Officer, what else?"

   Sid asked if we were new in the district. We explained that we were assigned to the area just for the night and that we were part of a new crime-fighting unit and that if he needed any help, we would be close by. During all this conversation with Sid, it was kind of hard to keep our eyes off the cockroaches that were playing tag on the kitchen sink and the bread on the rear counter. Bill suggested that we hit the street and earn our pay as he swiped a roach off my sleeve.

   Bill suggested that maybe we should hang around the corner of Forty-eighth and Langley because there was a Stop sign. We were on foot, which was a big disadvantage. When a car would stop at the Stop sign, we would be able to see if the car had a city sticker. If it didn't, we had reasonable grounds to stop the car and talk to the driver and check his driver's license; and if the driver seemed nervous, we could make a search of the vehicle for contraband. If the search proved negative, we could give the driver a ticket for not having a city sticker. That sure sounded like a plan to me. "Let's do it."

   Sure as hell, in about ten minutes, one of the cars that stopped at the sign didn't have a city sticker on the windshield, and we spoke to the driver, who was a twenty-two-year-old black guy and couldn't produce his driver's license. He said his name was Tyrone Wanamaker, and he surrendered his license to a policeman who gave him a ticket for speeding. He stated that it was not his car, that he had borrowed it from his cousin Willie Johnson. Tyrone told us that Willie lived on the West Side of Chicago. My partner told Tyrone to get out of the car and to let me look to see if I could find the sticker on the floor or the glove compartment. Under the front seat, I found a loaded .38 blue steel revolver and a box of .38 ammunition. In the meantime, Bill had searched Tyrone and had him handcuffed before I even told him what I found. I asked him how he knew the guy was dirty. "Just a gut feeling, Don," he said. "Like the old saying, sometimes you get the bear and sometimes the bear gets you."

Tyrone was placed under arrest and continued to deny that he knew anything about the gun and that it must belong to his cousin Willie. About this time, we began to notice that a crowd had gathered around us and some guys were making nasty remarks about our heritage and that we were racists as well as other things.

Under the circumstances, Bill suggested that instead of waiting for a wagon to transport the prisoner to the district lockup, maybe we could drive Tyrone's car to the station and then we wouldn't have to wait for a tow truck. Tyrone agreed that he would appreciate it if we didn't tow his car because he didn't have the money to pay the towing charge.

Tyrone was charged with a weapons charge, UUW, and failure to possess a city sticker. He was processed by our detectives, and I signed a complaint and would be the complaining witness against Tyrone in racket court.

By the time the processing was over, so was the shift; and we were relieved. We were told to report back to 1121 South State Street same place, same time the next day. It was also a Friday night, and a full moon was expected to be out; so be ready for an interesting night.

The next day, we were sent to the Eleventh District, which was located on the West Side of Chicago; and whoever said that Friday night in the ghetto with a full moon was going to be interesting sure knew what they were talking about. My partner and I were assigned to the area of Roosevelt and Pulaski Road. The first hour we were on the street we heard a squad coming, with lights and siren on; and it turned into an alley around the corner from us. It seems that an elderly black man in his sixties had been strong-armed and robbed by two gangbangers who took the sweater off his back and $7 USC. Apparently they were not satisfied, so they cut his neck and part of his ear. If we had been walking in that direction, maybe we would have caught the two punks in the act. Who knows?

I recall that night very well, because when we checked into the district station to use the washroom, we spoke to the desk sergeant who had a police radio on and asked him how things were going out in the street. He said that he would be glad when the shift was over in three hours and he could go home because everybody was going a little nuts because of the full moon. There already had been nine shootings, three of which were fatal; five stabbings, only one fatal; and two rapes; seven stickups; and numerous fights. He also suggested that we get back out in the street because we sure as hell weren't gonna catch any bad guys in the station. "Yes, sir," we said and got the hell out of there, back to our assignment. With us being in uniform and on foot, it was a little tough for us to get near any of the dope dealers who were on almost every street corner. I also learned a valuable lesson that night. It wasn't a good idea to walk underneath any apartment building windows that were located on Roosevelt Road because it seemed that more than a few beer and wine bottles would be dropped accidentally or on purpose out the windows whenever a cop would pass by.

There was also an abundance of bars and lounges in the Eleventh District. Talk about loud music. It seemed that everybody was having a good time, smoking dope and drinking. Oh well, I found out that there were more than two zoos in the Chicago area. There were three. The Eleventh District was the third.

For the next couple of years, I did about every job a cop could do in a district. I worked the desk; relieved on squad cars, the wagon, the three-wheeler, the lockup, and more school crossings; as well as directed traffic.

On November 10, 1956, I got married to my girlfriend, Genevieve Langer. She had put up with me all through the police academy, put up with all my bitching about the job; and if it wasn't for her, I probably would have quit and got a job with the gas company. To tell the truth, there were times in the future that I think that she kind of had the same thoughts.

My first two years on the job I must admit were really not that bad, except for a few bad experiences I had on some of these details. During that time, I and another cop whom I had worked with on occasion became good friends and were to become partners on a squad car, as well as when Commander Mike Foley made us vice detectives. His name was Bob Peters. Believe me, it is very important to have a good partner on this job, 'cause a lot of times your life depends on him. Bob was ten years older than I was but came on the job about a year after I did. He was an air force veteran of World War II, and flew a lot of missions over the mountains in Burma, which was known as the Hump. Bob was a hell of a guy and a great partner.

We would talk about teaming up and try to get assigned to a squad car together so we could get out in the street and do some serious police work. Prior to Superintendent O. W. Wilson taking over the Chicago Police Department in 1960, there were thirty-eight police districts in Chicago with a police captain in charge of each who owed his allegiance to the ward boss in which the district was located. In the Twenty-eighth District we only had three squad cars, one sergeant's car, one paddy wagon, and some three-wheelers; so obviously getting assigned to a squad car was not the easiest thing to do. But miracles happen, I guess, because at the end of 1957 the two guys who were assigned to car 121 were made detectives, and Bob and I were assigned to car 121 on a trial basis to see what we could do.

The men assigned to the same squad car must have confidence in each other. They take turns driving, and it is important that they have confidence in his partner's driving ability. Partners must be compatible since they spend a great deal of time together. I was lucky, we got along just fine, until I would mention that he was ten years older than I was.

Chapter 12

The Puerto Rican Connection

During the summer and fall of 1957, we had a rash of house and apartment burglaries at the east end of our district, which happened to be in our section. All these burglaries happened during the day watch, and the bad guys were really having a field day and making some real good scores. The only clue we had was that some witnesses thought that they had seen a couple of Spanish-looking guys in the area, but they weren't sure.

Needless to say, my partner Bob Peters and I took this stuff personal, and whoever was hitting these places were pissing us off. We finally caught a break one day when someone reported a couple of suspicious men at 4346 West Augusta Boulevard. We happened to be close by and damn near caught the bastards, and would have if the guy who called the police didn't tell them that the cops were on the way. "You better get out of here," he told them. They had just broken in a second floor apartment and were about to clean the place out when the witness, Frank Ruzika, did his good deed.

When we found that they had fled the scene of the crime, we scoured the neighborhood with some other squads, but to no avail. The witness described the two guys as Spanish looking and about twenty-five to thirty years old; they had to be our guys. He also told us that they ran east on Augusta Boulevard. And it seemed to him that they were running toward a yellow-and-white 1953 Chevy that was parked across the boulevard, and kind of hesitated for a second but seemed to change their minds and didn't try to get in the car. We checked out the car, which was locked, but we could see a Puerto Rican newspaper on the front seat. The witness told us that he had never seen the car before and that it didn't belong to any of his neighbors, as far as he knew.

Bob and I informed our patrol sergeant, Bart Hines, about the Chevy and that it was a good chance that it was their car, but they didn't have enough time to get in it when they were told the cops were on the way. We asked Sergeant Hines if the car could be kept under surveillance because they had no idea that we knew it was theirs, and they would come back for it later when things cooled off, and we could bust the bastards. Unfortunately, Sergeant Hines didn't agree with us and had us call a tow truck to bring the car into the Twenty-eighth District for further examination. After the detectives got in the car, they found in the trunk a couple of mink coats wrapped in a bedsheet, two sets of silverware, and a coin collection. Obviously, it was loot from other scores they made earlier.

A letter from a car dealer, Mars Oldsmobile, was found under the front seat that thanked a Francisco Soto for purchasing the Chevy in May 1957. We contacted Mars Oldsmobile, and the manager told us that the Chevy had been repossessed by them a week ago and was supposed to be in their used car lot. They gave us Francisco's address as 1942 North Cleveland Avenue, Chicago, Illinois. We also told the manager that they had better check their cars more often because some burglars in our district were using the Chevy.

It just so happened that Bob and I were off duty the next two days; but wouldn't it be nice if we could grab these two rats and lock them up for giving us all this aggravation the last couple of months? Officially we didn't notify our superiors as to what our plans were. We were sure that they would frown upon our off-duty activity. *The hell with them, what we're going to do gives me another shit detail, forget about it.* Next stop, 1942 North Cleveland Avenue. We spoke to the landlord, who told us that he thought Mr. Soto had moved out as he hadn't seen him around the last couple of days. He consented to let us search the apartment, maybe it was because we let him believe that Soto was a child molester and attacked a ten-year-old girl. Looking around the apartment, we found a couple of photographs on a shelf that apparently had been overlooked. The landlord identified Soto in one of the photos and also identified the guy in the photo with Soto as Santiago Herrera. He told us that the two of them were always together and had seen them in a yellow-and-white Chevy a couple of times. He also remembered that they both talked about how tough it was being waiters on the night shift in some downtown restaurant.

The following day, we made arrangements to show the photos to the witness, Frank Ruzika, who positively identified both men as the crooks he saw. Next stop was the Waiters Union at 205 West Wacker Drive, Chicago, where we identified ourselves as police officers to the secretary of the union, Mr. Red Sanders. He revealed that Santiago Herrera's last address was 710 North Clark Street, Chicago, Illinois, but that he hasn't worked lately, and he hadn't seen Francisco Soto for a while either.

Well, when you're hot you're hot, so it was on to 710 North Clark Street, Chicago, Illinois. Santiago was nowhere to be found, but his wife, Onidi, still lived there. She told us that her husband had gone back to New York because there was more work there, but had forgot when he had left or what address he would be staying at in New York City. We found a letter on the kitchen table that was addressed to Santiago Garcia at that address and asked Onidi if that was another name used by Santiago? She admitted that he did use the name *Garcia* on occasion.

I again contacted the waiter's union and informed Mr. Sanders of the name of Santiago Garcia also, and asked him if he would contact us in the event he heard of Soto, Herrera a.k.a. Garcia turned up at the union hall in New York City. He agreed to notify us if he heard anything about the two subjects.

After a few days of waiting, we became impatient, and I decided to make a call to the waiter's union in New York City. I spoke to E. Sarni Zucca, the secretary of Local 1 at 140 West Forty-third Street. Sometimes, a white lie is necessary in a situation like this to get cooperation from someone who really has no concern about the problems of Chicago. I told Mr. Zucca that the two bad guys we were looking for were child molesters of the worst kind and had fled the Chicago area because they knew we were closing in on them and they probably felt safer in New York City where they could get lost.

At that point, he begged me to give him their names so that he could check and see if the bastards were union members in New York. I gave Zucca their names, and he told me that he had four children of his own and hated child molesters and would love to see them locked up. Checking his records, all of a sudden he started laughing and said, "Yes, sir, they both just renewed their union dues the other day and have to report to the union hall every day for an assignment." We thanked Mr. Zucca and requested that he keep this investigation confidential so that the molesters are not alarmed; he agreed but requested that he be allowed to kick the shit out of both of them before they were arrested.

The next thing we had to do was to inform the detectives assigned to the case so that warrants could be obtained for Herrera and Soto. The detective bureau in New York was informed of the facts in the case, which would now be handled by our detectives and their detectives. A silly thought did flash through both our heads about just maybe we could go to New York and transport the prisoners back to Chicago to face charges; after all, we did have a little to do with the investigation. Famous last words were, "FORGET ABOUT IT."

The good news is that the detectives in New York went to the union office one morning and busted or "collared," as they say, Herrera and Soto when they reported to the union office for work. The only way we found out they were busted in New York was because Bob and I drove our "dicks" goofy, asking them every time we saw them if they had heard from New York.

Finally one day they said, "Oh, didn't we tell you, they got locked up in New York and are going to be extradited back to Chicago next week." They then showed us a report concerning the clear-up reports on numerous house and apartment burglaries committed by Herrera and Soto; of course, our names were not mentioned anywhere.

We were a little pissed off about that, but at least we had self-satisfaction knowing that if it wasn't for us snooping around, they probably would never have been caught. It was just another learning experience about being a Chicago cop.

Chapter 13

Teens, Guns, and Murder

On November 19, 1959, about 1:30 AM, my partner Bob Peters and I were cruising north on Pulaski Road toward North Avenue; that's when we saw the post man, George Leslie, who was assigned to that area, walking a beat. George was in his own car and seemed to be following a 1959 Chevrolet station wagon. We pulled alongside him and asked him what was up; George shouted that he thought the guy driving the wagon had abducted a girl who was in the car with him. When the station wagon saw us behind him, he took off north on Pulaski Road at a high rate of speed. The chase was on. He blew the light at North Avenue and was doing about 90 mph when he approached Armitage Avenue, which was four blocks away; he managed to slow down enough to make the turn and go east on Armitage Avenue. This time I was driving, and Bob was on the radio, telling the squad operator that we were involved in a high-speed chase of a '59 Chevy wagon, which could be involved in the abduction of a female. Bob kept the operator apprised of which direction we were headed. When the wagon got near Central Park Avenue, which was four blocks east, he made the turn to fast and rolled the wagon. The wagon skidded on its roof for about one hundred feet. When we got around the corner, the bad guy was running down the middle of Central Park Avenue, pulling the girl with him by her arm. At this point, I was running down the street after them, and that's when I realized that the bastard fired a few shots at me, but missed. I was so frustrated that I couldn't return fire because I was afraid I would hit the girl. Bob had called in that a policeman needed help, and we would have additional cars in the area real soon.

When the bad guy hit an alley at the end of the block, they ran east, which was a T-alley, and then ran around the corner of the T-alley. At that point I was running toward the T-alley when I got the surprise of my life. The bad guy was waiting for me just around the corner of the T-alley when he showed himself between a telephone pole and a brick wall; he had his arm around the girl's neck and a .45 automatic pointed at her head. He told me to stop where I was or he would blow her head off; that's when he cocked the .45 and told me to drop my gun. I told him, "No fucking way, pal." I also told him that I would stop and let him go if he would release the girl. He was grinning at me. He had that .45 pointed at my head and I thought, *Oh shit, this is not working out.* I could see that he was about sixteen or seventeen, and his hand was shaking a little. Then he stuck the .45 back on the girl, who also looked like a kid, and said that he was going to back around the corner and that if anyone followed him, he would kill the girl. I told him, "No problem, just let the girl go, don't hurt her, no one is going to follow you." Squads were pulling up all over the place, including the deputy chief, James Hackett, also known as Captain Midnight by the real police. We told him what had happened and that the guy had fired at us. The whole area was cordoned off, and I thought for sure that we would find the bastard before it got light out; but forget about it, he got away with the girl.

The good news was that some of the items found in the wrecked car he was driving led to his apprehension the next day, by the detectives. And surprise, surprise, he wasn't alone; he was with the same girl who was allegedly his hostage. Her name was Jerry Norwich, age fifteen and a pretty good actress; she sure fooled the hell out of my partner and me and also George Leslie, who had started the whole thing. At least the bastard couldn't shoot straight, so I got lucky anyway.

The reason that they ran from us the other night was because they had just stuck up a tavern at 4747 West Lake Street and they thought we knew that they had pulled the job. They were part of a teenage robbery crew of eight punks: Gary Horton, age seventeen; fifteen-year-old girl Jerry Norwich, whom we had chased in the station wagon –

she participated in the robberies also and displayed a .32 revolver. The rest of the crew was Robert Renteria, age seventeen; Ray Ocasio, age eighteen; James Potter, age seventeen; Joseph DiGiacomo, age seventeen; Angelo Contrerez, age eighteen, and J. Duran, age sixteen. The victims of robberies in Chicago and Oak Park, Illinois, identified them all. All were indicted and received prison sentences except for J. Duran and Jerry Norwich, who were juveniles and were turned over to juvenile hall.

The next time that a police officer ran into Gary Horton, who was now twenty-five years old and was recently released from prison, was on March 29, 1967, at about 10:00 PM. Horton and a female companion, Dahlea Jones, age twenty-three, were in a car traveling north on Cicero Avenue. Sergeant Gerald Doll, age thirty-eight, stopped Horton's car at about 2132 North Cicero Avenue. When Sergeant Doll was exiting his marked squad car, Gary Horton also got out of his car armed with a sawed-off shotgun and shot Sergeant Doll at point-blank range, critically wounding him. Though badly wounded, Sergeant Doll managed to return fire, wounding Horton seriously. Sergeant Doll then collapsed on the street and died. Horton was badly wounded, fled the scene on foot, and was found in a gangway of a house a short distance away. He was in a sitting position and was dead.

Gary Horton was a total nutcase and deserved to die. I thought of how lucky I was that he didn't have a shotgun the night I confronted him in that dark alley. I was lucky, and Sergeant Doll wasn't. When Horton's companion, Dahlea Jones, was questioned as to why Horton shot Sergeant Doll, all she said was that Horton hated the police because they had put him in jail in the past and he wasn't gonna go back.

Chapter 14

Willie Simpson and the Pink Ribbon

We had a stickup guy who was operating at the east end of our district and was getting everybody crazy. This guy robbed, beat, and terrorized people, but only operated on Friday night. He would pick on people who were parking their cars in the garage behind their house; they would most likely be alone, and Friday was also payday for most people. It got dark early in the late fall of the year, which was an advantage for him as well. His modus operandi was to wait in a dark alley for some unsuspecting soul to park their car in their garage; at that time he would enter the garage with the victim, and when the victim closed the garage door, he or she would be at his mercy. The stickup guy would then stick a gun or a switchblade knife in the victim's face and relieve them of all their valuables. Usually the victim had probably been paid that day and had cashed his weekly paycheck. He also took watches, rings, and anything else of value the victim may have had in their possession. On a couple of instances when the victim was a female, he would fondle them and had even raped two of them as well as rob them. He was also known to beat his victims if they didn't cooperate with him. Needless to say, the people in the area were petrified, and a lot of them refused to park their vehicles in their garages for fear of being robbed and beaten. The bad guy was described as black, six foot two, 200 pounds, between thirty and thirty-five years old, and had a six-inch scar on the left side of his neck. He would also wear some kind of stocking mask and always told his victims that if they told the police what had happened to them, he would come back and kill them while they were sleeping in their beds.

One of the victims who happened to be a woman had a very expensive wedding ring on her finger, and the bad guy told her to take it off. The woman tried to take the ring off, but she was unable to do so. She pleaded to the bad guy to please let her have the ring as her husband was dead and it was all she had to remember him by. At that point the bad guy stuck a handkerchief in her mouth so she couldn't scream, and then cut her ring finger off so he could get the ring.

Sometimes the bad guy would rob two or three different people on the same night, but he only seemed to strike on Friday night for some unknown reason. When I worked the four-to-twelve watch, which came around every third month, that was the only time that we had to try and catch this bastard. During our watch in November, he hit at least eleven different victims and obviously got away clean every time. No matter what we did to try and catch this guy, nothing worked. The robbery unit from downtown set up surveillances in the neighborhood on Friday night, but to no avail. The crook would still pull off a robbery; it really got to be an embarrassing situation. I know that you can't take these things personally because it will make you nuts, but this son of a bitch was getting to me, and I was getting very frustrated. One day I got an idea that after we got off the four-to-twelve watch, we were going on days. So I went home after work on a Friday and took off my uniform, had dinner with my wife, Gen, made some small talk, and then told her that I was going over to one of the guys' house to play cards for a few hours. I had a friend who knew about radios fix my car radio so I could get police calls on it. That way, whenever I was in my own car, I would respond to any hot calls that were close by. I would just say that I happened to be passing by the scene so I thought I would stop to see if I could be of any help. That way, I would be able to hear a call of anyone who had been robbed in the area, and just maybe I could get lucky and grab the bastard. I positioned myself around some alleys around Ohio Street and Homan Avenue, and hoped that maybe if I kept my eye on any car that would pull in an alley, I would see the black guy go in the garage with them, and I could grab him.

Well, after three weeks, my undercover surveillance did not work, and I was really getting aggravated now. It was bad guy seven robberies, and Herion zero. One Friday night Bob, my partner, had called my house looking for me; my wife told him that I was playing cards at a friend's house, which was fine. Bob knew me pretty well and knew that I didn't play cards that much, so he became suspicious right away. The next day when Bob asked me how the game was and if I had won, I screwed up and without thinking I said, "What game?" His next question was, "Where the hell do you go on Friday night, pal? I know damn well you're not playing cards, that's for sure." I decided to tell him about what I had been trying to do about the stickup man. He said, "Why the hell didn't you tell me? I hate that son of a bitch as much as you do. Besides, four eyes are a lot better than two, and we can cover more territory."

So the next Friday we both positioned ourselves in such a manner that we could cover four alleys and still keep each other in sight so that we could signal each other with a small flashlight if we spotted the guy. Well, it was another dry run even with my partner sneaking around the area. And to make it worse, the bastard robbed an old lady in her garage about four blocks from where we were staked out. The next Friday we decided to move around more frequently, so maybe the odds would be better for us. Well, guess what, while I was watching a car pull in the alley that I was covering, I could see the driver very plainly, and he was an older man in his sixties. When he got out of his car to open the garage door and pull his car inside, I saw a dark figure come out of a yard and enter the garage with the old man. The garage door closed, and the light inside went off. I could see that the guy was black, six foot two, about 200 pounds, and sure fit the description of the stickup man. I immediately signaled my partner, who was covering the next alley, and he joined me in the yard across the alley from where the stickup guy had gone. If high fives were popular then, we would have been doing one right then and there in that yard, that's for sure.

We were sure we had the stickup man right where we wanted him; we had a problem. We decided not to go in the garage like John Wayne because we would have to use the service door, and we would be silhouetted against the light that was in the yard. We knew he carried a knife and a gun, and would probably use them if he were cornered in the garage. We were also aware that up to this time he had never killed anyone yet, so we decided to wait until he came out and then we would take him down. Hopefully, the old guy in the garage wouldn't try to fight the guy and maybe get himself killed while we were standing around in the alley. After a few minutes, which seemed like an hour, we heard the service door open; the stickup guy came out and stuck a .45 in his belt, and then started counting some money that was in an envelope.

Do to the fact that the stickup guy wore a mask while he was robbing people, Bob and I both brought plastic masks with us and put them on for a joke when we confronted the bad guy in the alley.

Plastic mask Bob Peters and I wore when we caught Willie Simpson, the garage bandit, he really thought he was being robbed.

As soon as he opened the gate with his right hand, we knew that he couldn't get at his gun; we told him to put his hands up and ordered him not to move or we would blow his fucking head off. Now this mutt knew what it felt like to have a gun pointed at your head. He didn't know whether to shit or go blind. He just kept saying, "Don't shoot, oh please don't shoot. Take my money, please. For some reason we didn't say, "POLICE, GET YOUR HANDS UP," so this idiot probably thought that we were stickup men and he was being robbed. We handcuffed him to a cyclone fence then searched him and recovered a loaded .45 cal. automatic from his belt, a switchblade from his jacket pocket, as well as a watch, ring, and a wallet with ID from the victim he just robbed. Also, a check stub with cash in an envelope from a currency exchange was also recovered. I asked him his name, and he said Willie Simpson and that he lived at an apartment hotel on Hamlin Avenue by Lake Street. All the time he kept pleading for his life and for us not to hurt him. The next thing we heard was the guy who got robbed coming out of the garage, yelling for his wife, Marie, and for her to call the police to report that he had been just robbed. We knew that some fellow officers would soon be on the scene so we thought that we would play a joke on them also. We pulled Willie's pants down around his ankles and stuck the loaded .45 under his pants where he couldn't get at it. We then put the victim's personal belongings under his pants and told him that if he moved one toe, we would set him on fire. I saw some wrapping paper and pink ribbon in a nearby garbage can. I wrapped the pink ribbon around Willie's head and made a nice bow. He looked like a present for somebody. Before we left him, we told him that if he told anyone that he was robbed, we would find him and nail him to his own bed. When the police cars pulled up in the alley and they saw Willie handcuffed to a fence with his pants down and a pink ribbon around his head, they looked a little befuddled, because Willie was screaming that he had just been robbed by two guys with Halloween masks on. Then out of the house came our real robbery victim, yelling that he had been robbed, and when he got to the alley he pointed at Willie and told the police that he was the guy who robbed him; now our pals were really confused. We had intentions of coming out of our hiding place and tell our buddies what really happened and that Willie was the garage bandit everyone was looking for, but we were having such a good time watching all this confusion we decided to just remain anonymous.

The police recovered the .45 automatic, switchblade knife, and all the victim's possessions under Willie's pants and decided that Willie was indeed the garage bandit, and they arrested him and had a showup at the station where Willie was identified by seven different victims as the stickup guy. We understand that Willie swore that he was framed by two guys in Halloween masks and demanded to see a lawyer, because his rights had been violated. Bob and I never laughed harder in our lives watching this whole charade. The main thing was that the bastard was off the street, at least for a while anyway. The two guys who made the arrest on Willie were made detectives for their good work, but Bob and I got self-satisfaction; that's all that mattered to us. This was kind of like vigilante work. I kind of liked this way to operate; I wish I would have worn a Zorro mask though. Simpson pleaded guilty in court and was given eight to ten years and was sent to Statesville Penitentiary.

Chapter 15

Midnights Are the Best

On May 13, 1958, my partner Bob Peters and I were working the dogwatch, otherwise known as midnight's, on our assigned car 121. Bob and I always liked the dogwatch because it got us away from school crossings and all the other bullshit jobs that come up when you're on days. Besides that, there always seemed to be a good chance to catch a few crooks that may be driving around, looking to make a score. We were in the habit of checking alleys and stores on our assigned post; sometimes it got a little monotonous I will admit, but the anticipation of catching somebody at any given moment sure helped the long night pass by. As I recall, we had just checked the rear of a few stores east on Chicago Avenue; when we came out an alley around Hamlin Avenue and started heading west toward Pulaski Road, all of a sudden a car sped across Chicago Avenue on Harding Avenue heading southbound. By the time we got up to Harding Avenue, we had every intention to chase the unknown car that headed southbound, but on the northeast corner of Harding and Chicago Avenue a car was on fire and was totally consumed in flames, and it seemed to also light up the sky. We notified the fire department immediately of the location of the fire; we tried to see if anyone was in the car but due to the flames and smoke, it was impossible to tell. We hoped that the fire department would get there right away and put out the damn fire before the gas tank blew up. They arrived in a couple of minutes and extinguished the fire, and that was when we saw a very gruesome sight. There was a body on its knees on the passenger side in the front seat; it was so badly charred that you couldn't tell if it was a man or a woman. I did notice a small hole on the top of the victim's head that appeared to be a bullet hole; besides that, a drop of blood was dripping from what was left of its nose about every five seconds. There weren't any license plates on the car either, and things seemed to be leading us to believe that maybe this person was murdered. We called the detectives in the station and told them what had happened, and they came out and met us in about ten minutes. Detectives Doherty and Dolan remembered the car because of the front grill that was missing and thought they were pretty sure that the car belonged to a small-time burglar who had a gimpy foot and wore a special shoe. When the wagon took the body out of the car, sure enough, he was wearing a built-up shoe on his right foot. The detectives told us that they had interrogated the guy a couple of days ago about a few burglaries that had happened in the district. Bob and I wondered that if we had only been a minute earlier, maybe we would have bumped into the car that we saw headed south on Harding Avenue. It might have been the hit men, who knows?

We went back to our regular routine when we got through with the guy in the burned-out car and hit a few alleys on North Avenue and then started cruising south on Pulaski Road. Like they say, sometimes you get the bear and sometimes the bear gets you; only this time, it was our turn.to get the bear. When we drove past 1115 North Pulaski Road, which at the time was a National Food store, we both saw some broken glass on the sidewalk next to the entrance door, along with a brick. A closer look revealed that a pane of glass about sixteen by twenty-six inches had been broken, probably with the brick that was lying next to the door. A carton had been placed against the area where the glass had been broken out on the inside of the window. Obviously, the bad guy or guys were still inside the store. We called for another car to cover the rear of the store, and Charlie Mueller and his partner responded on car 160. Bob and I got in the window the same way the crooks did, and we began searching the store. As we got near the south wall, a fella we now know as Henry Degrazio, age thirty-one, stepped out from behind a counter with his hands in the air and said, "We're clean, don't shoot." We asked where his accomplices were, and two other guys stepped out from behind another counter with their hands in the air also. They identified themselves as James Cosmano, age twenty-five, and Sam Scully, age twenty-seven. They were searched for weapons at this time, but none were found. I asked them what they were going to take out of a food store, and they said nothing. We found shopping bags filled with various cartons of cigarettes, which they had placed near the rear door. All three men were charged with burglary, were subsequently indicted, and faced trial in the criminal court at 2600 South California Avenue. My partner and I appeared in criminal court on this case eleven different times before we went to trial. The burglar's lawyer continued the case for so many different reasons, like one of the defendants had a cold, or had to go to a funeral, or get examined. The lawyer also couldn't appear in court because he was in another court, or his kids were sick; it went on and on and on. Finally, on our eleventh appearance, the case was heard in front of a judge named Weiss on a bench trial; they didn't want a jury, no way. Bob and I testified as to the facts in the case and how we caught the three bad guys hiding in the store at 2:45 AM when the store was closed. The bad guys told the judge that they happened to be walking down the street past the National Food Store at 1115 North Pulaski Road when they saw some broken glass by the entrance to the store and observed a hole in the window, which was probably caused by a brick that was on the sidewalk. At this time, they stated that they thought maybe someone had broken into the store through the broken window and that if they went inside maybe they could catch the thieves in the act and turn them over to the police. The next thing they knew was that the police came into the store also and held guns on them and accused them of being burglars and arrested them. Well, guess what, the Honorable Judge Weiss then asked them if they had been drinking earlier in the night and maybe they didn't realize that they could be in an embarrassing position if the police found them in the store. The judge then made his decision – discharged as there were no witnesses who saw the three wise men break the glass in the store; he had no other choice. From that point on, I have never ceased to be amazed at some decisions made in court. I guess it's all part of the game.

Chapter 16

Hey, Guys, I'm One of You'se

Working the midnight shift at four in the morning on a weekday is usually very quiet. Normally, all there is on the street are rats, cats, and some stray dogs. All the saloons are closed, but you can probably find an all-night grill open if you look hard enough. All the drunks seem to congregate at the grills to get a bowl of chili or black coffee before they go home. Of course, there are some other folks out in the street. They're called burglars, stickup men, car thieves, rapists, and some very ugly streetwalkers. Some of the streetwalkers may be female impersonators, and their customers will never know the difference. Last but not least, when the drunk drivers hit the street, they think they're are at the Daytona 500 speedway.

My partner Bob Peters and I were working car 121, just cruising east on Division Street about fifteen miles an hour. Bob was driving the last four hours of the shift, and I was just looking around at some of the businesses for any possible break-ins. As we were just approaching Kostner Avenue, this newer Oldsmobile came flying around the corner at Kostner and headed westbound on Division Street right past us. He must have been doing about seventy miles an hour, and we could see that the driver looked at us when he blew by us, obviously he didn't give a shit because he gunned it and really took off. We could see that there were two people in the car when they passed us. While I was saying, "Get that son of a bitch," Bob was already in the middle of a U-turn, and the chase was on. I got on the radio and told the squad operator that we were in pursuit of a newer dark-colored Oldsmobile and were headed west on Division Street from Kostner Avenue at a high rate of speed. I also told the operator that all we knew about the Oldsmobile was that the driver was committing traffic violations. The Olds blew a red light at Cicero Avenue, going about fifty miles an hour; luckily, there weren't any cars coming the other way. That goes for us too because we also went through the same red light about sixty. Bob and I both knew that chasing some crazy bastard that was going through red lights at 50 mph was a very stupid thing to do. But most cops do it anyway, because for some reason, all your common sense leaves you. By the time we hit Central Avenue, which was one mile west, we hit eighty-five miles an hour, and we couldn't gain on the bastard. We had our red mars light on, our headlights were blinking high and low, our spotlight was on him, and our siren was blaring away. We hoped that other cars would see us and hear us coming and get the hell out of our way, because we were really pissed off at this bastard and were not going to give up the chase. We were really getting pissed at this guy now. All that mattered was we had to get him.

Then there is always the possibility of the car you're chasing may hit another car, causing some innocent person or persons to get killed or injured, or worse yet, you may hit some other car and kill somebody or even get killed yourself. And believe me, I would rather be driving the squad car than sit in the passenger seat; for some reason it is more nerve racking just sitting there. We didn't have seat belts or air bags back then either.

The chase continued west on Division Street, through the suburb of Oak Park, past Harlem Avenue, where he blew another red light going at least eighty-five miles an hour. We were now going through the suburb of River Forest, that when I happened to look down at the speedometer and saw that we were going 105 miles an hour, but we weren't gaining on the bastard and I'm shouting at Bob to go faster like a goof. I had kept the squad operator appraised of our position and which direction we were headed; he was also notifying the other police departments in the area.

We couldn't seem to gain any ground on this guy so I suggested to Bob that maybe if we turn off all our lights and siren maybe he would think that he lost us and slow down. He agreed. We sure didn't have anything to lose at this point. We were aware that Division Street ended at Thatcher Avenue, and that he would have to go either north or south. Well, for some unknown reason, the goofy bastard put his right turn signal on and went north toward North Avenue. That stretch of road started winding around a little, so when we turned north at Thatcher we couldn't see the car at all; but after the last bend in the road at North Avenue, there was our Oldsmobile stopped at a red light. It was the only red light that he didn't go through during the entire chase. We still had our lights out, and when we were about one-half block behind, the light changed and he started moving north again. At this point, we put our lights on and forced the car off the road; we came out of the squad with our guns out – ready for anything – and told the driver to get out first with his hands up and the passenger to put her hands on the dashboard. At that time about six suburban squads showed up – some had sirens on, all of them had their mars lights on, and it looked like New Year's Eve. We were now in Elmwood Park, and their squad car showed up with three guys in it, and all of them got out of their cars with guns in their hands. When the driver got out of the Oldsmobile, he said, "Hey, guys, I'm one of you'se," and flashed a Chicago Park District Police star; he was drunk out of his mind. The passenger then got out, a floozy blond broad and appeared to be as drunk as the cop. The driver said that his name was Vince Moretti and that he was a Chicago policeman and wanted to apologize for any inconvenience he may have caused.

Vincent Moretti

Well let me tell you, everybody there wanted to kick the shit out of this guy, and a couple of suburban cops told us that they would have let a few rounds go at this jagoff if it had been them chasing him. Right then and there, we should have arrested this clown for drunk driving and for a hundred other traffic violations he committed during the chase. But we decided to turn him and his broad over to the suburban police, who told us that they would handle it.

   A funny thing happened to Bob and me when we were getting back in the squad car; we both tried to light a cigarette, but our hands were shaking so much it was hard to do. It was then that my legs started shaking also. I guess that's kind of an aftershock or something. On the way into the station, we discussed how stupid the whole thing was and that we could have gotten killed chasing that son of a bitch or caused someone else to get killed or injured. When something like that happens, you just lose it; and the only thing that matters at the time is to catch the bad guys, no matter what.

   When we got back in the station, everyone knew that we were involved in a high-speed chase and wanted to know where the crooks were. We decided to tell them that the suburban police were handling the case, and we did neglect to tell anyone that the guy was a Park District cop.

   As things turned out during my time on the job, I did get involved in other high-speed chases, but none of them were as scary as the one with Vince Moretti. The Chicago Police Department's policy on any chases today is different. If you get involved in any chase at all, you must notify the squad operator as to why you are chasing the subject, and the operator will notify your supervisor, who will probably tell you to terminate the chase unless the subject committed a major crime. The supervisor will be held responsible for anything that goes wrong involving the chase.

   Vince Moretti, it seems, was not your all-American police officer; he was a burglar, as well as a few other things. Vince had a twin brother named Salvatore; they both were Chicago Park District policemen. Vince's future was not good. It seems that Vince and several other burglars had burglarized a prominent jewelry store on North Clark Street in Chicago in November 1977. When the owner, Harry Levinson, discovered that he had been robbed, he almost had a heart attack. The burglars had taken over $1 million worth of his best jewelry. He had installed the very best burglar alarm system, and his store windows were in public view. No doubt, this was a professional crew of thieves. The investigating officers were unable to find any clues; it looked as if the crooks had gotten away clean.

It seems that Levinson had a friend by the name of Tony Accardo whom he could go to. Levinson and Accardo had known each other for years; the biggest bookmaker in town, Hymie Levin, had introduced them to each other. When Levinson and Accardo met at a restaurant called Chez Paul near Rush Street, Levinson told Accardo what happened to his store. Accardo told Levinson that he shouldn't worry about this matter and that he would see what he could find out.

A couple of days after the meeting, Levinson got a phone call from a familiar voice, who told him to make sure that he was at his store that afternoon. That afternoon, a million dollars worth of jewelry was returned to Levinson, who became a very happy man. An informant revealed that Tony Spilotro, who was in Las Vegas and who was a jewel thief himself, suggested to the boys in Chicago that only a guy by the name of John Mendell could defeat the sophisticated alarm system that was in Levinson's jewelry store. Two days later, the jewelry was returned to Levinson.

Then an unbelievable thing happened. Tony Accardo's house had been burglarized. Accardo and his wife were in Palm Springs, California, when the crime occurred. Accardo also had a very high-line burglar alarm system defeated. It was January 9, 1978, when Accardo contacted Jackie Cerone, his protégé, who was running the outfit for Accardo. Cerone brought Tony Spilotro back from Las Vegas to take care of things. On January 20, 1978, a man by the name of Bernie Ryan was found in his 1976 Lincoln parked on a side street in Stone Park; he had been shot four times and had his throat cut from ear to ear. A known burglar and pal of Ryan, Steve Garcia, was found on February 2, stuffed in the trunk of a rental car in a parking lot of the Sheraton O'Hare Hotel on Manheim Road. His throat had been cut from ear to ear, and he had been stabbed numerous times.

On February 4, 1978, our speed demon pal who said "I'M ONE OF YOU'SE," Vincent Moretti, was found with Donald Swanson a.k.a. Donald Renno. Moretti's and Swanson's bodies were found in the backseat of Swanson's Cadillac in a parking lot of a restaurant called Esther's Place at 5009 South Central Avenue in Stickney, a suburb of Chicago. It seems that Moretti's face was burned off with an acetylene torch; he was also disemboweled and castrated. Swanson's throat had been cut just like his burglar buddies.

The electronic expert, John Mendell, who had beaten the alarm systems at Levinson's and Accardo's houses was next in line. On February 20, 1978, Mendell's body was found in the truck of his 1971 Oldsmobile that was parked in the 6300 block of South Campbell Avenue, Chicago. He was also tortured, and his throat was cut from ear to ear.

Any normal person would now figure out that if he were involved in Accardo's burglary, maybe he should take off for Argentina or join the French Foreign Legion, or at least get out of town. John McDonald apparently thought otherwise. On April 14, 1978, his body was found in an alley behind 442 North Racine Avenue; he was shot in the head, and of course, his throat was cut from ear to ear. This neighborhood was known as a strong mob hangout. McDonald had once been tried for burglary with Bernie Ryan; and the two were close friends. On April 26, 1978, another well-known burglar was found murdered; Bobby Hertogs was his name. Bob and I had busted Bobby for burglary when he was about eighteen years old. He had been shot numerous times, and of course had his throat cut as well.

The moral of the story is, if there is heat in the kitchen, get the hell out of town.

Chapter 17

Vice: How It All Began

In 1961 we were living in an apartment at 4752 West North Avenue; my wife, Gen, and our three children lived on the second floor above Joe's Barbershop. Joe was a good barber and also a good bookmaker, and ran a few parlay cards in the neighborhood. I was still working squad car 121 with Bob Peters, and we couldn't wait to get to work every day. At this point, I knew that this was what I wanted to do for a living. I even had my radio fixed on my own personal car to hear police calls. I guess that was a little extreme, but what the hell, I liked it, so the hell with everyone else. One of the things that I had learned in the short time I had been on the job was to always keep your eyes open and be aware of what is going on around you, for your sake as well as others.

Traffic was very congested at the intersection of North and Cicero Avenue, so a police officer was assigned to that corner for traffic control. There also was a school crossing at the corner, so that also was part of the officer's duties. The cop assigned to the corner was a friend of mine named John, his last name ended with ski so all the guys called him John the Polock. John didn't care about that; he was a really good guy and liked his job on the corner as much as I liked my job in a squad. When traffic was light and there weren't any children crossing the street, John would take a break and hang around a greasy spoon restaurant on North

Avenue, across from my apartment. When I worked the four-to-twelve shift, I would go over to the restaurant and shoot the breeze with John in the afternoon before I had to go to work. On occasion, John and I would play a game of rummy in the kitchen area of the restaurant, which was a good place because there was a two-way mirror and you could see everyone that came in the restaurant. And it wouldn't look too good if John were seen playing gin rummy in uniform.

One afternoon, while John and I were involved in a close gin rummy game, the cigarette man came in to fill up the cigarette machine; he had double-parked his truck in front while he made his delivery. That's when I noticed a green four-door Buick with three guys in it park across the street and seemed to be very interested in the delivery truck. One of the guys got out of the car and stood in my doorway, which had a small hall, and the other two guys in the car left. When he got out of the car, I recognized him as a guy Bob and I busted for fencing stolen goods; his name was Ellis Young. Ellis was a well-known burglar, fence, and thief and belonged to a group of hillbilly crooks that worked the district pretty good.

The deliveryman decided to get a cup of coffee and sat down at the counter after he had filled the cigarette machine. I kept my eye on Ellis Young and saw him signal somebody down the street, which was probably where the green car had gone. I knew that they were going to hijack the truck, which was loaded with cigars, cigarettes, and a variety of sundries. Here I was without my gun. I usually carried it whenever I went out, but not today; what a dope. The name of the truck was Commercial Delivery Inc. I told John what I suspected and not to show himself because he might spook them and they wouldn't try and make the truck. I figured that we had to get one of them in the truck to make a case, because you can't bust a guy for thinking about committing a crime. I asked John if I could borrow his gun, because I was in civilian clothes and could sit near the front window where I could keep an eye on them, and if they tried to make the truck, we could bust them in the act.

Well, for some unknown reason, the bad guys didn't try and make the truck; the deliveryman finished his coffee and got back in his truck. We didn't tell him anything about our suspicions because that might get him very nervous and he might screw up the whole thing. Ellis Young jumped in the green car, and they took off east on North Avenue. Oh well, I almost made a good pinch; but what the hell, these guys may be back tomorrow, and this time I'll have Mr. Smith and Wesson with me. It was a good lesson for me to never leave your piece at home when you go out in the street, because you never know when the shit will hit the fan. When I got to work that afternoon, I told my sergeant what had happened and that these guys were going to hit that truck just as sure as there are steers in Texas. Just then, Mike Foley, who was the district commander, happened to walk by, and the sergeant told me to tell him what I suspected was going to happen to that truck. I repeated my story to him – without the gin game of course – and added that if someone were to keep the truck under surveillance tomorrow or the next day, they would make a good grab. He looked at me and said uh-huh and that he would make a note of it. It was obvious to me that he thought I was a little melodramatic about the whole incident and probably imagined everything. Well, guess what, the very next day when I reported to work, the sergeant grabbed me and told me that the commercial delivery truck had been hijacked at Pulaski Road and North Avenue, one mile east of where I had told them about the day before. It seems the driver left the truck to make a delivery, and that was the last time he saw his truck, which was loaded with thousands of dollars worth of cigarettes, cigars, and other sundries. The truck was found abandoned in a vacant lot about two miles away, empty of course.

After roll call the sergeant told me that the district commander wanted to see me in his office upstairs right away. When I walked in his office, all he said was, "Herion, it looks like you may know what the hell is going on out in the street, and even call shots before they happen. That's exactly what I have been looking for, so tomorrow you are to report to work in civilian clothes, because you are now a vice detective." I told him that I was really happy doing what I was doing and had a good partner and that I sure didn't know anything about being a vice detective. His reply was, "Where it says the patrolman tells the district commander what he wants to do? And if it will make you feel any better your partner, Peters, will also be a vice detective with you, and you can call it the blind leading the blind. All you have to handle are narcotics, gambling, prostitution, liquor law violations, and a lot of other little things. Good luck. I know you guys will do a good job. Get out there and lock up all the dope fiends, bookmakers, hookers, and the bars that are selling liquor to minors." That was the beginning of my vice career. I had no clue what the hell I was getting myself into, but as things turned out, this was a more challenging job than working a squad car. Vice detectives' hours were 0900 to 1700 on the day shift and 1700 to 0500 at night. The good news was that my partner Bob and I were still together.

Chapter 18

You Are Now a Vice Detective

When the district commander told me that I was going to be a vice detective, I told him I was happy working the street in a squad car. That's when he reminded me that a patrolman doesn't give orders to the district commander. To be honest with you, I found out that wearing casual clothes instead of a uniform wasn't such a bad way to go; you could go into a restaurant, and people wouldn't stare at you as if you were some odd ball. And having an unmarked squad car to drive around in wasn't bad either. When I told the commander that I didn't have any idea what a vice detective's duties were, he told me, "You'll learn just like everyone else, Herion." After the Summerdale District scandal, Mayor Daley dumped the police commissioner Timothy O'Connor and replaced him with Orlando W. Wilson, and gave him a new title of superintendent of police. He told him to straighten out the Chicago Police Department and make it the best in the country. The mayor gave O. W. carte blanche and told him, "Money was no problem. Just do what you have to do." Well, O. W. changed the color of the patrol cars to blue and white; we also had a blue-and-white checked band on our uniform hat. Where a district had three or four squad cars before, they now had fifteen or more. The ranks of the patrol division were changed to district commanders instead of a captain; other ranks got new titles, as well. He also transferred the district detectives out of the district into detective areas. There were no more detectives in the district; that's when vice units were formed in each district. A sergeant was appointed as the vice coordinator, and he ran the vice detectives. Usually, he reported only to the district commander.

Being a vice detective means that you were responsible for all vice activities in your district, such as narcotics, gambling, prostitution, and all liquor violations. I had never been too concerned about that type of police work; all I wanted to do was bust burglars, stickup guys, rapists, and murderers. I did remember the Guzaldo brothers' poolroom though and put them at the top of my list as places to bust.

The hours of a vice detective were a little different; there were two shifts – 9:00 AM to 5:00 PM and then 9:00 PM to 5:00 AM at night. The main problem at night was the prostitutes, fights in taverns, and selling of booze to minors. There also was gambling, card games in clubs, policy operators in the black areas, and, of course, narcotics, which operated twenty-four hours a day. The dividing line between the Twenty-eighth District and the Thirty-first District was North Avenue; we lived on the Thirty-first District side of North Avenue in an apartment building. There were eight apartments in the building as well as four stores on the first floor. It so happened that an older couple lived next door to us, Bob and Lil. Bob and Lil operated the newsstand on the NW corner of North Avenue and Cicero. They took turns taking bets at the newsstand; one would be in the apartment taking bets on the phone and the other one would be taking action at the newsstand. Underneath our apartment was Joe's barbershop. Joe was my barber; he was also a bookmaker and ran football parlay cards in the neighborhood. Across the street from our apartment was Olson's Trainmen's Supply, which was a store where the motormen and conductors on the streetcars and buses hang out between their shifts. The proprietor also was known to take a few bets in the store. On the SE corner of North Avenue and Cicero was a sundry store; the owners were a guy named Shoes and a Chicago policeman named Jimmy. Jimmy worked at the Thirty-first District as a patrolman and was a silent partner in the store. It seems that Shoes took a little action on the horses on occasion from the fellas that worked at the streetcar barn. Anyway, now that I was a vice detective and had been given the job of busting bookmakers, I had a dilemma. What if someone from downtown busted Bob and Lil and Joe the Barber? I would sure look like a dope. I couldn't bust them, that's for sure; all I could think of was warn them that the FBI was working on them and they had better go out of business before they got grabbed. Joe the Barber and Bob and Lil told me that they were giving up the business and not to worry, that they wouldn't put me in such an embarrassing position. Here I was in this new job, and already I had problems. Now I was concerned about the other locations on the corner. I knew Shoes and Jimmy, and Pete who ran Olson's, and I told them that I was now a vice detective in the district with orders to bust everybody that was involved in illegal gambling. Well, the response I got was that it's all bullshit, and every once in a while some heat comes down and then everything is back to normal. I explained that there was a new commander in the district, and any gambling would not be tolerated. I explained that the commander had requested that some police assigned to a vice-detection unit downtown be sent to the Austin District so that they would investigate any reports of gambling going on. If they do find evidence of that, they would then notify the vice control division of the organized crime division, and they would come out and raid these locations. I explained that this is a new ball game, and there wasn't anything else I could do about it. Shoes did heed my advice and moved his bookmaking operation out of the sundry store and put it in a towing outfits office two doors away. Well, that lasted about one week before Downtown came in and raided the place. Shoes was now a believer. Pete, in the trainmen's store, decided that it wasn't worth it to get locked up at his age and went out of the booking business.

I did explain my situation to Mike Foley, the district commander at the time, and he understood my dilemma and told me that I handled it fine and not to worry about it. I told the commander about the problem that I had when I was detailed to Guzaldo's poolroom after they had been raided by the gambling unit of the organized crime division. His reply was, "Don't you think that you and a few of the other guys should drop in and say hi to Tony and Phil, maybe you might find them dirty, it would be nice to lock up two guys like that for a start wouldn't it?" Well, he didn't have to tell me twice. I got hold of Bill, the coordinator Bob and Wally Goebbert, who had just been a vice dick and explained the situation to them and what would be the best time to pay our respects to the boys. I also told them about the trick table they had to hide the bets in, and the phone booth where Tony or Phil just may be sitting when we walked in. There was also the problem of my old black friend, who was the lookout with his mirrors, and we would have to get in the poolroom in a hurry. I decided to borrow a bicycle and put a baseball hat on and park the bike in front of the door and just walk in like another dope in the neighborhood. When I got in, the rest of the guys could join me, and we would shake the hell out of the wise guys before they knew what hit them. Everything worked out just as I thought. The black lookout didn't pay any attention to me on my bike, and I was in before anyone could yell or even try and lock the front door. My partners joined me. And sure as hell, Tony was in the phone booth taking bets so fast that he never even saw us in the place for five minutes; when he did, he was in shock to see that the district vice unit was busting the place. We found a large quantity of wagers in the phony table, which was just great. Tony and Phil were busted, put in handcuffs, and thrown in the wagon, and taken to the lockup at the station. I guess that old saying really is true, "What goes around comes around." Revenge was sure sweet, just listening to old Phil and Tony whine and snivel on the way to jail was better that winning the lottery.

```
New Vice Detectives - Blind leading the blind
Don Herion ^Jim Griffin  Austin District 1961
```

Nov 1963

Find Hoodlum's Body in Trunk of Auto on West Side-

I'm the guy in the crew cut checked jacket checking out body of Leo Foreman Vice Detective in action

[TRIBUNE Staff Photo]

Police examining body in trunk of rented auto parked at 5204 Gladys av. Victim was identified in morgue as Leo Foreman, 42, of 4817 Neva av., convicted swindler and associate of syndicate figures. Foreman had been beaten and knifed several times and much of his clothing was gone. Wife told police Sunday that Foreman had been missing since Thursday. *(Story on page 1)*

SLAIN, BODY IN CAR TRUNK

SHOT, STABBED BODY FOUND IN TRUNK OF CAR

Hoodlum De Stefano Sought for Quiz

[Continued from first page]

parked nearby for several days.

Orsi found a trunk release button in the glove compartment of the car and pressed it. The trunk sprang open and revealed the half-clothed body. A briefcase containing Foreman's papers also was there.

Identification of the body was made at the county morgue thru fingerprints and by the victim's wife. Also called to view the body was Samuel Cavallo, 35, of 3815 Huron st., office manager for the LeFore company. Cavallo told police he rode to the office Thursday with Foreman.

Cavallo is free on bond pending a hearing on charges of grand theft arising from his arrest in July while transferring $40,000 worth of high fidelity phonographs from a stolen truck in a parking lot at 510 N. Harding av.

Gang Killing Hint Given

"This looks like another gangland slaying," said Coroner Andrew Toman, who went to the Gladys avenue scene. Foreman had been stabbed four times in the lower left back, once in the chest, and once in the right arm. He had been shot once each in the left buttock and the right forearm. The head bore cuts and bruises.

Police said no blood was found in the trunk, an indication Foreman had been killed elsewhere. The rest of his clothing was missing.

Twenty Arrests Listed

Police records show that Foreman had been arrested 20 times since Aug. 6, 1939. The charges included passing worthless checks, forgery, confidence game, embezzlement, swindling, and perjury. He pleaded guilty to charges of confidence game and embezzlement in 1955 and was sentenced to a year and a day in Joliet prison.

He last was arrested Oct. 22, for impersonation of a bondsman. He was released. Foreman was a former bondsman. His arrest records showed he used several aliases, including Leo Wilson, Leo Foreman, and Leo Seymore Foreman.

The car in which the body was found was rented by Foreman in February from the Courtesy Motor company in the name of the LeFore company. Officials said it was to have been rented for two years and was equipped with a telephone.

Hoodlum's Friend Shot and Stabbed

(Pictures on back page)

The body of a convicted swindler who was a friend of hoodlum Sam De Stefano was found shot and stabbed last night in the trunk of a rented car parked at 5204 Gladys av.

The slain man was Leo S. Foreman, 42, of 4817 Neva av., who was reported to be president of the LeFore Insurance company, 7050 Belmont av.

He had been stabbed six times and shot twice. The body was dressed in underclothing, with the undershirt pulled over the head. Only one leg of the trousers remained on the body.

Seek to Quiz De Stefano

Police said they are seeking De Stefano to question him about the death. They said

Leo S. Foreman

Foreman was reported to have played cards with DeStefano on Thursday, the day Foreman last was seen alive.

Police said they also were informed that DeStefano, a crime syndicate loan shark, threatened Foreman during a quarrel over money a year ago.

Chapter 19

The Mob and the Numbers Racket

After I became a vice detective, I discovered this was a whole new ball game that involved a different way to fight crime. This was a fight against the crime syndicate, which involved busting up their gambling operations as well as narcotics and prostitution. One faction of gambling involved a game called policy, which is a numbers game operated exclusively in black areas.

Policy, a nickel-and-dime lottery, preys on Chicago's poor and makes its operators rich. It is controlled by the mob, which became aware of the huge profits being made by this type of gambling when Sam "Momo" Giancana got himself convicted of bootlegging and was sentenced to prison in Terre Haute. There he met Eddy Jones, a black numbers operator. Giancana – who grew up in the "Patch" (Taylor Street area), where he became a member of the notorious "42 gang" – was viewed as crazy by fellow members of the 42s such as Felix "Milwaukee Phil" Alderisio, Marshall Caifano, and Sam "Teets" Battaglia. Before Giancana went to prison, he was just a wheelman who drove a getaway car and was a chauffeur for Paul "the Waiter" Ricca, a top mob boss.

Meeting Jones was probably the best thing that ever happened to Giancana. Jones, who was then a South Side policy king, told Giancana that he and his brother George made so much money from their policy wheels that they had to spread the cash to twenty-five banks. This was a shocking revelation, particularly since Giancana had previously dismissed policy as just a small-time nickel-and-dime racket. When Giancana was released from Terre Haute in December 1942, he imparted his new intelligence to Accardo, who advised that Giancana not create any heat in his attempt to take over this gambling empire. Giancana's attempt to take over some of the smaller policy operators by a series of beatings and bombings failed. When Jones was released from Terre Haute in 1946, he was kidnapped and was held captive in the basement of Giancana's new home in Oak Park, Illinois. Jones's family paid $100,000 in ransom to get him released; the brothers decided to get out of Chicago and move to Mexico.

Their top lieutenant, Ted P. Roe, was left behind to fight the mob, which he did for six years. In June 1951, the outfit attempted to kidnap Roe. A gun battle broke out, and Lenny Caifano, a brother of Marshall Caifano, was killed. About a year later, Ted P. Roe was shotgunned to death. The rest of the policy kings got the message and quickly fell in line, and the mob added policy to its long list of lucrative rackets.

In 1954, the Chicago Crime Commission estimated that Chicago's policy racket netted $150 million for the outfit, and this is a game that can be played for as little as nickels and dimes. Basically, a player can pick any numbers from 000 to 999. He can bet three digits, play the numbers straight, or box the numbers; he can also bet the digit system, and so forth. Betting three numbers is called a gig, two numbers played is called flat, four numbers played is a horse, and five numbers played is called Jack.

The low men on the totem pole are called writers or runners; they are in the street and take wagers from the bettors, or they go door to door also. The runners turn in their wagers to a person called a field man, who in turn takes the wagers to place called a bank. The wagers are evaluated to see which numbers are getting a lot of action. Of course, any numbers that were played a lot never seem to be chosen when the drawing takes place. There are two drawings every day – the AM drawing usually held at 2:30 PM and the PM drawing at 10:30 PM. The winning numbers are picked from a keg, which is a cylindrical drum, and then they are printed on policy result tickets, which are distributed to the runners, who disperse them to the bettors so they can see if they won or lost. The policy wheels have weird names, such as Win-Place-Show, Windy City-Comet-Neptune-Atlas to name a few.

We became involved in policy when the southeast end of out district around Madison and Kildare Avenue began changing from white to black; naturally, the policy racket also came into the district. The workers were black, of course, but the majority of the money was going to the outfit. Needless to say, our vice unit didn't have too much experience working the policy racket, so we had to learn how to catch these guys by trial and error.

The black bosses who controlled the policy in our area were fellas by the names of Thomas "Shaky Tom" Anderson and his flunky enforcer, James "Kid Rivera" Williams, a 325 pound terrorist. After we had busted a couple of runners for the policy wheel called Comet-Neptune-Atlas that belonged to Anderson, we learned that he had knocked out some competing independent or "wildcat" operators. They were trying to establish more business in our district by setting up policy operations. They had both been questioned and released by detectives investigating the murder of Alderman Benjamin F. Lewis. The police had signed statements from several persons that the pair had threatened Lewis. Both passed lie detector tests. The slaying remains unsolved. We had busted a dope dealer at Kostner and Madison Street who wanted to become an informant for us if we could get the state attorney to be lenient with him on his pending case in court. We called the guy Adolph because he had a mustache like Hitler; he proved to be very helpful in our endeavor to bust the policy racket. We locked up writers, runners, and fieldmen every day; and before we knew it, we were getting a reputation, and weird stories were going around about the Austin District vice men. The goofiest one that I heard of was that some runners were saying that we would put a dog's noose around their necks and made some of them walk into the lagoon at Columbus Park by the golf course and then we would shoot at them. They didn't believe that we were trying to hit them though, or maybe we were the worst shots on the police department. I remember one runner we locked up brought up that lagoon story in court; the judge just looked at him as if he was drunk and said that was the worst story he had ever heard. We never did see that guy again in our district. Who knows, maybe he really believed that story. We were really getting pretty good at this policy racket; every day and night we would lock up a few guys. Before long, we were finding it very difficult to find any people connected to policy in our district. Whenever we made any raids, we put them in a raid book; of course, our raid numbers were very high every month. Now that the policy people stopped coming into our district, we found it tougher to make any arrests; but then that was our job, or so we thought. Naturally, the statistics went down every month on gambling raids. John Neurauter, our district commander, told us that a deputy chief downtown wanted to know why our raid numbers were going down. He even insinuated that maybe we weren't doing our job and maybe it was possible that we became friends with them. The commander really got pissed off when he heard that remark and told the chief that he should get off his dead ass and come on out to the district and try and find any policy people. No one ever took him up on that one though; maybe they were convinced that if you really try, you could put a dent in this type of operation.

An indication of how much money was involved in this nickel-and-dime operation came to light when an old-timer by the name of Lawrence Wakefield, who was a small time policy operator, had a heart attack and died at his home. His wife called the fire department inhalator squad for help, but it was too late. On these types of calls, a squad car is usually assigned to assist the ambulance. When the officers noticed a large quantity of money wrappers and a bag of money on the table, they notified the district, and a search warrant was obtained to make a search of the premises. In a bedroom, they found bags of money stacked to the ceiling. The total amount of money in the bags was over $763,000. They also found two policy wheels, eleven policy presses, and seven guns. The name of Wakefield's wheel was Erie-Buffalo; it was reported to have grossed over $21 million in two years.

There was an attempt by at least ten policy wheels to get into business in the Austin area. Runners for several of the wheels were depositing "business cards" in apartment house mailboxes. They had an intensive sales campaign to get the business in a new area. The cards bear the names of the South Side and West Side managers and field agents of the wheels. "Deposit your stocks and bonds with this bank. Stocks and Bonds is the name of the wheel. "Call us anytime . . . day or night," read another. This card offered twenty-four-hour service in which players phone bets in to be recorded by an "electronic secretary." A runner whom we locked up – Roy Combs, age twenty-seven – told us that he worked for Kid Rivera. "I see him every day at the company when he brought in his collections. He's the boss. He works for Mr. Anderson." He added that he didn't know the name of that white fella at the top. Combs told us that the kid hired him and gave him 10¢ on every dollar he collected. The kid also gave him the phone number of a bondsman and an attorney who handled most of the policy arrests for the wheel. Combs told me that up to two weeks before the kid hired him, he worked for the Missile Orbit wheel, and they had told him to stay out of the Austin District because everybody gets busted there. But the kid, he didn't tell the boundary lines. "I didn't even know that I was in the Austin District," he said.

We identified Anderson, who was a holder of a university degree in accounting, as the link between the policy operators and three crime syndicate hoodlums – Gus Alex, Marshall Caifano, and Ralph Pierce. While Kid Rivera was less educated – his schooling ended in the fourth grade – the policy operators no less feared him. He was a former professional heavyweight boxer. As the crime syndicate pressure increased, so did Austin's vice and gambling unit. My partners – Carlo Cangelosi, Andy Giacalone, Wally Goebbert, Bob Houghton, Frank Kelly, and Bill Maloney – just kept locking them up. We proved a point that the harder we worked, the luckier we got; and we did stop the policy racket for a while anyway.

August 2, 1963

Austin Cops Thwart Policy Bosses' Bid

BY ROBERT WIEDRICH

The crime syndicate has opened a drive to expand policy wheel operations into the Austin police district.

But in their bid for the patronage of Negroes moving into a changing neighborhood in the extreme southeast corner of Austin, the hoodlums are getting a bloody nose from police.

"Shaky Tom" Moves In

Leaders in the attempted expansion of the multi-million dollar racket are Thomas [Shaky Tom] Anderson, 54, and

Anderson (left) and Williams

James [Kid Riviera] Williams, 37, a 325 pound terrorist who serves as Anderson's enforcer.

Details of Anderson's attempt to invade the Austin district were obtained from one of his runners in an interview. The runner works for Anderson's Comet-Neptune-Atlas wheel, which has spread across the south and west sides.

Thru Anderson's connections with the syndicate, this wheel has knocked out competing independents or "wildcat" operators.

Anderson and Williams start-

Area (shaded) into which syndicate is seeking to expand policy operations.

ed their drive last spring, soon after they were questioned and released by detectives investigating the Feb. 27 murder of Ald. Benjamin F. Lewis [24th].

Police had signed statements from several persons that the pair had threatened Lewis. But both passed lie detector tests. The slaying remains unsolved.

The two hoodlums have sought by various means to force the syndicate dominated racket into new territory.

But they are being harassed steadily by police under Commander John Neurauter of the Austin police district and Sgt. William Maloney, head of Austin's vice and gambling unit.

Anderson's runners are arrested and warned to stay out of the district.

A Never Ending Fight

"We tell them to get out of Austin and get out of the city," Neurauter said.

But it is a never ending fight as runners for at least 10 policy wheels move westward into Austin in an effort to pour additional thousands of dollars into crime syndicate coffers.

Runners for several of the wheels are depositing "business cards" in apartment house mailboxes. Theirs is an intensive sales campaign. The cards bear the names of the south side and west side managers and field agents of the wheels.

"Deposit your stocks and bonds with this bank," reads one card. Stocks and Bonds is the name of the wheel.

24-Hour Service

"Call us anytime . . . day or night," reads another. This card offers 24 hour service in which players phone their bets to be recorded by an "electronic secretary."

In the forefront of the hoodlum invasion are runners for Anderson's Comet-Neptune-Atlas wheel. Not far behind are those of the Windy City and B & O wheels, both long time

[Continued on page 4, col. 6]

Policy Racket Runs Into a Snag

Austin District Police Waging All-Out War

[Continued from first page]

established sources of revenue to the syndicate.

"I work for The Kid," Roy Combs, 27, of 1510 S. Keeler av., a runner, told a TRIBUNE reporter. "I see him every day at the 'company' when I bring in my collections.

"He's the boss. He works for Mr. Anderson. I don't know who that white fellow is on top.

"Every day I meet him in different places—different every day. I went to work for him two weeks ago. I used to work for the Missile Orbit.

"But the Kid, he gave me this stop so I could make more money. I get 10 cents on every dollar I collect."

Combs gave Sgt. Maloney an insight into the organization of Anderson's operations which the runners term "the company."

Tells of Double Cross

Combs paid a compliment to Maloney and his companions, Vice Officers Don Herion and Frank Kelly. He also indicated he had been double crossed by Kid Riviera.

"The fellows at the Missile-Orbit told me to stay out of Austin," he said. "They said everybody gets arrested there. But the Kid, he didn't tell me the boundary lines. Honest, I didn't know I was in Austin."

Kid Grows Fat, Prosperous

Combs also gave police a more personal report on Kid Riviera's physical condition.

"The Kid, he's so fat," said

Combs. "He justs sits over there collecting the money and huffin' and puffin'."

But Kid Riviera and his employer, Anderson, are no laughing matter to Neurauter and Maloney. They know that if they let up on the pressure for just a brief period, policy runners will descend on their district.

Link to Caifano, Alex

Undercover detectives have identified Anderson—holder of a university degree in accounting—as the link between the policy operators and three crime syndicate hoodlums, Gus [Slim] Alex, Marshall Caifano, and Ralph Pierce.

While Kid Riviera is less educated [his schooling ended in the 4th grade], he is no less feared by the policy operators. He is a former professional heavyweight boxer.

Detective Donald Herion (standing) and Sgt. William Maloney searching Roy Combs for policy game evidence.

Another Policy runner going to jail!!
Adam Romanowski ând myself on the hunt for bad guys, win again

Chapter 20

The Right Place at the Right Time

It was June 1962, and I was working vice in the 015th District; my partner was Carlo Cangelosi, who was a good old Italian from the West Side of Chicago. Carlo and I got along fine, I would call him Carlos, and he would call me Harry. Of course, he smoked those Parodi cigars all the time; and I swore that he inhaled the damn things, but he would never admit it. We were working from 9:00 PM to 5:00 AM and were concentrating on a policy operation that was trying to get a foothold in the east end of our district. We had kicked their ass before, but the word on the street was, they were starting to sneak around us again. Our boss, Commander Mike Foley, wanted to keep the policy racket out of our district; we were doing a pretty good job and had locked up quite a few runners. A couple of runners that we caught even apologized to us, saying that they didn't realize they had crossed over the district boundary lines, and to please don't keep them in jail for three days. They told us other operators had told them that we also confiscated their cars and put sugar in their gas tanks, so that they couldn't get around to take their bets or drop off policy slips. We did confiscate their vehicles, but that was bullshit about the sugar in the gas tanks. On occasion we did play let's-make-a-deal-with-a-few-runners and didn't confiscate their vehicle if they turned us on to a competitive policy operator that was trying to get some business started in our district.

    Carlo and I were parked in our unmarked Ford squad car in the 4500 block of Jackson Boulevard. It was a dark night, and the leaves were on the trees, which blocked the streetlights, making it all the darker. It was around midnight, and we were waiting for a red Cadillac to show up on the next block where two guys were dropping off result slips to a couple of houses in the 4400 block of Jackson Boulevard. The two guys were supposed to be working for the Windy City policy wheel, which was one of the biggest on the South and West Side of Chicago. Oh yea, another clue that we were given was that the Cadillac only had one headlight. I told Carlo that if we didn't find this car, we better find another line of work; little did we know what was in store for us before this night was over. About 2:00 AM we saw a car pull up to the corner of Kilbourn Avenue and Jackson Boulevard facing north. We were able to see that a white male was driving the car, and he stopped in the crosswalk and kept looking east on Jackson Boulevard. After about a minute, he drove across Jackson Boulevard and kept going northbound. We thought that maybe the guy was lost or drunk or maybe was looking for a hooker, which has been known to frequent the area. We didn't think too much about it until a few minutes later when here came the same car back again, pulled up to the corner, and kept looking eastbound on Jackson Boulevard again. We both had a gut feeling that this guy was wrong. About this time, we heard fire engines in the distance, and they were getting closer. Sure as hell, they pulled up to a building near the end on 4400 Jackson Boulevard. When the fire engines got closer, our guy pulled across the street on Jackson Boulevard and parked his car, got out, and started to walk back toward the fire. When he got away from his car, Carlo and I got out of our car; and while keeping him under surveillance, we looked in his car. The car smelled of fuel oil, and there were some tools on the floor of the car. I picked up a wrench, and it was covered with oil; there were also oil-soaked rags on the floor as well. If this guy wasn't a mechanic and gave oil changes for a living, he sure was sloppy.

    We watched the guy walk down to the fire, which was now going full blast in the rear of a three-flat building at 4419 West Jackson Boulevard. Our suspect was standing across the street from the fire, and I swear he had a smile on his face while he watched the flames shooting up to the sky. While Carlo kept an eye on our guy, I spoke to one of the firemen who just came out of the rear of the building. I identified myself and asked him if he knew the cause of the fire. He said that it was arson, and they had found an oil pipe in the basement that had been disconnected from the oil tank. When the oil leaked on the floor and reached a hot water heater, it caused an explosion and fire. Luckily, a tenant who lived in a basement apartment smelled oil, and when he looked out his rear door, that's when the explosion occurred. He immediately called the fire department. Luckily again, there was a firehouse six blocks away, and they were able to put the fire out before the entire building was destroyed and killed someone.

I told Carlo what I had learned, and he told me that our guy reeked of fuel oil. We identified ourselves to our new friend and asked him how his trousers got so full of oil. He said that he had changed the oil in his car earlier and some had spilled on him. We took him back to his car, and I checked the oil, and it was almost muddy. He identified himself as Sam Papalia, fifty, and said that he lived at 4121 West Adams, which was about four blocks away. He also said that he was in the construction business and admitted that he had money coming from the owner of the building for work he had performed on an addition. The owner, Ernest Speranza, had been renovating the building for the past several months and had just gotten it back in excellent shape. Papalia denied that he had anything to do with the fire but admitted there was "ill will" between him and Speranza, and that he still owed him money for work he had done on the building. At that point, we placed Papalia under arrest and transported him to the district station. We also confiscated his oily tools as well as his pants, and sent them to the crime lab for analysis to match up the fuel oil at the fire with the oil that was on his pants and tools. We charged Papalia with arson, and he was brought before Judge Walter Kowalski in felony court; and the case was continued for two weeks, pending the results of the crime lab investigation.

The crime lab results came back in a week, and the report stated that the oil from the oil tank at 4419 West Jackson Boulevard matched the oil on Papalia's tools as well as his trousers – heating oil number 2. The state attorneys decided that they wanted to get Papalia indicted as soon as possible, and I was notified to report to the grand jury the next day to present all the evidence in the case. I testified to all the facts involved in Papalia's arrest and the positive results from the crime lab matching the oil found at the crime scene, with the offender's tools and trousers. A female juror asked me a question I thought was silly. The question was,

"Did you see Mr. Papalia disconnect the oil pipe in the basement"? I felt like saying, *Hell yes saw him disconnect the oil pipe, then I walked away until the explosion started a fire and waited until the fire department showed up to see how prompt they were.* Of course, I told the truth and said, "No, I did not see Mr. Papalia disconnect the oil pipe, as my partner and I was a block away, sitting in a squad car." Well, guess what, after a few minutes, the state attorney came out of the grand jury and told us that the grand jury refused to indict Papalia, because there were no witnesses that saw him disconnect the oil pipe; and the case against Papalia was over. All Carlo and I could do was shake our heads, swear a little, and light up, him a Parodi and me a Lucky Strike. We would have been better off looking for the policy runner with his red Cadillac that night, I guess. Oh well, just another bump in the road. Like they say, sometimes you get the bear, and sometimes the bear gets you.

Blaze Ruins Improvement

Ernest Speranza, 76, went to bed a happy man last Wednesday.

As owner of the three-flat at 4419 Jackson, he has been busy the past few years putting the building back in shape. Neighbors who have visited the building have marveled at the improvements he has wrought.

Wednesday was special because that day marked the completion of a three-room apartment he had built on the back—all perfectly legal.

Maybe now he could take things easy. After all, at 76 it's nice to be able to feel that you are "caught up" in your chores for a little while, at least.

This was not to be for Ernest, however.

* * *

BEFORE 2 a.m. fire engines from the 23rd battalion were screaming down the boulevard bound for 4419 Jackson. Flames were leaping from the basement of Speranza's building.

Fortunately, quick action by firemen under Chief Robert Colburn limited damage to the basement and first floor. The fire report said $500 damage, though it is doubtful if Speranza will be able to make all the necessary repairs for that small a sum.

By a strange quirk of fate, however, Speranza may gain some satisfaction from the fire. Firemen listed arson as a possible cause of the blaze and police have charged a contractor who worked on the three-room addition with starting the blaze.

Pablo Rodriguez, a basement tenant of Speranza's, said he saw someone in the basement fooling around with an oil pipe just before the explosion and fire. Firemen found a pipe leading to the oil heater disconnected. They surmised that the fire was started by permitting oil to leak on the floor and then throwing a match into it.

* * *

THE "QUIRK OF FATE" occurred when Officers Donald Herion and Carlo Canselosi of the Austin station pulled up in the 4400 block just before the fire broke out to investigate a policy wheel reportedly operating in the area.

As they pulled up Herion and Canselosi saw Sam Papalia, 50, 4121 Adams, park his car at Kilbourn and Jackson. After the fire they saw him come back, get into his car and drive into the 4500 block of Jackson, where he parked the car and left it.

Suspicious, they stopped Papalia and talked to him. They said he "reeked" of fuel oil.

Papalia denied he started the fire, but admitted there was "ill will" between him and Speranza. Papalia claimed he had money coming for work on the addition. Speranza said he had already paid the contractor $2,000.

* * *

SPERANZA said he had handed over the money before the work was completed because Papalia told him he needed it for lumber and hospital bills. Papalia had asked him for more money, Speranza said, but he told him he had paid him enough and refused to give him any more.

Police decided to charge Papalia with arson and took him before Judge Walter Kowalski in Felony court Friday. The case was continued to June 19.

Chapter 21

This Eldorado Was Not a Cadillac

Being assigned as a vice detective in the 015th Police District was a very interesting job. A vice detective's responsibility is to investigate violations of the gambling, narcotics, prostitution, and the liquor laws. He is also expected to assist in any in-progress calls such as robberies, burglaries, shootings, rapes, and other serious crimes in the district. Usually there is a sergeant in charge of the vice unit, and the unit can have anywhere from eight to ten men. The sergeant reports directly to the district commander, who then handpicks the men in the vice unit. We would work two shifts – 9:00 AM to 5:00 PM on days, and 9:00 PM to 5:00 AM on nights. On day watch, the main thing we would work on would be bookmakers; every commander emphasized gambling as a top priority and wanted gambling arrests. It seemed that the boss's downtown always rated each commander on how many gambling raids he made. The night shift seemed to have all the other vice categories as well as gambling.

On April 23, 1963, my partner that day was Bill Maloney; we were working days and had plans to bust a bookmaker at a newsstand at Chicago and Cicero Avenue. We had been watching this guy who was taking horse bets from everybody in the neighborhood. Bill had eight children, and I only had four at that time, so he would always tell me that he was twice as good as I was. I did try to catch him, but I only had two more. When we reported to work that day, little did we know that we were going to make the acquaintance of Anthony "Pineapples" Eldorado, also known as Tony Pineapples, Frank Eldorado, and a bunch of other aliases too long to mention. We were assigned to investigate two teenage girls who were arrested for being drunk the night before at Congress and Cicero Avenue. The girls told the arresting officers that they had met two boys in a car and that one of them purchased a bottle of vodka in a hotdog stand at 5463 West Madison Street. They said that the man that sold them the vodka had to get it from the second floor above the hotdog stand. They described him as male, white, fifty years old, five foot nine, 190 pounds, and balding. When we got to that location, we found that the stand was undergoing some construction, but we saw a man that fit the description of the man that sold the teenagers the vodka.

We entered the stand and identified ourselves to the man as police officers and explained why we were there and asked him for his identification. His first reply was, "I don't know what the fuck you're talking about. Besides, if you want to talk to me, let's talk outside." Bill and I looked at each other, and we both knew that this was going to get interesting; but we told him, "OK, let's talk outside." As soon as we got outside, he began calling us vile names and started saying things about our mothers and other nasty things. That was enough for us; we told him he was under arrest for selling liquor to a minor. Well, when we said the magic word *arrest* he went ballistic. He shoved Bill and tried to hit me, but lucky for me I ducked; he was as strong as a horse, and before we got through dancing with him and got him handcuffed, we were a little tired. It must have looked very funny rolling around the ground with this nutcase; the only thing we couldn't figure out was why he went goofy when we told him he was under arrest. Maybe he had something to hide, we thought. Checking his ID, we found out that his name was Anthony Eldorado and his address was 6100 block of South Knox Street, Chicago, Illinois. We told him that we were going to check the second floor above the hotdog stand to see if there were any other bottles of liquor. After we persuaded him, he decided to accompany us to the second floor.

When we got upstairs, we found a three-room apartment, with one bedroom, front room, and kitchen. At this point, Eldorado was really fuming, and I was glad that we had handcuffed his hands behind him.

All the time we were searching the apartment, he was calling us Irish motherfuckers and screaming about being in Nazi, Germany. He must have been calling Maloney those foul names because I'm not Irish; of course, we were mentioning things about his Italian heritage also. When we walked in the bedroom and began looking around, he sat on the bed near the nightstand; that's when I noticed the bulge under a towel. I took the towel off and found a loaded .45 cal. automatic. At that point, he gave me a look and said, "You guys are lucky sons of bitches." And you know what, he was right. If he had given us a bad time downstairs, we never would have put the cuffs on him and who knows what would have happened when we got upstairs. It only shows that sometimes cops get lax in their job, and that's when some bad things can happen. When we brought Eldorado into the station and charged him, we checked his record; that's when we found out that there was a fugitive warrant for Anthony "Pineapples" Eldorado for an outfit murder in Lyons, Illinois, a suburb of Chicago.

Eldorado's arrest record dated back to 1936 when he was arrested for armed robbery in Detroit, Michigan, and was given a sentence of three to twenty years in the Jackson, Michigan, penitentiary. He had numerous other arrests including investigation of murder, battery, resisting arrest, and was known for his explosive disposition as a police fighter. He was reputed to be an enforcer for the crime syndicate and a juice collector. He was reported to be involved in a horsemeat racket with crime boss Fiore "FiFi" Buccieri, who reported to Sam "Mooney" Giancana and Tony Accardo.

When we appeared in court with "Pineapples," Judge Fitzgerald ruled that the evidence was insufficient to support a charge of resisting arrest or assault. A charge of unlawful possession of a weapon was dismissed because we didn't have search warrant, so was the charge of selling liquor to a minor.

The murder case involving Eldorado fell apart because all the witnesses had disappeared; it seems that the murder happened five years ago.

In January the next year, a cache of guns and ammunition was recovered in a South Side warehouse in a locker rented to Tony Eldorado. The police conjectured that this may be Tony "Pineapples" Eldorado but couldn't prove it. Naturally, I thought that Tony would have gone straight after Maloney and I arrested him. Am I nuts or what?

ANTHONY ELDORADO

The police report refers to him as one of FIFI BUCCIERI'S handymen.

680-79-15	In a report of April 24, 1934, TONY ELDORADO, 17, 1441 Flournoy, was arrested April 17, 1934, and charged with tampering. The automobile was found to have been stolen and used in a burglary. He was discharged when there was no evidence that he was doing anything with the car at the time.
65-224-40	In an American clip of June 30, 1951, TONY (PINEAPPLES) ELDORADO, 35, 619 S. Loomis, was questioned by the police concerning the slaying of LEONARD CAIFANO.
6A-23-145	In a Tribune clip of January 21, 1952, ANTHONY ELDORADO, 36, 619 S. Loomis, was arrested as keeper of a dice game at 655 S. Paulina. (He was freed in court January 22, 1952.)
60-184-366	In an American clip of March 27, 1952, attorney, ANTHONY CHANPAGNE informed the State's Attorney's office that he would surrender FIORE BUCCIERI and TONY ELDORADO for questioning in the horsemeat investigation.
60-48-1036	In a Tribune clip of February 24, 1963, MICHAEL TENORE, secretary treasurer of the FRONTIER FINANCE CORPORATION, 5131 Madison, said that TONY (PINEAPPLES) ELDORADO used a back room of the finance company to make phone calls to get a mortgage on a restaurant he way buying, but that he did not work for the finance company.
60-319-38	In a Sun Times clip of September 23, 1963, it was indicated that the Chicago Police listed TONY ELDORADO in the West Side Syndicate family in testimony before the U.S. Senate Committee investigation.
60-55-1915	In a Tribune clip of January 15, 1964, a cache of guns and ammunition was found in a South.side warehouse, in a locker rented to TONY ELDORADO c/o JOHN ELDORADO. The police conjectured that this may be TONY (PINEAPPLES) ELDORADO, 49, an ex-convict, who had a last known address at 5456 W. Madison.
65-166-564A pgs. 1 & 16	In a police report of June 21, 1964, w/r ACCARDO-HAWLEY, TONY ELDORADO was observed at the reception at the VILLA VENICE, and he was also seen at main gate of the restaurant and lounge to make sure that the gates were left open.
60-55-2220	In an inquiry made by a Federal Agency regarding ANTHONY ELDORADO, two addresses were given: 5643 W. Madison and 6107 S. Knox, on July 12, 1965.

FIST SWINGING HOOD REVIVES MURDER QUIZ

BY WILLIAM JUNEAU

Lyons police reopened their investigation yesterday into the 1957 gangland slaying of Willard O. Bates, a tavern owner, with the arrest by Chicago police of Tony (Pineapples) Eldorado, 49, a hoodlum and associate of the murdered man. Eldorado, an ex-convict who has served time for robbery in a Michigan prison, was arrested Tuesday evening by vice district detectives from the Austin police district in a hot dog stand he intends to open at 5463 Madison st., and under the apartment where he lives.

Sgt. William Maloney and Donald Herion sought to question Eldorado about peddling bottles of vodka from his home. They were unaware of his name and did not know that Lyons police had been searching for him for six years.

Eldorado, long known by police for his explosive disposition, attacked Maloney and Herion, when they questioned him. The policemen warded off the wild swings by the gangster and took him to the Austin station.

The leader of Chicago's crime syndicate, Anthony Accardo, would like to retire but can't.

Other major figures in the Chicago outfit: Joseph Aiuppa (top picture), Accardo's elderly lieutenant. At bottom left, Anthony Spilotro (in a 1960 photo), who wants Accardo's job; at right, Anthony (Pineapples) Eldorado, onetime chauffeur and bodyguard for the late Fiore (Fifi) Buccieri.

Chapter 22

The Blue Dahlia: Where Men Were Women

The Blue Dahlia was a lounge at 5640 West North Avenue on the northwest side of Chicago. Emil "Moe" Monaco was the owner of the place; he was a small man, about five foot six, 145 pounds, bald, and wore glasses, and was pushing fifty. Moe used to own a pizzeria on the east end of our district but got tired of his hands being in dough all day long and a hot oven blasting heat in his face. Moe wasn't married, so when he decided to change careers, he didn't have to get an OK from a wife. Moe bought the Blue Dahlia in the early 1960s and thought that he would give the bar business a try, even though he didn't have any experience selling booze. I was working in the 015th District as a vice detective, and the vice unit was responsible for any investigations that would occur where liquor was sold. Every now and then, my partners, Bob Peters and Carlo Cangelosi, would stop in the Dahlia to see how things were going with Moe. Sometimes when we stopped in there at night, Moe would be sitting at the bar, watching the news on a portable television set. The place was empty, and obviously Moe was not doing very well in the bar business. He told me that he even reduced the prices on his drinks, had a happy hour where he had free food, and the drinks were two for one; nothing seemed to work, he said. That's when he said that he had an idea of turning the place into a female impersonator club. I told him that I didn't think that that was the way to go, as the Blue Dahlia was located in a residential area and the people in the neighborhood would surely raise hell when they found out about it. I told him that I would have to inform the district commander about the change he wanted to make and that I would get back to him.

The commander wasn't too happy about Moe opening a female impersonator show, especially in a residential neighborhood, but he said that there wasn't anything we could do until he broke the law. We told Moe what the commander said and told him that if he went ahead with his plans, he had better run a straight place or he would get busted. Moe went ahead with his idea, and within two weeks, he had hired five female impersonators for his show. The star of the show was a young man by the name of Gale Sherman; he was about five foot eight, weighed 125 pounds, was in his early twenties, and was a good-looking male. When he dressed up as a female, you couldn't tell the difference; and he put on a terrific show. The other members of the group were also foolers, and when they dressed up in their gowns, they all looked like beautiful women. There lip-syncing of popular singers of that time like Doris Day, Peggy Lee, and Sarah Vaughn was perfect. Of course, all of them were gay, and they loved their work. Naturally, they attracted a lot of other gay people to the Blue Dahlia, but there wasn't any trouble involving them at all. A lot of straight people came to see the show also, and most of them couldn't believe that the women they saw on the stage were really men. Within a month's time, people were lined up outside, waiting to get in to see the show. A lot of them were senior citizens from the neighborhood that probably wanted to find out what the lines were outside the Dahlia. A couple of times, when we were checking on the place, we overheard some of the customers talking about how great the show was, but they were not convinced that the performers were really men.

Moe was the happiest guy in town; people were flocking to see the show from all over town. The star of the show was Gale Sherman, who was from St. Louis and the son of a bandleader. Sherman's goal in life was to have a sex change operation so he could really be a woman. "Everybody thought he was anyway, so what the hell was the difference," he said.

We had been working on a bar on North Central Avenue that was booking horses; we busted the place for gambling and locked up a young man who was taking the bets in the place. He told us that the boss of the tavern was a woman by the name of Rose. She wasn't on the premises at the time so we couldn't arrest her. It seems that Moe had been going out with a blond named Rosie, but we didn't connect her to Rose who owned the tavern we busted. Rosie didn't care for us too much under the circumstances, but what the hell, thats showbiz. Eventually Moe and Rosie got married – much to my surprise – and she sold her tavern and began working in the Blue Dahlia as the hostess. Rose had a terrible temper, as I remember. One afternoon Rose and Moe had a terrible argument; she went totally berserk and jumped though the front window of the Dahlia. She only suffered minor cuts, believe it or not, but I guess she proved her point that if you run into a plate glass window hard enough, it will surely break.

One night my regular partners were off, and I was working with a new man on the vice unit, an African American cop by the name of Willie Johnson. Johnson was a good man and had never seen a show like the one at the Blue Dahlia, so I decided to make a routine premise check. I neglected to tell him that the performers were men and not women. When he saw the acts he said, "Boy, are they good looking' women." They sure fooled the hell out of Willie. While Willie was watching the show, I noticed a girl and two men seated at the bar; they were just acting a little strange and not watching the show. The place was really crowded so I was able to stand real close to them without them becoming aware of my presence. I overheard the woman tell one guy that she could show him a real good time if they left now. I thought that the broad was a hooker and she was working the bar, so I told Willie, who was mesmerized watching the show, to follow me out when I left. I was on to something.

The girl and the two men left and got into the victim's car. When they left, three men in another car followed them. We began tailing the two cars to see just what the hell was going on. I knew at that point that this guy was in trouble and that he wasn't going to get lucky; he was probably going to get robbed, or worse. We followed the two cars to the area of Montrose and Narragansett Avenue where they pulled into a side street. We were able to see the girl and two guys in the soon-to-be victim's car, and they didn't appear to be assaulting him. The three guys in the second car joined the guy and the girl and appeared to be scaring the hell out of him. After a couple of minutes, the four guys and the girl got in the second car and started to drive away, leaving the victim in his car. I blocked their exit and with our headlights in their eyes, we identified ourselves as police officers and told them to keep their hands in a place where we could see them. I'm sure they could see the shotgun and .38 we had pointed at them; that, along with calling them a lot of vile names, convinced them that we were serious about blowing their heads off if they made a wrong move. After we got them out of the car and spread-eagled on a garage wall, I walked back to the victim's car and found him lying on the floor, shaking. I identified myself as a police officer, and all he could say was, "They told me to lie on the floor for ten minutes," and that was what he was going to do. I asked him what happened, and he said that he was just robbed by four men and a girl of his wallet and money. When he finally got off the floor and saw the five bandits spread-eagled against the garage wall, he believed that Willie and I were the police. We told him that we would have to keep his wallet for evidence and that he would have to appear in court. The bandits were just getting into robbing guys after the girl, who was nineteen, picked them up. The others were twenty-six, twenty-five, nineteen, and nineteen, all old enough to go to the penitentiary for robbery.

The funny part of this whole charade was when the victim told me that he thought that the good-looking girl was really a man. He said that he was a homosexual, and when he found out that the girl was really a girl, he was devastated. What the hell, it takes all kinds, I guess.

We went back to the Blue Dahlia after the paperwork was done, and told Moe what had happened. He said, "You can't blame me for that, Don. I try my best to watch everybody that comes in the place, honest to God." I told him, "No problem, but with this kind of entertainment you have to keep your eyes open because there are a lot of weirdo's out there."

At the time the Blue Dahlia was in business, the performers in the show lived for one night a year – that was Halloween. That was the day that they could wear anything they wanted outside and not get arrested. They had a Halloween ball at the Aragon ballroom, and it was really something to see if you were into that sort of thing. They would wear gowns fit for a "pardon the expression" queen, and rent limos for the night. When the limo would pull up to the ballroom, the driver would get out and open the door for the passengers; at this time about ten white doves would fly out followed by two guys dressed up like the queen of England and Princess Margaret. They also had hired four or five photographers, with their cameras flashing, catching their every move. The whole thing looked like a Hollywood premiere. There was also a contest to see who had the best-looking gown; the prize for first place was, I don't think you really would want to know.

Meanwhile, Moe and Rosie bought a very nice ranch home at 7100 West Wabansia Avenue and were living high on the hog. The Blue Dahlia was still drawing people to see the show. In fact, I saw some tour buses that would make the Dahlia one of their attractions in Chicago. Moe lived a little west of Sam DeStefano, who was a nutcase and an outfit juice collector, as well as a suspected hit man for the mob. Sam was a member of the 42 Gang, who were a bunch of burglars and thieves. Sam Giancana was also a member of the gang, as well as a lot of other mob guys who were running things in the outfit. A friend of mine, who was a detective at the old Thirty-first District, Cragin told me a story about DeStefano, which he swore was true. It seems that a black man had been waiting for a bus at Cicero and Grand Avenue on his way to work. He said that a white man offered to give him a lift in a Cadillac; he was running a little late for work so he accepted the ride. The next thing he knew, the man pulled a gun on him and told him to be quiet so he wouldn't get hurt. He said that they drove westbound and then down some side streets, where the man pulled into a garage of a very expensive house. The man forced him to enter the house, where he saw a nice-looking lady. The lady was Sam's wife; at gunpoint, he forced his wife and the black man to have sex while he watched. Mad Sam, as he was known, then drove the black man back to Cicero and Grand Avenue and told him to get out of the car. The Thirty-first District was only about a block away, so the black man walked into the station and told the station detectives what had happened to him. They didn't believe him at first, but when the man told them he could take them to the house, they put him in their squad, and he pointed out Mad Sam's house. He then added that if they would look under the seat on the passenger side of the Cadillac, they would find his lunch. They looked, and sure as hell the lunch was under the seat; now they believed him. Sam and his wife both denied ever having seen the black man before, and that was that. Moe, who had bought part of a restaurant in a Far Western suburb, told me about his partner, who was ripping him off, and he was really pissed off about it. He said that had known Mad Sam for a few years, and he made a mistake of telling him about his problem. He said that Sam told him point-blank that he would be glad to whack the guy for him, but Moe would have to help him dig a hole to bury the guy, as his back hurt him. Moe said that he almost had a heart attack when he said that and told him that no thanks he could handle the problem himself.

It seems that Mad Sam had two daughters who were really nice girls, and they owned a couple of dogs. Sam hated the dogs and threatened to kill them if the girls didn't get them out of the house. Rosie, who knew the girls, volunteered to take the dogs off their hands. One of the dogs was pregnant and was about to have pups. When the pups were born, Moe asked me if I wanted to take one of them. I said yes and went over to his house to pick one out. As things turned out, I took two of the pups and brought them home to my wife and children. I was a hero with the kids, but it took about an hour before my wife started smiling at me. The dogs were snoodles, a mixture of schnauzer and poodle. I named one of the dogs Sam and the other one Mr. Bates. As things turned out, it was one of the best things I ever did.

In May 1966, my commander was transferred downtown to 1121 South State Street; he was going to be the director of the vice control section of the organized crime division. The new commander who took his place was Mark Thanasaurus, who had a bit of a reputation. My partner Bob Peters and I had broken in Mark when he was made sergeant a few years before. He rose rapidly through the ranks and was now a district commander. My old commander requested that I transfer downtown to the gambling unit, and under the circumstances, I agreed with him. I was gone the next day.

It seems that Moe had to join a club that Mark set up; actually, it was very similar to paying street taxes. Moe said the membership for him was $500 a month. Rumors were floating around about a tavern club in the 015th District where the owners had to pay monthly dues. The U.S. Attorney's office started an investigation in the district, and Moe had to appear before a federal grand jury, where he was given immunity to either talk or go to jail. Moe testified, as did other tavern owners in the district; and as a result some policemen went to jail, including Commander Mark Thanasaurus. A few years later, when Mark got out of jail, person or persons unknown assassinated him on the North Side of Chicago. Moe and Rosie stayed in business for a few more years and then moved to Las Vegas, Nevada, where Moe bought Jimmy the Greek's house, who was a famous gambler and television star. Sam DeStefano got a surprise on a Saturday in the summer of 1973, when two guys wearing masks walked up to him while he was in his garage and shotgunned him to death.

Gale Sherman was reported to have had a complete sex change, moved to Hawaii, and married a major in the United States Air Force.

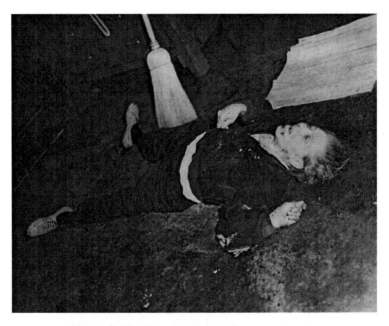

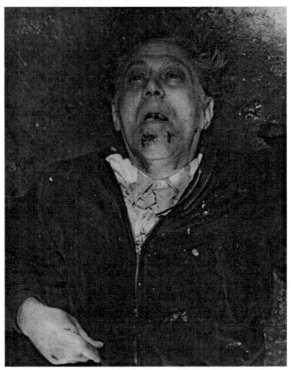

*Photos of mobster Sam DeStefano murdered
Source: Chicago Police Dep't*

Chapter 23

Car Chases

A car chase may be one of the most dangerous experiences that could happen to a police officer. It is also a lot of other things as well, such as exciting, nerve wracking, satisfying if you catch the bad guy, and deadly to yourself as well as to other motorists or pedestrians. Normally, a car chase begins with a traffic violation; when a police officer observes the driver of a vehicle commits a traffic violation, he will attempt to have the driver of the vehicle pull over to the side of the road. At this point, all he knows about the driver is that he committed a traffic violation; if the driver attempts to drive off and try to elude the officer, you better believe that the officer will be right on his tail. It is just human nature, I guess.

According to rules and regulations of the police department, the officer must notify the communication center and inform them that he is in pursuit of a vehicle, and give them his present location, direction of travel, as well the make of the vehicle and the reason he is pursuing the vehicle. At that point, the dispatcher will notify the officer's supervisor that the officer is chasing a vehicle for traffic violations. When the supervisor learns that the offender has only committed traffic violations, he will more than likely terminate the pursuit. This, of course, pisses off the pursuing officer, but he had better obey the order because if he doesn't and something goes wrong, he will be held responsible for his actions.

If an officer becomes involved in the pursuit of a motor vehicle that he has reason to believe the occupants have committed or attempted to commit a forcible felony, or is attempting to escape by the use of a deadly weapon, or otherwise indicates that they will endanger human life, or inflict great bodily harm unless arrested without delay, they are justified in pursuing the vehicle. But they must still notify the communication section of the pursuit and to inform the supervisor the reason for the pursuit. In any police chase, an officer must use common sense and good judgment and evaluate the driving of the fleeing felon. It is possible that the vehicle will go through red lights and stop signs at a high rate of speed, which could cause endangerment to life and property. The police must continue to evaluate the ongoing chase with respect to its danger, and make a judgment whenever necessary to terminate the chase. The prime objective of the police is the safety of the public, as well as their own safety. There have been cop shows on television that will show car chases, and normally the offender will always be apprehended after a wild chase scene. California seems to be on television more than any other part of the country in wild police pursuits. In my opinion, the key to apprehending a fleeing felon is the use of police helicopters, which is a great advantage for law enforcement. Helicopters can even notify the police of the whereabouts of a fleeing offender that abandons his vehicle and tries to escape on foot; they are equipped with searchlights that can track the offender at night.

The Chicago Police Department no longer has helicopters, so things have to be done the old-fashioned way. The odds are that anyone who attempts to escape from the police will be successful because police officers involved in car chases have to be extremely careful of other vehicles on the street as well as pedestrians. The fleeing felon doesn't care about other vehicles that may get in his way and will do anything to keep from being apprehended by the police. A lot of chases turn out in favor of the bad guys; good guys sometimes are left in the dust. Another chase we got involved in, we lost the bad guys due to traffic conditions we got caught up in. We didn't get the bad guys, but we did get revenge. We were involved in a mob-connected gambling investigation, which was again in the area of Grand Avenue and Racine on Chicago's West Side known as the Patch. It was early December, and the streets were very slick from a recent snowfall; it was not the time to get involved in a chase. We had been looking for two outfit guys in the neighborhood, but we didn't know what kind of car they were driving, but whatever it was we knew they would be dirty. We had three excellent unmarked cars in the area looking for them; we knew that on occasion they would frequent a card room at the southwest corner of Grand and May Street, so we set up surveillance on the card room.

This neighborhood was very difficult to set up surveillance on anything because most of the people in the area were very suspicious of any strange vehicle that didn't belong there. This time we got lucky when we spotted our two mutts pull up in a black Oldsmobile and park in front of the card room. The passenger, whose name was Vito, got out and went in the card room while the driver, Paulie, remained in the car. We were able to observe Vito hugging a couple of guys in the card room who appeared to be refugees from *The Godfather* movie. After a few minutes, Vito returned to the car and got in. They had been facing east on Grand Avenue so we set up on their car to go east; forget about it, Paulie made a U-turn and started going west on Grand Avenue but got caught at a red light at Ogden Avenue. This gave us just enough time to pull around and almost surround their car – one car on their right, one behind them, and my car next to the driver's side. We rolled down our window and identified ourselves as police officers and told them to pull over to the side as soon as the light changed. I was really happy that we finally found these two wise guys.

Paulie looked at us and said, "Fuck you." He then proceeded to drive through the red light, where they almost got flattened by a large semitrailer, which managed to stop before it hit them. This move really took us by surprise, but we should have known better, I guess. Here we go again, another chase. We had to go around the semi that partially blocked the street, and a car going east on Grand Avenue almost whacked us. The Oldsmobile started hitting a few side streets off Grand Avenue, and before we could get on their tail, they were gone. This turned out to be one of the shortest chases in history. We didn't even have enough time to get on the air and notify communications that we were involved in a chase, which would have been embarrassing, to say the least.

We started looking in alleys and side streets for the Oldsmobile; we knew they couldn't have gone too far out of the area. We finally got lucky and found the car in a vacant lot behind a row of houses; of course, the bad guys were gone. We checked the license plate on the car, but it was registered to a vacant lot. At this point, I thought that an examination of the Oldsmobile was needed. We got under the hood and pulled out every wire we could find as well as pouring dirt in the carburetor and gas tank. Someone came up with an ice pick that worked well on the tires. Needless to say, we lost the chase, but self-satisfaction may be better in the long run. I would like to have seen the two mopes' faces when they got brave enough to return to their car.

Usually, police agencies will have officers take a driving course. Since an officer will spend the majority of patrol time behind the wheel of a car, the officer will need extensive training in emergency vehicle driving. Some large-city law enforcement agencies average over one police equipment accident per day. Not only is it expensive to repair these cars, but an accident often results in injuries to officers and civilians, and the distinct possibility of a court case against the officer and the department.

Because the instructors assume that officers already have some average or better-than-average behind-the-wheel skills, the driving portion of police training usually focuses on emergency techniques to help the officer during high-risk pursuit-type operations. This includes "speed" braking, driving in reverse, turn driving, high-speed turning, and skid control – because the officers spend so much time behind the wheel and a moving car can be just as much of a deadly weapon as a gun. It is essential that the officer is aware of their responsibility every time they operate a police vehicle in a normal or emergency situation.

The news networks love car chases; it's like giving Krispy Kreme donuts to a dieter. You know that they are bad for you. You know that you should resist. But man, they're so tasty. I recall seeing CNN, Fox News Channel, and MSNBC showing pictures of a car, its hood torn off, stuck in gravel alongside a rural California highway. The police had it surrounded and were preparing to unleash a dog to subdue the driver. It was the end of a chase on Los Angeles highways followed by helicopters with cameras trained on the runaway vehicle that wound up on a rural road. I'm sure that the television audience wondered who the driver was. What motivated him? No one knew, or frankly, cared. Yet the chase was enough to push other news like the Middle East crisis, the sex scandal in the Catholic Church off the TV screens.

The reason became obvious; checking with the networks that viewed the chase, we learned that Fox News Channel nearly doubled its typical daytime viewers for the ninety minutes the chase was on to

1.38 million people. CNN had 900,000 viewers compared with its April daytime average of 555,000. MSNBC's audience was reported to be 60 percent higher than normal.

The networks say that it is kind of human drama; it's the good guys versus the bad guys that fits the definition of news. They marvel at how the viewers suddenly materialize when a car chase comes on the air. One media watchdog said the televised car chases further blur lines between news and entertainment. "News judgment about what is important takes second place to what is exciting viewing. Eventually, CNN judged the May 6 chase newsworthy because it snarled traffic throughout a major metropolitan area and, with the police standoff, lives were at stake. The viewing audience let the network know that they think car chases are news, and that's why they show car chases. A word of advice about getting involved in a chase: An officer must use common sense and think about the consequences. If the car you're chasing crashes into another car or a bystander and kills or injures them, you are probably going to be held responsible. Or God forbid your squad car hits another vehicle and you kill or injure someone, or worse yet, you and your partner wind up injured or dead. A good thought would be, if they get away what did you lose? It's possible that you got the license number anyway, and tomorrow is another day.

Chapter 24

Bookmakers – The Mob – Who Cares?

    In 1939, I grew up in an apartment building at North Avenue and Cicero. I lived with my mother, sister, an uncle, and sometimes my grandparents. Things were pretty tough in those days, and my mom was having a bad time; my dad had gotten sick and was in a hospital, so things were kind of rough on her. My mom got some help from my grandparents and my uncle, but it wasn't enough so we had to rent a room out to a friend of my uncle's; his name was Shoes. My uncle Earl was a horse player and worked for the streetcar company as a conductor; the barn was right across the street from us. As I was growing up, I learned about horse bettors from watching him try and pick a winner every day. When he won, I was told about it; but when he lost, it was usually kind of quiet around the apartment.

    When the Japs bombed Pearl Harbor on December 7, 1941, we were involved in World War II, and there was work for everybody in war plants and all the other businesses involved in the war effort. There was also an increase in gambling around the neighborhood. The newsstand on the corner was running a book as well as the barbershop underneath our apartment, which was booking and dealing in football parlay cards. Also a train men supply store across from my apartment on North Avenue was also booking horses and running card games in the back room for the motormen and conductors that drove streetcars and were working split shifts. When there was heat on gambling in the neighborhood, Jerry, the newsstand operator, wouldn't take any bets from anybody at the newsstand; he would have all his bettors call his wife, Lil, who lived in the apartment next to ours. On Cicero Avenue, there was a cigar store that booked and ran poker games as well in the back room.

Actually, my father-in-law would make a stop in the card room from time to time, and was known to even place a horse bet on occasion. To make a long story short, there were at least seven bookmaking operations going on just at the corner where we lived. It seemed that the more money people made, the more they bet, which holds true to this day.

When I was growing up and going to school, I was like everybody else; I would bet on a parlay card with Joe the Barber every week for a dollar. It was kind of fun watching the scores in the newspapers to see if you won. All you had to do was pick three teams; they all had to win with the point spread, and you would get back $6. Parlay cards were all over town – in schools, factories, and offices. I never won; but what the hell, what was $1. I never gave a thought about who was booking the cards or how much money he was making. Who cared? Nobody. But every now and then, I would see a guy in the barbershop who looked as if he just walked out of *The Godfather* movie. He never got a haircut; he would walk in the backroom with Joe, stay a few minutes, and then leave. Of course, another guy smoking a cigar would pick him up in front in a big old black Cadillac. I remembered seeing these two guys at the other book joints in the neighborhood from time to time. But then, like I said, who the hell cares anyway? – just like today.

I was sixteen in 1945 and decided that it was time to quit school, because what the hell did they know anyway? I changed my birth certificate from 1929 to 1928, and joined the Marine Corps for four years. Well, that lasted for one week, and they found out how old I was and told me "nice try" and sent me home. World War II ended, and all the GIs were coming home to find jobs, get married, and live a good life. A friend of mine named Horney got discharged from the Marines after serving twenty-eight months in the South Pacific and called me up and wanted to buy me a beer to celebrate his discharge. I told him that I would take a ride with him but that I would have to drink Coke. He picked me up in a 1938 Pontiac, and before I knew it, we were in Cicero, Illinois, at a bar called the 4811 Club on Cermak Road. The joint was really jumping at 2:00 PM. There were two very big burly bouncers at the door. They didn't check anybody's ID; they were just there for any problems that may come up, I guess. I had never been in a place like this. There were at least four tables going with card games. Money was all over the tables. There were a couple of phones ringing with a couple of mustaches taking horse bets right in front of everybody. The beer cost $1 for a small bottle. There were also dancing girls walking around the place, winking at everybody, wanting you to buy them a drink. It was so crowded that Horney only had one beer and wanted to leave the place.

I found out later that the bar was owned by the crime syndicate and that the boss was a mob guy by the name of Joey Aiuppa and his partner Joe Corngold. But like I said, who the hell cared who owned the place; as long as there was a chance to gamble, that's all that counted.

Cicero, Illinois, was approximately six square miles and had about 150 saloons scattered around town, a lot of them went twenty-four hours a day with prostitution and gambling. The town was controlled by the outfit, and that's where all the money went. So what, I sure as hell didn't care and never gave it a thought; every now and then you would hear about somebody turning up in a trunk somewhere or some guy that got his legs broke with a baseball bat. I was like everyone else, as long as it didn't affect me personally. So what if they kill there own people? I could care less.

Because I grew up in a neighborhood that had a few bookmakers around, I was used to it. I never really gave a thought to the Chicago mob running the whole thing. When I got out of the army after the Korean War in 1953 and started to hang around a couple of the bars in the neighborhood, I found out from one of the owners of Bruno's at North and Cicero that he had to take his jukebox from a certain company. That also held true for a shuffle board game that he had; he had no choice in the matter. One time he tried to get a bumper pool game in the bar and was bringing it in the front door when a couple of wise guys told him to get it the hell out of there, that if he wanted a pool game they would send him one. But that wasn't my business so I really didn't give it a second thought, but I was getting an education about the outfit.

It wasn't until I went on the job in February 1955 that I began to realize just how powerful the Chicago mob was. Part of my education was when I was detailed to that poolroom to make sure that the boys weren't making book in the place. Some old-timers explained certain things about the outfit that I wasn't taught in the police academy. They asked me how many times did I hear an alderman in our district complain to the police or the newspapers about gambling operations in his ward. They said that there was a reason for that; the alderman needed campaign contributions to take ads out in the newspapers that they were running for office. They also controlled liquor licenses in their ward, as well as jobs and a lot of other things. They were trying to explain to me that politics and the outfit go hand in hand, that one needed the other to exist in Chicago. They also told me that if I arrested the wrong guy, there was a chance that I would be transferred to another district; all it took was a phone call. I found that out myself in 1979 when I was transferred out of the organized crime division back in uniform, looking at the fish in Montrose Harbor on the midnights. I guess at that point I wasn't surprised. Because I had busted so many bad guys, I didn't know whom to get pissed off at.

I did find out what happened though. We had been making a lot of raids in Cicero, Berwyn and other Western suburbs, which, I was told, embarrassed the Cook County sheriff. His name was Richard Elrod. I didn't know if he was on the square or maybe he was naïve as to his vice control unit. We were getting a lot of publicity on some of the raids we made in Cicero because of its past reputation as being a mobbed-up town, going back to Al Capone. When Sheriff Elrod asked the commander of his vice unit, "how come the Chicago police can find gambling going on in the suburbs and you guys can't?" the answer he got was "Herion was wiretapping, and they weren't." Elrod then reported this news to the Chicago police superintendent, who became very upset. He then chewed out my lieutenant's ass about this. My lieutenant at the time was Ed Berry, a standup guy who denied the accusation. He told him that if the sheriff's vice unit got off their dead ass and opened their eyes, they may have better luck. As things turned out, the deputy superintendent who chased me had been a good friend of some bosses in the sheriff's office and did them a favor; but a new superintendent took over and transferred me back to the organized crime division. Some people assigned to the sheriff's vice unit wound up getting busted by the FBI and went to prison.

Chapter 25

Zagorski's Rathskeller: Was It Lottie or Louie?

Lottie Zagorski was a name I heard of for years when I was a vice detective in the 015th District. Lottie ran one of the biggest bookmaking operations in the Chicago area in some tavern on the Near West Side. Due to the fact that the tavern was in another district, I really didn't care too much about it; we had enough action in our own district to try and bust. When I was transferred downtown to the organized crime division gambling unit, I remembered all the stories that I had heard from people through the years about Lottie Zagorski; only now she was in my jurisdiction.

Lottie's tavern was called Zagorski's Rathskeller at 1925 West Cortland Avenue. It was a neighborhood bar and catered to the area residents as well as a lot of other people who wanted to make bets on horses or sports. Lottie was reported to be a woman and always wore a dress, but there were rumors that Lottie was really a man who dressed like a woman. The correct name for that would be a hermaphrodite, half man and half woman. I had a couple of informants who also said that Lottie was the nicest person you would ever want to meet and always helped out anyone who needed help. That's OK with me, but I didn't care if Lottie was really a Louie; if they were booking in the place, I was going to bust them. Lottie was also reported to be running about twenty other bookmaking operations and was associated with gambling boss Andy "the Greek" Lochious, who worked for Joseph "Joe Gag's" Gagliano, who reported to Jackie "the Lackey" Cerone.

I had enough probable cause to get a search warrant for Zagorski's Rathskeller, so my partner – who at the time was Wally Goebbert – and the rest of our crew paid Lottie a visit at the noon hour, which was the busiest time of the day for bookmakers. The bar was packed with people; some of them were drinking and eating, and some were perusing scratch sheets. There was a woman behind the bar wearing a long print dress and earrings; she appeared to be about fifty-five years old and had shoulder-length salt-and-pepper hair. When we approached the bar, she said, "Hi, fellas, what can I get you? She had a very deep voice, just like a man's. I had to look at her twice to make sure that she was the one who said "hi, fellas." We identified ourselves as police officers and gave her a copy of the search warrant. Some men who were sitting at the end of the bar were so interested in their scratch sheets that they didn't even know that the police were on the premises. There were a couple of card games going on; the players in the games just kept playing and obviously they did not realize that the police were watching them. A phone booth was toward the back of the room, and a male was on the phone, taking horse bets from anonymous bettors.

In a rear room back of the bar, a woman by the name of Phyllis, age forty-four, came out carrying some papers in her hand; she didn't know that we were there either. The papers were bet slips, which we confiscated after placing her under arrest along with Lottie. Another bartender, Peter Martin, age fifty, was searched; and he also was found to be in possession of bet slips. He was arrested as well. While we were on the premises, the telephone rang numerous times in the phone booth. We answered the phone and took horse bets from a variety of bettors. Some of them asked for Lottie, and others didn't seem to care who took their bets; as long as they got to make their bets, they were happy. Behind the bar was a picture of Lottie in a blue dress; another picture showed a few men who appeared to be politicians. There were rumors that local politicians frequented the Rathskeller and had parties in the basement, which went on all night. Lottie donated the basement for fundraisers to help people in the neighborhood who ran into money problems or had sickness in the family.

When we transported Lottie down to the gambling unit at 1121 South State Street, I asked her the big question, are you really a woman?

Lottie said yes she was and that I could ask anyone in the neighborhood if I didn't believe her. I have to admit that Lottie Zagorski was one of the nicest persons I have ever met, and I was convinced that she was a he and that she really believed that she was a female. It was a shame that she couldn't talk like a woman as hard as she tried; she sounded like Peter "Columbo" Falk. When we got in the office, we had numerous messages waiting for us from people who called on Lottie's behalf. A couple of judges, police captains, a ward committeeman and an alderman. Lottie was sure well liked, that's for sure. When we checked her record, we found that the first time she was arrested for bookmaking was back in 1952. Her next arrest was in 1963 when she was indicted by a federal grand jury for failure to possess a $50 federal wagering stamp. Lottie hadn't been arrested for three years until we got her in 1966.

The biggest problem we had was which lockup we were going to send her to to be processed. If we sent her to the men's lockup, that could cause a bit of a problem because she had her long print dress on and woman's shoes with earrings and a necklace. Lottie knew what we were trying to decide and had a look on her face of total panic when she heard the phrase *men's lockup*. To make a long story short, we sent her to the women's lockup because we didn't have the guts to send her to the men's lockup. When she found out where she was going, all she could say was, "God bless you, boys, you've made an old woman happy," in the lowest men's voice I've ever heard. Lottie was busted a few more times in the Rathskeller before she passed away of natural causes on January 20, 1973, at the age of fifty-nine. They say her funeral procession was a few blocks long, attended by her old cronies, cops, firemen, aldermen, priests, and a lot of bookmakers. I still never really found out if it was *Lottie* or *Louie*.

Turning a blind eye was business as usual in 1930's Chicago and at Lotties business was extremely "usual." Only a few feet under the seemingly laid back corner grocery store/tavern, Lottie presided over the kind of den of iniquity that legends are made of - the Rathskeller. Lotties was the portal to a basement world of craps, cards, off track betting and women of the night.

Lottie was a legend in Bucktown. The neighborhood residents just didn't know the whole reason why. There was something peculiar about her looks and the way she handled herself. This hulking 6' man-like person looked rather odd in a floral-print dress, but her charm allowed her to move in all circles. Whether she was schmoozing the local politicos, handing out dollars to school kids or tossing someone out of the joint, she was always respected.

Rumors went flying around the city about the alleged goings-on in the basement but nothing ever stuck. The bottom finally dropped out in '66 when the Feds moved in. Lottie was forced to close her doors but certainly her spirit, and some say, even her ghost remains at the place that still bears her name.

LOTTIE or LOUIE?

"Miss Zagorski was taken into custody after the discovery of a large number of betting records and other Gambling paraphernalia in her sleeping room at the rear of the tavern and in an ice box behind the bar."

"Police said the wireroom and tavern gambling operations were part of a wide-spread near NW side ring operated under the auspices of Andy (The Greek) Lochious, a lieutenant of Joseph (Joe Gags) Gagliano, a crime syndicate gambling and loan shark boss."

"Arrested as leader in the bookmaking ring was Miss Lottie Virginia Zagorski, 52, who held a similar role when the tavern was last raided Oct. 27 1966."

Chicago Tribune, Dec. 14, 1967

"More than 10,000 football parlay cards and two 16 gauge shotguns were seized."

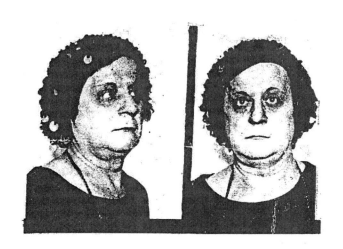

NAME:

ADDRESS:

ALIASES:

DOB: 19 November 1915   SS#: 356-28-6127

R#: 134331   FBI#: 709 292 E

ILLINOIS
DRIVER'S LICENSE #:

CRIMINAL ACTIVITY:

Wireroom & bookmaking overseer in conjunction with Andy "The Greek" Louchious, near northwest side of Chicago, has (1) previous conviction for gambling.

AREAS FREQUENTED:

Active in the 13th. &
14th. Police Districts.

Location and dates
of previous arrests:

1925 W. Cortland 6 May.'66

1925 W. Cortland 27 Oct.'66

1925 W. Cortland 13 Dec.'67

1925 W. Cortland 21 Mar.'68

Chapter 26

1968 Democratic Convention

The 1968 Democratic National Convention turned into the Battle of Chicago; some newspapers said that it was a police riot, and the Chicago Police Department had overreacted. Well, they must have been covering a different convention than the one I was at because a lot of Chicago police officers got hurt from flying bricks, rocks, nails clubs, and chunks of concrete that was thrown at them. The flower children, as they were called, or yippies also hit us with bags of human excrement. Another favorite weapon of theirs were pieces of tiles they had taken off washroom floors and scraped on the cement so that their edges were sharp and then sail them at us. This radical sons of bitches injured 198 policemen, as well as some National Guard soldiers who were also on the scene. A few of us wound up in the hospital, suffering from concussions and cuts and bruises, but then why would the Chicago police get angry over this type of behavior? It was amazing to me that not one person was shot or even shot at for that matter. We had seventy-three squad cars damaged; thirty-eight police helmets were also wrecked as well as numerous torn uniforms and other police equipment.

The Chicago police arrested 653 adults during the disorders – 573 men and 77 women and 28 juveniles. Some 253 were from Chicago, 98 came from other parts of Illinois; 292 were from out of state and 10 were from out of the country. The largest number, 348, were between twenty and twenty-nine years of age; 220 were from seventeen to nineteen; 54 were from thirty to thirty-nine; 20 from forty to forty-nine; and 11 were over fifty.

Grant Park and the Conrad Hilton hotel and other downtown locations were the scenes of 383 arrests. Around 211 were arrested in Lincoln Park and the Old Town areas, while 59 were arrested at the International Amphitheater and various other locations.

Charges against the defendants included criminal trespass, unlawful use of weapons, assault, battery, use of narcotics, criminal damage, theft, burglary, resisting arrest, failure to disperse, curfew violations, and fornication. The new media, which was stationed everywhere, kept calling these rabble-rousing bastards "the children," and were being attacked by the Chicago police.

Mayor Daley, who fought to get the convention in Chicago, knew that protesting groups would try to create havoc. But in his mind he thought that Chicago was better equipped to maintain order than any other city. Security preparation began days after Chicago was named the convention site. Scores of police officers were assigned to gather additional intelligence about the militants, who were the leaders of the protesters. Some officers were even sent to army riot training camps.

The FBI, Secret Service, and all security forces coordinated their work, but the nation's militants began holding informal meetings to coordinate the protests, which most of them felt they had to make during the convention.

Three hundred of them held an organizing meeting at a YMCA camp near Lake Villa early in April. They made plans for various demonstrations, which would all climax with a gigantic march on the International Amphitheater on August 28, 1968. Over 100,000 militants were expected to come to Chicago.

Five of the top leaders are as follows:

RENNIE DAVIS: The Chicago chairman of the National Mobilization committee is chief planner of the Center for Radical Research, organizer of Resistance Inside the Army, and was engaged in the program of disruption of the Students for Democratic Society. He made an illegal trip to Hanoi, North Vietnam, in November 1967 at the invitation of the Hanoi government.

THOMAS E. HAYDEN: He was an organizer and member of the Students for a Democratic Society. He was also an organizer of a group known as the Newark Community Project, which was very active during the Newark, New Jersey, riots that took place on July 12 through July 17, 1967. Hayden was referred to as the "Maoist" Messiah from Michigan in the newspapers. He served behind the scenes at the Columbia University riots and rebellion. Hayden also made a visit to Hanoi in North Vietnam, against United States policy. His encounters with the police in Chicago included resisting arrest and battery on August 27, 1968, obstructing police officers, and resisting arrest and disorderly conduct on August 26, 1968. He was considered a violent revolutionary.

ABBIE HOFFMAN: He was one of the organizers of the Youth International Party (YIP). He served as a coordinator of the proposed Festival of Life to be sponsored by the yippies during the convention. Hoffman was also part of the Students for Democratic Society disorders at Columbia University. On May 18, 1967, Hoffman participated in protest marches in New York City to protest police brutality and to prove that the streets belonged to the people. He also sponsored protest demonstrations in Times Square, Washington Square, and then to the United Nations in New York. This march was part of a group known as PTA (Protesters, Terrorists and Anarchists).

JERRY RUBIN: Another yippie leader who devoted his time and talent to bring disruption in the city during the Democratic National Convention was Jerry Rubin. Rubin was a member of the National Coordinating committee to end the war in Vietnam, which is Communist infiltrated. Rubin visited Cuba during 1964. He was arrested for participating in a demonstration against General Maxwell Taylor on August 24, 1965. He was also arrested in Washington DC for disorderly conduct on August 19, 1966, and in Oakland, California, for criminal trespass on November 30, 1966. He was convicted in a student sit-in at the University of California in Berkeley on January 28, 1967. On August 28, 1968, we arrested him at Madison and Dearborn streets for having a large group of yippies who had entered the downtown area and commenced throwing trashcans and garbage cans into store windows and the street. As I remember the little son of a bitch, he had the word *fuck* printed on his forehead with lipstick.

DAVID DELLINGER: He was chairman of the National Mobilization Committee. He was convicted in 1939 and 1943 for violations of the selective service laws. The Washington DC Police, jailed him for ten days in 1961 after staging a demonstration against the Central Intelligence Agency. He visited Cuba during the May Day Celebration in 1964, which is a big Communist holiday. Dellinger was arrested during a demonstration of the "Assembly of Unrepresented People to Declare Peace in Vietnam" held in Washington DC in 1965. He also visited North Vietnam in 1967 to oppose the United States policy. He allegedly admitted to being a communist. David Dellinger and Hayden held a press conference on June 29 and were quoted by the *Guardian* magazine as saying, "We are planning tactics of prolonged direct action to put heat on the government and its political party. We realize that it will be no picnic, but responsibility for any violence that develops with the authorities, will not be the fault of the demonstrators." They also were quoted that their direct action can include street barricading, fire bombing, seizure of buildings, and massive confrontations with the Chicago Police Department.

Hayden went on to say that the Chicago Police must not try to stop his shock troops if they invade the convention hall, block traffic, or make exits and entrances impossible. Hayden stated that these tactics were first tested at the Pentagon when ten protesters actually managed to penetrate the Pentagon. More than one hundred antiwar groups mustered for the march on the Pentagon, which was attended by an estimated 55,000. For Chicago, that number could easily triple or even total 250,000 protesters. Chicago newspapers carried daily stories, enlarging on protest plans and detailing ways that dissidents could make it unpleasant and even impossible for the convention to transact its business. Richard Strout, writing in the *Christian Science Monitor*, observed, "The news media in this city could be indicted for inciting to violence. The mildest parade of young people brings a TV camera crew like a hook-and-ladder truck to a three-alarm fire. Any youngster who will denounce the authorities finds himself surrounded by a ring of extended microphones. The press was talking so much about violence that they had their back against the wall and had to come up with some type of demonstration or violence or they would look silly."

On July 13, a meeting was held at 407 South Dearborn Street where Rennie Davis presided over a meeting with the National Mobilization Committee. Davis stated that plans were being made to bring in 100,000 protesters to the convention and also tie up two army divisions and make surface transportation to the convention site impossible. On August 9, leaders Rennie Davis, Tom Hayden, and others met Abbie Hoffman, the yippie organizer, to discuss plans for demonstrating during the convention. Classes in street fighting and guerrilla tactics taught by Hoffman were scheduled to begin on August 20. They also planned strategy to force the Chicago Police Department to spread itself over a large area. Rennie Davis appeared at another meeting of the Chicago Peace Council at the Lawson YMCA, where he displayed two large three-by-three-foot maps of the area surrounding the International Amphitheater. Locations were noted where police, National Guard, FBI, and other security forces would be situated during the proceedings. He stated that if trouble started at the Democratic National Convention, among other things "the loop will fall," implying demolition of the downtown Chicago area.

The primary targets are listed below:

- Federal Courthouse, 219 South Dearborn Street
- Chicago Police Headquarters, 1121 South State Street, plus all other police facilities
- United States Armed Forces Induction Center, 615 West Van Buren Street
- First National Bank of Chicago, 38 South Dearborn Street
- Chicago Title and Trust, 111 West Washington Street
- Illinois Institute of Technology, 3300 South Federal Street and 10 West 35th Street.
- Cook County Jail, 2600 South California Avenue
- Hallicrafters Co; 4401 West 5th Avenue and 4400 West 45th Street
- Motorola Inc. 9401 West Grand Avenue, Franklin Park, Illinois, and 1450 South Cicero Avenue, Chicago, Illinois
- Radex Corporation, 2076 North Elston Avenue
- Dow Chemical Corporation, 3636 South California Avenue and 6000 West Touhy Avenue
- Zenith Radio Corporation, 1900 North Austin Avenue and 1500 North Kostner Avenue

When the Chicago Police learned of schemes to assassinate Senator Eugene McCarthy, Vice President Hubert Humphrey, Mayor Richard

J. Daley, and other political and civic leaders, the mayor of Chicago immediately put into effect stringent safety measures to guard the lives of these men during their stay in Chicago and while attending the Democratic National Convention.

The most unnerving rumor was the one about a plan to murder a young female supporter of Senator McCarthy and blame it on the police. The police did not want to publicize any of these plots and rumors of plot for fear of planting the idea in others' minds.

In spite of the unpopular views espoused the dissident groups and the notorious backgrounds of their leaders, the City of Chicago still sought to protect their constitutional rights of freedom of speech. Meetings were held with representatives of all the groups in Mayor Daley's office. At these meetings, it was pointed out that all the public facilities in the City of Chicago would be made available to the members of these groups with the understanding that they would be used in a peaceful and lawful manner. They were informed that no one would be allowed to sleep in the park because of an 11:00 PM curfew. In regard to routes of march and places of assembly, the city's position indicated that the area immediately adjacent to the International Amphitheater could not be used for a mass assembly of persons because of security preparations of federal and local authorities. An invitation to submit plans for marches and assemblies that would not conflict with these security precautions was made and continuously reiterated to the group's representatives to make sure they understood the game plan.

Applications for parade and assembly permits signed by Rennie Davis indicated that 200,000 persons would march on August 28, 1968. A second application indicated that 150,000 persons would march and assemble at the amphitheater also on August 28. The duration of the marches would be from eleven in the morning until twelve midnight. Another application requested the use of the Grant Park band shell for an assembly of 150,000 persons on August 28, 1968. In light of these projected figures, traffic and security considerations precluded any street rally point in the vicinity of the amphitheater. The city stated that the purpose for the march and assembly, which was ostensibly to point out criticisms of the country's policy in participating in the war in Vietnam, could be achieved by a march in the downtown area and assembly at Chicago's Grant Park band shell.

The National Mobilization Committee filed a suit in the United States District Court, which was dismissed by Judge William Lynch.

In a similar lawsuit, the Youth International Party sought permission for "thousands of persons" to sleep in the public parks of Chicago, especially at Lincoln Park. This suit was also dismissed. Judge Lynch cited recent decisions of the United States Supreme Court, holding that local governments are entitled to regulate the use of their streets and other public places. The prevention of public disorder and violations are important objects of legitimate state concern when protest takes the place of mass demonstrations and parades. The court also cited that the City of Chicago suggested alternate places of public assembly and numerous alternate routes, and concluded that the city and the Park District acted in a reasonable and nondiscriminatory manner. The court held that it would be a novel interpretation to hold that the First and Fourteenth Amendments require municipal government to provide a public park as sleeping accommodations for persons desiring to visit the city.

Chronology of events of convention week from Sunday, August 25, 1968, to Friday, August 30, is as follows. At twelve noon, Rennie Davis and Tom Hayden led a group of approximately three hundred marchers south on the sidewalk on Clark Street from Lincoln Park to Monroe Street, then east on Monroe to Michigan, south on Michigan to Balbo, where they were diverted to the east sidewalk because of a crowd that already had assembled in front of the Conrad Hilton.

Later that afternoon, the demonstrators, who now numbered about five hundred, began another march back to Lincoln Park. They marched north on State Street and strung out about two blocks. They turned west on Ohio Street to LaSalle Street and then to Lincoln Park. We were keeping them under surveillance with orders from the high command to make sure they remained orderly. No arrests were made. However, during their march several times, they sat in front and obstructed the driveways of gas stations on their route. When advised by the police that they would be subject to arrest if they didn't move on, the yippies continued on with their march. At Lincoln Park, about two hundred protesters gathered and had various assemblies in which they discussed their leaders' trips to North Vietnam and how they had intended to stay in the park and what they would do in case the police forced them to leave.

Rennie Davis and Tom Hayden told the members of the crowd they had two alternatives: either leave, or form bands of seven to ten and resist. About 10:00 PM, Tom Hayden was caught letting the air out of a police vehicle. The officers placed him under arrest; he began yelling to the crowd of three hundred, who responded by surrounding the police and allowing Hayden and his companion to escape. The odds being 150 to 1, it seemed as if the sensible thing to do at the time was let them go; they could both be grabbed at a later time. At about 11:30 PM, another group gathered in the vicinity of Lincoln Park. About six hundred persons were concentrated around North LaSalle and about six hundred around North & Wells. About four hundred yippies still remained in the West Side of Clark Street and LaSalle. Most of the crowd west of Clark Street at Wells and LaSalle had left the park when the police began announcing its closing around 11:00 PM over bullhorns. At this time, we formed small groups and were walking through the park, and of course, the crowd called every vile name that you can think of. Shortly after 11:30 PM, there was a general movement of much of the crowd back into the park. I thought that this was going to get very interesting very fast. We observed several members of the news media in the front of the yippies, and we thought that they might have been even cheering them on.

About 11:50 PM, we got out of the park and joined other police to form a skirmish line in Lincoln Park about 1,000 feet long, running north and south from the General Grant Statue, then extending parallel to the Outer Drive, about 150 yards inside the eastern boundary of the park. An announcement was made several times over the bullhorn: "This would be a final warning, the park is closed, and all persons in the park including any news media are in violation of the law and subject to arrest. The police have information that there are persons in the park who intended to injure police officers. The police will take what steps are necessary to avoid injuring anyone. This is a final warning, you are in violation of the law – move out. NOW." Well, we might as well have been talking to deaf-mutes because we didn't scare anyone. The only thing that happened was that the mob, which totaled about 1,500, began throwing rocks and pieces of tiles that they pried off the floors in the washrooms. We had watched them rubbing these tiles on the cement earlier that day; now we knew what they were going to do with them. Firecrackers were also being thrown at us, like M-80s; at least, we hoped that the noise we heard was from firecrackers and not guns. The mob began chanting, "Hell no, we won't go," and "Kill the pigs." Of course, the word *pig* was the mob's vernacular for the word *police*. Our skirmish lines reached the west edge of the park at about

12:30 AM. The yippies had now lined the west edge of Clark Street opposite the park, screaming invective at us. "Kill the pigs," "Fuck the pigs," "Your wife sucks –" are typical examples of the chants being used. Rocks and bottles were flying at us from all over. We were in civilian clothes, and we didn't have enough sense to bring our helmets with us; fortunately, we knew how to duck. When the skirmish lines moved across Clark Street to the West Side, the mob began to run north and south on the street still screaming and taunting the police. We affected some arrests when we caught some of the demonstrators damaging police squad cars with rocks and bottles. A reporter from UPI and a reporter from the *Chicago American* were also arrested for violating the park curfew during this incident. The reporters were brought into the district station, where things cooled down and a station adjustment was made, i.e., no formal charges were filed and they were released. Both participants were able to see more clearly each other's point of view. The police were able to recognize that the newsmen, in order to gather a news story, must be close to where the action was taking place. The newsmen realized that when the police were deployed in a skirmish line it was virtually impossible to make distinctions among demonstrators and newsmen, none of who have the legal right to be in the park after curfew.

Monday, August 26, 1968: At about 2:45 PM, a march of about one thousand yippies and hippies left Lincoln Park and began marching down the middle of Dearborn Street toward the loop, picking up rocks along the way. The few police present managed to keep the marchers on the sidewalks. They had a loud speaker, a red flag, two Vietcong flags, a black flag, and many obscene signs, most of which said "Fuck the Draft," "Fuck the Pigs." The marchers continued on to police headquarters at Eleventh and State Street and then on to the Hilton Hotel on Michigan Avenue where they assembled on the east side of the street. The march was uneventful, except for the constant chanting of slogans, "Hell no, we won't go," "Kill the Pigs", "Peace now," and "Free Hayden". Hayden had been arrested earlier in the day as the result of events that took place on Sunday, August 25, 1968, when he had escaped from police. He was charged with obstructing police officers, resisting arrest, and disorderly conduct. The single exception occurred when some demonstrators climbed a statue (General Logan statue) at about opposite Tenth Street and east of Michigan Avenue. About fifteen yippies climbed on the statue with the red flag and the

Vietcong flag, and remained on it for about ten minutes. When we went up to the knoll on which the statue stands to clear the yippies from it, the marchers who had not climbed the knoll ran back toward it in a large group and rushed the hill. We surrounded the statue, and all the demonstrators climbed down, except one who refused. This asshole mounted the statue's head where he gave the "peace" sign to great cheers from the other yippies and hippies. We did finally pull the idiot down from the statue and arrested him. Of course, a scuffle ensued, and the police struck no one.

A man was observed sitting on the grass with his back against the tree. The man had a bandage in his lap and was having a conversation with three men who had camera equipment. He then leaned back, put the bandage to the left side of his head – where there was no visible injury – and the cameraman began taking pictures. A United States attorney who was present and was observing the action approached the men and asked them their names and for whom they worked. They all scurried off without answering.

I don't mind telling you that after two days of this type of activity, I began to wonder what country I was in and what the hell was going on. I must admit, on occasion I have used some cuss words in my time, but these yippie bastards made us look like choirboys. They kept screaming obscenities, and there were incidents of both male and female demonstrators spitting on the police. They began leaving the area and around 9:00 PM, about one thousand of them began marching back to the north side to Lincoln Park. The rock throwing continued, and they set trash baskets on fire and then threw them in the street. The police confronted this group, and a melee erupted during this attempt to clear the streets and open them so traffic could move. Some newsmen claimed they had been injured during this incident and made complaints, charging police misconduct. At about 11:00 PM, the crowd at the Hilton had dispersed, and within an hour, the demonstrators at Lincoln Park numbered about three thousand.

They had constructed a large barricade of picnic tables, snow fences, park benches, and trashcans. The barricade was about 6 feet high and about 100 feet across in a half-moon shape. It was located in the same area where we had assembled the night before. Rocks were being thrown at private cars leaving the park. The barricade was mounted with a red flag, Vietcong flags, and the black flag of anarchy;

they also had bullhorns and a bugle. We all knew that this was going to turn into quite a party; at least we had our helmets with us this time. The bullhorns were chanting with the crowd, "Kill the Pigs," "Fuck the Pigs," "Hell no, we won't go." Lincoln Park was pitch-black where the demonstrators had gathered, except for an occasional fire in a trashcan, so it was hard to see anything that was thrown at us. Then it started all at once, a virtual of rocks, building tiles, cans filled with sand, cherry bombs, and half bricks were being hurled from behind the barricade. All of a sudden, to our amazement, we saw the outline of a car driving toward the demonstrators; it was a uniformed, marked squad car and was moving very slowly. Apparently, this guy didn't realize where he was headed; but when he did he put his lights on and tried to get the hell out of there, they hit that squad car with bricks, bottles, and rocks and even set the car on fire. It happened so fast that we couldn't do anything to help the poor guy, but he did get the squad out of there; and he was lucky, he didn't get killed.

That was about all we needed to really get pissed off. We formed another skirmish line and made the same announcement that we had made the night before. It was given four times in about five minutes just before the skirmish line moved out at about 12:25 AM. Five or six officers ran toward the demonstrators and fired teargas canisters. One policeman was struck in the head with a brick; when he went down, the crowd cheered. When the gas approached the demonstrators, they broke and ran to the west across the park. A small group of about twenty-five ran north to the north end of the police line, and that happened to be where we were. Some of them had Nazi helmets on their heads, and one guy was carrying the black flag of anarchy. When we introduced ourselves to them after two days of listening to all the nasty things they were calling us, I have to admit that we were a little angry with them for saying things about our wives and mothers. After a few minutes, some of them were whining and sniveling because they had somehow fallen off a small bridge and into a pond and were screaming about their rights being violated.

The teargas was all over the park, and the wind was blowing it toward Clark Street and into the homes on the west side of the park. The teargas was nasty stuff, and all of us were crying as well as the yippies and hippies. Two of the yippies that we apprehended had small tiles in their pockets, the same kind that was being thrown at us for two days. To make sure that they didn't have any more weapons on their persons, we had to strip them of their clothes to be sure. One of the officers who was with us found a can of spray paint on a hippie he had searched, and we made good use of it. I LOVE COPS was printed on their backs, and their hair also got tinted with the red spray paint. At no time did we physically abuse any of the demonstrators whom we had apprehended, at least to the best of my knowledge. I often wonder what happened to the yippies that we spray painted that night; we gave them a break and didn't lock them up, but they sure did look silly running through the woods naked, calling us fascist pigs.

Tuesday, August 27, 1968: Bobby Seal, Black Panther militant, harangued another crowd of 1,500 in Lincoln Park at about 8:00 PM. About eight hundred headed for the Hilton Hotel; the other seven hundred went to a bus barn at 2600 North Clark Street, which was the Chicago Transit Authority, and joined the striking workers. The crowd at the Hilton built up and became unruly and began to throw rocks at the police. This type of shit was really getting old about this time, and a lot of police officers were about ready to lose their patience. Other projectiles included glass ashtrays thrown from the windows of the Hilton, Pepsi-Cola cans filled with urine, and the beer cans filled with sand. Golf balls with nails driven through them – another favorite weapon of the demonstrators – were thrown at us. Plastic baggies also filled with urine were coming down on the police from the hotel windows; some of the same tiles that had been thrown at us at Lincoln Park were again sailing at us.

At about 9:00 PM, a black militant by the name of Dick Gregory was observed leading a march of a group of about five hundred down LaSalle Street. The marchers had their arms locked and headed back toward the park.

We were ordered back to Lincoln Park at about 11:30 PM and found that another barricade had been put up on Monday night. When we again formed a skirmish line, about fourteen photographers joined the line with us. Police cars made the same announcements as before, and both vehicles were stoned. There were also some assistant United States attorneys with us, and they witnessed about twenty young men throwing bottles and rocks at the police. A person on a loudspeaker, thought to be Benjamin Ortiz, was urging the crowd to hold fast, and the crowd was screaming every kind obscenities at us. Two trucks joined the police line and were immediately stoned. At that point we released the gas again, and the demonstrators broke and ran and congregated at Clark and LaSalle Street on the west side of the park. Two squad cars were trapped in the middle of the mob, and they began to break the windows on the cars by throwing rocks and bottles. Again, the gas was all over, and many of the demonstrators had gas masks or makeshift masks on. One of the squad cars got out of the crowd; while we fought our way to get to the other one, the two officers got out of the car, which had to be abandoned. For the first time, to my knowledge, guns were drawn to keep the crowd at bay. The officers took refuge in a passageway where we got them out of there. The mob continued down LaSalle Street toward Division Street, setting fire to trash baskets and throwing them in the street. There were two empty squad cars with all their windows broken out on LaSalle near Germania Place. What appeared to be gunfire was heard on Division Street. Another abandoned squad car, which had three bullet holes in its windshield, was standing south of Division on Wells Street. We were making numerous arrests and used Mace on a lot of offenders to subdue them. Every day, this thing seemed to be getting worse, and the police were getting madder and madder.

In the meantime, the Hilton Hotel scene was again getting out of hand. Missiles were flying; obscenities and taunts never stopped coming. One policeman had human excrement thrown at him by a girl. Rennie Davis was haranguing the crowd this time. The mob continued to build from Lincoln Park and the coliseum crowd, which had let out. There were now about five thousand demonstrators massed in front of the Hilton and getting really rowdy by the minute. Police Commander John Mulchrone, Assistant Corporation Counsel Richard Elrod, and United States Attorney Thomas Foran went into the crowd in an attempt to talk to Davis and other leaders. They were surrounded by hippie types, who kept calling them every vile name you can think of. They were not permitted to talk to anyone and returned to the police lines. We finally were relieved about 3:20 AM on the twenty-eighth when the National Guard began to replace us after about fourteen hours of putting up with these yippie bastards. Seven hundred guardsmen were brought in. The crowd began to diminish and was virtually gone at 5:30 AM.

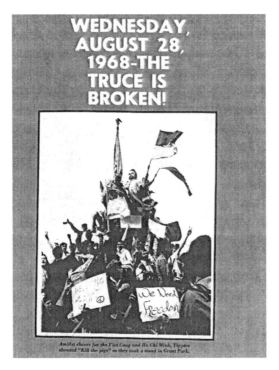

PAY, QUIT, OR DIE

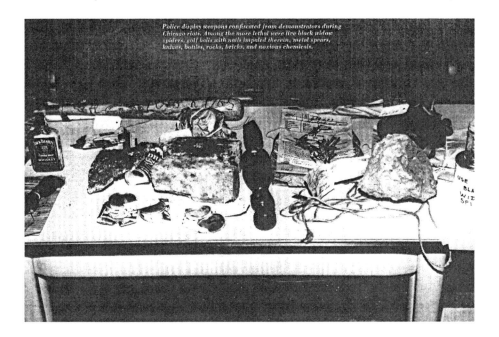

Police display weapons confiscated from demonstrators during Chicago riots. Among the more lethal were live black widow spiders, golf balls with nails impaled therein, metal spears, knives, bottles, rocks, bricks, and noxious chemicals.

WEDNESDAY, August 28, 1968: We were instructed to report back to Grant Park at 2:00 PM. This whole operation was like a zoo, with a bunch of people left over from Halloween. A large crowd had been gathering at the Grant Park band shell; it was estimated at about ten thousand. Thousands of pamphlets were handed out by the police, informing the crowd that the band shell assembly was illegal, no permit had been issued nor would any march or parade be allowed. At about 3:00 PM, some punk bastard about twenty-two years old began to lower the American flag from the main flagpole. His companions were ready to substitute a black flag of anarchy when the police became incensed, and eight to ten police prevented them from doing so, and the punk was arrested, and the others dispersed with firm kicks in the ass. Well, that started a barrage of bottles, sticks, rocks, and other objects being thrown. Assistant United States Attorney John Simon, who was at the flagpole, got hit with a plastic baggie filled with a mixture of paint and urine. A squad of about forty police rushed through the crowd, swinging their nightsticks; and after another barrage of various kinds of debris, the crowd seemed to quiet down again. From 2:00 PM to 5:00 PM, different speakers addressed the crowd, trying to incite them. Bobby Seale of the Black Panther Party, Rennie Davis, Tom Hayden, Norman Mailer, David Dellinger, and Sydney Peck all tried their best to get these idiots on the rampage. Their main topic was that they urged the crowd to march to the amphitheater no matter what the police said, and that they were ready for arrest or death. And if there was any violence it would be the fault of the police. Then the chants started, "KILL the PIGS,' and then they cheered for the Vietcong and Ho Chi Minh. We were standing about fifty yards from the crowd, and every now and then a rock would come flying into our ranks. Then a number of crowd "marshals" assembled immediately in front of the police and formed into their Japanese snake-dance style. These marshals were equipped with a variety of helmets and looked like a rough-looking group.

Dellinger instructed the crowd to form into two groups. One group was to head south led by the marshals, and the other group was to head north into the loop. The group that was heading south were the ones who were ready "to be arrested or to die" and those going north were to be peaceful. In the meantime, about two thousand people, mostly normally dressed people, had assembled opposite the Hilton. A large crowd had assembled behind the police line along the east wall of the Hilton. The crowd was heavily infiltrated with yippie types and was spitting and screaming obscene insults at the police. A United States attorney, McDonnell, and a police officer named Walsh were sprayed in the face with oven cleaner; this occurred about 5:00 PM. I don't know how true this is, but rumor has it that the three offenders who committed this crime were apprehended later, and the spray cleaner was used on them. Also they received a severe "scolding." Well, actually, they got the shit kicked out of them and got thrown into Lake Michigan.

The group that was marching south with there usual bullhorn and Communist flags were screaming and raising hell as usual; they were met at the corner of Balbo and Columbus. The police had formed a line directly in front of the head of the march. On the west side of Columbus Drive, there were spectators and, of course, the press. The National Guard was also on the scene. Dellinger and Peck were doing most of the talking. They announced that Rennie Davis had been arrested at the flagpole and had been badly injured. This was not true insofar as the seriousness of the injury was concerned. The marchers sat down on the sidewalk, and some negotiations were started. Deputy Superintendent Rochford and Assistant Corporation Counsel Elrod told the crowd that if the march were to continue, it would go to the area across from the Conrad Hilton. Dellinger stated that the purpose of the march was to go to the amphitheater. Dellinger was again informed that the march was unlawful and would not be permitted.

At 6:00 PM, the crowd that had drifted away going north was crossing the bridges at Monroe and Jackson Boulevard over the railroad yards. They tried to penetrate the guardsmen's line at the Congress Bridge. There were two full battalions of guardsmen along the streets and around the Hilton Hotel along with hundreds of us. The guardsmen were instructed to sheathe their bayonets, to carry rifles at "high port" braced across the chest when moving to break crowd formations. Their orders were to avoid using rifle butts on demonstrators unless it became absolutely necessary. Above all, they were clearly made to understand the chain of their command – to wait for orders and never break ranks. The CS-1 teargas was liberally supplied, but the standard operating procedure was that only the platoon commander's "lieutenant" and above could order the use of gas.

It was a lieutenant platoon commander who released the gas at the Congress Street bridge that drifted over Grant Park and into the hotels on Michigan Avenue. Lt. Col. Donald Lapsley, the executive officer for the guard's Thirty-third Infantry Brigade, explained his men had been told not to deny passage across the bridge into Michigan Avenue to people coming across in small groups, which was the technique the demonstrators were using to leave the park. "We knew it might drift," said Major Thomas Reynolds, operating officer for the brigade. "But sometimes you just can't maneuver your battlefields into position. There was no choice."

Here we were again, the third night in a row that we were gassed; the only difference this time was that the National Guard did it. We had been working sixteen hours a day since Sunday and were being called every vile name you can think of. We were hit with bags of urine, human excrement, bottles, rocks, tiles, nails in golf balls, and a variety of other objects. To say the least, some of us were losing our patience with the "children."

The guard took some criticism from some newsmen because they released the gas. Some of the poor fellas got a few good whiffs of the teargas that evening and didn't like it. Colonel Lapsley explained that he was proud of the guardsmen, that as far as he knew, none of the young troops broke ranks, and that there were no clubbings or beatings attributed to guardsmen in the encounter that took place at the Congress Street Bridge – this despite the stream of invectives and objects thrown by demonstrators at his troops. The clubbing and beatings that took place between the police and the demonstrators in full view of the television audience could not be blamed on any of his guardsmen. Well, thanks a lot, Colonel, if it wasn't for the Chicago police, your troops would have had their bayonets stuck up their ass. The night wasn't over quite yet; the Southern Christian Leadership Conference mule train came south on Michigan Avenue. It had a police escort. There were two mule carts and about eighty people. They seemed to have no idea what they were getting into, but they were immediately surrounded by this huge crowd, totally engulfing Michigan Avenue – the sidewalks on the east and west sides and a lot of the park on the east side of Michigan up to the tracks. They had flags and a loudspeaker with the mule train in the middle of the crowd. The crowd was a mixture of hippies, yippies, newsmen, cameramen, and a mobile TV truck. The TV lights were on the canopy of the northeast corner of the Hilton Hotel.

Many speeches were now being given by the leaders of the march. Rev. Ralph Abernathy of the Southern Christian Leadership Conference was in the midst of the crowd, but was not an active participant. The crowd kept inching toward the police lines; the tension was enormous. The demonstrators were chanting in unison, "Let's go, let's go to the amphitheater, and don't stop! You can't stop us!" At this time the vice president reportedly came back to the hotel, and a call was received that the amphitheater was to be blown up. There were speeches calling Humphrey a pig, warmonger, and a racist. The person leading the chants was Benjamin Ortiz from Camden, New Jersey – a rabble-rousing son of a bitch. The cameramen turned on the TV lights and were running around as if they might miss something. Dr. Abernathy was let through the police lines, and he informed Deputy Superintendent Rochford that he was in charge of the mule train and that he wanted no part of the mob. He said that he had eighty people with him and that included old people and children, and he wanted to get them out of the mob. Now the mob was screaming foul language of every type at the police, about their families and themselves. They were spitting on them and daring them to come and hit them. The police got the mule train out of the crowd and in front of the Hilton when several objects came flying out of the crowd that hit some police officers. The guy next to me got hit with a bagful of urine, and the crowd was going nuts. The chanting got louder and louder; "Let's go, let's go" became a roar. Their flags, which were in the forefront of the mob, surged forward, and the violent disorder began. The policemen at the surge point began to shove back and hit with their nightsticks. More missiles came flying out of the crowd, and the rest of the police line charged into the crowd, swinging their nightsticks; many arrests were being made. The arrestees were struggling and screaming. One man was carried by four policemen, and he grabbed one of the lead policemen and all four of the policemen fell to the ground. The police got up, and one of them gave the guy a few whacks with his nightstick. The policeman whose leg had been grabbed was yelling, "The bastard is biting me." It took two other policemen and an assistant corporation counsel to disengage the police's leg from the mouth of the prisoner.

There was a great deal of violent action at this time. The arrestees were being literally thrown into vans. Missiles were coming from all over, from the north and from the east and south of the police line where the crowd in Grant Park was being held back by other police. An elderly woman was being escorted away from the mob. Simultaneously, the crowd next to the east wall of the Hilton on the sidewalk north of the entrance began to surge to the south and to the east onto the sidewalk. Some of the mob that had been around the loud speaker was pushing the crowd to the south. The police were pushing them north. Two windows were smashed in the east wall and about six of the crowd jumped in through the windows; some police began swinging their nightsticks. On Michigan, at the site of the initial clash, the street was littered with shoes, hats, rocks, Pepsi-Cola cans filled with sand, a black duffel bag filled with rocks.

As the crowd moved north, they pelted the police with missiles of all sorts, rocks, bottles, firecrackers. When a policeman was struck, the crowd would cheer. We were trying to dodge the debris that was being thrown at us, but we weren't having too much success. A group of cameramen started a trash fire in the street behind police lines and put a Welcome to Chicago sign on the fire and then took pictures of it. Some of us wanted to bust them for starting a fire but were talked out of it by some lieutenant of police. A police van was in the center of the street at Jackson and Michigan, and was being bombarded with missiles by the portion of the crowd that was going north on Michigan. The last thing we saw of the van was that the driver probably said "fuck this" and put the pedal to the metal and got the hell out of there. I guess he made it, and we didn't see any yippies lying in the street.

THURSDAY, August 29, 1968: A crowd of five thousand had assembled opposite the Hilton in Grant Park by about 3:30 PM. They were addressed by a number of persons including Senator McCarthy about 4:15 PM. At the end of his speech, they started to march to the amphitheatre. Two thousand marchers arrived at Sixteenth Street and State Street. They were met there by the police, and they changed their minds and returned to Grant Park.

Mr. Gregory showed up again at Grant Park. He had a conference with General Dunn, who agreed to let the crowd march to Eighteenth and Michigan for further conference. At about 6:00 PM, a group of about forty demonstrators, delegates, and newsmen reached Thirty-ninth and State Street. Much to our surprise, they found out that they were not in a friendly neighborhood. The black youths gave them a cold reception, and in fact, a few scuffles broke out at Forty-first and State; the demonstrators had a change of heart and returned downtown and seemed very confused.

At 6:50 PM General Dunn asked for a meeting of the Chicago Police, Secret Service, and the United States Attorney at Eighteenth and Michigan. At 7:20 PM the crowd opposite the Hilton began marching south on Michigan Avenue. The crowd was now about five thousand and met resistance from guard units at Eighteenth Street and Michigan. The dangers of this crowd going to the amphitheatre, passing through the Robert Taylor Homes, were discussed. Mr. Gregory, "a rabble rouser," came through the crowd with Corporation Counsel Mr. Elrod, Deputy Rochford, and Mr. Foran, the United States attorney. A conference was held, and possible alternatives were discussed. Deputy Rochford offered to lead the delegates to the amphitheatre. He also offered to transport a reasonable number of guests to Gregory's home for dinner. I never could figure out that one. Gregory's reply was that he wanted all five thousand to come to his house; another wise-ass answer. Suggestions were made concerning alternate routes, such as Martin Luther King Drive to Thirty-fifth Street, or Michigan to Twenty-second Street and back downtown, or Eighteenth and Indiana and over to the band shell. Gregory would not consider any alternatives. He insisted on marching to Fortieth and Michigan, and then he would decide whether he would take the crowd to his house or to the amphitheatre. Obviously, this whole meeting was turning into a goddamn joke.

At 9:15 PM, Gregory and nine delegates – there were sixty delegates in all – intentionally disobeyed police and National Guard orders and peacefully submitted to arrest. One yippie tried to fight when he got in the police wagon. Mr. Ortiz, another instigator, started shouting on a loud speaker, "Let's go, we die here. To the amphitheatre." The crowd surged forward, and the front ranks of the National Guard were sprayed with a liquid that caused a burning sensation. The guard pushed them back with rifle butts then released teargas. The crowd dispersed; some of them returned downtown. A lot of "medics" treated people's eyes for teargas. The crowd kept throwing missiles at us and continued cussing us out; every other word was motherfucker and worse. The National Guard lined up on the east side of Michigan in force.

The singing and speechmaking continued; only now, more missiles were being thrown at us from the windows of the Hilton. This went on until about 2:45 AM when a bag containing caustic powder was thrown from a window of the hotel. It landed on a parked jeep; a guardsman called Assistant U.S. Attorney McKenzie to examine the powder, and it blew in his eyes, causing temporary blindness and great pain. He was taken to Henrotin Hospital for treatment. Missiles began coming more frequently from the hotel, which included ashtrays and cans both filled and unfilled. All this led to an incident in the McCarthy Hospitality Suite about 3:00 AM and an interview with Senator McCarthy in the lobby. The National Guard set up a number of observation posts on the east side of Michigan Avenue to try and pinpoint with certainty the offending room. With assistance from hotel employees, it was clear that the missiles were coming 1505A and 1506A, which were connected. This area occupied the eastern tip of the hotel wing; the hotel rented the room to J. K.Galbraith, J. H. Lynford, and Peter Sturgis. This floor housed supporters of Senator McCarthy. The commanding officer of the National Guard that was present was Colonel Robert Strupp, who requested that the police clear out rooms 1505A and 1506A because of the fact that someone could be gravely injured by the many objects that were being thrown from these windows. The objects being thrown were many beer cans – some filled with various liquids, some with human waste. Also heavy glass ashtrays, cocktail glasses, a metal coffee pot, and ball bearings. The hotel lowered five window awnings on the first floor below the rooms in question to give protection to Guard personnel and the police. After getting a hotel security guard and some National Guard personnel, fifteen of us went to the fifteenth floor, where about thirty-five people were either standing or sleeping in the hallway, and some drinking highballs. One young broad told us that she was the "jiggers" person and warned the others that the police were on their way. The door to room 1506A was open where we found about twenty men and women; in the adjoining room, 1505A, two young women passed out on a couch with beer cans all around them. One of them appeared to have thrown up all over the rug and on her shoes. A police captain who was with us told the group in a very quiet voice that because of the many objects that were being thrown from the windows, the suite was going to be closed. All persons who were not registered in the hotel would have to go down to the main floor; they didn't go for this at all, and at first they refused to move. After some convincing from the police, they began to move to the elevators. One goof did lift a table above his head and struck a policeman with it on his chest; when he raised the table again, he got decked with a baton and fell to the floor. He refused medical attention and called us all motherfuckers and Communists. Two other guys attacked some officers and had to be Maced. Afterward, some of the persons removed from room 1506A threatened a sit-in the main lobby of the hotel, but after a few minutes the were persuaded to leave the hotel. Hotel personnel described the condition of the rooms as being the worst-appearing room that they had ever seen. There were 14 fifths or quart-size liquor bottles that had been filled with whiskey, gin, and vodka; numerous beer cans food had been strewn on the furniture and carpeting. There was evidence of recent burns caused by cigarettes and cigars all over the carpet and drapes. On the following day, Mr. Quigley of the McCarthy staff refused to permit a press photographer to take a picture of the room.

It was estimated that four thousand out-of-town newsmen came to Chicago to report the Democratic National Convention and surrounding events. Also, the city had about two thousand local newsmen who hold press cards issued by the Chicago Police Department. During the period of the convention, complaints were made to the department that thirteen newsmen were assaulted by police officers. These complaints were investigated by the internal investigation division as well as nine other allegations of attacks on newsmen, which were reported in the press but not officially reported to the police department.

CBS newsman Dan Rather said that he was struck by a Chicago Police officer, but investigation revealed that it was a security guard that struck him (who claimed that it was accidental). CBS dropped the matter. Mike Wallace, another network newsman, admittedly grabbed the face of a Chicago Police captain. The captain hit Wallace in self-defense. After the incident, the participants shook hands and agreed to drop the matter.

The real problems began when the petitioners requested the City of Chicago to be able to assemble and demonstrate against the war in

Vietnam across the street from the site of the convention center, the amphitheatre. The petitioning groups did not want to assemble or march anywhere except to and around the amphitheatre. Their requests were denied because of the unreasonable size and duration of the marches proposed and the security measures necessary on the convention premises. Alternate sites were offered. The only specific request for an assembly area that was accepted was for the Grant Park band shell on Wednesday, August 28. It was after this assembly, as a matter of fact, that the protesters massed at the Hilton directly across the street from Grant Park, and the major disorder occurred. The agitator's main goal was to disrupt the convention and the city. They used the war as an excuse to demonstrate, but they really wanted to topple what they considered to be a corrupt society – educational, governmental, etc. – by impeding and, if possible, halting their normal functions while exposing the authorities to ridicule and embarrassment. Needless to say, it was unclear what replacements they envisioned.

The guerilla and psychological warfare tactics that were used by these revolutionaries erupted in numerous incidents; the main one was the eighteen-minute encounter in front of the Hilton Hotel. The news media responded to these tactics, which were incredibly misused. The success the revolutionaries achieved in their ultimate objective of fomenting hatred and ridicule among the citizenry against the authorities was in large part attributable to the almost sympathetic coverage extended by reporters to the revolutionary leaders, understandably to the idealist but unwary young people who unwittingly lent them assistance and camouflage.

For us in Chicago, the aftermath involved investigations and the assessment of the performance of the Chicago Police Department, military units, and government officials. Due to the negative reporting of the news media of the Chicago Police, calling the convention a "Police Riot" did not help matters. We were very concerned about injured newsmen, injured police officers, injured civilians, injured protesters, injured reputations, but most of all we were concerned about the lack of public awareness of the significance of the departing words of the yippie and "mob" leaders: "We won" and "The revolution has begun."

As things turned out, the citizens of Chicago gave their overwhelming support to the Chicago Police Department and the actions that they took to protect life and property in the City of Chicago. The calls and letters that came into city hall on one day were 41,185 supporting Mayor Daley and the Chicago Police, and 4,290 not approving of our action.

Chapter 27

This Keg Is Not a Barrel

Nick "Keg" Galanos was quite a guy; he got his nickname because of his stature. Nick was five foot five and weighed over 400 pounds, and he closely resembled a barrel; so I guess instead of calling him Barrel, they called him Keg or Kegee. Kegee also happened to be a bookmaker; he took action on horses, sports, and also handled football parlay cards. But Kegee had another fault besides overeating, he was a degenerate gambler himself, he would bet on anything, he loved the action. He told me one day that he bet a guy $100 on two roaches that were on a counter in a restaurant; the bet was which one would walk on the bagel that was on a plate behind the toaster. Kegee said that he won that one. I believed him because if he had lost, the bet was so dumb he never would have told me about it. I think he wanted to impress me as to the knowledge he had about quick-moving roaches.

I remember the first time my partner Bob Peters and I ran into Kegee; it was in a restaurant at Madison Street and Cicero Avenue called Howell's. It was a nice, clean place, and different types used to frequent the place. At the time, we were working vice in the Austin District, and we decided to get some coffee at Howell's; we were in soft clothes, and no one in the restaurant knew who we were anyway. We sat at the counter and got our coffee and I walked toward the back to use the restroom. I saw the giant of a man seated by himself at a table at the rear; the table was loaded with all kinds of food, and this guy was going at it with both hands. When I walked by him, I saw an open valise on a chair next to him; and in it was a scratch sheet, some envelopes with money sticking out of them, and a large quantity of football parlay cards.

I walked back to my partner and told him what I had observed and that we were going to bust this guy for gambling. Being Friday night, it was parlay card turn in time, so we decided to wait awhile and see if anyone approaches our human barrel in the back. Sure as hell, in a matter of fifteen minutes, eleven different guys walked in the restaurant and walked directly to the barrel and gave him envelopes. The barrel seemed to be a very jovial guy; he joked with the bettors as well as the waitresses, whom he tried to cop a feel every time one of them would walk by. We waited until he was through with his business and looked as if he was ready to leave when we sat down with him and gave him the good news that we were the police and that he was under arrest for bookmaking. He just stared at us and then said, "Well then, the least you can do is pick up my check, guys." I said, "You really are a funny guy. By the way, what's your name?" That's when he said, "Nick Galanos, but everybody calls me Kegee. Why, I don't know." We let him pay his check, and we acted as if he was a friend of ours, and we left the place, and no one knew that we just busted him. Kegee told us that he appreciated it and that he owed us one.

As it turned out, Kegee was a City of Chicago employee in streets and sanitation, and I told him that we would have to report that he had been arrested for being involved in illegal gambling. Kegee said that if we forgot to do that, he would owe us one and give us some good information about some hookers and other book joints. I told him that he owed us two; and from this point on, this was going to be the beginning of a beautiful relationship.

Kegee was a real piece of work; I found out a couple of days later when a friend of mine who hung around Howell's restaurant told me an interesting story. He said that the night we busted Kegee, he was supposed to make a juice payment to a juice collector named Sam. It seems that Kegee was behind in his payments and would be in a world of shit if he didn't make a payment that night. Kegee, who was desperate, had gone to the racetrack earlier and made some bets on some long shots to try and get lucky and get some money; but of course, he lost. But when we busted him, he had an excuse for not having the dough to pay the juice man, because he told him that the cops took all his money, that he had to make his payment. He also told them that they didn't give him a receipt either, and that the dirty bastards probably stole it.

Well, when I heard that story, I really got pissed off at Kegee and let him know so in no uncertain terms. He apologized and said that was all he could think of on the spur of the moment to tell Sam, the juice guy. He said that Sam and company were about to break his legs with a baseball bat and sew his mouth up so he couldn't eat if he was late making his payment one more time. I warned him never to tell anybody again that the police, especially me and my partner, stole his money. We sure as hell didn't need that type of bullshit going around, that's for sure. But then in the business, everybody thinks that you're stealing money anyway, I guess.

Every now and then I would get a call from Kegee and he would give me some pretty good info on some mob gambling and juice operations in the Chicago area. Whenever he told me anything, he always begged me to never tell a living soul how I got my leads or ever mention his name to anyone, not even to my other partners, because he would surely wind up in a trunk. When he said that, I said, "There is no way that you would ever wind up in a trunk, maybe a truck but not a trunk,.Only kidding, Kegee, relax." We made a lot of good raids with Kegee's help, and I'm sure that we were aggravating the outfit, and they were trying to figure out how the hell we were doing it. One day Kegee called me, and I had to meet him at North Avenue and Harlem in a Sears parking lot at midnight. When I met him, he was very nervous; he always thought that he had a tail on him for some reason. He proceeded to tell me about a couple of guys who were booking big-time in a restaurant at Roosevelt Road and Austin Boulevard. One of the guys was a midget named Jesse Testa; the other guy was called Frank, and he had to use crutches to get around. The next day, I staked out the restaurant during bookmaking hours; and sure as hell, Kegee was right, they were both in their using a pay phone at the back of the place. Jesse had a low sinister voice, while Frank had a high-pitched voice. Jesse was standing on a stool, talking to somebody in a very menacing tone; the conversation was about some bets the guy made and lost, and was coming up short with the money. Jesse was threatening him with all kinds of violence if the guy didn't pay up. Obviously, the guy didn't know what Jesse looked like, but he sounded as if he was six foot two and weighed 240 pounds; it sure was a comical scene.

We kept Jesse and Frank under surveillance for a couple of days and found out that they were moving their operation to an apartment on Austin Boulevard in Oak Park, a suburb on the West End of Chicago. It seemed that their business had grown so much they had to get a couple more phones to handle the volume. A few days later, we raided the apartment and found that Jesse and Frank had some outside help and had hired a guy named Frank Jerome and another guy named Gus to help them on the phones. We confiscated four phones, a ton of gambling records and names and addresses of all there players; the raid also hit the newspapers, and our boss gave us an attaboy.

Our guy Kegee must have had a clout somewhere because he was made a foreman and worked out of a city trailer on South Western Avenue. I overheard that he might also be taking some action in the trailer, but I ignored that tip because we were too busy working on things that Kegee gave us, so we didn't have time. Like the crap game he gave me being run by the outfit on Thirsty-first Street East of Wentworth Avenue on the South Side. He said that the game had been going on for years and never got busted because they were getting protection from somebody in law enforcement. After a little snooping around Thirty-first Street, we found the storefront where the game was being run and that they had lookouts in the area; some of them were riding around the area in a van with walkie-talkies to warn the game if there were any strangers in the neighborhood. We wound up raiding the game, and Kegee was right about the protection idea. The lads running the game indicated that everything was supposed to be cool with everybody and that they were a little shook up getting busted by us. I must admit that I was very secretive about us working on the game, and I didn't let everybody know that we were going to hit it when we did; but that's show business, I guess. Maybe some heads would roll over this I thought. Who knows, it could be mine? But let the chips fall where they may.

Being constantly paranoid was one of Kegee's big problems, as I said; he always thought that the bad guys as well as the good guys were watching him all the time. One night, I got a call from him, and he told me that we had to meet right away about something. I told him to come over to my house and park in the alley, and I would come out. When he showed up, I walked out and got in his Cadillac, and I could tell he was panic-stricken by the look on his face. He said that he had been followed, but he thought that he lost the tail when he ran a red light at North Avenue and Austin. I said, "Let's take a ride by LaFollette Park and see what happens." We drove around the park where you could see everything within a two-block area, and I was certain that we weren't followed. I told him to quit watching television and to get out of the booking business if all of this bullshit was making him goofy. He agreed with me, and then that's when he told me about a new game in town.

It seemed that two mob guys from Taylor Street were starting a street tax for bookmakers that would allow them to operate in the Chicago area without any problems from the outfit. The first guys they shook down were Jesse Testa and his partner, Frank the Gimp. They were told that they had to pay $300 a month to continue to operate. The rules were "Pay, Quit, or Die." Kegee also thought that they were also charged retroactively and had to pay for six months that they had been in business. The two bad guys were Harry Aleman and William "Butch" Petrocelli. They were the current strong arm men for the mob in Chicago, which was at the time being run by Joe Ferriola a.k.a. Joe Nagall. Kegee said that Aleman was a nephew of Ferriola and was very trigger-happy.

In the months that followed, Harry and Butch killed quite a few bookmakers in the Chicago area, and the bookmakers that stuck around the area now belonged to them, one way or another. Kegee had been told to pay $400 a month and was also told that he had to lay off some of his bets to an outfit-run bookmaking operation, and they would split the profits fifty-fifty. Kegee liked to frequent places in Forest Park, where he had some of his customers, but the mob told him that he was barred from entering that suburb. I had heard that Kegee had a small store in Forest Park where he was involved in buying merchandise from a crew of shoplifters, and he stored all the stolen stuff in the store and would sell it at a later time. This might have been one of the reasons that Kegee got whacked.

I didn't hear from Kegee for months, until one day, I got a phone call from a guy who called himself Nick. I asked, "Nick who?" and then he said, "Galanos, you dope." He told me that he had to see me right away and not to be shocked when I saw him. I agreed to meet him in the Burger King parking lot behind my house in ten minutes. What I didn't know was that Kegee had made the phone call from inside Burger

King and that he was seated at a table by the front window watching me. After about ten minutes, I was about to leave when this guy came out and said, "Hi, Sarge." I looked at him and couldn't recognize the guy. He said, "It's me Nick," then he said, "Galanos." I stared at him and couldn't believe my eyes – he must have lost 225 pounds – and I said, "Kegee?" He shouted, "No, not Kegee, I'm Nick. You said that if I lost some weight, you would never call me that stupid name again, remember?" After the shock wore off, I called him Nick and told him what a great job he did, and that obviously he had quit eating, and that all he had to do now was quit gambling. I told him I was proud of him, and he smiled at me and then said, "I'm working on something really big, Sarge. I'll call you in a couple of days." Then we shook hands, and he left. Two days later, while I was getting ready to go to work, I heard the local news talking that a man by the name of Nick "Kegee" Galanos had been the victim of an outfit hit. He was found in the basement of his home at 6801 West Wabansia Avenue, Chicago, Illinois. He had been shot seven times in the back and head; the murder happened the evening of August 30, 1975. Nick Galanos was murdered by the Chicago Outfit; he was one of many who got killed because they were involved in gambling. People say that gambling is a victimless crime, and why should the cops waste their time chasing these guys, when they should be out hunting terrorists or Communists? Well, I've seen a lot of gangland hits, and there aren't any more vicious people than the Chicago mob. They kill in a lot of different ways, and most of the victims are tortured before they die – and that includes their own people who screw up. Anyway, Kegee – I mean Nick – lost all that weight for nothing. What a shame, he was really proud of himself and did one hell of a job. There are times when I think about Nick telling me that he was being tailed and I told him it was his imagination. I hope it was his imagination, and that he didn't get hit because he had been seen talking to me. Nah, no way.

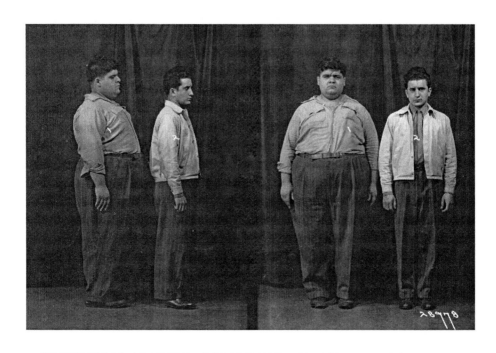

Crime figure Galanos slain on Northwest Side

By William Griffin

NICK [KEGEE] GALANOS, a figure in a 1969 investigation of the crime syndicate's infiltration of legitimate businesses, was found slain Saturday in his Northwest Side home.

Galanos was shot seven times in the head, back, and chest, police said. Several 45-caliber shell casings were found near the body in a basement recreation room in the home at 6801 W. Wabansia Av.

Police believe Galanos, 43, may have known his assailant since there were no signs of forcible entry and only the victim's wallet was taken.

GALANOS' BODY was found by his brother in law, George Colectis, who went to the home when Galanos had failed to keep an appointment, according to Sgt. Gene O'Connell of the Shakespeare homicide unit.

O'Connell said Galanos, a bachelor who lived alone, was probably shot late Friday or early Saturday. Colectis told police that he and his wife had visited Galanos in his home Friday evening but left at 10 p. m., O'Connell said.

Galanos' body was dressed Saturday as he had been the night before, and there was no evidence that the victim had gone to bed, O'Connell said.

POLICE HAVE determined no motive for the killing of Galanos, a city garbage dump foreman who had an interest in a Broadview discount store.

In 1969, Galanos testified under subpena before the Illinois Crime Ivestigation Commission, which was probing the mob's entry into legitimate businesses.

Following his appearance, Galanos created a stir outside the hearing room when he fled from a state's attorney's policeman who was attempting to serve him with a grand jury subpena.

The subpena was served when Galanos was caught several floors below.

Chapter 28

What Are Friends For?

When Ray Rice started working for me in the gambling unit of the vice control division in 1972, he had previously worked in the narcotics section for a few years and needed a change from that type of police work. Ray was a damn good cop and did a hell of a job for me in the gambling unit. He was reliable, honest, and always showed up for work ready to kick ass. Ray never smoked but was known to have a drink off duty on occasion, which incidentally didn't make him a bad guy.

Ray's hobby was boating, and he owned a thirty-one-foot boat, which was anchored at Montrose Harbor. On a couple of occasions, Ray took me and the rest of the crew out for a cruise on Lake Michigan. We would have a supply of beer and pretzels and spend a pleasant afternoon cruising up and down Lake Michigan, admiring the Chicago skyline. When we were out far enough, we would have target practice shooting at empty beers cans, which was a very tough thing to do, I might add. Every November, Ray and his wife would head for Islamorada in the Florida Keys on his annual furlough. They had been going to the same location for years and knew everybody in the area. Ray told me that when he pulled the pin, he was going to move down there and just go fishing and swimming. One day, Ray stopped in the local lounge to have a cool one when two of his pals, a fella named Skip and another guy named Al, asked Ray if he wanted to take a ride in Skip's new boat. Ray, who loved boating, said, Let's do it," and all three of them got in the speedboat and headed out to sea with a supply of beer. While they were cruising around, Skip pulled up to a buoy, which was a few miles out, and he asked Ray to hold the boat steady for a few seconds while he retrieved a bundle that was tied to the buoy. Ray asked Skip what the hell he was doing, and Skip told him he was doing a friend of his a favor and that Ray should not worry about it. Ray saw that the bundle was wrapped in plastic and was waterproof; there were also some numbers written on the bundle. Skip took the bundle and put it below deck where the engine was located and told Ray and Al not to be concerned and that everything was OK.

Al, who had a few beers, asked Ray just what the hell was going on, and Ray said, "Beats the shit out of me. Let's just head back to shore and get the hell off this damn boat." Ray had a bad feeling that the bundle Skip had picked up was narcotics, and being in the narcotics unit in Chicago, he had seen packages of dope wrapped very similar to this package. He told Skip, "Let's get the hell back to land. I don't know what the hell you're doing, but I don't want any part of it."

At this time a small ship appeared in the distance and was headed right for them; a closer look of the ship revealed a name they didn't want to see – United States Coast Guard. As the ship came closer, a sailor with a bullhorn instructed us to stop Skip's boat and prepare to be boarded for an inspection. Ray told Skip to cut the engine and wait until they boarded. Skip said, "Screw you, pal, we have to get the hell out of here, because if they find that bundle, we're all in deep shit." Skip hit the throttle, and the boat took off so fast that Ray and Al almost fell down, with the Coast Guard in hot pursuit.

The chase was on, and Skip's boat seemed to be pulling away from the Coast Guard cutter. That's when the sailor with the bullhorn warned Skip to stop or they would be fired on. Well, this warning didn't bother Skip at all; he just continued cussing the Coast Guard and telling them that they should be chasing terrorists or Communists and not law-abiding citizens. The Coast Guard was good at their word and commenced firing across the bow of Skip's boat. That's all Ray and Al needed; they both grabbed Skip and called him a dumb son of a bitch for running, and they turned off the engine. They told him that they would throw him in the ocean if he gave them any more trouble.

Needless to say, Ray and Al feared the worst. The bundle that Skip picked up from the buoy had to be narcotics, and the Coast Guard was laying in wait for some smuggler to retrieve the dope; and they were the smugglers. Ray saw his whole life flash before him; he was a Chicago cop who worked in the narcotics section and was still in the vice control section working gambling, which is all associated to organized crime. Nobody was going to believe that he didn't have a thing to do with the bundle and was an innocent guy just out for a boat ride.

Four sailors boarded the boat with automatic weapons and told Ray, Al, and Skip to sit down and shut up while they made a search of the boat for any possible contraband. The bundle was found, opened, and a lieutenant made a field test of the white powder that was in the bundle. Of course it was 98 percent pure cocaine; and Ray, Al, and Skip were placed under arrest, handcuffed, and read their rights. The lieutenant told them that they were going to be charged with smuggling and possession of cocaine and would probably get twenty years in the federal penitentiary for these offenses. Ray was protesting his innocence, and Al pleaded that he had only been along for a boat ride and didn't know anything about the dope. Skip told them to be quiet until they get a lawyer and everything would be OK. When one of the sailors searched Ray, he found his Chicago police identification and told Ray that he could kiss his job good-bye and that he was a disgrace to law enforcement. A petty officer took over Skip's boat, and they proceeded to head for shore. The lieutenant was overheard talking over the radio to the local police chief about the arrest they had made and that three people were in custody for smuggling cocaine and that this was a major drug bust.

Ray was a total wreck and felt like throwing up. How could something like this happen to him? Al was pleading his innocence on bended knees, denying any knowledge of the bundle or what was in it. No one paid any attention, and they were ignored.

As the Coast Guard cutter and Skip's boat neared shore, Ray could see some TV cameras, and a large group of people had gathered on the pier to get a glimpse of real dope smugglers. Still in handcuffs, Ray, Al, and Skip were marched down the pier to the awaiting press and TV cameras. Ray got a glimpse of his wife standing next to the chief of police in the crowd; she looked as if she was crying and had a handkerchief up to her face. A closer look, Ray could see that she was laughing, and then he saw the chief of police start to laugh so hard he had to turn around. Then the owner of the local lounge, who was also laughing, displayed a sign in red letters saying, "April fool in November Ray, we gotcha." This entire operation was a conspiracy by Ray's wife, Skip, Al, the chief of police, and even the United States Coast Guard. The bullets were blanks, the bundle was flour, and the TV camera crews were also in on it. When they all looked at Ray's face, they could see that he wasn't laughing yet, but he did seem relieved that he wasn't going to jail or blow his job. They decided to leave Ray's handcuffs on him until he had a couple of cocktails, just for safety's sake. All Ray could keep saying was unbelievable, unbelievable, over and over again.

The Strange Games Adults Sometime Play

Narc Rice and steel merchant Ault worridly avoid press photographer Herman.

Ault and Rice contemplate their future in the hold of the cutter. Everyone else strives to maintain their composure.

EXTRA

The News Gazette

WEATHER FORECAST: UNCERTAIN—and nothing can be done about it!

SPECIAL EDITION

ALL THE NEWS THAT'S SAFE TO PRINT!

PAGE ONE

HERION LEAVES GAMBLING UNIT
CICERO DECLARES LEGAL HOLIDAY

U.S. Missile Passes Test
CAPE CANAVERAL, Fla. —A Redstone missile, similar to the one that will carry the Mercury astronauts on short space trips, was recorded a successful 300-mile flight.
The Army said Monday night's firing was composed of last night meeting changes in the rocket. An informed source reported it also was a maximum of instrumentation to be used in Project Mercury shots.

Hammond Is Cited for Fire Safety
In his annual report released today, Hammond Fire Chief Edward J. Speiech said the total fire loss for the past for Town amounts to a record low $186,935.
"This is not only a record for Hammond, but also a record for cities of comparable size in the state and nation," Speiech said.

Official Urge Federal Aid To Colleges
WASHINGTON — In the nation's colleges and universities face a major crisis because of increasing enrollments, Secretary of Welfare Arthur S. Flemming urged Congress to approve federal aid construction programs for them.
Flemming estimated that institutions of higher education...

MY CREW GAVE ME THIS PAPER AT MY "DUMP" PARTY _ BACK IN UNIFORM TO 019 DISTRICT 1979 THANKS TO DEPUTY SUPT. Wm. HANHARDT _ to many raids

Death Toll end of 1959
INDIANAPOLIS — Traffic in cities are receiving an 1960 death toll ahead of last City deaths are three as high in the first 17 days as in the most period a year.
A police report of persons killed this year up to Monday 24, compared with 20 in the period last year.
In 12 cities and towns with as 6 to 18 in the period, the total score dropped from ... 19.

Smoking Isn't Only Cause Of Lung Cancer, Doctor Says
WASHINGTON — The director of the National Cancer Institute believes that excessive cigarette smoking is one of the causes of lung cancer.
Dr. J. R. Heller told a House subcommittee on tobacco that scientific evidence published today by reputed with Surgeon General Lever are about cigarette smoking.
Heller was asked by subcommittee Chairman John E. Fogarty (D-RI) whether he was "positive" on the various causes in treating ... requires more research, he said. The tobacco industry contends there is no direct link between cancer and cigarette smoking has been established.
Heller predicted that more research will be able to cure all cancers. He noted that the research...

Chapter 29

The Best of the Best

There are bookmakers, and there are bookmakers, but Ted Veesart was the sharpest, most cunning operator I ever met. Ted and I met kind of by accident; we were working on a North Side guy by the name of Louie Parrilli in the downtown area of Chicago. Louie was an outfit bookmaker for years and ran a few newsstands in the North Side El stations. We didn't have any idea whom Louie was reporting to in the outfit, so I decided to tail him around and maybe we would learn something. We had three squads on him when he left home in the morning, and because Louie wasn't a very observant guy, he never made the tail. We were able to track him to El stations, where he would pick up some action from his newsstands, also a few bars in the loop area as well as several restaurants. In the early afternoon that day, Louie picked up a guy who just came out of a bank on Madison Street. Being a Tuesday, which was usually pay-and-collect time for bookmakers, I decided to give Louie and his pal a street stop and see what they had on them.

Because we had observed Louie pick up a few bets earlier in the day at an El stop, that was all the probable cause that I needed. We pulled them down and gave them the old excuse that we were looking for a vehicle that was used in a burglary a short time ago. Well, Louie went for it and started producing all his ID as well as proof that he did own the car and that they were nowhere near the area where the burglary took place. The other guy looked at me as if saying, *Who are you bullshitting, pal,* and he identified himself as Theodore Veesart of Westchester, Illinois. At that time, we searched Louie, and sure as hell, he was dirty with the bets that he had picked up earlier. Ted Veesart was as clean as a whistle; all he had on him was money, over $12,000 in hundreds that he just withdrew from the bank. When he found out that Louie was dirty, he got a look on his face that would scare Dracula himself, because he knew that he was going to jail with Louie. We placed them both under arrest and took them to our lockup at Maxwell Street. I took Ted with me so that I could talk to him about his relationship with Louie. Ted was so pissed off he didn't think to clearly, I guess, because he called Louie the dumbest bastard on earth and said that he was going to fire the son of a bitch. Of course, Ted probably thought that we knew that Louie worked for him, but we sure as hell didn't. The money that Ted had on him wasn't comingled with anything illegal so we couldn't prove that it was being used for gambling. I could have confiscated it, but he would only get it back in court, so I thought I would make a deal with him. I told him I would ignore the money, but he owed me a few favors in the future. Much to my surprise, he agreed and gave me a phone number to call to reach him and we would get some coffee next week. That was one of the best deals I ever made. Ted was a fountain of information.

When Ted's criminal history came back, it showed that he had been busted a few times in the past for running bookmaking joints in Chicago and the suburbs. I checked him out with some informants I had, and they verified that he was running some bookmaking operations for Joe Gagliano and Willie Messino, who worked directly for Jackie "the Lackey" Cerone a top mob boss in Chicago. I thought that this was going to be a very interesting relationship if Ted was a man of his word. The first thing I would have to do is convince Ted that I was a sincere, honest, and trustworthy cop. If he didn't trust me, then he would only talk bullshit to me and I would never get anything worthwhile out of him. Not that I would blame him, 'cause if he got caught being friendly with me, the odds are he would wind up in a trunk with his throat cut.

I called Ted the next week and met him at a restaurant called Russell's at North Avenue and Thatcher Road. To be honest, I really didn't expect him to show, but I was wrong; he showed up at 11:30 as planned. We sat at the rear of the place, and we both got barbeque sandwiches and root beer. There was an informant meet form that I made out about where I was meeting an informant. It also had to be time stamped; this was all to protect me in case someone was following Ted – like the FBI – and they saw me meeting an outfit guy, they would probably think that I was getting a payoff or something. By the same token, Ted had to be careful meeting me because if some outfit guy saw us together, they might think that he's giving me information on mob operations, which could be hazardous to his health.

After some small talk about things like cops and crooks and how do you know if you can trust anyone, Ted asked me if I was wearing a wire. I told him no and asked him if he was; we both laughed at that one. That's when he said I did a little checking on you and found out that you could be trusted, otherwise I wouldn't be here. I said, "The feeling is mutual, Ted." Then, of course, he said, "Don't take this the wrong way, but is there anything I can do for you to kind of not go looking for me in the future?" I said, "Ted, if you can help me out with some information about some other people out there, then I guess I'll be too busy to even think about you, right?" "Gotcha," he said, "this could work out very nicely." Ted then said, "I'm sure you've heard of Tony Spilotro, haven't you?" Then he proceeded to tell me a very interesting story. It seems that Spilotro is the behind-the-scene boss of at least three Las Vegas Nevada hotels – the Stardust, Hacienda, and the Fremont. There was a fourth, but it has since been sold; it was called the Marina. Ted went on to say that a man by the name of Allan Glick, out of San Diego, California, borrowed $100 million from the teamster's union to purchase the above hotels for Tony Spilotro and the Chicago Outfit. Ted added that a bookmaker by the name of Frank" Lefty" Rosenthal from Chicago was one of the overseers of these hotels along with a guy named Simarella and a Bobby Stella. Ted said that anything that goes on in these hotels has to be cleared by Spilotro and Rosenthal. I told Ted that all of this was really interesting and that I appreciated it, but I'm from Chicago and need a little information about some local operations. All this conversation took place in the summer of 1977. Ted said, "OK, Sarge, I'll see what I can do. I'll call you next week." When we left the restaurant, we both were looking all over the place, hoping that we wouldn't see any familiar faces. When we got in the parking lot, Ted took something like a garage door opener out of jacket pocket, pushed a button, and his car started up automatically. "Can't be too safe, if you know what I mean." Obviously he was talking about a car bomb, which was a very common tool used by the outfit in Chicago to do away with someone they didn't like. I asked him if he was paranoid, and his reply was, "In this business, who the hell knows? See you around, pal."

I didn't see Ted until the next week, and we met at Russell's again. Their sandwiches were pretty good, and there didn't seem to be any bad guys around; besides, Ted felt relaxed in the place. But then you never know, sure as hell, who walked in the place with a blond broad but Phil Tolomeo a.k.a. "Philly Beans." He was a bookmaker and collector for the outfit. Phil and I happened to go to the same grade school and high school. Phil played end on the Austin High School football team. He wound up joining the Chicago Police Department, but he only lasted for a few years and then became a small-time outfit guy. Ted said that he had met him once before through Willie Messina and there was a good chance that he may remember him. When Phil went to the washroom, that was our time to get the hell out of there; no sense taking any chances. Ted went out one door and I went out another. I could see that this could get a little nerve-racking at times, but what the hell, God hates a coward. I got the feeling that Ted liked all this intrigue too and maybe he had a score to settle with some of the boys he had to deal with.

During the coming week, we had made a few raids on the North Side, and one of the raids was an office that was connected to Ted. The guy we busted was half Hawaiian; his name was John Mann and would not tell me anything about anything. I got the impression that if we had caught John in a closet with a smoking gun in his hand and we just heard a shot fired with a body on the floor of the closet, John would say, "What gun? What body? I don't know what you're talking about." But John screwed up, and he didn't destroy all his gambling records before we knocked down his door, and I found Ted's private phone number, the same one that he had given me. I found out later through Ted that John was laying off to Ted on occasion, and also that John was born in Hawaii and had watched the Japs bomb Pearl Harbor on December 7, 1941. Thinking back, I think I came very close to asking John if he was Japanese the day we busted him; that wouldn't have been a good idea under the circumstances.

The next time Ted and I met, we decided to change places, so we met at a restaurant called the Paddle Wheel on North Avenue in River Forest, Illinois. This meeting went well, and Ted gave me the names of a couple of bookmakers on the West Side of Chicago that were not connected to him in any way. He also told me about the time he was busted in Melrose Park, in the suburbs. He said that he was told that he was protected and that there was no chance he would ever be raided, but Ted said that he learned years ago that the only person you trust in this business was yourself. Ted said that he had two-by-fours barricaded against the doors and also had a fifty-gallon drum in the room so that in the event of a raid, he would be able to burn his gambling records before the cops got them. Well, the day came, and the police were beating on both of his doors with sledgehammers. Ted decided that he would start a fire in the fifty-gallon drum he had, but then he got a brainstorm. Whenever records are destroyed in a raid and the bettors find out about it, they all seem to make claims on the games that they had bet because the records have been destroyed and the bookmaker can't remember every bet that he took during the day. Ted grabbed all the bets that he had taken in and stood on a chair and put them in the ceiling light fixture, and then he burned some more newspapers and told the police if they would stop beating on the doors he would open up. When the police came in and saw the fire in the drum, they just assumed that Ted had burned all his records and didn't bother to make a search of the premises. Ted had also cut the phone lines, so the phones were immobilized also. They arrested Ted, but he was able to make bail in a couple of hours and, of course, return to the apartment he had been booking at and retrieved all his gambling records. Ted was proud of this little trick he had played on the cops, but it taught me a lesson that sometimes all things are not what they seem to be, and never under estimate your enemy, because if you snooze you lose.

 Ted told me that one night he had been invited to go out for a few drinks with his bosses; he said that this was a very uncommon thing and that he never really socialized with these people. But here he was drinking with Joe Gags, Willie Messina, Jackie Cerone, and another guy he only knew as FiFi. They were in a bar on West Madison Street in Chicago, which also belonged to Joe Gags. Ted said that everyone was having a good time and was having more than a few drinks. Ted said that he was drinking a certain brand scotch at the time, but they ran out of this brand so he started to drink wine. The other boys were getting smashed on booze, and the conversation was flowing freely. Besides, talking about the juice and bookmaking business and how good things were going, the talk changed to a trip Jackie Cerone took to New York with another guy to hit a Mafia boss. This was a favor to the old man Tony Accardo who was running the Chicago Outfit at the time. Ted said that Cerone was half laughing and half talking when he described how they hit this guy while he was sitting in a barber chair with a towel over his head. He told how the guy's legs were flopping around like a chicken when they blasted him out of the chair. He also said that Cerone got a lot of respect from the old man after that job. All Ted could think about while he was sitting with these guys who were drunk out of their mind was that they would remember what they were talking about the next day when they woke up and realize that Ted overheard everything that was said. And maybe they would whack him just to be on the safe side. Ted said that he didn't sleep well for two days after that session; but when he ran into Gags and Willie a few days later, they didn't even mention anything about being out drinking, so he slowly felt better about the situation. But he added that he was glad that he had that automatic car starter on his car and used it all the time, just in case. "Remember," he said, "if you snooze, you lose."

Ted was also the kind of guy who believed in taking precautions; he said it's kind of like an insurance policy, and in his business, a guy can never be too careful. He told me an interesting story about how he had set up his wire rooms. Some were in apartments, some were in storefronts, and he even used pay phones in hospitals. But the key to his insurance policy was a guy he befriended in the telephone company. Ted would only set up his rooms in one area of the city and only use the telephone exchanges in that area, of course. Ted said that he had taken care of his friend in the phone company for years; his friend just happened to be the guy in charge of security, and he gave him a hundred dollars a month as a token of his appreciation. All he had to do was to call Ted and let him know if anyone came in with a court order to tap his telephones. Ted made sure that the security guy had all of Ted's wire room numbers, of course. Well, one day, Ted said that he got a call from his friend who wanted to meet him right away, and guess what the friend said to Ted: The FBI had just given him a subpoena with Ted's phone numbers on it, and the wiretap was to begin the next day. Ted said that when he heard this, he, of course, discontinued all the phone numbers and decided to go out of business for a while. Ted figured that if they had all his numbers, they probably knew a lot more about him and his operation than he thought, and obviously they had some good informant information. *No sense pushing his luck*, he thought. One thing was for sure though; all the money that he gave his friend in the phone company for years for nothing paid off. I recall being out with some FBI agents on some raids that we made, and a few of them were talking about what a good case they had going on some outfit guy when the whole thing went sour for some unknown reason.

They said they knew who the operators were and all they needed was a good wiretap on the phones and they would put them all in the penitentiary. I guess Ted was right when he said, "If you snooze, you lose."

Chapter 30

Armored Wire Room – Chicago Style

    It was 1980, and we had just moved into a twenty-five-year-old three-bedroom house on the northwest side of Chicago. I was still working in the gambling unit of the organized crime division at 943 West Maxwell Street. The old neighborhood at North Avenue and Cicero was a lot closer to work, but due to the increase in crime in the area, my wife and I thought it best to take the six kids and move to a safer neighborhood. Being a sergeant, I was assigned an unmarked squad car to use because I usually worked a lot of nights, and the hours were crazy. If you want to be successful busting gambling operations and hurting the outfit, you have to work when they do – that usually meant nights and weekends. The majority of homes on the block we lived on were single-family homes, with several two flats at the north end of our block. One day, I was driving past one of these two flats when I saw a familiar face exiting the front door. I recognized this person to be a guy I had busted in the past for operating a large-scale sports wire room. His name was George Columbus, and I recall that he had the basement apartment that he was working out of barricaded. The doors had plywood behind them and fortified with two-by-fours, and of course, he had destroyed all the evidence, which was written on soluble paper. George was about sixty years old, and his eyes were not that good as I recall, but they were good enough to run a wire room for the outfit, that's for sure. I pulled around the corner to try and see what kind of car George was driving, but he just kept walking for about two blocks where there was a liquor store and bar. It was only about 11:00 AM on a Thursday in December, and I knew he wasn't going to any wire room at this time of day, so maybe old George needed some liquid refreshment. I waited around for about two hours when George came out of the liquor store with a brown bag in his hand that looked like some kind of booze; he was wobbling down the street and appeared to have been overserved. He managed to find his way home OK, so I ended my surveillance of him for the time being.

When I got to Maxwell Street, I got a hold of my partner Carlo Cangelosi and told him about how I happened to run into George and that we were going to have to give George a little closer look when there were football games scheduled. The odds were that George was back in business because he hadn't been busted in a few years and probably felt cool. Carlo and I have worked together for over twenty years off and on; he put some time in homicide for a few years and then the prostitution unit, but now we were back together again working gambling. I couldn't ever find a more reliable partner than Carlo; if ever the shit hit the fan when we worked in uniform or as district vice dicks, he was right there to do what needed to be done. I remember working together in a uniform squad car. I smoked cigarettes, and Carlo smoked Parodi cigars in the winter with the windows closed. When we opened the door of the car to go on a job, someone once told us that there was so much smoke coming out that they thought the car was on fire. Carlo was two years older than I was, and shorter. I told him that was from those damn Parodi cigars.

We decided to check on George on Monday because of Monday-night football, to see if he was back up to his old tricks. Carlo hadn't been on the raid with Columbus, so he didn't know who Carlo was, which was in our favor in case this turned out to be a close surveillance. There was always the chance that George wouldn't even leave his apartment, and maybe he was booking there; we would soon find out. At about 4:00 PM, George exited his front door, and instead of getting into a car, he walked a block away to Central Avenue where we thought just maybe someone might pick him up. Much to our surprise, he got on a southbound bus, so we tailed the bus to Jefferson Park bus terminal where he got off and walked to an eastbound El station. At that point,

Carlo got out of the car and followed George to the El station. At this time, we did not have any communication set up to talk to each other. The only thing I had was a pager, so we set up a quick plan for him to get on the El and stick with George until he got off, and do the best he could to see where he was headed. When he got off the El, Carlo could page me at a pay phone and tell me where he was so I could pick him up. Wouldn't you know it but the weather started getting nasty, and it began sleeting and snowing, and things got messy during the rush hour. George got on the eastbound El and so did Carlo with other passengers, which was good. I had no idea where the hell George was going to get off naturally; all I could do was to head east and wait for Carlo to page me and let me know where he ended up. About thirty minutes later, Carlo paged me and told me that Georgie Boy got off at Grand Avenue and Halsted Street and walked westbound on Grand Avenue. As far as he could tell, he entered an Italian social athletic club at the southwest corner of Grand and May streets. He then reminded me that it was sleeting out and to get my ass down there and pick him up, as he was too old for this shit. It was now about 4:45 PM and maybe George was just going to play cards in that place, who knows? I picked up Carlo twenty minutes later, and he looked as if he had been through a car wash. The first thing he did was get in the squad and lit one of those damn Parodi cigars and blew the smoke in my face. "Not a bad job for an old guy huh, Herion?" Then he laughed.

We got a break with it being December; it was dark out and the weather was for shit, but we decided to pick a spot to watch the club and to see if George was going to come out and go to some other location. This neighborhood was one of the toughest in Chicago to maintain surveillance; it was mostly Italian, and any strange cars in the neighborhood would be detected as cops. I told Carlo somebody had to walk past the damn club and make sure that George was still in there and that he didn't sneak out the back door. He looked at me as if I was nuts, and I said, "Does that look mean that you're not going to volunteer?" All he did was stick his middle finger in the air and smiled. I put on an old golf hat and put my collar up and walked the half block to the club; when I walked past, I could see George still there, talking to some young guy at the rear of the place, where some guys were playing cards. By the time, I got back to the car, I was as soaked as Carlo was, I told him we were still in business, and if George was in business, he would have to leave shortly because it was almost 6:00 PM. As everyone knew, the

Game started at 8:00 PM on Monday night. At 5:50 PM George and the younger guy he had been talking to leave the club walk across Grand Avenue on May Street and then walk west in the first alley past Grand Avenue. We had been set up down the street on May, so we couldn't see where they went in the alley. We waited for about ten minutes, and then we looked in the alley to try and see any footprints, but the snow was melting, and we had no idea where they went; but we were sure that they were in business that's for damn sure. We called it a day and decided to try and set up on them next Monday night where we could cover the whole alley and put them in there wire room.

The weather the following Monday night was almost as lousy as last week, but that was OK, this time we had a jump on George and his partner and maybe we would get lucky and put them in there office. During the week we picked out a couple of spots on the rear porch of a couple of apartments that gave us a view of the alley they had walked down last Monday. We made sure they were in the club, and sure as hell at 5:50 PM they came out – same routine – crossed Grand Avenue, walked north on May to the alley, and then east in the alley. We were on two rear porches on the third floor, and we were able to see them enter a door at the end of the *T* alley, which looked like an abandoned factory. When they were walking down the alley, their heads were turning around all the time to see if they were being tailed. We got out of there, and after we got in the car, we lit up, me a cigarette and Carlo a damn Parodi; but this time I didn't mind it at all. I thought that they now belonged to us, but it would be nice to see what time they came out of the place. It would probably be about game time 8:00 PM. We got back up on the porches about 7:45 PM and waited; and sure as shit, about five minutes after, they came out the door and walked back to the club. We got the hell out of the area but checked the address in the front of the place they had been in. It was 517 North Racine Avenue and appeared to be an abandoned two-story warehouse.

The next day we made a request through Illinois Bell security to get a listing of any telephone numbers listed to that address. Illinois Bell indicated that they had no records of any active telephones at that location. Carlo and I looked at each other and just shook our heads, but then maybe George and his friend were just playing blind man's bluff in the place. There was no way that we could get a search warrant for the place so we had to improvise. It just so happens that an outfit guy lived across the street at 530 North Racine Avenue. His name was

Jimmy Cozzo who, was connected to Joe Lombardo, a boss in the outfit. I decided to give it a try on Monday night December 15, 1980. The plan was that we would maintain a surveillance of the rear door where they would come out of, and question them about maybe they were burglars breaking into this abandoned warehouse. At 8:05 PM they came out and appeared to be slightly shocked by our presence. When they opened the door, we could see that it was pitch-black inside, and we couldn't see anything. We identified ourselves as police officers and asked for their identification, as if we didn't know who they were. George identified himself, looked at me, and recognized me from the last time he got busted. "I thought you were transferred out of the gambling unit, Herion," he said. I said, "I was, George, but I'm back as you can see." The younger guy identified himself as Philip Cozzo, twenty-three years old, of 530 North Racine Avenue. He said that his father was Jimmy Cozzo, and that's the last words we got out of him.

Accompanied by the two bad guys, we entered the building, where we observed that the door had a dead bolt lock and two two-by-fours that could be used to barricade the door. Above the door was a newly installed ADT alarm system. We traced the wires from this alarm system on the door to a concrete walk in safe with a seven-foot steel safe door, with a combination lock located at the center. This appeared to be a vault similar to a bank door where someone would hide their valuables. Entering this walk in safe, approximately ten by twelve feet in size we observed a six-foot table with two chairs. Four telephones were also located on the table with telephone numbers on each phone. The phones belonged to Illinois Bell and were active. We also found a quantity of water-soluble paper and marked sports schedules with the latest football lines with some wagers written on them. A large bucket of water was also next to the table.

The vault also contained a ventilation system, electric heater, and the ADT alarm system was set up inside the vault, which was connected to the front and rear doors of the warehouse. In the event of someone entering the premises they would be warned of the intruders and would destroy any gambling evidence they had. A closer inspection of the vault revealed that once inside the vault the offenders had a safety latch on the inside of the vault door which would make it impossible for anyone to gain entry from outside the vault.

We arrested Columbus and Cozzo on gambling charges, but, of course, we didn't have a search warrant for the premises so the case was kicked out of court. I did notify the telephone company of the four telephones that we happened to find in the vault, and asked them if they knew they were missing. But things turn out for the best sometimes, I guess, because if we had a search warrant for that warehouse, the bad guys would have been warned we were coming anyway. And then we probably wouldn't have believed that they were inside an armored vault because they couldn't breathe. But then again if they were inside, we would still be beating on that damn vault door. Oh well, the main thing is that we put them out of business at that spot. Some people said we got lucky to find that place, and said that we had a good informant. It's the old saying, The harder you work, the luckier you get."

The interior of this armored wireroom was equipped with a burglar alarm system (ADT), heat, air conditioning, ventaling system a radio and TV set. There was also a large bucket of water and a supply of water soluble paper. 4 telephones were on a 6' table. I had checked with Illinois Bell security for a listing of all telephones installed at 530 N. Racine Ave. I was informed that there were no records of any telephones in the building.

We arrested two men at that location. George Columbus and Phil Cozzo. Columbus was a known associate of Joe "Clown" Lombardo, Cozzo was the son of Jimmy Cozzo mob gambling boss.

Chapter 31

Bears-BettorS-Bookies

Soldier Field, Chicago, as the monsters of the midway wage their traditional gridiron clash with the Green Bay Packers, my partner Carlo and myself were in the center of a mass of humanity that had gathered around a series of pay phones that were scattered around Soldier Field.

We're bundled up in winter clothes and were perusing football sports schedules for the games that were going to be played that day. The Bear-Packer game was starting at 12:00 PM; it was now 11:00 AM and every bookmaker in the country was now open to take bets on all the pro games to be played that day. Everyone waiting in line was studying a sports schedule of some kind to make up their minds on what teams they were going to bet; we were pretending to do the same. A common thing for a bettor to do was to write down the phone number of their bookmaker at the top of the schedule so that they don't make any mistake when they called in their bets; of course, that's good for us. When they punched in the bookmaker's phone number, we memorized the numbers and recorded them down on our sports schedule. A lot of times the bookmaker's phone was busy, and the bettor had to redial the number more than once, so if the number was not on the sports schedule, we got it anyway. The bettor usually had an identification

FOOTBALL SEASON SOLDIER FIELD
BILL MUNDEE PLAYING THE PHONES

Gambling losses consume many victims

Most Americans consider gambling a victimless crime, yet authorities say it's the primary contributor to official corruption, embezzlement and the perpetuation of organized crime:

• Gambling was ranked as the No. 1 reason employees embezzle from their employers, according to a survey by the Chicago Crime Commission of the nation's top surety companies.

"Some companies estimated that gambling [by] employees has been responsible for 30 percent of the losses of those companies. Other companies blamed gambling for as high as 75 percent of their total losses," the commission said. One company noted that "gambling losses in large amounts are more frequent now than 10 years ago."

• "I knew a man who lost a small bus company he owned" because of gambling, Chicago Police Sgt. Don Herion said. "Others have lost houses, another a car dealership, another a clothing factory."

• Two months ago, a vice president of Bear, Stearns & Co., a blue-chip investment firm, was sentenced to two years in prison for embezzling $3.3 million from his company over two years to pay his gambling debts. Walter Gola, 44, of Elk Grove Village, married for 19 years with two children, never before had been charged with a crime.

• James Bittman, agent in charge of the Chicago IRS criminal investigation division, said organized crime figures often will look for other kinds of repayment from indebted gamblers.

"You suddenly have a new business partner or new owner. You're told to start buying goods from a particular supplier. You've had a good credit rating until now, but then it's ruined."

"This is not a victimless crime. There are a lot of victims in it because we find people all the time who are in way over their heads," Chicago Police Vice Unit Lt. Ronnie Watson said. "I'm talking about losing $200, $300 per game per day. The guy who gets into that has nothing but problems."

Toni Ginnetti

Chicago Police Sgt. Don Herion says losses have cost bettors their homes and businesses.
SUN-TIMES/Barry Jarvinen

---

number such as number 102 or any other number so that the bookie knows whom he was talking to. The bad guys have a lot of tricks they use to keep from getting busted, but as they say, sometimes you get the bear and sometimes the bear gets you.

Bookies in the Chicago area were usually open on Sunday from 11:00 AM to 12:00 PM and then from 2:00 PM to 3:00 PM for the later games. We picked out the bettor who was making the biggest bets, which sometimes range up to $5,000 a game. I call home and gave the number that we copped off of the guy to my wife, Gen. She then called the number to see if the phone was busy, or if a guy answered, or maybe she could hear another guy in the background taking bets. Gen called me back and told me that she had to call the number five times before she could get through, and that a guy answered and said, "Go ahead." She, of course, asked for her aunt Mary, and the guy called her a bad name and hung up on her. The good news was, she heard another phone ringing in the background. This guy was in deep shit, and his door would come tumbling down around him very shortly. We checked the phone number with the telephone company and learn that the subscriber lived on the fifth floor of an apartment complex on the Gold Coast. This should be a pretty good operation to bust, so we got a search warrant and proceeded to the suspect wire room location. We hit the elevator and located the suspect's apartment, knocked on the door, and announced that we are police officers with a search warrant and to open the door, "Now." We got a surprise when a woman answered us and told us to wait a minute. This is usually a delaying tactic used by bookmakers so that they can destroy the evidence before the police can get it. I said, "Screw this," and told the woman to open up right now or we were going to kick it in. The woman got the hint and opened the door, pleading with us not to break it down. We think that she probably flushed the evidence down the toilet. But we got a surprise; on the dining room table, there were two phones and numerous sheets of paper with bets recorded on them along with sports schedules, payout sheets and water-soluble paper. There wasn't anyone else in the apartment, and she told us her name was Anne Ceremi and she lived there with her husband, John, and she didn't know where he was. A further search of the apartment revealed a balance beam scale, some glassine bags, and some cassette tapes under a bed hidden under some shoeboxes. I noticed a window that was slightly ajar in the bedroom and a trace of white powder on the sill. I looked out the window and saw a glassine bag with white powder on a garage roof just below her window. Now I knew why she told us to wait a minute; she was worried about the dope being in the apartment and she tossed it out the window, but she didn't have enough time to get rid of the gambling evidence. We decided not to ask her any questions about the narcotics and to let her think that we were just a couple of dopes and missed it.

We sent her down to the gambling unit in a wagon and then went back to the garage roof to confiscate the suspected narcotics. Carlo and I flipped a coin to see who was going to climb up on the roof to get the dope. I lost the flip, so I had to be the monkey and get the bag, which turned out to be about 12 ounces of 95 percent pure cocaine. We knew that there was no way we could prove that Anne Ceremi had tossed the bag out her window on to the roof or that she even had it in her possession in the apartment. The narcotics was inventoried and sent to our crime lab for analysis, which proved to be positive and good-quality stuff. Needless to say, we thought that John Ceremi would sure be a good guy to keep an eye on in the future because he had over $200,000 in wagers, and was a pretty good dope dealer beside. I kept playing the cassettes we found, which were tapes from John's telephones. I guess he liked to record the bets that he took so there wouldn't be any claims from his bettors. The tapes revealed that John had a partner named Alex, who also booked with him. The tricky talk was about a delivery of

"Pepsi Cola" they were expecting in a week or so and that a lot of their friends were really thirsty. Alex seemed to be giving John directions of a meeting place they were going to meet a friend of theirs the next day, and Alex kept saying, "You know where we're going to meet. Remember the bar where you met that blond broad?" John didn't seem to remember, so Alex, being a real slick guy and secretive about the meeting place, believe it or not, spelled the name out – G-I-A-N-O-T-T-I; of course, anyone listening in would never figure that code out would he?

Some outfit guys, Don "Angel" Angelini and Dominick "Big Dom," owned Gianotti's restaurant, Cortina, which specialized in sports bookmaking and was a very popular place to go. It's also a hangout for some of the wise guys in Chicago, and believe it or not, a lot of straight people go there because they think they will see some gangsters; and they probably will. It's located just outside of Chicago, in Norridge, Illinois, on Lawrence Avenue. It's a real nice place to keep under surveillance because there was a large parking lot across the street in a shopping center. It was a good thing that I grabbed a snapshot of John when we were in his apartment, so at least we knew what he looked like; but we had to find out who his partner Alex was. The good news was that John or Alex didn't know what we looked like, so we had a small advantage. We set up a surveillance on John's apartment, and we would let him lead us to Alex. "Sounds like a good plan to me," Carlo said. But he added that wouldn't we need someone to hang around Gianotti's in case we lost John in traffic; being Italian, Carlo volunteered for this tough assignment because he wouldn't look out of place, he said. I had to agree with him; besides he was getting old and his driving made me nervous anyway.

Stakeouts are very boring, and you better not drink a lot of coffee, because you can't leave your subject for a second, because sure as hell that's when he will leave. Come to think of it, I can't ever remember a movie with a police stakeout where the cop had to go to the bathroom. After the third day, we tailed our guy John to a restaurant in Lincolnwood, Illinois, called Myron & Phil's on Devon Avenue, which was another well-known hangout for outfit guys like Lenny Patrick, Mike Posner, Tony Spilotro, Joey DiVarco, and a lot of other wise guys. Our guy John tried to make everybody think that he was Humphrey Bogart or James Cagney; he was wearing more gold that Sammy Davis Jr. and was buying everybody drinks at the bar, except me that is. The owners of this place used to run a cafeteria in the market around Maxwell Street, and they themselves were bookmakers. I think they went straight after they opened this place which was a pretty nice restaurant.

Johnny Boy also was a kisser. Whenever he would greet another guy, especially if he was Italian, Johnny Boy would kiss him on both cheeks. I started to think that I was part of *The French Connection* movie. My problem was to try and figure out who "Alex," his partner, was; that is, if he even showed up. Oh well, all I could do was keep my eyes and ears open. I was on my third vodka and tonic, so I hoped that I could identify "Alex" before I got stoned or somebody that I had busted in the past recognized me. Finally, Johnny boy decided to eat, and he was joined by three other guys at a table toward the back of the restaurant. I figured I was dead 'cause there was no way that I would be able to hear any of their conversation. The three guys all could be Italian or maybe Greek. Alex was a Greek name, so maybe my mystery man was Greek. I was on my fourth vodka and tonic now, so I figured I had to do something pretty quick, because if I finished that drink, I wouldn't even know who the hell I was.

I figured that I had to try the old phone call trick. I had used it in the past, and it worked most of the time. I got to a pay phone near the entrance and got the phone number to the restaurant from a book of matches. I called the number and either Myron or Phil answered the phone, and I told him that I was a friend of John and Alex who were having dinner with some friends. I said I had to talk to Alex about an important matter and would he please ask him to come to the phone. I also told him that I was on a mobile phone and my battery was going out so could he please hurry. He said, "You must mean Alex Salias. Sure, pal, hang on I'll go get him. I watched him go to John's table and talk to one of the guys with Johnny Boy, and it wasn't the guy that I thought it was. Alex got up and walked up to the phone by the cash register. I hung up before he got there. He probably thought my battery had gone dead. Who gave a shit, chalk one up for the good guys; now we knew who Alex the mystery man was. I felt like Ron Santo, the third baseman for the Chicago Cubs who used to jump up and click his heels when something good happened.

But this game was not over, all we had to do now was to wait and see what kind of a car Alex was driving and give him a tail; this could turn into a very long night. About two hours later, John and Alex came out of the restaurant; they probably were watching the Monday night football game to see how much dough they made for the night.

After a brief conversation, their cars were brought to them, and they left. Alex was driving a new Audi; we got his plate and gave him a tail home. Home was in an apartment complex in Park Ridge, a suburb just west of Chicago; he parked inside the building and probably went to his apartment through the garage. We checked his license plate, and sure as hell, the car was listed to Alex Salias at that address. One of the guys checked the mailboxes in the lobby, and his name was also on the mailbox along with his apartment number. It's just like they say, the harder you try, the luckier you get. Alex now belonged to us.

Now that we knew who we were dealing with, we had a chance to bust up a pretty good gambling operation as well as maybe catch them with some dope as well. I started checking with some informants I had whom I could trust and asked about our guy Alex Salias, and also John Ceremi his partner. We found out through reliable sources that both John and Alex were high rollers and threw a lot of money around town. They were big tippers also and it appeared that Alex was the brains of the outfit; it seems John had a big mouth and talked too much and he was told to shut up by Alex on a few occasions when they were out drinking around Rush Street. We also learned that John was dealing very big in quaaludes and would give some to a few of the waitresses in the bars he frequented. Alex was the Cocaine guy and it was rumored that he was working for an outfit guy by the name of Marco D'Amico, who handled a lot of the gambling on the northwest side of Chicago and suburbs. What I didn't understand was the outfit giving an OK to a couple of guys who are booking, and they also had cocaine in the same place, like John had. But then maybe the outfit didn't know that Alex and John were involved in dealing in cocaine and quaaludes. They all knew that if they were raided by the local police and got caught with all the gambling records, the worst thing that could happen to them was a small fine and supervision. But if they got grabbed with dope, they would have a good chance of hitting the shithouse for a long time.

I knew Marco D'Amico ran a lot of gambling for the mob and that he reported to John "No Nose" Difronzo, who was a top outfit boss in Chicago. But to my knowledge, the outfit didn't approve of a gambling and dope operation being run at the same place. But then again, who the hell really knows where they draw the line.

I remembered Marco from the past when he ran a couple of hotdog stands in Chicago. I busted him on Armitage Avenue where he was booking sports and horses and also at Fullerton and Austin where he would meet a lot of his players to straighten out their winnings or losses. All he was then was a small-time operator, but he was suspected of being in on a couple of outfit hits, but that could never be proved. Luckily, one of my informants was betting into Alex and gave me his wire-room phone numbers; he told me that he called two different numbers and that two different voices answered the phones. He thought that the numbers went to two separate locations, because he heard some other voices in the background. These numbers were checked with the phone company and a phone listed to Alex's apartment was one of them and the other one was listed to a heating and cooling company in another suburb. The informant also told us that on occasion he would buy some coke from Alex. I told him that when he makes some more bets with Alex he should ask him if he could get some of the other action as he was all out. Alex told him that everything would be fine by next Monday night and to give him a call then and he would meet him somewhere and take care of the problem. I was also told by a reliable source that Marco had full knowledge of what Alex and John were into with dope and he got a cut of the dope money as well as the gambling proceeds.

I wondered if his boss John "No Nose" Difronzo knew Marco was involved in the narcotics trade. I had a hunch that he would find out one way or the other, you follow what I'm saying? I was sure that it was about time that we got the ball rolling with Alex and John, because we had enough reliable informant information to get two search warrants for gambling. I decided to execute the warrants on Saturday night because most bookmakers were looking to get raided during the day and maybe we could catch them with their guard down; it was worth a try. We hit both locations simultaneously and we got lucky. The heating and cooling company in Elk Grove Village was pretty hard to get into; the two clowns that were operating the wire room there managed to get rid of most of there gambling records which were recorded on water-soluble paper, man, I really hate that stuff. Alex's brother Dave, forty-three, was running this operation with a guy named Mark Behman, twenty-nine, of Palos Hills. It has been rumored in the past, that when a bad guy destroys his gambling records in a bucket of water, this same bucket of water is poured over his head. The water gets very mucky from the soluble paper and looks weird in the guy's hair that's what I have been told anyway. These two clowns were handcuffed and sent down to Maxwell Street in Chicago charged with syndicated gambling.

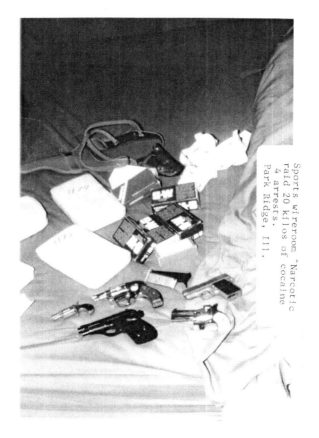

Sports wireroom "Narcotic raid 20 kilos of cocaine 4 arrests. Park Ridge, Ill.

At Alex's apartment we used a ruse to get Alex to open his door, so I used a police woman to knock on his door and tell Alex that she was sorry, but she accidentally backed into his Audi when she was parking her car. It worked like a charm, you could hear the deadbolt locks on Alex's door being opened, and Alex was saying, "How the hell did you do that?" We got in the apartment and our guy Alex was not alone; two guys were standing in the kitchen area next to a kilo of suspect cocaine when had been slit open and they had been testing the quality of the dope. Another guy was coming out of a bedroom at the rear of the apartment and he looked very surprised to find that they had company. All three of these fellas still had their coats on; they must have just arrived before we got there. They were all spread-eagled on the floor and handcuffed. A search of the apartment revealed another nineteen kilos of cocaine on the bed along with six handguns. With all this going on, would you believe that Alex wanted to go down to the garage and see how bad his car had been damaged by the woman who knocked on his door; obviously, Alex was not with the program. The bottom line was we found over $400,000 in wagers, $75,000 in cash and twenty kilos of cocaine.

Tony Basase, fifty-two, of Toledo, Ohio, was the mule that transported the dope from Miami up to Alex' apartment. The two other guys were dealers and distributors, Donald Greco, thirty-two, of Chicago and Joe Pace, thirty, of Mount Prospect, Illinois. All four men were charged with possession of cocaine with intent to deliver, and Alex and Pace were also charged with syndicated gambling. I told Alex, "Sometimes you get the bear, and sometimes the bear gets you." The surprise of this whole operation was that our boy John was nowhere to be found.

At the time of this seizure, it was one of the biggest dope raids in the Chicago area, believe it or not. But it wasn't over yet. Everybody arrested, of course, made bail and they were out of jail the next day. I told my boss at the time, Lieutenant Ronnie Watson, that in my opinion Alex was in a world of shit with his bosses because he got caught with a load of dope at the same place that he was running a wire room. The raid was in all the papers as well as all the television and radio stations, which referred to the seizure of the narcotics and gambling evidence as a mob controlled operation. It was obvious that the raids created a lot of heat for the outfit, which they didn't need. I suggested that Alex be kept under surveillance by the intelligence unit because there was a good chance that he may get whacked for causing all this heat, and there was also the chance that he was dealing in narcotics with out there approval, which was a no-no.

Watson took my advice and told our commander, Mike Hoke, about my opinion, and he agreed and a surveillance team was assigned to keep Alex under surveillance day and night. This kind of assignment could get very boring for whoever got the job, but luckily a good crew was assigned and Alex didn't know it but he was being protected by his Chicago Police Department and had his own personal bodyguards. Alex kept to himself for the few days and didn't leave his apartment much, but one day his car was observed leaving the parking area with what we thought was Alex driving the car. The driver, which we thought was Alex, drove in a very suspicious manner; he went slow then drove through some yellow lights, and then speed up. All of his precautions didn't mean shit, because the surveillance team kept him in sight at a safe distance as to not alert him that he was being tailed. Alex's car finally drove to a parking lot at the rear of a Howard Johnson's hotel at Irving Park Road and Manheim Road. The driver got out of the car, and that was when they saw that it wasn't Alex at all but some other older guy. He parked next to another car, and the driver of this car got out and they shook hands, said a few words. Then he opened the trunk of his car and took out a suitcase and closed the trunk and they both got in Alex's Audi and left the area. They then returned to Alex's apartment complex and started to enter the parking area of the building. At this time the surveillance team stopped the car because they thought that maybe Alex had been the victim of a crime and he may have been locked up in his own trunk. The two guys in the Audi tried to run away but they were apprehended before they could do so. A search of the Audi and the suitcase that was put in the car revealed ten kilos of cocaine in the suitcase. The two bad guys identified themselves as Bob Wilson and the other guy said his name was Don Smith. They both proved to be close friends of Alex and that's who the dope was for.

The Drug Enforcement Administration was contacted when we raided Alex with the other dope and they were in the process of trying to track the source of the cocaine. When they were told about the second seizure they really got interested and assigned a full time crew to the case. Bob Wilson and Don Smith were both charged with possession of cocaine with intent to deliver; they, of course, both were bailed out by Alex. Tom Thompson, who was in charge of a DEA group and a veteran narcotic agent, was the best thing that could have happened to this case. Most of the people that were assigned to his squad were Chicago Police officers, and they all knew what they were doing. As thing turned out, we learned that Don Smith jumped bail and was now a fugitive. Bob Wilson, who had been in the joint before, indicated that he didn't want to return. After Tom talked to him, he proved to be helpful to our investigation and things started to come together. The "mule", Tony Besase from Toledo Ohio had transported the cocaine up to Chicago from Miami, Florida. Besase had an especially built compartment in the car he used where there was enough room to hide twenty kilos of dope behind the rear seat. He installed a special switch under his dashboard, which released the rear seat cushion; there was no way that the police would find that compartment if they were searching the car. Besase told us that he got the dope from Smith who lived down in the Florida Keys, and that Smith had a connection to Colombia in South America where he had been getting all the dope that he needed. Thompson was very familiar with this type of operation as he worked on a few cases in the Florida area and had even been to Colombia working on other large-scale dope operations. This case was turning into a large-scale operation, and I was sworn in as a temporary DEA investigator so that I would have access to any federal information that DEA uncovered.

During the course of this operation, surveillance was still maintained on Alex as well as John, as John had not been charged with any narcotic violations up to this point. Sure as shit, here was John still running their bookmaking operation, only now he had gone to a suburb out West in Des Plaines, Illinois, in an apartment complex. Alex's surveillance revealed that he had rented an office in Park Ridge, Illinois, and was using this as a place where he could continue his dope operation. A reliable informant told me that he knew for sure that the money that Alex was going to make from his narcotic dealings for the outfit was going to be used to finance a feature film about the mass murderer, John Wayne Gacy. It was hard to believe that Alex and John would still be conducting the illegal enterprises, even though they had both been busted and were awaiting trial. Talk about balls; they both had them or maybe they didn't give a shit about going to jail. As things turned out, I got a phone call from Johnny Boy who wanted to meet me to discuss what he could do to help himself. A friend of mine, Larry Evans, who worked with me in the gambling unit a couple of years ago, had since been detailed to the DEA and was assigned to Tom Thompson's squad. I called Larry, and we both met Johnny boy at a restaurant parking lot at Belmont and Manheim roads in the suburbs. The meeting turned out to be very fruitful and John told us about the biggest quaalude dealer in Chicago as well as other gambling operations that belonged to the outfit. While all this was going on, Alex went out and bought a new Mercedes and started making his own coke deliveries just like nothing happened. This son of a bitch wasn't worried about anything or anybody, least of all, us.

With Johnny boys help we hit an apartment on North Sheridan Road where the quaalude dealer was operating and busted some dingy looking bearded bastard who also was involved in taking photos of small boys and girls. This guy was the scum of the earth; just looking at him made me sick. He even had red gravy in his beard and wore these little yippie glasses, which reminded me of the sixties. The Vietnam war was going on and every jagoff in the country came to Chicago for the Democratic Convention, and they all looked like this goof, but that's another story. Shortly thereafter, Larry Evans and I came up with a connection to this dope ring in Los Angeles, California. Thompson suggested that we take a trip out their and check it out as it was possible that some of the dope coming into the Chicago area was coming from Mexico through La-La-land. We had a name and address of a former girlfriend of Alex who was supposed to be the connection from LA back to Chicago.

Larry and I obeyed orders and went out to LA on official business and checked out this broad's involvement with Alex. She convinced us that she was no way involved with Alex and was leading a pure life and was in the process of getting married in the next month. While we were out there, I called a friend who worked in the movie business, Tony Borelli, who lived Sherman Oaks, a suburb of LA. Tony invited us to a movie lot he was working at and told us to just ask for him at the front gate and he would get us in the studio where they were making a western with James Garner and Bruce Willis. Well, when we drove up to the gate the next day and asked for Tony, the guard told us that he wasn't on the set right then and we would have to come back later. At that point Larry and I showed the security guard our DEA credentials and the guard started calling us sir and to please wait a minute. Two minutes later some guy came out and said that he was an assistant director and could he help us. I explained that we were friends of Tony Borelli, and we just wanted to say hello to him. At this point the director said just a second and went back into the movie set, which was inside a large studio. Larry and I knew that we had made a lot of people very nervous because we were from the Drug Enforcement Agency and they didn't really know what we were doing at their movie set or maybe who we were really looking for.

Larry and I decided to get real official looking and started to stare at everybody. Finally, an assistant producer came out and invited us onto the set inside; it seemed as if everybody involved in making this movie was staring at us. Some of them were smiling, and others seemed to be avoiding us. We had been standing outside of the set they were filming when James Garner came out and was getting ready to do his thing in this old time western bar they had. He took one look at us and walked over to us and said, "You fellas are Narcs, I'll bet." I have been a fan of Jim Garner ever since he did a series called *Maverick*, besides that he was a hell of a golfer. Then he said, "You know what, I was wondering what the hell was going on around here when I heard a lot of toilets flushing, there had to be Narcs somewhere." We told him that we were just there visiting a friend of ours, and we weren't looking for anybody. He said, That's OK," and stood there and talked to us for about forty-five minutes. Before he left, he told us to keep up the good work and he hoped that everybody that had anything to do with dope on his movie was shitting in their pants, not knowing who we were looking for.

Garner wanted us to kind of stare at his costar, Bruce Willis, but we thought that maybe we would be pressing our luck, so we told him that we had other plans for him. "Only kidding, Jim." Tony Borelli finally showed up, and he showed us around the whole movie lot, which was very interesting. I had met Tony when he was in Chicago working on a film called *Raw Deal* with Arnold Schwarzenegger. I was the technical advisor and even got a small part in the movie as a desk sergeant. I wore my own uniform, of course. Larry and I went back to Chicago and learned that we were going to bust "Alex" again, in his office in Park Ridge.

We executed a federal search warrant on Alex in his office in Park Ridge and found more cocaine which was hidden in the ceiling. This time he almost had a heart attack because he knew he was finished. Alex lost his Mercedes also, which was confiscated by DEA and it was used by Tom Thompson as a work car. The government also confiscated his condo in Park Ridge which was worth about $300,000 and all the rest of his assets. Alex was found guilty and sentenced to twenty years in a federal penitentiary; Johnny boy got six years, and all the others were sentenced to lesser terms. Alex was a standup guy though, because he never gave up his boss Marco D'Amico; probably because he would have gotten whacked if he did.

Obviously, whenever the Bears played at home we went to the game, a lot of bad guys hit the shithouse because of some dope using a pay phone and not paying attention to his surroundings – thank goodness.

Courtesy of Don Herion

Chapter 32

Racetrack Messenger Service Nightmare

The first racetrack betting messenger service in Chicago was called "Pegasus"; it was located in the loop on South Dearborn Street, on the second floor. This business was started by a group of slick dudes who wanted to make quick buck in a hurry; a couple of them were attorneys. It all started in 1976 and proved to be the biggest headache for me, and I know it was for my boss at the time, Lt. Edward Berry, head of the Chicago Police gambling unit.

I remember getting a call in the office on Maxwell Street where the vice control division was located. An attorney affiliated with the messenger service informed us that they had just opened for business the day before and were in the business of accepting horse wagers for races that were run at Sportsman's racetrack in Cicero. They explained that they would accept these wagers and charged the bettor 10 percent of whatever they had bet. The attorney, Mickey Kaplan, explained that these wagers were then brought to the racetrack where the wagers were bet through the windows at the racetrack. The mutual clerk would give the messenger the tickets for the bets they had made, the messenger would then return the tickets to Pegasus where they would be kept on file. Kaplan stated that the tickets would be checked to see who had won or lost their bets. If the bettor had won, he would be paid according to the results of the races. Kaplan explained that they only provided a service to customers that liked to bet the horses and were unable to get to the racetrack. The only profit they made was the 10 percent they charged for providing this service. At that point he actually invited us to make an inspection of the premises and check out their operation to see that they were not bookmakers.

I got my crew together and I explained where we were going and what we could expect to find. Of course, we all knew that this was just another scheme dreamt up by some slick dudes to make a fast buck and circumvent the law. What a sight we were in for, there were people standing in line waiting to make their bets at makeshift windows. Pegasus provided racing forms and scratch sheets for everyone including pencils. They even had free coffee and rolls for there customers. The results of yesterday's races were on the walls, which showed everyone who had won or lost. I found the manager of the place, and told him who we were and that we had been invited to make an inspection of the premises to see their operation. The manager, who I'll call Benny, showed us where all of the receipts of bets made at the racetrack were kept and said that they operate on volume and only make 10¢ on every dollar that they handle. He went on to explain that they stop accepting wagers one hour before each race so that they have enough time to get to the racetrack and place there wagers through mutual clerks.

Upon checking all the receipts against all the wagers they had accepted, they matched up and I must say that everything they told us was true. The only problem was in my opinion they were still bookmakers, and Lt. Berry agreed with me so we arrested the manager for being a keeper of bets and keeper of a gambling house. I think that this is what they really wanted anyway, to make this a test case in the circuit court. At the time we knew that we had a problem if this type of gambling was going to be declared legal, we had no idea what the future held.

While the case against the Pegasus raid was pending in court before Circuit Court Judge David J. Shields, other messenger services began to pop up all over town, which, of course, was no surprise to us. They all had different names, such as Western Messenger, Stretch Runner, Mr. Lucky's, Finish Line Express, Turf and RTM Messenger services and on and on and on.

We would make wagers in the Messenger services ten minutes before the first race was scheduled to go off at Sportsman racetrack. We would then keep the place under surveillance to see if anyone would leave the place to go to the track and place the bets at the pari-mutuel windows, which had been set aside for the messenger services. Obviously there was no way that they could get to the track in time to make the bets, unless of course they had a helicopter. They were very careful when it came to handling bets on trifectas or daily doubles. If someone would win a trifecta bet and they were holding the bet they could get hurt and have to pay out a lot of money. So they had a confederate standing by near the racetrack by a phone where they would call him and give him the trifecta or daily double bets and he could lay these bets off in the track windows.

Surveillances were also set up at the racetrack at the pari-mutuel windows that had been set up just for the messenger services to see who showed up to make there horse bets through the windows. At first some people did show up but that didn't last to long, after a few weeks nobody showed up at all.

We began making raids all over Chicago and locked up a lot of people that were involved in this type of gambling. Most of these establishments had a counter, some tables, chairs, and provided free coffee and rolls as well as scratch sheets and racing forms for their customers. I knew that the outfit was operating a lot of these messenger services, such as Mr. Lucky's and Finish Line Express. I also knew that they were booking all the bets that they were handling, except the trifecta and daily double wagers. They usually had a confederate standing near a pay phone outside the racetrack so that they could call him and give him all the trifecta and daily double wagers they had, then he would lay these bets off at the windows in the track. That way, they wouldn't get hurt if one of their customers hit a big trifecta or a daily double. In a few of the places we raided, we discovered that they were also taking bets over the telephone, they of course told us that they only did that as a convenience for a customer that was sick and couldn't make it to there messenger service. And that the customer's wagers were placed at the racetrack windows.

The suburbs began to notice that messenger services were opening up in their towns, and they would call us for advice on how to deal with this problem. We had a few meetings with some police departments and even went along with them on a few raids. This had to be the biggest scam the outfit ever put together. They were booking horse bets, like they always did anyway, but now they were also collecting 10 percent on every dollar they handled. One day we raided eight different messenger services. At each one a policeman made bets with someone at the messenger service ten minutes before post time at the racetrack. A surveillance was maintained at each location to see if anyone left the premises to bring the wagers to the track. Of course, that was a joke, not one person left any one of the services we made the bets in. These cases were also pending in court, which was turning into another joke.

There were a few honest people that opened a messenger service thinking that the money they would make some money by charging 10 percent on a dollar. They were the only people that would show up at the racetrack and place the bets that they had taken in. They, of course, didn't last very long and eventually they went out of business. And guess who would take over their location, a mob connected messenger service of course. They just changed the name on the place and it was business as usual. There was at least one independent operation, Track Shack Messenger service that was taken over by two guys that were believed to have crime syndicate connections, Bernard "Pepe" Posner and William McGuire. They were eventually indicted for extortion by the federal government in 1978.

Finish Line Express at 506 West Van Buren Street was the headquarters of this operation. There were twenty women working telephones on the second floor of this place where all the wagers from their fifty-four locations in the city and suburbs were tabulated. Dominic Cortina, reportedly a lieutenant to crime syndicate boss Jackie Cerone was observed at this location on numerous occasions. Pepe Posner and William McGuire also visited this location frequently. Another big operation was called Mr. Lucky's; there main offices were located at 1867 East Seventy-first Street and 2130 South Indiana Avenue. They reportedly had twenty-one locations, most of which were located in black areas. There were at least twenty women also operating telephones at the Seventy-first Street location, where all their wagers were tabulated from throughout the Chicago area. For two years we lived with this headache; all the while the outfit was making millions. We raided these places every chance that we could, but believe me, it was like trying to put out the Chicago fire by pissing on it. We had occasion to make a raid at 2654 North Long Avenue in Chicago in a vacant store, where we found two wise guys operating four telephones, taking bets from other messenger services. This operation was set up to make sure that in the event of a raid, the police would confiscate all the wagers and the messenger service wouldn't have records of the bets made that day. I guess you could call this a type of insurance policy.

Eventually the Internal Revenue Service, the FBI, and the Illinois Department of Law Enforcement joined us in our quest to put these places out of business. In April 1977, we affected three raids at the nerve centers of the Finish Line Express and Mr. Lucky's. In Mr. Lucky's office on

Seventy-first Street, we found twenty female clerks answering telephones and recording bets from other messenger services. The other office of Mr. Lucky's on South Indiana Avenue revealed thousands of dollars of horse wagers that were supposed to have been sent to the racetrack. The Finish Line Express at 506 West Van Buren Street, Chicago, was the biggest nerve center of all. Twenty-five females were answering telephones on the second floor and recording wagers, the wagers they had taken in from their other locations. When we made the raid at 506 West Van Buren Street, we found Dominic Cortina trying to hide behind a desk; he looked kind of silly at the time, being a big time mob guy like he was.

Finally in 1978, the federal grand jury indicted fourteen persons on charges of conspiracy, gambling extortion, and operating an illegal business in connection with the messenger services in the Chicago area. Dominic Cortina, Richard "Big Man "Piekarski, Bernard "Pepe" Posner, and Ralph Carbonari were arrested along with ten others.

Other investigations involving messenger service operations in Chicago from January through June 1978 resulted in raids conducted on seven locations. The raids were on May 19, June 15, and June 19, 1978, resulting in the recovery of large sums of money and voluminous gambling records. These raids led to the indictment of Anthony John Spilotro for Interstate Transportation in aid of racketeering and gambling; James Inendino for Eetortionate credit transaction. Spilotro and Inendino have been reported to be organized crime. Eventually James Inendino was sentenced to twenty years in the penitentiary. Anthony Spilotro, of course, was murdered with his brother Michael and buried in a cornfield in Indiana. They both had been beaten to death, probably with baseball bats.

Years later when I would run into some of the guys who were in the messenger service business, all they would say was that that was the biggest money-making scam they had in recent years. Well, for me, and a lot of other people in law enforcement, we were just as glad to see them close up.

Of course, we did get a letter of appreciation from the agent in charge of the FBI in Chicago, John E. Otto. He simply stated that the efforts of the officers involved weighed heavily in the successful culmination of these investigations. We also got an attaboy from the superintendent of police, James O'Grady.

PS: As aggravating as the messenger services were, we would find that the boys had come up with another money-making machine; it's called video poker. But that's another story.

Police arrest 10

8 bet service offices closed

THE MUSHROOMING racetrack betting messenger services face a new roadblock after eight were shut by Chicago police raids.

Ten persons were arrested on charges of transmitting gambling information by phone, and nine of them were also charged with being keepers of bets and gambling houses.

The mass raids Wednesday came as a surprise, since Chicago police have been raiding new messenger service locations once for the record and then leaving them alone until their legality is decided in the courts.

THE EIGHT locations, all operating under the name of Western Messenger Service, had been raided once.

But Lt. Edward Berry, head of the Police Department's gambling unit, said surveillance showed that the eight were not operating only as messenger services, which are supposed to take all bets to the track for placing. Berry charged that the eight accepted bets and held the money, as illegal bookies do, or transmitted the bets by phone.

He said his men went into each of the offices Wednesday and placed bets on the first race at Sportsman's Park racetrack in Cicero. They then placed each office under surveillance.

By 1:30 p.m., when the first race at Sportsman's was run, no Western Messenger Service employes had left to take the bets to the track, Berry said.

POLICE SAW one Western runner leave his home, go to a pay phone, and then go to the track twice, Berry said, but he placed bets only at the Daily Double and Trifecta windows.

The eight raided locations are at 7054 S. Western Av., 5752 S. Pulaski Rd., 6057 W. Belmont Av., 4757 N. Clark St., 5140 N. Elston Av., 7116 W. Higgins Rd., 6007 W. Irving Park Rd., and 6848 W. Grand Av.

The individuals charged were identified as Thomas Sullivan, 46, of 2189 S. Lowe Av.; William Tenuta, 48, of 2716 N. Neva Av.; Joseph Duran, 46, of 5752 S. Pulaski Rd.; Vince Bavuso, 28, of 7517 W. Fullerton Av.; Larry Furio, 25, of 7049 W. Windsor Av.; Michael Sabatino, 30, of 2325 N. 74th Av., Elmwood Park; Peter Loverde, 65, of 2620 W. Huron St.; Susan Kahoun, 42, of 4807 W. 96th St., Oak Lawn; Burton Turf, 27, of 175 7th St., Wheeling; and Louis Matroci, 51, of 9140 W. Grand Av., Franklin Park.

LOVERDE FACES the single charge of transmitting gambling information by phone. All were freed on $1,000 bond.

A test case filed against Pegasus, the first messenger service to start operations in Chicago, is before Circuit Court Judge David J. Shields for trial.

It was rumored that Judge Shields continued these cases for two years for one reason or another?

Two-year project
Grand jury indicts 14 in betting service probe

By Ronald Koziol
and John O'Brien

FOURTEEN PERSONS were indicted by a federal grand jury Thursday on charges of conspiracy, gambling and tax law violatons, extortion, and operating illegal businesses, in connection with off-track betting messenger services in Chicago.

Investigators said as much as $100,000 in daily wagers was handled by the controversial services, which were outlawed last July by the Illinois Supreme Court. Since then, many have resurfaced as private social clubs to circumvent the ruling, according to investigators.

Thursday's 15-count indictment was announced as 50 federal, local, and state law officers fanned out to arrest the defendants.

The action culminated a two-year investigation by the Federal Bureau of Investigation and Internal Revenue Service, in cooperation with the Chicago Police Department's vice control division and the Illinois Department of Law Enforcement.

The indictment returned by the February 1977 grand jury identified the defendants as:

DOMINIC CORTINA 55, of 1758 N. Normandy Av., reportedly a lieutenant to crime syndicate boss Jackie Cerone.

Richard "Big Man" Piekarski, 48, of 1373 Reichert Rd., Crete.

William "Charlie" McGuire, 53, of 745 S. East Av., Oak Park.

Ralph Carbonari, 49 of 7702 Woodard Av., Woodridge.

Bernard "Pepe" Posner, 59, of 3300 Carriage Way, Arlington Heights.

Raymond Brown, 49, of 7447 S. Lake Shore Dr., Chicago.

Vernon Cotton 24, of 1533 E. 65th Pl., Chicago.

Leonard Danner, 44, of 5000 S. Indiana Av., Chicago.

Frank Esposito, 50, of 3700 E. 171st Ct., Lansing.

Michael LeDonne, 34, of 121 W. 167th St., Calumet City.

Leonard Mondia, 32, of 2222 S. 58th Av., Cicero.

WALTER RHODES, 51, of 30 E. Division St., Chicago.

Jacqueline Ross, 38, of 6532 N. Francisco Av., Chicago.

Brenetta Bates, 6528 S. Evans Av., Chicago.

All were connected with either the Finish Line Express, with headquarters at 506 W. Van Buren St., and offices at 54 Chicago area locations, or Mr. Lucky's Messenger Service, 2130 S. Indiana Av., which conducted operations at 21 locations.

Rhodes was identified as president of Finish Line, and Brown as president of Mr. Lucky's.

The indictment charged the two services operated as "fronts" for illegal gambling and took in at least $1 million a month, authorities said.

WHILE OPERATORS of the services purported to take bets to tracks, the indictment charged "the defendants well knew a large number of wagers placed were not taken to Chicago area racetracks and bet at the pari-mutuel windows, but were 'retained' or 'booked' by them in violation of state and federal law."

The indictment charged that from July of 1976 to July 14, 1978, Cortina, Piekarski, McGuire, Carbonari, and Posner conspired to participate in racketeering activities to collect unlawful debts and conspired to operate controlled bet messenger services through a pattern of racketeering.

At least one independent operation, Track Shack Messenger Service, was taken over by Posner and McGuire through extortion, according to the indictment.

BROWN AND RHODES were also charged with perjury and obstructing a grand jury investigation by failing to produce records of the services.

Chapter 33

Harry "Hit Man" Aleman

Harry Aleman, Butch Petrocelli, Louis Almeida, James Inendino, and Lenny Foresta were some of the members of the infamous "Survivors Club" on Taylor Street near Racine Avenue. All it was a storefront, there wasn't anything fancy about it except that some of the members were hit men, home invaders, burglars, juice collectors, and extortionists. They were called the "Taylor Street Crew" and members of the Chicago Crime Syndicate. They reported to Joseph "Joe Nagall" Ferriola who at the time was reported to be the number two man in Chicago's Organized Crime Syndicate. Ferriola reported to the number one guy at that time, Jackie "the Lackey" Cerone, who was reported to be quite a guy with a shotgun, knife, or a Louisville slugger when he was working his way up the ladder in the Chicago mob.

The first time that I ever heard of Harry was about 1970, when Nick "Kegee" Galanos told me about him, William "Butch" Petrocelli, and James Inendino. They were terrorizing bookmakers to pay a street tax to the outfit for the privilege of bookmaking. They simply told them to "pay, quit, or die."

I was a detective sergeant assigned to the gambling unit of the vice control division, working out of 943 West Maxwell Street, which was only a few blocks away from Harry's hangout on Taylor Street. Kegee told me that two guys he knew that were booking, were approached by Harry and Butch and were told that it would cost them $300 a month to operate. The two partners were a midget named Jesse Testa and a crippled guy named Frank. They were also told that they had to pay a penalty for the past six months that they were in business, $1,800. I asked Kegee what they would get for there $300 a month, without blinking, Kegee said they would get to stay alive.

Aleman wasn't a big man, he was about five foot eight, weighed 150 pounds, but he had the eyes of a dead shark; and when he told you that he would blow your head off if you didn't pay your "street tax," you knew he meant it. It is believed that Harry's first hit was on a gambling boss on Taylor Street, Sam "Sambo" Cesario who was shot to death by two men wearing masks while he was sitting in front of his home at 1071 West Polk Street. The first time we busted Aleman was when he was running a crap game in the basement of a building in the 1000th block of Polk Street, which just happened to be across the street from Sambo's house.

At the time we had thrown a fifty-gallon garbage can threw the front window of the store to gain entry. We locked up twenty-five guys, and I made Harry the keeper of the game. I recall Aleman was telling everybody to calm down and that he would get them out on bail in an hour. Aleman never asked to see a search warrant, which was OK by me, because we didn't have one. Aleman pleaded guilty in court to the charge of keeper of a gambling place. I was surprised by that move because all his lawyer had to do was ask to see our search warrant, and the case would have been thrown out of court in two minutes. I wondered just how sharp Harry was, if he didn't get any smarter, he sure wouldn't last to long. Aleman, Petrocelli, Borsellino, and Jimmy Inendino were going all out lining up every bookmaker in the Chicago area and they were making tons of money. They had some cute ways to find out about any independent bookmakers they may have missed. It seems that they had a friend in racket court at 1121 South State Street where the gambling cases are tried. The friend would get a list of the people that were locked up for bookmaking or running a card or dice games and would turn over this information to Harry or Butch. At that point these people would get a visit from Harry and Butch and the facts of life would be explained to them. Very simply, "pay, quit, or die." I was also aware of the mob making gambling raids on some bookmakers. One such person told me; "just before he left town" about how a couple of mob guys had kicked in his door of the apartment he was using to run his sports wire room. At first he thought it was a police raid and he destroyed all his wagers which were written on flash paper. This infuriated the mob raiding party, because they wanted to know how much action he was handling. They proceeded to give this person a beating as well as sticking an ice pick through the hand that he wrote with. It seems that this bookmaker had been paying his street taxes on time, but he lied to Aleman and Butch about how much he was really booking. His payments were doubled from $500 to $1000 per month, with a warning that he wouldn't be able to take too many bets if his tongue was missing.

The '70s was a busy time for Aleman who was terrorizing a lot of people in the Chicago area and was really making a name for himself as the main suspect in a lot of murders. The second murder he committed happened on September 27, 1972, on the street at 5916 West Walton Street. The victim was William Logan who was a Teamster shop steward, Logan who had been going to work in Cicero when Harry gunned him down with two shotgun blasts. It was reported that Logan had been involved in a vicious custody battle with his ex-wife who was reported to be Aleman's second cousin. She also testified that after their divorce she had an affair with Butch Petrocelli, Aleman's rat partner. The investigation revealed that Logan sealed his fate when his ex-wife warned him to stay away or she would talk to Aleman about him. Logan was reported to have said, fuck that dago bastard. A short time later, according to Aleman's good friend and associate, Louis Almeida, he drove Aleman to Logan's home where that waited to ambush Logan when he came out. As fate would have it, a man by the name of Robert Lowe, a neighbor who lived across the street, had been out walking his dog and came face to face with Harry as he stepped out of the hit car, immediately after the shooting. Lowe was to be commended for identifying Aleman as the killer of Logan that night. Bernard Carey, who was the states attorney of Cook County at that time, announced the indictment of Aleman with great fanfare. It was a rare occasion when a crime syndicate murder had been solved in Chicago. It looked as if this was a slam-bang case, and Aleman was finally in a world of shit.

Robert Lowe, the good citizen who identified Harry Aleman as the assassin of William Logan in criminal court, felt that the case would be over and he and his family could return to a normal life. Lowe and his family had been in protective custody at an undisclosed location, miles from Chicago. Louis Almeida who had turned informant and was cooperating with law enforcement, testified in court that he was with Aleman when he murdered William Logan, and he drove the getaway car. This case was a lock and Aleman would certainly be found guilty and be executed or go to jail for the rest of his life. As they say, "FORGET ABOUT IT," not in our courtroom.

The presiding Judge in this murder case was Circuit Court Judge Frank J. Wilson who proved to be a disgrace to the judicial system. Another witness who was a neighbor of William Logan and heard the gun shots the night of the murder told Judge Wilson that she was offered a $10,000 bribe by Aleman if she would lie in court. The woman, Ella DeMarco, happened to be a niece of Alderman Vito Marzullo, a powerful West Side politician. Prosecutors did not consider her testimony of much importance because she did not see the actual murder or the killer. But, by chance she was also acquainted with Harry and his brother Anthony; she had dated Anthony and had gone to grammar school with Harry when she lived in the Taylor Street neighborhood as a child. Anthony contacted Ms. DeMarco and he said that he wanted her to testify that she saw the killer, but it wasn't his brother Harry. When she refused, Anthony got very angry and told her, "You'll have to look over your shoulder the rest of your life." Sources say that Ms. DeMarco responded with a threat of her own. Besides being the niece of Ald. Marzullo, she is also the niece of several other men considered to be of importance in the crime syndicate. And, the sources say, she told Anthony Aleman that if she was bothered, her uncles would put the Aleman brothers in the ground.

Later, she said Harry Aleman himself telephoned her about the case. She said that she was sure that it was Harry on the telephone because they had gone to school together and she asked him several questions, based on their acquaintanceship that only he could have answered. She said that he too asked her to say that she saw someone else on the scene of the murder, and offered her $10,000 to do so. She refused, and instead reported the alleged bribe offer and threat to investigators. The States Attorney's Office tried to have her testify in court about those conversations. Judge Wilson listened to the state attorney's request in his chambers, out of hearing of the press, spectators, and relatives of the murdered man. However a court reporter transcribed the in-chambers conference and lawyers for both sides were present.

After being told what Ms. DeMarco was prepared to testify about, Judge Wilson ruled that she could not because the conversations were hearsay. He impounded the court reporter's record of the conference and ordered lawyers not to talk about it. When Ms. DeMarco finally took the witness chair, all she could say was that on the night of the murder, she heard a voice through her open window say, "Hey, Billy," then heard the shots. While she testified, Harry Aleman stared at her and tapped on the side of his head with a forefinger.

Throughout the trial, prosecutors said that was virtually unheard of for a citizen to come forward and identify the alleged killer in a gangland slaying. They considered Lowe's testimony as well as Louis Almeida's testimony that he was present when Aleman gunned down William Logan on September 27, 1972, to be their trump cards in this murder case.

But on Tuesday, May 24, 1977, Judge Frank Wilson told a jam-packed courtroom, that Robert Lowe had "lied on the witness stand," and that Louis Almeida's testimony was subject to suspicion because he was under a grant of immunity. Long before Judge Wilson got to the words "Not guilty," assistant states attorneys Nicholas Iavarone and Joseph Claps must have known what was coming. Both began to slump in their chairs and Iavarone slowly shook his head. When Wilson concluded, "The defendant is found not guilty," Logan's sister, Joanna Dietrich, cried out "Oh my god, no!" Aleman stood up and grasped his attorney's face, grinning from ear to ear. After a few minutes the Logan family spoke to the disappointed prosecutors, they expressed fear for the future of Robert Lowe and his family. He jeopardized his wife and kids, all for nothing.

When I heard the verdict, I couldn't believe the outcome either. I thought if this case wasn't fixed there ain't a steer in Texas. I wondered, just how in the hell are we ever going to get witnesses to testify in court again? Oh well, Chicago, the city that works, right?

I remember that night when the word hit the street that Harry was a free man, we took a ride over to the Survivors Club on Taylor Street, and a lot of Harry's goombas were there celebrating his victory. MaMa Sue's restaurant and bar at Taylor and Loomis was packed; it looked like New Years Eve on Taylor Street. Harry was married to Ruth, a widow with four children. Ruth's first husband, Frank Mustari, had been a hit man too, but met his end in 1957 when the tavern owner he was stalking was tipped off by a growling watchdog, drew, and shot first. Ruth was a devoted wife and has been at her husband's side for years. When Harry was indicted for Logan's murder in 1976, she came to the Cook County jail with a suitcase containing $250,000 to bail him out, not realizing that she only needed 10 percent of the bail, $25,000. Aleman is suspected to have committed or participated in other murders in the Chicago area and has gained a reputation of being Chicago's top crime syndicate killer. Some of the murders are listed below.

December 20, 1973: Richard Cain, forty-nine, a top aide to Mafia boss, Sam "MoMo" Giancana; two masked gunmen shot gunned Cain at point-blank range in Rose's Sandwich Shop, 1117 West Grand Avenue.

February 24, 1974: Socrates "Sam" Rantis, forty-three, a counterfeiter; found with his throat cut and puncture wounds in his chest in the trunk of his wife's car at O'Hare airport.

April 24, 1974: William Simone, twenty-nine, a counterfeiter, found in the backseat of his car near 2446 South Kedvale Avenue, with his hands and feet tied and shot in the head.

July 13, 1974: Orion William's, thirty-eight, a suspected mob informant; found shot gunned to death at 70 East Thirty-third Street, in the trunk of his girlfriend's car.

September 28, 1974: Robert Harder, thirty-nine, a burglar and jewel thief who had become an informant; found shot in the face in a bean field near Dwight, Illinois. Harder had been a target for assassination in the past when Aleman and his partner, James Inendino tried to kill him, but he escaped.

January 16, 1975: Carlo Divivo, forty-nine, a mob enforcer; two masked men shot him with a shotgun and a pistol as he walked out of his home at 3631 North Nora Avenue.

May 12, 1975: Ronald Magliano, forty-three, an underworld fence; he was found blindfolded and shot in the head in his burning home at 6232 South Kilpatrick Avenue.

June 19, 1975: Chris Cardi, forty-three, a former police officer who loaned money to gamblers at high interest rates; he was shot nine times by two masked men as his wife and children looked on inside Jim's Beef stand in Melrose Park, Illinois.

August 28, 1975: Frank Goulakos, forty-seven, a federal informant, shot six times by a masked gunman when Goulakos walked to his car near DiLeo's Restaurant 5700 North Central Avenue.

August 30, 1975: Nick "Kegee" Galanos, forty-eight, a bookmaker; he was found shot seven times in the head in the basement of his home at 6801 West Wabansia Avenue. Kegee had been an informant of mine for years and was the first person to tell me about bookmakers being made to pay street tax to the outfit. The collectors were Harry Aleman and Wm. "Butch" Petrocelli.

October 31, 1975: Anthony Reitinger, thirty-four, a bookmaker, shot to death in MaMa Luna's Pizza at 4846 West Fullerton Avenue in front of a lot of children who were in costumes trick or treating on Halloween night. Aleman and Petrocelli, armed with a shotgun and a rifle, wearing ski masks, almost blew Reitingers head off.

January 31, 1976: Louis DeBartolo, twenty-nine, a gambler deep in debt; found shot in the head, and a broken mop handle stuck in his neck. He was found in the rear of the store where he worked at 5945 West North Avenue.

May 1, 1976: James Erwin, twenty-eight, an ex-convict who was suspected in the murders of two other reputed mobsters; cut down by two masked men with a shotgun and a .45 caliber pistol. He was shot thirteen times as he stepped out of his car at 1873 North Halsted Street.

July 22, 1976: David Bonadonna, sixty-one, a Kansas City, Missouri, businessman; fatally shot and found in his car trunk. His murder was one of several unsolved mob related slayings that year in an apparent mob attempt to infiltrate nightclubs that featured go-go girls.

March 29, 1977: Charles "Chuck" Nicoletti, sixty, a top mob hit man; shot three times in the back of the head while sitting in his car parked at the Golden Horns Restaurant, 409 East North Avenue, Northlake,Illinois.

June 15, 1977: Joseph Frank Theo, thirty-three, a burglar involved in stolen auto parts; found with two shotgun wounds to the head in the backseat of a car parked at 1700 North Cleveland Avenue.

Even before the Logan murder, Aleman was involved in burglaries, robberies and home invasions. He had Louis Almeida and a petty criminal, Lenny Foresta burglarize a home in south suburban Oak Lawn where Aleman believed $40,000 in cash was kept in the basement. Alemeida and Foresta terrorized a woman and her baby, but all they got was $1,800 and some jewelry. In another heist in November 1973, which turned into another botched job, Aleman, Almeida and Foresta used a Cook County sheriff's badge to gain entry to a home on the

North Side where Aleman believed a coin collection valued at $70,000 was kept. They tore up walls and searched all over the place to no avail, rather than leave empty handed Aleman grabbed a camera so thing wouldn't be a total loss.

They made some big scores too, a home invasion in Indianapolis in 1973 netted $25,000 in furs, cash and jewelry, and in 1974 Aleman and Petrocelli burglarized the home of a neighborhood drug dealer and walked away with $25,000 in cash, Almeida said.

In January 1974, Aleman, Inendino and Almeida were in a work car and Aleman parked in an alley at Harrison and Racine avenues. The car they were in could not be traced and was used strictly to commit crimes, Almeida said. Aleman got out of the car and walked to another car where he pulled a shotgun out of the trunk. Almeida suspected that his death was imminent and pulled out his own .38 caliber pistol and left. From that point on he avoided Aleman. Almeida didn't know it but his freedom was about to end. In March 1975, he was arrested in Ohio when he was on the way to Pittsburgh to assassinate a labor official. He immediately "flipped," became a government witness, and implicated Aleman in the murder of Logan. The case was reopened and the police came to Robert Lowe who had lived across the street from Logan and witnessed Aleman murder Logan on September 27, 1972. Aleman was found not guilty by Judge Wilson in May 1977 and was a free man, but not for long. A federal grand jury indicted Aleman and Lenny Foresta for three of the home invasion-robberies in late June 1977. The next year, both were convicted, largely on the testimony of Almeida, and Aleman was sentenced to thirty years in prison. Aleman was to spend the next eleven years in federal prison in Oxford, Wisconsin, where he was reported to be a model prisoner.

While Aleman was in prison, Petrocelli disappeared on December 30, 1980. His body wasn't found until nearly three months later on the floor of his car on the southwest side. Somebody was really pissed off at Butch because they tortured him, stabbed him a couple of times in the throat, and then wrapped him up in a sleeping bag. Then they poured lighter fluid all over his face and set him on fire. The fire died out because there wasn't enough oxygen in the car, if a window had been left open slightly Butch would have been cremated. A fellow inmate of Aleman's who befriended him in Oxford said that Aleman bragged that Petrocelli was Aleman's lifelong friend who he had killed because he feared Petrocelli was going to be a federal witness against him.

Aleman was released from Oxford in 1989 and moved in with his family in Oak Brook, Illinois. It was reported by reliable sources that Aleman was given $100,000 in cash as specified by mob boss, Joe Ferriola, who had died two months before Aleman's release. Aleman began working for his son-in-law in the concrete cutting business as a personnel manager. That job would only last for nine months before he was back in custody when he was indicted by a federal grand jury in February 1990 along with nineteen others, including Ernest "Rocky" Infelise for racketeering and gambling conspiracy. He was jailed without bond as a flight risk. Aleman made a public statement in a bid to be released on bond, stating that there wasn't enough money in the world to make him run away from his family. His plea was rejected. Shortly after, Aleman pleaded guilty and was given a twelve-year sentence that ends in the year 2000.

Plans for freedom in the year 2000 hit a snag in 1993 when a Cook County grand jury reindicted Aleman for Logan's murder, alleging that his first trial had been a sham because the verdict had been bought with a $10,000 bribe to Judge Frank Wilson. Aleman's lawyers lost a legal battle over whether a retrial for the Logan murder would violate the constitutional protection against double jeopardy and, finally, last fall, he returned to the Criminal Courts building. The trial, which began September 1997, was a dramatic and historic event. For the first time in the history of American jurisprudence, a defendant was being tried for the second time after being acquitted initially.

Almeida and Lowe returned from the anonymous lives they had lived for the past two decades, but Robert Cooley, a former mob lawyer also emerged to describe how he carried the $10,000 bribe to Wilson to ensure Aleman's acquittal in 1977. Wilson had retired shortly after the 1977 trial amid a firestorm of criticism. In 1990, Cooley, who was now an undercover federal informant, visited Wilson in his Arizona retirement home in a futile attempt to record admissions about the bribe. Wilson walked into his back yard and shot himself to death with a pistol.

Ruth Aleman and an entourage of other family members crowded daily into the courtroom of Criminal Court Judge Michael Toomin for the trail. This time it was a jury trial, and when the jury announced it" verdict of guilty, they were distraught, but Aleman remained stoic and hugged his weeping wife. Aleman had been transferred to the federal penitentiary in Memphis Tennessee, where he spends his days painting and reading. When his federal time is up in the year 2000, he will be transferred to the Illinois prison system to serve the 100-to-300-year term for the Logan murder. The conditions in a state prison will be a lot tougher for Aleman.

A key witness in the Logan murder, Bobby Lowe, disclosed that because of fears of reprisals, he was forced to change his name, move his family and fight years of bitterness over the first trial in which Wilson branded him a liar in acquitting Aleman. When Lowe heard the sentence Toomin imposed on Aleman, Lowe said Wow, then he added that he should have gotten the death sentence.

The state attorneys who prosecuted the case against Aleman presented several witnesses, including two federal prosecutors and a former cellmate of Aleman's during the sentencing hearing in an attempt to link the defendant to the shotgun murder of Anthony Reitinger in 1975. Reitinger had refused to pay tribute to Aleman and other organized crime figures and he died for it.

There is no doubt in my mind that Harry Aleman got pleasure out of killing, he might have even loved it. But if he had any real guts he could have gone in the service and volunteered for Vietnam, the only difference there is that some son of a bitch is going to be shooting back at you. He knew how to ambush somebody that's for dam sure, but it's all over now.

Aleman

EYES OF A KILLER

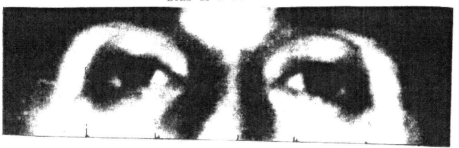

HARRY ALEMAN

ALEMAN HANGOUT ON TAYLOR STREET
SURVIVORS CLUB

Joseph "Joe Negall" Ferriola: Described in 1970 as the mob's No. 2 man in Chicago, Ferriola oversaw several crews, including Aleman's Taylor Street crew. In the early '70s, he and nephew Aleman started demanding "street taxes" from independent gambling operations.

Louis Almeida: Aleman's right-hand man became an informant after escaping what he believed to be an attempted hit by his boss.

Ferriola

Aleman's hit parade: Here is a list of murders that Harry Aleman is alleged to have committed or participated in, according to law enforcement officials and the Chicago Crime Commission.

Logan

Cardi

Nicoletti

Oct. 19, 1971: Samuel "Sambo" Cesario, 53, clubbed and shot to death by two masked men as he sat with his wife in lawn chairs in front of 1071 W. Polk St.

Sept. 27, 1972: William Logan, 37, a Teamsters union shop steward and ex-husband of Aleman's cousin, shot to death with a shotgun in front of his home at 5916 W. Walton St.

Dec. 20, 1973: Richard Cain, 49, a top aide to then-high-ranking organized-crime boss Sam "Momo" Giancana, shotgunned at point-blank range by two masked men in Rose's Sandwich Shop, 1117 W. Grand Ave.

Feb. 24, 1974: Socrates "Sam" Rantis, 43, a counterfeiter, found with his throat slashed and with puncture wounds in his chest in the trunk of his wife's car at O'Hare airport.

April 21, 1974: William Simone, 29, a counterfeiter, found in the back seat of his car near 2446 S. Kedvale Ave., with his hands and feet bound and a gunshot wound in the head.

July 13, 1974: Orion Williams, 38, a suspected mob informant, found shotgunned to death at 70 E. 33rd St., in the trunk of his girlfriend's car.

Sept. 28, 1974: Robert Harder, 39, a jewel thief and burglar who had become an informant, found shot in the face in a bean field near Dwight, Ill. He once escaped an assassination attempt by Aleman and a partner, James Inendino.

Jan. 16, 1975: Carlo Divivo, 46, a mob enforcer, cut down by two masked men who opened fire with a shotgun and a pistol as he walked out of his home at 3631 N. Nora Ave.

May 12, 1975: Ronald Magliano, 43, an underworld fence, found blindfolded and shot behind the left ear in his burning home at 6232 S. Kilpatrick Ave.

June 19, 1975: Christopher Cardi, 43, a former police officer who made high-interest loans to gamblers, shot eight times in the back and once in the face by two masked men as his wife and children looked on inside Jim's Beef Stand in Melrose Park.

Aug. 28, 1975: Frank Goulakos, 47, a federal informant, shot six times by a masked man who stepped out of a car as Goulakos walked to his car near DiLeo's Restaurant, 5700 N. Central Ave., where he was a cook.

Aug. 30, 1975: Nick "Keggie" Galanos, 48, a bookmaker, found shot nine times in the head in the basement of his home at 6801 W. Wabansia Ave.

Oct. 31, 1975: Anthony Reitinger, 34, a bookmaker, shot to death in Mama Luna's restaurant, 4846 W. Fullerton Ave., by two masked men.

Jan. 31, 1976: Louis DeBartolo, 29, a gambler deeply in debt, found shot in the head and with his neck punctured four times with a broken mop handle in the rear of the store where he worked at 5945 W. North Ave.

May 1, 1976: James Erwin, 28, an ex-convict who was suspected in the murders of two other reputed mobsters, cut down by two masked men with a shotgun and a .45 caliber pistol. He was shot 13 times as he stepped out of his car at 1873 N. Halsted St.

July 22, 1976: David Bonadonna, 61, a Kansas City, Mo., businessman, fatally shot and found in his car trunk there. His murder was one of several unsolved mob-related slayings that year in an apparent mob attempt to infiltrate nightclubs featuring go-go girls.

March 29, 1977: Charles "Chuck" Nicoletti, 60, a top mob hit man, shot three times in the back of the head while sitting in his car parked at Golden Horns Restaurant, 409 E. North Ave., Northlake.

June 15, 1977: Joseph Frank Theo, 33, a burglar involved in stolen auto parts, found with two shotgun wounds to the head in the back seat of a car parked at 170 N. Cleveland Ave.

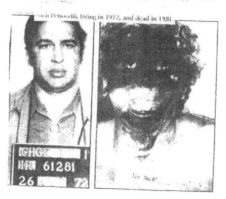
Orion Williams, living in 1972, and dead in 1981

Wm. Butch Petrocelli
Hitman - Hitman got hit

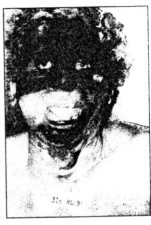

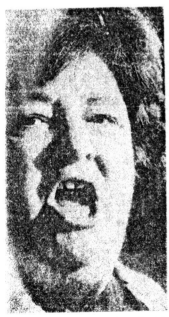

Reputed syndicate hit man Harry Aleman is escorted to his car by Edward Whalen, nephew of his attorney Frank Whalen, after he was acquitted of the murder of William Logan, a Teamster official. Joanna Dietrich (above) sister of William Logan, reacts with anger to the not guilty verdict. (Daily

whack Reitinger."

Rizza said Aleman planned to kill Reitinger on Halloween because he would not attract much attention wearing a mask. On that night, Rizza was at home watching a television news report about Reitinger's death. Then, he recalled, "The phone rings. It's Harry Aleman: 'We killed that [obscenity]. I told you we would kill that guy.'"

As an added source of income, Aleman organized Almeida, Foresta and, at various times, others to commit home invasions and burglaries. Each participant was paid $500 for his work and the proceeds were turned over to Aleman, according to Almeida.

Foresta was a career petty criminal. By 19 he had already been imprisoned for larceny and at age 20 he was arrested for robbing a woman of $42 in her apartment lobby. By 1970, Almeida, a dropout who couldn't get past the 6th grade, had served time for armed robbery, grand theft, burglary, and bond jumping. When he was released that year, he immediately sought out Aleman, who advanced him a $2,500 loan and put him to work as a personal aide, trailing Aleman to the driving range, the shooting range, restaurants and the Survivor's Club.

"I went and got his wife's car," Almeida testified in 1978. "Drove it to May and Taylor [Streets], had it fixed. I had tires put on the car. I did other odd jobs. . . . I used to get my ammunition from Harry. He used to make his own ammunition in the garage of his house."

Some of the Aleman-directed heists were less than successful. On Sept. 16, 1972—11 days before Logan was murdered—Aleman directed Almeida and Foresta to burglarize a home in suburban Oak Lawn where Aleman believed $40,000 in cash was kept in the basement. But after tying up a woman in the home and terrorizing her baby, Almeida and Foresta left with only $1,800 and some jewelry.

Another heist, in November 1973, was almost a complete flop. Aleman, Almeida and Foresta used a Cook County sheriff's police badge as a ruse to gain entry to a North Side home where Aleman believed a coin collection worth $70,000 was kept. After ransacking the place and ripping boards from a basement wall turned up no coins, Aleman grabbed a camera rather than leave empty-handed.

There were big hauls, too. A home invasion in Indianapolis in 1973 netted $25,000 in furs, cash and jewelry, and in late 1974 Aleman and Petrocelli burglarized the residence of a neighborhood drug dealer and walked off with $25,000 in cash, Almeida said.

The beginning of the end for Aleman surely can be traced to January

From gofer to government witness

At first, Louis Almeida was Harry Aleman's errand boy, a gofer assigned to such mundane tasks as putting new tires on Aleman's wife's car.

Later, the short, stocky man with a high-pitched raspy voice moved up in the hierarchy of organized crime to become Aleman's accomplice in murder.

Ultimately, though, Almeida carved out a niche in the annals of crime as Aleman's nemesis—a snitch turned protected witness who provided testimony that helped convict Aleman of the 1972 murder of Teamsters union shop steward William Logan.

In an interview in a suburban hotel room, Almeida, 45, offered his insights on the man authorities call Chicago's deadliest mob hit man.

"We grew up together near Taylor Street and Racine. He used to hang around on Bishop Street and I used to see him and talk to him," Almeida recalled. "Everybody looked up to him because his family was supposed to be in the Mafia. We hung around in the pool hall, in the park. He liked to bet on the horses and I think he was bookmaking, too. He always had money . . . nice clothes. We called him 'The Sheik' because he dressed nice.

"He said he had it rough at home, that his father beat him, handcuffed him to a radiator. I don't know how much of it was true," Almeida said.

Smiling as he recalled how Aleman met his wife, Ruth, whom he married in 1964, Almeida said, "She worked in this club on State Street. We used to go there quite a bit. Everybody loved Ruth, she was beautiful.

"Harry broke off an engagement to an Italian girl from the suburbs to marry Ruth and he was thrown out of the house because she was a cocktail waitress," he said. "It was a terrible argument. His father wanted him to go to college, to marry this other girl. Harry didn't want to."

Aleman was a strict father to Ruth's four children by a previous marriage, Almeida said. "One of his sons, he wanted me to beat up one time. The kid was getting drunk and staying out late and Harry didn't want to beat him up because Ruth would feel hurt.

"So I gave him a couple of light taps on the head with a rope," Almeida said. "I was going to scare him, tell him I was going to tie him up with a rope and throw him in the trunk."

In the mid-1960s, Almeida went to prison for robbery and, upon his release in 1970, received a $2,500 loan from Aleman to get back on his feet. In return, Almeida became Aleman's personal aide, driving Aleman to a shooting range in Lyons and a golf driving range in River Grove, and generally running errands.

"He told me, 'Come around, don't get lost,'" Almeida said. "He was looking for armed robberies and burglaries and was trying to get people to go on them. He was also bragging that he wanted to be a hit man.

"I guess he had to announce to everybody that he was starting to kill people for money or kill people who didn't listen to him."

In 1971, shortly before Sam Cesario was murdered—a hit authorities attribute to Aleman—Almeida said Aleman announced that he and his close friend William "Butch" Petrocelli were going on a hunting trip to Montana.

"Harry did like to hunt," Almeida said. "I don't know if he actually went that time or not. He had a stuffed bobcat, a deer head. He shot a moose one time."

Was Aleman, as authorities say, involved in as many as 18 murders?

"I don't know," Almeida said. "He liked to kill things. But sometimes, the police, if they didn't know who did a hit, I think they would just put it on Harry."

What kind of car did Aleman drive as a young man?

"I don't know—you mean legit cars?" Almeida said, chuckling. "I don't know, everybody drove stolen cars."

Almeida participated in at least three home invasions for Aleman, earning $500 each time. And he was Aleman's driver on the Logan hit. Almeida also was involved in several bombings along with Petrocelli.

Ultimately, Almeida said, he broke away from Aleman after three incidents. The first, he said, occurred in 1972, when, standing outside Aleman's Melrose Park home, Aleman told him he had just talked by phone with two of his robbery crew members and learned they had abducted Hillside Police Officer Anthony Raymond, taken him to Wisconsin and tortured him to death.

"I said, 'What are you telling me this for? I don't want to hear it. I don't want to be involved,'" Almeida recalled. "That was one of my bigger mistakes. Harry didn't like that. He just looked at me. I thought he was going to have me hit."

In 1974, Almeida said he was sitting in the front seat of a car next to Aleman pal James Inendino. Aleman was in the back seat.

"Harry put a gun to my head," Almeida said. "I looked back and he put the gun down. He and Inendino started arguing and then it seemed Harry sort of forgot about it. The person we were there to shoot didn't show up. I never really trusted him after that.

"Another time, right after that, we were in an alley and Harry got out of the back and got a shotgun out of another car. He told me to look straight ahead," Almeida recalled. "All I could see was windows with white shades drawn down. I really believed he was going to try to hit me. I left and I went my own way."

—M.P.

Louis Almeida (right) with a police detective in 1963.

1974, when Almeida, Aleman and Inendino parked in an alley near Harrison Street and Racine Avenue. They were in a "work car," a car that could not be traced and was used to commit crimes, Almeida recalled.

As the car rolled to a halt in the alley, Aleman got out and walked to another car where he pulled a shotgun out of the trunk. Almeida, suspecting his death was imminent, drew his own .38 caliber pistol and left. From then on, he avoided Aleman.

Almeida had only about a year of freedom left. In March 1975, he was arrested in Ohio while driving to Pittsburgh to assassinate a labor official. He immediately "flipped"—became a government witness—and implicated Aleman in the murder of Logan.

Though Aleman would ultimately be suspected of nearly 20 murders, the slaying of Logan would be the only one for which he would be

The crew: *These Aleman associates have been linked to burglaries, shakedowns and murders.*

Joseph "Joe Nagall" Ferriola: Described in 1970 as the mob's No. 2 man in Chicago, Ferriola oversaw several crews, including Aleman's Taylor Street crew. In the early '70s, he and nephew Aleman started demanding "street taxes" from independent gambling operations.

Leonard Foresta: A career petty criminal, he committed burglaries for Aleman and was convicted of three of them in 1978.

Foresta

William "Butch" Petrocelli: Aleman's closest mob friend and suspected partner in many killings. He was found slain in 1981; police say Aleman may have ordered him hit.

Petrocelli

Louis Almeida: Aleman's right-hand man became an informant after escaping what he believed to be an attempted hit by his boss.

Ferriola

Almeida

Tribune file photos

James Inendino began to flex their muscles, according to law enforcement officials. Foresta and Inendino ultimately would be convicted of home invasions or gambling activities. Almeida, who became Aleman's driver and all-around gofer, would eventually break from Aleman in 1974 after escaping what he believed was an attempted hit by Aleman and Inendino.

It was Almeida who, after his arrest in Ohio in 1975 en route to a murder job in Pittsburgh, began cooperating with law enforcement and became a key witness against Aleman. Almeida's testimony in 1978 was key to Aleman's first conviction, and his testimony last year played a part in Aleman's conviction for Logan's murder.

Logan, authorities believe, was Aleman's second murder and the second done for family reasons. According to evidence at Aleman's trial last fall, Logan was killed while involved in a bitter custody battle with his ex-wife, Phyllis, who testified that she was Aleman's second cousin and that after divorcing Logan, she had had an affair with Petrocelli.

Investigators have been told that Logan sealed his fate when his ex-wife warned him to stay away or she would talk to Aleman. "[Obscenity] that guinea," Logan reportedly replied, using a derogatory term for an Italian.

Shortly thereafter, according to Almeida, he drove Aleman to Logan's home where Aleman ambushed Logan as he left for work at a loading dock in Cicero. Logan was cut down by two shotgun blasts on Sept. 27, 1972.

Aleman's first official hit was on his own uncle, Samuel "Sambo" Cesario, according to authorities. The deed was handled with the help of Petrocelli and occurred on Oct. 19, 1971, according to O'Rourke. Two men wearing masks walked up to Cesario as he and his wife sat in lawn chairs in their front yard at 1071 W. Polk St., and Cesario was clubbed and shot to death.

The reason? Cesario, according to authorities, had secretly married the girlfriend of Felix "Milwaukee Phil" Alderisio after the Wisconsin gangster went to prison.

By day, Aleman, Petrocelli and others hung out at the Survivor's Social and Athletic Club, a dimly lit and nondescript storefront on Taylor Street, just west of Racine Avenue. The club was their headquarters for a reign of terror that included bombings, murders, home invasions, beatings and shakedowns, according to authorities.

It was sometime in the early 1970s, authorities say, that Ferriola and Aleman decided to reorganize gambling, particularly sports betting operations, and force independent bookmakers to pay tribute or "street tax" for the right to operate.

One of those was Vincent Rizza, a Chicago police officer who worked Loop traffic duty until he resigned in 1976 after he was ousted from Mexico following his arrest for trying to buy cocaine. While still a police officer, Rizza branched out into the bookmaking business. After news accounts reported that one of his wire rooms was raided by Chicago police, in late 1974 or early 1975, Rizza received a visit from Aleman and Inendino.

Sitting in a restaurant on Chicago's Southwest Side, Rizza recalled that Aleman and Inendino sat across from him and, at first, said nothing, fixing him with ominous stares.

It was a look for which Aleman would become well-known. Though he is a slightly built man—5 feet 8 inches tall and 145 pounds—Aleman's public face is a grim look, marked by depthless coal-black eyes.

As Rizza recalled, Aleman began the conversation. "Harry told me I owed him street tax . . . 40-some thousand dollars."

Aleman said Ferriola had instructed them "to organize Chicago the way it was back in the '30s and '40s. Those were his exact words," Rizza said.

Worried, Rizza paid a visit to his own clout in the ranks of organized crime. Angelo LaPietra, the boss of the Chinatown neighborhood, and explained his plight. "Angelo said it is a very serious situation I had gotten myself into," Rizza recalled. He said he gave LaPietra a paper sack stuffed with several thousand dollars that LaPietra promised to deliver to Aleman in an attempt to negotiate a deal.

In fact, Rizza said, such a deal was hammered out; Aleman and his pals got 50 percent of his winnings and agreed to pay Rizza's losses, and Rizza paid $1,000 a month in street tax. Though the terms seemed harsh, Rizza continued to operate at a profit.

And he continued to see Aleman and Inendino, almost daily, after they recruited him to help them ferret out other independent bookmakers that they could take over, Rizza said.

It was Rizza who first telephoned Anthony Reitinger to advise him that Aleman was demanding street tax from Reitinger's $100,000-a-month bookmaking operation.

When Reitinger responded with an obscenity and said he would never pay any street tax, Rizza reported back to Aleman. "He said he would kill that [obscenity]." Rizza tried again to persuade Reitinger to change his mind, but Reitinger dug in his heels. "He said he wouldn't pay. He wasn't interested," Rizza said.

Rizza then met with Aleman.

"I told him it's a dead deal, that Reitinger wasn't coming in," Rizza recalled. "Aleman told me to forget about it, that Reitinger was a dead man. . . . He said he was going to

---

grandkids—this gives me hope."

Family members have been staunch in their defense of Aleman, calling him a loyal and loving father and husband. In an interview in the office of [Al]lex Salerno, one of Aleman's [la]wyers, Ruth Aleman and her oldest [da]ughter, Terri Amabile, described [Al]eman as a stern but caring man who [wa]s continued to be a source of [st]rength despite his imprisonment.

"He was wonderful to my children," [Ru]th Aleman recalled. "He took the [ki]ds to Kiddieland, to dinner, on pic[ni]cs, camping. He always had time for [th]e kids."

Amabile, her eyes brimming with [te]ars, recounted how Aleman washed [h]er hair and her sister's in the kitchen [si]nk. "We had long hair and he was so [ge]ntle, getting the tangles out."

As a teenager, she remembers her [fa]ther lurking outside of school and [ch]urch dances to see whom she was [le]aving with and to ensure that she was where she had promised she would be.

"He guarded those kids like Ft. Knox," Ruth said.

Dinners were a family affair. "We had to be together," Amabile said. "No phone calls were accepted. He used that time to find out what was going on and we could talk about what was bothering us. I remember sitting at the table until 8 or 9 o'clock some nights. We wanted to be there."

Aleman's rise in organized crime was simultaneous with that of his uncle, Joseph "Joe Nagall" Ferriola, who had married a sister of Aleman's mother. In 1970, Ferriola was described as the No. 2 man under Jackie "The Lackey" Cerone, then believed to be the operating head of the Chicago crime syndicate.

It was as a member of organized crime's "Taylor Street crew" that Aleman and his pals such as Petrocelli, Louis Almeida, Leonard Foresta and

brought to trial. After Almeida implicated Aleman, the case was reopened and police came to Robert Lowe, a gas station manager who had lived across the street from Logan. Lowe told investigators that he had been out walking his dog and came face to face with Aleman as he stepped out of the car immediately after shooting Logan.

With great fanfare, then-Cook County State's Atty. Bernard Carey announced the indictment of Aleman in the fall of 1976. The case came to trial in May 1977 before Cook County Circuit Judge Frank Wilson. After a week of testimony, Wilson, hearing the case without a jury, acquitted Aleman, reinforcing his reputation as a mob untouchable. Days later, Aleman, ever the brazen killer, took part in the murder of Joseph Theo, a burglar involved in the stolen auto parts business, authorities say.

But Aleman's freedom was short-lived. A federal grand jury indicted him and Foresta for three of the home invasion-robberies in late June 1977. The next year, both were convicted, largely on the testimony of Almeida, and Aleman was sentenced to 30 years in prison. As he left the courtroom, Aleman paused to speak to O'Rourke.

"He came up to me, as a gentleman," O'Rourke later said. "He said, 'Agent O'Rourke, I just want to tell you: No hard feelings.'"

It was that sort of attitude that earned Aleman respect in the federal prison in Oxford, Wis., where he was to spend the next 11 years. "Harry has always been a gentleman and gotten along with the inmates and guards," said Marc Martin, one of Aleman's attorneys. "He has taken college courses, painted and been a good inmate."

On Dec. 30, 1980, Petrocelli disappeared. His body was found nearly three months later on the floor of his car on the Southwest Side. He died a horrible death; his face had been burned beyond recognition and he was stabbed twice in the throat, authorities said.

Some lawmen believe he was murdered for stealing mob money, some suspect he was trying to take over gambling operations that belonged to someone else, and still others suspect Aleman ordered his death.

In 1994, Monte Katz, a career criminal who befriended Aleman while both were imprisoned in Oxford, provided grist for the latter theory, telling authorities that Aleman bragged that "Petrocelli was [Aleman's] lifelong friend who he had flattened—he meant killed" because he feared Petrocelli was going to become a government witness against him.

Aleman was released from Oxford in 1989 and he moved in with family members in Oak Brook. His finances

Aleman painted this landscape at the federal prison at Oxford, Wis.

were bolstered, authorities say, by the delivery of $100,000 in cash, as specified by Ferriola before he died two months before Aleman's release.

Aleman, who began working for his son-in-law's concrete cutting business as a personnel manager, would later describe the next nine months as "the best time of my life." It was, family and friends agree, a time for Aleman to be as close physically to his family as he is emotionally.

"We were whole again," Ruth Aleman said. "We cooked together, shared meals—years ago. Harry taught me how to cook, how to make the gravy for the meatballs."

Amabile said her son Sam was devastated at age 9 when Aleman was imprisoned in 1978.

"From the time my son was old enough to walk, he was at my father's side," Amabile said. "A great love grew between them, a love that has withstood the test of time and hardship." When Aleman was released in 1989, he instructed that Ruth and Sam be the only ones to bring him home.

Amabile recounted how Aleman stood a bedside vigil for a baby grandson who underwent surgery. "When the baby came home, my father spent every moment with his grandchild, except for the times when he would leave to work," Amabile said.

During those months after his release, Aleman drove one grandchild to piano lessons, made breakfast for the children in the morning and attended parent-teacher conferences, she said.

"Our family has one common goal and that is to keep each other strong and one day bring my father home for good," Amabile said. "We count ourselves lucky to have such a man for a father."

Sharon Kramer, another of Aleman's lawyers over the years, said,

"The love in that family is genuine. He has tried to do his best to make sure they stay on the straight and narrow."

But Aleman was back in custody in February 1990 when a federal grand jury indicted him and 19 others, including Ferriola's successor, Ernest Rocco Infelice, on charges of racketeering and gambling conspiracy. Jailed without bond as a flight risk, Aleman made perhaps his only public statement in a bid to be released on bond.

"I love my wife and kids," he declared. "And that is my stability and predictability. There isn't enough money in the world to make me run away from my family. Throughout my years in prison, I survived for my family and they have stood by me."

His plea was rejected. Shortly after, Aleman pleaded guilty and was given 12 years, a sentence that ends in two years. At the time of sentencing, Aleman disclosed that he had taken up painting with oil, concentrating primarily on landscapes, and asked to be returned to Oxford to continue taking art classes. That request was granted.

Plans for freedom at the millennium hit a snag in 1993 when a Cook County grand jury re-indicted Aleman for Logan's murder, alleging that his first trial had been a sham because the verdict had been purchased with a $10,000 bribe to Judge Frank Wilson. Not long after, a guard at Oxford watching Aleman meeting with two men, including his stepson Jeff, saw Aleman pass notes to the pair and say, "The two will be taken care of if this goes to trial, one after the other."

Authorities theorize that Aleman could have been referring to witnesses poised to testify against him. His exact meaning is unknown because the notes were destroyed before guards could seize them.

Aleman's lawyers lost a legal battle over whether a retrial for the Logan murder would violate the constitutional protection against double jeopardy and, finally, last fall, he returned to the Criminal Courts building. The trial, which began last September, was a dramatic and historic event. For the first time in the history of American jurisprudence, a defendant was being tried for a second time after being acquitted initially.

Not only did Almeida and Lowe return from the anonymous lives they had lived during the past two decades, but Robert Cooley, a former mob lawyer, also emerged to describe how he carried the $10,000 bribe to Wilson to ensure Aleman's acquittal in 1977. Wilson, a veteran jurist with more than 1,000 trials, retired shortly after the 1977 trial amid a firestorm of criticism. In 1990, after Cooley, then acting as a federal undercover informant, visited Wilson in his Arizona retirement home in a futile attempt to record admissions about the bribe, Wilson walked into his back yard and shot himself to death with a pistol.

Ruth Aleman and an entourage of other family members crowded daily into the courtroom of Criminal Court Judge Michael Toomin for the trial. When the jury announced its verdict of guilty, they were distraught, but Aleman remained stoic, offering a hug to his weeping wife.

Since being transferred to the federal penitentiary in Memphis, Aleman spends his days painting and reading, as well as listening to opera and classical music. The family visits frequently, but pays the emotional price. "The leaving is hard," Ruth Aleman said. "Walking out the door, down the hall, I told the kids I never want Harry to see us cry. And then, when we're outside, the tears are rolling down."

The side of Aleman that law enforcement sees is invisible to the family. "If he's such a criminal, where's all the money?" Ruth said. "I don't believe a word of what they say. It's garbage."

Two years from now, when Aleman is to be released from the federal prison system, he will be transferred to the Illinois prison system to serve the 100- to 300-year term for the Logan murder. Conditions in a state prison will likely be much harsher.

It is a prospect eagerly anticipated by some law enforcement officials, who view Aleman as a man who has yet to pay the proper price for murder. Aleman was not eligible for the death penalty because it was not in effect in 1972 when Logan was killed.

"Even if Harry tried to commit a crime in federal prison, I would do my best to see he wasn't prosecuted," said a federal law enforcement official. "I want to see him in a state prison for the rest of his life." ■

Chapter 34

Hookers, Craps, and Augie

When William Joseph Petrocelli, a.k.a. Butch Petrocelli, failed to show up at his Forest Avenue residence in Hillside, Illinois, a suburb west of Chicago, in December 1980, his girlfriend, Nancy, reported him missing. Butch, who had been an outfit guy for a long time and rat partner of the infamous mob hit man Harry Aleman, usually let his girlfriend know if he was going to be late getting home. At the time, Harry was in the joint doing thirty years; so if anything happened to Butch, nobody could blame Harry. I got word from an informant that Butch might be in a little trouble because of money problems he was having with his bosses.

Harry and Butch allegedly had whacked a few guys together when they were shaking down independent bookmakers for street taxes in the Chicago area, one of which was a bookmaker by the name of Tony Reitinger, who got shot in MaMa Luna's Pizzeria on West Fullerton Avenue on Halloween night, 1975. Harry and Butch had set up Reitinger by making bets with him through a friend and bookmaker, George Sommers. Reitinger, who had a lot of players, was betrayed by Sommers who set up a meeting with Reitinger in the pizza joint to give him a large sum of money that he, Harry, and Butch had lost the previous week. Only Reitinger didn't know that Harry and Butch had been making large bets through Sommers, and he had no chance of ever getting paid. It seemed that Harry and Butch had tried to collect street taxes from Reitinger when they met him in a restaurant in Greek Town a few weeks previously. They explained to Reitinger that they knew that he had been booking for at least three years and that at a $1,000 a month Reitinger owed them $36,000. Reitinger told them that he didn't have that kind of money and that he would have to get back to them. After a couple of days he was contacted by Harry and Butch again about the money he allegedly owed them; he told them to go to hell and let them know that he wasn't afraid of them or of their dago bosses.

George Sommers, who had been betting and laying off to Reitinger, told him that he had a couple of businessmen that were big players and that he would guarantee any money that they lost if he could lay their action off to him. Reitinger agreed, and that was the beginning of the end for him. When Reitinger showed up at the restaurant that fateful night, he expected to meet Sommers, and when he didn't see him, he sat in a booth at the rear of the restaurant. Of course, there were kids in various costumes who were entering and leaving the restaurant, doing their tricks or treats. So when two guys with masks entered the pizza place, they didn't attract a lot of attention until you saw a shotgun and a .30 cal. carbine in their hands. It really was trick-or-treat night; only Reitinger was the guy who was going to get tricked. The first guy blasted Reitinger with the carbine, and the other guy stuck the shotgun in Reitinger's ear and blew his head off, which splattered all over the wall. Of course, this mob hit is still unsolved on the books.

Butch was also suspected of being on a lot of other mob hits such as William "Billy" Dauber and his wife, Charlotte, which occurred in Will County, Illinois, on Manhattan Moony Road on July 2, 1980. Another mob hit man named Gerry Scarpelli and Butch, who was accompanied by three other outfit guys, killed them both in their car. Scarpelli was in a van driven by Gerry Scalise, and he and Butch were seated in the rear of the van. Another "work car" was driven by Frank Calabrese and another bad guy. When the road seemed clear of traffic, Calabrese pulled in front of Dauber's car and deliberately slowed down. At that point, Scalise pulled the van alongside Dauber's car and Petrocelli, and using a .30 cal. carbine fired out the passenger window into Dauber's car. Scarpelli also fired his 12-gauge shotgun, hitting Billy Dauber and his wife. The car then swerved off the road into a field and struck a tree.

Petrocelli ordered Scarpelli out of the van to make sure they were dead. Scarpelli, who was wearing a ski mask, fired two shots from his 12-guage shotgun into the Daubers to make sure they were done. Scarpelli then returned to the van, and both vehicles left the scene. Scalise drove the van out of the area and parked it off the road in some bushes, where they exited the van with their weapons. Petrocelli then sprayed lighter fluid in the van and set it on fire in an effort to destroy the van and any fingerprints or physical evidence. The three men got into the "work car" driven by Frank Calabrese and drove back to a parking lot in the Joliet area, where they had another van stashed.

 This van did not have any windows. They switched to the van and drove back to Chicago. The weapons were broken up and the pieces thrown into the Cal-Sag Canal when they drove over the bridge on Illinois Route 83, after that they all separated on the South Side of Chicago. The reason that Dauber was hit was that Jerry Scalise had convinced Petrocelli that other auto salvage yards owners in the south suburbs of Chicago would get the message and start paying street taxes to the outfit. Scarpelli claimed that Scalise hated Dauber and that's why he told Petrocelli that the junkyards would begin to pay street taxes. Dauber's wife had to go because she was in the wrong place at the wrong time. That's the way it goes sometimes, Scalise said. Petrocelli had to have an OK from the boss, Joe Ferriola, or it wouldn't have been done.

 Butch Petrocelli was no choirboy. So when he had been reported among the missing, nobody gave a shit. In fact, a lot of people were happy about it, because the odds were that he had been killed for shorting his bosses. Sure as hell, our guy Butch showed up three months later on March 14, 1981; his car was found parked on the street at 4307 West Twenty-fifth Place in Chicago. He was wrapped up in a blue blanket, which covered everything but his feet and his nose and eyes, which had been burned; they stuck him behind the front seat on the floor. Butch had been tortured, his throat cut, and surgical tape had been placed over his mouth and nose. Two cans of lighter fluid were found in the car, whose interior had been partially burned; the fire had apparently burned itself out because there wasn't enough oxygen in the car. No telling how long it had been parked, but if it had been summertime, Butch would have been found much earlier, I'm sure. Butch and I had met on several occasions when I busted him for operating a couple of crap games with Harry Aleman and another mob guy by the name of

Jimmy Inendino. One of the games was in a storefront in the 1000th block of Polk Street on the West Side of Chicago, about a block from the University of Illinois Circle Campus.

We discovered that they had positioned a lookout down the street from the game, and that the lookout probably had a walkie-talkie with him. After a closer look at the guy, I recognized him to be a known wire-room operator by the name of Augie Galan, whom we had busted a couple of times. While we did attempt to get enough information for probable cause to get a search warrant to hit the game, I knew that the chances were pretty slim. So we would just play it by ear, as they say. We knew that with the people involved in the game, it had to belong to the outfit controlled by Joe Ferriola a.k.a. Joe Nagall at the time. Well, as everyone knows, "God hates a coward", so I decided to bust the game without a warrant; we call that direct pursuit. Obviously, we had to get to the lookout before he could warn the bad guys that we were in the neighborhood. It looked as if all the players were getting in the storefront through a rear door off the alley. After they were let in, you can bet your ass that the door was barricaded. The front windows were all painted, so there was no way to see anything from the front. I remembered that our lookout was probably bored just sitting in the car and just might like some female companionship to pass the time. So I told a couple of my guys, Jim and Tom, to take a ride over to Lake and Halsted streets and find a hooker and explain to her that we needed her help for about a half an hour. And if she agreed, we would take her back to her corner and not bust her for prostitution. They came back in fifteen minutes with a pretty, nice-looking hooker, who said her name was "Joey." I explained to "Joey" that we needed her services to help us arrest a known sex offender who was sitting in his car down the street and was known for making obscene phone calls to old ladies. I explained to her that all she had to do was walk down the street and get Augie's attention and get him to open the car door so that we could talk to him. This hooker didn't seem just right to me for some reason or other, and then I knew what was wrong. The hooker was a guy. Our girl "Joey" was really our guy "Joseph." But so what. At this point I didn't much care. As long as it would get Augie to open his window or car door, we were in business. Joey was a little disappointed that her secret was out, but agreed to go on with the show and even asked if Augie opened the door she would be glad to keep him company for a little while for the good of law enforcement. I told our female impersonator just to get him to open the door and that would be just fine. Anything further would make us pimps. Apparently, Augie was having illicit thoughts because when he saw our undercover agent approach his car, he opened his window right away. After a few words from "Joey" we saw the door open also. We were on him before he knew what the hell was going on, and grabbed his radio before he could warn anyone. At that point, "Joey" took off and was last seen high tailing it toward Halsted Street. I guess she didn't want a ride after all. I asked Augie what he was doing in the neighborhood, and he said that he was waiting for his girlfriend to show up when we grabbed him and scared her to death, so she took off. He then said that was his story and he was sticking to it. I told him that I didn't know he liked men instead of women, and explained to him that his alleged date's name was "Joseph" and would have probably kicked the shit out of him and robbed him if we didn't happen to be passing by. Augie wouldn't believe that "Joey" was really "Joseph." All he could say was, "You can't trust anybody anymore, if that were true." I asked Augie if he might just happen to have a key to the storefront down the street? His answer was, "What storefront, what street are you talking about? "OK," I said, "that's it. Cuff him, tape his big mouth and eyes, and see if he fits in the trunk of his car." I said, "It's showtime. Let's get this job going." I said we'd split up. I sent Jim and Tom to cover the rear of the store and grab anybody that came out. Ray Ron and Al and I would try to get in the front somehow. It was a good thing that our walkie-talkies were working so we could stay in touch with each other. As we were getting in position, sure as hell, we got spotted so it was now or never. We didn't have sledgehammer with us, so we had to improvise. There happened to be a fifty-gallon barrel in front of the store that was used for trash, so I said that sure looks like a key to me. So we threw it through the front window.

All we could hear was, "cops, cops, get the hell out of here." All this was coming from the basement, where the game was being held. We managed to grab twenty-five guys, including Harry and Butch. Dice were thrown all over the floor, and a large crap table had point cards on it along with chips and dice cups. Every player had money stuffed in their socks shorts and shoes, everywhere but their pockets. One goof was even trying to stick two folded $100 bills up his rectum, under the circumstances we let him keep his money. In a rear kitchen on the first floor, there was an area set aside for making sandwiches, like Italian beef and sausage and provolone. Also a fifty-cup coffee urn was making fresh coffee for the boys. We charged Butch and Harry with being keepers of a gambling house and operating a dice game and sent them down to be processed with the other prisoners. The weird thing about this raid was that nobody asked us if we had a search warrant. I guess they just assumed we had one when we broke the front windows in the store. Rumor has it that when cops make a raid like this, they become excited and have to urinate sometimes and just maybe that fifty-cup coffee urn would have contained fifty-two cups before we left the premises. I left one of the older players on the premises to watch the place because of the two TV sets and other things that could be stolen by thieves in the neighborhood. I've often wondered if he or anyone else had any of that coffee after we left. During all the confusion, I almost forgot about our lookout, Augie, locked up in his trunk. We took off his cuffs and the tape and noticed that he had wet his pants. I thanked him for being so cooperative and told him he could leave. We weren't going to lock him up. Well, Augie couldn't believe that I was going to let him go. He started begging to be busted, because Harry and Butch would probably think that he told us about the game and they would kick his ass up and down Taylor Street or worse. I hated to see a grown man whine and snivel, so we accommodated him and locked him up also. But I told him that he owed me a favor.

Chapter 35

Al Capone – Joe "Fifke" Corngold – Cicero, Illinois

The year was 1974, and my crew and I began terrorizing the town of Cicero, Illinois. Cicero, Illinois, is one of the most famous towns in the world because of Alphonse Capone who, ran the crime syndicate for years before he was put away for income tax evasion. Capone was sentenced to eleven years in prison on October 24, 1932. He spent time in federal prisons in Atlanta, Leavenworth, and Alcatraz; he was released on November 16, 1939, suffering from syphilis of the brain. While Big Al was gone, the mob didn't miss a beat; gambling and prostitution still ran rampant in Chicago as well as Cicero, Illinois.

Joe "Fifke" Corngold, who was an associate of Capone, got busted in the Lexington Motel, on Twenty-third and Michigan avenues on April 21, 1930. He described himself as just a bookmaker; he was thirty-five years old and a resident of Cicero, Illinois. Corngold was kind of a low-key guy, but he had a couple of partners in the bookmaking business who were well-known mob figures, Louis Campagna and Mops Volpe. Corngold had book joints at 5912 West Cermak Road, Cicero; 4807 West Cermak Road, Cicero; and 5937 West Roosevelt Road, Cicero, in the 1940s. In October 1943, Corngold and twenty-three other defendants, including officers of the Cicero Police Department, chief of the Cook County Highway Police, were indicted by a Cook County grand jury for conspiracy to violate gambling laws. The breakdowns of the indictments were ten police officers and fourteen gamblers, including Corngold. The case was nolle prossed on April 3, 1944, because the court ruled that the raids on which the indictments were based were illegal because they were made without a search warrant. In 1944 a Chicago newspaper reflected that Joseph Corngold, age forty-eight, was the refuted gambling boss of Cicero.

The old story that crime doesn't pay is really bullshit. Corngold's partner, Louis Campagna, declared in 1947 on his income tax profits from two gambling joints in Cicero, the El Patio, 5914 West Cermak and the Austin Club, as being $204,152 for the years 1937 to 1940. Campagna shared this profit with our guy Corngold. Corngold wasn't a secret to a federal grand jury, where he testified in 1948 as an associate of Paul "the Waiter" Ricca, Louis Campagna, and others. Campagna was sentenced to federal prison in 1943, and Corngold was still running things as usual. Information from reliable sources revealed that Corngold had from ninety to one hundred slot machines in Cicero as well as his book joints and had a friendly relationship with the police.

Corngold lived in a house at 1828 South Fifty-ninth Court in Cicero; his wife, Edith, age fifty-three, was taken from that house to a hospital where she died apparently from an overdose of sleeping pills. She was reported to be distraught because of her daughter Edith, age twenty-nine, was subpoenaed by a federal grand jury to testify about what she knew of involving organized crime.

Corngold also had a partner in his gambling operation that was unknown also; his name was Willie Heeney. Corngold and Heeney were known to frequent a hunting lodge near Hayworth Wisconsin, which was owned by a Claude Haddox alias Johnny Moore. Also in attendance were Joey Aiuppa, Rocky DeGrazio, Ralph Capone, and John Capone.

In 1952, Corngold was named in a criminal information suit filed in the Federal Court of Chicago for failure to buy a federal gambling stamp for the El Patio at 5912-14 West Cermak Road and the Austin Club at 5941 West Roosevelt Road in Cicero. Two others were also involved in the operation of these bars; Manny Weinberg and Harry Belcastro were also charged with failure to buy a federal gambling stamp.

Corngold managed to stay out of the limelight until 1961 when a story appeared in the *Chicago Tribune* naming Corngold as syndicate vice and gambling boss of Cicero. He appeared in criminal courte where he invoked the immunity statute eight times in a case involving a raid a

5941 West Roosevelt Road, Cicero, Illinois. He only gave his name and address, which was 1828 South Fifty-ninth Court, Cicero. Corngold was arrested on May 1, 1962, in a gambling raid at the El Patio, 5914 West Cermak Road, Cicero, by the States Attorney's Office, and the *Tribune* called him the boss of prostitution and gambling in Cicero.

On May 22, 1962, Corngold was questioned by the States Attorney's Police about the murder of Peter J. Bludeau, a Cicero gambler. But Corngold refused to cooperate with the police and would only give his name and address on the advice of his attorney. Another interesting sidelight is that a Chicago visitor to Cuba in the pre-Castro days, who cashed checks in the hotels that housed the plush gambling casinos, learned, after his checks cleared the bank, they were countersigned by Joe Corngold of Cicero, Illinois.

Joe Corngold and his partner Joe "Doves" Aiuppa ran a poker game in Cicero that sometimes ran twenty-four hours a day. They had dealers around the clock that handled three felt-covered poker tables. The dealers were professional, and they cut $1 from each $20 in the pot. The game was in some back room in Cicero and provided refreshments and had a wet bar for the customers, who were truck drivers, gangsters, females, and some affluent men who loved the action. It was reported that in its heyday, the game netted the mob from $20,000 to $25,000 a week; but now it was probably only providing $10,000 a week profit. There were three outfit guys present at all times to provide juice loans to anyone who needed money. Larry Rassano, Max Inserro, and Jack Gross worked for suburban boss Fiore "FiFi" Buccieri. Buccieri had four enforcers under him who would collect the loans or terrorize the poor dope who made the loan. They were refuted to be James and Angelo LaPietra, Vito Spillone, and John "Apes" Montelone. Only seven-card poker was played with a maximum limit on bets of $2, with no limit on raises; if a pair is showing, the raise is limited to $4. The big poker game was played on Sunday and was open to only the big money players; the bets were limited to $3 or $6 and raised from $5 to $10. When there wasn't any police pressure, the game went around the clock, and the profits reached $25,000 a week. Not bad for our guys Corngold and Aiuppa; they even got a cut of all juice loans made by their customers.

The minimum juice loan was $25, although some borrowers received loans of $2,000. Old customers and friends were granted an interest rate of 2 ½ percent a week; others were required to pay weekly interest rates of 5 to 10 percent a week. The interest must be paid first and the cash value never decreased, regardless of the decrease in the principal. Thus, if someone borrowed $200 at 5 percent weekly interest, he would pay $10 a week in interest even if the principal were reduced to $5. The most important thing to remember was, "Collateral for a juice loan is the borrower's life." During the time that we were raising hell with bookmakers in Cicero, we never heard of Joe Corngold, the only real bad outfit guy who was running Cicero was Joey Aiuppa as far as we knew. We started to pick up some intelligence from a few of the raids that we made about a guy named Phil Sheehan. I decided to give Sheehan a closer look and started to tail him. Sheehan showed up at every newsstand in Cicero as well as a lot of saloons and even some factories. He had a regular route every day; without fail he would go to Joe Corngold's house at 1828 South Fifty-ninth CT in Cicero, between 1:30 and 2:00 PM. It was obvious that Sheehan was running things for Corngold and giving him the wagers or totals for every day.

We learned from a few of the raids on wire rooms that we made in Cicero that they were using water-soluble paper to record their bets on. That being the case, we had to figure out a way to get Sheehan and Corngold together with the evidence. If we waited for Sheehan to get in Corngold's house and we knocked on the door, you can bet your ass that the evidence would be destroyed before we got in. So we had to get in Corngold's house just before Sheehan showed up with the bets. The only way that I could think of was to have two guys masquerade as gas company employees who were checking the houses in the neighborhood for a gas leak. I thought, what the hell, we didn't have anything to lose all we needed was a few props. We borrowed a couple of orange helmets from a construction guy I knew and two defoggers from another friend of mine at the park district. What were the odds that Corngold knew what a gas detector looked like?

It was the policy of the Chicago Police Gambling Unit to take along the local police when we were going to make a raid in their town, but my lieutenant decided that maybe we should just take the Cook County Sheriff's Police with us instead. We obtained a search warrant for Corngold's house, and I made a call to the sheriff's police vice unit to have two men meet us at Cermak Road and Austin Boulevard at 1:00 PM. It was September 5, 1974, and we were all set to hopefully pull off our trick of the week. All my guys wanted to go to Corngold's house, so I had them draw straws to see who would get the job. Ray Rice and Ron Kirby won and we were all set. The Sheriff's Police vice men showed up on time, and they asked me what we had going. I told them we had search warrant for a house at 1828 South Fifty-ninth CT and that we were going to send Ray and Ron in ahead of time dressed like gas company troubleshooters to fool the guy in the house. That's when the sergeant from the vice unit asked me who was the guy in the house. I, of course, told him "Joe Corngold," and that we were waiting for another guy to show up at the house with all the gambling records; that's when we were going to bust them. At that point the sergeant asked me what the date was, and I told him it was the fifth of September. He said, "Shit, I thought it was the fourth. I've got a court case on the fifth in Maywood this afternoon. We're going to have to leave." I told them, "No problem, we'll do the best we can." That's the last time I saw them.

Ray and Ron looked pretty convincing when they walked up to Corngold's house with their defoggers; we saw them knock on the door and go in. All we needed now was for Sheehan to show up on time. At 1:55 PM he showed up and parked in front of the house and knocked on the door and went inside. We got to the house and found the front door unlocked and went in. Ray and Ron had Corngold and Sheehan against the wall and were searching them; there were two females and another male seated in the front room. There wasn't anybody else in the house. Ray came over to me and said that he couldn't find anything on Sheehan or Corngold. Because of the females present, I told Ray to take Sheehan in another room and strip-search him. Corngold was as cool as could be. All he said was, "Obviously, we don't have to worry about a gas leak in the house, huh fellas." Then he started laughing and said, "You guys really had me fooled." Ray had taken Sheehan in another room to finish searching him; the closest room was the bathroom, which as things turned out was the wrong room. Ray called for me to come in the bathroom and when I did, I was surprised to see Sheehan's hair was all wet. Ray told me that he strip-searched Sheehan and found nothing; he then told him to take his shoes and socks off. Sheehan took his shoes off and gave them to Ray; at that point Sheehan who had hidden the wagers and totals in his sock took them out and threw them in the toilet. Of course, the evidence was on water-soluble paper. Ray tried to get the papers out of the toilet but he couldn't. He was able to see some wagers on the papers before they dissolved though. At that point Sheehan must have slipped and his head went in the toilet, which caused his hair to get wet. A systematic search of the house revealed bail bond slips from Corngold's dresser; the slips were for everybody that we had busted the past year in Cicero. We also found some wagers that were hidden away in one of Corngold's shoes, so we had enough to arrest the both of them on gambling charges. When I told Corngold and Sheehan they were under arrest and they were going downtown to the gambling unit at 1121 South State Street, he said, "Hey, that's OK. I haven't been downtown in years." When we got Joe and Sheehan up to the office, there were a few of the guys doing paperwork. A couple of them said, "Who the hell is that guy?" All I said was, "Aw nobody, just the gambling boss of Cicero, that's all. He was one of the last members of the original."

Telephone FRanklin 2-0101

CHICAGO CRIME COMMISSION
79 West Monroe Street
CHICAGO 3, ILLINOIS

ORGANIZED AND ENDORSED BY THE CHICAGO ASSOCIATION OF COMMERCE

March
Twenty-nine
1954

SUMMARY

Re: Joseph Corngold alias
Joseph Fifke

The following information is contained in the files of the Chicago Crime Commission concerning the above named individual:

A Chicago Evening Post clip of April 21, 1930 reflects that police raided the Lexington Hotel, 23rd and Michigan Avenue, and arrested JOSEPH CORNGOLD who described himself as a former handbook operator. The article indicated that the police expected to round up a number of Capone hoodlums.

In 1940 and through 1943 CORNGOLD had a partnership believed to be a handbook at 5912 W. Cermak Road, Cicero, with LOUIS CAMPAGNA and WILLIE HEENEY. During these years he named those persons as his partners but thereafter he was in a partnership but did not name his associates.

It was known that on October 4, 1943 CORNGOLD, using the name FIFKE while at 5914 W. Cermak, stated that he had a handbook operating at 4807 W. Cermak Road, Cicero.

On October 7, 1943 reliable information was received that the address 5914 W. Cermak, Cicero, was the headquarters for the syndicate and the hangout for MOPS VOLPE and CORNGOLD known as FIFKE. The place at 5914 W. Cermak Road, Cicero, appeared to be operated by WILLIE HEENEY and was connected with a place at 5937 W. Roosevelt Road, Cicero.

On October 30, 1943 CORNGOLD and 23 other defendants, including officers of the Cicero Police Department, Chief of the Cook County Highway police, were indicted by the Cook County Grand Jury for conspiracy to violate gambling laws. This case was nolle prossed on April 3, 1944.

A Tribune clip of October 31, 1943 sets forth the story regarding indictments returned on October 30, 1943 against 10 police officers and 14 gamblers, JOSEPH CORNGOLD included as an operator of a gambling place in Cicero.

In 1944 JOSEPH CORNGOLD lived at 1828 S. 59th Court, Cicero, Illinois, which address was good as late as 1948. He could usually be found at 5937 West Roosevelt Road or making book in a tavern next door west. He also operated the El Patio, 5914 W. Cermak Road, Cicero.

Information concerning JOSEPH CORNGOLD and his family was secured in March of 1944 as follows: JOSEPH CORNGOLD - born December, 1895; EDITH CORNGOLD - born October, 1894; EDITH R. CORNGOLD - born October, 1928.

March 31, 1964

MEMORANDUM

Re: JOSEPH CORNGOLD
SUMMARY REPORT

The information set forth hereinafter supplements a summation of information concerning this individual dated March 29, 1954.

In a memorandum of November 23, 1951 it is indicated that JOSEPH CORNGOLD's wife's name is LEONORE.

In a "Tribune" clip of October 8, 1955 it is noted that JOSEPH CORNGOLD, 57, reputed Cicero gambler, was fined $500 in Federal Court for failure to buy a $50 tax stamp for his handbook. CORNGOLD, of 1828 South 59th Court, Cicero, entered a plea of guilty to an information complaint.

In a memorandum of October 3, 1958 it was indicated that the JOE CORNGOLD family of Cicero was known to visit CASPER CIAPPETTI at the latter's residence in the 1600 block on West 94th Place, Chicago. CIAPPETTI had been reporting from $20,000 to $30,000 monthly as gross income on which he paid 10 per cent tax.

In a memorandum of June 24, 1959 it is stated that JOE CORNGOLD was known to be around the El Patio, 5914 West Cermak, Cicero, of which JOHNNY CARR is the manager.

In an "American" clip of May 1, 1960 in an article concerning vice and gambling in Cicero, the statement is made that "CORNGOLD is another syndicate figure reportedly connected with Cicero gambling. An interesting sidelight here is that a Chicago visitor to Cuba in the pre-Castro days, who cashed checks in the hotels which housed the plush gambling casinos, learned, after his checks had cleared his bank, that they were countersigned by JOSEPH CORNGOLD of Cicero, Illinois.

In an "American" clip of March 22, 1961 it is stated that the "big three" in Cicero underworld are JOE CORNGOLD, JOEY AIUPPA and BOBBY ANSANI.

In a letter from the Tucson, Arizona, Police Department dated July 10, 1961 it was indicated that JOE CORNGOLD had been a visitor in Tucson for the past several years during the winter months. He lived at 6888 Casas Adobes Drive in a subdivision north of the city limits in a better-than-average neighborhood. The

Joseph Corngold - Page 2

In Cook County criminal case 43-1465, indictment for conspiracy, included police officers and gamblers. Concerning this indictment, on April 3, 1944 Judge Rudolph DeSort entered a nolle prosequi order against the 24 defendants. The court had ruled that the raids on which the indictment was based, were illegal because they were made without a search warrant. CORNGOLD was one of the persons named in this indictment.

The Cook County Grand Jury, inquiring into the question of gambling in the county, had CORNGOLD before them for questioning on May 26, 1944.

A clip from the Chicago Sun of June 13, 1944 reflected that JOSEPH CORNGOLD, age 43, reputed gambling boss of Cicero, only opens his gambling establishment when he has an okay, he is reputed to have told Chief John J. McGinnis, County Highway police, when he was placed under arrest over the week-end. Chief McGinnis picked CORNGOLD up at a tavern at 5914 W. Cormak Road, Cicero, with a companion FRANK CAVALLO, age 42, 1119 N. East Avenue, Oak Park.

Herald American clip of March 27, 1945 recites that the Appellate Court reversed Judge DeSort in that he had no right to order the Sheriff to return the roulette wheel to JOSEPH CORNGOLD, after the Sheriff had seized it on October 17, 1943 in a hunt for gambling equipment which had disappeared from a syndicate gambling joint known as the Dome.

Tribune Clip of October 1, 1947 recites that LOUIS CAMPAGNA had declared in his income tax profits from two gambling joints in Cicero; the El Patio, 5912 W. Cormak and the Austin Club as being $204,152 for the years 1937 to 1940; that he shared profits from the clubs with JOSEPH CORNGOLD and WILLIE HEENEY.

Daily News clip of February 7, 1948 recites that EDITH CORNGOLD, daughter of JOSEPH CORNGOLD, residence 1828 South 59th Court, Cicero, was subpoenaed by the Federal grand jury.

Tribune clip of February 10, 1948 shows a photograph of EDITH CORNGOLD, daughter of Joseph, when she answered subpoena before the Federal grand jury.

News clip of February 27, 1948 with headline "Capone's Gone, But His Mob Still Runs Cicero Joints" mentions in the article the gambling place at 5941 W. Roosevelt Road, operated by JOSEPH CORNGOLD.

In March of 1948 CORNGOLD testified before the Federal grand jury in Chicago which had under investigation the paroles of Paul Ricca, Louis Campagna, Phil D'Andrea and Charles Gioe. It is not known what his testimony consisted of.

On March 9, 1948 WILLIE HEENEY, testifying before the Committee of the House of Representatives, regarding the parole of Campagna et al, stated that he owned the tavern at 5914 W. Cormak Road, Cicero, and had been in business with Campagna in handbooks and also had JOSEPH CORNGOLD as a partner from about 1936 to 1943 when CAMPAGNA went to prison. He testified that they had 90 to 100 slot machines also; that they had the El Patio, 4914 West 22nd Street and the Austin Club, 5937 W. Roosevelt Road, and that the profits were divided as follows: Campagna — 60%; Heeney - 25%; Corngold — 15%. He said that CORNGOLD took care of having the law enforcement officers lay off raiding the clubs.

Chapter 36

The Gold "N" Greek

December 1980, Nick is in a small town in Greece visiting relatives; he is with his current girlfriend, Anita, who works for TWA Airlines back in Chicago. Nick is what we call an associate of some outfit guys back in Chicago; he's not a mob guy, he just happened to have some business dealings with a few of the boys and they trust him, maybe more than they trust some of their underlings. Solly Bastone, who has a high position in the Chicago Outfit, has a lot of faith in Nick and knows that Nick will help him if he asked him to.

The town that Nick is in is so small that it only has a switchboard in a store to send or receive telephone calls to anyone in the village. On a cold day in December, Nick is notified that he has a telephone call from Chicago, the man's name is Solly. Nick answers the call as soon as he can, and it's Solly Bastone, who asks Nick how his vacation has been going, and if he was having a good time. Before Nick can answer him, Solly tells Nick that his services are needed in Paris, France, and that he should leave Greece and be on a plane no later than tomorrow. Nick was given an address in Paris and was told to meet a man named Aaron at that location. Nick was told that Aaron lived in the penthouse of an eight-story building in the center of town.

Solly also tells Nick that when he meets Aaron, he is to tell him that he represents the friends back in Chicago and not to make any kind of move unless Aaron clears it with Nick first. At this point, Nick doesn't have a clue as to what the hell is going on, but he knows that he will be fully informed about his assignment when the time is right.

Nick, who is a very smooth talker, now has to explain to his girlfriend that an emergency situation has come up and that he will have to leave on the next plane to Paris. Anita understands the situation, and they both make arrangements to leave Greece. Anita flies back to London and catches a plane for Chicago. Nick catches a plane for Paris, still wondering what the hell he was involved in now. When Nick arrives at the Paris address, he finds that the penthouse has its own private elevator, which goes to the penthouse and down to the parking garage. The doorman in the building calls the penthouse and announces that Nick has arrived. Nick takes the elevator to the top-floor penthouse, which opens inside the apartment. A man in his late thirties greets Nick and introduces himself as Aaron. Aaron introduces Nick to his bodyguard, Jimmy, and another man that Nick recognizes as Vinnie from Taylor Street in Chicago. Aaron also has two secretaries and a chauffeur at his disposal. Aaron shows Nick to his bedroom, which is the biggest bedroom Nick has ever been in; it has its own personal bathroom and shower, and everything is in gold and very impressive. Nick is told that there are ten rooms in the apartment, which at one time belonged to a Greek shipping magnate. Aaron tells Nick that he only leases the apartment part of the year when he is in town.

The following day Nick receives a call from Solly Bastone, who is in Chicago. He is told that he is in charge of the people in the apartment and nothing happens unless Nick gives the OK. Of course, Solly will be directing Nick through this entire operation. Nick is to inform everyone in the apartment that he is in charge and to clear everything through him, even if they want to go to the store. Solly tells Nick that he will get a phone call from him on a daily basis with instructions as to what to do involving the sale of certain gold certificates that are currently in control of Aaron. Bastone tells Nick that in the near future the certificates will be sold; it all depends on the market.

Nick is still uncertain of the entire set up but he knows that if Bastone is involved in it, it's got to be big. He also knows that he has been chosen to be the muscle guy because he is unknown in that kind of business, and is unknown to law enforcement. As the days go by, Nick tries to get some clues about Aaron's part in this business deal. Aaron isn't a very friendly person, and Nick can tell that Aaron is afraid of him and stays out of Nick's way in the apartment. Aaron has en extremely large office set up in the apartment where his two secretaries are kept constantly busy answering phones and watching the stock market reports. Aaron is on the telephone constantly, and Nick can hear him speaking French to some one and Spanish to someone else. Obviously, Aaron is a very sharp guy, but Bastone probably doesn't trust him to handle this business deal by himself.

As the days go by, Nick is starting to get cabin fever, so he gets tells Vinnie that he has to meet someone down the street and asks Vinnie to accompany him. As long as Aaron's bodyguard is with him, there shouldn't be any problem. Vinnie jumps at the chance to get the hell out of the apartment and is all smiles. Nick and Vinnie hit a few nightspots in town and meet a couple of the local beauties; a good time is had by all to say the least. When they return to the apartment, Aaron asks them how the meeting went; Nick tells him that the guy wasn't ready yet so they are going to have to meet him again. Like I said, Nick was a good actor.

Bastone contacts Nick every day without fail, checking on how things are going. He then tells Nick that if the price of gold hits $950, he is to tell Aaron to sell immediately.

A couple of day's later, gold hits the magic number, and Nick tells Aaron to sell the gold. Aaron tells Nick that they are making a mistake and they shouldn't sell at that price. At that point Nick knows that if he doesn't convince Aaron to sell the gold and the price of gold drops, Nick is going to be in a world of shit with Bastone. Nick decides to go into his maniac act and he tells Aaron that he is going to sell the gold right now or suffer the consequences, as he walks him to the balcony and Nick looks down at a lot of traffic passing by there building. Aaron tells Nick that he gets his meaning and scurries off to the office to start making arrangements to sell the gold.

The next day, Aaron tells Nick, Vinnie, and Jimmy that they have to go with him to the Russian Embassy to get visas so they can travel to Moscow and carry out the rest of the transaction involving the gold sale. Nick tells Aaron that there is no way that they will be able to get visas on such short notice especially to a place like Moscow Russia. Aaron assures Nick that there won't be any problem and to let him handle everything. At the embassy Aaron goes into the ambassador's private office while Nick, Vinnie, and Jimmy wait in an outer office. After about an hour, Aaron exits the office and motions for them to follow him as they leave the embassy, escorted by Russian soldiers. Aaron tells them that the visas will be delivered to the penthouse in the morning and for them to be prepared to stay in Russia for a few days. The next morning the visas are hand delivered, and all of them leave for the airport where they board a Russian airliner for Moscow. Nick, Vinnie, and Jimmy are in awe of Aaron and wonder what the hell is going to happen next; nothing surprises Nick anymore.

Well, that's not true, when they land in Moscow, they are directed by a Russian diplomat to four limousines, one for each of them. They are driven to the Cosmos Hotel in Moscow, which was very exclusive at that time. They find out that they have private suites. Nick and Vinnie are together, and Aaron and Jimmy are in the other one. At this point Nick is telling Vinnie about how nice everything has been since they arrived and how great they have been treated by the Russians. Vinnie, who is a little soft, starts to bitch about the Russian communists bastards and says that you can't trust them. Nick kicks him in the leg and motions for him to shut up while he checks out the suite for any wires that the Russians may have planted. Sure as hell, Nick finds a transmitter in the chandelier; and when he points it out to Vinnie, tough guy Vinnie has panic all over his face and starts to shake. Nick writes "Siberia" on a piece of paper and Vinnie gets tears in his eyes and remembers what he had said about the Russians.

Aaron tells the boys that this deal may take a few days and to take it easy, just to remember where they are and not to get any goofy ideas, just behave. Finally after ten days, Aaron informs them that everything has been completed and the deal has been finalized. They will leave the next day for Paris and then home. Back in Paris, Aaron and Nick go to a French bank where the vice president of the bank assures Aaron and Nick that the money has been transferred and everything was fine. Nick calls Solly, who is well aware of the business deal being completed and things are fine in Chicago and to come home. Nick gets the next plane out of Paris for Chicago and is glad the assignment has finally ended. That was the last time that he saw Aaron or Jimmy; he did run into Vinnie once in a while, and when he did, neither one of them ever talked about Paris or Russia, or anything involved in that job.

I remember Nick from my old neighborhood years ago; he owned a hamburger joint and did a little booking on the side. He was always

Paris France

kind of a guy that liked the fast life, and I think he had the philosophy of live fast, die young, and leave a good-looking corpse. He was a pretty slick guy and kept changing his bookmaking operation so that I couldn't catch up with him. There was a rumor that he also ran a couple of card games in the area as well as pull-tabs, otherwise known as a jar game. When Nick came back from Paris, an informant told me that Nick had a couple of hundred spots in the suburbs that he provided the pull tabs for and that he was associated with Solly Bastone and Joey "Doves" Aiuppa, a top organized crime boss in Cicero, Illinois. Nick allegedly also had a lot of poker machines in places in the Chicago area that he took care of for Bastone.

Around August 1980, Nick got word from Bastone that the FBI was looking for him, and it had something to do with him threatening the life of a guy named Aaron. Bastone told Nick that they were sending him to Guatemala and that he was going to be put in charge of there South American amusement machine business – poker machines. Nick asked Bastone if he could think about it overnight and he would give him an answer in the morning, if it was OK with him. Nick refused the offer and decided to leave the country and go back to Greece.

Nick, who had good connections with people in the right places, got a passport under a different name; he was now Gus Mannos. He got a first class ticket on KLM Airlines and was personally escorted to the plane by the boss of KLM and headed for Greece and away from the G. Bastone told Nick that he was to lie low, never rent a car, and stay out of trouble. Before Nick left town he left his jar game business in the hands of his brother-in-law. After six weeks, the brother-in-law called Nick to tell him that Bastone had taken over all their stops and that he was going to stop him from doing it. Nick told him, "Forget about it, if you like walking around, there was nothing they could do about it, and its all part of the game."

Nick had also contacted some people in the right places to find out if the FBI was still looking for him after three years. Well, the truth of the matter was that they were never looking for him in the first place. The whole thing was all bullshit from the beginning; they just wanted him out of town so that they could take over his little gambling operation. Well, that's nothing unusual for the outfit; that's the way they do things. Nick eventually came back to the good old United States and finally realized that he can work and live and be on the square, and he told me that I could give up trying to bust him because he was Mr. Clean now.

Chapter 37

Nick, Sal, and Red

My guy Nick was a very busy fella and had a lot of things going for him, and they all involved gambling in some form or fashion. Nick liked to associate with the boys – meaning the outfit, of course – and was a trusted soldier. At one point when he left town because the outfit told him that the feds were after him, he turned down an offer to go to South America to run all the outfit's gambling operations down there. It seems that the Chicago mob had all of the video poker machines down there under their control, and the overseer of these operations was a Chicago Outfit guy by the name of Hymen "Red" Larner. Larner was a well-known south suburban gambling boss, who got out of Chicago when the heat came down on him and his close friends, Sal and Carmen Bastone. Nick turned the offer down and took off for Greece to lie low while the alleged heat was on. As Nick tells it, he was the guy who started video poker machines in Chicago and suburbs for Sal Bastone, and made the boys a lot of money. In the late '70s, these damn machines were turning up all over Chicago. Nick even had ten machines in the back of his West Side restaurant and made a fortune. The machines themselves were legal to have and were licensed by the city; the only time that they were illegal was when the people that have the machines pay off players for getting a certain number of units. Forty units on the machine would get you ten bucks. When the machines first came, out you could play them for a quarter, and then they became too popular that they changed the units so that you could insert bills in them, $1, $5, $10, $20, up to $100.

Larner was the boss of all the pinball machines, illegal slots, and other gambling devices in the southern suburbs in the '60s; he also was rumored to be involved in gambling operations in London and Panama. He was currently reported to be the guy in Panama and lived in a house on top of a hill outside of Panama City. Allegedly he was taking care of Noriega, who ran all of the narcotics that was coming through Panama to the United States. Larner also had his hand in the jukebox industry in Chicago and the suburbs – the Lormar Distributing Company, which was run by the outfit. The owner was a killer by the name of Chuck English, who was a front for Sam Giancana, another outfit boss. Both of these guys would get whacked themselves later on. At a senate rackets committee hearing, Larner was asked how he maintained two homes, one of which was a mansion in Miami Shores. Also he bought two Cadillacs, two Mercury's, and a cabin cruiser, which was insured for $34,000. All this on an income of $34,800 for the past four years. Our boy Hymen, of course, took the Fifth Amendment. Sam "Mooney" Giancana as well as Chuck English and other big guys also took the Fifth. It seemed that the outfit was forcing jukebox operators to buy records from the Lormar Distributing Company. They were selling counterfeit disks and had a monopoly in Chicago, parts of Wisconsin, Minnesota, and Ohio. The operators purchased the records under threats of violence from the Chicago Outfit. Another method that was used was the taverns would be picketed by Local 134 of the Brotherhood of Electrical Workers, which was controlled by Juke Box Smith, a so-called business agent. Smith sold the operators union labels to paste on their machines, which guaranteed the union would protect the operators and their locations would not be bothered. Of course, this protection cost $1 a month per machine. Anyone who didn't join this organization had their machines chopped up or ruined with acid by two terrorists, Jimmy Rini and Alex Ross. Both of these thugs would wind up in Statesville Penitentiary for there misdeeds, and when they were brought back to be questioned by the McClellan committee, they both took the Fifth Amendment as all the other wise guys.

There was a third member of this terrorist crew; his name was Frank Musteri, and he could not appear at the hearing because he was shot to death on July 29, 1957, while the three terrorists were laying in ambush to murder a guy named Willard Bates in Brookfield, Illinois. Bates managed to escape only to have his head blown off a short time later in Lyons, Illinois. An outfit boss by the name of Edward "Dutch" Vogel hired the three terrorists to terrorize jukebox and coin machine operators, of which they did a good job. The committee counsel at this time was Robert F. Kennedy.

When video poker machines came into existence in the Chicago area in the late '70s, Nick was asked to do the bad guys a favor. Sal Bastone, the current outfit guy and overseer of all the video poker machines in the Chicago area, asked Nick to meet a guy that would fly into O'Hare field from Miami Florida on the first of every month. The Miami flight was the last one of the day to come into Chicago, and the guy they were meeting would be the last guy off of the plane. Nick was told what the guy looked like and that he would be carrying a valise full of money. Nick was to drive the courier to a motel on North Avenue in Melrose Park, Illinois where Bastone would be waiting in a room. The courier was instructed to give the valise to Bastone; at that point, Nick was to drive the courier to a house in Chicago Heights, Illinois. Nick was all for the job and agreed to be the chauffeur anytime any place; besides he said the money was pretty good, and it made him feel important.

The first time Nick met the plane, he thought that the guy wasn't on the plane because everybody got off including the pilots and stewardesses, but then here came this little Italian guy with a valise smiling at Nick. He told Nick his name was Alberto and that he always waited until the last person had left the plane before he got off; he said that he stayed in the lavatory which no one checked. He did that in case some federal agents may be waiting for him, they would think that he didn't get on the plane in Miami and would leave. Nick drove Alberto to the designated motel on North Avenue in Melrose Park, and Nick and the courier went to the motel room that Bastone would be waiting in. The courier then gave Bastone the valise, which he opened and placed on the bed. Nick said that for some reason Bastone let Alberto and him stay in the room while he made several piles of money and explained that this was some other guys share and he had to divide it up and give one of the shares to Joey. Nick found out later that "Joey" was Joe "Doves" Aiuppa, who was Bastone's boss at the time. Nick found out from Alberto that he was a relative of an outfit boss in Chicago Heights and that the house he was going to was his sisters. He also said that he lived in Miami now and that he would return to Miami the next day and he would see him on the first of next month. Alberto also said that Sal Bastone's brother, Carmen, has been exiled to Spain temporarily to supervise the video poker machine factory they had there. Nick was never able to find out the amount of money that was in the valise each month, but he was told by Sal Bastone that the money was coming from Panama and other parts of South America that had their video poker machines. The big guy down there was Hymen "Red" Larner, who had left Chicago years ago to avoid some heat from the senate hearings that were going on.

Video poker machines turned into one of the biggest sources of revenue for the outfit in years. The outfit flooded Chicago as well as the suburbs with them; although the machines were in itself legal, every bar and restaurant that had them paid off on them. I remember raiding six different places in one day, and confiscating thirty machines or more; but you know what, the machines were replaced back in the places we raided with in four hours. What a joke that was! After I left the gambling unit in Chicago on Maxwell Street in 1992, I was requested to work for the Sheriff of Cook County, Mike Sheahan, to help him solve a problem he had concerning gambling operations in the county. It seems that he was afraid that there wasn't enough enforcement of the gambling laws by his vice unit and needed some help along those lines. The former Under Sheriff, James Dvorak, had been accused of being on the payroll of mob boss Rocky Infelise for $10,000 a month to over look gambling operations in Cook County. Dvorak pleaded guilty to other charges of bribery but did not admit that had had ever accepted bribes from Infelise.

I remember raiding six different places in one day, and confiscating 30 machines or more, but you know what, the machines were replaced back in the places we raided with in four hours, what a joke that was. After I left the Gambling Unit in Chicago on Maxwell Street in 1992, I was requested to work for the Sheriff of Cook County, Mike Sheahan, to help him solve a problem he had concerning gambling operations in the county. It seems that he was afraid that there wasn't enough enforcement of the gambling laws by his vice unit and needed some help along those lines. The former Under Sheriff, James Dvorak, had been accused of being on the payroll of mob boss Rocky Infelise for $10,000 a month to over look gambling operations in Cook County. Dvorak pleaded guilty to other charges of bribery, but did not admit that had had ever accepted bribes from Infelise.

This photo of Hy Larner, taken during his testimony before the McClellan Committee in 1959, is the only known published picture of the Chicago Outfit's "mystery man." Larner would go on to become what many FBI insiders believe was one of the most powerful—and least recognized—individuals in organized crime during the twentieth century.

Hyman `Red' Larner

Sal Bastone

POKER MACHINES

We take out 5 at 10:A.M.

They get 5 more at 1:00 P.M.

Being interviewed by

The boss on the street

Yale Amusement

David Leader
busted 3-14-1997
Mia's Restaurant
1960 W. Irving Pk. Rd.

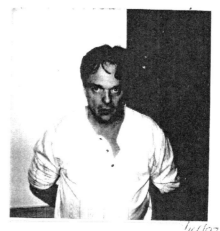

Jesse Yale distributor
and collectorfor 200
Poker Machines
Busted with David Leader

Chapter 38

Calvin Sirkin: Bookie with a Heart

Calvin Sirkin was a thirty-eight-year-old North Side bookmaker, who wouldn't quit taking bets even though he had massive heart attack and was confined to a bed in a hospital. Sirkin was a pretty slick fella and always took precautions to keep his base of operations a secret from the police. We began intermittent surveillance's of Sirkin when he left home in the morning, he would drive up and down alleys, go through parks, and use evasive techniques to elude any surveillance of him. Sirkin's bookmaking hours were from 5:00 PM to 6:30 PM during the week so we had to try and tail him until he got to his wire room. The way he drove you would think that he had 100 kilos of cocaine in his car; he was that careful. The key to tailing somebody is to keep him from making the tail, that's the tough part of the job. I had been using three unmarked cars to follow Sirkin but that wasn't working so I got five cars to see how that would work.

Sirkin left his home about 11:00 AM and drove south on Lake Shore Drive. He left the drive at Irving Park Road and then he began his routine of driving through alleys and sometimes even going through red lights that had just changed. This time I got lucky and was following him from in front; the rest of my crew was either behind him or parallel to him, so we managed to keep him in view. He stopped at a few restaurants a health club and sometimes he would just sit in his car and take a nap. We were sure that he didn't make us yet, and it was after 4:00 PM so we were in good shape at this point to take him to his place of business. About 4:30 PM Sirkin made a U-turn in front of a large tractor trailer truck and drove down an alley heading south; needless to say, he caught us by surprise, and we lost him in the area of Lincoln Park. After a lot of profanity, kicking tires, and punching the dashboard, I knew that we were very close to where he was operating because of the time. It was 4:50 PM when we lost him, so I decided to drive up and down every nearby street to try and locate his car; if we could find it, we would be in good shape to locate where he was running his wire room.

This guy was really frustrating the hell out of us, and we all would have liked to give him a slap for making us look like fools. But then we had to give him credit for out sharping us; that was his job, and so far he was winning this little game of hide and seek. It was the beginning of March 1976, and it was still getting dark early so we didn't have much time to find Sirkin's car. Well, believe it or not, we got lucky and found his car parked in the driveway of the Augustana Hospital on Lincoln Avenue. I thought that just maybe he was using the pay phones in the hospital, which was not an uncommon occurrence for bookmakers. We checked the pay phones all over the damn hospital, but no Calvin. There was only one other place to check, and that was the emergency room. There was Calvin lying on a table with a couple of nurses and doctors working on him; he was getting oxygen, and it looked as if he was in bad shape. I asked one of the nurses of Calvin's condition, and all she would say was that it was serious and that they suspect that he suffered a heart attack. I thought, *What the hell, this guy's beats us every time, one way or the other, but he was carrying this one a little to far.*

Calvin Sirkin had an interesting background; he had been sentenced to five years in the federal penitentiary in Leavenworth for a mob-connected scam in Des Moines, Iowa, in 1969. The scam was set up by a mob enforcer by the name of Phil Alderisio a.k.a. "Milwaukee Phil." Calvin could have walked away without doing any time if he would have told the FBI who he was working for at the time. But Calvin was a stand-up guy and went away and served three years of the five-year sentence. Alderisio was known as "King of the Scams" for his technique of moving in on legitimate businesses to run "controlled" bankruptcies for vast profits. He was also involved in burglary, extortion, mayhem, loan-sharking, and murder. He was a prime suspect in at least fourteen murders for the mob, and it has been reported that he was a loose cannon and that Tony Accardo, syndicate leader, could not control him.

This particular scam in Des Moines, Iowa, involved the purchase of a business where Alderisio had a man by the name of Bob Wolcoff buy the business and had his name on the license. Then Alderisio had Wolcoff along with Sirkin buy $500,000 worth of appliances, which were shipped to Chicago by the mob, where they were sold at half the price. The checks used to buy the business bounced, of course, and the appliances that they bought were paid for by check, which also bounced.

Milwaukee Phil pulled off another scam in 1964 when he had an outfit guy named Alan Rosenberg buy a travel agency from an older couple in the Chicago Board of Trade building in 141 West Jackson Boulevard. The old couple wanted to retire and travel to Europe so they sold the agency to Rosenberg for a $15,000 down payment and the rest would be given to them on their return from Europe. Alderisio then had Rosenberg purchase $300,000 worth of airline tickets through the travel agency, which was still in the old couples' name. They sold the airline tickets at bargain basement prices, of course, which was all gravy. The women who worked in the office were paid by check from the new owners, and they cashed their checks in a currency exchange owned by Mr. Myron Cohen also in the Board of Trade building. Needless to say, the payroll checks bounced also, which caused Mr. Cohen to be very upset; but there wasn't much that he could do about it under the circumstances. The old couple never got the rest of their money, nor did the airlines.

About a week after Calvin went in the hospital, I found out that he did have a massive heart attack and he was in room 204 in the Augustana Hospital. We also found out that in October 1975 the FBI unearthed evidence of Calvin's unlawful behavior and the Justice Department obtained a restraining order from Federal Judge Abraham Marovitz, instructing Sirkin to cease and desist further gambling. As things turned out, that order had about as much effect on Sirkin's activities as the heart attack. I again returned to the hospital the following week about 6:00 PM and found that Sirkin was still in room 204. When I got near the room, I could hear a phone ringing in the room, but it only rang once and was answered by Sirkin. I decided to hang around the door outside his room and make sure that Sirkin was behaving himself. Forget about it, the son of a bitch was sitting up in bed, talking on the phone, and giving out the basketball line. I heard him repeat back the bets that he took, such as, "New York minus three for two dimes." A dime was a thousand dollars; two dimes, of course, was two thousand dollars. A nickel meant five hundred dollars, and a dollar meant one hundred dollars. While I was standing there, he took in about $20,000 in a half hour. I thought about walking in on him, but maybe I would give him another heart attack, so I backed off and decided to get a search warrant to make everything legal.

Sirkin was in a two-bed room, so I thought about having one of my guys make off he was a patient in the next bed and really give him a surprise. I did notice that Sirkin had a bedpan on a table next to him, which was probably filled with water, and he sure as hell would try and destroy the bets which were written on water-soluble paper. The next day, we obtained a search warrant signed by Circuit Judge Robert Cusack, and we departed for the hospital late in the afternoon at a time when Sirkin would be hard at work. The hospital administrator said yes to a search of the room. Sirkin's physician said no. The shock of such a police invasion might be too great a strain for the bookmaker's heart, he said. While we were awaiting the doctor's decision, several of us waited outside of Sirkin's room; and there he was clad in a hospital gown, perched on the edge of his bed, bare feet dangling, as he was busy taking numerous basketball wagers on his private phone. He took bets for more than an hour and appeared healthier than any of us. Sirkin beat us again; we had to admit that this time he went to extremes to do it, but he did it. But there is and old saying, "It's never over until the fat lady sings."

Chapter 39

The Day We Busted Mob Boss, Joey "the Clown" Lombardo

In the fall of 1980, during the football season, my crew and I had been doing a lot of surveillances of big-time bookmaking operations. The two guys we were zeroing in on were a mob-connected bookmaker Jimmy Cozzo and the biggest independent bookmaker in the Chicago area, Hal Smith. Cozzo's father was a bookmaker and was from the Italian section of Chicago at Grand and Racine Avenue. We had a lot of success in that neighborhood and busted up some parlay card press operations and knocked out the whole crew from that neighborhood. Cozzo lived at 530 North Racine Avenue in an odd-shaped building with a swimming pool in the ground, which was a rare sight in Chicago. An eight-foot brick wall that made it difficult to see anything surrounded the building. Cozzo allegedly was running a large-scale bookmaking operation out of his house and also was suspected of having a lot of guns in his possession. I guess he felt secure because he was behind his big wall, and no one could get to him. I even had an aerial photo taken of Cozzo's house that gave us a good look at what he had behind the wall. I contacted the FBI and told them what we had going, and they asked if they could assist us if and when we made a raid because Cozzo was connected to mob boss Joey "the Clown" Lombardo. That information was not exactly earth-shattering news to us, but I told them that when we hit Cozzo's house, they could come with us.

Hal Smith wasn't as hard to work as Cozzo was; he lived in an exclusive residential area of Prospect Heights at 315 East Kenilworth Avenue. Hal was living the good life, and his house was somewhat of a show place, with four white pillars in front with a circular driveway. Hal hadn't given me any information for a while, so it was time to give him a visit. We had enough probable cause to get search warrants for Hal's house as well as Cozzo's. I picked Saturday, October 25, 1980, to raid both places; Saturday was usually one of the busiest booking days of the year.

I contacted an agent friend in the FBI, Darryl O'Donnell, and told him what my plan was, and requested he bring along a van so we could use it to scale Cozz"s eight-foot wall. O'Donnell said, "No problem, just tell us where to meet and what time." I picked out a spot about a mile away from Cozzo's house, because that was a very tough neighborhood to make surveillances in. I decided to just park the van next to the wall and then jump on top and figure out a way to get down afterward. I was thinking that this was the strangest way I ever got into someone's house.

Everything worked fine as far as the entry was concerned; we got in the house with no problem, but the bad news was that Cozzo was not home. We made a search of the premises and recovered a large quantity of sports schedules, sports bets, and other gambling paraphernalia. We also found a silencer for a pistol and a quantity of ammunition.

The real fun began when some of us left the building and observed Lombardo sitting in a black Pontiac; he was sitting next to the driver, Jimmy "Legs" D'Antonio, who was a known burglar and jewel thief. When D'Antonio spotted us, he threw the car into reverse and sped backward; the chase was on. We began chasing D'Antonio up and down a dozen streets; of course, our squads as well as the agents' cars, were unmarked. We were on the air describing to the squad operator what kind of car we were chasing and what direction they were going. The chase came to an abrupt halt at a police barricade. Of course, two uniformed officers at the roadblock had their guns drawn and covered everybody who was at the barricade; the detectives and agents had their guns drawn as well. While we were identifying ourselves to the uniformed police, Lombardo attempted to walk away from the scene in the confusion. D'Antonio remained behind the wheel and was observed throwing a quantity of small glassine bags out his window; the bags were of the type used by jewelers to put diamonds in. Lombardo managed to get to the corner when he was ordered to stop, which he did. Lombardo leaned against a fence but was observed to throw two notebooks over it. The notebooks contained names and phone numbers as well as license plate numbers and descriptions of the police cars that were involved in the chase. D'Antonio told the police, "Gee, that was fun, let's do it again sometime." Lombardo also had $12,000 in cash in his pockets and shoes, including 104 $100 bills.

The case was tried before Judge John R. Ryan in traffic court on April 15, 1981. Lombardo testified that he thought the detectives and the Federal Bureau of Investigation agents pursuing him were stickup men or killers out to get him. Lombardo said he was merely "going for cover" when he fled from a police roadblock at the end of the chase. Judge Ryan found Lombardo guilty of resisting arrest and fined him $500. James "Legs" D'Antonio was convicted of reckless driving and was also fined $500.

The verdicts and fines, however, was not the end of the day's events. As soon as Judge Ryan left the bench, D'Antonio bolted from the courtroom, looking for a way out for Lombardo, who previously wore a newspaper mask to keep from being photographed by reporters. The public doorways were already closed, but the resourceful D'Antonio found a way out through the basement, then across the tracks, and up a wooden ladder, ignoring posted danger signs. He was followed closely by Lombardo, then a defense investigator, then by out-of-breath defense lawyer, Mitchell Caplan, and finally by three reporters, all ducking to escape mud flung from the shoes above them on the ladder. A photograph of Lombardo, D'Antonio, and his associates climbing the ladder appeared in the *Chicago Tribune* the next day; the bad guys looked kind of silly trying to elude the reporters, maybe they just liked being in chases.

Lombardo was back in the headlines again in May 1981 when a federal grand jury in Chicago returned an eleven-count indictment charging five defendants with conspiracy to bribe Senator Howard Cannon of Nevada and to defraud the Central States Pension fund of the Teamsters. The defendants were Joey Lombardo, the mob boss, charged of overseeing Tony Spilotro and also the pension fund; Roy L. Williams, then the president of the International Brotherhood of Teamsters; a Chicago businessman who was the director of labor relations for the fund; and a Chicago trucking company executive who was a trustee of the pension fund. A court-authorized microphone that was installed by a special squad of the FBI in Dorfman's Amalgamated Insurance Company office obtained the evidence. This type of investigation went on for two years, with FBI agents monitoring the conversations of Dorfman, Lombardo, and others.

In 1982 a jury trial began in Chicago. All the defendants were found guilty and received lengthy prison terms. Lombardo was convicted for attempting to bribe Senator Cannon of Nevada to derail trucking regulations. Shortly thereafter, he was also convicted in Kansas City with Chicago mob leaders, John "Jackie" Cerone and Angelo "Hook" LaPietra, and Cleveland mob boss, Milton "Maise" Rockman, for skimming $2 million from Las Vegas casinos. Lombardo was sentenced to fifteen years; he was released from prison in 1992, but the dual convictions left confusion about when his probation ended. A hearing was held in December 1999 before U.S. District Court Judge Robert Gettleman about Lombardo's status. The prosecutors convinced the judge that Lombardo must stay on probation until 2002. The probation meant that Lombardo had his travel restricted and was forbidden from associating with any criminals or suspected organized crime figures, and faced the constant threat of having his probation revoked and being sent back to prison.

Lombardo and Tony Spilotro were suspected of being two of the four gunmen who murdered Danny Seifert, a twenty-nine-year-old president of a company in Chicago that was utilized to divert much of the money from the Teamster pension fund. Seifert was a key witness against Lombardo, Spilotro, Dorfman, Irv Weiner, DeAngelis, and two others. In September 1974, Seifert was with his wife and four-year-old son in their factory in a suburb of Chicago when four masked men walked into the building. Seifert ran away from his family to keep them out of harm's way when they caught him; they shot him in the head with a shotgun, and when he was lying on the floor, they blew his head off in front of his wife. When the case came to trial in April 1975, a jury, due to lack of evidence, found all the defendants not guilty.

Lombardo was also suspected to be involved in the outfit hit of Richard Cain in Rose's Sandwich Shop, which was located at Grand Avenue near May Street on December 20, 1973. Two masked men entered the shop with masks on and blew Cain's head all over the ceiling with a shotgun; the other alleged killer was Tony Spilotro. Cain was a former Chicago cop as well as a boss with the Cook County Sheriff's Office, and was Chicago mob boss Sam Giancana's closest confidant and traveling companion. Cain was allegedly an informant for the FBI.

Lombardo got his nickname from the press because of his zany behavior and cheesy jokes. At one interview, Lombardo explained to reporters that a piece of his jewelry was made from "canarly ctone." "You canarly see it."

Currently, Lombardo has been indicted along with thirteen others, who are part of the Chicago outfit, for alleged organized crime activities, such as racketeering, conspiracy, or gambling charges, which makes money for members and associates through illegal activities.

Lombardo is currently on the lam as his pal Frank Schweihs, an enforcer, collected and imposed "street tax" for himself and other members. In April 2005, Lombardo sent a letter through his attorney to local newspapers, explaining how innocent he was. The latest news about the clown is he is now in the slammer in a federal tier in downtown Chicago. He was captured hiding out in Elmwood Park, Illinois; he was charged with murder as well as a lot of other violations.

Screeching car chase

October 26, 1980

2 top mob figures arrested

By Manuel Galvan

TWO TOP CHICAGO syndicate figures were arrested Saturday when they were caught in a police net closing in on a West Side gambling operation, police said.

After a screeching car chase and brief struggle, police captured Joseph [Joey the Clown] Lombardo and James [Legs] D'Antonio.

"The funny part is, if they hadn't been so paranoid they wouldn't even have been pinched," said Lt. James Dvorak, commanding officer of the Vice Detection Section.

After three months of observation by officers of the Intelligence Section and agents of Federal Bureau of Investigation, Dvorak, who had a search warrant, and 12 men went to the home of James Cozzo, 530 N. Racine Av. Cozzo was not home, and several officers left for an unrelated gambling raid in Prospect Heights.

THOSE WHO STAYED removed gambling paraphernalia, a rifle, a shotgun, and a small-caliber handgun with a silencer from Cozzo's home. As the police were leaving, they noticed Cozzo's son, Phillip, talking to two men in a parked car.

Police recognized Lombardo, 53, reputedly one of the top five mobsters in Chicago organized crime. Police said they thought the other man in the car to be Cozzo.

When police approached the car, D'Antonio [whom police mistook for Cozzo], the driver, sped off and led the officers on a six-minute chase. It ended when patroling squad cars closed in on the car at Western Avenue and Fulton Street.

Lombardo, of 2210 W. Ohio St., a passenger in the car, was charged with battery and resisting arrest for allegedly punching a policeman. D'Antonio, 52, of 5242 W. Crain in Skokie, a reputed gem fence with a long burglary arrest record, was charged with reckless conduct, reckless driving, speeding, and eluding police.

BASED ON THE EVIDENCE recovered at Cozzo's home, police Saturday issued a warrant for his arrest.

The six police officers who left Cozzo's home first met with officers from the Illinois Department of Law Enforcement and Prospect Heights sheriff's police. They then raided the Prospect Heights home of Hal Smith.

Smith, 44, and his son, Michael, 24, both of 315 Kenilworth Dr., were arrested. Police confiscated gambling paraphernalia, $40,000 in cash, and records that indicated Smith's operation was generating between $500,000 and $1 million a week in bets. He was charged with gambling, being the keeper of a gambling house, transporting bets, and syndicated gambling. His son was charged with obstruction of justice.

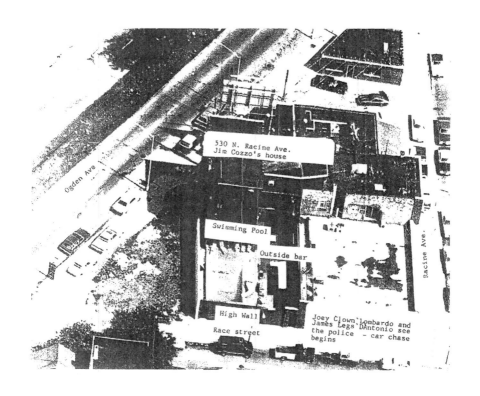

Source: Chicago Police Dep't

The outfit controlled it all

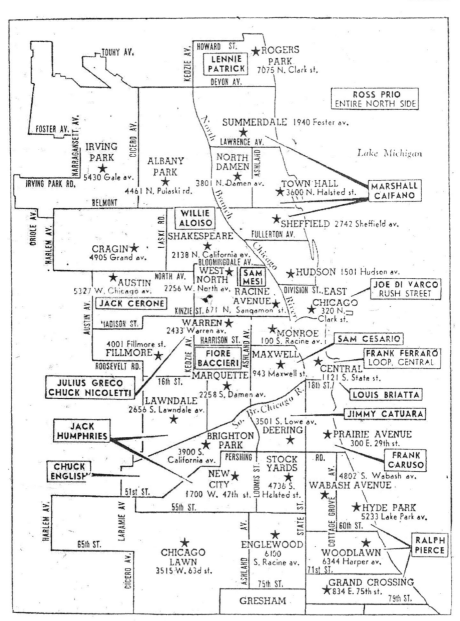

Legends on map link syndicate hoodlums with the police districts in which they control gambling and vice.

Source: Chicago Police Dep't

'The Clown' sounds funny, but the joke's on us

CAROL MARIN

e-mail:
cmarin@
suntimes.com

Joey "The Clown" Lombardo is quite a cutup as mobsters go.

Whenever he had to make his way through the lobby of a state or federal courthouse, he got a big kick out of making it difficult for those of us in the news trying to take his picture. Over the years we've seen him peering through a cut-out hole of a newspaper or walking by with a handkerchief draped over his face or other times wearing a goofy looking hat pulled way down.

When he wasn't pulling sight gags, The Clown tried his hand at other types of humor. Take for instance the ads he bought in three newspapers back 1992 just after he was released from federal prison.

It was to declare he was not a "made" member of the mob.

"I never took a secret oath with guns and daggers, pricked my finger, drew blood or burned paper (in my hand) to join a criminal organization," he wrote ". . . so if anyone hears my name in connection with any criminal activity please notify the FBI. . ."

What a card.

When FBI and IRS agents arrived at his door Monday morning to arrest him on racketeering and murder conspiracy charges, he must have gotten quite a giggle out of giving them the slip. As I write this, he and mob enforcer Frank "The German" Schweihs are still on the lam.

The fact is nothing about Joey Lombardo is funny or entertaining, and you and I pay the cost of him and the mob doing business.

Monday's indictment by federal prosecutors is hailed as a landmark organized crime case because never before have so many old, cold mob murders been bundled together for prosecution. Lombardo is one of a number of mobsters or mob associates tagged with those brutal crimes in which victims were buried or blow-torched or blown up or gunned down.

But though the unsolved mob murders are the red meat of this sweeping indictment, they do not occupy the main space.

What does?

Reputed gangster Joey "The Clown" Lombardo uses a Sun-Times to hide his face as he leaves court in 1981. He always got a kick out of making it difficult for the media to take his picture. —SUN-TIMES LIBRARY

Video poker.

For those of you who haven't hung out much at the corner tavern or neighborhood restaurant, picture this.

In many of these establishments, in the backroom, there are anywhere from two to 10 of these "recreational" machines. You put money in (some take $100 bills) and start playing poker. If you win, you pick up points, not money. These machines technically don't pay out. That would be illegal.

But if you are a regular customer and not suspected of being an undercover cop, at some point you go over to the owner or manager of the bar who does, in fact, "pay out." Your "points" are converted to cash.

Harmless fun, right?

A lot of people feel that it is. They can have a few drinks, stay in their own neighborhood and gamble.

But the poker machines in question are almost always operated by the mob, people like Jimmy Marcello and his brother Mickey, who were also indicted on Monday.

According to Cook County Sheriff Michael Sheahan, "A good machine pays out up to $2,000 a week."

There are, it's estimated, any-

It's a staggering amount of cash, and the Outfit takes half off the top.

where from 47,000 to 100,000 such machines in the state. Do the math. It's a staggering amount of cash, and the Outfit takes half off the top. The owner gets the other half. The state doesn't get a dime.

You would think that even those Illinois politicians who think gambling is the answer to all our revenue problems would be apoplectic about that. Not so.

"I've never had any politician come forward," says Don Herion, "saying hey, I have poker machines in my ward or district, I want something done about it. It never happened."

Herion worked for 40 years for the Chicago Police Department and then for the Cook County sheriff's police battling illegal gambling, especially poker machines.

"We'd go in, raid a place, take out four or five machines," he said, "and I knew that night, there'd be five more put back before we ever got downtown.

"Recreational" video poker machines are, to use Don Herion's words, impossible to regulate and "a joke, the whole thing is a joke."

A Joey Lombardo kind of joke.

He's not the only one who thinks so. Judge Aaron Jaffe, who is the new head of the Illinois Gaming Board, thinks so too. This week Jaffe will hold a news conference to outline his proposals to make the Gaming Board more independent and more relevant. He has a long list but a short staff. He faces pressure for new casinos, slot machines at racetracks and more. But video poker is somewhere on his list and I'm glad it is.

Until we put video poker machines out of business, the Chicago Outfit gets to stay in business.

Source: Chicago Police Dep't

Sunday Sun-Times, October 26, 1980

Mob boss Lombardo caught

By Lynn Sweet

Joseph "Joey the Clown" Lombardo, a top Chicago crime syndicate boss, was nabbed Saturday by police and FBI agents who spotted him outside a Near West Side apartment where they had just staged a gambling raid.

Lombardo, 51, of 2210 W. Ohio, was charged with battery of a police officer and resisting arrest after a high-speed chase from Grand and Racine to Western and Fulton.

Lombardo, reportedly the No. 3 man in the Chicago syndicate, in the past has been questioned about several organized crime executions, police said.

"No warrants for Lombardo were outstanding, so if he would have just stopped and talked with us, he probably would not have been arrested," said Lt. James Dvorak, a commanding officer in the vice-control section of the organized crime division.

"I was very surprised myself—a person as significant as he is in the crime syndicate," Dvorak said. "It shows their paranoia. They want nothing to do with police."

Today's OutFront column notes that Lombardo reportedly is in line to replace Anthony Spilotro, the syndicate's reputed top man in Las Vegas.

Also arrested was James "Legs" D'Antonio, 52, of 5242 W. Crain, Skokie. He was charged with reckless conduct, reckless driving, eluding police and speeding.

Police, who were looking for people taking bets in the apartment, gave this account:

On Saturday afternoon, a dozen Chicago police and FBI agents went to 530 N. Racine looking for a large gambling operation reportedly run by James Cozzo.

Cozzo, who reportedly works for Lombardo, was not at the apartment in the lavish complex, which includes an outdoor swimming pool, a cabana area and a 20-foot bar, all surrounded by a 9-foot wall, according to police.

Seized were records of sports wagers, a rifle, a shotgun, a gun silencer, a large quantity of water-soluble paper, and expensive, walkie-talkie-type telephone equipment.

Half the agents left the Cozzo home to go to another raid in north suburban Prospect Heights. When the other officers were leaving, an FBI agent recognized a man sitting in a car as Lombardo.

Hoping that Cozzo was in the car, police approached to question Lombardo. Cozzo was not in the car. The car took off at high speed, police said.

Minutes later, police stopped the car. Lombardo ran from it and threw away a paper that listed license plate numbers and descriptions of the officers who had left Cozzo's apartment, police said.

He allegedly struck a police officer while being arrested.

Lombardo and D'Antonio, who was driving the auto, were being held in a lockup at 11th and State.

The raid in Prospect Heights, conducted in cooperation with Prospect Heights police and the Illinois Department of Law Enforcement, closed down a bookmaking operation netting up to $1 million a week, Dvorak said.

Hal Smith, 44, of 315 E. Kenilworth in the suburb, was charged with syndicated gambling, transmitting wagers, keeping bets and keeping a gambling house.

Source: Chicago Police Dep't

Chapter 40

Butch, Harry, and Mama Sue's

The next time I ran into Harry and Butch was in a pizza place at the corner of Taylor and Loomis Streets called MaMa Sue's. I had heard that it was a hangout for some mob guys, so I thought we might take a look and see what we could see. Well, we sat in a booth and looked in the rear of the place and toward the kitchen, and there were Harry and Butch glaring at us. Butchie walked up to me and told me that he would like to talk to me for a minute, alone. I said sure, and we walked to the back by a jukebox, which was playing very loud. I guess this would keep anyone from overhearing our conversation. Then he asked me why we were hitting their gambling operations all the time, and why we didn't bust the Jews on the North Side or the Greeks on Halsted Street. I told him that we bust anybody anywhere we find illegal gambling operations going on, including his, and that it's all part of the game.

He then asked me why I was trying to whack him. I just stared at him, and then I said, "Are you kidding me, me hit you? What are you, nuts or what? Just why in the hell would you think something like that?" Then he said that my crew and I were on his tail the other night going west on the Eisenhower Expressway and that he could pick up conversation on his radio, because he just happened to have been tuned into our frequency. He said that he heard at least two cars communicating to each other and describing what lane he was in and heard one guy say, "I think Butch made us when we got on the ramp going west." Another cop then said, "He just got in the left lane, Don, do you see him up there?" He then heard, "Don, reply, I can't get a clear shot at him, just hang on, I'll get him if he doesn't hit the off ramp up there." Butch went on to say that he had been heading home to Hillside, a suburb west of Chicago, when this stuff took place. He became very nervous and got off the highway and went through a couple of traffic lights and side streets until he was sure that he wasn't being followed. I told him that if he was being followed, it sure as hell wasn't by me or any of my crew, because if it was, he never would have made us, that's for damn sure. He then described that when he got on the street where he lived, he found all the streetlights were out, and that's when he really became concerned. I could see in his eyes that he wasn't kidding around and was dead serious, and he really thought that he was going to get hit that night. At that point, I explained to him that he must have been watching *Hill Street Blues* or some other goofy cop show, and that he was getting paranoid. Butch then said, "Oh yea." He said that he wasn't in the house more than five minutes when the phone rang and when he answered it, a male voice said one word, *morta*, which means death in Italian. I tried to explain to him that I had no reason to hit him, and that the only interest I had in him was his involvement in gambling and juice, and that I will bust him every time I can catch him dirty. He just stared at me as if he was trying to figure out if I was bullshitting him.

Then he told me that he knew where I lived. That did it for me. I told him that I knew where he lived and ate and where he hung out, and that we had better get the rules straightened out right now. The next thing that could happen might be an OK Corral situation if that's what he is looking for. Butch then said that if it wasn't me on the expressway the other night, who the hell could it be? I told him that it wasn't me, but he had better find out who the hell it was before he might get a surprise.

At that time, Butch said he had to go and meet somebody for dinner in Chinatown, and he left. I told my guys what the nutcase had said and suggested that maybe it wouldn't be a good idea to eat a pizza in the place. Harry was in the kitchen and I didn't feel like eating roaches or flies or any other ingredient they felt like putting in it. As we were leaving, the phone rang, and the waitress said the call was for me. It was Butch on the phone, and he asked me if we could hang around until he got back, which would be in a few minutes. I told him we would be back, and we would see him later, in the meantime, he had better keep looking in his rearview mirror becuase something might be gaining on him. I was surprised to find that nobody had flattened the tires on our squad car while we were in the pizzeria. The next time that I ran into Butch was at the Maywood Park Racetrack in Melrose Park; he, of course, was with Harry Aleman. I was working security at the track at the time. I just happened to turn a corner in the dining area, and there they were – they both had their hands out and were smiling at me. Before I could recover from shock, I found myself shaking hands with the both of them and figured that somebody had me on candid camera or something. Here, I was caught shaking hands with the biggest hit men in Chicago. What a dope I was. Oh well, shit happens.

Strange things happen though. I guess Butch was right about someone trying to whack him, because that's just what happened. He was reported missing by his live-in girlfriend in December 1980. Butchie was subsequently found in the backseat of his own car abandoned on the street at 4307 West Twenty-fifth Place, Chicago, Illinois, on March 14, 1981. Butch's hands were bound with tape, his throat had been cut, surgical tape had been placed over his mouth and nose, and his face had been burned with lighter fluid. Apparently, the bad guys, or good guys – however you look at it – tried to set the interior of Butch's car on fire, but all the windows were closed so the fire burned out for lack of oxygen. Two cans of lighter fluid were found beside Butch's scorched face. Word on the street was that Butchie Boy had not been giving his boss all the money that he had been collecting on the street. Big mistake.

William "Butch" Petrocelli: Aleman's closest mob friend and suspected partner in many killings. He was found slain in 1981; police say Aleman may have ordered him hit.

Petrocelli

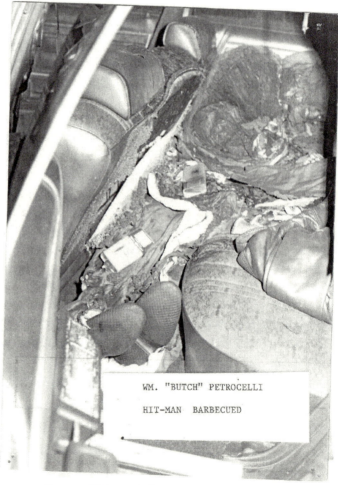

WM. "BUTCH" PETROCELLI
HIT-MAN BARBECUED

Source: Chicago Police Dep't

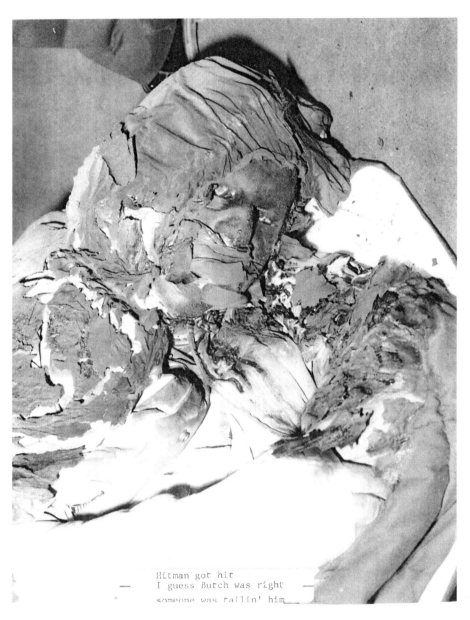

Hitman got hit
I guess Butch was right
someone was tailin' him

Source: Chicago Police Dep't

Chapter 41

Felix "Milwaukee Phil" Alderisio – Mob Hit Man

Phil was born in Yonkers, New York, on April 26, 1912. He drifted to Chicago, where he became a member of Sam Giancana's crew. His arrest record dates back to 1933, which reflects an arrest for murder as well as extortion, auto theft, and narcotic violations. Philly Boy was very active in the "juice" racket as well as other illegal activities. He reportedly was the liaison between the Milwaukee mob and the Chicago Outfit, and controlled the prostitution racket in Milwaukee. Intelligence sources have reported that he was only answerable to Sam Giancana, the boss of the Chicago Outfit.

Alderisio landed a job as a wheelman in the beginning of his career and drove getaway cars for the Capone mob. When he wasn't driving, he hammered his way into the inner circles of the outfit by terrorizing those who resisted it. In the four decades spanning the '30s to the late '60s, Alderisio was arrested thirty times. As he grew older, he turned to finance, mob style, and was indicted for phony bankruptcy schemes and nationwide stock manipulation. The two mobsters that crossed him in the stock deal didn't live to gloat over their achievement.

Alderisio's associates in the mob were high-line outfit guys, such as Sam Giancana, Jackie Cerone, Paul DeLucia a.k.a. Paul "the Waiter"

Ricca, Marshall Caifano, Albert Frabotta, Anthony Accardo, Alan Rosenberg, Joe Fischetti, and numerous other mob guys.

In May of 1962, Alderisio and another mob hit man, Chuck Nicoletti, were arrested by some alert Chicago policemen when they were observed crouching on the floor of an automobile, later described by police as a souped-up "hit car." Under the dashboard, police found three switches. Two of the switches controlled the taillights and a device to roll over the license plates. The third switch activated an electric motor, which opened a hidden compartment in the backrest of the front seat. The compartment was fitted with brackets to hold shotguns rifles and pistols. There was also room for a submachine gun. The car also had reinforced shocks, armor plating on all sides, and bulletproof windows. The last vehicle that had all those goodies on it belonged to Al Capone in the '20s.

In a *Chicago Tribune* clip in June 1962, a list of thirteen men were named as "contract killers" for the Chicago Outfit, and Milwaukee Phil led the list. He was described as a swaggering gangster, age forty nine, who has been seized by the police for questioning in dozen gang murders in the last decade. A reliable source advised that Marshall Caifano, Albert Frabotta, and Milwaukee Phil had murdered Louie "Russian Louie" Strauss in 1953. Information was also received that Alderisio was connected to the murder of John D. Trepani in Milwaukee in 1954. The lists go on and on.

Felix Alderisio was also a debt collector for the outfit as well as a hit man. He and another mobster were sent to the offices of a Colorado lawyer named Sunshine. Sunshine had allegedly mishandled some investments, causing significant monetary losses for Phil's bosses. "We're here to kill you," Phil announced blithely to the petrified attorney. Sunshine pleaded with his would-be killers, explaining that he had not cheated them and that it was an honest loss. Milwaukee Phil was contemptuous of such delaying tactics. He said that the only way for the lawyer to avoid death was to hand over the dough instantly or the execution would go forward. Still, the lawyer persisted, and for ninety minutes, he brought ledger after ledger to demonstrate his honesty. Argument and logic could sway even the likes of Milwaukee Phil at times. "It's a little irregular," he said, "but to show that there are no hard feelings, I'll do it. If he (Phil's mob superior) wants to cancel the hit, it's okay with me. I'll get paid anyway." A long-distance call was placed, and Phil came up with one less-than-lethal offer. If the lawyer would agree to pay the principal of $68,000 plus interest at the rate of $2,000 a month, he would be permitted to continue breathing. It was an offer Sunshine could not refuse, and it was a happy ending all around. As one mob leader put it gleefully, the deal Milwaukee Phil had arranged meant, "We'll be collecting from this sucker for the rest of his life. As things turned out later for Phil, Robert Sunshine and Denver attorney beefed on Philly boy and his rat partner, Americo DePietto, and they were indicted in the United States District Court in Denver Colorado on charges of conspiracy to murder Sunshine. Alderisio was found guilty, but DePietto was found not guilty.

Alderisio also tried to get involved in the fight business for the outfit and picked on a man by the name of Bernie Glickman. Glickman was the manager of Sonny Liston and Ernie Terrell, the heavyweight champs, and Virgil Akins, the former welterweight champion. It seemed that the mob had controlled boxing nationwide. It was reported that they controlled such fight managers as Blinky Palermo in Philadelphia, Charley Black in New York and New Jersey, and Frankie Carbo on the West Coast. There was reported to be connections between Chicago mob guy Ralph Pierce and the International Boxing Club's Jim Norris and Truman Gibson. Bernie Glickman was the owner of Kool Vent Awning Company and had installed awnings on Tony Accardos home in River Forest, which was an affluent suburb of Chicago. That is when he and Accardo became close friends. Glickman would go to Accardo's home every Sunday morning where he would bring lox and bagels and they would have breakfast together. This habit went on for years, and during this time Glickman installed awnings on a lot of other mob members homes, for the right price of course. Glickman was also the owner of the Hickory House Restaurant in the Rush Street area of the Gold Coast and had testified at the trial of Accardo when he had been indicted for income tax evasion. It seems Glickman perjured himself when he testified that he indeed buy Foxhead 400 beer from Accardo and on occasion would observe Accardo drive up in his Mercedes in order to sell beer. This testimony was extremely helpful to Accardo because he had been charged with making false deductions for the use of his car. There were other witnesses that testified that they had never seen Accardo selling beer in his car or out. Apparently, the jury didn't believe Glickman on the first trial and there had to be a second trial, Accardo was finally acquitted of the charge and never spent one night in jail in his lifetime.

Independent of his friendship with Accardo, Glickman began investing in prizefighters. Soon he had Sonny Liston and became his manager. There wasn't any connection between Glickman and the mob as far as his ownership in prizefighters. But Glickman had one big problem that would soon catch up with him; he liked to hang around with the wise guys. This would prove to be his downfall.

Bernie had a serious problem involving one of his fighters; it seemed that the New York Crime syndicate was trying to steal Ernie Terrell, his heavyweight champ. Bernie decided to tell Accardo his problem one Sunday morning over lox and bagels. Accardo made a decision to try and help Glickman; he would send Milwaukee Phil Alderisio to New York with Glickman to meet the mob guy that was causing all these problems. Glickman also wanted the Terrell-Clay fight to be held in Chicago and not in New York.

Glickman felt that he was in pretty good shape at this point because his friend Accardo had sent Alderisio with him to New York to straighten out the mob guy that was giving him all this trouble, Frank "Funzi" Tieri. After all, Alderisio was a well-known Chicago killer for the Chicago Outfit, and they would certainly fear him. Forget about it, by the time Alderisio was through meeting with Tieri, Glickman was lucky to come home with the clothes on his back.

We have to keep in mind that Accardo sent Alderisio to New York to speak on Glickman's behalf, or so Glickman believed anyway. By the time the meeting was over between Tieri and Milwaukee Phil. Who reportedly was soon to become the boss of one of the five New York families of the LCN, Glickman's future in the boxing business was just about over. When Alderisio reported back to Glickman about the meeting he threw $30,000 on the bed in Glickman's room and told him that that was his share of Ernie Terrell, and that he had better take it. Glickman, at this point, knew that he had been had and refused to take the money, that's when Alderisio informed him to stay away from Terrell and that the Clay-Terrell fight was going to be held in New York and not Chicago. Glickman was learning real fast how the outfit operated, and by the time the new year came around Glickman was in for some more surprises. They returned to Chicago and Glickman informed Accardo of the disaster that happened in New York and how Alderisio had really screwed him around. Glickman, of course, believed that Accardo was going to straighten out Alderisio and put him in him place. Again, forget about it. Accardo's only reply to Glickman was, "He's a loose cannon, Bernie. I can't control him anymore, end of story."

Bernie Glickman failure to heed the mob order to stay away from Ernie Terrell prompted Alderisio to attack and beat Glickman savagely. At this point, Glickman finally realized that he had been playing with fire with these mobsters and feared for his life. He immediately sought help from the FBI and sought protection from the outfit; he was put into protective custody. Glickman related to the FBI about the mob's influence in boxing nationwide and how Chicago Gambling boss Ralph Pierce was involved. Glickman related to the FBI that professional boxing was under the strong influence of the mobs across the country, especially New York, Pennsylvania, New Jersey, Illinois, and California. He recalled how a prominent bookmaker by the name of Farr who hung around the Morrison Hotel in Chicago was a close friend of Chicago mob boss and fixer, Gus Alex and Ralph Pierce. He told about fixed fights that these people arranged in Chicago. Gus Alex, a top member of the Chicago Outfit was known to bet heavily on these fights because he knew the outcome in advance. Pierce was identified as the Chicago connection between the International Boxing Commission who set up matches across the country. The commission was so strong that almost all fight managers in the country did it's bidding. They set up fixed matches where the outcome was never in doubt in order to be able to get decent fights for their fighters the managers cooperated. Norris and Gibson of the IBC were very close to Ralph Pierce and they fed him valuable information about these matches. Pierce, of course, would then utilize this information in making bets.

Glickman cooperated with the FBI and agreed to appear in front of a federal grand jury and repeat everything that he had told them about Alderisio, Frank Tieri, and the involvement of organized crime in boxing. This was not enough for the FBI; they wanted Tony Accardo, as well. Due to the fact that Accardo had ordered Alderisio to accompany Glickman to New York to meet with mob boss Frank Tieri to straighten out the boxing problem, he was involved in a conspiracy. "No way," Glickman replied. Accardo did what he did as a friend, and he had no part in this mess. He was double-crossed just like I was. Finally the FBI agreed to leave Accardo out of it and settle for what they did have.

Glickman began to wonder about his future, if he was to have one after he had testified against Alderisio and Tieri the New York mob boss. The government was not really equipped to handle informants at this point in 1965 to keep them safe and out of harms way. Glickman was a valuable witness and could break the mob's hold on boxing in the United States so it was imperative that he be protected. It was decided that Glickman would testify against Alderisio, Ire, the Madison Square Garden matchmaker, and three other mob guys that were involved; but Accardo had to be left out of the case at the insistence of Glickman or there wouldn't be a case.

After Glickman's meeting with the FBI, he wanted to go home and tell his wife what he was going to do. The FBI felt at this point that Glickman was in no danger and no one had any reason to be suspicious of Glickman so they let him go home. Of course, this was a fuckup by the FBI, because Alderisio beat the living hell out of him, and left him battered and bruised. Glickman was given medical attention and then taken to the federal building, where photos were taken of him for future court appearances. It was finally decided that Glickman had to be protected so for his safety he was brought out to Fort Sheridan, and army base on the North Side of Chicago. After a few weeks at Fort Sheridan, it was determined that Glickman was now a witness of the Justice Department and they and not the FBI had jurisdiction over him and his safety. U.S. Attorney Hannah ordered the U.S. Marshals to transport Glickman to St. Louis where they threw him into a county jail.

This was not a good place to keep a cooperating witness like Glickman; besides, his health was not what it should have been. After weeks of preparing for a federal grand jury case, Hannah decided to bring Glickman back to Chicago so he could interview him prior to his appearance at the grand jury. Apparently, there had been leaks in the Justice Department about Glickman being a cooperating witness because the newspapers had been full of news about Glickman exposing the mob influence on boxing in Chicago and the rest of the country. This, of course, was followed by stories about a mob contract on Bern's life to prevent him from testifying against Alderisio and the other Mafia guys throughout the country. When U.S. Attorney Hanrahan was informed that in no way was their anything involving Tony Accardo in this case, Hanrahan agreed and accepted the deal.

Hanrahan personally took Glickman into the federal grand jury room; after about an hour, Hanrahan and Glickman returned to Hanrahan's office where two FBI agents familiar with the case were waiting for them. Hanrahan was livid and began screaming about Glickman and said that the case was over. When the startled FBI agents asked Hanrahan what had happened it seemed that Glickman had testified about the involvement of Alderisio, Tieri, the fight matchmaker, and three other mobsters and everything had gone very well up to a point.

Apparently, Hanrahan either forgot or misunderstood the agreement with Glickman, because he asked Glickman about what roll Tony Accardo had in this conspiracy. Glickman remembered the agreement and lied about Accardo's involvement. He told the grand jury that Accardo was in no way involved in the conspiracy. The question is, why did Hanrahan even bring up Accardo in this conspiracy when all these facts were pointed out to him prior to his entering the grand jury room. Glickman perjured himself and was at that point discredited and was of no further value as a witness against Alderisio, Tieri, and the others. Hanrahan was furious and told the FBI that Glickman was no longer a federal witness and to get him out of his office. As a last resort, the FBI asked for the cooperation of the Chicago police to help keep Glickman in a safe place and guard him while some other arrangements could be made to keep him protected from the mob.

The word on the street was that Alderisio and his crew were hunting for Glickman to kill him. Apparently, Accardo was the man that had ordered Glickman killed when he learned that he was talking to the feds about the mob's involvement in boxing. As things turned out, when Accardo found out that Glickman would not implicate him in the mob's conspiracy to take over boxing and had perjured himself at the federal grand jury when asked if Accardo was involved in the conspiracy, Glickman replied, "Absolutely not." Reliable sources reported that Accardo stopped the contract on Glickman; Glickman was of course relieved and wondered why in the hell he ever got involved in this shit in the first place.

Bernie Glickman left Chicago and moved to California where he lived for the rest of his life; he passed away in 1986 of natural causes. Alderisio, who was convicted of conspiracy to murder Sunshine in Denver, Colorado, was free on appeal of that case and was up to his same old scam operation; it was business as usual for Philly Boy. A scam can be big or small, complex or simple. Sometimes a small one will be complex and a big one will be simple. But no matter, it is always fast and thorough, as George Hoyt the owner of a travel agency discovered in 1965. Hoyt met a connected mob guy who was an associate of Milwaukee "Phil" Alderisio; his name was Alan Rosenberg. Rosenberg had conned Hoyt into thinking that he knew the travel business and wanted to get involved. Hoyt said that Rosenberg agreed to sign a "hold harmless" contract, relieving Hoyt of the responsibility for his operations once he took over. Rosenberg paid Hoyt $15,000 in cash and promised another $45,000. He asked Hoyt to wait until he had obtained his own bond that was required by the airlines because of the ticket stock; and he took a cooperate note, about $45,000. About June 1, 1965, Hoyt went away on a trip to Morocco, with his assurances that he would notify the Air Lines Traffic committee of the change of ownership, get his bond straightened out, finish up the transfer of Hoyt's stock to him.

When Hoyt returned twenty days later, he discovered that Rosenberg "had done none of the things he promised." Then the company checks started bouncing and Rosenberg disappeared. On June 22, agents of the domestic airlines appeared at the Croydon Travel Agency and removed all of the remaining tickets. They informed Hoyt that he was still the owner of records and that the Corydon Travel Agency owed the airlines almost $100,000. The foreign airlines claimed "at least $50,000." And there was even worse news the next day when the operators of a commercial factoring agency informed Hoyt that they had paid Rosenberg $236,000 for accounts receivable represented by various types of travel tickets given to customers on credit. Then they displayed a stack of checks valued at $35,000 which had been returned marked "insufficient funds." The factoring agents said that Rosenberg had paid right on the dot the first eleven days in June and as a consequence they had introduced him at the National Boulevard Bank and had guaranteed Corydon's checks at that institution. Rosenberg had then taken that guarantee to a number of currency exchanges throughout the city and had cashed Corydon's checks "made out to real people who had, however, no claim to the money." With this device, Rosenberg managed to drain $165,000 from the bank in ten days. The last item was $28,000 from customer's deposits and prepayment for travel.

In a period of twenty days, Rosenberg and Alderisio parlayed a $15,000 investment into nearly $500,000. These are the odds the outfit appreciates. At the time he was scabbing Corydon he was under two federal indictments in New York City, one in Bettendorf, Iowa, and another in Kentucky. While all this was going on, federal authorities in Chicago were investigating Rosenberg and Alderisio for four other scams. The take from all these scams ran into the millions. Of course, all good things come to an end, and that's what happened to Rosenberg on March 16, 1967. He became Chicago's 1,003rd gangland victim. Rosenberg was found in his Cadillac. His hands were handcuffed; he had been beaten and shot seven times. Reliable sources say that he had shorted Alderisio on some money and that was a no-no.

Alderisio, who was known for being a good moneymaker for the Chicago Outfit over the years through his many money making scams, finally got unlucky. After his lengthy appeal was denied over the Sunshine case for threatening to kill him, he was imprisoned in 1969 for five years and sent to Marion, Illinois, federal penitentiary to serve his sentence. Alderisio, fifty-nine, died of a heart attack while walking in the grounds of the jail on September 25, 1971.

I have to add a few things concerning our involvement with Alderisio. Like all wise guys, Phil attended wakes to bid farewell to some other wise guy that may have passed away from natural causes or from a bullet in his head. He would also attend a meeting now and then at Meo's Norwood House at 4750 North Harlem Avenue. Norwood Park, Illinois. One night, we found Phil's car parked in the rear of the restaurant as well as Jack Cerone's, and a bunch of other outfit guys. They were probably planning their next hit. It was the end of January 1968 and it was cold and dark out as I recall. My partner Wally Goebbert and I decided that Philly would have a hard time driving his car with a couple of flat tires. I took care of the left front and Wally took care of the right rear. I will admit it was a good feeling watching the tires go flat; self-satisfaction is a wonderful thing.

On a couple other occasions we found Alderisio's car parked in the lot of the Granata Funeral home at 1857 North Harlem Avenue, and the Montclair Funeral Home at 6901 West Belmont Avenue. Both of these funeral homes seemed to be used a lot by the outfit when they were bidding farewell to there mob pals who passed away. One of these guys was a fella by the name of Red Altieri; it seems that one of Red's last requests was to be laid out on a couch in the funeral home. I didn't see Red, but a reliable source told me that Red had four Cuban cigars in his lapel pocket and his hands were joined together holding a scratch sheet. It seems that Red and his brother worked for the Chicago mob as bookmakers at the racetracks and made the outfit a lot of money.

At both of the above locations, Phil's car seemed to develop flat tires, and it was always the left front and the right rear. Being a sharp wise guy, he probably began to think that this was too much of a coincidence, or just maybe he was running into some bad luck. We did hang around at the Montclair Funeral home to watch his reaction when he found that he had two more flat tires, it was a sight to behold. The first thing he did was kick the right front tire and then began screaming, "I'll get you son of a bitches." He was yelling at anybody and anything that was near him. We were parked across the street and watched him beating up on his car, kicking and punching it; it was probably the first time that he beat something up that he couldn't be arrested for I imagine. Just to really piss him off, while he was ranting and raving we drove past him, blew the horn, and waved at him and gave him the finger; what a way to make a living. To tell the truth it was the best "sometimes."

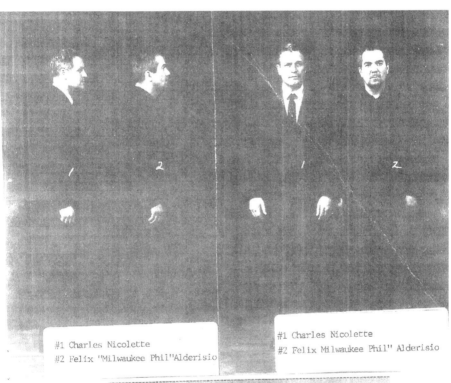

Source: Chicago Police Dep't

Chapter 42

Life and Death of a Bookmaker – Hal C. Smith

Hal C. Smith was quite a guy; he was a lot of things and led a very interesting life. I first met Hal when we kicked in the front door of a house he was booking in on the northwest side of Chicago. He did not use soluble paper, which was a surprise to me. He used yellow legal paper and had bets from a couple of days before as well. The total amount of wagers we recovered was in excess of $400,000, as well as a lot of code numbers his bettors used. Hal also had a list of telephone numbers that were listed next to each bettors name and code number; this was very surprising to me, because the bookmaker was supposed to protect his bettors identity at all times. Hal didn't seem to mind getting busted. In fact, he cracked jokes about it and said it was all part of the risk bookies take in this kind of business.

Hal got into bookmaking business in a common way, he was a degenerate gambler and lost more bets than he won. In the late '60s, Hal was working as an office manager for the First Finance Company in the area of Grand and Harlem avenues. Of course, he was betting and losing, so he began embezzling money from his company with fake loans to anonymous people. Being office manager, Hal was able to accomplish this quite easily; it lasted for a while, but of course Hal got caught. The company fired Hal and wanted to prosecute him if he didn't refund the money he embezzled, but Hal got lucky this time, and the bonding company made full restitution to the finance company. The bonding company made a deal with Hal, where as he would reimburse them; the payment would be $15 a month until he paid off the debt. As you can guess, Hal was a very likeable guy, and everyone felt sorry for him and wanted to help him.

You would think that Hal would have learned his lesson and quit gambling, forget about it. The next job Hal got was working for Coca-Cola; he had a driver and made deliveries throughout Chicago and suburbs. Of course, he started betting again and started to cheat Coca-Cola to get extra money to pay off his gambling debts. Hal did quit gambling for a short time, a real short time; he just couldn't help himself.

One day he ran into a bookmaker that he still owed some money; he told him that he would like to make a few plays with him. The bookmaker told Hal that the only way that he would take a bet from him was for Hal to put up $1,500 front money. Hal said "fine" and put up the money; of course, he lost as usual. Hal then put up another $1,500 and lost that money as well. The bookmaker made a mistake and let Hal bet $2,000 more. Hal, of course, lost those bets. To make matters worse, Hal, who had been stealing from the Coke company, got caught and they fired him on the spot.

The independent bookmaker knew that Hal was married with four children and felt sorry for him and asked him if he wanted to work a phone for him to make some money to support his family until he could get a job. Hal readily accepted and began taking bets on a telephone for the bookmaker. Hal was told that for safety's sake he was not to give his telephone number out to anyone; he was to call all the bettors. That way, the police would not be able to trace him through his phone number. Hal agreed to the rules, and he was in business. Things went along fine for a while, but all good things come to an end. One day, Hal met a man who he had been calling; the man had seven losing weeks in a row, which was unusual. The man was nice to Hal and always paid on time, but told Hal that he would appreciate it if Hal would give him his telephone number he could give him more action and it would be more convenient for him. The man's name was Roger Riccio, and he was an associate of people connected to the Chicago Outfit. When Hal gave Riccio his home phone number, he made a major mistake. Hal, who had been using a lady friend's telephone to call all of his bettors, got a visit from the FBI. It seems that the FBI had been working a case on Roger Riccio and a man named Tony from Taylor and Racine avenues. Their wiretap picked up Hal booking as well as identifying Hal through the home phone number that he gave Riccio. Hal's benefactor was also implicated in this investigation and was in deep shit. When the bookmaker found out that Hal had gotten busted, he assumed that Hal was taken to 1121 South State Street for processing. When he learned that Hal had been taken to the federal building, he knew something was wrong. At this point, Hal agreed to cooperate with the FBI about his gambling connections. When Hal was released from custody, the bookmaker met Hal and told him that he should stop booking and avoid any further trouble. Hal told the bookmaker that they were just harassing him and there was no problem. The FBI wiretap revealed that Riccio a man named Tony who owned a tavern at Taylor and Racine avenues; his bartender Joe, Hal; and the bookmaker were involved in a gambling conspiracy and were indicted by the federal government.

While the case was pending, Hal started to book on his own in 1975; he had a few of his own customers when he was working for the bookmaker and accumulated more as he went along. The bookmaker stayed in business himself while his case was pending. That's when he had a meeting with Harry Aleman, Butch Petrocelli, and Tony Borsellino in a restaurant called the Belden on North Clark Street. The bookmaker was told that he had to pay $1,200 a month in street taxes or else. He agreed and would meet Borsellino every month and give him the money. The bookmaker who was still friendly with Hal told him that eventually the outfit was going to find out about him and would probably want street taxes from him also. He told Hal that maybe if the bookmaker told the bad guys that Hal was working with him, he could probably just have to come up with $300 a month and he would be OK. The bookmaker, who was also employed by an insurance executive named Bill Haines, was also a big bettor. Haines got a visit from two FBI agents who wanted to inform him that the bookmaker was associating with organized figures and he should be careful. Haines told the bookmaker about his visitors and what they said. The bookmaker couldn't figure out how the FBI knew that he was meeting Aleman, Petrocelli, and Borsellino. Then it hit him that the only person that he told about the street taxes he was paying was Hal, and he must be an informant for the FBI. He then called Hal and told him to forget about the deal he talked to him about. The bookmaker felt that Hal was probably going to give him the $300 for street taxes, and he would then give Borsellino the $300 which would implicate him with the outfit. Hal was notified to report to the federal grand jury, and he asked the bookmaker what he should tell them, the bookmaker told Hal to "tell the truth," and he believed Hal was probably wearing a wire and Hal wanted to get him on tape, telling him to perjure himself.

Hal and the bookmaker were still friendly, and one night they went to the Arlington Hilton Hotel to watch a Muhammad Ali fight on close circuit television. Another gambler by the name of Calvin Sirkin was also with them. These three wise men, who had been involved in gambling all their lives, were about to be taken by one of the oldest scams in the book. They were walking down the hall in the hotel when they noticed a door open to one of the rooms, inside they were able to se four guys involved in a make shift crap game on a bed. There was money lying all over the bed and it appeared that this was a very nice game. Of course, they asked the men in the room if they could join them; naturally, the answer was "Yea, come on in." The four men in the game seemed like nice guys, they didn't notice until after they had been cleaned out that the men could have been gypsies. Between our three world-wise gamblers, they dropped about $5,000 in less than two hours. About a month later, the bookmaker happened to be at the racetrack and saw a couple of the guys that were in the game. He asked one of the mutual clerks if he knew them; the clerk said, "Sure, they belong to a group of scam artist gypsies who are real mechanics with dice and cards." The bookmaker thought about how dumb they were at the hotel. Who the hell leaves a door open in a hotel if you're shooting dice? The answer is, "Nobody, sucker."

My next encounter with Hal was in the summer of 1975 when we caught him booking big time; he still wasn't using water-soluble paper, and we caught him with all the bets, sports schedules and slough sheets. This time Hal asked me if there was anything we could do to forget about him for a little while. I told him that if he could keep us busy busting other people that he knew were booking, we probably wouldn't have too much time to chase him around. Hal thought about that for about two seconds and then gave me information about three other bookmakers in business in Chicago. I told Hal that whatever he told me would be between him and I, and nobody would know that he was cooperating with us.

The federal case involving the bookmaker, Hal, Roger Riccio, Tony, and the bartender named Joe went to trial in front of Judge Decker in federal court. The trial lasted for five days, and the judge decided to release Riccio for lack of evidence. The only defendant that got hurt was the bookmaker who was sentenced to two years. He served his time between Sandstone and the Marion penitentiary. Of course, when he got out he proceeded to go back in business. By this time Hal was going big-time and making a lot of money. Everybody knew how big he was getting, including the outfit, so he was in for a visit from the boys. Hal used to meet his customers at several different restaurants and bars in Chicago; sometimes there would be ten guys that he would meet to settle up with. One of his favorite places was the Club Lago at Orleans and Superior Street. They would all have drinks and lunch; of course Hal would pick up the check. After lunch Hal would either pay or collect from his players who were business men, some were stock brokers, doctors, and even truck drivers. Hal carried large sums of cash in an attaché case he carried; some times he would have a .38 cal. pistol in the case also just for protection, he said. The owner of the bar didn't care if Hal took care of his business in his place because he was a small-time bookmaker himself and gave Hal some action that he couldn't handle himself. We busted Hal in the bar as well as the owner of the place and confiscated about $45,000 in cash and his .38. Hal was not keeping us very busy at that time, so we had to remind him on occasion to give us a call more often. He was a very likable guy, and it was hard to get really made at him.

Roger Riccio who had escaped jail time when he was indicted with the bookmaker. Hal and the others was now moving in much larger circles. Riccio moved a lot of money from Las Vegas and New York; some days he would bet six or seven games with Hal, at $20,000 a game. Hal didn't blink an eye at those kind of bets; he loved the action, and most of the time he was the winner. The problem was that the outfit found out just how big Hal had gotten. Hal was a very outspoken guy and didn't care who he told how he felt about the outfit. He told me that the dagos could go and fuck themselves; he wasn't going to give them any more money. He said that he was giving them $2,000 a month, and that was all they were going to get. He hated Harry Aleman and Butch Petrocelli and another wise guy by the name of Salvatore "Solly D" DeLaurentis, who ran some gambling in Lake County. I remember how we would all be sitting around in the gambling unit at Maxwell Street, making bets on how Hal wouldn't be around for the new year, that the mob had to hit him to make a point of that old deal, "pay, quit, or die."

Hal didn't seem to care about who knew that he was a bookmaker; he drove a Cadillac with his name on the license plate and would have a few drinks on occasion and get stoned and talk about his business in front of anyone. Of course, he would always play the part of a playboy and buy everybody drinks and flash a lot of money. One night, we were tailing another bookmaker who went to a restaurant called the Golden Ox on North Avenue. The guy went into the dining room and met two other guys who we didn't know. They didn't know us either so we sat at the bar and kept them under surveillance. The next thing we know is that the bartender is giving us a drink from an admirer, he says. Of course, it's Hal who was sitting in another part of the restaurant with a blond; he saw us when we came in, but we didn't see him. He walked up to me and said, "So now you know another place I straighten out in." I told him that we just happened to stop in for a beer and that we weren't following him. Needless to say, he didn't believe us; he just accused me of getting old and careless and then said its all part of the game sarge.

The more times Hal got busted, the smarter he got; he started hiring other guys to run his wire rooms, because his business was getting bigger and bigger. Pretty soon, all Hal did was pay and collect at various parts of the city and suburbs; he would also stay in touch with his wire rooms and adjust the line on certain games. I knew on certain days Hal would stay at home and handle a few bets himself, that was because he was probably out the night before and probably got over served and had a hangover. He lived at 315 East Kenilworth in an exclusive neighborhood of Prospect Heights. He was living the good life and enjoyed every minute of it.

Hal's information was not getting to good so I thought it was time to reintroduce myself to him and let him know that I was not slipping and was still on the job. On October 25, 1980, a Saturday, we paid Hal a visit at home. He opened the door and was still in his pajamas when I said, "Good morning, Hal. We have a search warrant for you and the premises." All he said to me was, "Did you bring any aspirin?" We made a search of the house, and in his office we found about $1 million in wagers that he had taken in for the week. We charged him with syndicated gambling, transmitting wagers, keeping wagers, and keeping a gambling house. We brought him to our lockup at Maxwell Street and then sent him to the main lockup at 1121 South State Street for processing; he couldn't make bail until Monday morning. All he asked me was what were the final scores of the Notre Dame and Indiana games; he needed them both for a nice day. What a guy.

Hal was classified as the biggest independent bookmaker in Chicago; he knew it, we knew it, and the mob knew it, which was not good for Hal. He had a son "Mike," who was getting involved in Hal's operation and would pay and collect from Hal's customers on occasion. Mike had an appointment to meet someone at Sherman Goldman's hotdog stand on Pulaski near Devon Avenue one day. Sherman was also a bookmaker I had busted twice in the past. Mike got a little surprised when he got out of his car; two guys with masks on stuck a gun in his belly and robbed him of $25,000 cash. The question was, who knew that Mike had a meet at the hotdog stand that day and time, Hal, Mike, and one other person? The problem was Hal couldn't even report the robbery, so he just wrote it off as part of the game. The same thing happened to Mike on two other occasions; we knew that the outfit was behind these robberies, but Hal couldn't make an official report about it. The mob was going to get their street taxes from Hal one way or the other. The bookmaker who was out of jail now and back in business himself told me that he had a friend of his that was a plumber and was doing a job at Hal's house one day when he saw something very interesting. The plumber said that Hal was booking on the telephone while there were two other men present; they were FBI agents, and they were carrying on a conversation with Hal and laughing in between his phone calls. The bookmaker knew that Hal was working with the FBI in the past and obviously he still was cooperating with them.

Hal was in for another surprise when he got a visit from Internal Revenue agent on March 19, 1983, at his house in Prospect Heights. The raid was the beginning of the end for Hal C. Smith; the agents found $606,000 in cash stuffed in a gym bag in Smith's garage. The IRS confiscated the cash, along with Smith's Cadillac and house, citing a federal law that allows the government to seize assets derived from the profits of illegal activities. Smith temporarily won the vehicle back, until it became his coffin. The house later was relinquished to his widow.

In the spring of 1984, Hal had a meeting with Solly DeLaurentis in Tony's bar in Arlington Heights. Solly told Hal that he wasn't paying enough street tax. Hal was going to have to come up with a lot more money every month if he expected to continue operating. When solly told Hal that, Hal lost it and called solly a greaseball mother fucker and told him that he wasn't going to give him anymore money. Hal then told Solly to tell your fucking boss, Rocky that he can go to hell with you. Solly, who was also yelling loudly, told Hal, "you're trunk music, pa,." and left the bar. On February 10, 1985, his body was found stuffed in the trunk of his 1983 Cadillac Seville. He had been beaten, tortured, and had his throat cut. The Cadillac had been left in a parking lot of the Arlington Hilton Hotel. Hal who had defied the mob's demand for more street taxes had gambled and lost. Smith's execution was a message to all bookmakers as much as to the forty-eight-year-old man, who had made a fortune treading on the outfit's biggest business. His operation included almost a dozen wire rooms manned by clerks who could record as much as $200,000 each in bets on a single night. By the end of 1984, it was estimated that Smith's operation grossed $140 million in wagers annually. I remember Hal telling me that he netted $200,000 on one sports contest that was because he was a gambler as well as a bookmaker. He would often change point spreads or lines on games to his own satisfaction. Bookmakers have told me they consider a successful operation to be one that nets 1 percent of the gross wagers. Smith reportedly realized 2 to 3 percent of his $140 million gross, which would amount to an annual income of between $2.8 million and $4.2 million.

Smith signed his own death warrant when he refused to pay any more street taxes to Rocky Infelise and his crew; it was now all a matter of time before they would kill him. Infelise asked William "BJ" Jahoda a bookmaker that controlled all of Infelise's gambling operations to show him where Smith lived. Thereafter, Infelise and two of his lieutenants, Louie Marino and Bobby Bellavia, went looking for Smith so that they could observe him. In the fall of 1984, Infelise instructed Jahoda to keep in touch with Smith. On February 5, 1985, Infelise ordered Jahoda to make a meet with Smith and to bring Smith back to Jahoda's house. Jahoda made arrangements to meet Smith at a bar on February 7, 1985. Jahoda informed Infelise of this meeting and told Infelise that he would try to get Smith to come back to his house. On February 7, 1985, Infelise, Marino and Bellavia came to Jahoda's house. Infelise told Jahoda that only he and Smith should come to his house, preferably in Smith's car. Smith should enter the house through the kitchen; Jahoda should not go in the house. Later that day, Jahoda and Smith met at the bar and Jahoda brought Smith back to his house in Smith's car as instructed. Jahoda told Smith to go in through the kitchen while he pretended to go to his mailbox. Jahoda was able to see Infelise, Marino, Bellavia, and Bobby Salerno in the house after he arrived with Smith. The last time

Jahoda saw Smith, he was dazed and slumped on the kitchen floor with Infelise, Marino, Bellavia, and Salerno surrounding him.

Later that evening, Jahoda returned home and found his house was empty. He noticed that part of the kitchen floor had been mopped. Infelise then called Jahoda and told him to look for a cigar and glasses which Marino thought that he had left behind. Jahoda searched for these items but could not find them. Both items were later recovered from Smith's car, by the Arlington Heights Police. Jahoda left for Mexico the next day. After Jahoda returned from Mexico, he met with Infelise. Infelise told him that they were all "hot" because of "that thing," and that Jahoda was particularly hot. Jahoda began to realize that he was expendable and in a world of shit. When special agent Tom Moriarity of the organized crime unit of the IRS got through talking to Jahoda, he convinced him that he would be better off if he would cooperate with the government. Jahoda agreed to wear a wire and was instrumental in bringing down Rocky Infelise and his crew and clearing up the murders of Hal C. Smith and Robert Plummer another bookmaker murdered by Infelise and his crew.

Source: Arlington Hts. Police Dep't

Bookie was the best in business: police

July 19, 1985

by Anne Burris
Herald staff writer

Independent bookmaker Hal C. Smith was perhaps the best in the business, handling as much as $140 million a year in bets and personally netting between $3 million and $4 million, according to investigators trying to figure out who murdered the Prospect Heights resident.

"His was the biggest independent operation in the area," Sgt. Donald Herion of the Chicago Police Department Gambling Unit said Thursday. "He had 10 gambling ventures that I know of."

Smith was 48 years old when his beaten, slashed body was found in the trunk of a car at the Arlington Park Hilton last February. Police immediately suspected the bookie had been murdered by members of the crime syndicate eager to pass along a message to other independents — pay up or else.

Investigators believe Smith's demise came from his refusal to pay all of the dues or "street taxes" demanded by the mob. They said Smith paid some street tax, but he apparently refused to allow the mob to completely take over his operation.

Detectives investigating the murder have delved deeply into Smith's gambling business, which covered a territory that included Northwest Cook and Southern Lake counties. They paint a portrait of a bookie who was well-respected by those who patronized his illicit operation.

"HE ALWAYS had a good reputation and was reliable as far as paying off on bets," Herion said. "The guy was a gentleman. If I caught him booking and locked him up, he wouldn't cry about it. He knew what he was doing and he knew he wasn't going to get his head chopped off if he got caught."

In fact, Smith suffered only slaps on the wrist from law enforcement authorities in his many arrests. For
(Continued on Page 3)

Murdered bookmaker had good reputation

Daily Herald Suburban - July 19, 1985

(Continued from Page 1)
the married father of four, the big risk came in dealing with the mob.

Herion disputes reports that Smith had fallen into league with mob boss Joseph Ferriola. But he said there was no question Smith knew he might be in jeopardy by failing to cooperate with the syndicate.

"Oh yeah, I tried to warn him," Herion said. "The guy had a lot of guts. I told him he was nuts. There was a time when you figured he wouldn't last 'til the end of the year."

HIS BUSINESS, which consisted of wire rooms and extensive sports betting operations, sometimes meant he was holding millions of dollars in bets at one time.

"When it came to holding a lot on a game at one time, he'd do it," Herion said. "He'd hold $200,000 on one game rather than pass it on to someone else. How would you like to bet $2,000 on a Cubs game and then have to sit and watch the game? It's got to be a terrible feeling. But like I said, he had guts."

Smith was perhaps best known for his reliability. He covered bets and met every week with his customers, treating them to dinner and drinks at local restaurants while they discussed business and made whatever financial exchange was necessary that week.

His conscientious running of the business — which he took over in the 1970s from a man he had worked for — meant Smith could afford a prestigious home in Prospect Heights and was "never broke," Herion said.

"The rule of thumb for someone like that is if he nets 1 percent of the gross, he's had a good year," Herion said. "Now Smith, with his gambling and other sporting events, it's estimated he'd net 2 or 3 percent."

Herion said there were a lot of expenses Smith had to pay. "And remember," he added, "these guys don't win all the time. They lose a lot."

The sergeant said there are some leads on who killed Smith, but he declined to give any details about that aspect of the investigation.

Source: Arlington Hts. Police Dep't

■ Hundreds of thousands of otherwise law-abiding sports fanatics don't think twice about breaking the law with wagers, lining the pockets of bookies and their killers. Hal Smith, a big-time bookmaker, was found dead in the trunk of a car in 1985 (left).

SPORTS BETTING TERMS

Line: The betting line (also known as the point spread) is set by bookies. A favored team will "give" so many points, meaning it must win by more than that amount for a person betting on that team to succeed. For example, in the Bears-Packers game Oct. 12, the Packers were 11 ½-point favorites. Since the final score was Packers 24, Bears 23, the person betting on the Packers would lose while the person betting on the Bears wins.

Cover: A favored team winning by more than the point spread is said to "cover." Using the above example, the Packers won but they didn't cover.

Over-under: A bet on the total numbers of points scored in a game. If the bookie sets the over-under at 40 points and the final score is 25-17, a person betting the over on the over-under would win.

Chasing: When a bettor loses early in the day or on a weekend, then increases his bets later in the day or on Monday night football, he is "chasing" his losses. For example, a $100-per-game bettor might lose all 10 of his games on Sunday, then decide to chase those losses by betting $1,000 on Monday night.

Dog: An underdog – a team expected to lose.

Chalk: The favorite.

Juice: Also known as "vigorish" or "the vig." Bookies typically charge 10 percent juice on all bets, meaning one must risk $110 to make $100. For example, two $100 bets are placed, one losing and one winning. The bettor pays $110 on the losing bet and collects $100 on the winning bet, for a net profit to the bookie of $10. This is why the betting lines are designed to achieve as many bets on one team as on another, thereby providing a profit for the bookie no matter who wins. Baseball betting lines, which are more complicated, do not operate on the same system of juice.

Nickel and dime: $500 and $1,000, respectively.

it used to be," said Sealy, who spends much of his time briefing college and professional sports teams about the workings of illegal sports gambling.

Herion said the modern mob, in which the old code of silence hardly exists anymore, has made most mobsters a lot more cautious.

"Everybody's ratting everybody out," he said. "Guys figure, if they threaten someone, that guy's going to get scared, go to the G [federal agents] and come back wearing a wire."

The potential for violence still exists, however. And most players aren't willing to test the resolve of their "guys." Meanwhile, bookies who aren't connected to the mob would just as soon have their customers think they are, he said.

Sealy noted that it is far more worthwhile to pursue a prosecution involving extortion than simple gambling. Bookies know this, he said, so they avoid making threats. They are now more likely to cut their losses.

But Herion said there are creative ways of making threats. He gave an example recently to a visitor in his office

"I might say: 'Look at the water cooler,'" he said, directing his eyes to the water cooler, above which is a large picture of a dead

with too much money bet on one team in any game, he often will place his own bets on that team with another bookie—much the way financial institutions use stock derivatives to hedge their investments against potential losses.

Hal Smith wasn't concerned about balancing his betting lines. He would gamble that his bettors were wrong. "Oh, my dad used to tweak the line all the time," Mike Smith said. "We'd start with the Vegas line. But if he thought it should move, he'd move it."

"If the line was 10 and he thought the Packers were going to come in and roll, he'd move his line to 14," Herion said.

Herion estimated that Hal

Sealy agreed.

"My sense is it's [casino bling] not taking a big bite sports betting. It's getting ger," he said.

One thing that fuels spo gambling is the perception is a victimless crime. It's a perception, Herion said.

"I've known a lot of play over the years, guys who w formants of mine, I've seen ple lose homes, lose everyt he said.

In Herion's office downs at the Rolling Meadows co house is a large glossy pict It shows a large, bloated m folded face down in the tru a car, the dead body of mu bookmaker Robert Plumm

Source: *Arlington Hts. Police Dep't*

Hal Smith's car
he was found in trunk
murdered

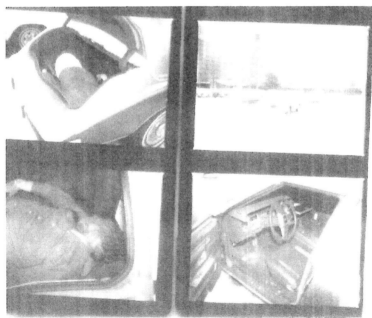

Hal Smith in trunk of
his cadillac
Feb 1985

Source: Arlington Hts. Police Dep't

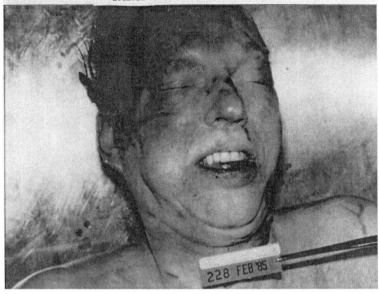

Hal Smith: Bookmaker "informant"
of mine. Brutally murdered
Stuffed in trunk of his own car

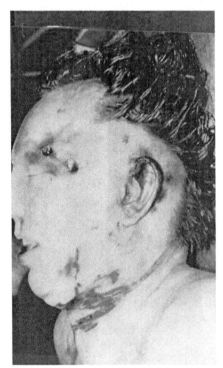

Source: Arlington Hts. Police Dep't

SCORECARD

EDITED BY ROBERT W. CREAMER

BAD ATMOSPHERE

The outrage people feel when college gambling fixes are exposed subsides with time, the initial shock dissipates; the residue tends to be a vague memory of some college kids getting into trouble because they listened to the siren song of a couple of modern gamblers. The fixes are pimples on the face of sport, ugly, but they go away. Rick Kuhn, the Boston College hoopster who was sentenced to 10 years in prison (later reduced to four; he hopes to be paroled in December) for his part in a point-shaving scandal, was asked last week in New York City at a gambling hearing of the President's Commission on Organized Crime if he felt his stern sentence had been a deterrent to others. "No, sir," answered Kuhn. "I don't think it's had a negative effect. I think people have become sympathetic toward me. They forget I committed a serious crime."

Kuhn also gave evidence that his bribers were more than jolly *Guys and Dolls* fellows, recalling a remark fixer Henry Hill made when Kuhn seemed uncooperative. "He told me I couldn't play with a broken arm," Kuhn said. "That's when I knew I was in over my head."

It's been suggested that big-time gambling, with whatever connections such gambling might have with organized crime, is involved with basketball fixing. Gary Kranz, a Tulane undergraduate arrested in the point-shaving fix there last winter and who has been charged with 22 counts involving sports bribery and cocaine, allegedly set up the fix with fellow undergraduate Mark Olensky, who pleaded guilty last week, in a plea-bargaining deal, to two counts of conspiracy. Olensky is the son of William Olensky, who runs a touting service in New Jersey. The senior Olensky, according to sources close to the investigation, took the Fifth Amendment after being subpoenaed in the Tulane case.

Edmundo Guevara, an FBI special agent and investigator with the President's Commission, says flatly that in every sports fix there is organized-crime involvement. Certainly, crime syndicates have ties with many neighborhood bookies. Illegal sports betting is said to rank second behind drug dealing as a source of mob revenue; it's an estimated $37- to $40-*billion*-a-year business.

Police sergeant Donald Herion of Chicago testified at the New York hearings that a bookie in Chicago named Hal Smith handled $140 million in bets annually (or roughly $400,000 a day); he took 2% to 3% of that handle for himself, or $3 million to $4 million a year (he had $600,000—probably "cash register" money—in a gym bag in his garage when the cops raided his place back in 1983). Herion said that a Chicago crime group known as the Outfit makes bookies pay a 50% "street tax" on their earnings. What happens if a bookie refuses to pay the street tax? "They usually give you three options," Herion said. "You can pay it, quit the business or die."

So far in 1985, three major Chicago bookies, including Hal Smith, have died, gangland-style.

season that Cincinnati's first baseman-manager is threatening to blow by Ty Cobb's career hits record.

COACHING GENIUS

The tentacles of bottom-line commercialism have long extended into college sports, and sometimes they get a little weird. At the University of Kentucky a mild controversy bubbled up when new basketball coach Eddie Sutton, late of Arkansas, signed a contract with Nike to have that company provide sneakers for the Wildcats next season. (Shoe companies supply shoes and pay handsomely for the assurance that every player on a squad will wear their brand.) In so doing, Sutton broke a long-standing Kentucky relationship with Converse shoes, dating back to the days of Adolph Rupp, the legendary Baron of Wildcat basketball.

Man in black faces sentence in mob-style hit

He was the ominous figure dressed in black that a government informant says he saw walk up behind bookmaker Hal Smith in the kitchen of a Long Grove house. Moments later, when he looked into the kitchen, mob turncoat William Jahoda said he saw Smith lying dazed on the floor, surrounded by Robert Salerno, the man in black, and three other mobsters. Jahoda was driven from the scene, but three days later Smith's body was found in the trunk of his car, fulfilling the warning of a top mobster that he would be "trunk music" for refusing to pay "street" taxes to organized crime. A jury deadlocked on Salerno's guilt or innocence at a 1991 trial, but he was convicted in a retrial last March, based largely on Jahoda's testimony. At 10 a.m. Friday, U.S. District Judge Ann Williams is to sentence Salerno in the Dirksen Building.

Sept-17-1995

Convicted in March, Robert Salerno now faces sentencing in the murder of bookmaker Hal Smith.

Chapter 43

Dissolvo – Spies – The Mob – Bikinis

There is one thing about bookmakers, they work goofy hours; usually they work when everyone else if off. They always work weekends and a lot of nights; on Saturday they have to work the day shift as well as evenings during the college football and basketball season. There hours are short, but they are always on the lookout to get raided. A lot of bookmakers hated the Chicago Cubs, because they only played day games back then, and of course they would have to handle the action, it was all part of the job.

But then when you're working on bookmakers; obviously you have to work when they work, and that's goes with the job. Believe it or not, one of the biggest action days of the year is on Thanksgiving Day. There are two pro football games, one at 11:00 AM and the other at 3:00 PM. Then there is a college game at night to top the day off. The bad guys usually work from 10:00 AM to 11:00 AM and then 2:00 PM to 3:00 PM; they probably would also take bets on the college game up to 3:00 PM and then close up. After all, they also celebrate Thanksgiving Day too. I used to make a habit of picking a target out to see what he was doing on Thanksgiving Day. I knew that we weren't going to eat dinner until about three in the afternoon, so instead of just lying around the house, I got on this guy I knew to be a major bookmaker.

He lived in a town in a Western suburb called Bensenville, which was about a twenty-five-minute ride from my house. I set up on the target, a "Marvin," who lived in a house with a side drive; his car was in the driveway when I got there at 8:30 AM, so I knew I was in business. It was showtime at 9:30 AM when Marvin left and drove westbound on Green Street. I was hoping that he would go east toward Chicago and be in my jurisdiction. No such luck, but I thought that I would tail him anyway even though I was out of Cook County. Marv drove to a gas station a few blocks away on Irving Park Road west of York Road and got some gas. He paid for his gas and then drove north on York Road to a side street, which was an industrial area, and then drove west to a flight service company where he entered this building by the front door which led to an office. Our guy Marv was right on time to begin booking at 10:00 AM; there were no other vehicles in this area because of the holiday. I think that Marv got a little lax in his driving habits and he never made me tailing him, shame on him. So far, so good, but now what?

I started thinking that maybe Marv was also a burglar and he used force to get in the building, I knew that he didn't work so he could be committing a felony by breaking and entering. I thought if only he was in Chicago there wouldn't be a problem, but I couldn't be so lucky. It was time to improvise, so I thought that it would only be proper for the local police to be notified of a possible burglary in progress in the flight service company. I got the address of the place and drove to a pay phone on Irving Park Road. There was a guy using the phone in a gas station, he sounded like a hillbilly and had a few beers in him. I then got an idea; maybe this hillbilly would make a call to the police, like a good citizen, and tell them about the burglary in progress. I decided to give him $5 for his help and told him he was an outstanding citizen. He agreed, smiled at me with his front teeth missing, and grabbed my five bucks. I gave him the address and told him to tell the police not to use their siren, as they may scare the bad guy away. He said, "Mister for ten bucks more I'll grab the bastard myself." All I said was, "Forget about it." Little did I know what an interesting day this would turn out to be.

It seems that one of the Bensenville police officers to show up was my son Tom, who was working a uniform car at the time; it's a small world, isn't it? Tom and his partner found Marvin in the office of the building and surprised him; I guess Marv never expected anything like this to happen on Thanksgiving Day. Tom saw Marvin trying to hide some wagers under a desk in the office and they arrested him on the spot. He was questioned as to what he was doing in the building and if he was a burglar. Marvin told them that he had a key and that he was a personnel friend of the owner of the business and the owner let him use the office from time to time to take care of his side job which involved a lot of paperwork.

While all this was going on, I was down the street minding my own business. When they took Marvin out and put him in their squad car, I knew that things were looking pretty good for the good guys. They took him to the station and booked him with violations of the gambling laws. I called Tom in the station and asked him what they recovered from Marvin, he said, "Boy, it's a small world, isn't it, father bumping into you on Thanksgiving Day? I, of course, explained the situation to Tom and what had happened on my end. He told me that they found a small amount of bets in the office where Marv dropped them and that was all. I asked if they would go back to the place and get their flashlight that they forgot there he said yea and that he paid a lot of money for it and he had better go back and get it. I asked him if he needed any help, and he said he sure did, so I met him back at the flight service ompany.

After a little scrounging around, Tom found more gambling evidence hidden in a dictionary on a table, but an added bonus was nine boxes containing thousands of sheets of water-soluble paper, otherwise known as Dissolvo.

Of course, almost every bookmaker in the country uses this paper, because in the event of a raid, they can throw it in water and it will disappear immediately. A closer examination of the boxes showed that the mailing address had been cut away with a razor or knife so we couldn't tell where the paper had been shipped to or where it was shipped from. This has always been a mystery to people in law enforcement, and has been very aggravating, especially when the wise guys destroy all their wagers in a bucket of water. In the state of Illinois, you must retrieve the evidence for a court appearance for any chance to get a conviction. But this time we got a break, Tom found a piece of cardboard that had been cut off one of the dissolvo boxes in a trashcan and it had the name of the company that had sent the boxes of dissolvo. The company was called Gilbreth International, 3300 State Road, Bensalem, Pensylvannia. Finally the good guys get a break. Like the old saying, even a blind squirrel gets an acorn once in a while.

Nation/world

Spies, mob use paper to wash away worries

By Bob Wiedrich
Chicago Tribune

BENSALEM, Pa.—Mafia bookmakers, Western intelligence agencies and the nuclear power industry have something in common—water soluble paper.

Even Las Vegas showgirls and magicians have found the product useful in their search for new ways to entertain audiences.

Mob bookmakers, who use the swiftly disintegrating product to record the identity of bettors and the amounts of their wagers, have frustrated police for years in their attempts to seize written records of organized crime gambling.

If the police approach, the ledgers can be dropped into a handy bucket of water, where they disappear in seconds.

According to a government document, the Pentagon began buying the product, known as Dissolvo, soon after the North Koreans obtained a wealth of secret documents when they captured the intelligence ship USS Pueblo in 1968.

Since then, some Dissolvo purchased by the government has been supplied to NATO countries, presumably for their own intelligence use, according to a spokesman for the product's U.S. distributor.

"It looks and tears like paper. You can write on it like paper. But it isn't paper," said Albert Miller, technical director of Gilbreth International Corp. of Bensalem, a Philadelphia suburb.

The company is the sole U.S. distributor of Dissolvo, said firm president William J. Spiegel. He said the product is made somewhere "outside of the United States," but he declined to identify its manufacturer.

Made from sodium barboxy methyl cellulose, the product contains wood fibers so it can be torn and calcium carbonate to give it opacity. It dissolves in three seconds, especially in warm water, leaving only a residue of fiber.

Developed about 18 years ago, the product's major ingredient is used as a thickener in ice cream, cake frostings and malted milk shakes, Spiegel said. It also is used to give body to hair preparations.

Spiegel said most of the Dissolvo his firm is used by the

nuclear power industry as a crucial element in the electronic welding of stainless steel pipe. It is put to similar use by chemical and food processing plants.

Less than 1 percent of the Dissolvo purchased is used for other purposes, including bookmaking, said Spiegel, who refused to disclose annual sales.

But police officials say use of the product poses a serious problem.

"Water soluble paper certainly impedes our efforts to win prosecutions of organized crime gamblers," said Capt. Fred O'Reilly, commander of the Chicago Police Department's vice control division. "We can find the bookmakers. But because many wirerooms are heavily barricaded, the physical evidence is gone before we can get in."

"I would estimate that 80 percent of the mob bookmakers use the stuff," said Sgt. Donald Herion of the department's gambling unit. "Without Dissolvo, we could get more convictions."

Usually sold in rolls or packages of 1,000 letter-sized sheets, the material costs about 10 times as much as conventional paper, said Frank Rable, manager of Dissolvo production. Depending on the quantity purchased, it sells for 10 to 15 cents a sheet.

Some buyers, he said, double those prices and include freight charges in retailing the product.

However, fragmentary records seized by Chicago police in recent gambling raids indicate that some retailers charge as much as 45 cents a sheet when selling to bookmakers.

For years, bookmakers have closely guarded their sources for Dissolvo. In those rare instances where detectives seized unused rolls or packages, the identity of the sender had been carefully cut out of the wrapping with a razor blade.

Last Thanksgiving Day, however, Bensenville police officers Thomas Herion and Michael Bratko seized six boxes of Dissolvo as they arrested Marvin Stellman on gambling charges in the offices of a flight service company in the Chicago suburb.

One package bore a delivery service stamp that police traced to

As the paper dissolves in a bowl of water, Sgt. Donald Herion of the Chicago Police Gambling Unit displays a sports schedule printed on Dissolvo paper. The schedule was seized in a raid on an organized crime sports betting wire room.

Gilbreth International.

"A number of years ago, I sat down with the FBI people and asked if we should just stop selling this product because of some marginally questionable uses," Spiegel said. "They told me absolutely not. It is an improper use of a legitimate product.

"We sell it to various distributors. How it is sold to bookmakers, I don't know. But obviously, we have limited control over the eventual user."

Dissolvo already is used in a variety of activities other than national security and bookmaking. Gilbreth officials are making a push for even wider usage by promoting the product at European and domestic trade shows.

Several years ago, a Las Vegas producer used Dissolvo to manufacture bikinis for a troup of showgirls he planned to have plunge into a pool, resulting in instant nudity.

Novelty makers use it in magic kits and automakers use it in a form to protect adjacent paint surfaces when installing chrome trim and other parts, Miller said. The tape then dissolves in a wash.

Gilbreth officials are investigating making disposable urinals and bedpans for contagious-disease hospital wards, Miller said.

The vessels would be specially coated so they would dissolve at 120 to 130 degrees Fahrenheit to "create the ultimate in disposable bedpans," he said. No body temperature is 98.6 deg.

The boxes of dissolvo were confiscated for further investigation and our guy Marvin would have his day in court. By the time this gambling raid was over, it was getting to be late afternoon; I had told my wife, Gen, that I would be back in two hours to watch the Detroit game. Needless to say, I was in as much trouble as Marvin was, but at least I wasn't in jail on Thanksgiving Day. I mentioned the story about the raid we made on Thanksgiving Day to a reporter friend of mine, Bob Wiedrich of the *Chicago Tribune*. I told him how we were able to locate the source of water-soluble paper, and that the company was in Bensalem, Pennsylvania. "Well," he said, "that's sounds good to me, let me explain the situation to my boss, I think that this would make a hell of a story and that we should both take a ride to Bensalem, Pennsylvania. and check out this company and see who runs it." I told him that I was packed and ready to go anytime. Well, the next thing I knew we were on a train headed for Pennsylvania, all expenses paid for by the *Chicago Tribune.* My bosses gave me the time off to make the trip so everything was A-OK. When we arrived in Philadelphia we had to rent a car because the Gilbreth International Company was located a few miles out of Philadelphia off of Route 95. I told Bob that he had better introduce me as a reporter also because they may get a little nervous talking to someone in law enforcement. Bob told the president of the company, Wm. J. Spiegel, why we were there and that we wanted to do a story on his company and Dissolvo. Spiegel explained that dissolve is made from sodium barboxy methylcellulose; the product contains wood fibers so it can be torn and calcium carbonate to give it opacity. It dissolves in three seconds, especially in warm water, leaving only a residue of fiber. It looks and tears like paper, you can write on it like paper, but it isn't paper. The company is the sole U.S. distributor of Dissolvo and added that the product is made somewhere "outside of the United States," but he declined to identify its manufacturer. Spiegel also told us that the Pentagon began buying the product, known as Dissolvo soon after the North Koreans obtained a wealth of secret documents when they captured the intelligence ship USS Pueblo in 1968.

Our government also supplies Dissolvo to NATO countries, presumably for their own intelligence use. Spiegel was asked if he was aware that Mafia bookmakers were using his product. He said that less than 1 percent of the Dissolvo purchased is used by bookmakers; he refused to disclose annual sales. The manager of Dissolvo production said that it is usually sold in packages of 1,000 letter size sheets and sells for 10¢ or 15¢ a sheet. But I recall making raids and found records indicating that each sheet cost as much as 45¢. He also said that he had a conversation with the FBI and asked if he should stop selling this product because of some questionable uses. They told me, Absolutely not. It is an improper use of a legitimate product." I asked Mr. Spiegel why his company has been such a secret as being suppliers of Dissolvo.

He then asked me if I was really a reporter, or was I a cop. All I did was smile at him and asked him if I could have a list of his customers that order Dissolvo in the Chicago area; I explained that all I needed it for was research of paper products. He said that would be against company policy, and that he was sorry that he couldn't help me. Mr. Spiegel also tried to explain that Magicians use the products as well as auto makers use it in tape form to protect adjacent painted surfaces when installing chrome trim and other parts. The tape would then dissolve in a car wash. The best one he came up with was a group of Las Vegas showgirls that used it to entertain audiences. Some producer used Dissolvo to manufacture bikinis for a troupe of showgirls he planned to have plunge into a pool and swim to the other end, when they emerged, it would be instant nudity.

Well, at least we found out what we wanted, and accomplished our mission, but I sure wish I could have gotten a mailing list of Dissolvo customer's back in Chicago. Weidrich wrote a nice story about Mr. Spiegel and his Dissolvo business and even sent a copy to Spiegel with a picture of me putting a football schedule made from Dissolvo into a bowl of water. Of course, half of the schedule had been destroyed in the water. By the way, the outfit is still using Dissolvo, and I don't mean in bikinis. Oh well, Bob and I got to ride on a train and see the sights in Pennsylvania as well as aggravating Mr. Spiegel, mission accomplished.

Chapter 44

Chicago's 42 Gang
"A Farm Team for the Mafia"

Chicago's 42 gang was the worst juvenile gang ever produced in the United States; their members were the biggest collection of crazies and killers who would supply Al Capone's mob for many years. The gang got their name from Ali Baba and the forty thieves, and they actually thought they were one better than the thieves plus Ali Baba. The gang was founded in 1925; some of the members were as young as nine years old, and they probably totaled no more than twenty-four members at that time, but over the years they actually did total about forty-two.

Their were other gangs in the United States that were considered bad such as the Jewish and Italian cliques of Brownsville and Ocean Hill, Brooklyn, New York, which fed Murder Inc., but for sure didn't supply anywhere near the numbers of soldiers for the national crime syndicate. It was for sure that no other juvenile gang gave the Chicago police as much trouble as the 42 gang did.

The gang originated around the Patch, or the Little Italy section of Chicago's West Side, Taylor, and Halsted streets. In the '30s, an in-depth studies by sociologists of the University of Chicago revealed some incredible statistics. Of members considered to be in the original 42 gang, more than thirty had be maimed, killed, or were serving time for such crimes as murder, rape, armed robbery, burglary, and other felonies. It was reported that they even broke into peddler's stables and stole their carts and killed their horses, hacking off the hind legs to supply certain outlets with horsemeat.

They were idolized by a lot of neighborhood girls who became their sexual playthings and were also used in some of the gang's criminal activity. The girls acted as lookouts and also at times they hid the gangster's weapons under their skirts if they were stopped and searched by the police.

The local press began writing stories about them, and the 42ers loved every minute of the publicity they were getting. Their ultimate ambition was to turn the heads of the big bootleggers, especially the Capone gang. They even pulled off a lot of robberies and then spend the money in places that were controlled by Capone. The first 42er accepted by the Capone gang was Sam "Mooney" Giancana; he had a reputation as being an excellent wheelman and who never became flustered under pressure. Tony Accardo took him as his driver. Later, as Giancana learned how to control his wild behavior, he moved up the syndicate ladder under the patronage of Accardo and Paul Ricca

Some of the other members of the 42 gang who were to make a considerable mark in the Chicago Outfit were Sam DeStefano, Felix "Milwaukee Phil" Alderisio, Sam Battaglia, Leonard and Marshall Caifano, Chuck Nicoletti, FiFi Buccieri, Albert Frabotta, William Aloisio, Frank Caruso, Willie Daddano, Joe "Little Caesar" DiVarco, Rocco Potenza, Leonard Gianola, Paul Battaglia, and Vincent Inserro.

Paul Battaglia, who was the older brother of Sam, didn't last too long. It seems that he had a bad habit about who he robbed; he was a fingerman for stickup guys who liked to rob horse-betting rooms and handbooks. In the '30s these operations belonged to the Capone mob, and it didn't take long to figure out who was responsible for these holdups. The end result was that Paul wound up with bullets in his head. This, of course, bothered Sam who had to make a choice; he could seek revenge or just go along with the boys. He made the right move because he later became the underboss under Giancana when he ran the mob.

Giancana was reported to be a snarling, sadistic psychopath who in time became the most powerful Mafia boss in the country. He was originally named "Mooney" because he was considered as nutty as a "mooner." Giancana didn't like that name so he changed it to "Momo," which was a much safer name to be used in his presence.

Giancana started his arrest record in 1925 and, through the years, was arrested more than seventy times. Some of the charges against him were for burglary, larceny, assault to kill, bookmaking, battery, suspicion of bombing, carrying a concealed weapon, and murder. He was the prime suspect in three murders before he was twenty; he was indicted for one of these when he was eighteen. He was released on bail and then never tried when the key witness somehow got murdered. He did three prison terms for operation of an illegal still, auto theft, and burglary.

By the early '50s a lot of the old Capone guys had gone by the wayside like Golf Bag Hunt, Guzik, Claude Maddox, Little New York Campagna, and Frank Diamond. Accardo and Ricca, who were running things for the Chicago Outfit, promoted Giancana to run the street operations. It was a changing of the guard, and Giancana brought a lot of the 42 gang with him; they were called the young bloods at the time. A guy like Sam "Teets" Battaglia succeeded because he always exhibited the same vicious outlook at his mentor. In 1924, at age sixteen, he was arrested for burglary. In all, he accumulated more then twenty-five arrests for burglary, robbery, larceny, assault, and attempted murder. He came into the public's attention for a bizarre crime in 1930. He was arrested for robbing at gunpoint the wife of the mayor of Chicago, Mrs. William Hale Thompson, of her jewels worth $15,000. Rubbing it in, he marched off with the gun and badge of her policeman chauffeur. A hitch developed in the case when a positive identification could not be made, and Sam insisted that he was watching a movie when the robbery occurred. He even produced half-dozen witnesses, who said that they were with him watching the movie. That robbery took place on November 17, and until the end of the year, Battaglia was a busy crook, being involved in one fatal killing and one attempted murder.

As time went by, Battaglia became involved in narcotics, mob extortion, fraud, and many more murders. He was known as the king of the outfit's loan shark activities and made judgments on debtors who owed the mob money. The juice victims were penalized by severe beatings or were killed. He was a major success in organized crime and was a millionaire several times over and owned a luxurious horse-breeding farm and country estate in Kane County, Illinois. But soon Teets' good fortune was to run out; in 1967 he was convicted of extortion and sent to prison for fifteen years. He died six years later.

Giancana brought up another 42er by the name of Fiore "FiFi" Buccieri; he was known as the lord high executioner of the Chicago syndicate. Giancana kept Buccieri very busy, not only as his personal hit man but as bomber, arsonist, terrorist, labor union racketeer, and loan shark. Debtors who owed Buccieri money were glad to pay up when their friends were told not to ride in a car with them because they were going to get hit. Buccieri scared the borrowers enough that they would steal money from their parents, their relatives, their friends, and their bosses. If necessary, they would put their wives and daughters on the street to make money to cover their juice payments.

He was known as the most monstrous killer in the Chicago Outfit. Federal agents picked up evidence of his dedication to the art of murder on a wiretap in 1962 in a house in Miami. Buccieri, Jackie Cerone, Turk Torello, Dave Yaras, James "Cowboy" Mirro, and Phil Alderisio had rented a house in Miami which the "G" had bugged. They had gone down there to "hit" Frank "Frankie the X" Esposito, union boss of five thousand city and county workers and sponsor for a lot of syndicate gamblers and hoodlums for city jobs.

In the evenings after a hard day's work of "casing" Esposito, the boys would gather in the living room to drink and talk shop. In 1961 a juice collector by the name of William "Action" Jackson, who weighed three hundred pounds, was the victim of a torture murder because he was suspected of being a stool pigeon. His body was found on lower Wacker Drive in the trunk of his car.

Buccieri brought up the subject of Jackson's murder during a discussion of techniques. Jackson's doom was sealed when Buccieri received word that "the fat slob" was a stool pigeon for the "G." Apparently Jackson had been seen talking with two FBI agents at the corner of Jackson and Laramie on Chicago's West Side. Buccieri and Torello talked about how they brought Jackson to a place called the "plant," a place described as having a large meat hook on the wall. Cerone then joined them, Yaras, and some others not mentioned by name. They shot him in the knee, stripped him naked, tied his hands and feet, and hung him on the hook for "a little bit of fun." Buccieri described the fun as using a cattle prod – a large battery-powered stick – which he placed against Jackson's penis. "You should have heard the prick scream," he recalled. While Buccieri was amusing himself with the cattle prod, others were playing around with such toys of torture as ice picks, baseball bats, and even a blowtorch. "Then," said Buccieri, "I shoved the fucking stick up his ass, and he shit all over the fucking joint. Boy, did he stink." Buccieri's account of this torture convulsed his audience into fits of hysterical laughter. A moment later, Torello became serious. "I still don't understand why he didn't admit that he was a stool pigeon." Buccieri ignored the remark. He related how sorry he was that the slob died so fast. "Jackson had lasted two days impaled on that hook. I'll never forget how he looked hanging there the fucking fat slob."

Cerone, at this point, said that he took credit for the cattle prod; he said that he got the idea from some "coppers who used the same thing on some hoods." Cerone then told how he attempted to kill Big Jim Martin, a West Side policy operator. I caught him real good with two blasts from a shotgun; the only problem was they had to go through a Cadillac. Joe asked me if the guy was dead, and I said, "Sure, didn't you see his head move?" The bad news was the headlines said the next day that the guy was only wounded and Martin would survive. Cerone said that it must have been the old ammunition I had, "Double O" buckshot, and that Accardo gave him the ammunition. Cerone then said that he returned to the shooting scene and mingled with the crowd, and talked to a couple of bystanders about how it was a shame the way that these niggers are always killing each other. The outfit got what they wanted anyway, because Martin left the country and fled to Mexico. They then took over all the policy and the numbers rackets in the black belt. It proved that Sam Giancana was right about how lucrative these operations would be, the annual take from these gambling operations was a large part of the mob's income.

Cerone was also a member of the 42 gang and his record dated back to 1933; he had been arrested for bookmaking, robbery, armed robbery, and was a prime suspect in at least four murders. He was an avid golfer, and I would see him and his underlings at White Pines Golf Course in Bensenville, Illinois. They would always have three or four golf carts and acted like they owned the place. I remember one day I was watching a group of guys hitting balls at a driving range on Fifth Avenue in Melrose Park. One of them was Jackie Cerone; he was kind of the main attraction with a bunch of other goombas who were oohing and ahhing every time he would hit a ball. I must admit that he was a pretty good golfer in his time. When a spot opened up next to them, I grabbed a few clubs and then checked to see if I recognized anybody that was with Cerone. I didn't, so I got a bucket of balls and started whacking away on the mat next to him. I have always had a hooking problem so when I began whaling away and watched the balls going left as usual I saw Cerone looking at me shaking his head. After a few more errant shots, Cerone spoke to me and said, "Pal, you got your left hand over to far on the club and you're bringing the club to far inside on the backswing." Then he said, "If you want to play this game, you better get rid of that fucking hook. When you get out on a golf course you could probably kill some poor bastard on the next fairway." When he said that, all his goombas started laughing. I said, "Yea, you're probably right. I'll give it a try because I sure wouldn't want to kill anybody, that's for sure. I'll be a son of a bitch if he wasn't right." After I moved my hand over and brought the club straight back, my hook disappeared. I began hitting the ball as straight as he was, and a lot farther. Cerone said see, what did I tell you, "Fuckin A." Cerone was still hitting balls when I expended mine; he had a very large basket with about two hundred balls in it.

I had hoped that I may have been in a position to overhear some interesting conversation from this group of Mafia guys but all the talk I heard was about golf. I then had a scary thought, what if the FBI was watching Cerone & Co. and they saw me getting golf lessons from one of the most feared assassins in the Chicago Outfit? That could be very embarrassing. But what the hell all was not lost; Cerone did straighten out my hook, which was the important thing I guess.

Needless to say, all the members of the 42 gang climbed through the ranks of the Chicago Outfit because of their skills, such as burglar's, stickup men, pimp,s bootleggers, extortionists, dope pushers, and murderers. All of them had extensive records and served time in jail, both state and federal penitentiaries.

Another stand out 42er was John Michael Caifano "Marshall." He legally changed his name to John Marshall in 1955. His arrest record goes back to 1929, when he was arrested for burglary. He was arrested another thirty-four times, for crimes like extortion, larceny, bank robbery, and interstate fraud, and was the prime suspect in more than ten murders. In 1958 he was cited for contempt of congress; he took the Fifth Amendment seventy-three times before the McClellan Committee. One noteworthy case was when Caifano was connected by the police to the murder of Estelle Carey, a Chicago cocktail waitress and beautiful girlfriend of imprisoned Hollywood extortionist Nick Circella. The outfit got the notion that Nick might start talking to get out of prison early so the mob sent over a killer to visit Estelle. She was tied to a chair, tortured, then covered with gasoline and set on fire. Circella got the message and kept his mouth shut.

Caifano lived about three blocks from me and used to go to "Rocky's" drugstore at LeClaire and North Avenue on the West Side of Chicago. He was like all the other bad guys, about five feet six inches, 150 pounds, and looked as if he could have been a jockey. But then a jockey with a gun or an ice pick will sure get your attention. Caifano had a brother they called Fat Lenny, who got killed in a shoot-out with a big-time policy operator on the South Side named Ted Roe in 1951; this was when Giancana wanted to take over all the black numbers operations. Roe was a hero on the South Side for a while because he took on the mob and won. This, of course, was not going to last to long, and sure as hell on August 4, 1952. Mr. Roe was blown out of his socks by a few shotgun blasts.

Chapter 45

Manny and Zeke vs. the Mob

Manny and Zeke were a class act and had more guts than a lot of outfit guys that I've run into working organized crime in Chicago. They were both good guys and had a similar problem; they both got involved in gambling, and sometimes that can get you involved in a world of shit.

I first met Zeke in the early '80s when I busted him for operating a sports and horse wire room on the North Side of Chicago on Lincoln Avenue. Zeke was handling a lot of action, utilizing two telephones in a vacant store he had rented for just that purpose. When we broke down his door, he kind of froze and wasn't able to destroy all the bets he had taken in. We knew that he was working for a guy by the name of Phil Janus and was probably making about three or four hundred a week. I knew that Janus was connected to a guy by the name of Joe "Pooch" Pascucci, and that he laid off all his action to him. Zeke turned out to be a nice guy, and I found out that he was Jewish, was married, and had a family, and was forty years old. He also said that he was just doing this kind of thing until he could find a better job. Zeke told me that this was his first pinch, and I told him that he was in big trouble and would probably get indicted and maybe go to jail. Of course, that is a joke, because no one goes to jail when you're busted by the local police. But what the hell, I thought if I scared him maybe he would want a favor and decide to cooperate with us as far as giving us information about other gambling operations in the Chicago area Is concerned.

I explained to Zeke that if he gave me some information that would help us, I would talk to the state attorney who was going to handle the case and maybe I could get him discharged in court. Zeke thought about the deal for about two minutes and agreed to cooperate with us if we agreed to keep him anonymous so no one would find out about him. I told Zeke, "No problem, pal," and we shook on it after I gave him my word of honor that no one would ever find out about him cooperating with me.

The next day in court, the states attorney agreed to discharge the case against Zeke and he also told me that Zeke had better keep his word or he would have the charges reinstated against him.

Zeke was a happy man and gave me a couple of telephone numbers to wire rooms that were taking big action; he told me that he thought they belonged to the outfit and to be careful when we bust them. I told him that they had better be good and I would let him know what happened when we kicked in their door. I told him, "Remember, the busier I am, the better for you because I won't have any time left to go hunting for you." He understood that kind of talk. The raid was good and from that point on Zeke and I developed a trust between us that would last for many years.

Through the coming months, Zeke's information proved to be reliable, and we busted up a lot of gambling operations in the Chicago area as well as places like Cicero, Berwyn, Melrose Park, and Elmwood Park, which had been the stronghold of the Chicago mob for years. When we made raids in the suburbs, we usually caught them with all the gambling evidence; it seemed as if they were very lax and didn't expect to be raided. When we made suburban raids, we notified the local police and invited them to accompany us on the raid and asked them to send a couple of detectives to meet us a designated corner; we didn't tell them where we were going or what we were going to hit. Sometimes they would send someone, and sometimes they said that they couldn't spare anyone as they were too busy.

Of course, we also made raids in the unincorporated area of Cook County, which was the responsibility of the sheriff's police. We also invited their vice squad to assist us in executing a search warrant, but most of the time they were tied up on other things and couldn't spare anyone; they just requested us to send them a report. We did run into problems though when the raids proved to be very successful and they appeared on television and the newspapers the next day. On one occasion, the Sheriff of Cook County, who at the time was Richard Elrod, had apparently asked his vice unit commander about these gambling raids and how come the Chicago Police Gambling Unit can make these raids in the county and his vice squad couldn't. I was told that the vice commander told him that Sergeant Herion was tapping telephones and that is how he is able to make all these raids, and they didn't do that sort of thing because it was against the law. I must admit that was a good answer to give too Sheriff Elrod, but needless to sayv it was total bullshit. Tapping telephones happens to be a federal offense and calls for five years in the joint, and believe me, there isn't a wire room on this earth that is worth going to jail for, that's for damn sure. But wouldn't you know it, I guess the sheriff believed his trusted commander because he contacted the superintendent of police, James Rochford, and told him about one of his sergeants in the gambling unit was wiretapping, namely Sergeant Herion. My lieutenant, Ed Berry happened to be walking into the lobby of police headquarters at 1121 South State Street when he ran into the superintendent, who told him about the allegation made by the Sheriff of Cook County. The lieutenant told the auperintendent that was all a bunch of hogwash and that maybe the sheriff had better check with his source of information because he may just have a problem with his vice unit.

It wasn't a short time later when we were notified that we would have to be sworn in as deputy sheriffs of Cook County if we were going to make any more raids in that area in the near future. As I recall, I believe we all had to have out photographs taken for an ID card to go along with the deputy badge. I'm sure that our photographs weren't passed out to anyone outside of law enforcement. Nah, no one would do that, would they?

I got a call one day from my guy Zeke, who told me that he was going to try something, and if it worked he would be in pretty good shape for a while. Zeke explained that no one was clearing him until about forty-five minutes after he closed up his wire room. So he figured that if he came up with a new player that bet into his office he would give him a code number and explain to his boss that the new guy was a good bettor and was a reliable payer if he lost. When someone works a wire room, all the bets are usually called in to another location so that there are duplicate records just in case of a raid or just to keep the wire room operator honest. This is usually done as soon as the wire room closes, that way they can't be past posted after the games are started. I told Zeke that I didn't think that was such a good idea, and to remember Murphy's Law: what can go wrong, will go wrong. Besides that, Zeke was the kind of guy that seemed to have a black cloud over his head all the time for some reason and always wound up in a world of shit.

After a couple of weeks of trying his scamb Zeke told me that he was going real small and was picking up a few hundred extra a week using his ghost bettor. He said that he had an edge of a full quarter in basketball and was able to get the scores of the games as they were being played. That would give him a very big advantage on any bet that he made. He said he had one game where he bet the underdog who was getting 11 points and they were winning the game by 10; he couldn't lose, and he didn't. He picked up a quick $200 bucks. "Boy, oh, boy," he said, "am I glad my old man came to this country. Whoopee." Needless to say, Zeke was in for a rude awaking, and the honeymoon was about to be over.

A few days later on a Saturday night, Zeke called me and told me that the impossible happened. Even though he still had a forty-five-minute edge on the games that were played that day, he said he went nuts and bet fourteen games for a thousand dollars each under the ghost's number. He said that even with that edge he lost thirteen out of fourteen games, and owed $13,300 to his boss, and of course he had no way that he could come up with that kind of dough. He said that he was thinking of jumping in the Chicago River or walking in front of a bus because when his boss found out about his scam he would wind up in a trunk anyway. Zeke was probably right about the trunk, but knowing Zeke, I knew that he would come up with an alternative decision when he came back to his senses.

The next day Zeke called me from a pay phone somewhere and told me that he was getting the hell out of town while he still could. I told him that I could talk to a FBI friend of mine about his situation and maybe if he cooperated with the G, he could go into the witness protection program. At least he would be taken care of and the bad guys wouldn't be able to get to him. Zeke told me, "Forget about it, pal." He decided to get out of town with his family and things would cool down after awhile and just maybe he could get the money that he lost and pay his boss back and all would be forgiven. He said that he thought that he might wind up out West somewhere and that I would be hearing from his when he got settled.

The next time I heard from Zeke was about a year later. He told me that he was working in Las Vegas and was doing OK. Then he told me he got friendly with a guy from the South Side of Chicago who came out to Vegas every couple of months and liked to bet sports. Zeke told me that the guy told him that he had a bookmaker back home he bet with, and he conned the guy into giving him his name and phone number. Zeke told me that the guy's name was Manny, and gave me the phone number that Manny was taking bets on. Zeke was still pretty good; even though he wasn't in Chicago. he still came up with good information, even I didn't know how good this thing was going to turn out.

My partner at the time was a great cop by the name of Bill Mundee who was from the South Side of Chicago and one tough son of a bitch. Bill had over twenty years on the job and was a University of Notre Dame graduate and should have made sergeant long ago. Anyway, Bill and I checked the phone number Zeke gave us and it was listed to a house in the Evergreen Park area. After some surveillances and further investigation, we got a search warrant and made a raid at a house and arrested a fella by the name of Manny. Manny turned out to be quite a guy and told us that he was in no way connected to the outfit. He did admit that he called some of his action into another wire room that he thought belonged to a bad guy, but as far as he knew, the wire room was located somewhere on the Far North Side. I explained to Manny that he was in trouble and could be indicted for operating a sports wire room, but if he would cooperate with us with information, we could cut him some slack in court, if he would give us the wire room number on the North Side of Chicago. He said, "You've got a deal," and gave us the information we wanted. The phone number he gave us was listed to a hotdog stand on a pier in Waukegan, Illinois. And the bookmakers name was Danny. Manny said that he thought that Danny was booking for a guy by the name of Joe Pascucci; some people call him Pooch. It just so happens that I had busted Pascucci and his nephew for booking in the past and that Pascucci lived in Wheeling, Illinois. Pascucci was also connected to an outfit guy by the name of Salvatore De Laurentis, who ran a lot of gambling in Lake County. He liked everybody to call him Solly D. He thought that was cool, I guess. The information that Manny gave us about Danny was passed on to the proper authorities in Lake County, because it was just a little out of our jurisdiction at the time.

In the coming months, Manny and I became pretty good friends, and he trusted Bill Mundee and me, and came up with some good gambling operations in the Chicago area. One day Manny told me an interesting story about a scam he got involved in with Danny, the bookmaker in Waukegan. It seems that Danny had asked Manny to do him a favor; he told Manny that he was going to add $1,000 to his figure for the week and that Manny could give him back the extra $1,000. Danny said there was no way that anyone would find out about scam because he controlled the figures. Manny agreed, and gave the $1,000 back to Danny the first week. The second week, Danny asked Manny to do the same thing, only this time Danny split the $1,000 with Manny, and he was beginning to like this idea. After several more weeks Manny said that his end of the scam was about $6,000. Danny's was more than that, he thought. He felt bad that he ever got involved in the thing, so he told Danny that he through. He was starting to get worried that the bad guys would find out about it, and he would get his legs broke.

In the meantime Joe Pascucci had been indicted by the federal government for gambling along with some other people and was sent to the federal penitentiary for a short period of time. At this point some outfit guys took over Pascucci's operation while he was incarcerated.

Out of the blue I got a call from Zeke who I hadn't heard from for a while. He said that he was still in Vegas and was playing poker a lot and was doing OK. Until the day when two guys that he had never seen before grabbed him and took him up to a room, they wanted to talk to him they said. Zeke said they told him that their names were Jim Peterson and Jim Bolling; they gave him a slap and then made him take his clothes off so they could check to see if he was wearing a wire. Zeke said that Peterson was about six foot two, 220 pounds, about forty years old; and Bolling was about six feet and weighed about 230 pounds, and was also about forty years old. They explained to Zeke that they had taken over the gambling operation that Zeke worked for back in Chicago and they knew that he had cheated his boss out of $13,300, and they wanted the money back or else. Zeke said that he never talked to fast in his entire life and was able to convince the two bad guys that he would be able to get the money for them if they would only give him a couple of days. Somehow he convinced them to give him some time, because they figured out that if they put him in the hospital they had no chance to get their money back. They told him that he was being watched and not to get any ideas about leaving town or he would wind up staked to the ground in the desert with his tongue cut out.

When Zeke described these two guys, I had no clue as to who the hell they were. But I suggested that if I could get a copy of the video tape that covered the area in the poker room in the casino, just maybe we would be able to identify them. I called the gaming commission and told them that I needed the tape in the poker room, but I didn't specify why, just that we wanted to identify some people that happened to be in the room that day. Believe it or not, they sent me the tape and we were able to make photographs from it of the two bad guys. Jim Peterson turned out to be a burglar and juice collector named James LaValley and Jim Bolling turned out to be a bookmaker by the name of James Bollman. Both of them were connected to the outfit in Chicago. LaValley was getting to be known as a real bad guy, and was known to be associated with Lenny Patrick and Mario Rainone, two killers from the Northwest side of the Chicago area. Lenny Patrick of course reported to the infamous Gus Alex, a longtime Chicago mob boss and close pal of Tony Accardo.

When I found out that LaValley and Bollman were for real, I notified Zeke that he was in a world of shit again; these guys were serious and he had better disappear for a while to be on the safe side. He agreed and said, "I'm outta here, Sarge, I'll keep in touch."

Before Joe Pascucci was indicted and sent to jail for violating the gambling statutes, Manny told me of a bar located on the Northwest side of Chicago on Northwest Highway. Manny said that he would go to this bar every Tuesday to meet Pascucci to settle up with him for the week. I had been keeping this bar under surveillance for a few weeks and had observed Pascucci as well as other men enter and leave the bar after only staying a few minutes. On one of my surveillances a goofy thing happened, I was sitting in an undercover car about a block East of the bar trying to be inconspicuous as I could, when I saw another guy sitting in a car just in front of my location. He had been writing on a yellow pad and every now and then would use some binoculars and look in the direction of Pascucci's location. Obviously, we were both watching the same target, so I decided to walk up to his car on the passenger side. I identified myself to him and could see that he has been writing down license numbers of vehicles that were stopping at the bar where Pascucci was. He seemed startled when I had approached him, and he didn't know what to say. So I told him that I was apparently watching the same target that he was, and that I was from the organized crime division and working on Joe Pascucci. Only then did he identify himself as an FBI agent and told me that he was in the area on an investigation but didn't tell me what. I explained to him that we had enough probable cause to get a search warrant for the bar and that I had intentions of raiding it the next day. I then asked him if that would screw anything up for him. "No problem," he said, "good luck," and then he left the area.

    The next day we obtained a search warrant for the bar, and there was still a lot of activity going in and out, and Pascucci was on the premises so we hit the bar. There turned out to be sixteen guys in the place, including Pascucci himself. Everybody was searched but all we could find was some sports schedules and cash. I searched Pascucci myself, and all I was able to find on him was a sports schedule and a lot of money; no bets were recovered on anybody in the place. Sports schedules are not illegal and neither is it illegal to have a lot of cash on your person. I was really pissed off at this point and told Pascucci in front of all of his friends that he was going to be my main target and that we were just going to work on his operation until he went to jail. At this point Pascucci went a little ballistic and started yelling about the fact that he was only a small guy and why we didn't bust Solly D. He was the son of a bitch that he had to pay street taxes to every month. Solly D., of course, is Salvatore DeLaurentis who is the right hand man of Rocky Infelise, who was running the outfit. Pascucci continued yelling that he had to pay that Dago $5,000 a month and that he should die of aids. I took Pascucci outside in front of the bar and told him that if he kept shooting off his mouth in the bar about paying street taxes to Solly D. some guy in the bar might tell him and he would probably get his head chopped off. I told him that I could make arrangements for him to wear a wire when he makes his next payment to Solly D. and we could get the bastard off the street. All of a sudden he calmed down and said that he couldn't do that because he would get whacked for sure. Due to the lack of enough evidence to arrest Pascucci or the others, I had to let them go. We went back to Maxwell Street and made out our necessary report concerning the execution of the search warrant and what had happened. The next morning when I reported for work, I was told to report to the commander's office for a meeting. There were two FBI agents with the commander with a pile of photographs they had been looking at. The photos were taken the day before of the bar that Pascucci was in when we made the raid. The two agents told me that they had identified everybody in the photos except this one photo which was of Pascucci talking to some guy by the front door of the bar. When I looked at the photo I almost broke out laughing. Of course, the photo was of Joe Pascucci and me; when I told them that, they had a very embarrassed look on there face. They said, "Oh yea, I guess that could be you." That was the end of that meeting; the two agents seemed a little embarrassed and left the building as fast as they could.

About two weeks later, I got a call from Manny about 9:00 PM, and he seemed very excited and scared to death. He said that I had to meet him right away because he was in big trouble and was almost killed by three big outfit guys about an hour ago. He told me that he was parked in the parking lot on the third level at O'Hare field and to please get there as soon as I could.

I told him to stay put and I would meet him in about twenty minutes. When I finally found Manny, he looked as frightened as a cat in a room full of bull dogs. When he finally calmed down, he told me that he had just left a meeting he had with three guys in the parking lot of the Cypress restaurant in Hinsdale at 294 and Ogden Avenue. Manny went on to explain that he was told by Danny the bookmaker in Waukegan that he was probably going to get a phone call to meet somebody concerning the scam that they had going with the extra money they were making. Danny told him that they knew what he and Manny were doing and wanted their dough back. Manny said that he was told where to go and what time to be there and just sit in his car and he would be contacted.

Manny said that he brought enough money with him to cover the $6,000 he made in the scam and thought that if he gave them $13,000 they would be satisfied. Manny said that he was parked in the lot for about forty-five minutes when a Black four-door sedan parked next to him. He could see that there were three men in the car, but they just sat there and stared at him for a few minutes, he thought that he was going to get killed right then and almost wet his pants.

All three of them got out of the car at the same time, and Manny said that he had never seen any of them before but they were really big guys. We found out later that the three guys were Jimmy LaValley, Jim Bollman, and Nick Gio. Manny said that when he got out of his car he noticed that the guy that got out of the backseat, Nick Gio" had a gun in his waist band; he began to panic and started to plead for mercy and told them that he was sorry. Manny said that LaValley grabbed him by his throat and told him that if he didn't come up with the money he cheated them out of he would stick an ice pick in his eye and beat him like a dog. LaValley released his chokehold on his throat long enough so that Manny wouldn't pass out. Manny told them that he only got $6,000 from the scam but he would give them $13,000 which was more than double there loss. He gave the $13,000 to Bollman who had been standing there laughing at Manny when he was pleading for mercy.

At this point the guy with the gun "Nick Gio" must of felt left out of the negotiations so he tells Manny that $13,000 ain't shit, and then sticks his gun in his ear and threatens to blow his head off. Manny said that he felt his heart stop and thought he was a dead man for sure. LaValley then told him that he still owes them $130,000, because that if how much he was ahead of them for the year. Manny tried to explain to the three monsters that he had won that money betting legitimately and that he didn't have that kind of money. LaValley gave Manny a crack across the face and broke his glasses. He told Manny that he had better get the money or else, and to get the hell out of there before they changed there mind and break his legs just for fun.

After Manny told me what happened to him in the parking lot, I asked him to describe the three bad guys. Two of them fit the description of the two guys that paid Zeke a visit in Las Vegas, the third guy was identified as an outfit wannabee by the name of Nick Gio. Gio was twenty-five years old about six foot one, 210 pounds, and thought he was the next mob enforcer in town. He was being instructed by one of the best, Jimmy LaValley who was getting to be well known around town as one mean son of a bitch.

Manny believed that the only reason that they didn't kill him was because they wanted the $130,000 from him. Manny asked me for a cigarette. I said I didn't know that you smoked; he said that he was starting right now. I told him to go home and that I would call him tomorrow after I had talked to a couple friends of mine with the FBI and find out a little more about these three bad guys.

The next day I told Bill Mundee what had happened to our pal Manny and that he was in a world of shit with the outfit and that we had a meeting with Tom Noble and Jack O'Rourke of the FBI. Mundee and I met with them and I explained that Manny was an informant of ours, and three guys had threatened his life over some gambling debts and that I thought that he would cooperate with us and just might wear a wire when he met them again. They said that they had heard about some guys in town threatening gamblers and people that were on juice, and added that they were real bad dudes and were working directly for Lenny Patrick. Patrick reported to the infamous Gus Alex, who was a bodyguard in the old Capone days for Jake Guzik. I told the FBI that we would get back to them after we tried to convince Manny that he was between a rock and a hard place and to trust us and everything would be OK.

The next night Mundee and I met Manny in a restaurant by the Evergreen Golf course on the South Side of Chicago. We explained the facts of life to Manny and went over his options. I told him that it would take a lot of guts to wear a tape recorder and that there would be some danger involved if he did. That there was always a chance that the bad guys would search him looking for a wire and that if they found one he could be in danger. But I also explained to him that he would not be alone and that we would cover him and see to it that there was no way that we would let them hurt him. The main thing is that he's got to trust us that we will protect him from any harm. I also explained to him that if he agreed to wear a wire, he would probably have to testify in court against the bad guys. Manny said that he had to think about it and told me that he would call me in a couple of days. Mundee and I both got the impression that Manny would not go for wearing a wire and that he just wasn't the type of guy to stand up against the mob, and to tell you the truth, their aren't a lot of people out there that would.

Well, were we wrong. Manny called me the very next day and said that he was not going to live in fear the rest of his life being afraid of those bastards, and that he wanted to get even with them. "Let's do it, Don." When I got off the floor, I called Mundee and told him what Manny said, his only reply was wow, that little guy sure has got some guts.

I called Noble and O'Rourke and told them that everything was go, and Manny was willing to due what ever was necessary to put those guys in the shithouse. That night we met in an alley near the University of Chicago on the South Side. We introduced Manny to Noble and O'Rourke, and this was going to be the beginning of a beautiful friendship. They explained the procedures involved in wearing a recording device and what was expected of Manny as a key witness in this operation. Manny was also told that there was a good chance that he would have to testify in open court against the bad guys. Manny said that he fully understood the situation he had gotten himself in and realized that he was going against the outfit. He also said that he wasn't a brave man and that when he had met LaValley, Bollman. and

Gio in that parking lot he was scared to death, and he firmly believed that they were going to kill him. He said that he never wanted to go through something like that again; but the more he thought about it. the angrier he got, and now all he wanted was revenge.

Manny was also informed that it was possible that his life could be in danger if this operation proved to be successful. The Federal Witness Protection program was also explained to him and how the program worked. At this point Manny refused to get involved in it, but asked to keep that option open in the event things started to get a little sticky in the future.

All we had to do now was wait for Manny to get a phone call from Jimmy LaValley to meet him somewhere. At that point we would get Manny wired up and be ready to go. The worse part of this whole thing was the waiting for the call, Manny was understandably getting a little more jittery as every day passed, which was not good. Finally LaValley called and told Manny to meet him in a parking lot of the Gossage grill, which was located on North Avenue just past Harlem Avenue that night. This happened to be in River Forest, Illinois, and located next to a gas station, which could give us a good spot to set up surveillance on the parking lot so we could cover Manny. Manny was rigged with the tape recorder, and he was given a code word to use in case he felt that he was going to be seriously injured or killed. I've got to hand it to Manny; he never used it even though at one point he thought LaValley was going to cut his throat. We had been set up in a van where we could keep Manny in view while we were recording the conversation between LaValley and Manny. I must admit that was a little nerve wracking watching LaValley, who was six foot two, 220 pounds, standing over Manny who was about five foot seven, 150 pounds. I can imagine how Manny was feeling. It was a hot night at the end of July, 1988, and that damn van was hotter than hell; we were all sweating, but not as much as Manny. At one point in the conversation, LaValley had threatened to stab Manny if he didn't hand over his driver's license. Manny was pleading with LaValley and even told him about his mother that was dying of cancer, that didn't do any good either and LaValley hit Manny in the face breaking his nose. Any second we expected to hear Manny give the code word *chocolate*, and we were ready to jump all over LaValley, but it never came. LaValley kept yelling at Manny about how he had cheated them, and that he had better come up with the $130,000 or, he was finished.

At one point I got nervous thinking, what if LaValley whacked Manny right in front of us that would really look good on the video tape, wouldn't it? Needless to say, Manny survived that scary night and lived to get his revenge, everything was on tape and LaValley was now looking at twenty years in the joint. When the tape was played in court at LaValleys hearing, it was so dramatic that the news media played it on the 10:00 PM news, which was really scary to listen to, and gave the public an idea of how the outfit works in Chicago.

8-16-90.

Gambler's pleas during beating heard on tape played in court

By John Gorman

In a dramatic tape played in federal court Wednesday, a debt-ridden gambler was heard begging for mercy as he apparently was being beaten by a mob enforcer in a River Forest gas station.

"Please, please, I'm doing the best I can," cried the gambler, identified as "debtor Number 3" by FBI special agent John O'Rourke.

The debtor's beating on July 7, 1988 was tape-recorded by FBI agents, whom the gambler had turned to for help when he was threatened by a mob enforcer, O'Rourke testified during a bond hearing for James F. LaValley, 46, of 5054 N. Delphia Ave., Chicago, and James William Bollman, 44, of 369 Mensching Ave., Roselle.

O'Rourke said he and other FBI agents and Chicago police watched and listened nearby as the debtor cried out in pain twice when the enforcer punched him.

Prosecutors charge that the 6 foot, 225-pound LaValley was the man attacking the 5-foot, 4-inch tall debtor.

"We had given him a codeword to use to use [to summon help] if he thought he was going to be seriously harmed," O'Rourke testified.

The debtor and another gambler had cheated a north and west suburban sports betting operation allegedly run by Bollman of an estimated $117,000, O'Rourke said. Bollman owns the Boulevard Tap Lounge, 297 S. McClean Blvd., Elgin.

In the bond hearing before U.S. Magistrate Joan Gottschall, O'Rourke also said that LaValley slashed the hand of a bartender who was $4,000 in debt to the betting operation.

Under questioning by Assistant U.S. Atty. Chris Gair, O'Rourke said that in late 1988, the bartender was accosted at the country club where he worked and ordered to deliver the money after the debtor was taken to an empty pro shop.

"LaValley struck him in the face, knocked him to the ground, beat him and stomped on him," O'Rourke continued. "Then he grabbed him by the left hand and slashed him with a knife behind the fingers. Blood began to spurt and gush from his hand."

Bollman allegedly took over the bookmaking operations of Joseph Pascucci after Pascucci was jailed at the Metropolitan Correctional Center, O'Rourke said. LaValley and Bollman were both arrested Tuesday and held overnight at the Metropolitan Correctional Center.

Over the objections of Matthew Lydon, LaValley's attorney, O'Rourke testified that LaValley, a convicted burglar, was connected with the Chicago crime syndicate. Bollman has no prior arrest record, O'Rourke said.

The hearing is scheduled to continue Thursday.

```
The truth of the matter is Manny was my informant andI· decided
to introduce him to FBI Agents Tom Noble and Jack O'rourke. I
talked Manny into cooperating with the FBI and to wear a wire
so we could nail the bad guys real good. Manny was a little
aprehensive about doing this but cooperated anyway. Manny Fred`
was a gutsy little guy and made a meet with the mobster Jimmy
LaValley near North Ave. and Harlem in a parking lot. Manny was
promised that we would be near by and nothing would happen to him
This meeting was video taped and recorded in cluding LaValley
hitting Manny in the face and threatening to stab him. Of course
when the facts of this case came out you would not have known that
the Chicago Police had anything to do with it. 'What else is new?'
```

Jimmy LaValley had always been known as a standup guy in the outfit, but when he realized the fact that he could go away for twenty years he jumped ship and became a federal informant to save his own ass.

Jimmy LaValley

He pleaded guilty to extortion charges and became one hell of an informant against the mob. He described how vicious Lenny Patrick was and how Patrick reported to Gus Alex, who had been the top mob fixer for the past thirty years. He even testified against his partner Jim Bollman. Bollman who was a Tavern owner in Elgin ran a large scale bookmaking operation and was with Jimmy LaValley on several occasions when they kicked and beat gamblers to collect money from them. On another occasion they threatened a gambler with castration if he didn't pay $150,000 that he owed Bollman.

LaValley testified in court that he was a burglar and was convicted of that crime when he was twenty-one, but did not become involved with the Chicago Outfit until he was forty-two; that's when he became a muscleman for the mob. LaValley who testified in the trial of Ernest

"Rocky" Infelise and four others said that it was his nature of refusing to take no for an answer when he was collecting money for the mob got him scolded from Salvatore "Solly D." Delaurentis, who was a Lake County mob boss. Solly D. told him that he was causing heat and to forget about the debt. LaValley admitted that his reputation often preceded him in the collection of mob debts. DeLaurentis was represented by, Bruce Cutler, who was John Gotti's attorney in New York City. Cutler had been very successful in getting Gotti out of three previous trials in New York in recent years. When I testified for the prosecution about numerous mob gambling operations we had broken up that belonged to Rocky Infelise, Bruce Cutler cross-examined me about my experience in making gambling arrests he became very dramatic as he always does. At the time I had been on the job for thirty-six years and had made over four thousand gambling raids and arrested hundreds of bad guys, so when I informed him of that he dropped the subject and told the judge that he had no more questions for me. When I left the stand, I looked at Cutler and he gave me a wink and half a smile, old Bruce was quite an actor all right.

While the trial was going on, my man in Las Vegas, Zeke, was requested to testify at LaValley and Bollman's hearing about the visit that LaValley and Bollman had paid him in Las Vegas many months before. The FBI had paid for his air transportation and hotel, but they didn't give Zeke any other spending money. When Zeke got in town he called me and I met him at Midway airport and he got a room at a motel across the street. Zeke told me that the FBI had promised him a certain amount of money for his cooperation and for being an informant in this case, but they reneged and said that they couldn't spare any money at that time. Zeke became very upset, because he felt that he was instrumental in identifying LaValley and Bollman at the beginning of this case which helped bring down Infelise, DeLaurentis, and the rest of there street crew. He felt that he risked great bodily harm to himself and his family in doing so. Then he told me that it was to dangerous for him to stay in Chicago and the fucking G sure as hell wasn't going to help him at all, so fuck them and the horse they rode in on. Zeke then booked passage on the first flight to Las Vegas, we shook hands and I told him that he did a hell of a job and one of these days I would be out to see him.

In my opinion, Manny and Zeke both showed that they had a lot of courage, and when the shit hit the fan, they did what they had to do and were very instrumental in taking on the Chicago Outfit, and beating them. James Bollman was sentenced to four years in prison, James LaValley received seven years and seven months. LaValley's time would probably be served on some military installation or other federal facility. U.S. District Judge Brian Duff, who issued LaValley's sentence, expressed grudging admiration of the turncoat mobster LaValley, who had pleaded guilty to extortion charges and admitted that he had stabbed, beat or burned with a cigarette numerous victims. U.S. Attorney's Mark Vogel and Chris Gair said that the transformation from a violent street hoodlum to a government witness was a remarkable development. LaValley's keen memory for details and the ability to articulate facts concerning mob operations was invaluable to the prosecution. But we must remember the fact that if LaValley hadn't been caught between a rock and a hard place due to the efforts of Manny and Zeke, he never would been put in a position where he had to become an informant for the government.

LaValley's information has helped indict or convict nearly a dozen members of organized crime in the Midwest. LaValley continued to cooperate in a grand jury probe of the outfit and he also testified in the trial of Gus Alex, who was a top mob figure for years in the Chicago area.

Chapter 46

Mob's Floating Crap Game

The Chicago mob's floating crap game probably ranked as the longest continuously running gambling enterprises in America, predating the legalized glitz of Las Vegas and Atlantic City. Since the mid-1930s, the game has drawn cosmopolitan clientele, with millionaire stockbrokers rubbing elbows with truck drivers, off-duty cops, judges, show-business personalities, restaurant owners, and convicted felons. Just like the Water Tower, the game has weathered the years well; its roots securely planted in the Capone era when the game had virtual immunity from arrest for at least the first twenty years of its existence. The game changed locations from Chicago to the suburbs two or three times a week and was very difficult to find. Usually, the game was set up in an industrial area in the suburbs so that the residents in the area would not be suspicious of a lot of traffic all hours of the night. One location the game was set up in was in an old warehouse where the mob provided underground parking.

I became aware of the game when an informant of mine told me that there was a huge crap game run by the outfit in the Chinatown area on the South Side of Chicago. He explained that the game was moved constantly to avoid detection by the police. Currently, the game was only open on Monday and Tuesday night, he said, and that there were lookouts with walkie-talkies in the area to warn the bad guys who ran the game of any impending raid. The informant also told me that he had never been to the game himself, but had heard some of his outfit friends talking about it when they had a little too much to drink. I asked him to ask his friends where the game was. He looked at me as if I was goofy by asking him to do that and said, "Sure, Sarge, I'll ask them and then the game gets hit, and they remember who had inquired about the game, and then I get hit. No chance, Sarge, my mother didn't raise a fool." By the way he said he thought he overheard them say that the game had some protection somewhere. I asked, "Just what the hell does that mean?" "Beats me," he said. "That's your problem, good-bye and good luck."

    My partner Carlo Cangelosi and I started looking through Chinatown for some kind of clue that would lead us to the game. It was the fall of 1982 and it was getting cold out at night, but what the hell, we could only look on Monday and Tuesday night, so it wasn't that bad. We tried walking through the area, eliminating a lot of the residential areas because we figured it would be too hard for the players to park their cars on side streets. The walking part was OK for a while, but we decided that riding would be a little better; they gave us a car, so it would be a shame not to use it. After about six weeks of scouring the area every Monday and Tuesday night, we finally got lucky. It's called being in the right place at the right time. We had stopped in an Italian restaurant on Thirty-first Street at Wentworth Avenue to get an Italian beef sandwich; as things turned out, we weren't the only ones that had a taste for a beef sandwich. While we were in the place, the guy behind the counter got a phone call for an order for twenty beef sandwiches and ten sausage sandwiches. It was 11:30 on Monday night, so being smart cops, we figured that some Chinese restaurant in the neighborhood was switching to Italian food or that there were thirty hungry crap shooters in the area. We left the restaurant and waited for somebody to come and pick up the order, so we could tail them. After about ten minutes, some wise-looking guy with a black leather jacket on, wearing a cap on his head, and smoking a very big cigar walked down the street, entered the restaurant, and picked up the order. He apparently was a friend of the counterman because when he left, they gave each other a hug and a big smile. We thought that the wannabee-wise-guy had parked his car around the corner because he was cautious in case there was any heat in the neighborhood. Forget about it; all he did was walk up to the first alley and go north to the end of the rear door of a store that was on the corner. The store's windows had been painted so there was no way to see inside from the street. This had to be the place where the game was; all we had to do now was to try and spot the lookout that had a walkie-talkie. Sure as hell, there was a guy sitting in a yellow van parked in a Shell gas station at 215 West Thirty-first Street, which was across the street from the game. He wasn't a very good lookout because it looked as if he was reading a newspaper and not paying attention to his surroundings, which was OK with us.

It was a good thing that it was winter and dark out, because the neighborhood we were in was mostly Italian, and it was a very difficult area to watch anything for any length of time because somebody would spot you; and that would be the end of it. From our vantage point, we were able to observe some guys leaving the store by the back door and walk down the alley. Other players would enter the store from the back also; no one would use the front door.

I remembered what my informant had told me about whoever was running the game had a friend that was in a position to warn them of an impending raid. I assumed that the unknown friend was probably in the gambling unit, as we were probably the only unit that would handle this type of work. Carlo and I did not want to take any chances of blowing this investigation if my informant was right, so I asked him if he would make an anonymous telephone call to the intelligence unit who could handle this type of raid if necessary. I instructed him who to ask for in the intelligence unit and to tell them about where the game was and all the other facts we had uncovered. I also told him to tell the lieutenant he was talking not to tell any other unit about any raid that they would make at 246 West Thirty-first Street on Chicago's South Side.

Carlo and I were conveniently off on January 11, 1983, at 10:30 PM when the crap game was raided by the intelligence unit. They broke down the door to get in the storefront where they caught thirty-two guys in the place. The first thing they did was take down the guy sitting in the yellow van with his walkie-talkie before he could give any warning to the guys in the game. They confiscated dice, point cards, poker chips walkie-talkies, and U.S. currency. The game was run by the outfit guys who worked for Angelo LaPietra, who has been a longtime mob gambling overseer. LaPietra was among thirteen reputed Mafia bosses awaiting trial in Kansas City, Missouri, on federal charges that they skimmed $2 million from a Las Vegas casino. He was found guilty of that offense and sentenced long term in a federal penitentiary.

We were happy that the game got hit and everything turned out the way we had hoped, but knowing the mob as we do, we knew damn well that the game would not be down for to long. At the beginning of April 1983, Carlo and I started snooping around on Monday and Tuesday nights again to see if our hunch was right. We tailed a known player who was busted in the game on Thirty-first Street, and guess what, he took us to another storefront which was a SAC Club at 254 West Twenty-sixth Street. These guys really got scared when they got busted a couple of months ago, didn't they? Forget about it. After finding the game was back in full swing, we had to try and locate the lookout they had in the area. Sure as hell, a red van kept driving around the neighborhood, but we were sure this guy would be more alert than the other guy who was supposed to be watching for the cops on Thirty-first Street. We checked out the back of the building the club was located in, and we saw that the back windows and rear door were all boarded up with plywood so no one would be able to get out the back door when he hit the place.

I informed my lieutenant about what we had uncovered and where the game was. The lieutenant said that we had better tell the commander about the game being up again. I explained that there was a lookout driving around the area in a van with a walkie-talkie and that the game would probably be tough to get near. The commander said he heard a rumor that some game was up and that there could be some politicians and policemen playing in the game. After discussing the situation further, it was decided that if there were police and politicians in the game, they were pretty stupid and deserved to get arrested. After another week of surveillance of the club, it appeared that all the players were getting in the place through the front door. That figured, because the back door was boarded up and they couldn't get in that way, which would make things a little easier for us, that's for sure. The front door was glass and appeared to be a two-way mirror as you couldn't see in the place. We had enough for a search warrant, so I decided to go on April 18, 1983, a Monday night.

We kept the club under surveillance for about an hour and counted twenty-one guys enter the place through the front door. A man was inside the front door and opened the door, which was locked, when a player would knock on the door. Carlo and I had split up, and our plan was to try and get in whenever a player would show up and knock on the door. We would be walking down the sidewalk from opposite directions, and with luck we would be close enough to get in the door with the player and grab the doorman before he could give a warning to the bad guys. We had six other men from the gambling unit set up close by, and we could tell them to come on in after we were in. The plan worked perfect, and Carlo and I got lucky and were close by when a player knocked on the door, and when it was opened we grabbed both guys and called for our backup.

When we got inside the club, we found that it was empty; all there was in the place were some tables and chairs, a couch, a television set, a kitchen sink, and a metal wardrobe closet. There were photos of famous Italian sports heroes on the walls as well as a blown up picture of Al Capone sitting in a box seat in a ball park. I thought that they were probably in the basement, and I started looking for a door leading to the basement. I asked the two guys we had in custody where all the other guys went. All they said was, "What guys? I didn't see any guys come in here." I looked in the wardrobe closet to see if their coats were hanging up in it. It was as empty as the clubroom, but one thing about the cabinet caught my attention, it was about four inches off the floor. When I looked closer I could see that part of the wall was cut along the sides of the cabinet. I found a latch on the side, turned it, and pulled on the cabinet; it swung open. The damn thing was on hinges. At that point I sent a couple of guys around the back just in case and told them to watch for anything. Behind the cabinet was a doorway that had just been built, and a plywood door, which led to a back room, was locked from the other side. It was sledgehammer time; we beat in the door and caught fifteen guys in the back room, with a crap table, point cards, dice, and U.S. currency still on the table. Apparently, they never knew that we were in the front of the club trying to find them when they were shooting dice. There was also a kitchen in the rear where they had sandwiches, beer, pop, and cigars.

We made another discovery at the back. The windows that were boarded up from the outside were also on hinges so that the players could have gotten out the back way if they had heard us in the front. I guess you can never be too sure about what you see. It goes back to the old rule: always expect the unexpected. This time we got lucky; it sure would have been embarrassing if we had come up empty-handed. There weren't any politicians or policemen in the game either – case closed.

After being involved in breaking up the floating crap game two times in the city, I wondered where they were operating in the suburbs. It was against the policy of the gambling unit not to raid anything in the suburbs except wire rooms. But there wasn't any rule that I knew of which prevented me from nosing around on my own time in the suburbs just to see if the game was up again. Every now and then, I would take a look at some of the people who I knew had been going to the game in the city. Who knows, maybe I would get lucky again and find out where they were operating. I knew that the game opened up on Friday night and also on Sunday in the suburbs. I started to follow a guy who drove a car with a vanity license plate Squeaks; he was a regular in the game, and after a few weeks I got lucky and followed him to a two-story warehouse at 1600 DiPrizio Drive in Melrose Park. The building was located at the end of a dead-end street, next to a set of railroad tracks. They had a lot of room for parking next to the building; they sure did pick an out-of-the-way spot to run the game. As they say today, "These guys are good." The only way it was possible to get a close look at the place was to get up on the railroad tracks, so that's what I did. That Friday night I counted forty-seven cars that drove down that dead-end street; they had a couple of lookouts with walkie-talkies, and they were sitting in a car near the end of the dead-end street. I checked the location again on Saturday, but there was no activity. But on Sunday afternoon and night, things were really rockin' and rollin'. I guess we didn't frighten anybody when we busted the game in Chicago; maybe they felt they were safer out in the boondocks.

I thought, *OK, wise guy, now that you found the game big deal, just what the hell are you going to do about it?* I knew they wouldn't let me hit the game in the suburbs, so I had to try and find another solution to handle this thing. I didn't think that the local police would be interested in the game, because they were to busy handling crime problems. The Illinois State Police were not getting involved in this type of activity either. All that was left was the sheriff's police; but from what I had heard, they didn't handle this type of gambling. I thought about another alternative. A friend of mine, Bob Wiedrich, was a well-respected reporter for the *Chicago Tribune*. I contacted him and told him about the game and where it was located. He knew the history of the game and told me that players within one-hundred-mile radius had been coming to the game and that the mob probably made a million dollars a year running it. I explained to him that I couldn't bust the game because it was out of our jurisdiction; he couldn't understand that part of it at all. He made a suggestion that maybe the FBI would be interested in hitting the game and that the special agent in charge of the Chicago office, Ed Haggerty was a close friend of his. I said, "That sounds good to me, go for it."

    The next day Bob called me and told me that Haggerty was very interested in the game because it belonged to the mob and was run by Jackie Cerone, a top echelon member of the syndicate. Bob said that he told Haggerty not to drive down the one-way street or go near the building because they might have lookouts during the day even though the game wasn't operating. At this point, I decided to tell my commander about the floating crap game and where it was in the suburb. He, of course, told me that we didn't have jurisdiction in the suburbs to conduct a raid; I told him that I was aware of that but maybe the FBI was looking into the game also. His only comment was, "That's up to them, Sergeant. They can go anywhere."

    That night, a Friday, Wiedrich and I got up on the railroad tracks so I could get him a better look at the game, and we were out of sight of the lookouts with the walkie-talkies. The parking lot was filled to capacity; cars were coming and going all the time. After about an hour, we got out of there and called it a night. The next Sunday, we got up on the tracks again and got the surprise of our lives. There were no cars in the parking lot, and the lights were off in the building; sure as hell, something was wrong. There were a couple of cars that parked in the lot, knocked on the door, and then left very confused. There was no mistake in my mind that the people running the game found out that there was heat on and decided not to open. The next day, Wiedrich talked to Haggerty about the game, and Haggerty said that he was so excited about hitting the game that he had to take a look at the building himself and took a ride to look over the location. Needless to say, I was really pissed off when Bob told me that. There were only four people who knew about the game – Haggerty, my commander, Wiedrich, and I. Oh well, another mystery, I guess. I'll just have to find the son of a bitch again, because they were not going to be out of business too long, that's for sure.

    Wiedrich told me that this game had been in operation for years and that in 1962 the mob moved the game to a Quonset hut, which was within two blocks of the Villa Venice nightclub near Northbrook. They wanted to cash in on a two-week appearance at the club by Frank Sinatra, Sammy Davis Jr., and Dean Martin. Fueled by the

Rat Pack's enormous popularity, the mobsters obligingly provided limousine shuttle service from the nightclub on Milwaukee Avenue to the Quonset hut on nearby River Road. During the two weeks, the mobsters reaped a $200,000 bonanza at the crap and roulette tables from the tuxedo – and evening-gown-garbed patrons. That the game was able to operate so openly came as no shock to those familiar with its operations over the years. For decades, sheriffs of three counties and local police appeared to be blind to what thousands of gambling patrons had no problems finding. The game was operated by Rocco Fischetti until his death in 1964; he was Al Capone's cousin and was the Chicago area gambling czar.

Well, here we go again, I thought, *if I find the game again, all I'm going to tell about it is my wife and six kids, well maybe Wiedrich, but I'll swear him to secrecy.* I gave them about a month to cool down before I went snooping around again. I was getting to like this snooping around stuff; it was like a challenge to me. It took me about two weeks to locate the game again; this time it was in an abandoned factory alongside another railroad embankment near Twenty-fifth Street and Lake Street in Melrose Park. A surveillance of the location revealed that the game was in operation only on Fridays and Sundays, just like the last place they had. A lookout was stationed in a black sedan outside the gate to the fenced in property, and he would have to know you or you would not get through the gate. He also had a walkie-talkie in his hand at all times. The license plates of the vehicles that frequented the game revealed that some of the players lived as far away as Antioch, Rockford, and Hammond, Indiana. At one point I had to park my car near the entrance of the block-long driveway with my hood up and a jack under my rear bumper and fake car trouble so I could get license plates of some of the players. The eight-foot-high metal lattice fence that surrounded the Mafia's premier floating crap game made it difficult to see clearly into the area where the game was being held. It was necessary for Wiedrich and I to get up on the railroad embankment, which would give us cover; and we could look directly down on the entrance and could even hear conversation between the lookout and people arriving to the game.

One night while I was up on the embankment, a couple of freight trains passed by me while I was trying to hide in some weeds. I guess someone spotted me and called the railroad police. All at once, two guys came out of the other side of the tracks and told me not to move and get my hands up. They identified themselves as railroad dicks and wanted to know what I was doing up on the tracks at 1:00 AM in the morning. I had no choice but to show them my police identification and told them that I was on undercover assignment watching for a couple of burglars who were supposed to be going to make a factory on the other side of the tracks. They finally put their weapons away and told me that an engineer on a passing train had spotted me on the tracks and that's when he called the railroad police. Luckily, the lookout didn't hear any of this conversation going on between me and the railroad dicks, so everything was still cool.

Syndicate's roving dice game roles into suburban hideouts

By Bob Wiedrich

A LOOKOUT guarding a crime syndicate dice game in Melrose Park jumped from his car when the first of a series of aerial bombs from a nearby neighborhood festival exploded overhead.

The fireworks illuminated the parking lot of the abandoned factory in which the game was operating at capacity, turning night into day as carloads of patrons arrived. From a railroad embankment across the street, the lookout could be observed identifying players as they emerged from their cars before admitting them. Those with whom he appeared more familiar were waved through.

The lookout lounged in his black sedan, parked just inside the gate of an 8-foot-high, metal lattice fence that safeguards the Mafia's premier Chicago-area crap game at its well-disguised location in the western suburb.

Hidden in a four-square-block industrial park near 25th Avenue and Ike Street, the game reaps at least $1 million tax free a year for crime syndicate keepers, according to sources familiar with the operation.

TO ACCOMMODATE customers from at least a 50-mile radius, the game used to float between the city and several western suburbs, operating six days a week until last

La Pietra   Cerone

year, when Chicago police raided the operation twice.

Its city locations then were abandoned in favor of the suburbs, first in another Melrose Park industrial building and later in a Stone Park motel. It switched to its present location several months ago, the sources said.

In a series of surveillances over several weeks, the game was found to be open only two days a week, an apparent consequence of pressure from law enforcement attempts to pinpoint it. Patrons were observed entering and leaving the building on Friday nights and Sunday afternoons and evenings.

Investigators say the dice game has operated for at least a decade in the city and suburbs, but it has been raided only in Chicago.

WHILE IN Chicago, investigators report, the game operated under the auspices of Angelo La Pietra, 64, whom they identified as a longtime mob gambling overseer. La Pietra is among 13 reputed Mafia bosses awaiting trial in Kansas City, Mo., on federal charges that they skimmed $2 million from a Las Vegas casino.

The suburban locations, investigators said, are operated by James Cerone, 64, a cousin of Jackie Cerone, 69, identified as the Chicago mob's second-in-command.

Jackie Cerone is also among those awaiting trial with La Pietra in Kansas City. Both Cerones were sentenced to five years in federal prison in 1970 after being convicted of conspiring with others to operate a multimillion-dollar-a-year interstate gambling ring.

The game is difficult to find and even more difficult to observe. Its location is a closely guarded secret among players.

The game's new location is along a dead-end drive serving the industrial park. The area is deserted at night and on weekends, making it easy to detect snoopers.

ON A RECENT night, an estimated 60 to 70 customers were observed pulling up in cars, some of them carrying as many as three or four male passengers.

A check of license plate numbers of some of the cars led to Chicago's

Continued on page 6, this section

City/suburbs   Chicago Tribune, Sunday, July 29, 1984

A dice game set-up as it was discovered by police after a raid last year at a social and athletic club on West 26th Street. In keeping with the floating game's tradition, the dice are thrown on a rug instead of on a more costly and less mobile crap table, an investigator said.

Dice game

Continued from page 1, this section

Northwest Side, as well as Bensenville, Schiller Park, Elmwood Park, Villa Park and Antioch. Three of the patrons identified were among 32 arrested at the game in Chicago in January, 1983.

In keeping with the game's tradition, the dice are thrown on a rug instead of on a more costly and less mobile crap table, an investigator said. "That way, they can roll up the rug and move in minutes," he said.

"That has occurred in the past, he said, when undercover investigators were suspected to be in the area. Lookouts use walkie talkies to communicate with confederates in the game.

Patrons play against the house. So do customers who make side bets on the roll of the dice. "Some players never touch the dice," the investigator said.

ALSO PRESENT are as many as three crime-syndicate loan sharks to extend instant credit at interest rates of 25 percent a week, he said.

The four to five employees of the game always pick up the dice after every throw to make certain no customer has substituted them with loaded cubes.

A metal lattice fence surrounds a suburban Melrose Park industrial area, site of the Mafia's premier Chicago-area dice game. The game takes place in the building located behind the two trailers.

A metal lattice fence surrounds a suburban Melrose Park industrial area, site of the Mafia's premier Chicago-area dice game. The game takes place in the building located behind the two trailers.

Wiedrich suggested that it would be nice if we could take a few photos of the building the game was in as well as the lookout and some of the players that were going to the game. He said that he had a photographer from the *Tribune* whom he had worked with before and had a camera that could take pictures in the dark. I thought that it was a good idea; maybe we could get a shot of Jimmy "Tar Baby" Cerone when he went in the game. Jimmy was the cousin of Jackie Cerone, who was in a federal prison at that time. We met the photographer "Phil," and got up on the railroad embankment; we instructed him to wear dark clothes so he wouldn't be spotted while he was up on the tracks. My friend, Bob Wiedrich, was dressed as if he was going to a formal dinner – shirt, tie, and cuff links; at least his clothes were dark, so I guess that was all that mattered. There happened to be a few freight cars parked near the entrance to the game, so Phil the cameraman was able to get on top of one of the cars where he had a great view of lookout and the front gate.

While he was on top on one of the cars, Wiedrich and I were sneaking around the weeds trying to overhear talk between the lookout and two other guys who were standing around talking to him. All of a sudden, we heard a lot of loud explosions and rockets flying in the air. It seemed that there was an Italian feast going on not to far away, and they always blew off a lot of fireworks. It sure shocked the hell out of us. I think Phil almost fell off the top of the freight car he was standing on. We decided to call it a night and got the hell out of there. Wiedrich had enough for his story about the floating crap game, and now we would also have photographs to go along with it. The story would appear in the paper the next day, so nothing mattered now. I had my son Don print a six-by-four-foot sign on white plasterboard that said in big red letters NOTICE – "CRAP – GAME," with eight red letters and a red arrow pointing at the building where the game was. It also gave the time the game opened – "Friday and Sunday, with refreshments and loans on the premises, J. Cerone – Proprietor." That night when we were leaving, I nailed the sign up on a telephone pole at the entrance of the driveway leading to the secret crap game.

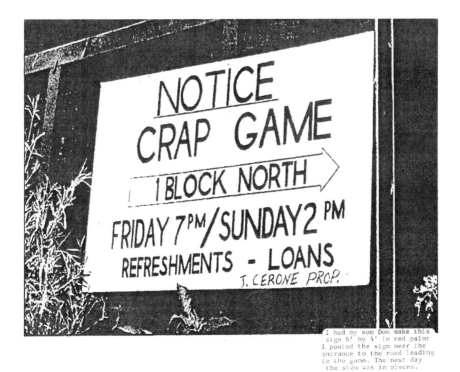

I had my son Don make this sign 6' by 4' in red paint I posted the sign near the entrance to the road leading to the game. The next day the sign was in pieces.

The next day Wiedrich did his story, and it hit the front page of the *Tribune*, including the sign that was posted. Everything was great except that the photographer forgot to put film in his camera; due to all the excitement, he said he just got nervous. Wiedrich explained the sign by saying that possibly a disgruntled player decided to give police a little help in finding the game. I still remained anonymous and the game was put out of business. Driving by the location the next day, I saw that the sign had been broken up into little pieces. Oh well, that's show business.

I really felt good about putting that game down and didn't even give it another thought for about six months. I started to get curious again and wondered if the game was up or maybe they went out of business forever. Are you kidding me? After two days, I found the game again, believe it or not; and it was still going full blast. It probably never went down at all. I was just kidding myself. This time it was in Maywood, Illinois, in a warehouse at 140 South Seventh Avenue.

The warehouse had underground parking, which was always good because no one would think anything was suspicious if they didn't see a lot of cars around.

MAYWOOD, ILLINOIS — ANOTHER PLACE THE MOB USED FOR — THE MIDWEST BIGGEST CRAP GAME

There was also a lookout posted inside the parking lot who opened the garage door for the players as they arrived. I called Wiedrich again and said, "Guess what?" He guessed it right away and said, "I'm on the way." I was using my own car for this surveillance, which was not a good idea; but that's all I had so I had to make the best of it. I picked him up a few blocks away and drove to a vacant lot that was about the only place to get a good look at the entrance to the warehouse. We copied a lot of license numbers down, and some were the same people that had been at the other locations. While we were watching the building, we noticed a jeep had been in the area a couple of times going around the block; we got out of there and decided to come back on Sunday night. It was the same story on Sunday. There must have been forty cars parked in the lower level of the warehouse. I was beginning to think that these guys couldn't take a hint. I called my son Don and told him that he was back in the sign business again, only this time make it four by eight feet, with some reflectors on it.

We checked the game again on Friday night, and everything was the same, including the jeep circling the block. We were about to find out who was in the jeep; the driver pulled in front of my car with his headlights on us, and he got out of the car. We could see that he was a black man and was pointing an automatic pistol at us. He said that he was a police lieutenant from Maywood and wanted to know what we were doing there.

Wiedrich explained to the lieutenant that he was a reporter for the *Chicago Tribune* and was investigating a crap game that was in progress in the warehouse across the street. Wiedrich requested that the lieutenant accompany us while we went over to the building. The lieutenant almost turned white and explained that he was off duty then but that he would inform the chief of police about it. We then asked to go to the station and talk to him, but the lieutenant said that he wasn't in now and told us to come back tomorrow. He then holstered his weapon and got the hell out of there. When Bob and I quit laughing, I got my sign and put it on the fence at the entrance to the parking lot. At one point I had an idea of grabbing the lookout and handcuff him to a streetlight, then drive his car down the ramp that led to the underground parking and throw his keys away. The overhead doors would be jammed, and the cars would not be able to get out of the

Mafia paid 2 cops off, probers told

By Bob Wiedrich

Two Maywood police officers received payoffs from the crime syndicate to serve as lookouts, often while on duty, when the mob's premiere floating crap game was held in a warehouse in the suburb, a former girlfriend of one of the officers has told authorities.

The woman, who said she routinely accompanied her boyfriend as he served as lookout, said she saw him accept the payoff money and turn over some of the cash to his alleged accomplice. She has told her story to Maywood police officials and the Cook County state's attorney's office, authorities said.

Maywood Police Chief Mac Woods said the two men, both of whom hold supervisory rank, have been subpoenaed to appear before a Cook County grand jury.

The woman, who insisted on anonymity during an interview in the office of her Loop attorney, Patrick Reilly, recounted the ritual in which her former boyfriend and his fellow officer patrolled the area of the Maywood-owned warehouse at 140 S. 7th Ave. to ensure against interference by fellow officers or by state or federal investigators who might have discovered the game's presence.

Every Friday and Sunday night for nearly a year, she said, the two police officers took turns patrolling the square block perimeter of the warehouse, checking on suspicious cars and monitoring police calls.

"I had a relationship with one of the officers from 1983 until the spring of 1985," she said. "I rode frequently with him on his patrols of the warehouse for nearly six months during 1984 and 1985."

Between them, she said, the officers divided equally the hours between 7 p.m. and 5 a.m., when the dice game attracted scores of players on the two nights a week that it operated.

The building, which is two blocks west of the Maywood police station, is owned by the village and leased as a warehouse to Vincent Falzone, a local resident.

In exchange for the patrols, she said, her former boyfriend received $1,000 from the gamblers and paid $200 of that to the officer he had recruited as an assistant for the mob moonlighting job.

Through her statements authorities said they are gaining a rare insight into how crime syndicate gangsters have been able to operate the crap game for more than 10 years in different parts of the Chicago area with almost complete immunity from po-

basement. I wouldn't do that, or would I? Weidrich told me that he found out that the lieutenant and a sergeant were the official mobile lookouts for the crap game and that the syndicate was paying them to provide that service. A girlfriend of the sergeant told Wiedrich that she often accompanied him while he was patrolling the area around the warehouse. She also said that the officers divided equally the hours between 7:00 PM and 5:00 AM when the dice game attracted scores of players on the two nights a week that it operated. She also said that she saw him accept payoff money and turn over some of the cash to an alleged accomplice; she also requested anonymity and was in fear of bodily harm. Wiedrich's story appeared on the front page again the next day. That morning I took a ride in my car to see if anything happened to the sign I put up. It appeared that someone was angry because the sign was in a hundred pieces all over the lot. Mission accomplished for now, but I think we will be back again.

Almost two years passed before I had a chance to see what was happening with our floating crap game. Up to this point, the only person who knew that I was the main culprit in heating up the game was Bob Wiedrich. I didn't know what would happen if any of my bosses found out about my vigilante work; they would probably think I was getting goofy.

After some more tracking and trailing, I got lucky again and found that the game had now set up in a one-story warehouse near Van Buren and Madison streets, across the street from a senior citizen's retirement home on the west edge of Forest Park.

It was difficult to keep the place under surveillance because of its location, so I got an idea to check out the retirement home with my wife under the ruse that we were looking for a place for an old retired uncle. We checked it out during the day, and I was able to take pictures of the warehouse across the street while my wife was keeping the manager of the home busy. I needed a room on the east side of the home, and Wiedrich was going to set up a video camera in the room to tape the activity going on across the street in the warehouse. No such luck; there were no rooms available so that the idea went down the drain, back to the drawing board.

I again called Wiedrich and filled him in on our new spot; he said that it sure took you long enough to find the damn game again. "I'm with you pal, only kidding," he said. We watched the game off and on for about two weeks, and everything was the same until one night when we passed by the place on a Friday night, we didn't see any cars in the parking lot next to the warehouse. It was a Friday night, and the place should have been jumping, but it wasn't; there was only one car in the lot and it didn't look as if anybody was around the place at all. I was still using my own car, but I had taken the license plate off the front so there was only a 50 percent chance somebody would get my license number if anyone became suspicious of us. We watched the place for about an hour, and I told Wiedrich that I was going to pull across the street and get a closer look at the building; maybe there was a fire in it or something. When I drove into the parking lot, a guy who had been sitting in his beat-up Chevy jumped out and asked us what we wanted. Obviously, he had never seen us before and seemed a little leery of us. I just asked him what we wanted to know, "We're here for the game, where is it?" He asked me my name and I told him, "Jimmy, I'm a good friend of Joey Morabito." He said, "You a friend of Joey's, okay. I had to check you out, you know." He said his name was Carmine. Wiedrich and I couldn't believe it, but here was a lookout for the biggest crap game in town guiding us, a cop and a reporter, to the new location of the game. Carmine drove to an industrial complex at Hannah and Harrison streets in Forest Park.

When he got out of his car, he pointed to a warehouse across the street and told us that we could get in through the back door of the building. I gave Carmine a $20 bill and thanked him for all his help; all he said was, "Keep your voices down because a cop lives down the street and doesn't like too much noise." Carmine was smiling from ear to ear with his $20 stuck in his pocket, and drove away. I asked Wiedrich if he was going to write about our meeting with Carmine; he said, "Are you kidding me?"

I was wondering how Carmine was going to be treated by his bosses when they find out he personally took us to the game.

The new location was a three-story warehouse with parking in the rear. But the game operators started using a shuttle service to get players to the game. They wanted to reduce the number of vehicles in the neighborhood, so they shuttled them in. There was a CTA parking lot at the northeast side of Harrison Street and Harlem Avenue, which was in Oak Park. The players were instructed to park their cars in the lot, and they would be shuttled to the crap game in other vehicles. I got a video camera and borrowed a van from a friend of mine and videotaped how the shuttle service operated in the CTA parking lot; this was really getting to be kind of interesting. This would really be a great raid, I thought, if only they would let me do it. I kind of hinted at another game that was

Mob's craps game rolled snake eyes

After 6 months, gambling vanishes

By Bob Wiedrich

Gambling patrons were milling around the street when the Chicago crime syndicate's premier floating craps game unexplainably shut down in Forest Park.

At the bar of a nearby restaurant, several disgruntled players speculated that "heat" from the police investigation of the gangland-style shooting of Teamsters official Dominic Senese might have prompted the mob to suspend the lucrative game.

"They could've left somebody to tell us what's doing," a player complained.

For at least six months, the craps game had been flourishing on Friday, Sunday and Monday nights in the western suburb, alternating between two locations and catering to patrons from within a 100-mile radius of Chicago.

At times, the numbers of patrons pulling in and out of adjacent parking lots caused passing uniformed police squads to hit their brakes to avoid accidents.

But the unusual nocturnal traffic flow failed to alert patrolling officers that something might be amiss, an investigator said.

On some nights, as many as 60 players crowded into the game at a single time, filling parking lots to overflowing.

An entire evening's patronage often totaled a hundred or more, an investigator estimated.

At first, the game operated in a one-story, warehouse-type building near Van Buren and Madison Streets, less than a mile from the Forest Park police station and across the street from a senior citizens' retirement home on the west edge of Forest Park.

Then several weeks ago, the game abruptly shifted to an alternate site in an industrial complex at Hannah and Harrison Streets, this time a half-block from a Park District Police facility.

It was while at this location that the game closed its doors in late January without warning customers, causing a minor traffic jam as players abandoned their cars on the street and pounded on the doors to no avail.

A mob institution, investigators say the crap game has floated from city to suburban locations for more than 25 years, generating an estimated $1 million a year for mob coffers.

After the game was twice raided by Chicago detectives five years ago, however, operations were transferred exclusively to the suburbs, where the gamblers believe police are less sophisticated in detecting the types of closely guarded facilities favored by the mob.

As at previous locations in Maywood and Stone Park, lookouts equipped with walkie-talkie radios were stationed outside the game in Forest Park to safeguard against police.

Investigators spotted more guards lurking behind windows partially blocked by cardboard.

"We're not going to tolerate it," declared Forest Park Police Chief Robert Conklin after being informed that the game had been operating in his town. He said he had been unaware of its presence. But he added:

"We were a little suspicious [of the Van Buren Street] location because there were so many cars there at night."

But, he said, local police made no investigation.

During weeks of surveillance of the two locations, investigators identified players frequenting the game from as far away as Rockford, as well as Chicago and a score of suburbs.

Several weeks ago, a player lost more than $25,000 in the high-stakes game, an informant reported.

And on several nights, the informant said, an off-duty north suburban police officer joined the crowds of patrons, who ranged from blue-collar workers to professionals.

To accommodate patrons, mob loan sharks were on hand to offer on-the-spot credit at interest rates of about 25 percent a week. Some customers played against the house while others made side bets, the informant said.

After the game moved to the Harrison Street complex, a mob lackey named Carmine was posted outside the game's previous site on Van Buren Street to direct customers to the new location.

Whenever a carload of customers arrived, he would lead them in his car to the game, after first questioning them to establish their credentials in an effort to screen out undercover investigators.

Unfortunately for his bosses, Carmine failed.

By claiming friendship with one of the game's most devoted players, an investigator persuaded Carmine to lead him to the Harrison Street site.

"Who do you know?" Carmine asked. "Sam Morbito," was the reply. "You a friend of Sam, okay," he said. "What's your name? I gotta check you out." "Jimmy," he was told. "Oh, okay, follow me," Carmine said.

After guiding the investigator, Carmine gratefully pocketed a $20 tip, then warned him to hold down his voice because "a cop lives down the block from here and doesn't like too much noise."

In keeping with that admonition, the game's operators started using several cars the next night to shuttle players between the game and a CTA parking lot at Harlem Avenue and Harrison Street to reduce the number of autos in the area.

A few days later, the game was gone for reasons known only to its operators.

going on in a suburb and asked if I could bust it; same answer, no way. At this point in time, I was getting a little desperate to get somebody to bust the game, so I talked to a friend of mine in DEA, Tom Thompson, and told him that I had heard there was a guy selling cocaine in a game in Forest Park. I would trust Tom with my life and knew that he would never say anything about the game to anybody. He looked over a list of names I had of the people who had been going to the game, and he happened to know one of them, who turned out to be an informant of his. He said he would find out if they were selling dope in the game, and if they were, he would get a warrant and hit it. After a few days, Tom called me and told me that he had enough probable cause to get a search warrant for dope, but if there were any other violations going on in the place, of course, proper action would be taken.

A plan was set up to make the raid at the end of the week. In the meantime, I had kept the place under surveillance from time to time and found that this was the busiest location I had seen yet. There had to be anywhere from seventy-five to one hundred people in the place at any given time.

The night we were going to hit the game, something had gone wrong. Some players had pulled up in their cars and parked in the lot next to the warehouse; they knocked on the rear door of the warehouse, but no one would let them in. This didn't look good at all. Some of the players walked to a nearby restaurant, and they were overheard saying, "If they weren't going to have a game tonight, why the hell didn't they call us and tell us before we drove all the way over here." They could have at least left somebody around to tell us what was doing. It was quite obvious that they had gotten wind of an impending raid, but they must have just been notified because they didn't have time to tell all their customers that they were down. Oh well, shit happens, I guess. Wiedrich got his story anyway, and it was all over the *Tribune* the next day. I thought we were going to outsmart them this time and put them all in jail and bust up their crap table with a sledgehammer. There were different thoughts on why the game had gone down so suddenly. When a federal agent obtains a search warrant, he has to have it approved by an assistant U.S. attorney, and then it has to be signed by a federal judge. The usual procedure is that the U.S. attorney will contact the FBI and inquire if they are involved in an investigation at the game's location. Rumor has it that an FBI agent had an informant who liked to gamble, so he called him up and told him not to go to the crap game that night. You can imagine what the informant did with that information. It may have been an innocent thing that the FBI agent did, but he sure as hell didn't use any common sense because the whole operation got totally fucked up.

Wiedrich received a lot of phone calls at the *Chicago Tribune* from persons who refused to identify themselves; one guy told him that he blew $25,000 in the game one night. Also, he said there were three or four loan sharks at the game who were happy to borrow you money. He said they all looked as if they were in the movie *The Godfather*; the rates were about 25 percent a week. Another guy told him that there were plenty of free sandwiches and pots of steaming pasta and meat sauce.

During the Ernest "Rocky" Infelise trial, it was reported that the chief of police of Forest Park was being paid off every month by mob bosses to look the other way. At the end of the 1980s, there were changes made in the administration of the Chicago Police Department, and certain restrictions were abolished concerning gambling investigations outside of Chicago. My new commander Michael Hoke and the deputy chief of the organized crime division Joe Shaughnessy gave me the go-ahead if I could find the elusive floating crap game. Well, that's all I wanted to hear; now it was my turn to get even with the wise guys. Instead of having my son Don print another sign to nail up at the game and walk away, somebody was going to hit the shithouse.

This time I got my whole crew out to help me find the game, if it was up. Det. John "Smooth" Kohles and I found the game in another suburb, Leyden Township, Cook County, Illinois. This was an unincorporated section of Cook County, under the jurisdiction of the sheriff's police. The game was on the second floor at 11223 West Grand Avenue. The building was two stories high. On the first floor was an Italian store that sold all kinds of imported cheese, pasta, olive oil, and sausages, among other imported items. The main entrance to the building was all plate glass with two glass doors that led to the Italian store and a stairway that led up to the second floor where the crap game was. Surveillances were conducted across the street from the building, and we observed anywhere from forty to seventy men enter the building when the game was on, which was Friday and Sunday. A red curtain was placed over the inside of the plate glass entrance so that passersby could not see inside the premises.

Two lookouts were stationed inside the hallway behind the red curtain; they had cut a hole in the curtain so that they could see who was ringing the front door bell, and admit them. The players then walked up some stairs to the second floor, where the game was.

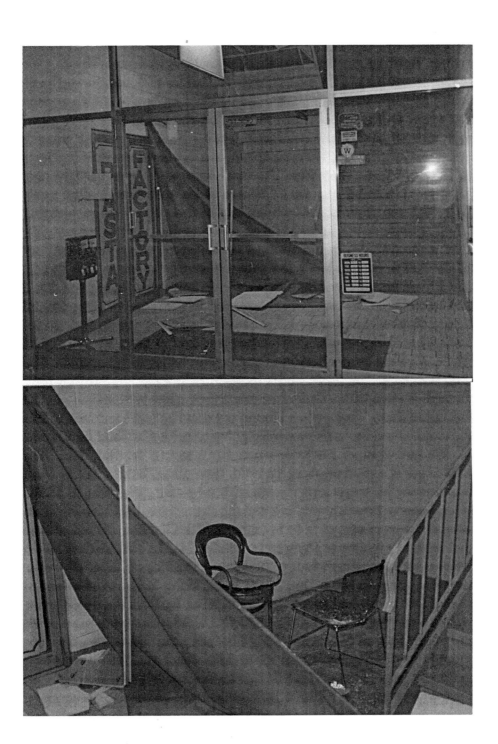

The sneaky bastards were still running a shuttle service to the game for some of the players. A guy named Vince Calvino was one of the shuttle drivers. Another guy who was shuttling players was Jamie Boyd. A lot of the players parked their cars in a lot at Twenty-fifth Avenue and Lake Street, Melrose Park. They were then picked up by the shuttle service and taken to the game. When players left the game, they were taken back to their cars. These guys were getting good at this stuff; practice makes perfect, I guess. We were able to identify two guys who had keys to the front door; they were Thomas Zizzo and Renato DiSilvestro.

It seems that Renato was a Chicago Police officer on medical leave. We wondered what his assignment was in the game; he was probably working undercover, right? I had an idea one day and I asked my wife, Gen, if she would help me out on a surveillance I was doing. I told her all she had to do was buy a few things in and Italian store. She agreed, and I took her to the Italian store, which was open during the day. I told her to keep the storeowner occupied while I tried to get up to the second floor with my camera. I just had to see what was up there so we knew what to expect when we hit the place in a few days. She did a good job keeping the owner busy, and gave me a chance to get upstairs. The door was locked up there, and it looked as if it would be tough getting through it, even with a sledgehammer. I took a few pictures and got the hell out of there. That's when I found out that she had spent over $50 in the damn store; looks like we were going to eat Italian food for a while.

We had enough probable cause for a search warrant, and John Kohles got it signed on April 12, 1989. Now all we had to worry about was keeping it a secret until the fifteenth, when we were going to hit the place. I was worried about a leak and the damn game disappearing again after all the work we put in on it. I suggested to Commander Mike Hoke that anybody who was going to be involved in the raid was not to tell anyone, including their wives, what we were working on, especially when we were going to hit it. Due to the game being in an unincorporated Cook County, we had to request a representative from the sheriff's vice unit to accompany us. The vice detective was instructed to meet us on the South Side of Chicago, a long distance away from the game. He thought we were going to raid some video poker machines somewhere in Cicero, he said later. The FBI also accompanied us on the raid.

I will admit that I was a little concerned about the game going down and we would find the building dark and empty, like the last time in Forest Park. These guys had eyes and ears all over the place, so nothing would surprise me. I told my boss, Lieutenant Stahl, that I was going out to Grand Avenue as soon as it got dark about 7:30 PM to see if everything was normal. When I got out there, the first thing I saw was the red curtain hanging inside the front hallway. There were also two cars that belonged to the shuttle drivers parked by the side of the building. I called the office and told them everything was A-OK so far, and it looked as if they were ready for business.

After midnight I counted at least forty players enter the front door after they were buzzed in by the lookout who was behind the red curtain. The only problem now was getting in as fast as we could. I suggested that we have one of the guys park an undercover van near the front entrance, and after the driver parked the van he should get out and walk away from it. There was enough room in the van for four of us; we would be in a position near the side of the building to be ready to get in the front door when some of the players would leave the game. A lookout stationed across the street could keep an eye on the front door and contact us by radio when someone was walking toward the door to leave the game. At that time we could get in and take care of the doorman before he could give a warning to people in the game. Hopefully, the door leading to the crap game on the second floor wouldn't be locked, and we could surprise them. If the door was locked, we would have to batter it down with a sledgehammer, which would cause mass confusion inside the room. Who cares, I thought, everybody in the room was going to hit the shithouse anyway. At about 1:00 am we were notified that three of the players were about to walk out the front door; we had the door to the van open, and as soon as the three came out, we grabbed them and the door man before the door closed. They were handed over to other officers who arrived; we then went up to the second floor, where we found the door open. We walked in and found a large group of men gathered around a crap table approximately twenty feet in length. No one in the room realized that the police were present and were able to observe the game for two minutes, at which time the other members of the raiding party arrived.

We observed a man we now know as Renato DiSilvestro handling the money from a "cut box" that was at the middle of the table. DiSilvestro was the Chicago Police officer on the disability pension roll.

He also was observed removing a semiautomatic pistol from the front of his belt and threw it to the floor. All the subjects were detained and placed on the wall to be searched.

Cop faces gambling charges

By Matt O'Connor

MAY 24 1989

A veteran Chicago police officer and four other people, all with alleged ties to organized crime, were indicted Tuesday on charges of running a gambling operation atop a pasta factory in western Cook County, authorities said.

Police arrested 37 patrons in a raid last month at the establishment and recovered more than $75,000 cash.

State's Atty. Cecil Partee identified the gambling operation's ringleader as Renato DiSilvestro, 46, an Austin District patrol officer who is on disability leave from the police force.

DiSilvestro, of the 5400 block of North Pioneer Avenue, was indicted by a grand jury on six counts of armed violence and seven gambling-related charges.

A Chicago Police Department spokeswoman said DiSilvestro is a 21-year veteran of the force, but she declined to disclose how long or why he has been on disability leave.

Acting on a tip, officers from the Chicago Police Department's vice control section, with the aid of Cook County sheriff's police and agents from the Federal Bureau of Investigation, raided the second floor of a building at 11223 W. Grand Ave. in unincorporated Leyden Township on April 15.

Police found James Moccio, 61, of 1255 W. Lake St., Roselle, and Thomas Zizzo, 55, of 1414 W. Flournoy St., selling poker chips at a craps table and DiSilvestro and Chris Serritella, 69, of 6306 W. 63d Pl., counting money, authorities said.

Police said Tony Mastro, 62, of 1820 N. 34th Ave., Melrose Park, guarded the door to the gambling den.

Partee said all five have ties to organized crime.

The grand jury indicted each suspect on one count of keeping a gambling place, a misdemeanor, and several felony counts of conspiracy to commit gambling.

Another Chicago Police officer was found on the premises; he was searched, and no weapon was found. He claimed that he was only observing the game and was not participating in it. A total of forty-two persons were arrested, and five of these subjects were charged with being keepers of a gambling house. Di Silvestro was one of these subjects. The other four subjects had connections with organized crime and have been arrested by me and other officers in the past.

We confiscated $75,000 in cash, thirty-six pair of dice, croupier sticks, point cards, a case of poker chips. The cut box contained $8,455. DiSilvestro told us he had no idea to whom the money belonged. The crap table was a real professional table, and it was probably the same son of a bitch I had been chasing all over Cook County in Melrose Park, Forest Park, and Maywood. It was a real pleasure breaking it up with a sledgehammer because I had been waiting a long time for that moment.

Commander Mike Hoke
smashing crap table with
his best swing

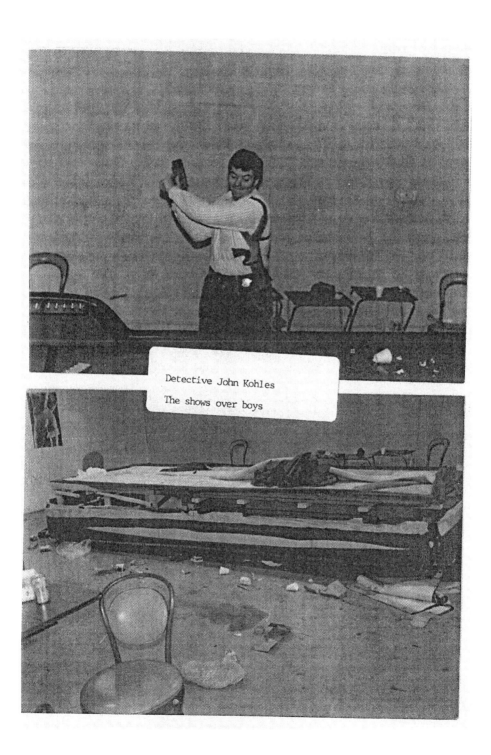

Detective John Kohles
The shows over boys

The game's operators collected from 2 to 5 percent of each pot as their end of the action. Individual bettors were wagering from as little as $25 to as much as $20,000 on a single roll of the dice. Hopefully, this raid put a crimp in their crap game operation, and they would go down for a while while they tried to figure out how they got caught. The Cook County Grand Jury indicted the five keepers of the game, which caused them a few headaches; all the other mopes went fined and went on their way. Renato DiDilvestro left the police department and had since moved to Las Vegas, where, rumor has it, he has taken over where Tony Spilotro had left off. To my knowledge, the infamous crap game has not reopened since we busted them in 1989. I would like to take credit for their demise, but to be realistic, the State of Illinois was really responsible for putting them out of business. The state issued ten riverboat licenses for casinos which allows you to gamble legally on slot machines, blackjack, and dice games, and video poker. We couldn't put them out of business by locking them up, so we legalized casino gambling. I think they finally got wind of who had been causing them aggravation all these years; at least I hope they did, it sure was fun while it lasted.

On a roll

ILLUSTRATION BY ROB PORAZINSKI

Inside the oldest established permanent floating crap game in Chicago

By Bob Wiedrich

Chicago's premiere floating crap game is like the Water Tower—a Windy City institution.

Obviously, the game is not as visible as the historic limestone pumping station, although during its nearly 60-year history, patrons have not had any trouble finding it.

Just like the Water Tower, the game has weathered the years well, its roots securely planted in the Capone-era corruption that ensured its virtual immunity from police intervention for at least the first 20 years of its existence.

Until 1959, the crap game had never been raided. Since then, it has been hit by police six times, still an enviable record among other gambling operations accustomed to suffering the occasional inconvenience of an arrest and a gentle slap on the wrist from a compassionate judge.

In its early decades, the game ranged through Will, Cook and Lake Counties, occupying spacious but thinly disguised quarters in a succession of posh supper clubs and road houses.

North Shore socialites and show-business celebrities helped pump profits into crime-syndicate coffers as they patronized such locations as a country club west of Deerfield, a sprawling white-frame mansion east of Half Day, and the Fort, a block-like structure then located on Lake Avenue, just east of the Glenview Naval Air Station. Even a swank restaurant in a rural area near Cary, in McHenry County, offered the game santuary on occasion.

To the long line of Mafia bosses whose lifestyles have been generously supported by the game, the operation has been a reliable stabilizer, says Sgt. Donald Herion of the Chicago Police Gambling Unit, who has spent many years hunting down the enterprise. "They pay no state, local or federal taxes, and they control their clientele through terror."

As American society changed, so did the game.

By the early 1960s, the luxury cars with their chauffeurs and sleekly dressed patrons were replaced by more modest sedans and imports. Only the dice survived.

And instead of being embraced by Victorian velour and tuxedo-clad hosts, players found the game in more utilitarian settings—warehouses, abandoned manufacturing plants, sometimes even quonset huts. The gourmet meals once served on fine china were replaced by cold cuts and paper plates and pots of steaming pasta and meat sauce.

The game lost its class but never its profits nor the lure it offered those addicted to the galloping dominoes.

The Chicago Mob's floating crap game probably ranks as the longest continuously running gambling enterprise in America, predating the legalized glitz of Las Vegas and Atlantic City.

Since the mid-1930s, the game has drawn a cosmopolitan clientele, with millionaire stockbrokers rubbing shoulders with truck drivers, lawyers, off-duty police officers, judges, show-business personalities, restaurant owners and convicted felons.

Until the 1960s, the mobsters shifted the game to various locations in the tricounty area surrounding Chicago, not so much to avoid detection by police but to accommodate the economic demographics of gambling patrons.

One week the pocketbooks of North Shore businessmen might be the target, the next the wallets of blue-collar steelworkers. Thus, the

1st Ward or Chinatown a day later.

Imagewise, the game had slumped into dog days as the mobsters sought less highly visible quarters than the supper clubs in which they had accommodated patrons in earlier years. But for one glorious period in 1962, some of that earlier opulence was restored when the gangsters moved the game into an abandoned quonset hut within two blocks of the Villa Venice night club near Northbrook to cash in on a two-week appearance at the club by Frank Sinatra, Sammy Davis Jr. and Dean Martin.

Fueled by the Rat Pack's enormous popularity, the mobsters obligingly provided limousine shuttle service from the night club on Milwaukee Avenue to the quonset hut on nearby River Road. During the two weeks, the mobsters reaped a $200,000 bonanza at the crap and roulette tables from the tuxedo-and evening-gown-garbed patrons. At times, the crush of gambling patrons was so great that traffic stalled along major arteries.

That the game was able to operate so openly came as no shock to those familiar with its operations over the years. For decades, sheriffs of three counties and local police appeared blind to what thousands of gambling patrons had no problems finding.

No law-enforcement figure ever went to jail for taking the Mob's protection money. But it was obvious that somebody besides the game's operators was making a buck. An outgrowth of more static Prohibition-era gambling casinos, the game was operated until his death in 1964 by Rocco Fischetti, Al Capone's cousin and Chicago-area gambling czar. Always at Fischetti's side was August Dierolf Liebe, a sad-faced, chubby man who served as the gambling boss' trusted lieutenant. Liebe, who died in 1970, was always good for a laugh, fending off with a scorching string of obscenities questions by Tribune reporters who, unlike some police officials, had no trouble unearthing the game. Both worked for a succession of Mob operating bosses including Jake Guzik and Sam Giancana. They're dead. And so are their bosses.

The game lives on, however, and continues to prosper, despite a string of bad luck that intermittently has plagued the operation since a balmy Saturday night in September, 1959. That was when a raiding party of state's attorney's police headed by then Chief Investigator Paul Newey used three battering rams to knock down the doors to the Viaduct Lounge in Cicero to arrest Fischetti, Liebe and 54 crapshooters in a raid that astonished mobsters accustomed to enjoying immunity from such actions. James Thompson, a young assistant state's attorney who later would become Illinois governor,

game was drawing crowds to a two-story building nestled in a Will County picnic grove, the Illinois Supreme Court ordered the money returned to Fischetti.

And in 1965, in another ironic twist of a capricious judiciary, a U. S. Tax Court judge in Washington ruled that the $25,000 a year Liebe had been paying then Mob boss Tony Accardo for permission to run the game was tax-deductible. The court held that Accardo performed services for the cash that included helping to bankroll the operation and "standing by" with resources to offset big winning streaks by patrons.

In 1962 Chicago police intelligence division and gambling unit detectives hammered down the armor-plated doors to the Nightingale Social and Athletic Club, then at 536 W. 26th St. in Chicago's 11th Ward to arrest 29 men. They just missed Liebe by minutes.

Liebe, however, fared less well the following year, when state's attorney's police arrested him and 39 other men in a raid on the game at the Tomahawks Athletic Club near 24th Street and Wentworth Avenue in the heart of Chinatown. It was then that the game embarked on another decade of virtual immunity

(Continued on page 38)

GIFTS FOR GOOD TIMES.

A. $1100 XL Camera. 35mm f/2.8 lens, multi-auto focus, auto film load/advance/rewind, sensalite flash, self-timer, LCD display.   SALE 159⁰⁰

B. $350 Special Outfit. 35mm camera with motorized advance/rewind, built-in flash. Includes film, case, batteries, lens tissues, $10.00 coupon book.   SALE 69⁰⁰
$10 Mail-in rebate. Details in store.

C. $900 Special Outfit. 35mm camera, telephoto lens, auto advance. Includes 2 rolls of film, batteries, lens tissues, case, $10.00 coupon book.   SALE 139⁰⁰
$20 Mail-in rebate. Details in store.
*Plus, official team football jersey coupon.

D. $500AF Camera. 35mm, auto focus f/3.5 lens, unique auto film pre-wind/advance, sensalite flash.   SALE 116⁰⁰

E. T-120 Videotape. 2, 4 or 6 hr. recording.   SALE 3⁰⁰

F. 3-Pack Film. 110 Gold 200, or 35mm 100, 24 exp. Includes 2 Supralife batteries at no charge.   SALE 7³⁷

G. 4-Pack Batteries. C or D with bonus keychain flashlight included. Or, bonus 8-pk. AA batteries. SALE 2⁹⁹

Gambling
Continued

from arrest as its operators imposed security regulations rivaling those at Ft. Knox, precautions that exist to this day.

Lookouts armed with walkie-talkies guard the doors and personally check out each player before he is admitted. Similarly equipped perimeter patrols, usually in vans or panel trucks, roll through adjacent streets to guard against prowling undercover cops. They also use police scanners to eavesdrop on communications.

"Then you've got a guy on the front door who can't be seen from the outside," Sgt. Herion says. "He unlocks the door if he recognizes you as a regular player. Otherwise, he doesn't show himself, and you don't get in. You just can't walk into the game if you're a stranger. A regular player has to vouch for you."

Depending on the location, the game is located in a large 1st- or 2d-floor room. The dice are thrown on an oversized, custom-made crap table, usually 20 feet long by 6 feet wide. And the house provides the dice.

Generally, four to five men oversee the play, one using a croupier's stick to recover the dice. Another exchanges chips for cash. The overseers monitor the bets and make sure nobody tries to change a wager after the chips are down. Always hovering in the background is at least one of the Mob's juicemen, a loan shark with bundles of cash to extend credit at astronomical weekly interest rates to tapped-out players.

Few fail to repay the loans. But if they do, the loan shark has musclemen ready to break a welcher's arms or legs. And in extreme cases, they'll kill a customer as an example to others who might think of defaulting.

The game's operators collect from 2 to 5 percent of each pot as their end of the action. Individual bettors wager from as little as $25 to as much as $20,000 on a single roll of the dice. In the course of an evening, depending on the crowd, as much as $200,000 can exchange hands.

In recent years, the game has usually operated on Mondays and Fridays, starting at 5 p.m. Sunday sessions begin as early as 2 p.m. Closing time is flexible, usually when the players are exhausted or they run out of luck and money. On occasion, the dice have been known to roll until dawn.

And, in rare instances when the players have been riding high, the house has gone broke and the game's bankers have had to dispatch $50,000 or $75,000 to replenish the coffers.

"The gamblers tell the players to keep their mouths shut about the game's locations and to not even tell their wives or girl friends where the game, somebody who will tell you where it's operating," Herion says. "The players don't want to spoil their fun. And, besides, they don't want their legs broken."

Thus, police must spend endless days and sometimes weeks following players who previously have been arrested at the game in the hope that they will lead them to it. On occasion, detectives will get lucky and detect a location, then spend endless hours taking down license-plate numbers of gambling patrons entering the premises, in the hope of tracking them down later and getting someone to spill the beans. Such firsthand evidence from someone who has witnessed the gambling is essential to obtaining a warrant with which to conduct a raid.

Even then, their efforts may come to naught. One of the surveillance cars may get spotted and the game will abruptly shut down. And the game's operators periodically move the now thrice-weekly game from location to location to further avoid detection.

Tracking down the game is not without hazards. Once, the crew of a passing freight train spotted a brace of investigators lurking in the bushes along a railroad embankment overlooking a warehouse where the game was operating. The crew radioed the dispatcher, who summoned railroad police because there had been recent thefts of beer from boxcars nearby. The investigators soon found themselves looking down the barrels of two .357 Mag-

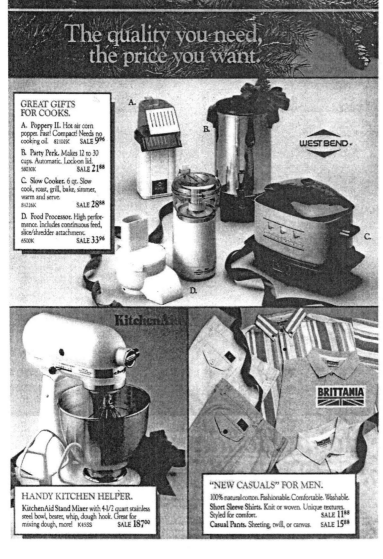

nums held by railroad detectives.

"The food's good, but the action's better," a veteran player says. "It's a lot cheaper than flying to Las Vegas, and nobody reports their winnings to the IRS."

Someone, possibly a disgruntled player, decided to give police a little help in finding the game.

"It's funny to watch. Some of the North Shore and lakefront swells —you know, the yuppie types— stand in the corner and try to make like the bad guys, talking out of the side of their mouths."

In 1983 the crap game ran into another string of bad luck that forced its current operator, James Cerone, 69, a cousin of imprisoned Mob boss Jackie Cerone, to move the enterprise to the suburbs. Twice within four months, Chicago police raided the game at locations at 246 W. 31st St. and 254 W. 26th St. A year later, investigators spotted it operating at two factory locations in Melrose Park, but it closed before the cops could gather evidence sufficient to get a warrant.

Someone, probably a frustrated cop or a disgruntled player, later posted a large, handlettered sign under a lamppost on Lake Street in the suburb that read in bold print: NOTICE. CRAP GAME—1 BLOCK NORTH. FRIDAY 7 P. M. —SUNDAY 2 P.M. REFRESHMENTS. LOANS. J. CERONE PROP.

As soon as the sign was spotted, the game again moved.

Once in the suburbs, the game again flourished. In 1986 an off-duty Maywood police officer shoved an automatic pistol in a reporter's stomach after he discovered him conducting a surveillance of yet another crap-game location in the suburb.

Maywood police never raided the game. But subsequently, department superiors said they suspected the cop and a fellow officer of being paid by the Mob to ride shotgun on the game. And an investigation showed that the Village of Maywood was the crap game's unwitting landlord. It owned the building and leased it as a warehouse.

Two years later, the game again surfaced in Forest Park, playing to hundreds of patrons a night who often created a traffic jam outside two locations in the suburb. Despite that nocturnal crush, however, uniformed patrol officers driving by somehow miraculously failed to suspect anything was amiss. After six months, the game again vanished.

However, last April 15, the game's steak of luck again ran out. A team of Chicago gambling unit detectives, FBI agents and sheriff's police waited until the door to a building in unincorporated Lyden Township was opened by a lookout to admit two patrons, and they crashed in beside them. A total of $75,000 in cash was seized, and 42 men were arrested. A veteran Chicago police officer on disability leave and four others were later indicted as operators of the game. They are awaiting trial.

"Gambling is the Mob's biggest moneymaker," says Commander Michael Hoke of the city's Vice Control Section. "The hoods run 90 to 95 percent of the illegal gambling in this area. Yet people try to call gambling a victimless crime.

Chapter 47

President's Commission on Organized Crime

The first time I had heard of an investigation on illegal gambling by the President's Commission on Organized Crime was in May 1985. I was working out of the gambling unit of the organized crime division at 943 West Maxwell Street in a downtrodden part of Chicago near the market place. My crew and I were just leaving the building to execute a search warrant in Cicero when my lieutenant called me in his office and informed me that I had to be interviewed by two staff members from the President's Commission on Organized Crime out of Washington DC. He told me that was all he knew about it and instructed me to be back in the office as soon as we were through with our raid. I never did like surprises like this, but I didn't have any choice in the matter.

We hit a house in Cicero and busted two guys who had four phones, going taking a lot of action on baseball and basketball games that were going to be played that night. They had the doors barricaded with two-by-fours, and of course, they had water-soluble paper, which they threw in a bucket of water. That really pissed me off, because if the bucket tipped over, they could possibly slip on the floor and that sticky stuff could get in their hair and ears. Oh well, you win some and lose some, I guess. When we got back to Maxwell Street, we had our two wise guys in cuffs; and when we were putting them in our lockup, I noticed two well-dressed guys sitting on a bench outside of our squad room. I had never seen them before, so I figured these might be the guys waiting for me. I wondered if they had seen the two bad guys we just put in the lockup with their hair all mucky looking; oh well, it's too late now.

When I finally got back to the lieutenant's office, there were the two guys waiting for me. They both told me they were from the President's Commission on Organized Crime, assigned as staff investigators. They explained that their main office was in Washington DC. Their names were Jack Leonard and John Walsh. Leonard said he was retired from the New York Police Department and was currently a staff investigator. Walsh was also a staff investigator, but he was a special agent with the Internal Revenue Service and was formally attached to the organized crime division in Chicago.

That's when they told me I had been recommended to them as an expert on organized crime gambling and was knowledgeable about how the Chicago mob operated. Then they asked me questions about my family and how many children I had, what kind of car I drove and where I lived. I answered their questions and then asked them why they had to know about my private life. They said it was just routine, and they had to ask these questions of prospective witnesses who may appear at the public hearings that were going to be held on the Chicago organized crime group outfit in June. They asked me how long I had been on the job, how long I had been working organized crime, and a lot of other questions about my career on the police department. After I answered their questions, they told me they had checked me out with the FBI and found that I had an excellent record, and that there was good chance that I would be asked to testify at the public hearings that were going to be held in New York on June 24-26. If I agreed to testify, I would be requested to go to Washington DC at 1425 K. Street to be interviewed by the executive director and chief counsel James D. Harmon Jr. I asked them just what I would have to testify about. All they said was, "Gambling, and how it works in Chicago. How the mob operates and what type of illegal gambling do they control." I told them that it sounded good to me if it was OK with my bosses. They said, "Fine, you will be hearing from us very soon." Jack Leonard then said, "Off the record, Don, what the hell did those two guys you just pinched have in their hair?" I just said that they had a lousy barber, I guess. They both laughed and just shook their heads. As they were leaving, I heard Leonard say, "I think we've got the right guy."

The following week I got a phone call from Jack Leonard. "Expect a subpoena in the mail along with round-trip plane tickets to Washington DC," he said. That day I got both, and the next day I was on a plane to Washington DC. Leonard picked me up at the airport and gave me a tour of Washington and all the points of interest in our nation's capital. The next day, Leonard picked me up and drove me to 1425 K. Street, Suite 700, for my interview. I was introduced to a lot of other commission investigators and was interviewed by the executive director James Harmon Jr. The questions asked by Harmon were all Mafia related – about the outfit's gambling operations in Chicago. When the session was over, Harmon shook my hand and said that he was convinced I would make an excellent witness at the hearings in New York City in June. Then he told me that I would probably be on a panel with two U.S. attorneys from Chicago, Mark Vogel and Judy Dobkin. "I believe that you were all involved in the Joseph "Caesar" Divarco case?" he asked. I told him, "Yes, that's true. Divarco was a top lieutenant in the outfit and a street boss in the Rush Street area, Chicago's nightclub district." That was that, and then he said, "We'll see you in New York next month, Sergeant."

Jack Leonard was really a great guy, and I found out that he was one of the most decorated cops in New York City. He didn't tell me that; someone else, who was also from New York, did. It seemed that Jack was on a rescue squad and got involved in all kinds of weird things, such as having to climb up on the Queensboro Bridge to bring a jumper down.

Jack told me this would be a great experience for me and that I would probably be in New York for about five days, from June 23 to 27. He said that some of the other witnesses were Daryl Gates, the chief of the Los Angeles Police Department; Howard Cosell, the famous sports journalist and the voice of boxing; and Stephen Wynn, the owner of the Golden Nugget Casino in Nevada. There also would be some outfit guys, who are in the witness protection program, and other notables from the United States. I asked Jack if that made me notable; he looked at me and started laughing, and then he said that I would probably be a star witness and become famous. He sure had the Irish bullshit.

On the plane ride back to Chicago, I started to wonder what the hell I had gotten myself into now. I hated to wear a suit and tie, but I'm sure that would be the correct thing to do. When I got back to work the next day, I told my lieutenant that I would have to go to New York for about five days in June to testify in front of the President's Commission on Organized Crime and tell them about the Chicago mob. "No problem," he said, "as long as the 'G' is paying your expenses, it sounds good to me." On June 16, 1985, I was served with a subpoena to appear in New York, New York, on June 23, 1985, at Twenty-six Federal Plaza at 9:00 AM. I also received round-trip airline ticket and hotel reservations at the New York Penta Hotel at Seventh Avenue and Thirty third Street. It was showtime. I will admit I was getting a little nervous about just what I was going to be asked at the commission hearing, but it was too late to worry about that now, I'd just play it by ear.

I left on June 23 and arrived in New York about 2:00 PM. I was picked up by Jack Leonard, who helped me get squared away. He drove me to the Penta Hotel, and I checked in. I asked Jack if he any idea what I was going to be asked at the commission hearing. He said, "Whatever they ask you, I know you can answer their question. That's why you're here, old buddy." "By the way," he said, "I think you're slated to testify tomorrow, along with the two U.S. attorneys." He said that most of the witnesses will have prepared written statements with them, and all they do is read from their notes, and it would be a lot more impressive if you just winged it instead of refer to notes every time you were asked a question. "By the way," he said, "there will be a lot of television cameras and reporters in the room, so don't get nervous. Some of the witnesses will be accompanied by armed guards and will be wearing hoods on their heads because they are Mafia guys who have turned stool pigeon for the government."

The next day, Jack picked me up at the hotel and drove to the federal building at Twenty-six Federal Plaza; we got there about 8:00 AM, where I had a meeting with Commission Deputy Chief Counsel C. Stanley Hunterton. He said he would question me about the Chicago mob and how they controlled gambling. He briefly went over some of the questions that I would be asked and made me feel a little more relaxed. I had no problem with the questions, and then I asked him if he was familiar with water-soluble paper or flash paper, which is what bookmakers use to destroy their wagers in case of a raid. I had some with me, so I demonstrated how they both worked. He thought that it would be an excellent idea if I would repeat the same thing for the commission members, as to give them an idea what the police are up against seizing evidence. He said he would have to find a bottle or something to put water in so that they could get a good look at the paper dissolving. I suggested that if he could find a small goldfish bowl, that would be fine. "No problem," he said, and then sent a deputy out to try and find one. The deputy really gave me a nasty look when he left.

The room where the hearing was being held was very impressive. Everything was very official looking; dark wood paneling and the emblem of the presidential seal was all over the room. There were eighteen commissioners seated next to each other at a very long bench; they each had their name in front of them. Below them were two dark leather chairs and another long bench where the executive director James D. Harmon Jr. sat alongside Deputy Chief Counsel C. Stanley Hunterton. The chairman, Judge Irving R. Kaufman, sat in the middle of the commissioners and gave a welcoming speech to the President's Commission on Organized Crime hearings. He said that today's testimony would explore the scope of gambling in the United States, the extent of organized crime involvement in this activity today, and the changing nature of criminal syndicates' illegal gambling operations in different regions of the country. He also said that we will hear from law enforcement experts who will discuss current strategy and assist the commission in devising new approaches to combat organized crime.

At this point I felt pretty relaxed and not too nervous about testifying, until I found out who the first witness was. Jerome Skolnick, professor of law at the University of California, Berkley, who has a distinguished record of publications including a book entitled *House of Cards: The Legalization and Control of Casino Gambling*. Here was a professor testifying before the commission, and guess what, he had a prepared statement he was reading from. But not me, I was just going to wing it. I just hoped I wouldn't embarrass myself too much when my turn came.

Chairman Kaufman asked Professor Skolnick if he was in favor of the legalization of sports betting on college athletics under any set of controls as a means of controlling organized crime. His reply was that his expertise was in casino operations, and he has not done a study of the legalization of sports betting but added that it is a subject that they should study. He also said that he could pick up any newspaper on the day of the Super Bowl and tell you what the odds are. The odds are announced on the airwaves. It would be very difficult for somebody who wanted to learn the odds on a sporting event not to find out about them in this society. How right he was.

The next witnesses were Frank Storey, assistant special agent in charge of the New York office of the FBI, and Joseph DePierro, the seputy inspector of the NYPD assigned to the public morals division of the organized crime bureau and has been on the job for twenty-nine years. The third witness was Lieutenant Robert Gaugler assigned to the

Organized Crime Bureau of the New Jersey State Police and has been on the job for twenty-three years.

Agent Storey testified about the FBI's organized crime program; he kept using the name La Cosa Nostra, instead of saying "the outfit" or "the mob." He said they have achieved successes in the fight against their number one priority, La Cosa Nostra, utilizing three major investigative techniques, namely, informants, undercover operations and, the Title III electronic surveillance's "wiretaps." Gambling investigations of organized crime groups are essential due to the fact that gambling and violence go hand in glove. LCN figures operating bookmaking rings generally protect their monopolies by savage acts of violence against those opposing them. This brutality stems from the underworld's all consuming greed and desire to eliminate competition. The most important asset the FBI has is Title III; if they took away that investigative tool, the FBI would be screwed, in my opinion.

The next witness, Joseph DePierro from the NYPD, testified about the different types of gambling organized crime controlled in New York City. It was, of course, bookmaking, policy, and illegal casinos. The casino is run as the casinos are run in Atlantic City, only on a smaller scale. He said they had roulette wheels, baccarat tables, blackjack tables, and crap tables. They also provided food and drink, and if the players ran out of money, the friendly loan shark would gladly borrow whatever you needed.

Depierro also described how the Cubans have been involved in policy or numbers in the past few years. There was a strong relationship between Cuban organized crime and the La Cosa Nostra. It was also believed that the Cubans were paying street taxes to the LCN or they would not be allowed to operate their gambling enterprise in New York. The police departments conducted a survey on how many illegal policy operations were in the city of New York. When he told the commission that there were 4,355 OTB parlor-type gambling spots in operation, I almost fell off my chair. The OTBs were storefronts and had Plexiglas put there to guard themselves against theft and problems. They had slots to pass the money back and forth; odds were posted all over the building. It was obvious that the place was only used for gambling. I thought we had a problem in Chicago when we had about 220 OTBs in operation; what a joke that was.

The next witness was Lieutenant Gaugler from the New Jersey State Police; he said that his main problem was video poker machines, Joker Poker, which was all over the state. He said that in March 1985, the New

Jersey State Police and the Essex County Prosecutor's Office conducted a large-scale raid, which culminated an eighteen-month undercover investigation. As a result of these raids, seventy persons were arrested on variety of charges: promoting gambling, theft by extortion, criminal usury, official misconduct, and possession of illegal gambling devices, and conspiracy. In addition to these arrests, over $90,000 in cash, ten vehicles, and over four hundred illegal video gambling machines were confiscated. The interesting part of this was that two of the men who were arrested, Ralph "Blackie" Napoli and Joseph Sodano, were identified as members of the Bruno crime family and associates of Nicodemo Scarfo, mob boss. Sodano had a criminal history of bookmaking, lottery, and robbery. He had been involved in narcotics trafficking and was also a suspect in two murders. The same story holds true for Chicago; there's no doubt in my mind that all the innocent video poker machines that are in hundreds of establishments throughout Chicago and the entire state of Illinois are controlled by organized crime.

The next witness was a commission investigator who had previously worked for the Internal Revenue Service as a senior special agent for over fifteen years. He presented a profile of the "Corporation" and Jose Miguel Battle Sr. known as the "Godfather." A comprehensive review of the files of various federal, international, state, and local law enforcement agencies and independent investigation by the staff of the commission clearly revealed the existence of a tightly knit, well-financed, armed, and powerful group of Cuban racketeers known as the Corporation. These individuals are sometimes CIA trained and anti-Castro sympathizers that had taken part in the Bay of Pigs Invasion.

The Corporation controls gambling operations with policy and lottery storefronts throughout New York City. Seized gambling records reflect a weekly gross take of over $2 million for the Corporation. The Corporation earned a minimum annual net profit of $45 million from New York City gambling operations alone. This net profit has been estimated as high as $100 million. The Corporation controls this gambling enterprise by means of violence, intimidation, arson, and homicide, with the OK from the Mafia. The Corporation, of course, paid the Mafia a percentage of the action and lay off some of the bets with organized crime. The Genovese Crime Family was instrumental in negotiating this alliance.

The Corporation, which Jose Battle directs, was conservatively valued at an estimated several hundred million dollars. When Battle moved to Florida in 1982, he, his wife, and son purchased various real estate for

$1,115,000, of which $805,000 was paid in cash. In April 1983, Battle's son was detained by the New York Port Authority Police after resisting a search of carry-on luggage while boarding a domestic flight to Miami. After some resistance, he submitted his luggage for inspection wherein $439,000 in U.S. currency was found wrapped in gift boxes. Battle Jr. denied ownership of the currency and would only indicate that he was a vice president of the Union Financial Inc. in Miami, Florida, he said that he was going to deliver it to a person in Miami. He said that he did not know the name of the person; all that he had was a description.

The Corporation also had a way to launder some of the gambling money that was through the Puerto Rican lottery. The Corporation let it be known that they were willing to purchase winning Puerto Rican lottery tickets for an amount greater than the amount provided by the winning ticket. This technique is used to provide a legitimate source of income for the Corporation members, who, in turn, redeem the "purchased" ticket. These individuals had no other means of legitimate income and are happy to pay the federal tax on their winnings, simply to legitimatize their expenditures.

All Puerto Rican lottery tickets sold in the United States are controlled by organized crime. The lottery tickets are transported from Puerto Rico to Miami on a weekly basis; they are then distributed to Chicago, New York, Los Angeles, Houston, and Tampa. All distributors of the tickets are informed to notify the Corporation immediately of a large winner. For instance, if an individual wins $125,000, he is contacted and is told that if he travels to Puerto Rico to collect the $125,000, certain reports have to be made out, and the Internal Revenue service notified, and the individual will only get a small portion of the winning ticket. The individual is offered $150,000 in cash for his ticket with no problems; of course, they always take the $150,000, and everybody is happy.

In Chicago, we had an organized crime guy by the name of Ken "Joe the Jap" Eto running the entire Puerto Rican lottery for the mob. We busted Eto for gambling a few times; apparently, the outfit thought that Eto was going to rat on some of the boys so they put three bullets in the back of his head. But he didn't die.

The two hit men who tried to murder Eto-Jasper Campise and John Gattuso – were arrested for attempted murder and were released on bail, which was a big mistake. They were both whacked for screwing up the hit on Eto and were found in the same trunk in a parking lot in a Far Western suburb.

Eto tells how mob set up botched 'hit'

By John O'Brien and Philip Wattley

ONLY HOURS before he was shot in a bungled gangland hit, mob figure Ken "Tokyo Joe" Eto had a premonition of death and told his wife to get his insurance papers in order.

This and other revelations, including Eto's dramatic naming of his two would-be assassins and his angry charge that he was 'set up' for murder, were made Friday to FBI agents in a tape-recorded statement from his hospital bed.

In addition, The Tribune learned, Eto provided an account of what he described as events leading up to his shooting, including a meeting with two of his bosses in the crime syndicate Thursday morning.

Eto, 63, of suburban Bolingbrook, was shot Thursday night as he sat behind the wheel of his car, which he had parked in a theater lot at 7229 W. Grand Ave. Bleeding from his wounds, he then managed to walk more than a block to get help at the Terminal Pharmacy, 7029 W. Grand Ave.

FRIDAY AFTERNOON, Eto, although listed only as in fair condition, was whisked

Continued from page 1

come increasingly under surveillance by police. The money used for drug purchases is believed to have come from gambling profits.

Eto's remarkable survival of three bullet wounds in the head and his realization of his betrayal left him furious and led to his startling break with the mob's code of silence.

Both developments prompted a beaming Police Supt. Richard J. Brzeczek to call the suspects' arrests "the break of a lifetime" for law enforcement.

"We may get a handle on organized crime," Brzeczek said. "The victim is still alive, and we need that kind of information. . . . There may be panic within organized crime. They're shooting people to keep them quiet."

ETO WAS WILLING to talk only after he received assurances of government protection from Chicago FBI chief Edward D. Hegarty, who rushed to Eto's bedside at 2 a.m.

By 8 a.m., the two men named by Eto as his assailants were in custody and charged with the attempted murder of the man regarded as the highest-ranking Oriental in the syndicate, overseeing bolita and other gambling rackets throughout metropolitan Chicago.

Arrested at their homes were Jasper Campise, 67, of 1535 Forest Ave., River Forest, a reputed syndicate "soldier," and John Gattuso, 47, of 1721 Sunset Ridge, Glenview, a Cook County deputy sheriff who worked as a process server.

Informed of the arrests, Sheriff Richard Elrod suspended Gattuso, pending a disciplinary hearing.

Campise was taken into custody by homicide detectives and members of the police intelligence division. Gattuso was arrested by Jules Gallet, commander of the division, accompanied by police officers assigned to the U.S. Drug Enforcement Administration.

Brzeczek identified Campise as part of the mob's north group, led by Vincent Solano, a union boss who controls rackets along Rush Street and as far north as Lake County. Directly under Solano are Joseph DiVarco, Joseph Arnold and Eto. Campise ranked under them.

THE TWO suspects were held on bonds of $500,000 each pending a hearing Saturday in Holiday Court. Arnold was later picked up for questioning but claimed no knowledge of the shooting and was released without charge. DiVarco could not immediately be found, and investigators said efforts to question him would be postponed.

It was learned that aides to State's Atty. Richard M. Daley intend to seek indictments in the case Monday. Daley reportedly has assigned the head of his organized crime unit, Stephen Connolly, and Assistant State's Atty. Paul Nealis to review police and FBI findings for presentation to the grand jury.

In Eto's tape-recorded statement, described as lucid and coherent, the veteran gambling figure said he feared for his life and had a premonition of death shortly before he was shot.

Eto said Campise was seated in the front seat next to him, Gattuso was in the back, and the shots came from behind.

FEIGNING DEATH, Eto said, he slumped forward and began faking convulsions before suddenly going limp. At that point, he said, Campise and Gattuso jumped out of his car and fled.

After a few moments, he cautiously peered from the car window and, seeing no one, got out of the car and began walking to seek help.

Eto said events leading up to the shooting began Wednesday night, when he received a telephone call at home from Arnold, directing him to meet with DiVarco the next morning.

Following that order, Eto said, he met both DiVarco and Arnold at 11:30 a.m. Thursday in a hideaway, "Oldsters for Youngsters," a spot frequently raided for vice and gambling, at 876 N. Wabash Ave.

Eto said it was there that DiVarco mentioned Solano's name, explaining that the mob overseer "wanted to have dinner with me." Also, Eto said, DiVarco had instructed him to pick up Campise and Gattuso at a veterans' hall en route to the meeting with Solano.

Leaving the meeting, Eto contacted his wife and told her of the conversation with DiVarco. "Tonight might be the last time I have dinner with anybody," Eto recalled having told his wife.

HE THEN TOLD her of his fears for his life and instructed her to "put together" his life insurance policies, and "fear for the worst."

Eto then kept his fateful appointment with those who tried to kill him, he said.

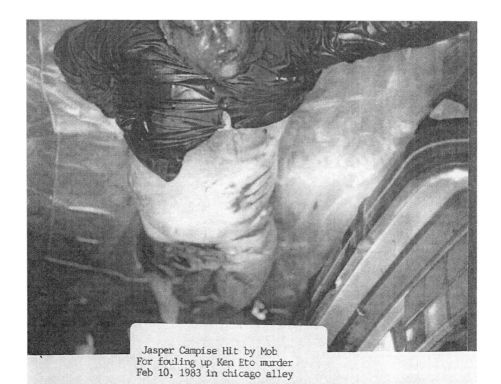

Jasper Campise Hit by Mob
For fouling up Ken Eto murder
Feb 10, 1983 in chicago alley

John Gattuso shot Eto 3 times
in the head with three .22 cal.

Eto went on to testify as a federal witness against the outfit and help put a lot of mob guys in the joint. He is still in the witness protection program, and it is rumored that he had some plastic surgery as well.

The last three witnesses really did a good job explaining the problems law enforcement was running into with different gambling operations in their areas, and how organized crime was behind all of it. I noticed that they all had diagrams, video tapes, and charts to demonstrate the different types of illegal gambling controlled by the outfit. I was starting to get a little nervous; no that's wrong, I was starting to get a lot nervous about giving my presentation to the commission. All I had was a damn fishbowl as an aid.

Chairman Kaufman asked Mr. Harmon to call his next witness. Deputy Chief Counsel Stan Hunterton then called for Sergeant Herion, Mark Vogel, and Judy Dobkin to step forward and be sworn; this was the moment of truth.

Mob tells Chicago bookmakers: "Pay or you're betting your life"

Is sports gambling a victimless sport? Not in Chicago where three bookmakers already have been murdered this year in a war with what is dubbed euphemistically as "The Outfit."

The mob's ultimatum to independent bookies is "pay, quit or die," Chicago police sergeant Donald Herion told the President's Commission on Organized Crime hearings here yesterday.

The three-day hearings on organized crime's gambling connection opened at 1 Federal Plaza yesterday. Sgt. Herion's testimony dealt in part with how the Mafia — also referred to as LCN for La Cosa Nostra — was putting the squeeze on the bookies with a "street tax" amounting to 50% of their business. One of the dead bookies apparently already had quit, but was hit because of his vocal opposition to the tax, Sgt. Herion said. He added that the mob also used its resources to steal customers from the independents.

Asked about some of the difficulties in fighting illegal sports gambling, Sgt. Herion cited "the availability of sports information." This included not only newspaper items with odds, weather and other pertinent information, but up-to-the-second coast-to-coast dope available by phone. "You can get it all for a 50 cent phone call," Sgt. Herion said. "It used to be a federal offense."

— Larry Fox

I noticed that Vogel and Dobkin both had notes with them, which they placed on the table in front of them; all I had were sweaty hands.

This was the way it went down. Mr. Hunterton, Mr. Chairman, Sergeant Donald Herion of the Chicago Police Department are seated to the commission's far right at the table.

A panel of law enforcement experts describes the connection between gambling and organized crime. Left to right: Judith Dobkin and Mark Vogel, prosecutors with the Chicago Strike Force of the Justice Department, and Sgt. Donald Herion of the Chicago Police Department.

He went on to say that I had been a member of the Chicago Police Department for thirty years and assigned to the organized crime vice vontrol section – gambling unit for twenty of those years, both as a working detective and now as a supervising detective sergeant. He has a thorough understanding of Chicago's organized crime group, and its control over illegal gambling in and around Chicago.

Mark Vogel was next; his background was impressive. I must say his education was a little better than mine. He was a graduate of Northeastern Law School in Boston and has been with the U.S. Department of Justice for the past thirteen years, the last five of those as a special attorney with the Organized Crime Strike Force, Chicago office. He was one of the prosecutors in the prosecution of the president of the International Brotherhood of Teamsters Roy Williams, Chicago racketeer Joey "the Clown" Lombardo, and the late Allen Dorfman. He will also describe a prosecution in which he took part, in which he was the lead attorney against Frank Balistrieri, the head of the Milwaukee LCN family.

Judith Dobkin, a graduate of George Washington Law and a holder of a master's in law from Georgetown, who has been with the Department of Justice for eight years and, like Mr. Vogel, with the Chicago Strike Force for five. She will describe *United States vs. DiVarco*, a gambling prosecution which, to anyone's recollection, produced the longest prison sentence ever handed out in the federal court. She has other experience in this area, having prosecuted race-fixing cases. I have to admit that her educational background was also a little better than mine, but being a graduate of Austin High School in Chicago was nothing to sneeze at.

The first question I was asked was, "Sergeant Herion, what is the outfit in Chicago?" Here I was sitting in front of a commission of judges, former U.S. attorneys, and other highly respected senators from the United States of America, you would think that I would have been nervous, wouldn't you? Well, you would have been right. A thought flashed through my head: I was in high school and had to get up in front of the class and recite something or other. I would automatically cut class to avoid that type of situation. There was nowhere to run now. I was out on a limb all by myself; it was either sink or swim.

I answered the first question by saying the outfit in Chicago is organized crime, also known as the mob, the Mafia, or La Cosa Nostra. After that question, I felt very relaxed and was ready for anything they could throw at me. I explained what part the outfit played in illegal gambling in Chicago, and that everyone involved in illegal gambling had to pay a street tax to the outfit for the privilege of operating in Chicago. In 1985, it was estimated that up to $40 billion was wagered on sports events annually. I agreed with that figure and added that that figure did not include numbers, policy, or horse wagering. I was asked to explain what vigorish or juice was involved in sports bookmaking. In Chicago we always called it juice; for instance, if a bettor bet $1,000 on a football game and he lost, he would have to pay the bookmaker an additional 10 percent, or $1,100. On the other hand, if he won, he would only collect $1,000. I understand that a bookmaker made between 1 percent and 2 percent of his gross handle a year; if he accomplished that, he has had a good year.

In Chicago, the outfit gave independent bookmakers an ultimatum – it was pay, quit, or die. Some paid, some quit, and some died. We had three major bookmakers murdered in Chicago in the beginning of 1985. Hal Smith, who happened to be an informant of mine, was beaten, stabbed, and strangled, and was found in the trunk of his Cadillac in a suburban parking lot. Lenny Yaras, who was considered part of the outfit, was shot to death in his car in front of his business, in broad daylight. His father, Davie Yaras, was an outfit assassin and a partner of another killer named Lenny Patrick, who turned against the outfit and testified against mob boss Gus Alex. Chuck English was gunned down in the parking lot of a restaurant; he was a top outfit guy and killer for most of his life and controlled a lot of gambling operations in and around Chicago.

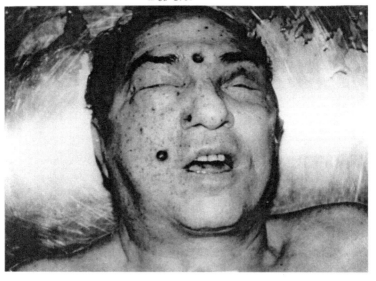

Charles C. Englesi
AKA Chuck English
Gambling Boss
whacked in Elmwood Pk.
Feb 1985

Commission member Strom Thurmond asked me what problems we ran into trying to bust up wire-room operations. I explained that a lot of bookmakers had moved to the suburbs due to the heat we had caused them in Chicago. They also used call forwarding, where they would have their calls transferred to other phones. They would utilize beepers and fax machines as well. Cellular phones were not that popular in 1985 and didn't work that well. But the thing that always worked for them was water-soluble paper and flash paper. The bets were written on that type of paper, and in the event of a raid, they would throw the soluble paper in water, which would dissolve and burn the flash paper.

The New York Times

NEW YORK, TUESDAY, JUNE 25, 1985

U.S. Panel Says Former Cubans Run a Bet Ring

New York Hearing Told Rivals Were Killed

By ERIC SCHMITT

A group of Cuban-American racketeers operates a $45-million-a-year illegal gambling syndicate in New York City and New Jersey, often killing competitors and burning down their businesses, a Federal commission on crime said yesterday.

A profile of the syndicate was presented at a hearing in lower Manhattan by investigators for the panel, the President's Commission on Organized Crime. The profile said the syndicate — called "the Corporation" — paid the Mafia a fee to run illegal numbers games in its territory in Manhattan, Brooklyn, the Bronx and northern New Jersey.

The commission is investigating organized crime's involvement in legal and illegal gambling operations as part of its nearly three-year mission to study organized crime and to recommend legislative and judicial ways to combat it. The panel can subpoena witnesses and make recommendations to authorities on prosecutions.

$1.5 Billion a Year

"In the tristate New York area alone, $1.5 billion is spent each year on numbers games, sports, bookmakers and other forms of illegal wagering controlled by organized crime," said the commission chairman, Judge Irving R. Kaufman of the United States Court of Appeals for the Second Circuit in New York.

Twelve of the 19 panel members attended the first day of a three-day hearing at the United States Court of International Trade at 1 Federal Plaza. The hearing will continue today and tomorrow.

The highlight of yesterday's hearing was testimony by a former member of the Cuban gambling syndicate who corroborated the information in the commission's profile.

Dressed in a monk's black habit, his face smeared in black to conceal his identity, the informer, who used to run an illegal gambling parlor, said 2,500 people in New York City worked for the crime group's "godfather." He identified him as Jose Miguel Battle Sr.

According to the commission, Mr. Battle is a former Havana anti-vice officer who was recruited by the Central Intelligence Agency to participate in the Bay of Pigs invasion.

Sgt. Donald Herion of the Chicago police demonstrating at hearing how operators of numbers games use paper that dissolves in water.

The gambling sites often resemble legalized off-track betting establishments and earn between $7,000 and $12,000 a day, the witness said, speaking through a Spanish interpreter.

When asked by James D. Harmon Jr., the chief counsel to the commission, how the Corporation dealt with its competitors, the informer said the organization's "enforcer" assigned men to "kill the people and burn down their stores."

He said the crime group had killed 20 people since it established a foothold in New York through Cuban and other Hispanic-owned bars and groceries. Ten to 15 other people died in the arson incidents, he said.

Mr. Battle, who was subpoenaed by the commission, was present in the courtroom, but in a letter from his lawyer had invoked his Fifth Amendment rights to avoid incriminating himself. Mr. Battle used to live in Union City, N.J., and now makes his home in Miami.

According to the commission's profile, the Corporation controls legitimate mortgage and finance companies, travel stores, banks and real-estate agencies in the Miami area that are worth "several hundred million dollars."

The profile also said that the Corporation laundered millions of dollars in illegal revenues through financial institutions and the official Puerto Rico lottery. Investigators estimated that $14 million a week was laundered through the lottery.

In other testimony, city, state and Federal law enforcement officials said racketeers used advanced telephone, computer and video devices to thwart police detection.

Video card games that operators can program as gambling machines are particularly vexing to the police, the authorities reported.

One game owner made $500,000 in 15 months from five rigged machines, Lieut. Robert Gaugler of the New Jersey state police told the hearing.

Sgt. Don Herion demonstrating Flash paper used by bookmakers to destroy their bets in event of a raid, to members of the Presidents Commission on Organized Crime in New York.

Courtesy of Don Herion

I explained that without the wagers, there was no way we could get a conviction in court. It didn't even matter that we operated the bookies' phones and took in thousands of dollars in bets; that evidence was inadmissible in court. The commission members were also surprised that in Chicago we were not allowed to use wiretaps; it was a federal violation to do so.

The chief counsel, Stan Hunterton, then asked me to demonstrate how water-soluble paper worked and how the bookmakers used flash paper. I demonstrated how the soluble paper dissolved in water first. The goldfish bowl was on a table next to me, so I wrote some bets on the soluble paper and then placed the bets in the water. All eyes in the room were glued to the fishbowl; when I put the paper in the water, I took in out immediately and all that was left of the paper was a mushy glob on my hand. For some reason, that seemed to get their attention. For my next trick, I held up a normal sheet of flash paper that looked like any other paper, and I lit a match to it. The paper had a golden flash to it and disappeared in midair without a trace. I guess that nobody in the room had ever seen anything like that before, because all I heard were oohs and ahhs. The goofy part of this whole demonstration was that there was a picture of me on the front page of the *New York Times* with my hand in the fishbowl, showing how the paper disappeared in front of everybody. It sure is strange what attracts people's attention sometimes.

Mr. Hunterton then asked me to explain an exhibit that was set up of photographs of a "Chicago armored wire room" that we had raided recently on the Near West Side of Chicago. I explained that this particular wire room was set up inside an abandoned warehouse, where the bad guys had built a room about ten by six feet. The walls were a made of cement, and the entrance to this room was through a six-inch-thick steel door, something like a furrier would have. When the door was closed, it would be impossible to get it open from the outside; there were no knobs or handles on the outside of the door. The room was equipped with an alarm system that was connected to the rear door of the warehouse; anyone who entered that door would set off an alarm inside the vault. They also had a small ventilation system set up near the cement ceiling. We found four telephones on an eight-foot table along with a twelve-inch television set, lighter fluid, as well as a quantity of water-soluble paper, flash paper, football schedules, and other miscellaneous gambling paraphernalia. It was quite obvious that had we attempted to raid the vault while the bad guys were in; it would have been an impossible feat to get them dirty. As things turned out, we were able to grab two of the bad guys when they were coming out of the back door. An older guy named George Columbus and an outfit guy's son, Phil Cozzo, who was twenty-one years old and learning the business at an early age and wanted to be a wise guy like his old man.

I explained to the commission about the problem we were having in court with these gambling raids. I told them that 90 percent of the bookmakers in the Chicago area used water-soluble paper as well as flash paper to record their wagers on. In the event of a raid, they would be able to destroy the gambling records by placing them in water where they would vanish or burning them with flash paper. In Illinois we had to recover the gambling records to make a case stick in court and get a conviction. Even if we took over the bookmaker's telephones and accepted bets from their customers, the court ruled this to be hearsay evidence and was not admissible in court.

Mr. Hunterton asked me if I had any other problems as a law enforcement officer working organized crime operations. I told them about the availability of sports information, such as point spreads on sporting events, weather conditions, injury reports on athletes, even which way the wind was blowing at Wrigley Field, which would, of course, influence the number of home runs that could be hit if the wind was blowing in or out. Most of this information can be obtained for a .50 cent phone call, and it is legal to obtain at this time. A few years ago this type of information transmitted across state lines was a federal offense. It seemed that we were making it easier for illegal gambling to operate and that the majority of newspapers printed the point spreads on sporting events as well as results on horse races across the country. I told them there wasn't any reason to print point spreads in the paper because the only place that you can make a bet on a sporting event was in the state of Nevada, as you well know.

I thought that I would also make the commission aware of the problem we were having in the Chicago area involving video poker machines. There are an estimated five thousand machines and 95 percent of the people that have them area paying off on them. The device itself was not ruled illegal in Illinois. The only way that we were able to make an arrest involving these devices was to observe someone being paid off after they accumulated a certain amount of points, or by us playing the machines and being paid off by the operator of the establishment. I had been acquainted with one person who operated ten poker machines, and his profit averaged $10,000 a week; the machines were in the rear room of a hamburger joint and had been rigged by the owner. There was no doubt that this was a major illegal enterprise operated by the mob or the Chicago Outfit. Mr. Hunterton then thanked me for my testimony, and I was excused.

Little did I know at the time but my testimony along with other witnesses' would be printed in a book and would be read by a movie director by the name of John Irvin. Irvin asked me if I wanted to be a technical advisor on a movie he was going to make in Chicago about the mob starring Arnold Schwarzenegger. I had one question, "Where do you want me to report and when?"

Chapter 48

Offshore Bookmaking Is Like Another Wall Street

Offshore bookmaking is the latest method used by organized crime to make millions. Just one such operation headquartered in the Dominican Republic is reported to handle over $1 billion a year with profits of nearly 20 million. I first became aware of this bookmaking operation at the end of 1989. We had our hands full trying to bust up local gambling operations that were using cellular telephones, which are very difficult to track down. Some evidence we recovered from some of these raids revealed that the gamblers were laying off bets to 800 numbers that were believed to be out of the United States. I convinced one of my informants to begin making bets through an 800 number that we learned was taking any kind of bet you wanted to make. He told me that he had to send $2,000 to a location in the Dominican Republic and then he would be OK'd to make wagers with them. He said that he was given a code name and two 800 numbers to call any time of the day or night to make his bets. They told him that if he won his bets, he would be paid by check, or on occasion someone would contact him to settle up. In the event he lost the $2,000, he would not be able to make any more wagers until he put up another $2,000 as front money.

My informant normally bet anywhere from $500 to $1,000 a game and was a pretty good handicapper. After the first week, he only bet three games for $300 each; he told me that he won all three games and had $900 coming. He also told me that whenever he would call the two 800 numbers, the phones were never busy even though he would call twenty minutes before the game went off, which is usually the busiest time for bookmakers. He also said that he could hear other phones ringing in the background and other voices that were giving out the betting lines or repeating bets back to other customers. The betting week usually ended on a Sunday, so he was waiting to get paid his winnings; and he told me that he probably would get screwed and that the whole thing was a scam. That Wednesday he received a check in the mail for his $900, and the envelope was postmarked New York, New York.

I figured as long as my informant was winning, he might as well keep betting; he agreed naturally, and for the next month he was up about $5,500. At one point I told him that all the money he won from betting would have to be used as evidence when we busted up this operation. Before he went ballistic, I told him I was only kidding and to keep up the good work.

I called an FBI agent friend who was assigned to the organized crime unit in Chicago. I told him about this massive bookmaking ring that was operating in the Dominican Republic. He said he would check on it and let me know if gambling was legal in the Dominican Republic, and what the government could do about this situation.

In the meantime we learned that the main operation was in Santo Domingo, the capital of the island. The island is located about 575 miles southeast of Miami, Florida. And the people are of Spanish and African ancestry and raise sugarcane, rice, and cocoa beans. Christopher Columbus discovered the island in 1492 for Spain. Well guess what, now the island has been re-discovered by the mob in 1989. It only took the boys 497 years to find the island, and their main product is not sugarcane. We learned that these guys will take bets on anything, including golf tournaments.

After a week, my FBI friend said that gambling was legal in the Dominican Republic, but that it was illegal to accept bets from the United States. Of course, it is illegal for anyone to bet on sporting events in the United States, except Nevada. My friend in the FBI told me that the U.S. Attorneys Office of the Northern District of

Illinois was looking into this bookmaking operation, and they were going to open a case on it. He also said that by checking with other bureau offices in the country, he learned that they also were going to look into this matter. This investigation took three years before the Dominican Republic Police, assisted by the FBI, conducted a raid on the headquarters of this bookmaking ring. Evidence recovered from the raid revealed that the alleged leader of the Santo Domingo operation was a Californian, Ronald "the Cigar" Sacco, forty-eight, a well-known bookmaker. A reliable source reported that they had sixteen 800 phone lines, and take action all day long. Other cities in the United States that are associated with this ring are San Diego, Los Angeles, San Francisco, Sacramento, Reno, Las Vegas, Tulsa, Dallas, Baton Rouge, Cleveland, Philadelphia, Canton, New York, Baltimore, Miami, and, of course, Chicago. All these cities have connections to organized crime in the United States.

A former clerk who had moved to Santo Domingo from New York to pay off his gambling debts said that the office he worked in was like a zoo. Everyone who worked in the office would be yelling and screaming when it was a busy day like a Saturday during the college football season. Their boss would be telling them to move the betting line on certain games with a lot of action. The clerk also said that computer terminals set up at each clerk's cubicle are connected to a mainframe, so they can keep track of the thousands of bets they had taken in and in part to prevent fraud within the organization. An example would be that a bet was made before a race or game, and all conversations are tape-recorded in case of any disputes.

Whenever a customer would call and make a bet, he would first have to give you his code name, then any bets that he made, you would have to write up a ticket, and then repeat the bets back to him. The office manager would pick up the tickets every once in a while and then put them in a lock box. One copy would go to someone called a "grader" in a separate room. The grader marks the totals on the balance sheets each night to adjust the betting lines in an effort to even out the bets on each game so the organization can make the 5 percent juice or profit on the overall handle. Bookmakers in Chicago charged 10 percent juice on losing bets.

The operation also took bets via computer and even via faxes, but this can be dangerous because the FBI can get copies by tapping into the lines for their computers or fax machines. The bookmakers had set up a ninety-foot tower nearby and two satellite dishes when they started the business a few years ago. They even had a phone company employee on their payroll, so in case something went wrong with their phones, he could make the necessary repairs so there wouldn't be any interruption of business.

The FBI has reported that Ronald "the Cigar" Sacco has admitted that he was a bookmaker, but that he didn't know anything about any Mafia connections. But the Justice Department described an electronically linked network of organized crime families as well as independent bookies. It was also alleged that Sacco was being taxed by the mob, especially the Gambino Crime Family in New York. Records that were seized indicated that Sacco netted more than $7 million and the "company" netted $19 million. The question was, who got the other $12 million? You can bet it wasn't the Salvation Army. The Justice Department brought a civil action suit against a man named Darryl Kaplan who operated a pawn and loan shop in the Mission District of San Francisco; they seized $1.2 million in cash and $118,000 in jewelry, claiming that it was used for illegal gambling. An IRS investigation claimed the shop handled more than $80 million worth of checks from 1984 to 1990. Kaplan said that his main businesses were cashing checks and making loans. He did readily admit that he was also a gambler, and bet pro football, and gave little regard to its being illegal. He also admitted betting with offshore 800 numbers and how was he to know if Sacco was a bookmaker or where he got the checks from that he brought in his shop. Gambling is more popular than it ever was; now we have the same type of bookmaking operations going full blast in Jamaica, Antigua, Costa Rica, and other places in the Caribbean. I know one bookmaker whom I busted for running a wire room in Chicago about twenty years ago has since gone to Australia and is still in business. His players are in Chicago, and they call him on an 800 number. The bookmaker has someone settle up with his players every week, and it's business as usual. When the FBI and the local police made the raid in Santo Domingo, they confiscated their telephones, fax machines, computers, and all their gambling records, which is normal procedure. But wouldn't you know, the bad guys apparently thought ahead and took the necessary precautions to make sure they didn't remain out of business to long. My informant, who had been making bets with this office, told me he was contacted by someone connected with Sacco's operation and was given two new 800 numbers to call if he wanted to make any bets. Obviously, they had an alternate location set up in case of a raid by the authorities; these guys didn't miss a stroke, and they were real pros.

This type of bookmaking is so far out of control, it's a joke. The government had better open their eyes and make this situation a top priority and do whatever it takes to try and put a stop to this type of activity. Believe me, organized crime is behind all of it. As the director of a vice detection unit of the Cook County Sheriff's Office we investigated organized crime gambling operations.

We learned of an illegal bookmaking operation that was utilizing 800 numbers. Our investigation of this operation found that the 800 numbers were in San Jose, Costa Rica. This sports book would take any kind of bet up to $25,000 and is open twenty-four hours a day. The interesting part of this case was that a guy by the name of John Scala of Berwyn, Illinois, was the main collector for the Costa Rica operation on the southwest side of the Chicago area. I had busted Scala in the past for running a sports wire room. Scala would meet bettors at various locations throughout the city and suburbs to pick up their winnings or pay off their debts. I decided it was time for Mr. Scala and I to renew our friendship; we executed a search warrant on Scala in the 200th block of South Racine Avenue while he was on his route. We found gambling wagers totaling $225,000, four cellular telephones, pagers, portable paper shredder, and $35,995 in cash; all these items were confiscated. I believe that Scala could be in a little trouble, because I think he was handling some action himself, which I'm sure was against the house rules. With Scala's arrest, it only proved to us that the mob was behind this offshore bookmaking operation as they are behind all the other offshore books. I believe that if enough pressure would have been put on some of these operations when they first started, we wouldn't have the problem that we have today with illegal gambling. In St. John's Antigua, a Caribbean island, there have been as many as twenty-five sports books on operation. One of them is called World Sports Exchange; they have twenty-five operators working their computers, logging bets from all over the United States. On Super Bowl day, they take in over 10,000 bets on that day alone. An ex-bookie from Boston named Eremian booked for eleven years; he then decided to move to the island and open up his book because he wouldn't have to worry about getting his door getting battered down. Another sports book called WorldWide Telesports has thirty-eight phone clerks – or "sports consultants," as the company calls them – seated in front of computers. Gamblers from all over the world, but mostly from the United States, call them. They claim that they can handle almost four thousand calls per hour, with bets ranging as high as $25,000 on a game. Located on the top floor of the tallest office building on the island, the company has eighty-five employees, including marketing, accounting, and systems departments. All the department heads are Antiguans, and the all female staff of phone clerks starts at $5 per hour. Antigua is a member of the British Commonwealth and has a population of 70,000; over 95 percent of the natives are black, and most white residents work either in the hotels or the sports books. Now the sports books are getting into online casinos, which allow customers to bet on interactive games, like slot machines, blackjack, and poker. Of course, the critics of these offshore books are the operators of casinos in the United States, who loathe the thought of gambling dollars leaving the country. Despite requests from some state attorney generals to put an end to the offshore betting operations, the Department of Justice so far has not acted. A Justice Department spokesman's reply was, "We have no jurisdiction." Well, it sure looks as if the tail is wagging the fucking dog.

John Scala was main collector for mob running gambling from the islands using 800 numbers

SEPT. 28, 95

Police uncover gambling syndicate

By J. Carole Buckner
Staff Writer

A regional illegal gambling figure is expected to appear in court today on charges he used an 800 number to Costa Rica to place illegal bets, authorities said.

The Cook County sheriff's police arrested John Skala, 55, 1624 S. East Ave., Berwyn, on Chicago's South Side Thursday, according to Don Herion, director of the vice division of the Cook County Sheriff's Department.

Skala was charged with syndicated gambling, Herion said.

Herion said Skala was the "main collector" for an elaborate international gambling operation that involved using an 800 number to Costa Rica where wagers of all types were taken.

Bettors used the 800 number to place their bets and then met Skala afterward at various locations throughout the city and suburbs to pick up their winnings or pay off their debts, Herion said.

"He was the main collector for the region," Herion said. Herion said the 800 gambling operation was "international" with connections "in the major cities throughout the country."

Police arrested Skala in the 200 block of Racine Avenue in Chicago about 12:15 p.m. Police said they confiscated $35,995 in cash from Skala's car. They said they also confiscated gambling wagers totaling $225,000, four portable phones, pagers, a paper shredder and a book titled, "Covering the Spread: How To Bet Pro Football" from Skala's house in Berwyn.

Offshore operation is 'like Wall Street'

Steve Wilstein
Associated Press

Packets of $100 bills, stapled inside magazines, arrive punctually each week by overnight courier to pay salaries at the bustling offices of the nation's largest sports bookie ring, headquartered in the Dominican Republic.

The pay is fantastic on this island, but it is a piddling expense for sprawling operation that handles $1 billion a year with profits of nearly $20 million, according to the FBI and sources working for the ring.

The FBI believes the operation is linked to organized crime and large bookie rings in New York, Philadelphia, Baltimore, Chicago, Cleveland, Dallas, Tulsa, Okla., Baton Rouge, La., San Francisco and Los Angeles. And it's still going strong, despite raids on several offices, more than two dozen indictments and guilty pleas.

Amoeba-like, the operation feeds on money and sports everywhere it exists, stretching from country to country in the Caribbean — the Dominican Republic, Jamaica, Antigua, Costa Rica — and city to city in the United States.

Dominican police, assisted by the FBI, broke up one Santo Domingo operation last year. Gambling is legal on the island, but it is illegal to accept bets from the United States. Yet nothing much changed except the address and the toll-free, rollover 800 numbers that were running up bills of $50,000 a month.

"We have about 16 '800' phone lines and we take bets all day,"

Please see BETTING, D-8

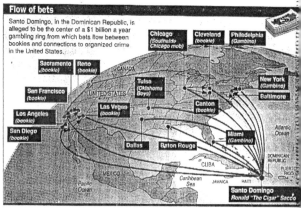

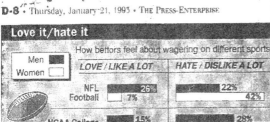

Love it/hate it

How bettors feel about wagering on different sports:

Men / Women — LOVE/LIKE A LOT — HATE/DISLIKE A LOT

- NFL Football: Men 26%, Women 7% / Men 22%, Women 42%
- NCAA College Football: Men 15%, Women 3% / Men 28%, Women 46%
- NBA Basketball: Men 13%, Women 3% / Men 25%, Women 45%
- NCAA College Basketball: Men 13%, Women 2% / Men 30%, Women 47%
- Major League Baseball: Men 13%, Women 4% / Men 24%, Women 43%
- NHL Hockey: Men 4%, Women 1% / Men 31%, Women 47%

*Figures do not add up to 100%, since some answered no opinion, like a little or dislike a little. Americans polled aged 12 and over.

Source: Associated Press/Sports Marketing Group-Dallas

BETTING: Sacco alleged leader

Continued from D-1

said Carl, a clerk or 'writer' who moved down from New York to pay off his gambling debts by working at one of the bookie houses in the Dominican Republic capital. "It's like Wall Street, everyone screaming and tense when there's a lot of action, the boss shouting to move the line when someone comes in with a big play because the bettors will try to dump you for half a point. They're a tricky bunch, the players. We have to be fast and accurate because mistakes cost money."

Computer terminals set up at each writer's cubicle are connected to a mainframe, in part to keep track of the thousands of transactions, and in part to prevent fraud within the organization — to prove that a bet was made before a race or game. All phone conversations are tape recorded in case there are disputes.

"The conversations are so bizarre," Carl said. "You're talking with someone code-named 'Eel' and you say, 'Yes sir, can I help you?' And he says, 'Yeah, I want a dime on the Niners,' and a dime is $1,000. So you'd write up a ticket

SPORTS GAMBLING

Tuesday: Americans oppose legalized sports gambling, but many can't wait to get a bet down, legal or not.

Yesterday: Bookmakers handled $10 billion in bets from four million Americans last year.

Today: A betting ring headquartered in Dominican Republic, linked to organized crime by the FBI, is only an 800 call away.

Tomorrow: Compulsive gambling exacts heavy toll, but treatment is not readily available and often misguided.

Saturday: Young bettors can find action on the college campus and in the high school classroom.

Sunday: Electronic gadgets help high-tech bookies zip bets around the world.

bino family in New York and the Southside Chicago Mob in the Midwest.

reveal where most of the money had gone. The figures indicated Sacco netted more than $7 million and the "company" seems to have netted $19 million.

"So who got the other $12 million I don't know. It's probably sitting somewhere in New York," said FBI agent Rick Smith in San Francisco.

The probe also involves allegations of horse-race fixing in Toronto, Chicago and San Francisco, and of a few college games. According to affidavits, two informants told the FBI that another Californian bookmaker in Santo Domingo, Anthony "Fatso" Labue, boasted of paying a referee to fix a college game, saying, "We own that whistle."

Sacco's attorney scoffs at the idea of any bookmaker fixing a game.

"The worst situation a bookmaker can be in is having to deal with a fixed game," Henderson said. "That hurts bookmakers. No bookmaker in the world would ever fix a game; that's a bettor's delight. It doesn't make any logical sense that even Labue or any of those guys would be involved in the fixing of any games because that's how bookmakers get wiped out."

While nearly all bookies lay off bets when they're handling too much action on one side, Sacco never does, as far as the FBI can tell.

The Justice Department brought a civil action to seize a pawn and loan shop run by Darryl Kaplan in San Francisco's Mission District, $1.2 million in cash and $118,829 in jewelry, claiming it was used for illegal gambling. An IRS investigation claimed the shop handled more than $80 million worth of checks from 1984 to 1990.

Yet, Kaplan hasn't been charged. Nor has he gotten back his money.

Kaplan's main businesses are cashing checks and making loans and his avocation is gambling.

"I bet mostly pro football, betting the middle, laying 6 and taking 7," he said, giving little regard to the illegality of his hobby. "I told the feds, 'You got something, arrest me. You want me to plead guilty to a gambling charge, I'll plead guilty. I'm a gambler. Give me my money back.' I don't need to launder money. I did bet offshore. I told them that, although I probably shouldn't have.

"But I cash checks all the time from lots of people. Am I supposed to know if someone's a bookie or how he got the check? Sacco's never been popped. I've never been arrested. But it's been a nightmare. How come I'm still

Chapter 49

Organized Crime, Gambling, and the Movies

When I appeared at the President's Commission on Organized Crime in New York, New York, on June 24-26, 1985, as an expert witness on the Chicago mob and their involvement in illegal gambling. I had no idea how that would effect me getting in the movie business. It seems that the government printed a book with the results of that hearing and the testimony of all the witnesses as well as photographs of the evidence presented to the members of the commission.

Some of the people who testified were college professors like Jerome Skolnick, who was a professor of law at the University of California, Berkeley. He had a distinguished record of publications including an authoritative 1978 work on Las Vegas entitled *House of Cards: The Legalization and Control of Casino Gambling*. Others were Daryl Gates, chief of the Los Angeles Police Department; Howard Cosell, attorney and noted sports broadcaster, who was the voice of boxing in the United States as well as *Monday Night Football*; and Stephen Wynn, owner of the Golden Nugget Casino in Las Vegas, Nevada. There were also numerous investigators from the various cities, states, as well as the federal agencies that were considered experts on organized crime gambling in the United States. Last but not least were college coaches as well as newspaper publishers and the ever-popular hooded witnesses who were in witness protection, such as Frank Cullotta and Ken "Tokyo Joe" Eto from the Chicago mob.

I was working in the gambling unit at 943 West Maxwell Street one day when I got an unusual telephone call from some guy with an English accent. He told me his name was John Irvin and that he was a movie director and would like to talk to me about helping him make a movie. I thought that this was a joke, of course, because cops love to play jokes on other cops. This director told me that he was calling from England and would be in Chicago in about a week and would like to meet me. I asked him how he got my name and knew where to find me. He told me that he had read a book about organized crime that the President's Commission on Organized Crime printed and had read my testimony about the Chicago Outfit and that I seemed to know what I was talking about. John Irvin then told me that he was going to make a mob movie about Chicago and was going to film it in Chicago and he needed someone to be a technical advisor that had knowledge of the Chicago Outfit and the way the Chicago police operated.

I still thought that this was some copper with a good English accent and was yanking my chain; I asked him just what a technical advisor did. Irvin explained that all I would have to do is to read the script, and when they were going to shoot a scene involving the mob or the police, I would make sure that it was done properly. I asked him if advisors get paid for that, and he said they sure do, but you will have to negotiate a deal with the producer. I still thought that the whole thing was some kind of joke, but I figured I might as well go along with it, as I had nothing to lose. Irvin told me that he would be staying at the Palmer House when he got in town next week and that he would call me when he arrived. I asked him who was starring in the movie, and without stuttering he said, "Arnold Schwarzenegger."

Much to my surprise, the following week Irvin called me at the office to tell me he had arrived and was at the Palmer House and would like to meet me. It just so happened that we had a search warrant to execute that night on an outfit wire room on the North Side of Chicago around Ashland and Montrose Avenue. I told Irvin that we had to bust down a door on an apartment and that I probably wouldn't be able to meet him. Irvin asked if he could go with us on the raid and that he would stay out of our way and wouldn't be any problem. It was against the rules to have a civilian with us, of course, but I thought, what the hell,

I would leave him in front of the building so that he wouldn't get hurt in case something went wrong.

I said OK and told Irvin that I would pick him up and asked him what he would be wearing and to stand by the front desk so I could find him. I was trying to picture what this guy looked like and wondered if he would be wearing an ascot or knickers and a tam. I found him all right; he was wearing jeans and a Windbreaker, was about six foot one, weighed 200 pounds, and about forty-two years old. There really was a John Irvin, movie director. We shook hands and told him that we had to leave and meet three other cops on the North Side so we could execute the warrant. I explained a few things that we were going to do and that he shouldn't be nervous at all. Irvin said that he would be OK and that he would stay out of our way. Little did I know at the time that Irvin and a cameraman had filmed a lot of stories for the BBC around the world. Most of the stories involved revolutions in areas around Saudi Arabia, such as in the Republic of Yemen, which borders on the Red Sea and Saudi Arabia. Irvin probably saw more fighting than an infantryman in World War II. He even did a documentary on the Marines in Vietnam at an outpost in the middle of the Vietcong. Irvin only talked about these things after a few beers. Needless to say, I felt a little embarrassed when I told him not to worry about the raid we were doing and that usually nobody ever gets shot.

The raid went off very well, and we locked up an outfit guy named Lamont "Woody" Howard and caught him with $200,000 in bets. The apartment he was using was a pigsty, with a lot of roaches crawling around, eating the garbage on the floors. I called Irvin up to the apartment to let him see what a scumbag apartment the guy was using and that we got lucky we found the bets and we wouldn't have to search the rest of the roach-infested apartment. He was going to sit down on a chair, and I stopped him and told him that he would probably have some friends running around in his shirt if he did. We took the prisoner back to Maxwell Street and processed him. Howard kept asking if Irvin was with the police department and if we were hiring English cops now. I told him that Irvin was from Scotland Yard in London and he was here to go on this particular raid because he had heard so much about Chicago gangsters. I don't think he believed me. We got rid of the paperwork and then decided to eat at a German restaurant on Southport Avenue.

Before the night was over, I found out that English directors could consume quite a bit of beer, whiskey, and wine – not necessarily in that order – and it didn't faze him one bit. I can't say that for the rest of us though, but that's all I'm going to say about that part of the night. We took Irvin back to the Palmer House after a lot of questions about the movie, which was going to be called *Triple Identity*, but they changed the name to *Raw Deal* for some reason. Irvin seemed to be a real nice guy and wasn't a bullshit artist, as far as I could tell anyway. We made arrangements to meet the next day at the Palmer House because he wanted to introduce me to the unit production manager and the producer as well as a few of the movie crew who were also in town.

The next day, Irvin – whom I was now calling John – told me that a part of the movie was also going to be shot in Wilmington, North Carolina, where they were going to blow up an oil refinery. Arnold was going to have a major shoot-out with about thirty bad guys in a gravel pit over a large cache of narcotics. I had to ask John how Arnold Schwarzenegger was going to infiltrate the Chicago Outfit as a bad guy with his heavy Austrian accent. He said, "Don, don't worry about it. This is all make-believe, and they can do anything in the movies." He was sure right about that, as I was to find out later. I was given the script, and it wasn't too bad a story. Arnold was going to play an FBI agent who got involved in a scandal when he beat the shit out of a child molester who murdered a young girl. The U.S. attorney gave him a choice – resign or be prosecuted. Arnold resigned and left Chicago with his wife, Amy. They ended up in a small town in North Carolina, where Arnold got a job as the sheriff in a town called Barrett, population 4,610. Arnold and especially his wife were not happy being stuck in this godforsaken place, but it was better than nothing.

Then one day, Arnold got a call from an FBI agent that he had worked with in Chicago; his name was Harry Shannon. Darren McGavin, who was a veteran actor, played Shannon. Anyway Shannon told Arnold that his son, who was also an FBI agent, was killed by the Chicago mob when he was assigned to guard a federal informant who could put the bosses of the Chicago mob in jail. Shannon told Arnold that he had $45,000 of his own money, which he would use to finance Arnold if he would accept the job to go to Chicago and infiltrate the Chicago Outfit. This would be an unofficial assignment, and the FBI or anyone else would know about it. Of course, Arnold accepted the challenge and off to Chicago he went.

Myself and Arnold ???
Movie called 'RAW DEAL'

I was told that the budget for the movie was $6 million and that Arnold was getting $1 million of it, not bad for about twelve weeks work. John Irvin introduced me to Arnold, and when we shook hands I expected to have my hand crushed, but it didn't happen; he was really a likable guy and was easy to get along with. He stayed at the Palmer House while he was filming in Chicago, and at the time he was engaged to Maria Schriver, who came to town to visit him on a few weekends. An actress by the name of Katherine Harrold had the female lead, and Sam Wanamaker and Steven Hill were the mob bosses.

At the time I was working out of 943 West Maxwell Street, which was the gambling unit of the organized crime division as well as intelligence and the prostitution section. My hours were flexible enough so that I was able to take care of my consulting on the movie as well as make gambling raids. We even used Tony Accardo's old mansion on Franklin Avenue in River Forest for the home of the mob boss, and it really looked good. There was a big shoot – 'em-up car chase on Navy Pier where another bad guy named Robert Davi played a hit man. These movie people worked about fourteen hours a day shooting this movie, and there was a lot of sitting around and waiting in between scenes; actually, it was pretty boring at times.

I got pretty friendly with the crew during the filming of the movie, and most of them were really great guys and knew their business. A lot of them were from England and a few were from Italy. The English guys said that the real power behind the movie was a producer by the name of Dino De Laurentis, who operated his own studio and liked to have a few Italians on the set. Some of them indicated that De Laurentis used to pay everyone involved in the making of a movie in cash, which led some of them to believe that he had an association with the Mafia in Italy. De Laurentis was married to a woman by the name of Martha Schumacher, who just happened to be one of the producers of the movie. Someone said that she was a former bartender from New York and just got lucky in showbiz. They also hoped that she was a better bartender than she was a producer because she didn't know shit about making a movie.

A real interesting bunch of guys in making this movie were the special effects people. The leader was a great guy by the name of Joe Lombardi; he had been in the business for forty years and knew everything there was to know about special effects. His son Paul was with him, as well as two other fellas who knew how to blow up anything and everything. Joe and I became good friends and even worked on another movie together entitled *Next of Kin*, with Patrick Swayze and Liam Neesan, which was also about the Chicago Outfit; but that's another story. I found out that Lombardi had been involved in special effects ever since he got out of the navy after World War II, and he was considered the best in the business. He worked on the *Lucille Ball Show* when television first started as well as *The Godfather* movies and *Apocalypse Now*, a war movie about Vietnam. There was a scene in the movie down in North Carolina where Arnold blew up an oil refinery to cover his exit from his sheriff's job. Lombardi had about two hundred 50-gallon drums set up to show what would happen when an oil refinery blew up. Well, when that thing blew, all you could see were these 50-gallon drums flying through the air with flames 200 feet high; it looked like a war zone. Lombardi told me later that maybe he had used a little too much gasoline for the explosion, but it sure looked great in the movie.

John asked me one day if I would like a part in the movie; at first I was a little surprised that he would ask me to act in a scene because I told him that I didn't know jackshit about acting. Then he said, "I think you can handle the part. It's playing a Chicago Police Department desk sergeant." "Besides all policemen are actors," he said. When I thought about it, I agreed with him and told him that yes I would give it a try; I had nothing to lose.

The set designer built a police station with a long desk and everything else that you would have in the station. I was fitted with a sergeant's uniform and began rehearsing my lines, or I should say, *line*.

My scene was as follows:

> I'm behind the desk walking toward a phone that is ringing at the end of the desk, at this time a driver with a hand cart comes walking in the front door of the station; the cart is loaded with pop and chips. He proceeds over to a pop machine and a machine that has chips and candy and begins to load up both of the machines. Being a sharp desk sergeant I know that this is not the regular deliveryman so that is when I say my line, "Hey! Where are you goin'?" He answers by saying, "I'm going to fill the machines. It's Wednesday, right?" Then I say, "Where's Bobby?" He answers with, "That's what the boss would like to know. Say, you guys bigger on potato or corn chips? The boys over at the Sixth don't even touch the corn." I then answer the phone on the desk, "Ninth District, Sergeant Moore." The best part is that I don't see this guy put a pop can loaded with an explosive in the machine. Of course, after the guy leaves, the station blows up and I'm killed, along with several other people who happened to be in the station.

Now to do this scene, the cameramen had a camera set up on a track behind the desk and another camera set up on the other side of the desk out of view of the one behind the desk. They had to film this scene of me walking behind the desk and at the same time film the deliveryman coming in the front door, so the timing had to be perfect to get us both. We had to do the scene four times because either I was walking too fast or the deliveryman was walking too slow, and they weren't able to get us both in the same frame. I found out later that sometimes they had to shoot scenes ten times to get it the way they wanted, so I guess we did all right after all. The director, John Irvin, said I did fine and that I really looked like a cop. That's all I cared about anyway. I must admit that it sure was funny to hear words like

"Quiet please," "Everybody, settle down," and then the words "ACTION," and "Cut," and "Print it." That means the scene is over and moves on to the next location. There is another part of this moviemaking that was interesting; everybody has to go to the makeup trailer before you would do your scene. I walked into the trailer, and there was a man and a woman who were putting makeup on a couple other "actors." I, of course, got the man, which made me a little nervous at the time. Anyway, he applied powder on my face and some other makeup to cover up any blemishes that would be seen on film. He seemed OK to me at the time, but he did seem to have some feminine mannerisms, when I come to think of it. He asked me how long I had been an actor; when I told him that this was my first time, he seemed shocked. He then told me that I would be eligible to join the Screen Actors Guild if I wanted, and then I would be in the union and they would have to pay me union scale. All you need to qualify to join the union is a dialog in a movie.

The original name of this movie was *Triple Identity*, but they changed it to *Raw Deal*. I also learned that they changed the first part of the movie because Arnold didn't like the scene with his "wife" cheating on him. It seems that Sheriff Arnold goes home a little early from work one day and finds his wife in the sack with another guy. Then he goes nuts and throws all her clothes out on the front lawn. Apparently, Arnold felt that no wife of his would possibly cheat on him, and it would be embarrassing in the movie. He changed the scene to him coming home early OK, but his wife was in the kitchen baking a cake and she was drunk out of her mind, and she throws the cake at him but misses. I guess that made Arnold feel better, and the studio went along with him.

Arnold was a pretty nice guy, and we got along OK. He told some funny stories about when he was in the Austrian Army when he was younger. The army made a big mistake one day when they told him he was going to be trained to drive a tank. He said that after the second day of his training, while he was at the controls of the tank, he made a wrong move and backed the tank up into somebody's house. His sergeant then thought Arnold would be better off in another unit.

Arnold had a deal with the studio that they would provide a room for his weights so that he could work out and keep in shape while he was doing the movie. I'm not sure if he also had it in his contract that he be supplied with the biggest Cuban cigars that they could find; he had a contact somewhere because he always had a stogie in his mouth except when he was shooting a scene.

Another actor who was very well known played an outfit guy in the movie and wound up getting killed in a shoot-out with other Mafia bad guys; his name is Steven Hill and has been in movies and TV for many years. He was staying at 400 East Randolph and had a nice apartment paid for by the studio of course. One day, when we were shooting a chase scene at Navy Pier, which is where he gets shot and his car blows up, he was so nervous after the chase scene – which was really convincing, by the way – he had to go home and lay down. There weren't any teamster drivers around at the time, so I gave him a lift home, and he thanked me and insisted that I accept a rare bottle of wine. I didn't want it, but he insisted, so much I just took it. I don't know jackshit about wine except that some are white and some are red. I gave it to the door man at 400 East Randolph, who looked as if he knew what wine was all about.

All in all, I found moviemaking to be very interesting; these people work long hours and in all kinds of weather. The major actors are really treated royally with their own house trailers on the set and a teamster driver who gets them whatever they want. They are picked up at their hotel and driven to wherever the scene is going to be shot that day. I had a few conversations with some of the teamster drivers who told me that a few of the actors liked to smoke a little wacky tabacci or whatever else they could get. Some of them indicated that they were helpful to the stars in that area.

The teamster drivers had a pretty good thing going in the movie business. It seemed that after they picked up the actors and delivered them to the set, they had nothing to do but wait until the actors were through with their scene. Sometimes that was twelve hours later, so they had to keep themselves busy by playing touch football, gin rummy, or just sleep. There was one guy by the name of Sal who always seemed to have a telephone in his hand during booking hours. I was pretty sure that he was booking a little action on some football games. I was never able to get close to him because he always had a few goombas around to warn him if I was anywhere in the area. Somehow I got the idea that if I busted this guy on the set, the teamster union might try to screw up John Irvin in some way and cause him some problems making the movie.

Arnold had another big action scene in the movie where he drives to a gravel pit in his Cadillac to confront half of the Chicago Outfit. His cover had been blown, so now it was open warfare. He armed himself with an MP-5K submachine gun – the devastating 9-millimeter blaster used by the U.S. Rangers and Britain's elite SAS commandos for overwhelming firepower; also 750 rounds of death per minute, and half a dozen 30-round magazines; a pump action Winchester shotgun with a box of three-inch Magnum loads and an ammunition belt; a pair of heavy Browning Hi-Power pistols with ten clips. He was now ready to go to war.

He drove toward Cicero, Illinois, where the gravel pit was located. He stopped in a gas station and got directions, and he found it without difficulty. The gravel pit was really in Wilmington, North Carolina, but this is the movie business so they made it look like it was in Cicero. The mob bosses' men were in a small corrugated-metal shed where seven of them were cutting and bagging heroin, sacks of currency rested on the floor beside them. They were all heavily armed and were ready for anything. There were lookouts posted all over the gravel pit and were also armed to the teeth. Arnold shot off the lock on the front gate of the ABC Gravel, and then he blew out the windshield of his Cadillac so that he could have total visibility that he needed; the game was on. When the scene began, you can see Arnold firing his submachine gun while he was driving the Cadillac at breakneck speed; then there was a cut. When you could see the car from a distance and the car was zigzagging all over the gravel pit, Arnold was not driving. The driver was a stuntman by the name of Joel Kramer, who doubled Arnold in any scene that could be risky and if Arnold could get injured. He could really drive that Cadillac while he was firing guns and killing all the bad guys. Fifteen bad guys were shooting at Arnold, and in the movie, he got nicked a couple of times, but he managed to kill all of them. But before they all died, Arnold got caught in the middle of a Terex Pit Truck and a massive Caterpillar loader; they had the Cadillac boxed in and Arnold "Joel" just managed to get out of the Cadillac before they crushed him. It sure did look as if Arnold was in the Cadillac all the time this action was taking place, but a lot of the time, Joel Kramer was doing his job. I talked to Joel about his stunt work, and he said it was a lot easier than it looked. He asked me if I was the Chicago cop who was the technical advisor for the movie. I said yes I was, and then he asked me if I had ever been in any high-speed chases in my career. I said yes I was, and that I hoped that I would never get in anymore of them as they can get pretty hairy sometimes.

He was a very interesting guy, and I found out that his uncles owned a restaurant just outside of Chicago, in Lincolnwood, Illinois. The restaurant was called Myron and Phil's on Devon Avenue. I had been involved in a few investigations involving a lot of wise guys who frequented the restaurant and were familiar with the owners. Myron and Phil and their father owned a restaurant on the South Side of Chicago in the Maxwell Street area and were involved in a bookmaking operation for a long time. They sold the restaurant and moved over to Devon Avenue and opened up Myron and Phil's, which was a very nice restaurant. As far as I know, they got out of the bookmaking business when they left Maxwell Street. As things turned out, they would turn out to be victims of mob threats on their lives and have to pay protection money to keep from getting their heads cut off by a guy by the name of Mario Rainone, who worked for mob boss Lenny Patrick. All those guys are now in jail, doing a lot of time.

Again, Joel asked me about the chases that I had been involved in and what rate of speed we reached. I told him the fastest chase I had was when we hit 105 mph chasing some idiot down Division Street toward the suburbs. Whenever a chase starts sometimes it gets out of hand and it becomes a personal thing between you and the bad guy. We could have been killed a few times during the chase and we could have killed some innocent person as well. I explained that all common sense leaves your head and you become stupid and do dumb things, such as going through red lights at 75 mph. Just because you have flashing lights and a siren blasting doesn't mean that all the other vehicles on the street can see or hear you coming. That particular chase happened at 4:00 AM so there wasn't much traffic on the street; besides at the time, we didn't give a shit if there was or wasn't. There was always the chance of the nut that you were chasing hitting some other vehicle; we didn't give a damn if he cracked up himself, but if he killed some innocent person or persons, that would be tragic.

The majority of chases begin because of a traffic violation by the bad guy; it's true that he is running because he just killed somebody or robbed someone or committed some other crime, but the police don't know this at the time. Today anyone that gets involved in a high-speed chase has to immediately notify the radio room and tell them that they are in pursuit of a certain vehicle. At that time the operator will notify the officer's immediate supervisor and advise him of the chase. The supervisor will ask the officers why they are chasing that particular vehicle. The officers will then inform the supervisor of the facts of the pursuit; the supervisor will make a decision either to continue or terminate the chase. If in fact the bad guys committed a felony, the odds are fifty-fifty that the supervisor will terminate. He will be held responsible for whatever happens involving this action.

Joel Kramer said that if he were one of the cops involved in the chase, he wasn't sure that he would obey his supervisor if he were told to terminate. I told him that no matter what happened in this pursuit, if he didn't obey his supervisor he would be in deep shit and could be suspended or even fired if things went haywire and someone got killed or injured. Then he said, "That really sucks. I would rather do all the stunts called for in a movie, it's a lot safer than being a cop in Chicago." I told him that the chase was bad enough, but when the bad guys are shooting at you during the chase, that really gets scary; naturally, you have to return fire, and it gets to be like a moving OK Corral shootout. Where all the bullets went would be a real mystery; probably all over the street and into somebody's house. I really didn't want to find out.

Believe it or not, I did join the Screen Actors Guild. The dues were $37.50 every six months; that made me equal to Marlon Brando, Robert De Niro, or Mickey Rooney, as far as voting goes, I mean. I had to get some eight-by-twelve headshots made and then get an agent. What the hell did I know about all this showbiz stuff? Nothing. I remember one day I got a call from my agent, who told me that I had an audition to go to for a part in a movie entitled *Hoffa*. The part I was going for was a deputy in a courtroom where Hoffa was to be tried by the federal government. The audition was to be held in a downtown hotel, where I was to read some lines for the part. I went to an office where the audition was to be held and sat down and tried to memorize a couple of lines that I had been given by a secretary. Then much to my surprise, the person who was going to interview me was Danny DeVito, who was directing the movie. Jack Nicholson was going to play Hoffa in the movie. DeVito was about as tall as a midget and smoked a big Cuban cigar. DeVito introduced himself, and we had a conversation about Hoffa, which didn't turn out to good for me. I told DeVito I had heard that Hoffa was a well-connected guy with the outfit and that he screwed up and got himself whacked and buried in the end zone of an NFL football field in New Jersey. I added no loss either. I had been working on mob guys most of my career on the Chicago Police Department, and it was a fact that the Teamsters had a few Mafia connections, and Hoffa was behind most of it. Needless to say, my dialog with DeVito didn't go too well as I found out that he was a long-time admirer of Hoffa and thought that he had done an outstanding job with the Teamsters Union. He thanked me for appearing at the audition and bade me farewell. Hell, I didn't even get a chance to read my lines. I did learn a lesson though; you never know who is a friend of whom, it's best to stay neutral in these situations. The only good thing that I did was not call DeVito a dwarf, which is what he is. Not that there's anything wrong with that.

We finished the movie *Raw Deal* in December down in Wilmington, North Carolina, and I thought it would have done very well at the box office. I guess it did fair, but was no big deal as far as blockbuster movies go. I found it very interesting and learned a lot about the inner workings of the movie business. John Irvin called me again to be an advisor in another outfit movie that was going to be made in Chicago, as I mentioned before. This one starred Patrick Swayze, Liam Neeson, Helen Hunt, Adam Baldwin, and Bill Paxton and will be the subject of another story that really was interesting. This time bunches of hillbillies were going to take on the mob because one of their own was killed by the outfit.

ZOOMING IN

Dual role for Don Herion

REAL COP POLICES A REEL FEATURE

DON HERION

BY MARILYN SOLTIS

"Freeze!" That familiar command used by every television cop may be just another Hollywood aberration, according to Chicago police sergeant Don Herion, technical advisor to, and an actor in, "Next of Kin."

Herion, a veteran tactical officer of the Chicago police force, said, "In 33 years I've never heard anyone say, 'Freeze!' when they were chasing somebody. What we usually say is 'Stop, you so and so,' or whatever comes to mind.'

On "Next of Kin," Herion uses his expertise to make the cops—star Patrick Swayze plays one of them—and the bad guys as realistic as possible.

Given his line of work, Herion, 55, is uniquely qualified to detail the differences between reel cops and the real McCoy. "My favorite is the typical scene with the two cops sitting right in front of the restaurant waiting for the bad guys to come out," he said. "That's nuts. But it's really the only way for the idea to come across."

The more likely scenario is the one Herion actually experienced. "I spent an entire night curled up in the trunk of a car doing surveillance through a hole in the tail light. That was real and it makes for a better story, but you can't film it very well."

Herion wasn't looking for a career in show business. In fact, he is still working 14 years after the 20-year retirement cut-off just because he likes his job. "I look at it as a kind of game," he said as he unbuckles his ankle holster to show the snub-nosed .38 he carries at all times.

The tall, graying and powerfully built tactical officer's beat is illegal gambling activities of organized crime. "I've been locking 'em up since 1961," he says. It was this expertise that led circuitously to his present involvement in film work. In 1984 and 1985 he was Chicago's expert witness on illegal gambling, and appeared with similar law enforcement experts around the country on the President's Panel on Organized Crime. Director John Irvin read the government-issued findings while he was researching background for his feature, "Raw Deal," with Arnold Schwarzenegger, part of which filmed here.

Irvin called Herion and asked him to be technical advisor on the film and gave him a small part in the Chicago scenes. While working on "Raw Deal," Herion got the bug, and that job led to some commercial and print ad work. "It's fun and the pay isn't bad," he said.

Herion didn't appear in "Crime Story," but he was a technical advisor during the scripting by the writing partners, one a former Chicago police officer.

When Irvin brought "Next of Kin" to Chicago, he tapped Herion as technical advisor a second time. Herion also was given the part of a hard-nosed, bigoted cop in an opening scene, in confrontation with Patrick Swayze's character, a rugged Kentucky police officer. "I told John that the part was a piece of cake," he said. "I just had to play myself. I found out that is very hard to do. The minute someone tells you to be yourself it's impossible." The interaction of the country boy against Herion's acerbic agression sets the tone for Swayze throughout the film. It is an important scene with which Herion is now satisfied, but it didn't come easy.

The rest of Herion's time was spent analyzing the details of the police actions. "I drove Patrick around in a squad car and showed him the proper way to call and receive calls on the car radio," he explained. "The script was entirely wrong. I know the way it's supposed to be and I know there has to be a happy medium. I advise so they won't get too far off but maybe the angles are too tough and it won't be dramatic enough."

Herion also taught Swayze how to wear an ankle holster like his own. Swayze put it on, walked around and said, "How can I pull the gun out fast enough?" Herion replied, "You're not supposed to—there are no quick-draws in this business. The real problem is how to get to your gun, period. All that quick-draw stuff is pure show biz."

Technical advice aside, Herion finds many standard script bits about police outrageously exaggerated. "One of the funniest Hollywood fantasies is calling for a helicopter from the squad car and it miraculously appears as they pull into the crime scene. They do it all the time in Hawaii Five-O," he says. "Do you have any idea how much paperwork it takes to requisition a helicopter for?"

He admitted to having been involved in car chases throughout his career, often at 100 m.p.h. through city streets. "I wouldn't bother with them anymore. They're too dangerous, and whoever you're chasing throws all the evidence out of the car while you're chasing them so you really can't ever get them on anything," said Herion.

The policeman/actor would like to continue his show biz career, but in the meantime he's still fighting organized crime, working out of the Maxwell St. Station. That's the same police station filmed for the opening of "Hill Street Blues." □

Kup's column

Irv Kupcinet

The Weekend PicKup: We predict George Bush and Michael Dukakis will each claim victory after their first debate. And with some justification. Each presented himself capably. ... Political fundit Mark Russell had a better idea: "I'm against a debate. I prefer a duel—the Pledge of Allegiance at 20 paces." ... Russell, who appeared here over the weekend, also reported former White House aide Michael Deaver, after receiving that slap on the wrist, a suspended five-year sentence, "had to be carried kicking and *laughing* out of the courtroom." ... President Reagan and his entourage will check into the Palmer House and Towers Friday for his speech at the Merchantile Exchange.

IT'S OUR ONE MAN'S OPINION that the solution to the Chicago Theatre problem may be a nonprofit operation, like the Auditorium Theater and Ravinia. No operator is coming forth to take over the theater in view of the tremendous costs, including $800,000 a year in rental. I recommend Mayor Sawyer and his staff give consideration to this nonprofit approach. The theater is too vital to the North Loop to remain dark.

PAT SWAYZE, filming here for "Next of Kin," in which he plays a Chicago cop, is planning to pay a condolence visit to the family of Patrol Officer **Irma Ruiz**, slain in the shootout the other day. ... Incidentally, a Chicago policeman, **Don Herrion**, serving as technical adviser on "Next of Kin," has a small role in the movie. Who knows? He could be the next **Dennis Farina**, who went from policeman to movie-TV star.

MICHAEL DUKAKIS is singing the praises of a longtime Chicago friend, steelman Andy Athens, his chief fundraiser in Illinois. Athens' efforts will enrich the Dukakis campaign coffers by an estimated $3 million, most of which will come from tomorrow's whopping fund-raising dinner here.

Pat Swayze

THE PARKING permits issued to Wrigleyville residents for the Cubs' seven night games may have to be discontinued. A New York court, in adjudicating a similar "parking permit" case in Albany, ruled that the residents "have no greater right to use the street for parking than any other member of the public." Meanwhile, Citizens United for Baseball in Sunshine (CUBS) has started an evaluation of the problems during the seven night games.

NEWEST STATUS SYMBOL: Flaunting a Bloomingdale's shopping bag. The Near North streets were jammed with the bag carriers over the weekend. ... Legal light **Jerry Gerson** is leaving the Rudnick & Wolfe firm to join Winston & Strawn as its real estate expert. ... Mike Kotzin, after directing

Mark Russell
He'd rather see a patriotic duel

has assured Payton he has no control over the franchisee's actions. So far, Buckingham Palace has taken no stand.

BILL PETERSEN, one of Chicago's foremost actors, is a victim of mononucleosis, which has temporarily halted production of his new TV movie, "The Kennedys and Fitzgeralds," a six-hour ABC mini-series shooting in Boston. Petersen, portraying Joe Kennedy, ages in the movie from a youth to a senior citizen. Producer of the film is former Chicagoan **Lynn Raynor**, whose father, **Ted**, is a former NU basketball player and also a moviemaker.

SPORTS ILLUSTRATED'S story about the estrangement of NBC's Bryant Gumbel and his mother, Rhea, was written before they had a "rapprochement." At least they're talking now, and he called her from Seoul the other day. Rhea is a City Hall employee. ... Adding a year: Channel 2's **Johnny Morris** and **Phil Ponce**,

It is a known fact that the New York mob was not going to let Robert Evans, who was the president of Paramount Pictures at the time, make *The Godfather*. The mob thought that the movie would make all Italians look like bad guys and idiots. I met Robert Evans in Chicago when he asked me to be a technical advisor on a movie entitled *The Cinch*, which was also about the Chicago Outfit. I, of course, asked Evans how he managed to do *The Godfather* if the New York mob was against it. He said he went to a close friend of his who was a lawyer by the name of Sidney Korshak. Apparently Korshak knew the right people because he called Evans the next day and told him not to worry about it as he squared everything with the mob. As things turned out, *The Godfather* movies were smash hits, and now every outfit guy I ever met acts like Sonny Corelone, the son of the Godfather. That's showbiz, I guess.

Myself and Wesley Snipe

Movie: U.S. Marshalls
Tech Advisor

UNTOUCHABLE SERIES

FEBRUARY 1993

Chapter 50

Lenny Patrick: Jewish Hit Man

When I first got involved in working on organized crime investigations back in 1961, I thought all outfit guys who ran things in Chicago were Italian, how wrong I was. I had heard of a guy by the name of Lenny Patrick for years, and that he was a killer and ran all the gambling on the North and West sides of Chicago in the Jewish areas. It seemed that Lenny had been rewarded for a hit he made on a fella by the name of James Ragen in 1946. Ragen owned and operated the Continental Press, a wire service that was in competition with the outfit's Trans-American wire service, which dealt in race results throughout the country. Lenny Patrick, Dave Yaras, and William Block had been identified by four witnesses as Ragen's killers and were indicted for it. But then one guy got killed himself, another witness got out of town, and the other two recanted their stories, so of course, the indictment was dropped. But Lenny Patrick and Dave Yaras both were in good shape with the mob and were trusted by them even though they were Jews.

Yaras was also a close associate of Jack Cerone, a mob boss and killer himself, and believed to be part of a crew that committed the torture murder of William "Action" Jackson a 300-pound juice collector in 1961. They hung him on a hook and used a cattle prod on him, as well as ice picks, a blowtorch, and a baseball bat. He did live for two days impaled on the meat hook but never did admit that he was a stool pigeon. They threw him in his car trunk and dumped the car under Wacker Drive. Jackson worked for Sam DeStefano, who ran the juice operations for Tony Accardo, who was the boss of the Chicago Outfit at the time. Sam was considered to be a maniac and also participated in Jackson's torture murder and offered to show photos of Jackson's body to one of his juice victims to intimidate him; it worked too.

Source: *Chicago Police Dep't*

On the West Side in the twenty-fourth ward there was a black alderman by the name of Ben Lewis who was controlled by our guy Lenny Patrick. Lewis couldn't even go to the bathroom without Patrick's OK. Patrick was getting 50 percent of all the illegal gambling operations in the ward and the people operating these illegal enterprises had to take care of any expenses out of their own pocket, such as protection from the law. The ward, which was 99 percent black, also had a lot of policy operations that had to pay Patrick for the privilege of operating in the ward. Then a strange thing happened: on the night of February 27, 1963, Alderman Lewis got whacked by person or persons unknown. He was found in his office shackled in handcuffs with three bullet holes in the back of his head. There were rumors that he had been linked to the policy racket in his ward and just maybe had a falling-out with our guy Lenny over payoffs. This murder is still unsolved. When you work organized crime gambling, you usually bust people who are taking the action in wire rooms, and on a rare occasion you may get a good informant who is upset with the mob and wants to cooperate with you. Ted Veesart was one of those guys as well as another guy who happened to be in a position that was associated with Lenny Patrick. We'll call him Harvey, who turned out to be an excellent source of information for me. I told my commander I was going to make Patrick a target just to see how far we could get inside his organization. My boss said that he thought Patrick was out of the rackets and retired. I told him, "I'll let you know in about a week, but I think he's still up to his ears in bookmaking, juice, and extortion. These guys never quit, they're too greedy."

Patrick lived in an apartment at 7425 West Belmont Avenue and drove a 1981 Maroon Oldsmobile that was, of course, registered to the Cosmopolitan Textile Rental Service at 5758 South Halsted Street. This is a common thing for bad guys to do; they never seem to have their name listed to anything. The first day of surveillance revealed a known bookmaker named George Sommers come out of Lenny's apartment; he was followed to another bookmaker's house at 2236 North Seventy-sixth Avenue in Elmwood Park. This guy was Ray Spencer another outfit guy and juice collector for Lenny Patrick. Patrick left his apartment and then walked up to Harlem Avenue where he made three calls on a public phone; after that he returned home. Now that was a normal thing for an old retired guy to do, wasn't it? Not exactly. Apparently, he was afraid that his phone was tapped, and he had some very private things to discuss with someone, or maybe he just needed the exercise. Forget about it.

The next time we saw Patrick was about 5:30 PM when he left his apartment and drove to 6400 North Cicero Avenue in Lincolnwood where his rat partner, Lenny Yaras, lived in Apt. 513. Coincidentally, the Sheriff of Cook County, Richard Elrod, also lived in the same apartment complex. George Sommers was then followed from 2236 North Seventy-sixth Avenue, Elmwood Park, to 7600 West Diversey Avenue where a men's social athletic club was located. This place was a known hangout of an outfit boss named Marco Di'mico and the rest of his crew of bookmakers and burglars. Lenny Yaras was the son of Patrick's old partner and fellow hit man, Dave Yaras, who has since got out of Chicago and went to Florida, where there was less heat – no pun intended.

I decided to take a look at Lenny Yaras and give him a tail from home to see what he was up to. Yaras left his apartment at 7:10 AM and drove to 4224 West Division Street, American & A-1 Industrial Uniform Company on the West Side of Chicago. Apparently, Yaras ran this place and had a piece of it with Lenny Patrick. After a couple of hours, he left and drove to Jack's Restaurant at 5200 West Touhy Avenue in Skokie, which was a known hangout for gamblers. He met another mob guy named Joe Pettit, and put his golf clubs in Pettit's car. They drove to a driving range on Route 21 in Half Day, Illinios, where they hit some balls, then to the Mid Lane Golf Course in Waukegan, Illinois. After a few minutes, a car parked next to Pettit's, and two guys got out with their clubs also – Marshall Portnoy, the right-hand man of Joe "Little Caesar" DiVarco, and a big time bookmaker named Warren Winkler. We had busted both guys in the past running a large-scale sports wire room for the outfit. After they had a meeting, they got on carts and played golf, and we called it a day. We sure were running into a lot of guys who were connected to Lenny Patrick; it would kind of make you believe that our guy Patrick was as busy as ever. Surprise, surprise! I informed my boss of what we had learned about Patrick and his associates and requested to keep an eye on them from time to time; he agreed and we got enough intelligence to raid some wire rooms that belonged to Patrick. We busted Portnoy, Winkler, and Sommers and eventually even got to Joey DiVarco, the top mob boss. A couple of other bad guys turned up on our surveillances at a meeting place in Melrose Park, at 4801 West Lake Street, Ninth Hole hotdog stand – Larry Pettit, Mario Rainone, Marvin Marks, and Jimmy LaValley, a muscle guy and juice collector for Patrick. Something went wrong with something though, because around the time DiVarco got indicted, Lenny Yaras got whacked in front of his place of business on Division Street.

A couple of guys shot Lenny in his car in broad daylight. It was too bad that we weren't tailing Lenny that day. Who knows, we may have caught a couple of hit men.

The background of Patrick was interesting in that he was a close associate of all the Italian outfit boys such as Sam Giancana, Joe "Doves" Aiuppa, Chuck Nicoletti, Turk Torello, Joe "Nagall" Ferriola, Ross Prio, Gus Alex, and Chuck English, to name a few. Obviously, the outfit trusted him because he had whacked a few people for them, but of course, that was a mistake, as they would find out later.

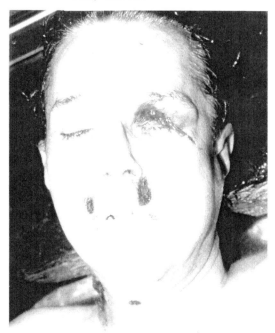

Lenny Yaras – Got whacked Jan 1985 in his car on Division St. Partner of Lenny Patrick

Source: Chicago Police Dep't

In November 1988, after fooling around with Patrick and gathering enough information, my partner Bill Mundee and I decided to get a search warrant for Lenny at his apartment for gambling. I decided to wait until he came out of his apartment so that he wouldn't be able to get rid of any evidence in his apartment. Good move, because we caught him flat-footed outside and he was kind of glad to see that we were cops and not hit men when we walked up on him. "You never know," he said, "there are a lot of nuts out in the street." Here was one of the biggest hit men in Chicago, and he was nervous about nuts out in the street. We found enough gambling evidence to arrest Lenny, who said he didn't know anything about gambling. I told him his nose was getting longer. What really was beneficial to us were the papers we found inside a secret compartment in the kitchen cabinet. Also an address book with dates and times, as well as facts and figures with some familiar names. Everything we recovered was turned over to the FBI for further investigation. When Lenny appeared in racket court on February 22, 1989, with an attorney named Stillo, he plead guilty and was placed under one year court supervision and was fined $400 by Judge Bowe. But that was only the beginning for our guy Lenny; bigger things were in his future. As everyone knows, the wheels of justice move slowly, especially the government wheels. But on December 18, 1991, Fred Foreman, United States attorney for the Northern District of Illinois, announced the return of a six-count indictment charging Gus Alex, Leonard Patrick, Mario Rainone, and Nick Gio with racketeering and extortion. The indictment charges stated that the four defendants were members or associates of the "Lenny Patrick" street crew, which shook down restaurant owners, car dealers, a theater, and the operators of illegal gambling businesses for extortion payments. The defendants used death threats, beatings, and even attempted to firebomb a theater. Our man Lenny personally collected $150,000 payment from a Niles IL. car dealership. Everything that Lenny did have to be cleared through Gus Alex, who received a share of the proceeds. Rainone assaulted business owners, threatened to cut the head off of one business owner, and "blow away" the children of another restaurant owner. Nick Gio, who was only twenty-five years old also administered beatings to reluctant victims and assisted in attempting to firebomb a theater; he even threw a hand grenade on the roof of the theater. The indictment also names James LaValley an underling to Patrick, as an unindicted coconspirator, who has agreed to cooperate with the government. Jimmy LaValley is another story, and I will explain how we set him up on videotape with a very heroic informant of mine, later on.

Mobster pleads guilty, set to squeal on pals

By Matt O'Connor

Leonard Patrick, a reputed top Chicago mobster since the 1930s, when Frank Nitti headed the Outfit, pleaded guilty in a surprise move Monday to racketeering charges.

Patrick, 78 and reportedly in frail health, also agreed to testify against co-defendant Gus Alex, an alleged associate of reputed Chicago mob boss Anthony Accardo, and cooperate in any other governmental investigations of longtime mob friends.

"He could be very damaging," a retired FBI agent said. "He could bring down just about everybody."

Patrick entered a guilty plea to extorting more than $300,000 from two restaurants and a well-known car dealership and attempting to shake down other businesses.

"He doesn't want to die in prison," David Mejia, Patrick's lawyer, explained to reporters after his client's plea, made in a gravelly, barely audible voice in U.S. District Court.

Under a plea agreement with the government, Patrick would be sentenced to 6 years in prison, making him eligible for parole in 2 years.

Law-enforcement authorities predict Patrick could shed vital intelligence on mob control and influence in political, legislative and judicial circles, as well as possibly clear up as many as two dozen gangland slayings going back half a century.

William Roemer Jr., a retired FBI agent who made a career out of investigating the mob, called Patrick "the most important mobster to ever turn against the Chicago mob."

In pleading guilty to racketeering, Patrick admitted he headed a North Side "street crew," or crime family, and personally collected an extortion payment of $150,000 from Ray Hara, the owner of King Nissan in Niles, in 1986.

Patrick also acknowledged sending reputed mob enforcer Mario Rainone in 1986 to shake down the owners of two restaurants, Billy and Company Restaurant in Wheeling and Myron & Phil's Steak, Seafood and Piano Bar in Lincolnwood.

Rainone is alleged to have grabbed William Moss, owner of

See Patrick, pg. 10

Chicago Tribune, Tuesday, April 7, 1992

Mobster pleads guilty, set to squeal on pal

By Matt O'Connor

Leonard Patrick, a reputed top Chicago mobster since the 1930s, when Frank Nitti headed the Outfit, pleaded guilty in a surprise move Monday to racketeering charges.

Patrick, 78 and reportedly in frail health, also agreed to testify against co-defendant Gus Alex, an alleged associate of reputed Chicago mob boss Anthony Accardo, and cooperate in any other governmental investigations of longtime mob friends.

"He could be very damaging," a retired FBI agent said. "He could bring down just about everybody."

Patrick entered a guilty plea to extorting more than $300,000 from two restaurants and a well-known car dealership and attempting to shake down other businesses.

"He doesn't want to die in prison," David Mejia, Patrick's lawyer, explained to reporters after his client's plea, made in a gravelly, barely audible voice in U.S. District Court.

Under a plea agreement with the government, Patrick would be sentenced to 6 years in prison, making him eligible for parole in 2 years.

Law-enforcement authorities predict Patrick could shed vital intelligence on mob control and influence in political, legislative and judicial circles, as well as possibly clear up as many as two dozen gangland slayings going back half a century.

William Roemer Jr., a retired FBI agent who made a career out of investigating the mob, called Patrick "the most important mobster to ever turn against the Chicago mob."

In pleading guilty to racketeering, Patrick admitted he headed a North Side ... crew," or crime family, and sonally collected an extortion ment of $150,000 from Ray F the owner of King Nissan in N in 1986.

Patrick also acknowledged s ing reputed mob enforcer M Rainone in 1986 to shake d the owners of two restaura Billy and Company Restauran Wheeling and Myron & Ph Steak, Seafood and Piano Ba Lincolnwood.

Rainone is alleged to h grabbed William Moss, owne

See Patrick, pg

Patrick
Continued from page 1

Billy and Company, hit him in the face, and threatened his family.

Moss and Phillip Freedman, Moss' father-in-law and co-owner of Myron & Phil's, eventually paid a lump sum of $100,000 and agreed to pay "street taxes" of $500 to $2,000 a month, Patrick ftted.

In revealing the names of the extortion victims, the government disclosed Patrick also ordered underlings to extort money from three other restaurateurs, but those efforts failed.

In one extortion effort in 1987, Rainone is accused of threatening to cut off the head of Dominick Gallo, owner of Francesco's Hole in the Wall Restaurant in Northbrook, Assistant U.S. Atty. Chris Gair said in court.

Gallo tape-recorded conversations with Rainone, Gair said.

Rainone also demanded $300,000 within 10 days from Marshall Bauer, owner of Father and Son Pizza in Chicago, or he would "blow away" Bauer's children, Gair said.

Rainone, 37, is to go on trial next month with Alex, 75, also a reputed longtime mob official who allegedly approved the extortions, and Nicholas Gio, 25, another alleged enforcer. All three have pleaded innocent.

Patrick's guilty plea marked another odd twist in the government's investigation of him. Patrick worked undercover for the FBI for a few months two years ago, secretly recording conversations with mob friends while wearing a body recorder and taping on his wiretapped phone.

His cooperation came to a halt when the government learned he continued to pocket money from

Leonard Patrick

illegal activities even after the FBI paid him $7,200 over two months.

Patrick was indicted in December on racketeering and extortion charges, and has been locked up since then.

The government took no chances of letting Patrick back out of the deal. When U.S. District Judge James Alesia raised a few concerns Monday morning about the plea agreement, prosecutors pressed him to set aside time in the afternoon to take Patrick's guilty plea.

The last time anyone close to Patrick's stature defected from the mob with high-level secrets was nearly a decade ago, when gambling boss Ken Eto began talking after surviving a murder attempt in 1983.

Among the gangland slayings Patrick could clear up is the 1983 murder of insurance executive Allan Dorfman, the mob's conduit into the pension and welfare fund of the Teamsters Union, law-enforcement authorities said.

And Patrick has long been a suspect in the 1946 murder of James Ragen, the owner of a racing news service who opposed mob efforts to take over his business.

Although reaching the mob's upper ranks, Patrick wasn't made a full member of La Cosa Nostra because he is the son of Jewish immigrants from England, Roemer said.

Patrick not only could provide damaging testimony at Alex's trial but also could provide details of Alex's alleged work since 1965 as head of what the FBI calls the corruption squad, the mob faction that corrupted public officials such as judges, police officers and labor leaders, Roemer said.

According to his plea agreement, Patrick was told several decades ago that he was "with" Alex, "that is, that he was required to report to Alex, to take orders from him, to obtain Alex's approval for criminal activities, and to share proceeds of criminal activities with him."

Patrick's criminal activity dates to the 1930s. In 1933, he was sentenced to 7 years in prison for bank robbery.

"He learned in the joint [that] bank robbery is not the thing to do," said Jerry Gladden, chief investigator for the Chicago Crime Commission and retired Chicago police sergeant. "Gambling is where you make money."

Authorities said Patrick ran gambling for years on the West Side before assuming charge of North Side gambling in the 1960s.

At Monday's hearing, Patrick, balding and bespectacled, thanked Alesia for clearing the way for him to receive his medication for heart trouble in the Metropolitan Correctional Center, where he has been since his indictment.

Mejia said Patrick reached his decision "on his own" and "against my recommendation."

Tribune reporter John O'Brien contributed to this article.

Source: Chicago Police Dep't and Donald Herion

CHICAGO SUN-TIMES, THURSDAY, DECEMBER 19, 1991

2 oldsters are veteran mobsters, U.S. charges

By Harlan Draeger
Staff Writer

Two aging figures from Chicago's colorful gangland past returned to the public spotlight Wednesday after being indicted on racketeering and extortion charges.

Gus "Slim" Alex, 75, and Leonard "Lenny" Patrick, 78, were accused of conspiring to extort $376,000 from businessmen and gamblers between 1983 and 1989.

U.S. Attorney Fred Foreman called the two "longtime members of the Chicago outfit" in announcing indictments against them and two other men.

Foreman said the charges demonstrate there is "no retirement, no pension" for veteran lawbreakers in their golden years.

Both men were confined to the Metropolitan Correctional Center after being denied bail during a lengthy detention hearing late Wednesday.

For Alex, publicly identified and pursued for decades as a major player in the crime syndicate, prison bars are a new experience.

First indictment

"He's never been convicted of a thing and never indicted," said his attorney, Carl Walsh. "It's very unfortunate that, when a man is 75 years of age, they decide to indict him."

But government prosecutors said the two had not changed their ways despite advancing age.

Alex, of the 1300 block of North Lake Shore Drive, is accused of sharing in the profits of a violent extortion ring called "the Lenny Patrick street crew." He faces one count of racketeering conspiracy and one count of conspiracy to commit extortion.

White-haired and erect, but slow afoot, Alex sat through the detention hearing without speaking or showing any expression.

Patrick, of the 7400 block of West Belmont, is charged with racketeering conspiracy, racketeering and four counts of extortion. He showed more life at the hearing, grinning at times and engaging his lawyer and Walsh in conversation.

Linked to '30s crime

Opposing bail, Assistant U.S. Attorney Chris Gair called Alex "a close associate of the highest levels of Chicago organized crime" since the 1930s.

Gair said that Patrick became boss of the extortion ring after a long career as a top syndicate gambling operator. Patrick received a 10-year sentence in 1933 for bank robbery and was jailed for contempt in 1977 after refusing to testify in a federal trial.

Also indicted were Mario Rainone, 37, formerly of Bloomingdale, and Nicholas Gio, 25, formerly of Niles. Named as an unindicted co-conspirator was James LaValley, 47, who pleaded guilty in 1990 to exortion counts and running a gambling operation.

Much of the government's case apparently grew out of LaValley's decision a year ago to cooperate with the government.

The indictment charges that Rainone, LaValley and Gio used death threats, beatings and an attempted firebombing to extort large sums.

Part of the indictment charges that Patrick ordered Rainone and LaValley to extort at least $200,000 from the owner of an Italian restaurant in Northbrook. It says that Rainone threatened to cut off the heads of the owner and his family if he did not pay. Similar threats were used to collect large sums from owners of restaurants in Lincolnwood, Wheeling, Chicago and Skokie, the indictment says.

Source: Chicago Police Dep't and Donald Herion

When Lenny Patrick realized that he was going to go to prison for the rest of his life, he decided to cooperate with the government and become a federal informant and wear a wire to tape conversations of his boss Gus Alex and others connected to the Chicago Outfit. Patrick who was in his late seventies didn't want to die in jail.

Patrick did a good job and recorded conversations of First Ward powerhouse, Pat Marcy, and ward committeeman, John D'Arco, who were indicted for corruption and other charges which ruined the First Ward. When Patrick appeared in Federal court as a witness against Gus Alex, he was asked how long he had been a member of organized crime. His answer was, "Fifty years." Patrick was the highest-ranking mob figure in Chicago to become an informant for the government. He outlined a half-century of mob murders and payoffs during the racketeering and extortion trial of reputed top mobster Gus Alex.

Reminiscing about the 1920s, Patrick said that at age fifteen he ran dice games. The reason for his first murder of gambler Herman Glick in 1931 was simple, Patrick said. "He hit me, and I killed him a week later." His next five murders through 1953 were done to take over lucrative mob gambling operations. One of the victims was former gambling partner Willie Murphy.

In 1952, Patrick said that he carried a message from mobster Felix "Milwaukee Phil" Alderisio to Charles Gross then acting Republican committeeman of the Thirty-first Ward. Patrick told him, "They don't want you to run. If you're smart, you won't run, or you'll get killed." Gross was found shot to death soon afterward.

Patrick wasted no time in identifying Alex as his boss who allegedly received a cut of his extortion and gambling profits for thirty-five years. He said that he handed over extortion profits to Alex at numerous rendezvous spots: Marshall Fields, Hamburger Hamlet, and Northwestern Memorial Hospital, to name a few.

Alex's lawyer, Sam Adam, attacked the credibility of Patrick, seventy-eight, who pleaded guilty to racketeering and extortion charges to avoid dying in prison. Adam said that by Patrick's own account, he has killed as many people as Richard Speck did in one night – eight. Unlike Speck though, Patrick was never convicted of any homicide. Patrick said that he did spend a month in the Cook County jail after Herman Glick identified him as the gunman on his deathbed, but he was released when prosecutors couldn't use Glick's statement. Patrick then told how he joined a robbery gang, robbing two banks in Indiana; he got caught in one holdup and was sentenced to ten years in an Indiana prison.

He was released in 1940 and began running Chicago's biggest dice game for the outfit. There he met top syndicate members Sam Giancana, Paul Ricca, and Felix Alderisio. In 1945, after working for William Galatz, a powerful West Side gambling boss, Galatz fired Patrick. Patrick then decided to kill Galatz; his partner, David Yaras, now dead, shotgunned Galatz.

MOB HIT CAR
Dumped in alley & burned

Patrick then took control of the mob's West Side bookmaking business, taking bets on baseball, football, and horse racing. He even started running poker and blackjack games, including bingo. Patrick controlled all the gambling in the Jewish neighborhood on Chicago's West Side; when the Jewish population moved to the North Side, Patrick got the approval of a top mob boss to take over all the North Side gambling. He said that he continued to pay off alderman and police for protection until the late 1960s. Patrick said he made as much as $850,000 from the sports gambling business in one year after paying off the mob bosses, like Gus Alex.

Patrick reacted with violence to any threat to his authority.

When he learned in late 1947 that Harry Krotish, twenty-nine, another West Side bookmaker, wanted to take over, Patrick said, "I shot him." Krotish died from four gunshot wounds. Patrick said that he ordered three other rival bookmakers killed – Edward Murphy in 1950, David Zatz in 1952, and Milton Glickman in 1953.

Patrick also admitted extorting money from some well-known businesses and people, including the Big Bear grocery store chain, the Black Angus Restaurant, and insurance executive Allan Dorfman, who was murdered in 1983.

Patrick said that he got $300,000 from Dorfman; he and Yaras split $75,000, and the rest went to mob bosses.

Ray Hara, a Chicago area car dealer, remembers being terrified when two unidentified men came into his showroom in 1986 and threatened to kill his children if he didn't pay $300,000. Hara thought that it was a fortuitous coincidence a few days later when Lenny Patrick, a friend from decades earlier on the West Side, called him for the first time in years to see how he was doing.

Hara said that he told Patrick his problem and asked if he could help him. Patrick told Hara that they were very bad people. "You're going to have to pay them." When Hara testified in court at Gus Alex's trial, Alex was charged with racketeering and extortion; he said that he never suspected that Patrick was the mastermind behind his extortion. Patrick made a deal with the bad guys for $150,000 and told Hara that he would never be bothered again. Patrick personally picked up a brown paper bag filled with $150,000, and that's when he thanked Patrick for helping him. When Patrick testified against his boss, Gus Alex, in federal court, the defense attorneys attacked Patrick's believability, noting that he admitted to extortion, bribery, and killing six people. When Alex was found guilty, some of the jurors said that Patrick's testimony and the tape recordings were the cornerstones in convincing the jury of Alex's guilt.

The deal that Patrick took, in return for his cooperation, included a request that he get catered restaurant food and a plentiful supply of prescription heart medication while he was in federal custody.

Auto dealer recounts extortion by the mob

By Matt O'Connor

Ray Hara, a veteran Chicago area car dealer, remembers being terrified when two unidentified men came into his showroom in 1986 and threatened to kill his children if he didn't pay $300,000.

Hara, owner of King Nissan in Niles, thought it was a fortuitous coincidence a few days later when hoodlum Lenny Patrick, a friend from decades earlier on the West Side, called him for the first time in years to see how he was doing.

Hara said he confided his problem to Patrick, a longtime mob gambling boss who was then in his early 70s, and Patrick offered to intervene.

"Oh, they're very, very bad people," Hara recalled Patrick telling him. "You're going to have to pay them."

In testimony Wednesday at Gus Alex's racketeering and extortion trial, Hara said he never suspected Patrick was the mastermind behind his extortion.

Alex, 76, a reputed longtime mob official, is on trial on charges he gave Patrick the go-ahead to extort Hara and other legitimate businessmen in the 1980s.

Hara testified that Patrick led him to believe he acted as a mediator and persuaded the extortionists to accept half of their original demand.

Hara said he raised the $150,000 by borrowing $35,000 from relatives, selling stock for $65,000 and collecting on a $50,000 debt owed him by another dealership.

Patrick personally picked up the paper bag that Hara had filled with cash, put it under his arm and told Hara the extortionists would never bother him again, Hara said. "I thanked him," Hara told Assistant U.S. Atty. Chris Gair.

Patrick, 78, the government's star witness, admitted his deception in Hara's extortion in earlier testimony.

Sam Adam, Alex's lawyer, hammered away at the fact that Patrick, who had employed Hara at his restaurant as a waiter 50 years ago, had repeatedly lied to Hara but had been able to convince him otherwise.

Adam contends Patrick has pulled off another con, convincing his "street crew" that Alex was his boss so he could pocket a bigger share of the extortion proceeds.

The defense has denied Alex has mob connections, admitting only that he was a longtime gambler.

But an FBI agent testified Wednesday that six years ago he photographed Alex meeting with Sam Carlisi, reputedly then mob boss in Chicago, in a parking lot of a McDonald's at Oakbrook Center.

Agent James G. Brown, on a surveillance in August 1986, said he saw Alex remove two shopping bags from his Mercedes and struggle as he carried them over to Carlisi, leading Brown to think there was something heavy in the bags. Both men peered into the bags before Alex put one or both bags into Carlisi's car, Brown said.

The defense has argued Patrick really reported to Carlisi, not Alex. Brown's testimony suggested they all knew one another.

In other testimony Wednesday, two elderly men, Max Zimmerman and Dr. Joseph H. Brown, admitted innocently acting as go-betweens for Alex and Patrick. Previous testimony indicated the two didn't talk directly on the phone together in case of FBI eavesdropping.

Brown, 79, who described himself as "a reputable and ethical doctor," said he frequently dined with Alex in two popular restaurants in recent years and had been Patrick's physician for years.

Brown said Patrick asked him to deliver messages to Alex several times, including one request for money for legal and other bills. Alex also once gave him a package to give to Patrick, Brown said.

Zimmerman, 82, longtime owner of Zimmerman's Liquor Store, said Alex, a customer for 10 years, asked him to take phone messages from Patrick on two occasions in 1990. " 'Tell Mr. Gus to meet me,' " Zimmerman said Patrick told him both times, without specifying a place or time.

Patrick testified he shared extortion profits with Alex at regular meetings, usually in a sixth-floor hallway at Northwestern Memorial Hospital and the book department in Marshall Field's flagship store.

Chapter 51

The Fall of Mob Boss, Gus "Slim" Alex

After Manny and Zeke did a number on Jimmy LaValley and we nailed him for extortion among other charges, little did we know how far this investigation would take us. When Bill Mundee and I busted Lenny Patrick in his apartment at 7425 West Belmont Avenue in November 1988, we found enough evidence to arrest him. The most important thing of the raid was the documents we recovered from Lenny's apartment. These documents involved other members of his street crew and certain intelligence that involved mob activities he was involved in with Gus "Slim" Alex who was Tony Accardo's closest friend. We turned over everything that we recovered to Jack O'Rourke of the FBI as he was working on the LaValley case, which was connected to Lenny Patrick. As things progressed with the LaValley case, he became a federal witness and things really came together when he ratted on his partners in crime as well as Lenny Patrick his boss. Then guess what, Patrick, who was now in his late '70s, decided that he did not want to go back to jail again because he would probably die there. So he decided to turn federal witness and wear a wire against his boss, Gus Alex. Of course, we didn't find out about this turn of events right away, the FBI likes to keep things on the hush hush if you know what I mean. Even though we were responsible for the LaValley bust which started this whole investigation, but that's showbiz, I guess. I better leave the subject alone for now.

Gus "Slim" Alex has been a top mob boss for years in Chicago and was called the most ruthless and vicious hood in the Chicago Outfit when he was questioned by Chief Counsel Robert F. Kennedy when he appeared before the U.S. Senate racket committee. Alex pleaded the Fifth Amendment at least forty times. Alex started out his career as a body guard for Jake "Greasy Thumb" Guzik who was a top mob fixer for Al Capone, Frank Nitti, and Tony Accardo, so you can see he was taught by the best outfit guys around. Alex, of course, was a Greek, but that didn't seem to make any difference to the boys. In the old days he was employed by the Atlas Brewing Company of Chicago, which was owned by the mob. They sold beer to every outfit joint on Rush Street, and Gussie was getting kickbacks from each place that had to buy the beer. Alex was in good shape and held in high esteem by his bosses, Nick Nitti, Paul "the Waiter" Ricca, and Murray "the Camel" Humphreys.

The owner and operator of the Continental wire service, which provided race results from around the country, was a big help to all the bookmakers. James Ragen, the owner, told the police that Gus Alex had threatened to kill him if he didn't turn over the wire service to the mob. Ragen said that he told the mob to go and fuck themselves, which turned out to be a big mistake. James Ragen was the victim of a shotgun attack in 1946 on the South Side of Chicago. The shooters were Lenny Patrick, Davy Yaras, and Willie Block. Ragen did not die immediately; when he was in the hospital, someone poisoned him that did the job. So you can see the connection between Lenny Patrick and Gus Alex goes way back; obviously, they trusted each other in murder, extortion, and a lot of other things, and that's what led to Alex's downfall.

Finally, through a chain of events that connected Manny and Zeke to Jimmy LaValley, which led to the downfall of a lot of mob guys, like Jim Bollman, Marion Rainone, Nick Gio, and the infamous Lenny Patrick, the good guys were winning. I recall when the indictments came out naming, Gus Alex, age seventy-five, and Lenny Patrick, age seventy-eight, as high-ranking members of organized crime in Chicago as murderers and extortionists, a lot of people were wondering why the government would even bother with senior citizens like this. Well, for example, Gus Alex had the Chicago Loop under his command for years and Lenny Patrick who was a convicted bank robber back in 1937 was an admitted murderer and controlled all the gambling on the West and

North sides of Chicago. I remember I was sitting in a restaurant and lounge on Devon Avenue called Myron and Phil's which was a known meeting place for outfit bookmakers. I was at the end of the bar watching a couple of wise guys exchanging money at a nearby table bitching about how they should have moved the line on the Bear game from 6 to 7. That's when Lenny Patrick walked in; he was all smiles, and sat down with the two wise guys. I was able to hear that Lenny did move the line, and his crew made a killing on the Bear game. While Lenny was sitting there the Owner Myron, walked over to him and bought him a drink and treated him like a king. Little did I know that Lenny was extorting money from Myron and Phil for years, which would come out later at the trial. Part of the conspiracy against Alex was Nick Gio and Marion Rainone, who were part of Alex's crew; they carried out orders from Alex. Rainone tried to extort money from a theater in Oak Park, Illinois, and threw a hand grenade on the roof of the Lake theater in an attempt to force the owners to give up a percentage of there business. Alex also ordered Rainone to threaten the owner of a restaurant in Northbrook, Illinois. To give him $200,000 or he would guarantee that the mans entire family would wind up in Mount Carmel Cemetery. Jimmy LaValley also testified that Lenny Patrick had ordered him to give a beating to a victim by the name of Al Tapper who owned a construction business in the suburb. LaVallay admitted that he and Nick Gio hospitalized Tapper, who is now dead.

When Gus Alex and Lenny Patrick were indicted in 1991 for approving extortion schemes, which involved threatening business people with beatings if they didn't fork over thousands of dollars, I did a dance like Walter Huston did in the Treasure of Sierra Madre when he discovered gold. Alex lived at a nice location at 1360 North Lake Shore Drive Apt 31B; in the winter months, he would travel to his other home in Fort Lauderdale, Florida. Both Alex and Patrick were held in the Metropolitan Correction Center in Chicago. Due to Alex being sickly, U.S. Magistrate Judge Joan Gottschall allowed Alex to be confined to his apartment on Lake Shore Drive. He had to wear a monitoring device at all times and was only allowed to visit his doctor or attorney. He also had to surrender his passport and the deeds to his two homes as well as post a $25,000 cash bond.

When Lenny decided to seek leniency, he already had worn a body mike when he was with Alex, so it was nothing new to him. When Alex and Lenny had decided to meet, Alex is the one that set the meeting place. Alex told Lenny to meet him on an upper floor in a hallway of the Northwestern Hospital on the Near North Side of Chicago. They would both go separately and enter at different entrances after they concluded there meeting they would leave the building separately also. Alex believed that his precautions would preclude any surveillance of there meeting. Alex never dreamt that his old friend Lenny Patrick was wired for sound. The statements that he made on the tape were very incriminating as well as the cash he got from the extortion's he had ordered. In exchange for leniency, Patrick agreed to testify against Alex to support the conversation that he had with Alex when he met him in the hallway at the Northwestern Hospital.

Gus Alex's trial was presided over by U.S. District Court Judge James H. Alesia, who was a former Chicago policeman and incorruptible. After Patrick's testimony, along with the other evidence against Alex, Judge Alesia sentenced Alex to fifteen years, eight months in prison. He also ordered Alex to pay $823,000 in fines and restitution. He also made Alex pay $1,400 a month for the cost to the taxpayers of his prison cell. Alex's attorney, Carl Walsh, appealed the verdict and sentence, but the appeal was denied.

Myron and Phil Freedman, the owners of Myron and Phil's restaurant on Devon Avenue, received $154,000 from Alex; and needless to say, they were quite happy with the results of the trial as were other victims who had been extorted and had their lives threatened.

A Chicago area car dealer, Ray Hara, who owned King Nissan in Niles, Illinois. recalled how terrified he was when two men came into his showroom in 1986 and threatened to kill his children if he didn't pay them $300,000, a few days after the threat, who walked into his dealership with his old time pal, Lenny Patrick. Hara thought that he really got lucky when he saw Lenny; it seems that they have been friends for fifty years and he knew that Lenny was an outfit guy and just maybe he could help him with his problem. When Hara told him his tale of woe. Lenny told Hara that they were very bad people and that he had better pay them because they were known to carry out there threats. Lenny told Hara that maybe he could talk to them and explain that Hara was a personal friend of his and just maybe they would do him a favor and cut the amount in half. When Hara heard from Lenny again, Lenny told him that he had good news and met him at his dealership. Lenny told Hara that he persuaded the extortionists to accept half of their original demand. Hara couldn't thank Lenny enough and told him that he would try and raise the money somehow. Lenny told Hara that the extortionists wanted Hara to give the money to Lenny and that would be the end of it. Hara said that he had to borrow $35,000 from his relatives, sell stock, and was finally able to get the $150,000. Hara said that Lenny personally picked up the cash which was in a paper bag, and he told Lenny that he couldn't thank him enough. Lenny said "no problem," and guaranteed Hara that the extortionists would never bother him again.

When the truth came out about the attempt to extort $300,000 from Ray Hara, of course, it was Mr. Slick, Lenny Patrick, who was behind the whole thing. He sent his street crew into see Hara and threaten him and then he acted as a mediator to cut the figure in half. Of course, this whole plot was with the approval of Gus Alex, who gave Lenny a simple warning: "Be careful." Judge Alesia sentenced Patrick to seven years in jail, which was still better than the fifteen years Alex got. Wouldn't it have been something if Gus Alex became an informant also? Boy, there's no telling how far this case would have gone. Oh well, things worked out pretty well after all, and a lot of outfit guys went to jail, and that's what working organized crime is is all about.

Gus Alex, 76, arrives at the Dirksen Federal Building Thursday, where he was found guilty of racketeering conspiracy and extortion. It was his first conviction.

Gus Alex faces prison, big fines for extortion

By Matt O'Connor

Gus Alex, reputedly the mob's chief political fixer in Chicago for decades, was sentenced Friday to 15 years and 8 months in prison and ordered to pay $823,000 in fines and restitution for approving violent extortions.

The sentence almost certainly ensures that 76-year-old Alex, frail and noticeably thinner since his conviction and imprisonment 4½ months ago, will die in prison.

A federal jury found Alex guilty last October of being the overseer of the Lenny Patrick street crew who approved violent extortions of legitimate businessmen with the brusque warning: "Be careful."

Assistant U.S. Atty. Chris Gair called Alex "the gentleman gangster," who outwardly appeared dapper and respectable but who spun "his evil web from his Gold Coast apartment, sending out legbreakers to do his bidding."

Defense lawyer Carl Walsh asked for mercy, saying Alex has lost so much weight since his imprisonment that "he is almost skin and bones."

But U.S. District Judge James Alesia imposed the maximum term on Alex, fined him $250,000 and ordered him to pay $376,000 in restitution to the extortion victims: four restaurateurs and a car dealer.

The jury that convicted Alex previously ordered him to forfeit an additional $197,000, his share of the extortion profits.

Alex reputedly headed for decades the "connection guys," the outfit's effort to corrupt public officials such as judges, police officers, politicians and labor leaders. His mob ties date to the 1930s, law enforcement officials said.

Alex's racketeering trial last fall was highlighted by the testimony of Patrick, the wisecracking former head of the mob's Jewish faction who admitted to six murders in his youth and to extorting businessmen well into his 70s.

Patrick, 79, became the city's foremost mobster to defect when he pleaded guilty in April and agreed to testify against his longtime boss.

Patrick's North Side street crew, which answered to Alex, did its work the old-fashioned way: approaching restaurateurs and car dealers and threatening them and their families with violence or death to extract huge cash payoffs of up to $150,000 at a time.

Walsh maintained Alex wasn't aware of the acts of violence, but Alesia was unimpressed, saying: "Why should he have? He was the organizer. He had plenty of underlings for that."

Chapter 52

The Dinty Moore Episode

    I remember one February night when we were on the five-to-one shift working out of Maxwell Street, Bill Mundee and I decided to stop for a drink on Halsted Street after work. We had a pretty good night making a couple of wire-room raids on Taylor Street, which was a stronghold of the outfit for the past fifty years. Actually I had a plan. I wanted to execute on a new bartender that had just started tending bar at Dugans, which was a cop bar and a nice place to relax once in a while. I told Bill that I would buy him a drink at Dugans; as soon as I said that. he looked at me suspiciously and said, "The last time you bought me a drink, the Cubs won a double header, what the hell are you up to?" Bill knew me pretty good by this time and knew that I had something devious up my sleeve; actually, he was right, only it was in my coat pocket not my sleeve.
    I said, "What, can't a guy buy a friend a drink?" Bill liked to kid around a little bit also and told me, "Who said I was your friend? I hang around with you because you're my sergeant and give me my efficiency marks, besides I'm doing your wife a favor by looking out for you. Just for that I'll buy you a cappuccino. Okay?" Bill was shocked. "You'll buy me a cappuccino?" "Yeah. You've got a good memory for being Irish, pal." "By the way," I said, "remember Dinty Moore?" "Oh

no," he said, "not tonight." I told him to act a little drunk when we walk in Dugans. "There's supposed to be a new bartender who's a wise ass and knows everything about everything, let's see if he knows Dinty Moore."

We walked in and took a couple of stools at the end of the bar and introduced ourselves to the bartender; he was about six foot two, 220 pounds, thirty years old, and wore an earring. We acted as if we had been overserved at another bar and were kind of abusive to the new guy. There were only six other people at the front of the bar, and they had a few bottles of beer in front of them; we didn't know who they were, but they could have been yuppies from the neighborhood. Bill and I ordered two martinis with a beer chaser; the bartender who we'll call Al looked at us and suggested that we had had enough for the night. We were stumbling around and slurred our words and did appear to be bombed out of our mind. When Al said that, Bill slammed his fist on the bar and demanded that we get our drinks, because we were nowhere near drunk. Bill wore a shoulder holster, and Al spotted the gun on Bill and figured we were a couple of drunken Chicago cops and nobody to fool with. The people at the front of the bar are watching us, now shaking their heads and whispering to each other.

Al brought us our drinks and just shook his head and walked back to the front of the bar and began talking to the other patrons. Now was the time. Bill asked me where Mr. Moore was. I told him to drink the damn martini or throw it on the floor; it was showtime. I brought out the baggy filled with Dinty Moore stew and when I was sure no one was looking. I poured it on the bar in front of Bill. Bill just looked at me as if I was weird and shook his head. I told him to start gagging and then grunt as if you're throwing up; he really liked this part of the scam. Bill let out the best vomit noise I ever heard; the bartender heard that familiar noise and hurried back to us. He saw the mess on the bar and started to gag himself. He yelled about how he told us that we had enough to drink; all the while Bill was still pretending to have the dry heaves. Al said, "Oh Jesus. Let me get a towel and clean that up." Now it's my turn. I told the bartender to wait a second. "Let me check this out." I pulled a spoon out and proceeded to eat some of the stew while I'm smiling at the bartender, saying, "Hey, it's not bad the second time around, want some? Bill said, "Yea, don't mind if I do." Bill helped himself. "You want some kid?" The bartender turned green, yellow, and then lost it, grabbing his heaving stomach. He raced to the men's room, not quite making it in time. Bill and I clunk our beers and drank. Mission accomplished.

Needless to say, the yuppies at the front of the bar also began gagging and made a hasty exit while calling us nasty names as well. We could hear Al the bartender gagging and still throwing up in the washroom when we were leaving the bar.

Chapter 53

Mob Boss Rocky Infelise Gets Wired

It was 7:10 AM on September 14, 1989, when mob boss Rocky Infelise and William "BJ" Jahoda had a meeting in Andrea's Restaurant, in Forest Park, Illinois. Jahoda ran all the mob's gambling operations for Infelise, but Jahoda was now an informant for the IRS and special agent Tom Moriarity. BJ was wearing a wire for the past few months and was wired for this conversation, which proved to be earth shattering and very informative on the workings of the Chicago Crime Syndicate. The tape of this conversation was played in federal court in Chicago during the trial of Infelise and others who were charged with gambling, racketeering, and conspiracy to murder. When the tape was being played, Infelise brought up the name of Herion and how he was working on getting the motherfucker transferred. Infelise was heard to say that he was using an unidentified police official with access to the superintendent of police to transfer Herion to a district on the South Side of Chicago or the subway detail. Infelise said that right now the superintendent can't do anything because he was working for the fucking G. The police official who talked to the superintendent told Rocky that the superintendent said that he inherited him and "maybe down the road, we'll see what happens." At that point Infelise said, "I guess we got to live with the motherfucker if we last that long, till the next election. Daley gets in for four years. Fuck it, he don't give a fuck." The following is part of that transcript that shocked the courtroom and made headlines in Chicago newspapers.

Rocky: I lay out $35,000 a month for guys that are away, and the coppers. That's not counting the worker, that's just the nut. You know it's getting rough.
Jahoda: Jesus Christ.
Rocky: Between you and me –
Jahoda: No, I mean, I knew you had ten with the –
Rocky: Ten goes to the sheriff.
Jahoda: Yeah, with the Bohemian.
Rocky: Yeah.
Jahoda: But I had no idea.
Rocky: Five goes to another guy.
Jahoda: I got no right to ask you the question. What the fuck do you get for $10,000 a month?
Rocky: Well, the sheriff never bothers us, BJ. Then we got a guy at the States Attorney's Office. We got another guy downtown. Then we got seven guys away, get $2,000 a month. The kid that's in England still gets money. Jerry, one armed Jerry.
Jahoda: I never met the guy, just heard about him. I can see coming up with the envelopes, but Jesus, get something for it. And you know, every Christmas it's another thing. Most of the whore, most of he strip joints are closed, aren't they?
Rocky: No, not in Cicero, there's a few of them still going.
Jahoda: I thought you had somebody, you know, a low level guy you had in the federal building.
Rocky: We had a guy there, but no more. He wasn't a low level guy, he was a supervisor.
Jahoda: Is that right?
Rocky: He got out of there on the skin of his fucking teeth.
Jahoda: What, they retire him?
Rocky: He retired. They were, I think they were getting close to him
Jahoda: Is that right?
Rocky: Gave us a lot of information. We paid for it; we didn't get it for nothing.
Jahoda: You're willing to pay anybody, that's the thing.

Rocky: A lot of guys don't want to come up. If you don't give, then you won't get nothing. They'll make up fucking stories and bullshit you. At least this guy with the sheriff's office, he sends me a lot of information. They only went on one pinch, they were called in after that fucking Herion and the G were already in the place. Now I'm working on getting the motherfucker transferred.

Jahoda: Oh, Herion and his gambling crew?

Rocky: Yeah, but the guy can't do nothing right now because he's working with the fucking G.

Jahoda: Is that right?

Rocky: That motherfucker Herion.

Jahoda: Yea, get him transferred.

Rocky: The guy was going to move him out, you know transfer him.

Jahoda: Put him on the CTA detail.

Rocky: The commissioner, pretty good guy, can't get him out. I didn't go to him. The guy that went to him, says listen, I'll do anything. He says the motherfucker is working directly for the G. He says I inherited him. And he says, maybe down the road, see what happens.

Jahoda: Yeah.

Rocky: I think we gotta live with the motherfucker. If we can last that long, 'til the next election. Daley gets in for four years. Fuck it, he don't give a fuck.

Jahoda: He looks good.

Rocky: You know we gave him a lot of fucking help on his last election.

Jahoda: He looks good. He's really coming across.

Rocky: You see how many votes Vrdolyak got, don't you? Three percent of the vote. We shut that down. When he first run for mayor, that's when he was in good, good taste, that DeBartolo. You know DeBartolo? From Cleveland, the guy that owns the 49ers, give him $600,000. Now we told him to back off on this election. We shut off and the guy balked, sent a guy there. Joe was too sick, and I was supposed to meet him, something happened. So I got hold of a guy in Pittsburgh, he's in the same district as DeBartolo. I said listen, son, you got to do me a favor. What is it? Tell that motherfucker, don't give him five cents. You got it? Another guy here, big banker you know. We shut him off in five spots.

Jahoda:	Is that right?
Rocky:	Like a mil, that's a lot of money. Over a mil. We worked against him. All the guys that were supposed to be working for him were working against him.
Jahoda:	He was a fool to run this last time.
Rocky:	Well, that's right; he's a jagoff and his own guys, Dvorak come and told us, you know, he says that fucking headstrong mother fucker that don't want to listen. So Daley sent word to us, through somebody, not himself, if we would help his brother. You know his brother's a nice guy. The brother went through a big union guy that's like this with him. And I tell you what B. I always thought he was a mother fucker. I still don't trust him. But when he was state attorney, the old guy was supposed to get a subpoena and everything. The state, they were going to make a big thing out of it. This guy went to him, quashed it right out.
Jahoda:	I think the kid is coming across 100 percent more than I ever thought.
Rocky:	It's just like the same story. Money talks and bullshit walks.
Jahoda:	That's what I mean, that's what I learned from you years ago.
Rocky:	Here, have the paper.
Jahoda:	Go ahead and read it, thanks. Which way you headed, buddy?
Rocky:	I got to go to the garage, and then I got to go to 0'Hare Oasis. I meet some guy there once a month. That's why I'm tired, really fucking tired, not physical, it's fucking mental.
Rocky:	Do that will you, B.
Jahoda:	Oh, yeah.
Rocky:	Help him every way you can.
Jahoda:	You bet.
Rocky:	All right, you know one way or the other I'll make it up to you.
Jahoda:	I'm not worried about that. Shit, Jimmy the Greek could make it up to me.
Rocky:	He will, he's not a bad guy.
Jahoda:	Cuz, you know, all you got to do is throw some action my way.
Rocky:	Catch you later, B.

James Nicholas (left) and Michael Zitello leave following indictments Wednesday.

20 linked to mob indicted

DeLaurentis   Infelice

Source: Chicago Tribune

In one of the largest crackdowns on organized crime ever in Chicago, 20 alleged mobsters were charged with using money, muscle and murder to run and protect the "Chicago Outfit's" lucrative gambling, extortion and juice loan operations.

Reputed mob chieftain Ernest Rocco Infelice and 11 others, including alleged hit man Harry Aleman were charged with using murder, other violence, threats, intimidation, and payoffs to witnesses and various public officials to protect their operations.

The group was called the "Ferriola Street Crew" by the FBI after the late mob boss Joseph Ferriola, who died March 11, 1989. Infelice, 67, picked up the reins after Ferriola's death, according to federal authorities.

The eight others were charged with operating a sports betting ring that ran for more than a decade.

The charges outlined in detail allegations of how murder and the threat of it were used to keep order among victims and workers and represented a deep penetration into what federal authorities call organized crime.

A key factor in obtaining the indictments was the cooperation of William Jahoda, 47, a key Infelice ally who turned to the government for protection a year ago and began spilling secrets, federal authorities said.

For example, the indictments said that last September, Infelice confided to Jahoda that he had paid $35,000 in monthly protection money to various public officials and to various jailed cohorts, presumably to keep their silence. Jahoda, formerly of Itasca, was among those indicted.

And that same month, Infelice and others conspired to lend $50,000 to a man they knew as Larry Weeks to pay off policemen in Walworth County, Wis., according to the indictment. Weeks, however, was an undercover agent for the Internal Revenue Service.

The indictments were the most significant attack on organized crime since the 1986 convictions of eight top Chicago mob leaders on casino-skimming charges. Wednesday's charges arose from an eight-year probe by the FBI, the Internal Revenue Service, Illinois State Police and Chicago police homicide detectives. They were announced by U.S. Atty. Gen. Dick Thornburgh.

"We've learned that a successful attack on the lawlessness of organized crime requires the coordination and cooperation of all of law enforcement," Thornburgh said.

The crew exacted "street taxes" from illicit businesses as well as "questionably legitimate businesses" as part of the racketeering activities, according to Acting U.S. Atty. Ira Raphaelson.

The investigation involved undercover operatives, wiretaps, informants and a meticulous examination of the federal income tax records.

James McKenzie, special agent in charge of the FBI office in Chicago, said the 102 pages of charges marked the first time that Chicago's crime family has been designated as a criminal enterprise under the federal Racketeer-Influenced Corruption Organizations Act. The law allows the government to seek stiff prison terms for those convicted of membership and to seek forfeiture of assets.

"Our goal is to dismantle the Chicago mob. This is a good case, but there are more good (mob) cases to come," McKenzie said.

The charges seek the forfeiture of Infelice's home at 1535 Forest Ave., River Forest. Also named in forfeiture demands was the home of an alleged lieutenant, Salvatore DeLaurentis, 52, located at 411 Lauder Lane, Inverness, and two other

20 linked to mob indicted -

DeLaurentis properties in Island Lake in Lake County. The charges also seek $3.7 million the two allegedly reaped.

Among the allegations were the murders of three gambling figures, including the Feb. 7, 1985, torture-slaying of independent bookmaker Hal C. Smith, 48. Barbara Smith told investigators her husband left home saying he had been summoned to a meeting with Jahoda at a Long Grove restaurant. Four days later his body was found in the trunk of his Cadillac, abandoned in the parking lot of an Arlington Heights hotel. The extent of Smith's operations became known when federal agents raided his Prospect Heights home and seized $611,000 in cash in 1983.

Infelice, DeLaurentis, Robert Salerno, 55, of 317 N. Aldine, Park Ridge, and Robert Bellavia, 50, of 1805 Kings Point Dr., Addison, were charged with conspiring to strangle Smith.

Infelice was also charged with conspiring with unnamed others to murder Robert Plummer, 51, whose partly decomposed body was found June 2, 1982, in the trunk of his wife's late model Lincoln Continental in a Mundelein parking lot. Once described as among the 10 top organized crime leaders in Lake County, Plummer, of Lake Forest, was bludgeoned to death on the stairway of a mansion that housed gambling operation in Libertyville, the indictment charges.

The indictment charged that Aleman, who was once acquitted of an alleged mob murder, was the group's enforcer. In the fall of 1975, Aleman orchestrated the murder of alleged bookmaker Anthony J. Reitinger Jr. "as an example" because he was not paying street tax, the indictments charged. On Oct. 31, 1975, Reitinger, of Chicago, was cut down by a shotgun blast as he dined in a restaurant at 4846 W. Fullerton Ave.

The indictments also allege that before he died, Ferriola ordered Infelice to pay Aleman $100,000. Aleman was released from prison last year after serving 11 years on a home invasion conviction. Sources said Aleman, 51, of 735 Forest Glen Lane, Oak Brook, was paid as a reward for keeping his mouth shut while in prison.

The indictments charged that between 1980 and 1982, Infelice, Louis Marino and others forced gambling kingpin Ken Eto to either pay a street tax or desist from his gambling activities. Marino, 56, of 11732 Brookside Dr., Palos Park, was among those charged with racketeering.

Eto was shot three times in the head in 1983 in a bungled mob assassination attempt in a Northwest Side parking lot and turned government informant.

Infelice, Marino and others also were accused of supplying money to James Basile to make juice loans ranging from $6,500 to $9,500 between 1985 and 1988. Basile, who joined the federal witness protection program as an informant, was not charged Wednesday.

Assistant U. S. Attys. Thomas Knight and Jeffrey Johnson, who will prosecute the case, said they will seek to jail Infelice, DeLaurentis, Aleman and five others without bonds at court hearings next week. The others were allowed to go free in lieu of $50,000 personal recognizance bonds.

Also charged were Michael Sarno, 32, of 1031 S. Mason St.; Edward Stevenson, 71, of 1826 N. 72nd Ct., Elmwood Park; Robert Covone, 34, of 33 N. Main St., Lombard; William DiDomenico, 47, of 1405 Park Dr., Mt. Prospect, and Michael Zitello, 35, 3225 Oak Ave., Brookfield.

Charged with conspiracy to conduct an illegal gambling business were Robert Garrison, 54, of 202 Prairie View Ave., Libertyville; Thomas McCandless, 56, of 3624 Dauphine, Northbrook; Paul Spano, 59, of 711 S. Lytle Ave.; Ronald DeRosa, 28, of 1509 N. 16th Ave., Melrose Park; Frank Maltese, 59, of 3818 S. Austin Blvd., Cicero; James Coniglio, 53, of 2107 Kenilworth Ave., Berwyn; James Nicholas, 47, of 716 Scarborough Dr., Hoffman Estates; and James Damopoulos, 34, of 3339 W. Barry Ave., Chicago.

[Illustration]
PHOTOS 6 Caption: James Nicholas (left) and Michael Zitello leave following indictments Wednesday. after being indicted. of 20 people Wednesday at the Dirksen Federal Building. Tribune photo by Chuck Berman. CAPTION: PHOTO: (Salvatore) DeLaurentis.

Reproduced with permission of the copyright owner. Further reproduction or distribution is prohibited without permission.

Abstract (Document Summary)

In one of the largest crackdowns on organized crime ever in Chicago, 20 alleged mobsters were charged with using money, muscle and murder to run and protect the "Chicago Outfit's" lucrative gambling, extortion and juice loan operations.

Reputed mob chieftain Ernest Rocco Infelice and 11 others, including alleged hit man Harry Aleman were charged with

using murder, other violence, threats, intimidation, and payoffs to witnesses and various public officials to protect their operations.

The group was called the "Ferriola Street Crew" by the FBI after the late mob boss Joseph Ferriola, who died March 11, 1989. Infelice, 67, picked up the reins after Ferriola's death, according to federal authorities.

Infelice plays tough guy in court
But judge gets last word, sentences hood to 63 years

By John O'Brien
TRIBUNE STAFF WRITER

19·AUG·93

It was a mob sentencing of the likes seldom seen in an American courtroom, and three convicted mobsters were at the center of attention.

There, wisecracking and telling off the judge who was about to sentence him to 63 years in prison, a defiant Ernest Rocco Infelice stood. He was spouting about his rights and beliefs along the lines of apple pie and motherhood and looking squarely at U.S. District Judge Ann C. Williams.

"I don't think we got a fair trial," Infelice said sharply, his bare forearms protruding from his well-worn blue jail jumpsuit as he gripped the lectern tightly. "We fought three prosecutors here, and you were the fourth. I don't think a judge should be the fourth prosecutor."

At 71, the convicted Chicago street crew boss was speaking up, something that until now he had left to his lawyers from his arrest 3½ years ago on racketeering and murder conspiracy charges through his lengthy trial.

And what was there to lose by such an outburst from someone given to silence as a way of life? The judge, after all, had let it be known she had intended to impose life sentences in the case.

Infelice would play a tough guy to the end, a James Cagney or Edward G. Robinson.

He even got off a parting shot at his nemesis, the prosecution's star witness, hoodlum-turned-infor-

SEE INFELICE, PAGE 10

Infelice
CONTINUED FROM PAGE 1

mant William "B.J." Jahoda, in a remark interpreted by law enforcement officials as a veiled threat.

"Rock," as Infelice is known on the street, a burly World War II paratroop veteran, began his verbal assault with his version of a Hallmark greeting.

"Mr. Jahoda's birthday is [this month]," Infelice said derisively, recalling a reference to when Jahoda gave a book as a gift to another mobster on his birthday.

"I would like to send him a happy birthday," Infelice said, mocking Jahoda, a former Cicero cardsharp who had managed Infelice's illegal gambling business.

Jahoda is now a protected federal witness whose appearance and identity have been changed. He once testified that Infelice would have nailed him through his tongue to a Cicero telephone pole, if he had the chance.

Facing a stern Williams, Infelice bellowed and chastised her for being a "prosecutor" who had ruled against the defense in favor of the team of government prosecutors led by Assistant U.S. Atty. Mitchell Mars.

He complained the judge hadn't resolved to his satisfaction allegations that unknown government agents eavesdropped on the defense's pre-trial strategy talks, when the mob figures huddled with their lawyers at the Metropolitan Correctional Center.

As for his beliefs, Infelice endorsed "law and order, justice, the jury system and the courts."

He also mentioned "defendants' rights," saying he hadn't gotten much of them from Williams.

Infelice's mention of the words "judge" and "prosecutor" in the same breath was greeted by a smattering of applause in the crowded courtroom. The noise came from supporters of the mob figures, among them Antoinette Giancana, daughter of slain Chicago mobster Sam Giancana and au-

Ernest Rocco Infelice

thor of the book, "Mafia Princess."

He then sat down, turned to look at the spectators and winked.

Infelice seemed pleased with his performance.

Williams glared back at him, unflinchingly.

An African American woman from the streets of Detroit, she had listened calmly to the criticism, a hand cupped under her chin. Then it was her turn to speak.

She declared in open court what she had told lawyers in the case: She had intended to sentence Infelice and co-defendants Louis Marino and Robert Bellavia each to life in prison for a litany of crimes, including a plot to murder bookmaker Hal C. Smith of Mt. Prospect because he had refused to pay street taxes, or extortion money, to the Infelice street crew.

But, she said, the law stayed her hand.

Infelice's sentence would be 63 years, she ruled, the total of a combination of terms for crimes ranging from racketeering to murder conspiracy to running an illegal horse and sports gambling business in parts of Lake and Cook Counties as well as tax evasion charges.

"The evidence is overwhelming," she said, "that Infelice was the mastermind."

There is no parole anymore in the federal penal system, so Infelice could be expected to serve up to 85 percent of his term, lawyers said.

Bellavia, 53, a former Bellwood businessman portrayed by his lawyer Kevin Milner as a family man, but convicted as a mob money collector and terrorist, was sentenced to 30 years in prison. He read from a handwritten statement in which he said Williams was "going to convict us no matter what the jury said. Don't be judge and jury."

Marino, 61, formerly of Orland Park, waived his right to speak, leaving that to his lawyer, George Leighton, a former federal judge who also criticized Williams. Marino got a 28-year term.

Chief prosecutor Mars, accompanied by Assistant U.S. Atty. Mark Prosperi, depicted Infelice, Bellavia and Marino as brutal and vicious men with no regard for human life. Any notion that members of organized crime are somehow "men of honor" is a cruel hoax, Mars said, a self-serving ideal of wannabe thugs whose only honor is one of greed.

Of the conspiracy to kill Smith, Mars said, "For the life of me, judge, I cannot comprehend where that evil comes from."

Williams observed that crucial evidence in the case included hundreds of secret recordings made by Jahoda of talks with Infelice and others. Such evidence, the very words of the mobsters, she said, left no question in her mind that what Infelice was doing was an extension of "the Chicago mob."

Defense lawyers said they would appeal the convictions while their clients serve their sentences.

Infelice defense gets its turn
Prosecutors wrap up 17 weeks of testimony in mob trial

21-Feb-92

By John O'Brien

After calling 105 witnesses to testify over 17 weeks, prosecutors rested their case Thursday in the racketeering trial of Ernest Rocco Infelice and four other reputed mobsters.

Defense lawyers immediately counterattacked, calling the first of several witnesses to discredit testimony by the government linking Infelice and co-defendants Robert Bellavia, Salvatore DeLaurentis, Louis Marino and Robert Salerno to two gangland murders.

U.S. District Judge Ann C. Williams later told jurors that closing arguments and verdict deliberations would begin next week.

The first defense witness, Donald Austin, a Northwestern University professor, took issue with claims by star prosecution witness William "B.J." Jahoda concerning the view into the kitchen of Austin's Long Grove home where prosecutors contend Mt. Prospect bookie Hal C. Smith was strangled in 1985.

Austin said Jahoda was renting it from him at the time of the killing. Jahoda claims he was outside the house but could see Smith slumped on the kitchen floor while Infelice and others stood nearby out of sight preparing to kill Smith. Austin told defense lawyer Terence Gillespie that he didn't think Jahoda could have fully seen anyone in the kitchen from that view.

Wrapping up the government's case, two FBI agents told of exploring the hidden "money room" in the Oak Brook mansion of the late crime boss Joseph Ferriola and of recording a conversation in which DeLaurentis, reputed Lake County underboss, is heard explaining to a gambler why he must pay street taxes.

Special Agent Thomas B. Noble said he didn't find any money in Ferriola's basement "money room" during a search in June 1991, two years after the mobster's death.

Noble's testimony was offered, prosecutors explained, to corroborate earlier witness statements that Infelice had gone into the basement after Ferriola died because "company [mob] money was down there."

Infelice's lawyer, Patrick Tuite, argued unsuccessfully that showing the jury enlarged photographs of the hidden room and the exterior of the castle-like Ferriola home had no relevance and was prejudicial.

In the street-tax recording, made at Alemar's restaurant in Palatine in 1986, Special Agent James Kuntzelman said he observed DeLaurentis and gambler John Katris in a terse discussion.

According to the recording played for the jury, DeLaurentis told Katris, who then ran a card game in Lake County, to pay the tax to the mob or shut down.

"I'm delivering the message to you," DeLaurentis said. "You weren't born yesterday. You know how that works. You're from Chicago, aren't you? Everybody pays. You can't skate for free."

19-AUG-93

METRO

Defiant Mobster Infelise Gets the Max – 63 Years

By Daniel J. Lehmann
Staff Writer

Mob crew leader Ernest "Rocco" Infelise on Thursday received 63 years in prison—the maximum term—from a federal judge who said he deserved a life sentence.

"I really don't think we had a fair trial, your honor, from Day One," an openly defiant Infelise, 71, told U.S. District Judge Ann C. Williams just minutes before she sentenced him and co-defendants Robert Bellavia, 53, and Louis Marino, 61.

But Williams returned Infelise's fire a few minutes later, saying that there was "no question in this court's mind ... that [the three men] operated as a part of the Chicago mob" and that they all deserved life sentences.

Restricted by statute from imposing that penalty, Williams instead sentenced each man to the maximum term for each count of their convictions and ordered that the terms be served consecutively. Bellavia received 30 years and Marino got 28 years in prison for their three-count convictions. Infelise was convicted on 20 counts.

Assistant U.S. Attorney Mitchell A. Mars labeled the three men "career criminals" who are "brutal, vicious ... violent parasites" for whom maximum terms were "the only sentences that are righteous."

Infelise, of River Forest; Bellavia, of Addison, and Marino, of Palos Park, were convicted last year in a complex four-month trial on charges of running an illegal sports bookmaking operation and collecting "street taxes" in Cook and Lake counties between 1974 and 1989.

Ernest "Rocco" Infelise

Infelise and Bellavia also were convicted on separate racketeering charges in a conspiracy to murder Hal Smith, a bookmaker. The jury could not reach verdicts on charges that they murdered Smith and found Infelise not guilty of murdering another bookmaker, Robert Plummer.

After Infelise finished nearly 10 minutes of remarks in which he bitterly denounced the trial process, several people in the packed courtroom applauded.

Bellavia was equally blunt.

"I thought I could get a fair shake in court. ... I was wrong," he said.

"Whatever the government wanted, they got. ... I feel confident finally I will receive some justice" in appealing the convictions, said Bellavia.

The three men were incensed by Williams' refusal to grant them bond after their arrests in 1990. They said they also were upset that during preparations for trial, their conversations with attorneys at the Metropolitan Correctional facility were taped.

Patrick Tuite, Infelise's attorney, added, "This case is a perversion of all we hold sacred in this country."

But Williams said there is "no evidence to support" allegations that prosecutors were responsible for the tapings at the Metropolitan Correctional Center.

Chapter 54

James LaValley – Mob Enforcer

On August 14, 1990, the Chicago Police and the FBI arrested James Frederick LaValley and his partner, James Bollman. They were both charged with knowingly conspiring to participate in the use of extortionate means, namely violence and explicit threats of violence to cause harm to the person of various individuals in order to collect and attempt to collect illicit extensions of credit, namely, illegal sports gambling debts.

This was a three-year-long investigation conducted jointly by the Chicago Police Department detectives from the organized crime division – gambling unit and the FBI. LaValley, forty-six, lived at 5054 North Delphia Avenue in Chicago, Illinois. Bollman, forty-four, lived at 369 Mensching Avenue, Roselle, Illinois. Bollman was the owner of the Boulevard Tap Lounge located at 297 South McLean Boulevard, Elgin, Illinois. Both men could be sentenced to prison for not more than twenty years and a fine of not more than $10,000 or both.

The first time that I had ever heard of LaValley and Bollman was when they visited a friend of mine in Las Vegas and had threatened to cut his life short if he didn't pay them $13,300 which they said that my friend "Zeke," owed them. LaValley said that his name was Jim Peterson, and Bollman said that his name was Jim Bolling. LaValley was about six foot one, 220 pounds, and Bollman was six feet, 230 pounds; both were in their forties. Zeke told me that LaValley and Bollman grabbed him in a casino poker room and took him up to a room in the hotel where they strip searched him to make sure that he wasn't wearing a wire and then slapped him around. They explained to Zeke that they had taken over the gambling operation that Zeke had worked for in Chicago and they knew that Zeke had cheated his boss out of $13,300, and they wanted the money back or else.

Zeke said that he had never been so scared in his life and started talking as fast as he could. He told them that he would get them the money, but they had to give him a couple of days to get it. Somehow he convinced them to give him some time, because if they put him in the hospital they had no chance to get their money. They told him that he was being watched and not to get any ideas about leaving town or he would wind up staked to the ground in the desert with his tongue cut out.

When they left, Zeke called me and told me about his meeting with these two guys and described both of them; he was sure that they had lied about their names. I had no idea who they were by their names or description, so I suggested that if I could get a copy of the videotape from the poker room there was a chance that we might be able to identify them. I made a few phone calls to some people whom I knew that were connected to the gaming commission in Las Vegas and told them what I needed. I didn't tell them why I needed the tape, but it would help me to identify some people who were in the poker room that day.

Much to my surprise, they sent me the tape and we were able to make a couple of photographs of the bad guys. That's when LaValley was identified as "Jim Peterson," and Bollman was "Jim Bolling." LaValley turned out to be a burglar and a juice collector for the Chicago Outfit. Bollman was a bookmaker from Chicago and was also connected to the outfit. They allegedly were part of a crew that worked for Lenny Patrick and Mario Rainone, two killers from the northwest side of Chicago. Patrick, of course, reported to Gus Alex, a long-time mob boss and close pal of Tony Accardo, who ran the Chicago Outfit. When I told Zeke who the two bad guys who paid him a visit were, he knew that he was in deep trouble and that these guys were serious. He agreed with me that it would be a good time to disappear and head for the hills, all he said was, "I'll keep in touch, Sarge, and hung up."

When Zeke was in Chicago giving me wire-room numbers, one of the numbers he gave me was listed to a guy who lived in a house in Evergreen Park on the South Side of Chicago. My partner at the time was a great cop by the name of Bill Mundee. Bill was a graduate of Notre Dame and had been on the job over twenty years. After we got enough probable cause to get a search warrant we arrested a guy who we will call "Manny." Manny was an independent bookmaker who got his kicks taking a few bets, but he earned his living by being involved in legitimate business. Manny told us that he liked to bet himself and would lay off some of his bets to a mob-operated wire room located on the North Side of Chicago. We convinced Manny that we could get him some help in court if he would give us the wire room number on the North Side; he agreed and gave us the number and told us that the guy running the wire room was a guy named Danny. He also said that he was pretty sure that Danny was working for Joe "Pooch" Pascucci, who ran a lot of gambling on the North Side.

I had busted Pascucci a couple of time in the past, so I knew where he lived and who he reported to in the outfit. Pascucci paid street tax to a mob guy named Salvatore De Laurentis who liked to be called "Solly D." DeLaurentis ran a lot of gambling in Lake County and was part of the Rocky Infelise crew. The North Side wire room operated by Danny turned out to be in Waukegan, Illinois, which was a little out of our jurisdiction so the information was turned over to the Lake County Sheriff's office vice unit.

I didn't hear from Manny for several weeks, until one day he called us and told us an interesting story about a scam he got involved in with Danny, the bookmaker in Waukegan. It seems that Danny asked Manny to do him a favor; he told Manny that he was going to add $1,000 to his weekly figure and then Manny could give the $1,000 back to him. Danny guaranteed Manny that there was no way anyone would find out about the scam because he controlled the figures. The second week, Danny split the $1,000 with Manny, who was beginning to like the idea. After a few weeks, Manny's end was about $6,000, but he was getting nervous about the outfit finding out what they were doing. He told Danny that he was through with the scam because he didn't want to get his legs broke if the bad guys found out what they were doing. While this was going on Pascucci got himself indicted along with some other people and they were all convicted and sent to prison. At this point, the outfit took over Pascucci's bookmaking operation while he was in jail.

About two weeks later, I got a call from Manny at about 9:00 PM and he sounded very upset and he told me that he was in big trouble and that three outfit guys almost killed him about an hour ago and would I please meet him. He said that he was on the third level of the east parking lot at O'Hare field and to get there as soon as possible. I got there in twenty minutes and drove to the third level in the parking lot. I knew what Manny was driving and finally found the car but I didn't see anyone in it which made me a little nervous. When I walked up to the car, there was Manny all curled up on the floor on the passenger side. When I knocked on the window, he said he almost had a heart attack. When he saw that it was me, he smiled and opened the door and asked me why the hell it took me so long to get there. I told him to calm down and tell me what happened to him.

Manny told me that he had gotten a phone call from Danny the bookmaker in Waukegan that he was going to get a call to meet someone concerning the scam that they had going. He told Manny that the outfit knew about their scam and how much money they had made and they wanted their money back.

Manny said that he got the call from an unknown man who told him to be at the Cypress Restaurant in Hinsdale at 7:00 PM and park in the parking lot where he would be contacted by someone. Manny said that he brought enough money with him to cover the $6,000 he made in the scam and brought an extra $7,000 to give to them maybe they would be satisfied with that. He said that he got to the meeting place a little early and about forty-five minutes later a black four-door sedan parked next to him. He could see that there were three men in the car; they just sat there and stared at him for a few minutes. He thought that he was going to get killed right then and there and almost wet his pants.

The three of them got out of the car at the same time; he had never seen any of them before, but they were really big guys. We found out later that the three guys were Jimmy LaValley, James Bollman, and Nick Gio, three enforcers for the mob. They told Manny to get out of his car where they searched him and asked him if he was wired for sound. Manny said the guy that got of the backseat had a gun in his waistband; he was identified as Nick Gio. Manny then began to panic and started to beg for mercy and told them that he was sorry and to give him a break. Manny told me that one of them grabbed him by the throat and told him that if he didn't come up with the money he cheated them out of; he was going to get an ice pick stuck in his eye and beat the dog shit out of him. This guy was identified as James LaValley. Manny said that he only made $6,000 out of the deal, but he would give them $13,000, which would double their loss. He gave the $13,000 to the third guy who was standing there laughing as Manny was pleading for mercy; he was identified as James Bollman. At this point, the guy with the gun, Nick Gio, must have felt neglected because he pulled out the gun and stuck it in Manny's ear and threatened to blow his head off. Manny felt his heart stop and he almost fainted he said he thought he was dead for sure.

LaValley then told him that he still owed them $130,000, because that was how much he was ahead of them for the year. Manny tried to explain that he won that money legitimately and that he didn't have that kind of money. That's when LaValley gave Manny a crack across the face and broke his glasses. He told Manny that he had better come up with the dough or else, and to get the hell out of there before they changed their minds and broke his legs just for fun.

When Manny told me what had happened to him and he described the three guys that scared him half to death; two of them fit the description of LaValley and Bollman the same two guys that paid Zeke a visit in Las Vegas. The third guy was identified as an outfit wanabee, Nick Gio. Gio was twenty-five years old, six foot one, 210 pounds, and wanted to make a name for himself as a mob guy. I explained the facts of life to Manny, that he was in deep trouble and these guys were very dangerous people and they might have whacked him in the parking lot if they didn't want the $130,000 from him. I suggested that he let me handle things and to let me call a couple of friends of mine with the FBI and I'll set up a meeting with them and decide which way was the best way to go with his problem.

The next day I told my partner, Bill Mundee, what had happened to our pal Manny and that I was going to set up a meeting with the FBI. I called Tom Noble and Jack O'Rourke, who were assigned to the organized crime section and explained the situation to them and that Manny might be willing to wear a wire. They told me that they had heard of some guys in town threatening gamblers and people on juice and they were bad dudes.

The next night, Mundee and I met Manny in a restaurant by the Evergreen Golf Course on the South Side of Chicago. We explained his options and made sure that if he were willing to wear a wire there would be some danger involved. There was always the chance that the bad guys would search him for a wire and if they found one thing's could get real serious. I explained to him that he had to trust us that we wouldn't leave him alone and we would cover his back so no harm would come to him. I also told him that in the event that he would wear a wire, he would probably have to testify in court against them.

Manny said that he would have to think about it because this move would probably change his entire life and he wanted to be sure about his decision. I'll call you in a couple of days, with that he walked out of the restaurant shaking his head. Mundee and I both agreed that there was no way Manny was going to agree to wear a wire; in a way, we didn't blame him.

Well, we were both wrong. Manny called me the next day and said that he was not going to live in fear for the rest of his life. "Let's get these bastards, Don, the sooner the better." After I picked myself off the floor in shock I called Mundee, and when I told him that Manny agreed to wear a wire he said wow, that little guy has got a lot of guts. At this point things were looking pretty good and we had a good chance to nail these guys and put them in jail.

I called Noble and O'Rourke and set up a meeting with Manny, Mundee, and I in an alley near the University of Chicago on the South Side. They explained the procedures involved in wearing a recording device and what would be expected of Manny as a key witness in this operation. Manny said, "Listen, I'm not a brave guy but I realize that I've got myself in a situation, and this was the only way out for him." He said that if he had known that he was getting involved with the Mafia he never would have started gambling, even the state lottery.

The FBI explained the Federal Witness Program to Manny and how it worked; at this point he refused to get involved in it right now but kept that option open in case things got a little sticky in the future.

All we had to do now was wait for LaValley to contact Manny for a meet, then we could wire Manny up and get the show on the road. As each day passed, Manny became more nervous and started to have second thoughts about what he agreed to do. Finally, LaValley called him and a meet was set up in the parking lot of the Gossage Grill located on North Avenue just west of Harlem Avenue for that night. Manny called me and we met the FBI and got him wired up for the meeting. We gave him a code word to use in case he felt that he was going to be seriously injured.

The grill was located next to a gas station where we could set up an undercover van and keep Manny under observation just in case. It was a hot night in July 1988 and the van was hotter than hell but then so was Manny. LaValley showed up in the parking lot, and Manny met him near the entrance. The conversation between Manny and LaValley was being recorded, and we could overhear LaValley tell Manny that he was going to cut his throat and to hand over his driver's license. Manny began pleading with LaValley and even told him about his mother that was dying of cancer; none of it mattered.

LaValley then punched Manny in the face breaking his nose and screamed at him about coming up with the $130,000 or he was finished. Manny began whimpering in pain and said, "I'm doing the best I can please don't hit me again." We started to worry that LaValley might whack Manny right in front of us on video, that would not be good. I was really concerned about Manny's well-being and had made up my mind that I was prepared to shoot LaValley if I felt Manny's life was in danger. We all expected Manny to say the code word *chocolate*, but he never did; he had some guts that's for sure.

Manny survived that scary night and got his revenge; everything that happened was recorded and LaValley was looking at twenty years in prison for being a tough guy. LaValley was busted along with Bollman and Gio. When Manny's tape was played in court at LaValley's bond hearing, it was so dramatic that the news media played it on the 10:00 PM news and the public was able to listen to the Chicago Outfit in action.

Testimony indicated LaValley was the muscle of the operation and described how LaValley burned one victim with a lighted cigarette, sliced a second man's hand with a knife, and threatened to cut and mutilate two other men for failing to pay gambling debts. LaValley was overheard to tell Manny, "Nobody robs us, if it gets out, then everybody robs us and we have to kill everybody." LaValley told another bettor that he had been involved in fire bombings and "clipping" (murdering) guys.

Jimmy LaValley had always been known as a standup guy in the outfit, but when he realized the fact that he could go to prison for twenty years, he jumped ship and decided to become a federal informant to save his own ass. He pleaded guilty to extortion charges and became a hell of an informant against the mob. He described how vicious Lenny Patrick was and how Patrick reported to Gus Alex, who had been the top mob fixer for over thirty years. He even testified against his rat partner, James Bollman, who had been with LaValley when they terrorized my friend Zeke in Las Vegas. On another occasion they threatened a gambler with castration if he didn't pay $150,000 that he owed Bollman.

When LaValley was on the witness stand in the racketeering trial of mobster Gus Alex, he described how he floored a man with one punch and then kicked him when he was down as LaValley's cohort Nicholas Gio, Alex's codefendant, sat on him, and beat him in the face. "This ain't the girl scouts," LaValley said. He also admitted that he threatened to cut off the remaining arm of an amputee who was a bookmaker.

LaValley told how at one time he took about eight years off from crime to own two legitimate businesses, LaValley ended up beating both his partners, one with a baseball bat. He claimed that he had been cheated of profits in separate schemes.

Some extortions were less successful he said when he belonged to long-time mobster Lenny Patrick's street crew. He described that he and Gio tried to firebomb the Lake Theater in downtown Oak Park in 1988 by hurling four jugs full of gasoline onto the roof from the street. To light the gas, LaValley threw a phosphorous grenade onto the roof, but it bounced and fell to the street burning intensely before he could retoss it. LaValley said that he and Gio then fashioned a Molotov cocktail, threw that on the roof, but no fire erupted.

LaValley recounted his life as a criminal, including more than fifty burglaries and countless beatings of people who didn't pay money to the mob. He acknowledged that his reputation often preceded him in the collection of mob debts. LaValley testified that he was a convicted burglar at twenty-one but that he did not go to work as a muscleman for the mob, a North Side street crew until he was forty-two.

LaValley was also a very good golf hustler, once winning $90,000 over three days from a professional golfer. Then there is the story about the day LaValley was playing in a foursome at the Brookwood Golf Course, which was a known hangout for the outfit. The president of the club was Jackie Cerone, a top mob boss. Someone in the foursome hit a ball onto an adjoining street and happened to break the windshield on a passing car. The driver stopped the car and proceeded to start swearing at LaValley and his companions, and walked toward them. LaValley told the man it was an accident and to get the hell out of there. Obviously, the man didn't know who he was dealing with and didn't stop. It was reported that LaValley beat the guy senseless and left him laying on the fairway.

LaValley became a key witness for the government and testified against mob bosses Gus Alex, Lenny Patrick, Rocky Infelise, Salvatore DeLaurentis, Mario Rainone, and many others. Rainone, accompanied by LaValley, was charged with assaulting business owners and threatening to kill them and members of their families if they failed to meet extortion demands. Lenny Patrick had ordered Rainone and LaValley to extort $200,000 from the owner of an Italian restaurant in Northbrook in 1987. Two days later after confronting the owner of the restaurant, Rainone phoned the owner and warned him that if he didn't pay the $200,000 his entire family would wind up in Mt. Carmel Cemetery.

LaValley did have some compassion at times; a friend of mine told me that when he came home from the army after being wounded in Vietnam, he had to use crutches to get around and decided to have a drink in a lounge called The Office on West Lawrence Avenue. LaValley happened to be running the place at the time and when he saw the wounded GI on crutches he told his bartenders that anybody that charges him would be fired.

LaValley, who had been in federal custody for two years while he was testifying against his fellow mobsters, was sentenced in July 1992. He was sentenced to seven years and seven months in prison for using terror tactics to collect gambling debts. He is now a free man, was given a new identity, and has started a new life.

JAMES FREDERICK LA VALLEY, aka
Jimmy La Valley,
"Angelo", "Panda"

Criminal associates:
JAMES WILLIAM BOLLMAN, aka
Jimmy Bollman
MARIO RAINONE
NICHOLAS GIO, aka
Nick Gio
GARY EDWARDS
LEONARD PATRICK, aka
Lenny Patrick
JOSEPH VENTO, aka
Singing Joe Vento
PHILLIP TOLOMEO, aka
Philly Beans Tolomeo
LEONARY CARDONE, aka
Lennie Cardone
MARCO DI'AMICO
RENATO DI SYLVESTRO, aka
Ray Di Sylvestro
VITO J. MAGGERISE

Source: Chicago Tribune

SEPT 15 1992

Chicagoland

Ex-enforcer tells jury of mob victims

By Matt O'Connor

With his size and his reputation as a mob muscle man, James LaValley's mere presence was sometimes enough to persuade people to pay juice loans, gambling debts or protection payoffs.

But when that didn't work, LaValley testified Monday in federal court, he threatened them and, in some cases, their family; displayed one of three knives he often carried; or resorted to violence.

In a full day on the witness stand in the racketeering trial of reputed mobster Gus Alex, LaValley recounted his long list of victims before he pleaded guilty to extortion and began cooperating with the government.

LaValley said he floored one man, on the hook for a friend's debt, with a punch and kicked him when he was down as LaValley's cohort, Nicholas Gio, Alex's co-defendant, sat on him and beat him in the face.

"This ain't the Girl Scouts," LaValley said.

LaValley admitted he knocked out a tooth of one victim, cutting his finger; cut the hand of a gambler who owed money; and threatened to cut off the remaining arm of an amputee who was a bookmaker.

Even when he took about eight years off from crime to own two legitimate businesses, LaValley ended up beating both his partners, one with a baseball bat. He said he had been cheated of profits in separate schemes.

LaValley also admitted he hustled golf, once winning $90,000 over three days from a professional golfer.

The extortions were sometimes less successful. LaValley, who said he belonged to longtime mobster Lenny Patrick's "street crew," testified that he and Gio tried to firebomb the Lake Theater in downtown Oak Park in 1988 by hurling four jugs full of gasoline onto the roof from the street.

To light the gas, LaValley threw a phosphorous grenade onto the roof, but it bounced and fell to the street, burning intensely before he could retoss it, LaValley testified.

LaValley said he and Gio then fashioned a Molotov cocktail, threw that on the roof, but no fire erupted.

Source: Chicago Tribune

Gambler names Alex enforcer in beating

By Matt O'Connor

A professional gambler testified Tuesday that two reputed mob enforcers beat him in a restaurant parking lot after he tried to stop running a mob-sanctioned poker game out of his home.

Scott Brooks, testifying for the government under a grant of immunity at the trial of longtime reputed mob official Gus Alex, identified Nicholas Gio, Alex's codefendant, as one of the two attackers in July 1988.

Brooks said he agreed to pay a "penalty" of $5,000 after the mob discovered he had begun hosting a poker game for 20 to 25 players in his Sheridan Road home twice a week. He was also ordered to pay $600 a week in "street taxes."

"I didn't think I had any other choice," said Brooks, who identified the mob contact as James LaValley, an admitted enforcer who testified earlier in the trial that he was a member of the Lenny Patrick "street crew."

By April 1988, with interest in his game subsiding and neighbors complaining about the noise, Brooks said he stopped hosting poker out of his home.

When he balked at mob demands he continue the game, Brooks testified, LaValley and Gio beat him for 15 minutes in the parking lot of Dapper's Restaurant, 2901 W. Addison St.

As the two punched him, Brooks said, LaValley warned him, "This is just the beginning. It could get worse."

Under questioning by Marvin Bloom, Gio's lawyer, Brooks conceded he didn't seek treatment and wasn't cut in the beating.

Earlier Tuesday, Patrick concluded 3½ days of often colorful testimony, repeatedly contending he was telling the truth and had nothing to hide.

Patrick, 78, the highest-ranking Chicago mob official to ever become a government witness, was the main witness against Alex, 76, reputedly the mob's chief political fixer for years. Patrick testified he shared profits of the street crew's extortion activities with Alex.

During 2½ days of cross-examination, Sam Adam, Alex's lawyer, accused Patrick of doing whatever was in his best interest, just as he did in half a century as a gangster.

"I'm testifying truthfully," Patrick insisted Tuesday. "I wouldn't lie, and if I do they're going to tear up the agreement, and I go to prison for the rest of my life. I'm not lying about anything."

Patrick pleaded guilty to racketeering and extortion and was sentenced to 6 years in prison, though he expects to serve just 2 to 4 years.

Told by Adam he could appeal to the Parole Board for an even shorter time in prison, Patrick replied, "I'm glad you told me. I don't know anything about it. I'm glad you told me."

Source: Chicago Tribune

Chapter 55

James "the Schemer" Nicholas

The first time I ever heard the name Jimmy Nicholas was back in May of 1989. It seems that Nicholas was a bookmaker in and around the Chicago area. A reliable source of mine described Jimmy to me and told me that he was frequenting the Sportsman's Park racetrack located at 3400 South Laramie Avenue in Cicero, Illinois. He also told me that Jimmy was driving an '89 Chrysler with license number 840910, and added that he did not like Jimmy because Jimmy was involved in promoting fixed card games and cheated a lot of Greeks out of a lot of money. The source also said that he thought Nicholas was connected to the mob, and he thought that he was a real bad ass. I thought, *What the hell, let's give this guy a look and see what we can come up with.* On May 5, 1989, John Kohles, who was a member of my squad, and I set up a surveillance at Sportsman's Park. I thought that maybe it might be a good idea to hang around the entrance of the parking lot, as long as we had his car and license number we might get lucky and see him drive in. That way we could give him a tail and see what he was up to. Well, like they say, sometimes you get the bear and sometimes the bear gets you. This time we got the bear; we spotted Jimmy drive in with his Chrysler, and when the driver got out. He fit the description we were given of James Nicholas. Of course, he valet parked the car, and

Judge Hett, recused himself during the summer of 1989 because he knew one of Jahoda's family members. After Hett's recusal, Infelise told Jahoda that Maltese had met with Hett and that Hett would have been given $7,500 to take care of the case. Maltese was one of the 20 mobsters indicted in Feb 1990. The state eventually dismissed the case on its own motion.

At this point in time, James Nicholas is still in Chicago and is reported to have snow-white hair because he doesn't dye it anymore. Greek town is still his haven, even though all the Greeks know that he had been cheating them all these years with his fixed card games, what a guy.

James Nicholas (left) and Michael Zitello leave following indictments Wednesday.

20 linked to mob indicted

By John O'Brien
and John Gorman

In one of the largest crackdowns on organized crime ever in Chicago, 20 alleged mobsters were charged with using money, muscle and murder to run and protect the "Chicago Outfit's" lucrative gambling, extortion and juice loan operations.

Reputed mob chieftain Ernest Rocco Infelice and 11 others, including alleged hit man Harry Aleman were charged with using murder, other violence, threats, intimidation, and payoffs to witnesses and various public officials to protect their operations.

The group was called the "Ferriola Street Crew" by the FBI after the late mob boss Joseph Ferriola, who died March 11, 1989. Infelice, 67, picked up the reins after Ferriola's death, according to federal authorities.

The eight others were charged with operat-

DeLaurentis   Infelice

than a decade.

The charges outlined in detail allegations of how murder and the threat of it were used to keep order among victims and workers and represented a deep penetration into what federal authorities call organized crime.

when he did the attendant said, "How ya doin', Jimmy?" We couldn't believe that this was going so easy; maybe we should play a few races as long as our luck was going so good.

Jimmy went up to the second floor in the Saddle and Sulky room, which is frequented by customers who have to pay an additional fee to enter. And guess what, Jimmy walked up to a booth that was occupied by three other individuals, Rocky Infelise, Louie Marino, and Solly D. DeLaurentis.

I was thinking that if this were a war, one hand grenade would take care of a lot of evil. Rocky was running things in the Chicago Outfit and Louie Marino was his right-hand man along with Salvatore "Solly D." DeLaurentis. Nicholas sat down with this triple trio and had appeared to be having a serious conversation with Rocky himself. After a few minutes, Nicholas left the booth and walked into the seating area where he was observed talking to a black man and his female companion who were seated at a table. The black man was studying a racetrack program and spoke to Nicholas, who proceeded to write some notations down on his program. The black man then gave Nicholas an unknown sum of currency; this all occurred a few minutes before the first race. Nicholas then left and met another white male who gave Nicholas a sum of currency. Nicholas called the man Phil; after a short conversation, Nicholas left and met two more men, who were black. After the race was over, Nicholas returned to the first black man he took money from and gave him an undetermined amount of U.S. currency, and stated something about his female companion must have brought him luck.

Nicholas returned to the Saddle and Sulky room frequently to converse with Infelise, Marinoc and DeLaurentis; it was obvious that Nicholas was taking orders from Infelise. At the end of the racing program, Nicholas was observed leaving the track accompanied by Phil and another unknown man; he dropped them off at another parking lot. Nicholas was driving a red 1989 Chrysler four-door with license number 840-910; he was tailed to Adams and Halsted Street in Greek town where he entered a Greek restaurant on the northwest corner.

Needless to say, we were very satisfied with the turn of events and we were sure that we had uncovered a large organized crime bookmaking ring that was operating on the racetrack. I questioned some sources I had about Phil, who was unknown to us at this point. I found out that Phil was called "Phil the Fruit" and was an on track bookmaker who was working for our guy Nicholas, who obviously was working for Rocky Infelise the top mob boss in the Chicago area.

```
Phil`the fruit, busted
for bookmaking with Jim
Nicholas - Sportsmans Pk.
Racetrack
```

I decided to get a couple more of my crew to assist Kohles, in an effort to identify as many other bookmakers on the track as we could. After numerous surveillances at the track of Nicholas and Phil the Fruit, we discovered that Phil was taking bets from bettors all over the track. Phil also had a few black helpers working the grandstand area, taking action. At no time did anybody connected to this bookmaking ring ever go to the windows to make and wagers. I wondered what the owner of the racetrack would think of this little operation; these guys were making a ton of money and the track was getting cheated. No matter what, Nicholas always checked in with Infelise after every race and Infelise always seemed to be giving instructions to Nicholas. I sure wish that we had a bug in that booth; I'll bet we would get a real education.

Nicholas always made sure that he talked to this one black man about fifty-five years old who was with a female companion. This guy wore a lot of gold and dressed like a dope dealer; he also wore a large hat. It is well known that dope dealers like to bet with on track bookies because they can launder their dope money that way. This black guy always bet no less than a few hundred on every race; he would tell Nicholas what he wantedb and Nicholas would make notations on his program. Nicholas never went to the betting window. We did manage to follow the black guy out of the track to his car so we could try and identify him, and sure as hell he was driving a brand-new Cadillac with Alabama plates. We checked the plates later, but of course, they were not in file yet – big surprise. Phil the Fruit was all over the track taking bets from everybody, so was the black crew he and Nicholas had working. I'm sure Rocky Infelise and company were well satisfied with this operation; whenever Nicholas would return to Rocky's booth to report how things were going, there seemed to be a lot of grinning and back slapping going on.

The next surveillance we had was a few days later, and this really turned out to be interesting to say the least. The first time we saw Nicholas was when he was sitting in the regular booth they always seemed to use in the Saddle and Surry restaurant. Nicholas was in the company of Louie Marino, who was Rocky's lieutenant. Mike Sarno, who was a juice and street tax collector for Infelise, joined them. Nicholas and Sarno left the restaurant and went to a pay phone in the lobby area; they both were studying a piece of paper that Sarno had. At this point, Louie Marino joined them and they had a serious discussion about the contents of the piece of paper. Sarno then made a phone call to an unknown party, which lasted several minutes; they then returned to the booth they had been occupying. A few minutes Marino left the restaurant and rode the escalator to the lower floor where he walked up to the express window and was observed making a lot of wagers on the eighth race. Several minutes later, Marino was joined by Mike Sarno and they continued talking. The goofy part was that when the race he had bet on started; he showed no interest in the race at all and didn't seem to care what horse was winning the race. When the race ended, he walked back to the clerk at the express window and gave him his tote tickets. The clerk was observed counting out a large amount of U.S currency in front of Marino, which Marino took and put it in his pocket. Marino then left the track and entered a black Cherokee jeep wagon, with license number FS 8607, which checked to Anthony Marano Co., 1811 West Fullerton Avenue, Addison, Illinois.

I informed my boss about everything that was happening at the racetrack and who was involved. He suggested that I call the IRS and maybe we could work this case together. I told special agent Tom Moriarity of our findings, and he agreed that this looked like a real organized crime scam and would work with us on the investigation.

The next day, I showed Tom who the bad guys were and what they were up to; he was very familiar with Infelise, Marino, DeLaurentis, Sarno, and Nicholas. A goofy thing happened when I was walking in the club house area. I spotted a lawyer whom I knew sitting close to the area where the bad guys were, and his name was Bob Cooley. Cooley usually handled bookmaking cases in court and I knew that he knew me. Cooley also had the reputation of being a degenerate gambler, and probably gave all of his action to mob bookies. I got out of the area as fast as I could because I was afraid that if he saw me moping around the racetrack he would tell Infelise. This could heat our whole investigation up. Little did I know at that time that Cooley had been wearing a wire for the FBI and was working for the Government against the outfit. Cooley would prove to be involved in a lot of fixed cases that involved the First Ward and was the pay-off man for a murder case involving the biggest hit man in the country, Harry Aleman; but Harry is another story. We set up a plan to grab Nicholas, Infelise, Marino, and Delaurentis when they were all together sitting in their favorite booth. The next day we were all set up with Tom Moriarity and a few other federal agents as well as my crew with John Kohles and Wayne Lloyd who had been with me on a lot of surveillances of Nicholas and company. This time the bear got us, because Infelise, Marino, and DeLaurentis didn't show up. We waited around for a few races hoping that they would show, but no luck. We had to go with what we had so Nicholas was grabbed along with Phil the fruit, and they were taken to the racetrack steward's office for questioning. The racing programs they had which had been marked in code identifying the horses that their customers bet on, as well as amounts of money, was confiscated. Photos were also taken of Nicholas and Phil the Fruit and they were warned that their actions would not be tolerated on the premises, and to leave the racetrack. If nothing else, I felt that we screwed up their little bookmaking operation and caused Nicholas and his boss Infelise some aggravation to say the least.

The next day I thought about how things had gone at the racetrack, and I began to wonder just how much of a scare we had given Nicholas and Phil the Fruit. After I analyzed things I decided to go back to the racetrack just to see if Nicholas paid heed to the warning he was given by the steward's office. Well guess what, about an hour before post time, here came Nicholas walking in as if he owned the place. The only difference was that he didn't go up to the Saddle and Sulky room; he stayed on the first floor and acted like nothing happened the day before at all. I'm sure that the racetrack security would keep an eye on Jimmy boy from now on, now that they knew who he was and what he was up to, right?

The next thing I found out about Nicholas was that he was running rigged card games for the outfit as well as running a bookmaking operation. Nicholas would put some shills in the game that were the best cheaters in the country. His main clientele were Greeks; most of them were businessmen and had money and loved to gamble. Most of the time, Nicholas would rent a suite in the downtown area and provide food and drinks as well as a few high line prostitutes that worked for the infamous Rose Laws. Laws was called the Gold Coast Madam and had been in the prostitution racket for many years. She was known to brag about the gorgeous hookers that she could provide, which cost a lot of money. Nicholas didn't care what they cost, because he would get that money back from the suckers he had coming to his high stakes rigged card games. Jimmy boy had some of the players meet at a Greek coffee shop on Halsted Street and then he would provide a limo to take them to his game, little did these guys know what they were in for. One of the most popular games that Nicholas ran was blackjack; it was quick, and Nicholas made a lot of dough for the mob running it. Of course, Nicholas was cut in for a share of the profits from the games he ran.

There just happened to be a grand jury investigation going on during this time that involved Infelise, Marino, DeLaurentis, and the Ferriola street crew. During the grand jury investigation of this case, James Nicholas and other crew members were subpoenaed to testify; they asserted their Fifth Amendment privilege. They were then immunized and still refused to testify before the grand jury. Ultimately, Nicholas and the others were incarcerated for civil contempt. Nicholas served eighteen months in the Metropolitan Correctional Center. While he was in custody, the outfit gave him $1,000 per month for being a standup guy. The other people that he was with also received various amounts of money from the mob. Nicholas was released in the summer of 1989; at that time he was given $75,000 for his end of the profits from his bookmaking operation that continued while he was incarcerated. In April 1989 B. J. Jahoda decided to defect over to the federal government and began wearing a wire. Jahoda was Infelise's main guy who took care of all the gambling operations for the mob.

Nicholas, along with nineteen other mob guys, was indicted in February 1990 for charges ranging from murder, gambling, extortion, and juice loans. Nicholas was released on his own recognizance from the charges placed against him. Nicholas, of course, got back into business right away; he ran an illegal card game at the Hellas Coffee Shop at 334 South Halsted Street in Greek Town. We had an undercover officer inside the coffee shop, and he observed Nicholas collecting a cut of the card games. We raided the coffee shop in May 1989 and arrested Nicholas for gambling as well as being a keeper of a gambling house. Shortly thereafter, Nicholas was incarcerated again for violation of his personal recognizance bond.

A jury tried James Nicholas in the criminal court at 2600 South California. Judge Thomas Hett Circuit Court of Cook County was the presiding judge. The undercover officer, Peter Domain testified along with Detective Wayne Lloyd, Lt. Guanineri, and yours truly. James Nicholas was found guilty by a jury of his peers, which put him in deep shit at the federal building involving his other indictments on gambling charges. Nicholas was sentenced to serve another six months in jail, which came to a total of about four years total. Judge Thomas Hett's name had been mentioned along with two other Cook County judges in the case involving B. J. Jahoda in 1989. Jahoda had been arrested for operating an illegal blackjack game at the Arlington Hilton in Arlington Heights, Illinois in February 1988. Infelise told Jahoda that he believed that something could be done on the case. Jahoda had a series of conversations with Infelise, DeLaurentis and Maltese regarding payoffs they were offering the three judges to fix Jahoda's case.

Judge Hett recused himself during the summer of 1989 because he knew one of Jahoda's family members. After Hett's recusal, Infelise told Jahoda that Maltese had met with Hett and that Hett would have been given $7,500 to take care of the case. Maltese was one of the twenty mobsters indicted in February 1990. The state eventually dismissed the case on its own motion.

At this point in time, James Nicholas is still in Chicago and is reported to have snow-white hair because he doesn't dye it anymore. Greek Town is still his haven; even though all the Greeks know that he had been cheating them all these years with his fixed card games, what a guy.

Tape links accused madam to mob

By Ray Gibson
and Matt O'Connor

A woman accused of operating a nationwide prostitution ring was surreptitiously videotaped last September when she met with a reputed organized crime figure and a key government informant in the federal investigation of alleged corruption in Cook County courts and City Hall, court records show.

Rose Laws, a woman authorities have dubbed the Gold Coast Madam, met for 40 minutes in the Lake Shore Drive apartment of a key government informant, William "B.J." Jahoda. Jahoda is a one-time overseer of the mob's day-to-day gambling operations who is now cooperating with the federal investigation.

Also at the meeting was James Nicholas, 47, of Hoffman Estates, accused in February by federal prosecutors of being a bookmaker and operating an illegal gambling scheme under the auspices of reputed mob chieftain Ernest Rocco Infelice.

Nicholas faces federal gambling and criminal contempt of court charges. He was among 20 reputed organized crime figures indicted in February as part of an investigation of mob figures, judges and politicians.

The disclosure of the meeting marks the first time that authorities have made public any connections between Laws and organized crime figures.

Nicholas and Jahoda are the second and third targets of the federal probe who investigators say were linked to Laws. A high-ranking Cook County judge, also a target of the probe, was told last year his name was found in a listing of clients of the ring.

Cook County prosecutors have filed court documents stating they intend introduce the videotape as evidence in pending prostitution-related case agai Laws. The prosecutors said they may c as witnesses two Internal Revenue Serv agents who secretly observed the meetin

Government sources said Nicholas a Jahoda both were customers of the ri and also hired the ring's prostitutes entertain at a Jahoda party and at ille blackjack games Nicholas allegedly op ated in Chicago's Greek Town.

A cassette tape of the meeting has be turned over to attorneys for Laws. C Walsh, one of the attorneys, declined comment. A judge has issued an ord prohibiting both defense attorneys ar prosecutors from discussing the case.

Walsh has previously denied the ri had any connection to organize crime fi

See Mob, pg.

Mob

Continued from page 1

ures.

According to authorities, the 200-woman ring brought prostitutes to Chicago from the East and West Coasts. Using eight posh apartments, the ring catered to Chicago politicians, judges and affluent businessmen, authorities have said.

Laws was arrested on prostitution-related charges in September 1988 and again in July 1989.

Nicholas, who was free on $50,000 bond from the February charges, was arrested again on May 19 in an early morning gambling raid at the Hellas Cafe, 334 S. Halsted St.

U.S. Magistrate Thomas Rosemond ordered on June 1 that Nicholas be held without bail after government prosecutors argued that Nicholas could flee to his native Greece where he would not be subject to extradition. Nicholas faces another federal bond hearing Friday.

When Chicago police raided the restaurant on May 19, they recovered $11,000 in cash, plus items used in gambling.

The February indictment accused Nicholas of operating a mob-run blackjack game and contended he was a horse racing and sports bookmaker who turned over some of his proceeds to Infelice.

Tribune reporter Ronald Koziol contributed to this story.

Testimony of cop is challenged

By John Gorman

The testimony of a masked undercover Chicago police officer violated the constitutional rights of alleged Chicago mob gambler Jimmy Nicholas to confront his accuser, Nicholas' lawyer argued in a federal court motion.

"There is no legal basis for admitting the testimony of Officer X [as the hooded officer was called]," Nicholas' attorney, William Theis, argued in the motion filed last week. "Receipt of this testimony would violate Mr. Nicholas' constitutional rights to confront his accusers and to due process as well as his statutory rights to cross-examine [witnesses]."

In what was described as an unprecedented event in a local U.S. District Court, the 17-year police veteran testified last month in an attempt by federal prosecutors to persuade Judge Ann Williams to revoke Nicholas' bond.

The undercover officer testified that he twice observed Nicholas collecting a "cut" of card games in May at a cafe at 334 S. Halsted St.

On the second occasion, May 19, Nicholas, 47, of 716 Scarbrough Circle, Hoffman Estates, was arrested when the cafe was raided. At the time, Nicholas was out on a personal recognizance bond on gambling conspiracy charges.

He was one of 20 alleged crime syndicate figures charged last February in a federal crackdown on crime syndicate activities. Others charged included Ernest Rocco Infelice and Salvatore DeLaurentis.

Assistant U.S. Atty. Thomas Knight told Williams in the July 1 hearing that the officer's undercover role would be compromised and his life endangered if he testified openly before Nicholas and his friends.

Williams ruled that the witness could testify while wearing the hood with the provision that Knight convince her later through written briefs about the legality of the unusual maneuver.

Nicholas denies he was engaged in gambling, Theis argued, "nor does he concede that Officer X ... was present in the Hellas [cafe] on May 18-19."

"If Officer X will not even show his face, Mr. Nicholas is stripped of any opportunity to call people who were in the Hellas that night and who could testify whether Officer X was also present," Theis contended.

Chapter 56

Bobby Johnson – Bookmaker – Suicide or Homicide

On June 7, 1993, Robert "Bobby" Johnson, a forty-three year old bookmaker, was found hanging in his cell; it was ruled a suicide. Johnson was incarcerated in a cell on the seventeenth floor at the Metropolitan Correctional Center, 71 West Van Buren Street, Chicago, Illinois. Johnson had been jailed on extortion and gambling charges. A jail guard found him at 8:45 PM hanging from a bedsheet tied to an overhead sprinkler pipe, Johnson of Palos Park, a suburb of Chicago. The Cook County medical examiner ruled the death a suicide.

My first encounter with Bobby Johnson was a few years earlier when we busted him and John Orsi on November 29, 1980 running a sports wire room at 11740 South Ridgeland Avenue in Worth, Illinois. Bobby also booked a lot of football parlay cards on the South Side as well. Johnson was about five foot ten, 220 pounds, and was a very powerful guy; he didn't give us a bad time when we arrested him. He said that it was just part of the game and shrugged it off. I asked him how much he had to pay the outfit a month in street tax to be able to book. He looked at me as if I was nuts, then said I don't give those jags a cent, and I never will. At first I found that hard to believe but after I talked to a couple of guys that knew him they said that he was tough enough not to pay the mob and they weren't surprised at all.

The thing that got Bobby in trouble was his alleged high pressure terror tactics in collecting gambling debts that eventually forced corrupt attorney Robert Cooley to turn federal witness. Cooley's testimony helped convict numerous judges and other high-ranking officials in future cases.

Johnson allegedly ran one of Cook County's most sophisticated gambling operations independent of organized crime. Johnson was charged on December 1, 1992, with extorting gambling payments; he was being held without bail pending trial. It was alleged that one time Johnson shot up an Orland Park man's garage and then set it on fire; he then beat the man unconscious because of a $40,000 gambling debt. Johnson informed the government that he never paid street tax to the outfit when he was in the bookmaking business; he simply refused to give them anything no matter how much they pressured him. To defy the mob when they were killing a lot of bookmakers who refused to pay them a street tax took a lot of guts on his part.

Cooley, who had been betting with Johnson, ran up a debt of $45,000, which he couldn't pay; that was when Johnson threatened Cooley with violence. Cooley informed the FBI and began working for them; the FBI paid off Cooley's debt to Johnson, which put him in a world of shit. That's when he was arrested for extortion and gambling. When Cooley became an informant he was invaluable in Operation Gambat (Gambling Attorney), which was named after him. The government set up a sting which resulted in convictions of former Alderman Fred Roti (First Ward), former state Senator John D'Arco (D-Chicago), former Cook County Circuit Court Judge Dave Shields, and Pat DeLeo, a former law partner of D'Arco.

Johnson had written his former wife from the MCC prison that he had heard that he was going to be "taken care of" while he was at the MCC. He said that four of mob boss John "No Nose" DiFronzo's associates were in prison with him; he added that they looked like a bunch of old men. Both the U.S. attorney and Johnson's lawyer asked him if he was paying the mob to book. They both called him a liar, and they didn't believe him. He told them that he had problems in the past but that he handled it; all they told him was he was full of shit.

Johnson had a multimillion dollar bookmaking operation for years and insisted that he never paid the mob street taxes. It seems that there had been a contract out on Johnson's life; allegedly; the FBI found out about it and notified Johnson's mother in 1986. If Johnson was telling the truth about not paying the mob any street tax; he was either the toughest man in town, crazy, or the outfit couldn't find him. I have had the opportunity to talk to a few people that knew Johnson and they told me that he could have been the toughest man in town. Also there was no way that he would ever commit suicide.

Johnson told some friends of his that he had heard that John "No Nose" De Fronzo told someone that Johnson was going to be "taken care of" while he was at the MCC. Johnson said that he was very concerned about this and he felt vulnerable while he was locked up. Four of Rocky Infelise's crew who were awaiting trial on murder, gambling and extortion charges were also on Johnson's floor which did not make Johnson feel any safer.

While Johnson was being held in custody at the MCC, he was examined from time to time by medical personnel. It seems that he exhibited a manifestation of a nervous condition that resulted in bleeding sores on parts of his body. The sores were diagnosed as anxiety and a nervous condition, and he was given medication for the sores.

On the day of Johnson's death, another prisoner who had been Johnson's cellmate for several weeks advised Metropolitan Correctional Personnel that Johnson was acting "weird" and had been throwing up. On the afternoon of June 7, the prisoner spoke to a MCC guard and asked for permission to move out of Johnson's cell because of Johnson's behavior. This permission was given, and the prisoner was moved out of Johnson's cell that afternoon. Johnson was now alone in his cell and not assigned another cellmate and was allowed to stay in his cell alone. A few hours later, Johnson hanged himself with his bedsheet from an exposed sprinkler system pipe.

There are people who do not believe Johnson killed himself; one of these was a guy with connections who suggested to family members that they get a copy of the prisoners that were on Johnson's floor when he died. A well-known attorney told the family that he would do this for them; but of course, he never did. Johnson did have a cut on the bridge of his nose but the FBI told the family that when the guards cut Johnson down he hit his nose on his bunk which caused the bruise. At this point in time, Johnson's death remains a suicide and will remain that way.

After Johnson was arrested, the government seized $2 million of his assets, including his Palos Park home, a house in Michigan and $1.7 million is stocks, bonds ands certificates of deposit.

lleged bookie found hanged in jail cell

Park man jailed on ex- gambling charges was ged to death in his cell ropoli- ctional SOUTHWEST thori- SUBURBS Tues-

"Bob- son, 43, of 12322 S. , was found by a jail ut 8:45 p.m. Monday om a bed sheet tied to an overhead sprinkler pipe, authorities said.

Johnson was rushed from his 17th-floor cell at the jail, 71 W. Van Buren St., to Northwestern Memorial Hospital, where he was pronounced dead on arrival.

The Cook County medical examiner's office ruled the death a suicide.

It was Johnson's alleged high- pressure terror tactics in collecting gambling debts that eventually forced corrupt attorney Robert Cooley to turn federal witness, officials said. Cooley's testimony has helped convict several judges and high-ranking government officials.

Johnson allegedly ran one of Cook County's most sophisticated gambling operations independent of organized crime, netting up to $2,000 a day in sports bets, authorities said. One FBI agent described Johnson Tuesday as a "vicious bully."

Assistant medical examiner Dr. Mitra Kalelkar, who performed the autopsy, said there was no indication of foul play.

"There weren't any other injuries or marks on his body. As far as I'm concerned, it's suicide," Kalelkar said.

Kalelkar said no suicide note was found in Johnson's cell.

Johnson was charged Dec. 1, 1992, with extorting gambling payments. He was being held without bond pending trial.

Federal prosecutors said Johnson once set fire to an Orland Park man's garage, fired shots into the garage and beat the man unconscious to collect a $40,000 debt.

After Johnson was arrested, the government seized more than $2 million of his assets, including his Palos Park home, a house in Michigan and $1.7 million in stocks, bonds and certificates of deposit.

Unlike other independent bookies, Johnson avoided detection by organized crime bosses and apparently paid no "street taxes" to the mob, FBI officials said.

Johnson drew the attention of FBI agents through his gambli dealings with Cooley, who at o time owed Johnson $45,0(Johnson's threats of violet against Cooley eventually p suaded Cooley to start worki for the FBI, which paid off C ley's debt to Johnson, FBI offici said.

Cooley's testimony has be crucial in the Operation Gamb convictions of former Ald. Fr Roti (1st), former state Sen. Jo D'Arco (D-Chicago), former Co County Circuit Court Judge Da Shields and Pat DeLeo, a form law partner of D'Arco.

Source: *Chicago Tribune*

Chapter 57

John "Schavoni" Santucci – Burglar

On July 3, 2002, I appeared at the federal building at 219 South Dearborn Street for the sentencing hearing of Gregory "Emit" Paloian before Judge Kocares in room 2547 at 9:45 AM. Paloian had pled guilty to a charge of gambling and racketeering.

Special agent Tom Moriarity of the IRS contacted me on July 1 and asked me if it were possible that I still had phone records from John Santucci's mobile phone. Moriarity had tried to get the U.S. attorney's office to investigate Santucci, who was taking money from bookmakers and guaranteed them immunity from arrest from me. Moriarity was aware that Santucci was an FBI informant, which was confirmed by his telephone records which had shown that Santucci had called the number 312-431-1333 numerous times. Santucci was also involved in a scam involving counterfeit beanie baby tags as well as other things.

Santucci's telephone records were almost three years old, but for some reason I had kept them along with other reports involving gambling raids that involved Santucci.

At the federal building, I spoke to Moriarity and U.S. Attorney Mark Vogel who asked me if I still had Santucci's telephone records. I told them I did as well as other reports concerning Santucci's involvement in gambling operations. Mark Vogel, Judith Dobkin, and I were together in New York in June 1985 as expert witnesses on organized crime in Chicago; we all testified at the President's Commission on Organized Crime gambling.

I asked Vogel why he needed Santucci's records now, and they didn't seem to interested three years ago when I was looking for some assistance. Vogel related that they had a situation where Santucci who had been an informant for the FBI for the past thirty-one years had gone bad. Apparently, Santucci was involved in a wiretap on a bookmaker I had busted named Anthony Giannone. Santucci, who had probably given the FBI probable cause to obtain the wiretap, had been overheard on the tap warning Giannone that his phone may be tapped which could be a problem for the FBI.

Vogel told me that Santucci was saying bad things about me and was probably telling them that he gave me $30,000 that he took from Belpedio. Who the hell knows? Vogel asked me if I would mind talking to FBI Agent Hall and Apecial Agent Terry Hake, who was involved in the Greylord scandal years ago. I gave Vogel my phone number and told him that I would be glad to talk to anybody. At that point he said that it was possible that I would be called before a federal grand jury sometime in the future.

I again had a conversation with Moriarity who told me that one FBI agent who used Santucci for an informant was Kevin Blair, who has since been transferred to Washington DC. Blair is a personal friend of my son Tom; I have played golf with Blair and my son Tom in the past. It is rumored that Blair was to testify in an organized crime case involving Mayor Maltese, but he was not allowed to do so for some unknown reason.

On July 8, 2002, I received a phone call from special agent Steve Hall of the FBI who requested to meet me sometime during the week if possible. I could either go to his office or I could pick a place that was convenient for me. The meeting concerned the problem that I had with John Santucci the past few years. I agreed to meet Hall at the Blue Angel restaurant at 10:00 AM on Friday, July 12, 2002. I arrived before Hall did and waited at the rear of the restaurant for him. I knew that he wouldn't come alone, and I was right. Terrence Hake, who is currently a special agent with the Department of Justice, walked in first and said, "Hi, Don, I met you at Sheriff Sheehan's golf outing a couple of years ago, we were introduced by Joe Shaunessey." Hake was a former states attorney for Cook County, who became disenchanted with the way things were run in the criminal courts building and became a mole for the FBI. He was responsible for the Greylord scandal that involved numerous judges, attorneys, court clerks, and others. He then joined the FBI and became a special agent and was assigned to the Chicago office where he works in the Inspector General's Office of the Department of Justice. He explained that he came along because Santucci had made accusations of FBI special agent Kevin Blair accepting money from the outfit.

Hall walked in with his female partner – I forgot her name – and we sat at a table. Hall said that he has been with the FBI for four years; his female partner was pregnant and also has been with the FBI a short time. I asked Hall why everybody seemed to be so interested in Santucci now and not before when I notified Jim Wagner who was the group boss of in the FBI and denied ever having heard of Santucci. Hall said that it was true that Santucci has been an informant for the FBI for the past thirty-one years, but he had turned bad and were currently working a case on him. I asked Hake about Kevin Blair and if he was in trouble because of what Santucci said. Hake said that that was the reason he was at the meeting because he had to make an investigation of Santucci's allegations and to find out what I knew about Santucci and his past. Hall said that they have a good case against Santucci who was overheard on a wiretap warning a bookmaker and dope dealer "Anthony Giannone" that his phone was tapped by the FBI. We had arrested Giannone at his house in the suburbs three years ago; he was a punk who acted like Joe Pesci from the movie the *Goodfellas*. Hall said they have an airtight case against Giannone for dealing in narcotics, bookmaking, and threatening someone's life. Giannone was the punk that introduced Santucci to Sinnase the printer who was hired by Santucci to print one million counterfeit Beanie Baby tags of which Santucci agreed to pay Sinnase $400,000. Under the circumstances, Giannone has agreed to cooperate with the FBI against Santucci and has been telling them everything he knows about him. He's smart enough to figure out that it would be better to rat on Santucci than spend twenty years in prison where he would probably wind up as some black guy's wife.

Santucci also told certain people that when we had busted Giannone for booking; he took care of the case through Herion and it was thrown out of court because he told Herion to tore up the evidence that we had confiscated from Gianonne. Hall told me today that that case was still pending in DuPage County after three years.

Hall asked me if I would appear at a federal grand jury against Santucci in the next couple of weeks. I said, "Yes, I would be glad to." He also indicated that they were going to be a lot of other witness's that are also going to be appearing at the grand jury against Santucci. They are going to interview Belpedio, his partner Sommesi, the printer Sinnesi, and others.

Nothing changes; the FBI is the slowest moving group of law enforcement people in the world. This all could have been taken care of three years ago. The only reason that they are moving now is that one of their own has been implicated with Santucci.

Chapter 58

Cook County Sheriff – Vice Detection

When I was working as a detective sergeant in the gambling unit, organized crime division of the Chicago Police Department I received a phone call from an old friend of mine, Pat Durkin. Pat had been an outstanding sergeant with the Illinois State Police, and we worked a lot of organized crime cases together before he left the job. Pat told me that he was a good friend of Michael, Sheahan who was going to be a candidate for the Cook County Sheriff's Office in the next election. Pat asked me when I was going to retire from Chicago and hang it up. I told him, "Pretty soon, old buddy, but why are you asking?" That's when he said, "In the event that Mike Sheahan beats the current sheriff, Jim O'Grady, would you consider coming over to the sheriff's office after you retire and help Sheahan out?" He explained that the current vice unit was under heavy scrutiny by the federal government and the unit needed a house cleaning and Sheahan sorely needed an experienced vice man to come in and make some gambling raids. It seems that the current vice unit hasn't been to active along those lines for one reason or another. This conversation took place in the summer of 1989.

Mike Sheahan ran against Jim O'Grady in November 1990 and beat him handily. O'Grady's regime was in the middle of a scandal involving his under sheriff, Jim Dvorak, who was accused of taking $10,000 a month from mob boss Rocco Infelise to ignore gambling and other vices in Cook County. Dvorak pled guilty to other charges and was sentenced to the federal penitentiary in Wisconsin for a few years. A tape that was played in federal court at the Infelise trial revealed that the "sheriff never bothered the mob"; the vice unit only went on one raid and that was with Herion and his crew. Infelise was heard on tape saying that he was trying to get Herion out of the gambling unit and transferred to the subway detail. It was quite obvious that the sheriff's vice unit needed some help as they couldn't seem to make any raids on their own.

I remained on the Chicago Police Department until August 27, 1992, and then retired after thirty-eight years on the job. In December 1992 Pat Durkin called me and said that he heard that I retired from Chicago and would I consider meeting Sheriff Sheahan and talk to him about the vice job that he had mentioned to me before the election. I told him sure, as I was getting bored being a man of leisure and we set up a meeting for the end of December at the Daley center in Sheahan's office.

I met the sheriff, and he seemed like a nice guy; he explained the problem he was having with his vice unit that was headquartered in Maywood. He said that there were still a few vice men that worked for Ex-Sheriff O'Grady and there were some new officers that didn't have a clue as to what they were doing in this type of work, but that they were willing to learn and were honest. He asked me if I would be interested in working for him and maybe putting together a vice unit that would make some gambling raids and do something about organized crime wire rooms in the county.

I explained to the sheriff that there were some conditions that would have to be met before I would consider taking the job. The first one was that I would be able to make raids not only in unincorporated Cook County, but in other towns such as Cicero, Berwyn, and Melrose Park, etc. The second thing I wanted to know was who would I have to report to, if anybody? The sheriff said that I wouldn't have to report to anybody, that all I would have to do was make a couple of wire rooms a month if I could. Then he said, "I don't want to know who you're working on or who you're going to raid. I don't want you looking at me if something goes wrong."

I then suggested to the sheriff that it would not be a good idea to have two vice units, because people would ask, "Why does the sheriff of Cook County have two vice units, doesn't he trust his vice unit in

Maywood?" If that's the case, he should transfer them out or fire them if they can't do the job. He agreed with me on that statement and asked me, "How can we get around that?"

I suggested to him that I set up a vice detection unit that had experienced men in it, men that I could trust and knew what they were doing out in the street. The vice detection's job would be to find the bad guys and the bookmakers and to get enough probable cause to get a search warrant for the location that they were operating at. At that point, I would notify the lieutenant in charge of the Maywood vice unit and request that he send two or three of his police officers to meet us at a designated location to accompany us on the raid or raids. When we made the raid, the police officers that accompanied us would be witness to what happened when we executed the search warrant. They would be able to testify in court as to who we arrested, where the evidence was and other pertinent facts involved in the case. They would then be responsible to take the prisoner or prisoners and properly charge them with the proper violations. They could then sign the necessary complaints against the offender and testify in court as what had transpired during the course of the raid. If someone challenged the search warrant, the member of the vice detection unit that procured the warrant would appear in court to testify about the facts of the search warrant and offer any other assistance needed.

The Maywood vice unit would get credit for the raid and if there were any newsworthy arrests, the lieutenant could take care of the publicity with the news media. At this point, the sheriff said that it would be nice to have some positive publicity in the area of vice arrests made by the Cook County Sheriff's Police, vice unit.

The sheriff agreed that it would look a little strange to have two vice units, but the way this would be set up, it seems like a good idea. I told him that I had an experienced retired IRS agent that I had worked with in the past that seemed interested in getting back in the game again; his name was Phil DiPasquale and he knew gamblers as well as I did.

I also said that maybe it would be a good idea if he would transfer one of his vice men from Maywood into the vice detection unit. There was one other thing I insisted on and that was that anybody that would get in this unit had to be hand picked by me and that politics were out as far as anyone getting assigned to my unit.

Illegal gambling persists despite widespread legalized forms

By John O'Brien
TRIBUNE STAFF WRITER

These days billboards advertise gambling, radio jingles promote it and some politicians proclaim it the salvation for financially sinking schools and other societal ills.

You find housewives and tradesmen elbow to elbow in casinos, like so many festivalgoers.

So the question might logically arise:

In an age of state-sponsored lotteries, off-track wagering and an ever-widening circle of legal betting activities, why do people like Don Herion even bother to try to crack down on illegal gambling?

And wreck their weekends in the process?

That, of course, is the busiest time of the week for gamblers, when betting action, running heavy on a seemingly unending schedule of collegiate and professional sports contests.

So that's when Herion, veteran undercover Cook County sheriff's investigator, and members of his police unit, simply named Vice Detection, are on the prowl for illegal gambling activity.

City watch:
Law enforcement

Chicago area.

Advances in telecommunications are making it harder for Herion and his sleuths to do their job. Like everyone else, bookmakers are using voice mail and call forwarding.

"The hours are terrible, and wives get upset. My wife still gets mad, and I've been doing this for years," Herion said from his office hidden away in a upscale northwest suburban area where gambling fever and disposable income abound

But Herion bristled at the suggestion that his job is somehow pointless or anachronistic in today's climate of gambling fever.

From behind his desk with its miniature sledgehammer, a commemorative of all the doors he's bashed down, Herion stepped quickly to a bulletin board, festooned with photographs of mob murder victims and a copy of a federal indictment against a suburban crime family, headed by imprisoned mob boss Ernest Rocco Infelice.

"Illegal gambling," Herion declared, "is not a victimless crime. It gets into deeper things like juice [high-interest loans] and murder. One thing leads to another. With them there always seems to be murder and mayhem."

"Them," he explained, are people like Infelice, convicted of charges arising from the torture killings of two independent north suburban bookmakers, Hal Smith and Robert Plummer.

Herion's bulletin board photos also depict the fate of two mob soldiers, a grim reminder of mob vengeance. Strangled and dumped in a car trunk, Joseph Gattuso and Jasper Campise paid with their lives for bungling the 1983 contract killing of mob gambling strategist Ken Eto.

For much of his 38 years in law enforcement, Herion has chased bookmakers, raiding betting parlors and investigating organized crime gambling rackets in the Chicago area.

"They could be lying on a beach somewhere while their telephone recorder is doing the work, logging bets from calls from bettors," Herion said. "All the bookies have to do is check their messages."

Herion's boss puts a high priority on pursuing illegal operations despite the proliferation of legal gambling.

"Illegal gamblers don't pay taxes," said Cook County Sheriff Michael Sheahan, ticking off a litany of reasons for enforcement. "They give bans out to fish, so to speak. They run loan sharking. It leads to corruption. Not only of elected officials but police departments.

"There was always a cloud with Operation Safebet," a federal probe of corrupt police in the 1980s, said Sheahan. "There were charges that vice officers were bigger than the problem itself in the county."

For that reason, Sheahan established Herion's unit in January 1993 to ferret out not only illicit gambling activity but also mob attempts to buy police protection.

Among his secret weapons is unit member Phil DiPasquale, a former Internal Revenue Service agent and master of disguises—he's been mistaken for a dozen nationalities—who Herion said has been critical in successfully bird-dogging targets.

Among their most recent success stories was the Sept. 28 arrest of a reputed mob payoff and bet collector that capped an investigation of a gambling business based in Costa Rica and accessed by local gamblers using a 1-800 telephone number.

Don Herion (left), director of the Cook County Sheriff's Vice Detection unit, and his secret weapon, Phil DiPasquale, a master of disguises who has passed for a dozen nationalities.

Source: Chicago Tribune

CHICAGO SUN-TIMES, FRIDAY, FEBRUARY 26, 1993

Michael Sneed

Hmmmmm....

New Dem National Committee chief **Dave Wilhelm** tells folks privately he thinks state Treasurer **Pat Quinn** is the best candidate to run against **Gov. Edgar**. Hmmm. Top political strategist **David Axelrod**, who has worked with Wilhelm, is this/close to Quinn. Hmmm. Quinn is hitting the same political trail as Dem gubernatorial hopeful **Dick Phelan**. It must be election time!

Brenda Edgar **Hillary Clinton**
Style may differ, but goals are similar

Theeeee First Lady...

Watch for low-profile **Brenda Edgar**, who is shy but savvy, to embark on a new effort on behalf of children next month. She'll touch on everything from immunization to drug abuse prevention to services protecting kids from abuse. She's more low-key than **Hillary Clinton** (whew), but on the same track.

Here's Eddieeee!...

Ed Vrdolyak tells Sneed he still owns a white horse—and rides it every once in a while. Banish the sight!

Police Blotter...

Pssst! Sneed hears Cook County Sheriff **Michael Sheahan** has created a special hush-hush unit to handle organized crime and gambling. And he brought in outsiders to run it.
• The stat: It's run by **Don Herrion**, a former Chicago vice cop who's highly respected. He's working with former IRS agent **Phil DiPasquale**, an expert on organized crime who testified in the federal trial of mobster **Lenny Patrick**.
• The chat: Since its recent inception, the unit has had two successful gambling raids in suburban Cook County.
• The kicker: The sheriff wanted a professional from OUTSIDE the department who would report ONLY to him. (Sheahan is placing a priority on organized crime and gambling.)

al **Neil Hartigan** and Cook County Assessor **Tom Hynes** before joining Clinton's campaign.

Luis Lore...

The reform candidate: Listen up! When House Speaker **Tom Foley** announced an across-the-board pay freeze for all members of Congress, guess who was smiling? The fella who introduced the freeze idea: Rep. **Luis Gutierrez**, who takes the CTA to O'Hare to fly to Washington every Tuesday.

The Rush Job....

Rep. **Bobby Rush** just got appointed to a "hit squad" of nine House members to line up votes for Clinton's economic agenda. The hit squad chief is deputy House Whip **Butler Derrick**.

Hopkins Hoopla...

Actor **Anthony Hopkins** was knighted by **Queen Elizabeth** Tuesday at Buckingham Palace. Sez Hopkins: "I didn't expect this and I hope I don't sound falsely modest, but I'm very honored. I can't quite take it in."

Anthony Hopkins

Sick Room

Brit actress **Emma Thompson** was supposed to hit the states to do interviews and meet the press before the Oscars next month, but she got a virus.

Cruise 'em...

Tom Cruise is to make his directorial debut on Showtime's upcoming short story series called "Fallen Angels."

Book Beat...

Oprah Winfrey's biographer, **Joan Barthel**, is working on the bio at Oprah's Indiana farm. It's due this fall.

Hackman Hoopla...

Gene Hackman sez he never feels confident, always feels like every movie will be his last and is surprised **Tom Cruise** didn't get an Oscar nomination for "A Few Good Men." Hackman, who did get one for "Unforgiven," is working with Cruise on the movie version of "The Firm." "I voted for him; he's a fine actor," Hackman reveals, saying Cruise and **Ann-Margret** are the two nicest people he's worked with in show biz.

Source: Sun Times

Sheriff Sheahan agreed to the terms that I presented, and said that I would be called a director of this unit and asked me when I could start. "How about January 4, 1993," I said. "I'll bring DiPasquale with me and we can get the show on the road." We shook hands, and that was the beginning of an experience that I won't soon forget.

The vice detection unit was set up in the basement of the Third District Courthouse at 2121 West Euclid Avenue. Rolling Meadows, Illinois.

Reporter from Current Affair interviewed me about the Super Bowl and gambling.

Phil and I started working on a few known bookmakers that worked for the mob and would be a good way to start the unit with two or three raids in one day. I interviewed a police detective from the Maywood vice unit who told me that he had a lot of experience working wire rooms and other gambling operations and had been a vice man for a few years. I accepted him and told him what I expected from him and that he would also be expected to work weekends because that was the busiest time of the week for bookmakers. I also interviewed two other young deputies that had never worked vice before but they seemed eager to learn and would be glad to work any time, weekends were OK with them also. We were set up and ready to go in a week's time, there was a little problem with undercover vehicles but that was straightened out with a phone call from the Sheriff who told the people that handled that stuff to give us whatever we needed to get operational.

Phil DiPasquale and I put together three big gambling operations that were connected to the outfit and we were ready to raid three sports wire rooms the first two weeks we were in operation.

It was January 16, 1993, I notified the lieutenant in charge of the vice unit that we needed three separate two man teams to meet us at three different locations in the county to join us on three wire room raids. The first raid was in Harvey, Illinois, a south suburb of Chicago, where three bad guys were running a sports wire room from a house. When we met the vice men from Maywood at the meeting place, I couldn't believe what I saw. The lieutenant had sent the sheriff's tactical team to meet us in a van; there were at least ten men all dressed up in jump suits, jump boots and had ever weapon that you could think of with them. There was also a lieutenant in charges of this unit, and these guys were ready for blood. They were all happy because they were getting paid overtime for this mission and thought that we were going to attack the house in force, they even had concussion grenades with them. I tried to explain to there boss that all this fire power wasn't necessary for this particular type of raid, but they all wanted to help out so what the hell I decided to let them all go, the more the merrier.

It was obvious that these people knew nothing about gambling operations or what was involved to take them down. The house was located at 843 West 167th Place in Harvey. We executed the warrant and busted all three guys with mobile telephones, sports schedules, sports wagers and other gambling paraphernalia. The three bad guys were taken to the Maywood vice office to be processed and the evidence inventoried. Their names were Alfred Troiani, Michael Wood, and Paul Herman and were charged with syndicated gambling.

The second raid went off just as well. Jimmy Kossar, another well known bookmaker who was sometimes called "Tiny," because he was six foot four and weighed 460 pounds, was arrested as he exited a wire room in a western suburb of Chicago, Franklin Park, Illinois. Kossar was booking in his Lincoln town car as well as a house at 2821 Edington Avenue. Aorund $13,370 in U.S. currency was confiscated from him as well as mobile phones, wagers, and other gambling paraphernalia. He was also transported to the Maywood vice unit for processing.

PAY, QUIT, OR DIE

Three men arrested in Harvey gambling raid

DONNA HORNIK
Staff Writer

HARVEY — Three south suburban men were arrested Saturday afternoon when Cook County Sheriff's Vice and Gambling Unit raided a home in Harvey.

Sheriff deputies also arrested two Chicago men during raids in Skokie and Franklin Park at the same time, according to Sally Daly, public information officer for the sheriff's department.

Deputies arrived at the Harvey home of Paul Herman, 42, 843 W. 167th Pl., with an arrest warrant around noon, Daly said.

They recovered a number of gambling sheets and wager records as well as cellular phones and an undetermined amount of cash, she said.

Herman was taken into custody and charged with keeping a gambling place, she said.

Police also charged Alfred Troiani, 60, 1320 S. Ashland Ave., Chicago Heights, and Michael Woods, 42, 16445 S. Halsted St., Harvey, with syndicated gambling, Daly said.

Both men were in Herman's home at the time of the raid, she said.

Gary Oliva, 46, of Chicago was arrested for operating a gambling business out of his car in Skokie and James Kossar, 48, of Chicago was arrested for operating a gambling business after leaving a house in Franklin Park, Daly said.

Altogether, police confiscated $13,370 in cash, two handguns with ammunition, five cellular phones and Oliva's car, as well as the gambling records, Daly said.

The raids were a result of a number of weeks of investigating and the gambling and wager sheets will be looked at in detail for possible leads to further raids, Daly said.

Metro BRIEFINGS

GAMBLING RAID NETS 3: Three suburban men were arrested Sunday in a gambling raid at a home in Berwyn, Cook County sheriff's police said. Anthony Orlando, 58, of the 2500 block of South Lombard Avenue, Berwyn; Demitri Stavropoulos, 25, of the 4500 block of Sunnyside Avenue, Brookfield; and Albert Galluppi, 34, of the 7800 block of Darien Lake Drive, Darien, were all charged with syndicated gambling and obstruction of justice, said sheriff's police spokesman Bill Cunningham. The latter charge resulted from the destruction of records of the operation, which took in as much as $500,000 in sports bets over a weekend, police said.

Police raid $3 million-a-week sports gambling ring in suburbs

By Ray Minor
Daily Herald Staff Writer

March Madness, that time when college basketball tournament games generate millions of dollars in bets, came to an early end Saturday for one Bloomingdale man, officials said.

Joseph Gianforte, 25, of 289 Royal Lane, No. 600, was charged with operating a syndicated gambling operation out of his apartment that generated an estimated $3 million a week in bets, said Sally Daly, spokeswoman for the Cook County Sheriff's Department.

Acting on a search warrant, Cook and DuPage counties vice police raided Gianforte's apartment at about 1:30 p.m. Saturday.

They confiscated eight cellular telephones and numerous betting sheets with about $1 million in bets already tallied, Daly said.

The betting ring focused mostly on college basketball, which is especially lucrative at this time of year with conference tournaments being played and the National Collegiate Athletic Association championship tournament brackets being announced, she said.

The third raid went of with out a hitch. Gary Oliva was operating out of his '89 Oldsmobile with a mobile phone. He would park in the middle of a shopping mall where he would hope that no one would see him booking, stay there for twenty minutes, and then drive to another location. He was finally busted in his car in Skokie, Illinois, another suburb of Chicago on the North Side. Oliva had two mobile phones as well as a large amount of sports bets that were on soluble paper. He was also transported to the Maywood vice unit. To say the least all three raids went off as planned, there were five bad guys in jail, and three large-scale gambling operations broken up that were connected to organized crime.

The sheriff asked me if there were any newsworthy raids, and asked me to call his press person, Sally Daly, and she would take care of notifying the news media. I notified Daly as to what had happened and how many raids we had made and suggested to her that the raids were worth some publicity. I tried explaining how a wire room operated and how the mob was involved in this type of activity, and she didn't have a clue as too what I was talking about. The outcome of this was that she suggested that I speak to the news media. I explained that I was not expected to talk to the press and that someone from the Maywood vice unit could handle that job, probably the lieutenant in charge, because he was on the scene at the time of the raids. As things turned out, Chief Burke of the Cook County Sheriff's Police was notified of what had happened and he held a press conference with the news media. I had to explain to him how the raids went down and other facts of the cases before he would appear on camera.

As things turned out, the three raids made by the vice detection unit and the Maywood vice unit appeared on all the local TV stations as well as the radio and the *Chicago Tribune* and *Sun Times* newspapers. The Maywood vice unit was given credit for knocking out three major gambling operations in Cook County. Some Maywood cops told me that this type of enforcement hadn't happened in the last fifty years. I found out later that some of the vice men didn't appreciate my unit telling them where to go or what to do or who to lock up. How true that was. They wanted the gambling raids in their raid book, but they didn't want to appear in court to testify as to what they saw at the time of the raid. These guys were a real piece of work. All we had to do was make the investigation, do the surveillances, the tracking and trailing, and get enough probable cause to get a search warrant when we found out where the wire room was operating. They didn't want to sign the complaints against the bad guys or appear in court. I didn't know what the hell they wanted, but one thing was for sure, they sure didn't like working with us.

In reality, if they were doing their job and busting up gambling operations themselves, the sheriff would never have hired me in the first place.

During the first year we were in operation we made a lot of good raids and got a lot of positive publicity for the sheriff's office and his Maywood vice unit. But as time went on, it seemed the more raids that we made, the madder the vice unit got. There were a few guys in the unit that liked what we were accomplishing but the others were totally against us. At one point the chief of the sheriff's police had to order the vice unit to cooperate with us or else, this didn't help matters at all. I guess that the police assigned to the vice unit didn't like to be told where to go and what time to meet us, the location of the raid was kept confidential until we met. Sheriff Sheahan agreed upon this method of operation and the chief of the sheriff's police, to keep any suspicion falling on the vice unit in the event something went wrong with the raid. It was not because the sheriff didn't trust his vice unit.

The sheriff's vice unit just couldn't understand why they had to go to court when they didn't have anything to do with the investigation. I tried to explain to them that they had enough knowledge of the execution of the search warrant, who was arrested, and what and where the evidence was when we made the raid. I again informed them if they had a problem in court about the search warrant being challenged by a defense attorney, all they had to do was to inform me of the court date and the officer that procured the warrant would appear in court to testify in the case.

Needless to say, the friction continued between vice detection and the vice unit. After a while, we were not receiving all of the court attendance reports, continuance dates, or the disposition of any of the cases that we made together. I also made a request to get a report of any case that was dismissed in court, and for what reason. I just couldn't convince them that if we signed the complaints against the people that we were arresting and appeared in court on every case that we made; we would never be out in the street making new cases, we would be spending all of our time in court. Besides that, what the hell would we need them for if we were doing the work, getting the warrant and making the raids.

As time went on, we became aware of several instances where the vice unit personnel appeared in court on some cases where the defense attorney challenged the search warrant, this made it necessary for the officer that obtained the warrant appear in court. The only problem was the vice-officer did not notify me or anyone in vice detection that the case had been continued or what date the case was continued to. So guess what, when the vice detection officer did not appear, the case was thrown out of court, which, of course, made the vice detection unit look incompetent. On some other occasions, I was informed that some vice officers who appeared in court testified that they knew nothing about the case; they only assisted the vice detection unit in executing a search warrant. This, of course, was not true, because the vice officer who signed the complaint against the arrestee was on the scene during the entire raid.

On March 25, 1997, I sent a report to the then acting chief of police of the Cook County Sheriff's Office, Thomas Fitzgerald. In the report I informed him of why the vice detection unit was started and how it was set up. The main purpose of the unit was to focus on gambling operations in the county and to put them out of business when and wherever possible. The best way to do that would be for the sheriff's police vice unit and the vice detection unit to cooperate with each other to accomplish that goal. The report led to a meeting between me and Inspector General Joe Shaughnessy and Thomas Fitzgerald in a restaurant in Forest Park, Illinois. Fitzgerald said that he understood the problem and would make an effort to straighten things out. In the months that followed, I didn't notice any change in the vice units operation or their cooperation with us. Oh well, I thought, we would just have to do the best we can and work with the Chicago Police Gambling Unit a little more.

In the first three years of our operation, we conducted raids on 193 gambling operations, most of which were wire rooms.

Numerous surveillances were conducted on organized crime bookmakers as well as independent gamblers. A lot of the targets we were working on were followed in their vehicles to wire rooms and who they would meet to pay or collect money from other gamblers. We were utilizing a device called Tele Trac, which was a small box-type object that would be attached to the chassis of a car by four magnets. The box was also equipped with a small antenna, which would send signals to a receiver that was located in the vice detection unit office. Tele Trac worked like a charm, and would give us the location of a vehicle within fifty feet. This also eliminated three or four vehicles, which would try and track and trail the bad guy to his base of operations. The device could only be attached to a vehicle that was parked on the public way; it couldn't be used on someone's private property. A search warrant was not needed to use this tracking device. Tele-Trac worked like a charm for us and proved to be invaluable in locating suspects anywhere within a fifty-mile radius. The only drawback to using it was someone had to attach it to the suspects vehicle, which usually was accomplished late at night or early in the morning when no one was around. Of course, the unit also had to be removed without anyone seeing you take it off. If the bad guy found the device on his car, he would naturally remove it and probably throw it away. There were no identifying marks on the unit so the suspect would not have a clue of who attached it to his car or what law enforcement agency was working on him. It was imperative that no one found out that this device existed or was being used by law enforcement to follow people. If the word got out, all the bad guy would have to do is look underneath his vehicle and remove it. The Tele-Trac unit cost $1,500, which, of course, could get very expensive if the devices were found and destroyed.

Cook County

Sheriffs collar suspected gambler

The Cook County Sheriff's Police Department charged a Palos Heights man with one count of gambling at 11:45 a.m. Tuesday, police said.

Undercover vice officers executed a search warrant against Ronald Antos, 49, of 7415 Ishnala Drive, Palos Heights, at a parking lot in the 9700 block of South Roberts Road, according to Penny Mateck, a spokeswoman for the Cook County Sheriff's Police Department.

Officers found two handwritten pages of bettors and debts, sports schedules and blank sports schedules after a search, Mateck said. A search of Business Antos Travel Agency, 7480 W. College Drive, Palos Heights, found accounts and balance sheets related to gambling, she said.

A piece of paper with a $15,000 bet on a New Orleans Saints football game was also found at the travel agency, Mateck said. It is believed the bet is for a coming game, she said.

During a hearing at Cook County 4th District Circuit Court in Maywood, a $1,000 deposit bond and a preliminary court date of Dec. 6 were set for Antos, Mateck said.

Cook County's top vice cop, Don Herion, holds a seized piece of paper recording $15,800 in bets.

Pay dirt for sports gambling

BY JOHN CARPENTER
STATE REPORTER

Thousands of Bears fans shook their fists in holy wrath two weeks ago when Erik Kramer's pass fell idly to the turf on a two-point try, dooming the home team to its seventh loss in a dismal season.

But more than a few of those fans still watched the clock tick down with smiles on their faces. The Bears had lost again. But, by golly, they had covered the spread.

Illegal sports gambling remains a thriving institution just outside the borders of legitimate society, a place where blue-collar beer drinkers and Rolex-jingling cigar smokers alike go to place their bets.

A former bookie and current "players," as well as the cops who chase them, offer a behind-the-scenes look at a multibillion-dollar underground industry.

Source: Sun Times

Cops' sting forces area gambling ring to fold

Times Staff Report

LANSING – A 41-year-old Lansing man was one of three charged Thursday night in a sheriff's police gambling sting.

Larry Pufahl, 3528 Madison St., was arrested and charged with being a keeper of bets at 5:20 p.m. Thursday after Detectives Phil DiPasquali and Bernie Riordan of the Cook County Sheriff's Police Vice Detection Unit served a search warrant at his home, police said. The detectives allegedly discovered Pufahl transmitting $5,000 in wagers for professional and college basketball games, according to a vice unit spokesman.

A Lansing man is among three arrested for taking thousands in bets.

"Through tedious work and information, we conducted an investigation that led to Mr. Pufahl," said Don Harion, director of the vice unit.

Pufahl allegedly used a voice mail system through his mobile telephone to receive bets, a system Harion said is the "latest method used by book makers."

"It's easier because you don't have to rent a room, you don't have to pay a clerk $500 a week, and the phone bill's not that high, so you eliminate a lot of overhead and decrease the possibility of arrest," Harion said.

According to Harion, Pufahl allegedly gave his clients his mobile telephone voice mail number and when they called it, they received the point spreads for the games. The clients then left messages to place their bets, and Pufahl allegedly retrieved the messages using a locked code number.

Vice unit detectives also arrested two men in the lobby of the Swissotel, 323 E. Wacker Dr., during Thursday's gambling sting.

Roger Riccio, 59, 1300 Lee St. in Melrose Park, and Robert Najman, 55, 1212 N. Lake Shore Drive in Chicago, were charged with syndicated gambling in the hotel lobby, police said. Syndicated gambling is a felony charge.

Riccio and Najman were apprehended after Harion and Det.

> 'It's easier because you don't have to rent a room, you don't have to pay a clerk $500 a week and the phone bill's not that high.'
>
> Don Harion, director of the Cook County Sheriff's Police Vice Detection Unit

James Kondilas allegedly observed them "with a big bowl of nuts, martinis and foot-long cigars, two mobile phones with extra batteries and sports schedules taking bets while seated in the lobby of the hotel in front of everyone," Harion said. The pair allegedly were taking bets on the Bulls-Pistons game.

Harion said detectives seized two mobile telephones, thwarted $50,000 in bets and seized $29,000 from Riccio and Najman

"Roger has been around for many, many years," Harion said. "I busted him 30 years ago, and he was arrested 14 times since then for the same thing.

"They were getting big bets between $2,000 and $4,000 a game," Harion said.

Raids net police $500,000 in gambling records

By Jim Allen
Daily Herald Staff Writer

Police said Tuesday they rounded up $500,000 in wagering records during raids in Cook, Lake and DuPage counties on four alleged bookmakers who reportedly used mobile phones and voice-mail systems to keep up with huge call volumes.

In one case, police said calls were coming in so rapidly prior to Sunday's noon football kickoff schedule that a bookmaker using a mobile phone in his car was apprehended when he had to return home to recharge his batteries.

"There's only so long those things will last, and we knew he'd have to come home sooner or later," said Don Herion, director of the Cook County sheriff's vice unit that led the raids Saturday through Tuesday with the help of county deputies in Lake and DuPage counties and police from Chicago and Highland Park.

Thomas E. Russell, 53, of Highland Park, was arrested after he returned to his apartment Sunday at 1988 Green Bay Road. He was charged with syndicated gambling, a felony, and was assigned a court date of Dec. 13 in Chicago, Herion said.

Russell had about $200,000 in wagering records and $2,100 in cash when he was taken into custody, authorities said.

At another raid Saturday at the home of a 52-year-old Lombard resident, police took $100,000 in wagering records. No arrest was made, pending further investigation by the DuPage County state's attorney's office, Herion said.

At the Lombard search, the alleged bookmaker had two mobile phones and a regular line into his apartment, Herion said. After police arrived, they took calls and bets, Herion said.

"These people are so goofy and they want to get their bets in before the kickoff, they'll tell anybody anything," Herion said.

One caller wanted to place $2,000 on Penn State against Northwestern, Herion said.

"Maybe he got lucky," Herion said, adding that such conversations often prove valuable in court.

On Monday, police targeted betting on the NFL schedule at the South Side home of Gary Reich, 33, who allegedly logged bets through a voice-mail system, Herion said.

Police seized $200,000 in betting records at Reich's residence at 2955 S. Emerald Ave., Herion said. Reich was charged with syndicated gambling and scheduled to appear in court on Dec. 1.

Early Tuesday, police raided the South Side home of James Kozik, 27, and seized another $1,800 in betting records and charged him with keeping a house of gambling, Herion said.

Local men charged in Waukegan gambling raid

By Leslie Ator
ASSISTANT MANAGING EDITOR

Jack Foreman, 59, of 1250 Park Avenue West, and Robert Powers, 23, of 1600 Grove Ave., both of Highland Park, were arrested shortly after noon Nov. 20 in the parking lot of Arlington in Waukegan, an off-track betting facility at 630 Green Bay Road, Waukegan, and charged with syndicated gambling, a Lake County investigator said.

Lake County Sheriff's Lt. Chester Iwan said Nov. 24 the men allegedly were running a college and professional football gambling operation from a Chevrolet Blazer. Police recovered $1,515, water-soluble betting slips and a bucket of water from the Blazer, Iwan said. Foreman and Powers did not have time to destroy the printing on the slips, he said.

The pair operated by using cellular phones in their vehicle and were hard to track, Iwan said.

The arrest was coordinated with Chicago and Cook County Sheriff's police after an investigation began more than a month ago. Authorities believe Foreman and Powers are part of a larger gambling operation that accepts $100,000 a week in football bets and is linked to organized crime, Iwan said.

Both men were released on $25,000 recognizance bonds Nov. 21 after appearing in Lake County Bond Court.

Metropolitan report

Cook County *11-SEPT-93*

Police raid sports betting operations

Cook County sheriff's police confiscated half a million dollars worth of football and baseball betting slips in raids Saturday.

During one raid, officers intercepted a call from someone who wanted to place a $5,000 bet on Saturday's Michigan-Notre Dame game, said Penny Mateck, a sheriff's spokeswoman.

In a raid at 11 a.m. Saturday at a house at 5800 N. Kilbourn Ave., Chicago, police allegedly confiscated $400,000 in betting slips, along with $6,379 in cash and 60 grams of marijuana, Mateck said. August Zymantas, 45, was charged with syndicated gambling and possession of a controlled substance.

Officers also raided the the A and Z Mail Center, 4949 W. Dempster St., in Skokie, a businses they say was operated by Zymantas where they confiscated $50,000 worth of betting slips.

On Friday evening, officers raided a house at 3360 N. Pioneer Ave., Chicago, and arrested James Loverdi, 33, on charges of being a keeper of a gambling house. Officers say they confiscated $40,000 in betting slips.

Don Herion, Cook County Sheriff's Vice Unit, demonstrates flash paper (left) and describes one way he's seen bookies use it:

"I dove across the couch but he just took his hand with the papers and moved it over to the candle. It was gone."

Courtesy of Don Herion

On May 3, 1996, I received a memorandum from the Chief of the Sheriff's Police, William J. Burke Jr. The subject was about Tele-Trac; it read as follows:

> It has come to our attention you are in possession of Tele-Trac equipment and other electronic surveillance devices. This equipment must be inventoried and inspected by the CCSPD Technical Services Unit immediately. Please turn this equipment over the Technical Services Unit representatives who present you with this order.

At that point I contacted Inspector Thomas Bohling of that unit and asked him what identifying marks would be put on the Tele-Trac units. He replied that CCSPD letters would be inscribed on each unit as well as an inventory number. I explained that inscribing those letters and numbers would defeat the purpose of Tele-Trac and was not necessary. He replied orders are orders; we have to keep our property in order. He then asked me to turn over another device called Triggerfish that he had heard we were using as another tracking unit. I told him that we didn't have Triggerfish in my unit, but I wish that we did have. Triggerfish is used for tracking cellular telephones, which would be a great asset for us to have, but it cost about $50,000.

I turned over the two Tele-Trac units we had as well as the receiver to the technical services unit and expected to get them back in a couple of days. Forget about it. The next time I heard from that unit was on June 6, 1996. It seems that Inspector Bohling had requested a legal opinion from the Sheriff's Office of Legal and Labor affairs, about the legality of the Tele-Trac equipment and how it was being used. There was a meeting between the legal and labor affairs department attorneys, Brian Flaherty and Dan Brennan who stated the following. After extensive research on the questions of whether the use of these tracking devices could cause constitutional concerns. It was their opinion that these devices should be used only when there has been prior judicial approval. Prior approval is only needed when the sheriff's police are attaching the device without the consent of the individual you are tracking. Now there is one hell of a decision. All I would have to do is to get the OK of the individual that we tracking, then we wouldn't need judicial approval.

After I was notified of that decision. I was shocked, to say the least. That was the dumbest decision I had ever heard of. I contacted other police agencies that were using Tele-Trac and asked them if they had to get judicial approval before they used the tracking device. They all said, "No, they didn't." As long as the vehicle was parked on the street or any other public place it was legal.

At this point I decided they could keep the tracking equipment, because I was not going to ask an individual I was working on, if I could attach a tracking device to his car so that we could follow him, the guy would think I was a nut case.

Another memorandum was issued concerning the use of the tracking device and procedures for having someone install it on a vehicle. The technical services unit was to be notified at least twenty-four hours prior to the actual request. A phone call with the location of the vehicle and the type of vehicle is needed. The type of vehicle is of the utmost importance in that the technicians must locate the same vehicle in order to locate a premium on the vehicle for placement of the transmitter. At the time of the installation of the transmitter there, will be at least two surveillance officers on the scene to provide security for the technicians. For one-half to one hour after the installation, an officer will keep the target vehicle under constant surveillance. This is done for the security of the installation.

Here comes the best statement of all. All investigators must note that the tracking instruments are an investigative aid only. All surveillance's are to be conducted in a normal fashion with the assistance of these devices. Technical equipment of this nature occasionally encounters operational difficulties due to weather conditions and the geographic area of the operation. Please consider the conditions when planning your operation. Know your subject; this device will aid you in your investigation, not conduct the investigation.

I have asked a friend of mine that was assigned to the Maywood vice unit if he had occasion to use Tele-Trac on any investigations. He told me in confidence, that as far as he knew, no one was using the tracking device. And that he didn't think that anyone could understand the receiver that was used to locate the vehicle they were working on.

I recall that I installed Tele-Trac on numerous vehicles with one other officer present. And there were times when I was by myself or had my wife or my son Don with me when I installed the device. I also removed the device on many occasions when I was alone, because the opportunity to do so presented itself. If in fact it would be necessary to have three or four vehicles following the suspect vehicle, which has a tracking device on it, what's the point of even using a tracking device? But then what the hell do I know? It sure has been an experience working with the Cook County Sheriff's Police; they are a unique group of men to say the least.

The next surprise that I got was when I was given a subpoena to attend a hearing concerning a vice grievance. The Sheriff's Police Union, who represented the Cook County Sheriff's Police vice Unit, instituted this grievance. The Union was the Metropolitan Alliance of Police, *Chapter 201 vs Cook County Sheriff,* and case No. 98 CH 4430. I was ordered to appear on the twenty-third day of September 1997 at 9:00 AM at the office of the Cook County State's Attorney, 500 Richard J. Daley Center, Second Floor, Board Room, Chicago, Illinois. To testify and give evidence at a hearing in a certain manner now pending and undetermined before Arbitrator Robert McCallister to give an opinion on the unions vice grievance.

The Maywood vice unit was upset with Sheriff Sheahan because he started the vice detection unit, while he still had a vice unit in Maywood Illinois at 1401 Maybrook Drive. According to the union, the collective bargaining agreement does not permit the Sheriff of Cook County to form another unit to do the work of the sheriff's police. The union insisted that this second or third generation collective bargaining agreement prohibit the sheriff from forming any unit that performs activities identical to those performed by the sheriff's police regardless if they were doing their job or not.

The union labels as pretext the county's efforts to justify the formation of the vice detection unit and notes that, while a county witness, Marty Walsh, who was in control of hiring or firing people that were employed by the sheriff's office opined that a "cloud' hangs over the sheriff's police. Walsh admitted there are no pending or prior indictments, discipline or investigations of sheriff's police officers. The union insists that since Walsh was unable to document his opinion, the arbitrator dismisses Walsh's testimony that the vice detection unit was created because the sheriff's police were untrustworthy and lacked the full confidence of Sheriff Sheahan.

At the arbitration hearing, a sergeant assigned to the sheriff's vice unit in Maywood was asked, "Does your unit ever do investigations with regards to bookmaking?"

A. Yes.
Q. How many investigations in the last year have you done with regard to bookmaking?
A. None.
Q. Do you have any investigations with regards to wire rooms?
A. I consider wire rooms and bookmaking to be the same thing. No, it would be none.
Q. What about in 1995?
A. There was some, yes.
Q. How many?
A. I don't recall.
Q. Was it more than five?
A. It may be, I don't know.
Q. What about 1994?
A. I don't know. Again, we could have investigated – all I can say is that in 1997 we have not investigated any bookmaking operations or wire room operations.

It was no wonder that Sheriff Sheahan asked me to help him set up a vice unit to try and make some organized crime gambling operations, the vice unit that he had sure as hell wasn't doing it.

I testified as to how the vice detection unit operated and how it was setup to assist the Maywood vice unit, not to be in competition with it. I explained where the unit was located in the suburbs and how many men I had working for me. I told them that there were three other fellas and I had two others on my payroll but they were detailed to other units. As a matter of fact, one of them was detailed to the Chicago Crime Commission and the other one was detailed to the U.S. Drug Administration. The union accused me of being involved in ghost pay rolling and a local reporter thought he had a scoop and ran the story on the10:00 O'clock news, which fizzled out and died.

I also informed the arbitrator at the hearing of what we had accomplished since we started on January 4, 1993, until June 1998. Approximately 510 raids, 462 of the raids were on organized crime wire rooms. There were also 44 raids on video poker machines, where we confiscated 153 machines and seized $14,921 in cash. Two parlay card presses were also put out of business with the arrest of the owners and distributors. Several of the business locations that we raided that had poker machines went out of business do to the numerous raids that we executed; some places were hit twice in one day. The bad guys figured that if they got busted in the morning all they had to do was replace the poker machines that we confiscated and it would be business as usual. WRONG.

I received a letter in June 1998 from Jacob M. Rubinstein, assistant state attorney of Cook County, informing me that the arbitrator had ruled in the union's favor. He said that although Sheriff Sheahan has the right to create new units, the arbitrator stated that the sheriff should cease using noncertified individuals to perform the work of sheriff's police officers. Sheriff Sheahan responded by saying that he would continue to operate both the vice unit and the vice detection unit.

It seems that the arbitrator, Robert McCallister, reached his decision December 23, 1997. A meeting was held with the union attorney Joseph R. Mazzone and Jacob M. Rubinstein, who represented the sheriff's office of Cook County on June 4, 1998. They reached an off the record agreement and took numerous steps to comply with the arbitrators award.

The following is what I was told what was decided by all parties concerned. The vice detection unit is not to perform the work of shcriff's police officers under any circumstances. In light of the award, vice detection personnel do not identify themselves as sheriff's police officers and do not use paperwork of the Sheriff's Police Department. Moreover I was informed that I was not to engage in investigation or intelligence gathering of any kind in *unincorporated* areas of Cook County, which is the primary jurisdiction of the Sheriff's Police Department. In the event that the vice detection unit personnel happen upon information regarding organized crime and or vice activity in unincorporated Cook County, I am to turn over such information to the Sheriff's Police Department vice unit. The vice detection unit has been informed not to perform the work of Sheriff's Police Officers in any respect

Sheriff Michael Sheahan tried to put a crimp in organized crime operations in unincorporated Cook County by hiring myself as well as other experienced retired police officers but as you can see by this report that maybe we did hurt some bad guys out there. I've been around these guys a long time and nothing surprises me on the different ways they can get things done. I'm sure that the vice unit will really go out there and kick some ass now that they have us out of the picture. Personally, I don't think that they could find a Jap in Tokyo.

OFFICE OF THE STATE'S ATTORNEY
COOK COUNTY, ILLINOIS

RICHARD A. DEVINE
STATE'S ATTORNEY

500 RICHARD J. DALEY CENTER
CHICAGO, ILLINOIS 60602
AREA 312-603-6440

BY FIRST CLASS MAIL

June 11, 1998

Joseph R. Mazzone
Schenk, Duffy, Quinn, McNamara,
Phelan, Carey and Ford, Ltd.
Iroquois Commons Office Park
1220 Iroquois Drive, Suite 204
Naperville, IL 60563

RE: *Metropolitan Alliance of Police, Chapter # 201 v. Cook County Sheriff*
Case No. 98 CH 4430

Dear Mr. Mazzone,

Pursuant to our June 4, 1998 off-the-record settlement discussion, please be advised that since the issuance of Arbitrator McAllister's decision dated December 23, 1997, management in the Office of the Sheriff of Cook County has taken numerous steps to comply with the Arbitrator's award.

First, we have provided a copy of the award to Don Herion, the Director of the Sheriff's Vice Detection Unit. Second, we have explained to Director Herion that, pursuant to the award, his unit is not to perform the work of Sheriff's Police Officers under any circumstances. In light of the award, Vice Detection Unit personnel do not identify themselves as Sheriff's Police Officers and do not use paperwork of the Sheriff's Police Department. Moreover, we have instructed Director Herion not to engage in investigation or intelligence gathering of any kind in unincorporated areas of Cook County, which is the primary jurisdiction of the Sheriff's Police Department. ~~In the event that Vice Detection Unit personnel happen upon information regarding organized crime and/or vice activity in unincorporated Cook County, they will turn such information over to the Sheriff's Police Department Vice Unit.~~ The Vice Detection Unit has been instructed not to perform the work of Sheriff's Police Officers in any respect. We anticipate no deviation from this directive.

When we made some noteworthy raids, the *Chicago Tribune* and the *Sun Times* printed the stories as well as some of the television stations made a big deal about the Chicago mob getting busted. Every couple of months I got an anonymous letter from a group of concerned citizens that the Chicago Crime Syndicate was taking over there small town called Naplate which was located next to Ottawa, Illinois, ninety miles from Chicago. They said that they had three taverns on the main drag and on Saturday and Sunday they handle up to $200,000 in wagers. They said that the three taverns handled football and basketball bets, parlay cards, tip boards and they also had video poker machines.

They explained that they had read a few stories in the *Chicago Tribune,* telling how the Cook County Sheriff's Vice Detection Unit was busting all these book joints and putting people in jail. They pleaded for help from us because the police in their area did nothing to stop this type of activity, and with the mob involved, "bad things could happen." It was signed, *Concerned Citizens, Thank You.*

I began to think about the problem they had and pleading for help and not getting any help from anybody, the local police, LaSalle County Police, the state police, or even Batman or Robin. I figured that what the hell, my hands are kind of tied right now so I'll just get back into the vigilante mode and see what I can do to help these concerned citizens.

— A call for help
Undercover again
90 miles away —

> Sir,
>
> We read your article on gambling in Monday's issue of the Chicago Trib.
>
> The town of "Naplate" is next to Sttawa, Ill. in LaSalle County. There is 3 taverns on the main drag. And on Sat. or Sunday, they handle at least 100,000 to 200,000 tip boards, football & basketball parley cards. 6 to 5 line, etc
>
> We feel the syndicate is involved & bad things could happen.
>
> Concerned Citizens
> Thank you

I knew that I couldn't make any kind of arrest down there if I found these three taverns bookmaking. I also decided that I would make sure that whatever I did it would have to be when I was off duty. I contacted a friend of mine who had access to an undercover camera that a person could wear under his jacket. The lens was about one sixteenths of an inch that would fit inside your jacket, which was connected to a battery pack that fit on your belt. I had used this type of camera before when I had filmed some mob guys on a riverboat paying and collecting money from other bookmakers, it turned out very well and they would up on some television stations very embarrassed. The bad news was that the security people on the riverboat got pissed off and because they were embarrassed that the mob was using there boat as a meeting place to straighten out their gambling business. Maybe they should be more observant about what is happening around them and start kicking somebody's ass.

I made arrangements to meet my friend whom I'll call J. R., who had the under cover camera, as well as a waist-length jacket with a small hole on the left side and an inside pocket that would hold the camera. The meeting place was a small cemetery just outside of Naplate.

The cemetery was not very big but it had a few large head stones to give us some cover in case someone showed up to visit the grave of their loved ones. Then there was always the chance of a funeral showing up, that would give us an audience that we didn't need. The Village of Naplate had a sign at either end of the village that said Population 620.

When I drove through the town I saw the three taverns that were mentioned in the anonymous letter that I got from the good citizens of Naplate. One was called Bones's Blue Line, Aric's Pub and Pizza, and the last one had a Budweiser sign with a couple of pictures of Popeye above the awning. I noticed a lot of pickup trucks parked all around each of the taverns, as well as a lot of cars. Being Saturday at the end of January and very cold out, it was a good day to look around each tavern to see if there really was gambling going on.

I went back to the cemetery to tell J. R. that I was ready to be outfitted with his undercover camera and battery pack. He asked me if I really wanted to do this and reminded me that I was a little out of my jurisdiction. I told him that this was no problem, and that I had my Levi's on as well my Caterpillar cap, my old army boots, besides they won't ever make me because I can talk like Jed Clampett if I have to. This shouldn't be any problem compared to working a few bars in Chicago in the Uptown neighborhood where they were loaded with crazy hillbillies and a lot of American Indians who thought that every white man they saw was related to General Custer. I told him that you have never lived until you hang around a few bars and have a bottle of wine in a place called the "Wooden Nickel." The word was that the place was owned by a Chicago police officer that worked in the local district. Actually, I did see him working behind the bar one day when I was working undercover, but who the hell cares anyway.

After J. R. set me up with the camera and the battery pack that fit by my lower back I was all ready to get the show on the road. I asked J. R. if he could see any bulges where he installed the camera, which was by my left breast where the lens was set up behind some lettering on the jacket. J. R. said, "Everything looks great, but don't get to close to anybody in the bar where they may bump into you and wonder what the hell you had under your jacket."

I told him, "No problem, pal, they're probably all half drunk anyway." I suggested that he visit a few grave sites as long as he was in the cemetery and when I got through I would meet him either in the cemetery or on the other side of town.

My first stop was called Bones Blue Line Tavern; it was located on the main street in a two-story building with parking in front of the bar and across the street. Of course, there were a lot of pickup trucks and vehicles were parked all over the street. It was tough finding a parking spot close to the tavern, but I got lucky when some guy came out of the bar and got into his truck. I could see that he had some sports paraphernalia in one hand and a bottle of beer in the other. After I parked in his spot, I walked in the bar, which was loaded with patrons. As far as I could tell, none of the good old boys even looked at the front door when someone came in.

I found an empty stool at the end of the bar, which was good, because I could see everybody in the place and what they were doing. I could have seen a lot better if it wasn't for the damn cigar and cigarette smoke. Being an ex-smoker, I hated that smell. I saw two women in the place all the rest were rednecks wearing coveralls, plaid shirts, and jackets, and shit kicker boots. Everyone had sports schedules, tip sheets, football and basketball cards. The tables at the front of the bar were covered with sports sheets, the odds of the games to be played that weekend. All the wagers that they were making out were then turned in to the big guy behind the bar who was also answering the telephone taking bets from other players. Most all of the rednecks were drinking beer; a few of them had six or seven bottles in front of them, all empty.

The bartender got off the phone, where he had been writing all kinds of bets on some yellow paper he had in his hand. He said, "Hi, partner, what's your poison?" I ordered a beer and a bag of pretzels; it was nice that I was able to see the bets he had in his hand, most of them were on basketball games. It looks as if the good citizens of Naplate were right about gambling in their village.

I had a small problem with the camera because I remembered that to get anything important on film; naturally, the lens had to be pointed at the subject matter, which meant I had to face whatever I was shooting. That was OK because most of the good old boys in the bar were engrossed in making their bets or were half in the bag; none of them paid any attention to a stranger walking among them or turning around on occasion.

Of course, they also had some video poker machines against the wall. All of them were occupied, some by old ladies. I figured that I had enough good stuff on film so I left and paid a visit to the next place down the road with was Aric's Pub and Pizza.

Aric's was a one story building painted yellow and faced the main street. There were also a lot of pickup trucks, station wagons, and some older beaters parked around the place. Aric's was also very busy, and all the patrons had some form of gambling paraphernalia, parlay cards, tip sheets, tab games, etc. The phone also rang quite a bit which was answered by the bartender, six foot, 185 pounds, about fifty years old, who smiles a lot. He would records the bets and then slip them under the bar.

A middle-aged woman was also behind the bar waiting on the good old boys. I ordered a bottle of beer and asked where the washroom was; she was kind enough to tell me. As I walked away from the bar and stopped to look at a couple of TV sets that were set up behind the bar. This gave me some freedom to move around and film some of the action that was going on in the place. When I left the washroom I also observed some more video poker machines in another part of the tavern and got them on film as well.

When I got back to the bar, the guy sitting next to me asked if I lived around their and that he had never seen me before. This guy was about six foot two, 190 pounds, and was wearing a T-shirt where he had a pack of cigarettes rolled up by his shoulder. Both arms had tattoos, one was a black snake coiled around what looked like a uniformed cop. He spoke with a heavy Southern accent and looked as if he had been chewing tobacco; some of it had drooled down the side of his mouth. I told him that I was looking for a place to go hunting in the area and stopped in to have a beer and take a leak. He told me that there was plenty of places around that I could go hunting and that I probably wouldn't even have to get a hunting license. I bought him a boiler maker Shot & Beer, and he offered me a "joint." For those uniformed, that is a cigarette made from the cannabis plant that is also known as marijuana, which is, of course, illegal.

I told my new friend "Billy Joe" that I had to give up smoking because I had a touch of emphysema. Billy Joe said, "Just take some Pepto Bismol, and you'll be back to normal." I thanked my new friend and told him that I had to go to the drugstore and get some Pepto Bismol.

I was glad to get away from Aric's pub and made my way to the Budweiser saloon a short distance away. Everything was the same in this joint, bookmaking was going wide open and nothing was any different then the other two bars, except maybe there was more smoke. I had another beer and even bought the bartender a drink; he had to put the phone down where he was recording bets and giving out the basketball line.

This sure was a learning experience for me; I wasn't use to seeing such wide open gambling going on, especially in taverns where they are taking a chance of blowing their license if they get busted. It was as if they just didn't give a damn about the consequences, but on the other hand maybe they didn't think the police had enough time to investigate violations of the gambling laws. Little did they know that they were going to be in the newspaper and on television very shortly.

Maybe this was a good thing and would open a can of worms about illegal gambling operations going on in small town USA. I'm sure the Chicago Outfit would be very interested in all the bookmaking going on and just maybe they weren't getting their end. I'm sure that they will make their own investigation about gambling operations down state and take the proper action.

TV links Mob, area gambling

By PEGGY SCHNEIDER
City Editor

A Chicago television station will broadcast a story tonight linking gambling in La Salle County with Chicago organized crime.

NBC Channel 5 News will air the report on the 10 p.m. news.

Police agencies investigating organized crime believe "outfits" are "moving their tentacles out to smaller towns" in La Salle, Kankakee, McHenry, Lake, Vermillion and Effingham counties, said reporter Dave Savini.

"The reason is that small towns have less resources to do special undercover investigations, and smaller (police) departments don't have a lot of time to spend" in such investigations, Savini said. La Salle County "seems to be the county they (sources) keep talking about," Savini said. "Whether or not the Mob is running the operations, they've more or less taken a piece of them."

Savini plans to air, as part of his report, a video provided by a police agency he would not identify. The video shows open sports bookmaking.

"They hand out betting forms like menus," Savini said.

Illegal gambling is going strong in Illinois, said Steve Hirsch, chief of criminal investigations for the Illinois Department of Revenue.

"We are getting more calls from people complaining their spouses have lost the entire paycheck," Hirsch said.

Also, video gambling machines are becoming popular because they generate easy profits and the risk of getting caught is smaller than some other forms of crime, such as narcotics trafficking, Hirsch said.

Organized crime followed the profits, Hirsch said.

"Organized crime involvement should not be a surprise. It exists not just in Chicago and cities, but is expanding to urban and rural areas where the money is," Hirsch said.

He would not confirm that La Salle County operations have ties to organized crime, but said investigation continues.

However, referring to a 1996 probe that led to 38 arrests in La Salle County involving gambling, Hirsch said, "We have received information that some of the locations are back in business."

Crime organizations became interested in Downstate communities decades ago, said Don Herion, director of the Vice Detection Unit of the Cook County's Sheriff's Department.

A mobster named Chuck English (who Anglicized his name) opened operations in La Salle County. English was famous in Chicago for running the Mob's amusement machine operations: pinball and poker machines and pool tables, Herion said.

English was killed about 20 years ago in a mob hit, Herion said.

The gambling can take the form of poker machines, "tip boards" or pull tabs.

Poker machines themselves are not illegal, but making payoffs to winners is, said Ottawa Police Chief Dale Baxter.

Catching a payoff can be difficult, Baxter said.

The machines accumulate points, and — to make the operation illegal — a proprietor would pay the winner so much money, a point.

A wary proprietor would only long-time customers, would be suspicious of newcomers or possible undercover agents, Baxter said.

"We have some poker machines around. I don't know the number," Baxter said.

"Possession of pull tabs and boards by other than licensed not-for-profit organizations is illegal, Baxter said.

"We've reduced possession those," he said.

"I have no doubt there is illegal gambling in La Salle County, but think it has diminished in October since the current administration has enforced gambling laws," Baxter added. "It's not entirely stopped, just like no other crime has, but it's decreased."

The film that I took got in the hands of Dave Savini, an investigative reporter for NBC Channel 5 News. Peggy Schneider, city editor of the *Daily Times,* ran a story about organized crime's tentacles moving to smaller towns in LaSalle, Kankakee, McHenry, Lake, Vermillion, and Effingham Counties.

It seems that small towns have fewer resources to do special undercover investigations and smaller (police) departments don't have a lot of time to spend on such investigations, Savini said. LaSalle County "seems to be the county they (sources) keep talking about. Whether or not the Mob is running the operations, they've more or less taken a piece of them."

Savini plans to air, as part of his report, a video provided by a police agency he would not identify. The video shows open sports bookmaking. "They hand out betting forms like menus," Savini said.

Illegal gambling is going strong in Illinois, said Steve Hirsch, chief of criminal investigations for the Illinois Department of Revenue. "We are getting more calls from people complaining their spouses have lost their entire paycheck," Hirsch said. "Organized crime follows the profits. Organized crime involvement should not be a surprise. It exists not just in Chicago, but is expanding to urban and rural areas where the money is."

The video that was taken of these three taverns located in Naplate is a very good educational exposure of wide open gambling that is going on all over these small towns in Illinois. The reason given by law enforcement is they don't have the resources to combat this type of illegal activity. I would suggest that they find a way to put a stop to these gambling operations before it's too late, because the next thing that may happen is that the mob will take over these places, if they haven't already, that is.

Come to think of it, it might be a good idea for someone to return to the scene of the crime and see if gambling still exists. The odds are that things are better than ever and its business as usual, after all that video was taken over four years ago. Hopefully, law enforcement did their job and busted these places, could be, huh? As they say on Taylor Street, "FORGET ABOUT IT."

Chapter 59

Audie Murphy:
War Hero vs the Chicago Mob

For some people that have never heard of Audie Murphy, he was the most decorated soldier of WW II. Some 16,353,659 service men and women served in the United States military during World War II. America had 405,399 killed in action and 671,278 wounded, as well as thousands missing in action before the war was over.

Murphy earned thirty-seven military awards, citations, and decorations, including every American medal for valor, including our nations highest – the Congressional Medal of Honor. He also was wounded in action three times, returning to his unit to fight again. When he enlisted on June 20, 1942, he was eigteen years old, five foot four, weighed 120 pounds; he looked about fifteen.

Before the war was over he rose from buck private to first lieutenant in command of his own company before he was twenty-one yrs old. He was credited with killing or capturing over 240 of the enemy in nine major battles he fought in. By the time his service was completed following the end of the war in May 1945, he had fought in North Africa, Sicily, Italy, France, and Germany.

Murphy was featured on the front page of *Time Magazine* on July 16,1945; that article and photo stirred the interest of movie actor James

Cagney. Cagney invited Murphy to Hollywood, took a fatherly interest in him, and helped him get started in the movie business. Murphy acted in a total of forty-five films. In 1955 he was voted the most popular actor in Western films.

Disaster struck when Audie Murphy was killed in the crash of a private airplane near Roanoke Virginia on May 28, 1971, at the age of forty-six. Murphy had survived two years of combat only to be killed when his plane crashed into a fog-shrouded mountain during a flight that probably never should have been taken.

Murphy's problems began in 1970 when he was in Las Vegas. He was reportedly introduced to two men who claimed that they were Buccieri gamblers from Chicago. They told Murphy that when he was unable to get a bet down he could call them as they ran a highly sophisticated bookmaking operation for a select group of patrons with excellent credit ratings.

They explained the rules to Murphy and told him that they would give him two telephone numbers that he could call in Chicago from anywhere in the country. He could make his daily bets strictly on a credit basis with cash changing hands only when it came time to settle up the profit and loss for the month.

Murphy accepted the arrangements with the bookmakers and became a client. He is reportedly to have wagered as much as $5,000 to 10,000 on a single race during the nearly one year that he did business with the men At one point, Murphy paid the Chicago gamblers $90,000 in cash that he lost on horse races and basketball games.

But a few months later, when Murphy had a winning streak and was ahead $112,000 in credit with the gangsters, he discovered his benefactors had suddenly become elusive.

Murphy hired a private investigator in an effort to help him locate the mysterious bookmakers and help him to recoup the money that he had won from the Buccieri brothers. The brothers were identified at Fiore "FiFi" and Frank Buccieri. FiFi was known as a top Chicago crime syndicate loan shark, gambler, arsonist, and in 1966 was named by federal authorities as the lord high executioner of the Chicago syndicate. Frank was an enforcer, juice collector, and gambler and was the operator of singer Vic Damone's Pizza Corporation with brothers Donald and Joe Grieco, juice collectors and enforcers.

The investigator said that Murphy was told at first that the bets he made had been placed too late for the races involved. Then he was unable to contact them through the numbers they had given him that were in a small loop office as well as public phones in parking garages, bars, and restaurants.

Angered, Murphy sought the help of a Los Angeles County Sheriff's detective with a reputation of a crime syndicate expert.

A reliable source related that Murphy had probably been dealing with Fiore "FiFi" Buccieri's brother Frank and a Cicero mobster Rocky Infelise.

Murphy became very angry at this point and asked the private detective to get FiFi Buccieri's home phone number. Murphy was no one to fool around with and didn't like getting cheated by the mob or anyone else. Murphy, who single-handedly killed or wounded fifty German soldiers in one battle in the Colmar Pocket in France January 26, 1945, telephoned the Chicago gangster at his hotel room in an effort to collect the $112,000 he thought Buccieri owed him. Murphy told Buccieri, "Hey, you son of a bitch, I've been betting with your people and you owe me $112,000."

Apparently taken aback, Buccieri is said to have first denied the debt, and then instructed Murphy to meet him at the office of a Hollywood talent agent on North Canyon Drive in Beverly Hills.

The agent was identified as a front man for a gangland-connected Chicago attorney who represents many movie stars.

Murphy went to the office, taking with him tape recordings of phone conversations he had had when he was making horse bets with "Frank" and "Rocky." Allegedly these tapes were turned over to the Internal Revenue Service and the Illinois Bureau of Investigation later.

Of course, Buccieri was a no show at the office, but Murphy played the recordings for the talent agent. The agent listened and then reportedly declared, "That isn't my client; now get the hell out of here." Murphy who was small in stature, swung at the agent, and hit the agent flush on the mouth, and the six-foot-four-inch man went down for the count.

Law enforcement authorities in Los Angeles aware of Murphy's efforts to retrieve his money wanted him to testify before a grand jury about his brush with the underworld. Instead Murphy sought help from the private detective he had used in the past.

Murphy explained the latest developments that had occurred and gave the detective the tape recordings of the bets he had made. It was determined that the voices on the tapes were not those of Buccieri, his brother Frank or Rocky Infelise.

Murphy provided additional information concerning these mob guys and through the help of a Chicago police sergeant assigned to the gambling unit. Organized crime division were able to identify the two men.

George Peara a convicted burglar and bank robber had left Chicago and moved to the Miami area of Florida. The other man was Carl Fiorito who had been arrested fifty times and was convicted of trafficking in heroin. Both men were associated with the Chicago Outfit. I had the pleasure of busting both George Peara and Carl Fiorito, two scumbags.

When questioned about their involvement with gambling and Audie Murphy, they both claimed that they were broke. In reality, the bets that they took from Murphy were never placed by the gamblers who took Murphy to the cleaners.

As things turned out it, was learned that Frank Buccieri was grateful for having the mess straightened out for which he was taking the heat. FiFi Buccieri thought that his brother was shorting him by not telling him about the money that he had won from Murphy. Brother or not, FiFi was not anybody to fool with when it came to money.

Chapter 60

Chicago Streets and Two Cops

What cops face eight hours a day can be unbelievable sometimes. I know it was for me. Cops worry about looking like a fool, of being weak, of being a coward. They're afraid of saying the wrong thing, or doing the wrong thing and getting their ass in trouble with the department – which is easy to do, believe me.

Working the streets of Chicago, cops run into things that are tragic, comical, pitiful, dangerous, and that can get deadly in a hurry. But that's OK, because most cops who work the street never know what's going to happen from one minute till the next because you're dealing with human beings from every part of society. Most of the cops I know just say, "Bring it on."

The only real way to learn about humans is to deal with them face to face. The problem, I'm sorry to say, is that most humans do not like the police, mainly because they just don't understand them or have any idea what they do.

Cops, of course, carry guns; there is a very good reason why they carry guns – to protect life and property of the citizens of Chicago and, of course, to protect their own life, which is more important. One of the jobs that a street cop does is work on a tactical team. Having worked on a TAC team myself in my early days on the job, I know what they have to do and what is expected of them on the street.

There were two such cops that worked TAC in the Austin District on the West Side of Chicago, sometimes called ghetto cops and the hardest working cops in the city; maybe that's what got them in hot water on occasion. I know for a fact that the harder you work, the odds are that you're going to get in a world of shit for just doing what you're supposed to do. That's just part of being a cop.

I had worked in the Austin District for eleven years, including five years on a TAC team, but we were called vice detectives back then. When I was promoted to sergeant in February 1970, I had to leave the organized crime division and go back in uniform and work as a street sergeant. It so happened that I was transferred back to the Austin District, which was fine with me. The only difference was, a lot of the district had changed from white to black.

While I was in the district, I was back in my old neighborhood, which was a plus because I didn't have a long way to drive to get to work. I would frequent a hamburger joint at Leclaire and North Avenue, which was about a block from my house. The owner was a guy called "Gus," who for some reason or other thought that the only reason I frequented his restaurant was to find him doing something illegal so I could bust him. Actually, I just liked his hamburgers, but I never told him that.

Gus was a police fan, and the cops liked him as well. That's where I got to know Tony and John; they worked on the TAC team and had a lot of street smarts for being fairly new on the job. They were chosen for their aggressiveness, dedication to duty, guts, and above all, common sense. They would dress in army fatigue jackets, Windbreakers, floppy hats, and, on occasion, carry two guns. They stopped and searched more cars on a tour of duty than the rest of their shift combined. They had been in at least nine shootouts. John got shot in the back on one occasion and was almost out of ammunition, but his partner Tony was positioned in precisely the right spot to save his partner's life and capture the two gunmen.

John and Tony had been working together for six years and between them had killed seven felons and wounded several others. Tony had never been shot but had been wounded twice. Once, a Doberman Pinscher bit him on his buttocks when he tried to subdue the guard dog's owner. On another occasion, he was dragged through a street after he reached inside a car window to snatch the ignition keys from the driver, a robbery suspect. It's a known fact that for some reason some cops are like magnets to crime on the street. It's also a fact that the harder you work, the luckier you get; that's why they were able to make fifty to sixty busts a month for guns and drugs. Tony, who was a former marine, and John were not only partners, but they were close personal friends as well. They always covered each other on the street and knew what the other was going to do in any situation that came up. They also have helped each other in small ways, such as breaking the cigarette habit. Each came from a blue-collar upbringing, and their families had some hard times, being on food stamps or welfare. They each had two years of college.

John was married and had a daughter; Tony didn't talk about his private life.

Tony liked to listen to disco music and read American history. John drives a truck on his days off and delivers cargo to Wisconsin "to clear his head." The two partners were cocaptains of the district softball team. John wore his blue team jacket on the job along with a railroad engineer hat. Tony was the "Wheelman" in a battered old yellow Dodge they used as their TAC car at the time. Half the time, it would stall and was not a very reliable vehicle, but it got the job done.

The squad was well known to all the scumbags on the street, but at night it didn't matter much because Tony and John would be on them before they had a chance to do something stupid.

One night they were called to a troublesome Division Street bar when a white punk in a fuzzy afro and with glazed eyes walked with his chest thrust out toward John. "Hello, John," he said in an almost teasing voice. "We saw your car pull up outside. We all know your car. It's a pretty color. We'll all be waiting for you guys someday." John, a beefy 230-pound Greek with a gregarious manner, smiled at him. "That's why we keep it yellow, boy. We always want you to know when were coming."

When John seemingly played with the punk's challenge, Tony was at the corner of the bar with two other youths, who owed him favors. They were telling him about some neighborhood burglaries and some drug dealers whom they didn't like.

They both have learned that if they took the job seriously, they would soon crack up. Just riding around in the district, which was mostly slums now, was depressing enough. Tony, who is Bohemian, grew up in the Austin area, which was mainly Italian, Irish, and Jewish. He remembered the area when it was fresh and pretty, not like it is now.

I remembered the area as well. You wouldn't find beer cans on the parkways; the streets all glitter with glass particles at night; apartment buildings with broken windows, some boarded up; streetlights were broken or just didn't work; and the street was filled with small craters. The sidewalks were deserted at night except for family moving furniture into a truck at midnight. It seemed that people always moved at night in the ghetto. You never see any grass or cats in the ghetto either; they seem to die off. What you do see are rats and packs of dogs.

Violence seems to be a way of life in the slums, and as a cop you have to learn how to deal with it; if you can't, you better look for another line of work.

"Being a cop means being in the right place at the right time, or depending on your perspective, being in the wrong place at the wrong time."

Police inquiries of the shootings that John and Tony were in were all ruled justifiable. The men killed were either in a shoot-out or involved in the commission of a crime.

Two such men were shot when they broke into a boutique on Madison Street at night. Tony and John were assigned to a stakeout inside the store after information was received that there was going to be a burglary take place. Tony and John were waiting for them with shotguns. They were both armed and decided to shoot it out with the good guys; obviously they lost.

Tony was off duty when two other shooting deaths occurred with in a five-month period. Tony was on his way to work when he spotted a heroin addict whom he had arrested in the past walking in a neighborhood that the addict didn't live in. Tony followed the suspect and saw him walk in between two buildings on the 1700 block of North Mayfield Avenue. Checking the building, he found the rear door of the second-floor apartment had been forced open, and the bad guy was ransacking the apartment. When the burglar saw Tony, he lunged at him with a knife. Tony shot him twice, once over the left ear.

The other off-duty shooting happened when Tony was in an apartment at 1600 North Leclaire Avenue. It so happened that a man who had entered a bar at 5005 West North Avenue, which was around the corner had been refused service because he appeared to already have had to much to drink. The man walked outside, pulled out a gun, and fired the pistol through the front window. A policeman inside the bar who was on medical leave fired back, and hobbled outside on a broken leg to pursue the gunman.

The gunfight resumed near the corner of 1600 North Leclaire when both men fired at each other from behind parked cars. Tony, hearing the gun shots, ran downstairs and found that the suspect had entered the building and was trying to break into a first-floor apartment. When the shooter saw Tony, he pointed his gun at him. Tony fired six rounds. Two of the three hits found the neck and right ear; it was all over.

Again we have the old saying of being in the right place at the right time, or being in the wrong place at the wrong time; it all depends on how you look at things, I guess.

Tony and John were interviewed by police officials after every shooting they were involved in. Joseph DiLeonardi, citywide homicide commander, agreed with police officials that the shootings were justified and the officers followed police procedure in every instance.

One thing that will never change, that is Monday morning quarterbacking. Cops are not very kind to one another at all. Whoever gets involved in something, there's always a bunch of guys who will tell you that you should have done it this way. Why did you do it that way? Terrible stuff. I did it myself a long time ago, but I after I thought about it, I realized that I wasn't there when it went down, so how the hell would I have any idea how it was. The important thing was the policeman didn't get killed or hurt; the bad guy did.

Naturally, whenever policemen get involved in situations that may involve a fight or a shooting, people want to believe that it was police brutality or the cop made himself judge, jury, and executioner. Make no mistake, it is a frustrating job at times, but then nothing is perfect, so you just learn to roll with the punches, because it can always get worse.

For example, Tony and John just happened to be a couple of blocks away from a robbery in progress in a store at Lake Street and Central Avenue. Some citizens who had passed by the store saw two guys with guns pistol-whipping the owner behind the counter. He called the police from a pay phone to report what he had observed.

As luck would have it, there was also a uniform beat car in the area with a rookie driving. Apparently, he hit the lights and siren and began speeding to the scene. When the two stickup guys heard the approaching siren, they ran out the rear door just as John and Tony pulled around the corner.

When they saw the bad guys who had weapons in their hands come out the back door running, they yelled at them that they were the police and to drop their guns.

One of the bad guys shouted, "Go fuck yourself, pig," and fired at them. At this point, things turned into a running gun battle, with the crooks running toward Lake Street. The cops were firing from behind parked cars as were the bad guys. John emptied his .38 at the one guy, and he went down stumbling on the curb. Tony cornered the other punk, and they both fired at each other. Tony was the better shooter and hit him in the chest. When it was over, there was one guy dead and one guy wounded; everything was in control, and things worked out for the best. It seems that they were responsible for other robberies in the area and identified by other victims of the stickup men.

When Tony or John would walked through the district station, they heard things like, "Hey, blew another one away huh, Tony, one for the good guys huh, John?"

The two men were popular with businessmen throughout the district, both black and white. They are visible reminders that there is some protection beyond a window grating and a gun under the counter.

The facts of life are cruel sometimes; even though Tony and John were doing an outstanding job on the Chicago Police Department and were given numerous awards for heroism and dedication to duty, they made some politicians unhappy. While they were partners on the TAC team, they became involved in nine gun battles on the street and had killed seven stickup men, murderers, burglars, and dope dealers who were trying to kill them. Police investigated every shooting officials ruled justifiable.

Apparently the politicians and police brass felt pressure from somewhere that they decided to split up Tony and John, Tony was transferred to the Youth Division, and John was sent to traffic. John also was given a promise that he would be promoted to sergeant in the near future. Obviously the real reason they were split up was because of the shootings they had been involved in; even though they were all ruled as good and they acted within the law, they didn't need them to get involved in any more. As things turned out, John was never promoted to sergeant and resigned from the police department in disgust. Tony stayed on the job and retired as a detective.

The fact of the matter is, "People do not like the police." Cops represent authority, and people do not like someone telling them what to do or how to do it. In my opinion, traffic tickets that cops give to people cause them to hate the police. But traffic enforcement is necessary; if we didn't enforce the traffic laws, the tail would be wagging the dog. Nevertheless, people despise getting a traffic ticket; they also despise the cop that gave it to them. Most everybody knows that when they go on the job, they just better get used to being disliked; it's a fact of life.

Chapter 61

Just Another Gangland Hit
"Las Vegas Style"

Herbert "Fat Herbie" Blitzstein was the victim of a gangland hit in his Las Vegas townhouse at 3655 Mount Vernon Avenue. The reputed Chicago mobster was found slumped over in a chair in his living room in January 1997; he had been shot in the back of his head. When I heard of his sudden departure, I wasn't surprised, because his clout, Tony Spilotro, was dead.

It brought back memories of his past history in Chicago and how we tormented him when he was a Rush Street cowboy. In Chicago, he liked the nightlife on Rush Street, and he hung around with some mob guys like Al Frabotta, Joe Arnold, Joe "Little Ceasar" DiVarco, Ken Eto, and a few bookmakers like Moe Shapiro, Sherman Goldman, Marvin Marks. He got friendly with Tony Spilotro, who would run the Chicago Outfit's rackets in Las Vegas.

Herbie and Moe Shapiro hung around a hamburger joint at 917 North Rush Street called "The Banquet on a Bun." The restaurant was located on the first floor of a two-story brick building; an office in the basement was set up as a sports wire room. The telephones that were installed were listed to a Sidney Boyanski – whoever the hell he was.

Tony and Michael's
grave in a cornfield
in Indiana.

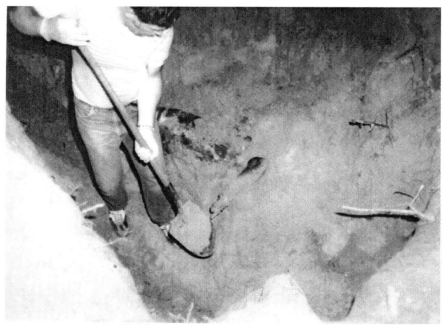

Source: Indiana State Police

Tony Spilotro Michael Spilotro

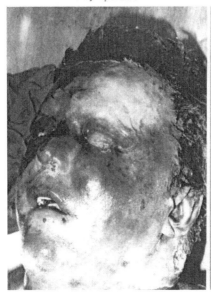
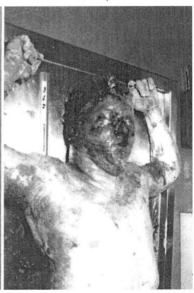

Source: Indiana State Police

When this photo appeared in the newspaper my commanding officer called me at home and asked me what I was doing at Michael Spilotro's house. He saw the man in the middle and was sure it was me. He told me that he called the Superintendents office and reported that Sgt Herio picture was in the newspaper at Organized Crime figure Spilotro who been reported missing with his mobster brother, Tony and feared they had been murdered. I told him that I had never been at Spilotro's house and he was crazy. I bought the Sun Times and looked at the photograph, a had to agree that the guy looked just like me. I found out later that the person was some union offical

Source: Chicago Police Dep't

After a lot of surveillances on that location and observing Fat Herbie and Little Moe, our investigation revealed our two guys were conducting a large-scale bookmaking operation in the basement. The bad news was they had installed a very big iron-barred door, which could give us a problem.

On June 5, 1970, we obtained a search warrant for the basement office and executed it at 6:15 PM. Of course, we had a tough time getting through the back iron door, but when we threatened to use an acetylene torch on the door, which we didn't have, that apparently convinced Herbie and Moe to open another door, which had been barricaded, as well as the iron door. We recovered gambling paraphernalia, telephones, and accepted bets from people calling into the office to make bets on baseball games.

Herbie was a big guy, six foot one, about 300 pounds, thirty-seven years old, while Moe was five foot six, 130 pounds, forty-three years old. Of course, they asked who ratted on them. I told Herbie that I would be glad to tell him if he would tell me whom he was laying off his bets too. He said, "What are you nuts, you want to get me killed?" We answered him by throwing them in a wagon and locking them. We busted him a few more times before he moved to Arizona to escape the Chicago heat, so to speak.

Fat Herbie moved to Las Vegas in the early 1970s and rose to be chief aide of the Chicago mob's top man in Las Vegas, Tony Spilotro. Tony and his brother Michael were beaten to death. Their mutilated bodies were found buried in a Northern Indiana cornfield in 1986.

Blitzstein allegedly owned Gold Rush Ltd., a jewelry shop that federal authorities believed to be a front for Spilotro's operations. Herbie was a member of Spilotro's Hole in the Wall gang. The gang was a burglary ring that operated with help from corrupt members of the Clark County sheriff's organized crime unit.

The FBI captured gang members in action on July 4, 1981. Herbie was indicted along with Spilotro on federal racketeering charges. Prior to this, he had spent several months in jail on contempt-of-court charges for failing to provide handwriting samples to a federal grand jury that was investigating Spilotro. That trial took place in the beginning of 1986 and was declared a mistrial when one of the jurors informed the judge that she heard two other jurors discussing a bribe. Before the second trial could begin in mid-June, Spilotro was murdered.

Fat Herbie got messed up again in 1987 when he pleaded guilty to four separate federal indictments including using counterfeit credit cards, receiving stolen government postage, and income tax evasion. He was sentenced to eight years in prison. His health was deteriorating due to weight and dietary problems. In addition to two heart bypass surgeries, doctors removed a few toes on his right foot.

He was released in 1991 and returned to Las Vegas. But now things were different. The stranglehold the Chicago Outfit had on Las Vegas had diminished due to pressure from law enforcement. Herbie found a new friend; his name was Ted Binion and belonged to the Binion family who owned Horseshoe Casino. Eventually, the Nevada Gaming Commission suspended Binion from operating the Horseshoe Casino because of his association with Blitzstein and because of a personal drug problem. Such associations are never good for business, particularly in image-conscious Las Vegas.

Blitzstein and Binion would get drunk on occasion and ride around in a limousine. On one of their binges, Binion spoke to a girl called Sandy and handed her $2,000; he said, "This is for you, honey." Sandy was a stripper in town and a smart-mouthed flirt. She looked at Binion and threw the money back in his face. "I don't want your fucking money," she told Binion. Ted had a problem with booze and drugs, and his personal fortune was estimated at between $30 million and $50 million, and Sandy Murphy knew it. Binion was immediately attracted to her and liked her style.

Binion, who had a ranch at Pahrump, Nevada, lived alone; his wife, Doris, had left him because of his heroin addiction and womanizing. Before long, Sandy Murphy spent some time on the ranch and entertained him; she was twenty-three, and Binion was fifty-one and rich. Binion got in trouble again when he instructed a Horseshoe employee to cash $11,000 in checks for his buddy Blitzstein, who, of course, was a known mob guy in Las Vegas.

Binion who had been told by the gaming commission to have nothing to do with the Horseshoe ignored their instructions. Binion had a problem because he had $7 million in silver coins and bullion in one of the Horseshoe's basement vaults; he would have to find another storage place

Binion ran into a thirty-two-year-old guy by the name of Rick Tabish in the men's room of another old-time Vegas joint called Piero's on Paradise Road. Tabish was an ex-con from Montana and had been in the construction business. He was married with two kids, and told his wife that he would send for them after he got established in Nevada. Binion took a liking to Tabish, and Rick became a frequent visitor to Binion's mansion. Of course, he met Sandy as well. Ted trusted Rick and asked him to build an underground vault near his ranch in Pahrump, Nevada, off a dusty road on a piece of property that Binion owned.

Tabish was glad to comply to help his new friend and dug the vault. On an evening in July, Binion and Tabish, along with members of Tabish's work crew, hauled 48,000 pounds of silver to Pahrump. It was reported that Binion had worn a bulletproof vest and two guns on his hips to protect his interest while they were moving the silver. Binion, who tried to turn his life around, started smoking heroin again and didn't realize that Sandy and Rick were getting to be very close friends.

On September 17, 1998, Sandy Murphy made an emergency call for medical help at Binion's mansion. The medics found Sandy to be hysterical; she told them that Binion stopped breathing. Binion was found dead in the den surrounded by foil wrappers and an empty bottle of Xanax. Sandy was so shaken that she had to be hospitalized and sedated. Thirty-six hours later, Tabish was caught in the middle of the night in Pahrump, having just excavated Binion's silver from the underground vault he had built.

It was a known fact that Binion had been a mean, abusive drunk. Sandy suffered beatings, black eyes, and a lot of bruises. If Ted would punch her, she would punch him right back, or kick him, or scratch him. She would then threaten to leave him. On one occasion after he busted up her face and pulled out a hank of hair, he got back in her good graces by buying her a brand-new $97,000 black Mercedes.

When Tabish was caught removing the silver bullion valued at $7 million, he told the police that he was moving some concrete. When the police discovered the silver in his truck, Tabish admitted that he had lied. He said that he was a friend of Binion's. He built the vault for Ted, who had asked him to make sure that when he died, his ex-wife didn't get her hands on his silver. Tabish even told the police that the sheriff of Nye County, Wade Lieseke, knew all about it. Lieske, it was reported, was very nervous and tried to talk the deputies out of arresting Tabish and his cohorts, according to the deputies. Sheriff Lieske claimed that he ordered the arrest and to charge them with the attempted theft of Binion's silver.

The Las Vegas police at that point did not consider Binion's death a homicide; but Binion's sister, Becky Behnen, did. She didn't believe that Ted died of an overdose of Xanax because according to her, he never used pills. Becky hired a former Las Vegas cop, Tom Dillard, to begin an investigation. Eventually, the police and the district attorney's office joined in as well. The investigation revealed that Binion was, in fact, murdered.

Nine months later, in June 1999, the metro police had enough evidence to arrest Murphy and Tabish for conspiracy to murder Binion by forcing him to ingest "a lethal combination of heroin and Xanax." Tabish had been out on bond from the silver robbery; his bail, $100,000, had been put up by Murphy. The motive, of course, was love and money. Murphy stood to inherit $300,000 and the Palomino Lane mansion. The prosecution had a mountain of witnesses and evidence against Murphy and Tabish.

I became involved when I got a phone call from an old friend of mine; Tom Thompson, a retired DEA agent who had been contacted by an associate of the private detective, Tom Dillard, who in turn had been hired by the Binion's to investigate the murder case. It seems that while Rick Tabish was incarcerated, he got a visit from Salvatore Galioto, who was from Chicago. No one knew who Galioto was, and thought it was strange that he would visit Tabish; of course, he may have been interested in the $7 million in silver.

When Thompson asked me if I had ever heard of Galioto, I told him that I knew that he's associated with some wise guys from Chicago and involved in gambling and the movie industry. His brother John was a known sports bookmaker, using cell phones that were listed to Local 225 4242 North Old River Road, Shiller Park, Illinois.

Thompson told Dillard that I knew a lot about these subjects and that if he came to Chicago, I would tell him what I knew about the Galiotos – about how Salvatore Galioto a.k.a. Sam Galioto operates.

Movies in Motion, a company specializing in supporting film companies operating in Illinois, was a member of Local 714, Teamsters Union. Galioto's father, William "Bill" Galioto (retired police officer), owned the building at 4242 Old River Road, Shiller Park, Illinois, where local 225, Liuna was located on the second floor. William Galioto is the brother-in-law of the convicted mob underboss, James Marcello, described to be the number 2 man in the Chicago mob.

The Galiotos tried to make a deal through Mayor Daley and the department of planning and economic development to build a movie studio at 2200 West Madison Street; it was to be known as Studio Works. The city had approved a $5.5 million low interest loan to associates of the Chicago mob. An investor in the project announced at a groundbreaking ceremony with great fanfare that the city was scrambling to kill the deal because it was learned from veteran alderman Ed Burke about possible mob involvement in the fledgling deal. Mayor Daley was embarrassed by the turn of events and issued orders to kill the deal, stating that he did not want the city doing business with people in FBI files associated with organized crime.

Needless to say, the Galioto family was connected. Could it have been possible that Sam Galioto was involved with Rick Tabish and the $7 million in silver? He was the only visitor that Tabish had while he was incarcerated. The Galiotos also owned a strip club called the All Star Gentleman's Club on West Grand Avenue in unincorporated Northlake, Illinois. They, of course, provided lap dances, as well as strippers and what has you Tom Dillard, his partner former DEA Agent Phil, and Tom Thompson in the place to get an idea of how business was. The place was jammed with the usual all-male patrons, some of them vanishing into rear rooms behind some drapes with a stripper/waitress.

After a few drinks, we decided to get the hell out of the place as we saw everything we needed to see. Tom Thompson and I offered to pay for the drinks, but Dillard told us he was going to take care of the tab as he was on an expense account from Jack Binion, the brother of murder victim Ted Binion.

The next day, Dillard took Thompson and I out to Jack Binion's Empress Casino in Joliet, Illinois, to meet Jack Binion. He turned out to be a regular guy and treated Thompson and I like kings. He was very interested in what I knew about the Chicago mob and the connection between his brother's murderer, Rick Tabish, as well as the Galiotos.

It seems that Binion owned other Horseshoe casinos in Bossier City, Louisiana; Tunica, Mississippi; and Hammond, Indiana. The combined annual revenues totaled $840 million.

As things turned out, Binion sold the Empress Casino in 2001 and the others to Harrah's Entertainment Inc. in 2003. Binion and his wife reside in Las Vegas, Nevada.

In November 2004, the Nevada Supreme Court, on a decision of four to three, acquitted Tabish and Murphy of murder charges but agreed that they were guilty of stealing Binion's millions in silver. They were supposed to be retried in the near future.

Herbert "Fat Herbie" Blitzstein's murder trial began in April 1999 in Las Vegas. Two men were on trial for authorizing the January 1997 slaying of mobster Fat Herbie Blitzstein. U.S. Attorney Eric Johnson gave the jurors a crash course on the workings of the Mafia and told them that the evidence in this case will demonstrate that there is a nationwide criminal conspiracy known as the La Cosa Nostra.

Authorities claimed Henderson residents Stephen Cino, sixty-two, and Robert Panaro Sr., fifty-seven, used their status as soldiers or members of the Mafia to sanction the killing of Blitzstein. The two men were indicted on a variety of charges in April 1997 as part of a broad federal investigation of organized crime in southern Nevada. Prosecutors later accused them of playing a role in Blitzstein's death. Three other defendants already entered into plea agreements and admitted their involvement in the contract killing. Mob associate Alfred Mauriello, seventy-two, of Las Vegas pleaded guilty earlier in the month to participating in racketeering activity, which included Blitzstein's slaying.

As part of his plea, Mauriello admitted receiving $10,000 from Peter Caruso to kill Blitzstein. He also confessed to paying Antoine Davi and Richard Friedman between $3,000 and $4,000 to carry out the murder for him. Peter Caruso, fifty-nine, died in January while awaiting trial. Joseph DeLuca, the owner of a Las Vegas auto repair shop, pleaded guilty to the same charge as Mauriello during a closed hearing in August 1997. DeLuca admitted helping the killers gain entry to Blitzstein's Las Vegas residence and admitted helping pay for the job.

He reported the killing to police on January 7, 1997; he attended Fat Herbie's funeral in Chicago as well. Reliable sources have said Blitzstein was killed by the outfit because they wanted to infiltrate his business activities in the Las Vegas Valley. Authorities described both DeLuca and Caruso as mob associates.

As part of their plea bargains, both Mauriello and DeLuca agreed to cooperate with prosecutors and to testify for the government at the trials of their codefendants. Davi, a thirty-one-year-old Henderson resident, had pleaded guilty about a week ago to murder in aid of racketeering activity; he too agreed to testify against his codefendants for a reduced sentence of twenty years.

Several other defendants in the case, including Carmen Milano of Las Vegas, were also scheduled to go on trial. Milano was described as reputed underboss of La Cosa Nostra's Los Angeles family but has not been accused in playing a role in the Blitzstein killing.

During the prosecutor's opening statement, he described Cino as a member of La Cosa Nostra's Los Angeles family and Panaro as a member of Buffalo, New York Crime Family. The prosecutor told the jurors Blitzstein "was a criminal associate and perceived friend" of those who killed him. That was no surprise, of course; that's the way the boys do things. They knew Fat Herbie was up to his ass in illegal activities, and he wasn't giving them their end.

The prosecution said that Blitzstein had a hidden interest in DeLuca's business and operated a loan-sharking business as well. He described how Caruso came to DeLuca and suggested killing Blitzstein. At first DeLuca was concerned about the chance of retaliation from Blitzstein's mob connections in Chicago. DeLuca agreed to go ahead with the plan only after receiving approval from Cino and Panaro; he would testify to these facts in court for a recommended prison term of 12 ½ years.

After a four-week trial in federal court, which featured mob guys fingering each other and few paid informants testifying against the bad guys, it was like a Chinese fire drill. Cino and Panaro were found not guilty of the charges of murdering Blitzstein. They were, however, found guilty of conspiracy to extort from him.

The final suspect in this fiasco, Richard Friedman, pleaded guilty to murder-for-hire charges, which left him facing a twenty-five-year sentence as opposed to a life term. Friedman was allowed to admit to receiving payment for participating in the crime, but denied being the triggerman.

Of the seven persons involved in the plot to kill Blitzstein, four pled guilty in order to receive reduced sentences. One died in prison awaiting trial, and two went to trial and were acquitted. As the record stands, no one officially killed Blitzstein.

The investigation into the murder of Fat Herbie Blitzstein started a two-year FBI probe called Operation Button Down. The investigation, which was targeting the Milano Crime Family from the West Coast, returned indictments on twenty-five individuals with a total of 101 counts. In the end though, only two men were tried for Blitzstein's murder, and they were acquitted.

Oh well, even though Blitzstein was shot in the back of the head three times, if no one pulled the trigger, then there was always the chance that Fat Herbie shot himself. He would have to shoot really fast though to shoot himself three times; then that would be classified as a suicide, wouldn't it?

Why they died: Las Vegas control

By Phillip J. O'Connor

Experts on organized crime said yesterday that hoodlum Tony Spilotro and his brother, Michael, probably were slain because Tony resisted efforts to replace him as the Chicago mob's boss in Las Vegas.

Bill Roemer, a former FBI mob expert in Chicago, said he believes the mob's new day-to-day operating boss, Joseph Ferriola, 59, wanted his own man as Las Vegas boss and Spilotro resisted being ousted.

Bill Lambie, the Chicago Crime Commission's former expert on organized crime, agreed with Roemer that Tony Spilotro's reluctance to surrender his Las Vegas post probably led to the double slaying.

"My guess is that he [mob] powers to be told him he wasn't running Las Vegas anymore," Lambie said. "He probably defied them. Michael was probably just there when they grabbed Tony and they killed him, too."

Roemer, a consultant to the Chicago Crime Commission, said Tony Spilotro's reluctance to be a contender for the mob operating chief's job, "wasn't doing the job" in Las Vegas and that's probably why Ferriola wanted to oust him.

Roemer pointed to the recent Kansas City, Mo., trial on charges of Las Vegas casino skimming that resulted in conviction of five mob

Anthony Accardo — Joseph Aiuppa — John Cerone — Allen Glick — Angelo LaPietra — Joseph Lombardo

leaders and 28½-year sentences for the Chicago mob's No. 2 leader, John Cerone, 71, and the mob's former operating boss, Joseph J. Aiuppa, 78.

Sentenced to 16-year terms in the skimming trial were Chicago hoodlum bosses Joseph Lombardo, 58, and Angelo LaPietra, 66.

"So many [mob-linked] people under Tony Spilotro's dominion became government witnesses against Aiuppa, Cerone and the others in that trial," Roemer said. "It was an indication he was not doing his job."

One of the government's star witnesses in the Kansas City trial was Allen Glick, a mob-linked financier who used two loans totaling $87.7 million from the Teamsters Union's Chicago-based Central States Pension Fund to buy and remodel the Stardust and Fremont casinos in Las Vegas.

Lambie said there are three basic reasons for mob murders: punishment, power, and to protect the mob "from people who might rat on them."

"I think this [double slaying] was strictly punishment," he said. "I think that Tony Spilotro defied them [mob leaders]. I never have believed that the Chicago mob engaged in assassinations to make power changes.

"Going back in history, you'll find [mob chieftain] Tony Accardo has never believed in that. He has always believed power changes could be made peacefully."

Lambie said he also doubted Ferriola would have ordered Tony Spilotro slain without consulting other mob leaders, including Accardo, the mob's elder statesman, and imprisoned mob bosses Cerone and Aiuppa, whom Ferriola replaced.

Lambie said, "Cerone and Aiuppa may be in prison, but they would have their say. I think they also would have a say in who will replace Tony Spilotro as the mob's boss in Las Vegas."

Accardo, who turned 80 in April and spends winters in Palm Springs, Calif., returned to the Chicago area in May to advise Ferriola and a new generation of mob leaders because of the power vacuum created by imprisonment of several top mob bosses.

The young bloods include riola lieutenants Michael Po 44, whose first assignment wa expand the Chicago mob's Wi sin operations, and Salvatore Laurentis, 47, whom Fer picked to replace him as County, Ill., gambling boss, inv gators said.

Tony Spilotro faced retrial Las Vegas racketeering trial. first Las Vegas racketeering ended in a mistrial in April a reports that someone attempte bribe a juror. He and eight ot were charged with conspiracy racketeering in connection wit burglary ring at Las Vegas ho and businesses in 1980 and 1

Robert Sheehan, deputy chie the Chicago police organized-c unit, said the Spilotro brothers been bringing the mob "heat" f law-enforcement agencies as a sult of pending charges aga them.

Michael was awaiting trial o another Spilotro brother, Victor the federal Operation Safe Bet vestigation on charges of shak down the operator of an ill credit-card setup who catered the sex-shop trade.

Investigators said mob bo may have considered Michael weak link" who might turn gove ment informer more easily t Tony, leading to a decision to Michael along with Tony.

Herbert `Fat Herbie` Blitzstein
Chicago Mobster whacked Jan 1997
in Las Vegas

Fat Herbie was former aide to Tony Spilotro

Source: Chicago Police Dep't

Chapter 62

Gambling: The Great American Sport "Just Ask the Mob"

Gambling means different things to different people. Some envision a racecourse with horses running around the final turn, with the crowd screaming encouragement. Others envision an elegantly clad cluster of men and women watching the movements of a croupier at a roulette wheel. Then others get a mental flash of a dozen crapshooters gathered around an alley game or a blanket in an army barracks. Then we have poker games in a guarded hotel room. Of course, we now have riverboat casinos and video poker machines in every other bar and grill. There are people that purchase lottery tickets and play jar games at their church while they are playing bingo.

Virtually, every ethnic group in a nation of ethnic groups has its own game run in its own neighborhood and in its own language.

The Mexicans and Filipinos have their cockfights, the Chinese have fan-tan, the Greeks have barbouth, the Jews gin rummy, and the Irish sweepstakes and bingo. Two games, policy and bolita, are called "numbers." Policy is a daily gamble with two drawings a day, patronized by blacks in their neighborhoods. Bolita is played largely in the Cuban and Puerto Rican areas.

Policy was brought to Chicago from the Deep South seventy-five years before the syndicate mobsters muscled in. Everybody thought it was just a nickel and dime ghetto game.

The outfit had no idea of its annual take. When Sam Giancana was serving time in a federal penitentiary Terre Haute, Indiana, with another prisoner, Edward P. Jones, Jones opened his mouth and told Giancana how he and his two brothers owned a few policy wheels on Chicago's South Side and how well they were doing. At this time Giancana was a lowly mobster, and Jones had no idea of whom he was talking to. He would soon find out.

When Sam got out of prison, he sold Paul "the Waiter" Rica and Tony Accardo, the two Chicago mob bosses, the idea of taking over Jones's empire. This idea helped Giancana rise up the ladder in the syndicate until he eventually became the boss. Giancana was advised not to create any heat in his attempt to take over this gambling empire. Giancane's attempt to take over some of the smaller policy operators by a series of beatings and bombings failed. When Jones was released from Terre Haute in 1946, he was kidnapped and held captive in the basement of Giancana's new home in Oak Park, Illinois. It was reported that Jones's family paid $100,000 in ransom to get him released.

The Jones brothers decided that it would be healthier to get out of Chicago and move to Mexico. Their top lieutenant, Ted P. Roe, was left behind to fight the mob, which he did for six years.

In June 1951 the outfit attempted to kidnap Roe; a gun battle broke out, and one of the mobsters was killed. Lenny Caifano, a brother of mob boss Marshall Caifano, didn't know how to duck obviously. About a year later, Ted P. Roe was shotgunned to death.

The rest of the policy kings got the message and quickly fell in line, and the outfit added policy to its long list of lucrative rackets.

In 1954 the Chicago Crime Commission estimated that Chicago's policy racket netted $150 million for the outfit, and this is a game that can be played for as little as nickels and dimes. All of this took place the first decade after World War II.

In the '60s, the outfit muscled in on the Puerto Rican – Cuban lottery called bolita. At that time, a mob boss named Fiore "Fifi" Buccieri was the outfit's man in charge on the local scene; Fifi collected 25 percent of the gross.

This area extended from Gary, Indiana, to Milwaukee, Wisconsin. It was estimated that no fewer than 85 percent of the Spanish population played bolita, which included five- or six-year-old children who were allowed to bet nickels.

Bolita is a simple lottery to play; any intelligent child can understand the game. Anyone can choose a three-digit number, anything from 0-0-0 to 9-9-9. All winners are paid in cash, of course. Since there are 1,000 numbers from which to draw, the odds against winning are 1,000 to 1, and the payoff is only 500 to 1. The facts are that the outfit controls the games, and the results are sometimes rigged. If too many bets are placed on a particular number, it is simple to fix the game so that a number cannot possibly come up.

Buccieri got a cut on the bolita games in Gary, Hammond, East Chicago, Whiting, Aurora, Naperville, North Chicago, Waukegan, Kenosha, Racine, Milwaukee, and Waukegan as well as in Chicago. Buccieri operated out of Cicero with Joey Aiuppa so he could run his bolita operations without any trouble; he had to cut in Ross Prio and Lenny Patrick of the North Side, Ralph Pierce of the South Side, and Chuck English on the West Side. All these mobsters are now deceased except for Lenny Patrick, who became an informant against the outfit.

Ken Eto, the crime syndicate's only Oriental muscleman, was put in charge of bolita operations. He, along with James "Kid Rivera" Williams, also ran the Win-Place-Show policy wheel, one of the two largest under the direct control of the crime syndicate. Eto was a loyal soldier for thirty years until the mob thought that he had turned informant; they attempted to assassinate him on February 10, 1983, in a parking lot on the northwest side of Chicago. Eto explained that mob bosses Big Joe Arnold and Joseph DiVarco, who met with Eto earlier that day, had set him up. He was told to meet Jasper Campise and Johnnie Gattuso that night when he was led to believe he was going to an Italian restaurant to discuss business with them. Gattuso shot Eto three times in the back of the head, but the shots failed to kill Eto. Campise and Gattuso were hacked to death and found stuffed in the trunk of Campise's car in Naperville. Eto also related that Vince Solano, a North Side crime syndicate rackets boss as well as president of local 1 of the mob, related that the laborers' union had given the order to have him killed. Eto, fearing for his life, entered the government's witness protection program and had been telling authorities all he knew about his career as a mob overseer of illegal gambling, particularly bolita.

In 1976 another form of gambling surfaced; it was called Racetrack Messenger Service. The first one that opened was called Pegasus. It was located in the loop on South Dearborn Street, second floor. A couple of attorneys were involved in the ownership of this scam, along with some other questionable characters. This proved to be one of the biggest headaches we would ever have. Mickey Kaplan, one of the attorneys, explained to us that they were accepting horse bets for races that were being run at Sportsman's racecourse in Cicero, Illinois. That's the only racetrack that they would accept wagers on. Kaplan explained that they were providing a service for anyone who bet. They would charge the bettor 10 percent of whatever they would bet. All the wagers were then brought to Sportsman's, and the wagers were bet at the windows at the track. The mutual tickets were then brought back to Pegasus, where they would be kept on file as proof that the wagers were in fact placed at the racetrack. The tickets would be checked at the end of the day to see who had won or lost their bets.

I knew one thing for sure: if this operation was being run by legitimate people, they must be paying street taxes to the outfit or the mob was running it. Regardless, we made a visit to Pegasus and found people waiting in line to make their bets at make shift windows. They were provided with racing forms, scratch sheets, pencils, and had free coffee and donuts.

The manager, whom I'll call Benny, gave us permission to check the wagers from the day before against the mutual tickets from the racetrack. They all checked out, and we couldn't find any discrepancies. Benny explained that they stopped taking wagers one hour before post time at the racetrack so that would give them enough time to place the wagers at the mutual windows. In my opinion, I thought they were bookmakers; my lieutenant agreed with me, so we arrested Benny for being a keeper of bets and keeper of a gambling house. Actually, I think this was what they wanted to make a test case in the circuit court. While the Pegasus case was pending in court before Judge David J. Shields, other messenger services began operating all over Chicago. The all had different names, such as Mr. Lucky's, Western Messenger, Stretch Runner, Finish Line Express, and on and on and on. We started to make wagers at as many of these messenger services as we could. We made our bets about ten minutes before the first race at Sportsman's Park; of course, there was no way anyone could get to the track before the race went off, and place the bets they had taken. We also kept the messenger services under surveillance to see if anyone left the place to go to the track. Forget about it.

Surveillances were set up at the pari-mutuel windows that had been set up at the track just for messenger services so they could place their wagers before the first race. At first a few runners showed up and made wagers at the windows, but that didn't last long. After a few weeks, nobody showed up at all.

They were very careful when it came to handling bets on trifectas, daily doubles, quinellas, etc. At this point in time, telephones were not allowed on the racetrack, and cell phones were not around yet. So the messenger services had some confederate set up at a pay phone in close proximity to the track where they would call him and give him all their trifecta bets and daily double bets and he would lay them off at the racetrack. That way they couldn't get hurt if there was a big winner.

There were some mob-controlled messenger services that just held on to the big bets, because if there happened to be a big winner, they just wouldn't pay off. They would tell the customer that their messenger was robbed on his way to the track and wasn't able to make the bet. There were some messenger services operated by what we called "Ma and Pa joints"; they actually did try and make a living on the 10 percent they would charge people to accept their bets. They didn't last too long. The outfit would then come around and make them an offer they couldn't refuse, and that was that.

I recall one of the independent messenger services that called themselves Track Shack messenger service. They were in a good location in the city and had a lot of customers. Naturally, the outfit just took it over with threats and intimidation. Both were well-known mob guys, Bernard "Pepe" Posner and an ex-cop William McGuire. They were both indicted for extortion by the federal government in 1978.

On the second floor of a building at 506 West Van Buren Street was the headquarters of the Finish Line Express messenger service. There were twenty women operating telephones on the second floor taking wagers from fifty-four different locations in the city and suburbs. Crime boss Dominic "Large" Cortina, a lieutenant to Jackie "the Lackey" Cerone, was observed at this location numerous times on our surveillances. Pepe Posner and William McGuire also frequented this location.

Another big operation was called Mr. Lucky's messenger service. Their main offices were located at 1867 East Seventy-first Street and 2130 South Indiana Avenue They controlled over twenty-one locations, mostly in the black areas. There were at least twenty women operating telephones at the Seventy-first Street location, where they were tabulating all the wagers for that day. We made raids at every messenger service that opened up; sometimes we would raid ten locations in one day.

One day we busted a vacant storefront at 2654 North Long Avenue, Chicago. Two mopes were answering four telephones, taking bets from some messenger services. This place was set up to make sure that in the event of a raid and when the police confiscated all the bets, the messenger service wouldn't have any records of them. Kind of an insurance policy, I guess.

Eventually, the IRS, the FBI and the Illinois Department of Law enforcement joined us in our quest to close these places up. In April 1977, we raided three nerve centers of the Finish Line Express and Mr. Lucky's. We recovered thousands of dollars of horse wagers that were supposed to be bet at the racetrack as well as forty-five women who were. accepting the bets over the phone, Dominic Cortina was found hiding behind a desk at Van Buren Street. Bernard "Pepe" Posner and William McGuire, who had both been linked to the crime syndicate, were also on the scene. Over $100,000 was seized as well. The Chicago Police's gambling unit had been hampered in the past from making raids at the same location more than once until their legality was decided by the courts. A test case filed against Pegasus, the first messenger service to start operations in Chicago, was before Circuit Court Judge David J. Shields for trial. It sure was taking a long time for this damn case to be heard. I always wondered about that.

On another occasion we raided eight messenger services operating under the name of Western Messenger Service. The locations were spread out all over the city: 5754 South Western Avenue, 5752 South Pulaski Road, 6057 West Belmont Avenue, 4757 North Clark Street, 5140 North Elston Avenue, 7116 West Higgins Road, 6007 West Irving Park Road, and 6848 West Grand Avenue.

Six people were indicted for operating this messenger service. Victor Spilotro, a brother of crime syndicate boss Anthony Spilotro, was indicted on gambling and tax charges. The others indicted were William Louis Tenuta, Louis Tenuta, June Martino, Penelope Riccio, and Emil Cibic.

After two years of investigation and aggravation with these bastards. A federal grand jury indicted fourteen persons on charges of conspiracy, gambling, and tax law violations, extortion, and operating illegal businesses in connection with offtrack betting messenger services in Chicago. The Illinois Supreme Court outlawed the services.

Some other raids that we had made in May and June 1978 where we confiscated large sums of money and voluminous gambling records resulted in the indictment of Anthony John Spilotro for Interstate Transportation in aid of racketeering and gambling. James Inendino for extortionate credit transaction. Inendino was sentenced to twenty years in the penitentiary. Spilotro, of course, was murdered with his brother Michael.

As aggravating as the messenger services were, it wasn't long before the outfit came up with another moneymaking scheme; it's called video poker machines. My guy Nick was involved with these machines and was the main culprit that started video poker machines in the Chicago area for his associates Sal and Carmen Bastone. These machines were all over South America under the control of the Chicago Outfit. Nick actually turned down an offer to run all the outfits gambling interests down there and stayed in town to get the machines operating here. It seems that the overseer of these operations was a Chicago Outfit guy by the name of Hymen "Red" Larner, who ran amusement machines until the heat came down on him and he went down to Panama.

As Nick tells it, video poker machines began showing up in the Chicago area in the late '70s. I remember it well. Nick had ten poker machines in the back room of his restaurant, and he made a fortune. The machines were legal to have and were licensed by the city. The only time they became illegal was when a bartender or anyone else pays off players for getting a certain number of points. Such as forty units on the machine would be worth ten bucks.

When the machines first came out, you could play them for a quarter. After they became popular, they changed the machines so that they would also accept $1, $5, $10, $20, up to $100 bills.

Larner was reported to be in charge of all the pinball machines, illegal slots, and other gambling devices in the southern suburbs in the '60s. He was also rumored to be involved in gambling operations in London and Panama. He was reported to be living in a house on top of a hill outside of Panama City. When Noriega was in power, Larner took care of him every month, according to reliable sources, because he didn't want any problem with his gambling operations.

When the video poker machines began to appear all over Chicago and suburbs, the mob was making a fortune not only in the Chicago area but in South America as well. My guy Nick was asked to do the bad guys a favor. Sal Bastone was the current outfit overseer of all the video poker machines in the Chicago area and was also connected to Red Larner in Panama. The outfit needed a reliable guy to meet a courier that would fly into O'Hare field from Miami Florida on the first of every month. The Miami flight was the last one of the day to come into Chicago, and the guy he would meet would be the last guy off the plane. Nick was told what the guy looked like and that he would be carrying a valise full of cash. Nick would then drive the courier to a motel on North Avenue in Melrose Park, Illinois. Bastone would be waiting for them in a certain room. The courier would give the valise to Bastone. Nick and the courier would then leave, and Nick would drive the courier to a house in Chicago Heights, Illinois. Nick took the job and agreed to be the chauffeur anytime to any place; besides, the money was pretty good, and it made him feel important.

The first time Nick met the plane, he thought the guy wasn't on the plane because everybody had gotten off, including the pilots and stewardesses. But then here came a little Italian man carrying a valise smiling at Nick. He told Nick his name was Alberto and that he stayed in the lavatory, which no one checked. He did this in case some federal agents may be waiting for him, and they would think that he didn't get on the plane in Miami, and they would leave.

All this secrecy was to protect the cash from Panama. Nick had started all the video poker machines for the outfit, and Sal and Carmen Bastone we're making a lot of money. Nick drove Alberto to the designated motel at North and Manheim roads in Melrose Park, Illinois. Nick and Alberto went to a room where Bastone was waiting for them. Alberto gave the valise to Bastone, who opened it in front of Nick and Alberto and piled the money on the bed and made several piles of money. Bastone told them that each pile was for a certain mob boss, and that he had to make sure that Joey got the biggest share of the proceeds. Nick learned later that Joey was Joe "Doves" Aiuppa, who was Bastone's boss at the time.

Nick drove Alberto to a house in Chicago Heights where he said his sister lived. He also claimed that he was related to a top mob boss, but that he now lived in Miami and was going back the next day. He told Nick that he would see him on the first of the month. Alberto told Nick that Carmen Bastone had been exiled to Spain temporarily to supervise the video poker machine factory the mob had there.

As hard as he tried, Nick was never able to find out how much money was coming into Chicago from South America. He was told by

Sal Bastone that the money was from Panama and other parts of South America that had video poker machines. The big guy down there was Hymen "Red" Larner, who had left Chicago years ago to avoid heat from the Senate hearings that were going on.

Video poker machines turned into one of the biggest sources of revenue for the outfit in years. The outfit flooded metropolitan Chicago with them, and things were good again. The machines were legal; every bar and restaurant that had them paid off on them. I remember raiding six different places in one day and confiscating at least thirty machines or more. But to be honest, I must admit that that crushing blow to the outfit's gambling enterprise was like pissing on the Chicago fire to try and put it out. Within four hours, they had replaced the machines in every place we had raided.

After I retired from Chicago I was asked to set up a gambling unit for the Cook County Sheriff's Police. It seems that Sheriff Mike Sheahan had a problem concerning gambling in the county. I accepted the assignment and for the next eight years caused some headaches for the mob. In 1996, for example, our vice unit effected 109 raids and confiscated 173 video poker machines as well as $89,798. That did not include outfit wire rooms. On a lot of our raids, we were accompanied my old friends in the Chicago Police Department's gambling unit. The more pressure we put on poker machine operations the smarter the bad guys got. They began to empty their machines every hour in case of a raid. Then there seemed to be a shortage of storage space where the machines were kept while the cases were pending in court. Then it was decided that we shouldn't seize the machines so there wouldn't be that problem. Another problem was that due to these arrests being misdemeanors, physical arrests were halted and replaced by the issuance of nontraffic summons. The reason given was that it was a cost-cutting measure and would free personnel to handle matters of higher priority in a department that was already overburdened.

It should be noted that these machines are all over the United States as well as other countries. I had occasion to be on a British Air Force base in Belize in 1990 and played the video poker machines that were there as well.

The state police in New Jersey completed an investigation on video poker machines, and reported that five machines alone generated $500,000 in net profit at one location in a fifteen-month period. I wonder if they had a storage problem.

In 1974, Illinois started the state lottery, which was supposed to reduce taxes, build roads, and improve the education system, and so on. Maybe it did help out the citizens of Illinois somewhat, but it also helped the Chicago Crime Syndicate enter a new way to make money.

It was easy; all they had to do was start taking bets on the daily lottery; pick three and pick four games. They would take bets from 5¢ to $5 to pick three or four correct lottery numbers. The winners were determined by the winning numbers of the Illinois state lottery drawing that was broadcast every night. One lottery ring operated for nine years on Chicago's South Side, West Side, the Southern suburbs, and in Gary, Indiana. Authorities said the enterprise was so sophisticated that it offered paid vacations and sick leaves to its employees.

Rueben Richardson, fifty-one, who headed an illegal lottery ring for eight years that netted more than $5 million from 1981-1989, pleaded guilty for his role in heading the illegal lottery ring. He became the ninth person to admit guilt in running the ring; the charges against Richardson carry a maximum penalty of ten years in prison and $500,000 in fines. Richardson and a Harvey resident, Linda Oaks, who previously pleaded guilty, were ringleaders of an organization that at its height employed fifty workers, and had a payroll of more than $30,000 a week, and acted as a credit union of sorts to employees granting them loans.

The ring paid out $600 for each dollar wagered on a three-number bet, $100 more than the state paid. Payout on a winning four-number bet was the same as the state's. However, the ring paid winners in cash and did not withhold taxes, making the illegal lottery more appealing than the state's.

The business operated from numerous wire rooms, which were often in private homes. Bettors gave their wagers to "writers," who worked the streets and collected bets wireroom clerks would then call the writers' daily.

Collectors picked up lottery receipts from the writers and paid off any winning wagers. The lottery ring kept $100,000 in cash on hand to pay off winning bets.

After we raided this operation numerous times in 1988 and 1989, Det Bill Mundee accumulated enough intelligence to execute search warrants at numerous locations throughout the Chicago area, which resulted in the enterprise's downfall. During those raids we seized more than $2 million in lottery wagers as well as shredding machines, telephones, tape recorders, and fax machines.

10 housewives, owner charged with gambling

By Bob Wiedrich

Chicago police couldn't believe what they found when they entered the basement of a home on the Far South Side Thursday evening: 10 women, all housewives, were operating a central tabulating center that was recording bets made on the Illinois State Lottery.

The housewives and the owner of the house were charged with syndicated gambling, a felony.

"We were so surprised by what we found, we almost didn't know what to do," said Sgt. Donald Herion of the police gambling unit.

Based on information from an informant, Detectives Bill Mundee, Dan Dugan and Mike Nealis of the gambling unit obtained a warrant to enter the basement of a single-family home at 9964 S. Winston Ave.

When they entered Thursday evening, they found 10 women stationed at 10 card tables, each recording and tabulating bets on the Illinois State Lottery.

Herion said records indicated that the tabulating center recorded bets from a citywide network of walking bookies taking wagers on the daily Illinois State Lottery games for as little as 25 cents each.

The women used tape recorders attached to the telephones to maintain permanent records of the bets.

After studying ledgers, police estimated the annual gross of the tabulating center at $10 million.

"I thought it was a Bible school session they were holding down there," said Rebecca Stoxstell, 64, owner of the home.

Later, she told police that she was aware of what was going on in the basement and that she rented the space for $300 a month.

"This is the most professional operation we ever have found," Herion said.

Posted on a bulletin board was a set of rules governing the conduct of employees. One rule warned that anyone reporting for work after 4:10 p.m. more than twice in a week would be "docked one hour, supervisors included."

"After 4:15 p.m. you'll be sent home without pay," the employees were admonished.

Still another rule governed vacations and days off for workers in the seven-day-a-week operation.

A suggestion box on the corner of a table contained one plea from a worker that the basement should be equipped with a microwave oven.

The women will appear in court Sept. 6.

4 DIGIT - PAY OFF

STRAIGHT — LIMIT .50

.05......250.00	.20.....1000.00	.35.....1750.00
.10......500.00	.25.....1250.00	.40.....2000.00
.15......750.00	.30.....1500.00	.45.....2250.00
		.50.....2500.00

BOX

$	LIMIT $12 24-WAY 1-2-3-4	LIMIT $6 12-WAY 1-2-2-3	LIMIT $3 6 WAY 1-2-1-2	LIMIT $2 4 WAY 1-1-1-2
.05	10.00	21.00	42.00	62.00
.10	21.00	42.00	83.00	125.00
.15	31.00	62.00	125.00	187.00
.20	42.00	83.00	167.00	250.00
.25	52.00	104.00	208.00	312.00
.30	62.00	125.00	250.00	375.00
.35	73.00	146.00	295.00	437.00
.40	83.00	166.00	333.00	500.00
.45	94.00	187.00	375.00	562.00
.50	104.00	208.00	416.00	625.00
.55	114.00	229.00	458.00	687.00
.60	125.00	250.00	500.00	750.00
.65	135.00	270.00	541.00	812.00
.70	146.00	291.00	583.00	875.00
.75	156.00	312.00	625.00	937.00
.80	166.00	333.00	666.00	1000.00
.85	177.00	354.00	708.00	1062.00
.90	187.00	374.00	750.00	1125.00
.95	198.00	395.00	791.00	1187.00
1.00	208.00	416.00	833.00	1250.00
2.00	416.00	832.00	1666.00	2500.00
3.00	624.00	1248.00	2500.00	
4.00	832.00	1664.00		
5.00	1040.00	2070.00		
6.00	1248.00	2496.00		
7.00	1456.00			
8.00	1664.00			
9.00	1872.00			
10.00	2080.00			
11.00	2288.00			
12.00	2496.00			

LOOK HERE! PAY-OFF AMOUNT: $600 — $1.00

DAILY LOTTERY
PAYMENT SCHEDULE

Amount	Straight	Box	6-Way Box	3 Way Box
.05	$ 30.00	$ .05	$ 4.50	$ 9.00
.10	60.00	.10	9.00	18.00
.15	90.00	.15	13.50	27.00
.20	120.00	.20	18.00	36.00
.25	150.00	.25	23.00	46.00
.30	180.00	.30	27.00	54.00
.35	210.00	.35	32.00	64.00
.40	240.00	.40	36.50	73.00
.45	270.00	.45	41.00	82.00
.50	300.00	.50	45.50	91.00
.55	330.00	.55	50.00	100.00
.60	360.00	.60	54.50	109.00
.65	390.00	.65	59.00	118.00
.70	420.00	.70	64.00	128.00
.75	450.00	.75	68.00	136.00
.80	480.00	.80	73.00	146.00
.85	510.00	.85	77.00	154.00
.90	540.00	.90	82.00	164.00
.95	570.00	.95	86.50	173.00
1.00	600.00	1.00	91.00	182.00
2.00	1200.00	2.00	182.00	364.00
3.00	1800.00	3.00	273.00	546.00
4.00	2400.00	4.00	364.00	728.00
5.00	3000.00	5.00	455.00	910.00

Limit $5.00

We also learned that this type of gambling in Chicago was also connected to Wisconsin, Minnesota, and Indiana, where they used computers to transmit gambling information. In Gary, Indiana, the illegal lottery would accept food stamps in lieu of cash, but if you wanted to make a dollar bet, it would cost two dollars in food stamps.

In July 1988 we were surprised at what we found in a single-family home at 9964 South Winston Avenue on the South Side of Chicago. Ten women, all housewives, were operating a central tabulating center that was recording bets made on the Illinois State Lottery. Each woman was seated at a card table with a telephone and tape recorder recording bets on the lottery from a citywide network of walking bookies, who took wagers as small as 25¢ each.

After studying ledgers that we found hidden in the basement ceiling, we estimated the annual gross of this tabulating center at $10 million. The woman who owned the house told us that she rented the basement to some women for $300 a month. They told her that they were holding Bible school sessions in the basement. All the women were charged with syndicated gambling, a felony. Rebecca, the owner of the house, was also charged with being a keeper of a gambling place.

There was no doubt that this illegal lottery was making millions of dollars and the State of Illinois was losing a lot of revenue because of it. We continued investigating this type of gambling and made numerous other raids in Chicago as well as Phoenix, South Holland, Harvey, Markham, Dixmoor, Dolton, and Calumet City. Of course, something like this had to have the OK from the Chicago Outfit for it to operate. The majority of the people we locked up claimed that all they knew was that their job was to take bets on the phones, and didn't know whom they worked for. But we did manage to get some information about who was really behind this gambling operation. The information we obtained was very reliable from sources who reported that two white guys who appeared to be of Italian descent would meet with a representative of the lottery operation once a month on the southeast corner of Seventy-ninth and Racine Avenue. At that time a money drop would be made. "Street Tax." How much money was involved was not known to our source.

We notified the gaming commission of the Illinois State Lottery that we were finding more evidence that people who played the lottery were placing their wagers with mob bookmakers. The fact of the matter was that it was more convenient for them to place their bets with a bookmaker who would come to their house if requested to do so. The bookmaker also paid better odds than the state, and there were no taxes involved. I suggested that law enforcement, the state police, should join forces with the Chicago Police's vice control division to try and eradicate this growing problem before it gets out of hand.

They agreed that it was a problem and that something should be done. They told us that they would try and put something together to combat this problem, and they would get back to us. I never did hear from them.

When the cases finally came to trial in 1994 before Judge Marvin Aspen in the U.S. district court, testimony revealed what a sophisticated illegal operation it was. The employees got paid vacations and sick leaves. The only thing they didn't get was a pension plan.

One ringleader, Reuben Richardson of South Holland, learned the tricks of the trade from his father, who has engaged in such activities his entire life. He was sentenced to twenty-five months in prison; his associate, Linda Oakes of Harvey, who ran the lucrative Indiana operation, was given a twenty-one-month prison term. Richardson's daughter Jacqueline and Quincella Stanley, both involved in the ring, were each sentenced to six months in prison and six months work release. The others involved received lesser sentences, depending on their positions in the operation.

18 CHICAGO SUN-TIMES, Friday, June 16, 1989

Cops seize 9 homes, store in lottery scam

By Phillip J. O'Connor and Adrienne Drell

Chicago police and U.S. marshals Thursday seized a liquor store and nine homes allegedly used in a multimillion-dollar illegal lottery on the South Side and in the south suburbs that employed dozens of workers.

The operation, a copycat of the Illinois lottery, siphoned off as much as $5 million a year that would have gone to the state, investigators said.

The $200,000 house of two alleged ringleaders, Reuben Richardson, 50, and his wife, Margaret Lockhart, 45, of 1109 W. 107th Pl., was among homes seized.

Also seized was their Lockhart Food & Liquors, 1139 W. 79th St., which served as "an administrative center" for the ring, according to an affidavit filed by Chicago police in U.S. District Court to support the seizures.

The affidavit identified the third ringleader as Linda Oakes, whose 10-unit apartment building at 14720 S. Page in Harvey also was seized.

No arrests were made at any of the locations because Lockhart tipped off residents of buildings to destroy any incriminating possessions, investigators said. Because no criminal charges had been filed against the couple, investigators said they didn't halt her calls.

Last November, police raided a $100,000 condominium at 500

Park Ave. in Calumet City, another property seized Thursday, and found records for an $11,000-a-week payroll of 37 ring employees, said Cmdr. Michael Hoke of police vice control.

Other properties seized Thursday on the ground they were used in illegal gambling were 9964 S. Winston and 1030 W. 108th Pl. in Chicago and 14906 Lincoln, Harvey; 241 Joliet, Dixmoor; 15529 S. Vincennes, Phoenix, and 3016 W. Nottingham, Markham.

Richardson and Lockhart were arrested last February in raids at their home and liquor store in which police found eight unregistered guns and utility bills that the couple paid for other locations allegedly used as bet collection centers, investigators said.

In the past year, Hoke said, police arrested a total of 40 people involved in the ring in other raids.

The ring's work rules were posted on walls at bet collection centers, along with days off and vacation schedules, Hoke said.

"They operated every day of the year except for Christmas Day," he said.

Ring members took bets ranging from 25 cents to $50, with winning numbers based on the Illinois daily and Pick-4 lotteries, police said.

Patrons preferred the ring's operation to the state lottery because winners were paid more and the Internal Revenue Service is not notified of winnings, investigators said.

Law enforcement officials seize Lockhart Food & Liquors, 1139 W. 79th St., Thursday for alleged illegal gambling activities.

```
LOTTERY LINE
976-2020
35¢ per call.*

WEATHER PHONE®
976-1212
25¢ per call.*

* Plus applicable tolls.
By Phone Programs Illinois, Inc.
```

29-March-94

Boss of sophisticated lottery pleads guilty

By Joseph A. Kirby
TRIBUNE STAFF WRITER

A South Holland man Tuesday pleaded guilty to two counts of conspiracy for his role in heading an illegal lottery ring that operated for nine years on Chicago's South Side, the southern suburbs and Gary, Ind.

Authorities said the enterprise was so sophisticated that it offered paid vacations and sick leave to its employees.

Reuben Richardson, 51, became the ninth and final person to admit guilt in the running of a business that authorities said took bets on numbers drawn daily in the Illinois State Lottery Pick-3 and Pick-4 games and netted more than $5 million from 1981-89.

The charges against Richardson carry a maximum penalty of 10 years in prison and $500,000 in fines. But Assistant U.S. Atty. Matthew Schneider, who prosecuted the case, said lighter sentencing guidelines could lower those penalties. U.S. District Judge Marvin Aspen set sentencing for June 16.

Authorities said Richardson and Harvey resident Linda Oaks, who previously pleaded guilty, were ringleaders of an organization that at its height employed in excess of 50 workers, had a weekly payroll of more than $30,000 and acted as a credit union of sorts to employees, granting them loans.

The ring paid out $600 for each $1 wagered on a winning 3-number bet, $100 more than the state lottery. Payout on a winning 4-number bet was the same as the state's. However, the ring paid winners in cash and did not withhold taxes, making the illegal lottery more appealing than the state's.

Authorities estimate the ring withheld more than $1 million in taxes from the IRS.

The business operated from numerous "wire rooms," which were often in private homes. Bettors gave their wagers to "writers," who worked the streets and collected bets. The writers would then be called daily by wire room clerks.

Collectors picked up lottery receipts from the writers and paid off any winning wagers.

The lottery ring kept $100,000 in cash on hand to pay off winning bets.

A series of raids by police in 1988 and 1989 resulted in the enterprise's downfall. During those raids, authorities discovered more than $1.75 million in gambling wager slips, a shredding machine and copies of the ring's formal operating rules.

Richardson's daughter, Jacqueline, 30, of Phoenix, Ill., who was in charge of the day-to-day operations of the ring, also has pleaded guilty.

Source: Sun Times and Donald Herion

Another form of gambling is commonly known as parlay cards. It's another way to bet your money on a game of chance where the odds are against you. Parlay cards have been around Chicago ever since I can remember. The most popular parlay cards are college and professional football games that are listed on the card with the point spread. There are also college and professional basketball cards and baseball cards, which are not that popular.

Football cards are normally printed on Monday or Tuesday at a secret location. The printer usually runs a legitimate printing business but makes a lot of money printing the cards for some outfit guy. Usually the outfit guy will get the point spreads on the coming weekend games and gives them to the printer. The number of parlay card runners will determine how many cards will be printed for the coming week. I've been involved in at least twenty different raids on printing presses where they were printing anywhere from twenty-five thousand to fivehundred thousand cards a week.

The cards are given to people who work in factories, offices, high schools, taverns, truck drivers, or anyone who would like to make 25 percent on whatever they booked for the week. The *Chicago Tribune* had some paper delivery drivers handling parlay cards and would distribute them to all the newspaper stands in Chicago and the suburbs.

The runners would give out the cards all week long to their players; the bottom part of the card had a stub and a number that would coincide with the number on the top of the card. The stub had to be turned in to the runner with his bets and money before the first game listed on the card begins. The minimum bet is three teams; all the teams have to win, ties lose. If your three teams win, you will be paid 6 for 1, if you bet four teams, you would be paid 11 for 1. You can bet up to ten teams, who all must win for you to get back 150 for 1. There is a consolation prize if you pick 9 out of 10, 20 for 1.

Bets usually run from $1 up to $50. The runner deducts his 25 percent off the top before he turns in the stubs to his boss. We have found that some runners handle up to $3,000 a week, which gives him $750 tax free, and he doesn't have to worry about the winners.

Investigating parlay cards can be an aggravating experience. It involves a lot of time, patience; a lot of tailing people is involved in the operation. The main target is the people printing the cards and the location of the printing press. Because the cards are distributed usually on Monday and Tuesday, they are the only days that you have a chance to follow a bettor to see where he gets his cards from. Once that is determined, a surveillance of the person or place that is dispensing the cards must be set up to try and learn how the person or place is getting their cards. This usually means hours of surveillance. The subject that you're watching must be kept under surveillance constantly until you find out who is supplying the cards to him. At that point, this supplier must be kept under observation until his source is found. This investigation can only be done on Monday or Tuesday when the cards are printed and distributed; obviously it will take weeks to locate all the bad guys involved.

The other part of the investigation involves finding who gets the bet stubs. The stubs have to be turned into the bookmaker "runner," usually on Friday night or Saturday morning. The runners who distribute the cards on Monday or Tuesday collects the stubs and the money. Some runners are in business for themselves and keep the stubs, but they have to worry about how many winners his bettors have weekly.

The runners who are in business for themselves buy the parlay cards from the distributor for anywhere from $20 to $40 per thousand; they distribute them and book all the bets they collect. Of course, they are running the risk of the mob finding out about their little enterprise and could probably catch a good beating, or worse. They would then have to pay street taxes, of course.

I remember one parlay card operation we broke up was in 1968. My partner at the time was a great cop, Jimmy Hanrahan. Jimmy and I had used our own private vehicles to tail people. The Chicago Police Department didn't have any undercover vehicles for that type of surveillance at the time; their unmarked cars all looked the same.

After weeks of tailing bad guys, we finally were able to find the boss of this particular operation and began following him around. His name was Big Tony Verlick, who liked to hang around downtown Chicago at Jackson Boulevard and Wabash Avenue.

To tail someone from downtown Chicago during the day was a real bitch, but we gave it a shot anyway.

The first time we tried it, we lost him within two blocks; that's after watching him for five hours. The next week we did a lot better and managed to follow him out of the Loop, which meant committing a lot of traffic violations, such as beating red lights and stop signs, and speeding. We also got extremely lucky and tailed him to 2421 Green Bay Road, North Chicago (Lake County). Vogue Printers was located at that address.

Source: *Chicago Police Dep't*

    This, of course, was way out of our jurisdiction, but we decided to keep Big Tony under surveillance from a safe distance away to see what we could see. Sure as hell, after a couple of hours, Tony began loading his vehicle with some large boxes that he put in the trunk. Some other vehicles showed up, and they too came out of the printer with large boxes and put them in their vehicles and drive away; one of the cars was from Wisconsin.

    The last vehicle to show up belonged to a man by the name of Leslie Sugarman at 2805 West Hollywood Avenue, Chicago, Illinois. Big Tony came out of the printers with two large boxes and gave them to Sugarman, who put them in the trunk of his car. We decided to follow Sugarman to see what he was going to do with the parlay cards. He drove south on Route 41 to Chicago and parked in front of his first-floor apartment. Sugarman carried the boxes into his apartment where he could be seen from the street.

    Sugarman's residence was watched, and from 4:00 PM to 7:00 PM we observed twelve different vehicles driving up to this residence and entering Sugarman's residence, staying a few minutes, and leaving with bags or packets. They then drove off.

The good news was this location was in Chicago, our jurisdiction. The Chicago Police Department wouldn't let us get involved outside the city limits. It didn't matter that the cards were flooding Chicago.

After explaining what we had uncovered to our lieutenant, he told us to call the FBI and to let them handle it. That was a real kick in the ass, as far as we were concerned, but orders were orders. I met with some FBI agents and gave them all the information we had about Big Tony and Sugarman, where the press was located, and about the vehicles that showed up at Sugarman's residence. My only request of them was that if and when they decided to raid this operation, if we could accompany them on the raids. No problem they said, we'll keep in touch and let you know when we do it.

Weeks passed and we didn't hear anything from the FBI, until one day we saw an article in the newspaper relating how the FBI had smashed a major gambling operation at the Vogue Printers in North Chicago. They confiscated five hundred thousand football parlay cards and made several arrests. There was no mention about the Chicago Police Gambling Unit being involved in the investigation. Surprise, surprise. When we gave the FBI the name of employees that worked at the Vogue Printers, we told them that a chief petty officer who was stationed at the Great Lakes Naval Center worked there on a part-time basis. The fact of the matter was that the FBI decided to interview the chief and requested his cooperation concerning the printing of the football parlay cards and Big Tony's involvement. Rumor had it that the chief was told to cooperate with the FBI or there was a good chance he could be shipped to Vietnam. The chief decided to be cooperative with the FBI, of course.

It seemed that the FBI also interviewed other people in places where Big Tony hung out and asked what they knew about him. Naturally, word got back to Big Tony that the "G" was asking about him and parlays cards. Well, Big Tony figured out that this was not a good thing and decided to do the last week and then close up. Big Tony notified the printer that it was the last week for the cards. At that point the chief heard about it and, not wanting to fight the Vietcong, called the FBI and told them that this was the last week for the cards. The FBI couldn't get a search warrant that fast so they went to the local police and asked them to get a warrant. Hence, the raid was made and the investigation was over.

I don't have any idea why the FBI interviewed people who were acquainted with Big Tony; it seems to me that there was a chance they might just mention this to him, which could alert him that the FBI had him under investigation. I was a little disturbed over this because we were about to bust Leslie Sugarman and twelve runners who were associated with his operation. Now that the printer got busted, Sugarman wasn't able to get his cards, so we weren't able to make any arrests.

Due to the fact that Sugarman didn't get busted by the FBI, maybe he thought that he was safe and that no one knew about him. Being a curious guy, I decided to keep Sugarman's residence under surveillance the following Tuesday evening. Well, guess what? Sugarman arrived home and removed some bundles from the trunk of his car and brought them into his apartment. Unless he had been grocery shopping at Dominick's, it looked as if it was business as usual. For the next two hours I watched the same cavalcade of vehicles park by his residence, enter his apartment, and come out with bags and packages, and then drive away. Obviously, Sugarman was back in business, and Big Tony found another friendly printer – money talks and bullshit walks.

I notified my lieutenant of what I discovered, and he again told me to call the FBI to make them aware of the situation. I called the FBI and spoke to Vince InSerra, the supervisor of squad C-1. I told him about Sugarman and the runners who were still dealing the parlay cards. He then told me that William Roemer, a special agent in his squad, had kept Sugarman's location under observation and reported that there wasn't any activity at all. Apparently, the FBI had rented an apartment across the street from Sugarman's residence to keep it under surveillance; maybe Special Agent Roemer was watching the wrong apartment. Special Agent Roemer was the author of several books when he retired; one was titled *Man Against the Mob*.

The following week, November 26, 1968, Jim Hanrahan and I set up surveillance on Sugarman's residence, with other members of the gambling unit set up in the area. When a runner would leave Sugarman's residence with his parlay cards, we would notify gambling unit squad which way he was going so that they could stop him several blocks away from Sugarman's residence to avoid any heat in the area.

Everything worked out as planned, with no screwups. We made ten raids and confiscated thousands of parlay cards and stubs along with a large amount of U.S. currency. It was a pleasure to put handcuffs on Sugarman, who turned out to be a full-time licensed pharmacist. He denied having any knowledge of parlay cards

The main bad guys were indicted for conspiracy to commit gambling and gambling. The others were charged with being keeper of bets and promoting a lottery. All were found guilty in circuit court.

Another form of gambling that is most lucrative for the outfit is poker games. Not video poker games but games like seven-card stud and Texas hold-em. The mob usually operates these games in private residences, mostly in suburban residential streets. The patrons are usually trusted and reliable people. They are given code names that they can whisper into the intercom to gain entrance.

The particular game I'm going to tell you about was located on the second floor of a yellow brick single-family home in a quiet residential neighborhood in a suburb of Chicago, Elmwood Park, Illinois. At the time, the game had prospered for about five years at the same location. A good friend of mine who liked to play poker verified this and played in a seven-card stud game there a few nights.

It was estimated that the gambling joint pumps between $2.8 million and $6.7 million annually into the coffers of gambling bosses. I had the privilege of raiding a few of these games through the years and busted mob guys like Harry Aleman, Butch Petrocelli, John Manzella, and Jimmy Inendino, who were running the games for the outfit. This game was only one of several such operations scattered throughout Chicago and the suburbs. The marathon game at the Elmwood Park house usually opened in the evening of one day and runs for three or four days round-the-clock. If the action gets hot, however, the game can last for as many as seven consecutive days, with the house providing customers hot meals, sandwiches, and even a couch on which to flop for a few hours' rest.

The staying power of customers, my friend said, is near Herculean as they indulge in such favorites as seven-card stud and Texas hold-em. The betting structure is from $10 to $20 on the turn of a card. Some of the players will remain at the table for as many as twenty-four hours without rest, pausing only to attend such necessities as going to the bathroom. Others though will sit in for only six to eight hours and depart when their luck goes bad.

The guys who stay and stay are usually the guys who are losing and trying to get back their money. 'The smart players get in and get out."

To an uninformed observer, the game doesn't sound like much – just eight to ten players seated around a large octagonal table in what ordinarily would be the dining room of a second-floor apartment.

The game represents a multimillion-dollar-a-year gold mine for the mob in exchange for a minimal investment. Here is how it works.

Each pot in the game averages $800, of which the house takes 5 percent, or $40, for services. It is estimated that there are, on an average, twenty hands playing an hour, generating twenty pots.

That much action yields the house $19,200 a day. If the game lasts only three days, the house grosses $57,600. A seven-day game produces $134,400. Those two estimates projected over a year, excluding the two weeks when the game traditionally is closed for vacation, result in potential annual gross profits ranging from $2,880,000 to $6,720,000, reported by a reliable source.

From that gross, expenses for salaries of the two to four house employees must be deducted, as well as the cost of refreshments, food, and other overhead. The house employees are reported to be paid about $50 for a ten- to twelve-hour shift, much of which they spend watching television or reading when not attending to the comfort of players.

During the early morning hours, when the number of players sometimes lags, one or two of the house workers will sit in on the game as shills so that interest in the contest doesn't lessen. They play with house money and often get to keep a share of any winnings as a bonus; my source told me about the well-stocked kitchen next to the card room that provides cold cuts, soft drinks, coffee, wine, and liquor. Most players don't touch the hard stuff, because they want to keep their wits about them.

The bad guys also provided transportation to customers, so there wouldn't be a lot of cars parked in the area of the poker game that might arouse suspicion. When I was with the Chicago Police Gambling Unit, we didn't have any jurisdiction at that time to investigate illegal card games, so the next best thing I could do was to give the information I had to a crime reporter, Bob Wiedrich of the *Chicago Tribune*.

He wrote a story about the secret game; I'm sure when it appeared in the *Tribune* the bad guys decided to find another place to operate. Sports gambling is by far the biggest source of revenue for the crime syndicate, and it's getting bigger. Internet gambling has caught on and is more popular than ever. There has never been a public outcry for law enforcement to eradicate gambling in any form; most people think it's a victimless crime, anyway. Well, if it is, I would like someone to tell me how all the dead guys I have seen in the trunks of cars got there.

I must admit that the outfit has slowed down a lot, and they don't whack as many people or associates as they used to. They realize it causes heat when bodies start turning up all over town. But then they could still be up to their tricks; if they whack somebody and don't want the body found, it won't be found. All it will be is a missing person case.

I busted bookmakers for forty years. A lot of them were connected directly with the mob; others were what we called independent bookmakers who split their action with the outfit fifty-fifty. Then there were independent bookmakers like Hal Smith or Bob Plummer, who were tortured and murdered and stuck in the trunk of their own car.

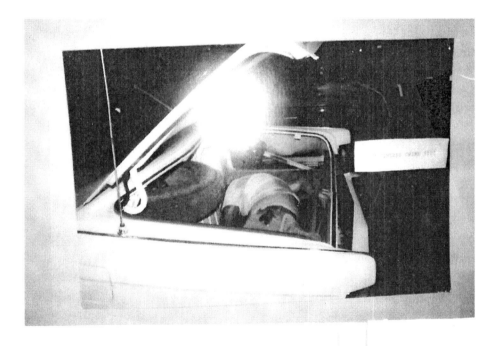

Bob Plummer
Whacked by Rocky Infelise

Source: Chicago Police Dep't

They didn't believe in paying the outfit "street taxes." There were a lot of other guys who were whacked by the outfit – some mob guys, some bettors, and some informants involved in gambling like Nick "Kegee" Galanos. Kegee was shot in the head numerous times in his own home. The sad part of it was Kegee was five foot five and weighed over 400 pounds; he went on a diet for health reasons and lost about

240 pounds. Maybe the mob didn't know that he had gone on a diet, that's why they whacked him at home. They probably thought there was no way to put him in the trunk of his car; he was too heavy.

Sports gambling is sometimes called a hobby with thrills. Betting is also referred to as "action." And action is what it's all about. Football is the most popular sport to bet on, both college and professional. The next would be basketball and events like March Madness. Baseball is not real popular for bookmakers, neither is hockey. But if you bet on the Internet, they will handle anything. Even though it's against the law to bet on sports anywhere but Nevada. The majority of the island bookmakers are part of the mob, such as the largest operation headquartered in the Dominican Republic. Their handle is $1billion a year with profits of nearly $20 million, according to government sources.

It is illegal to accept bets from the United States, nothing much changed after the raid, except for the address and the toll free rollover 800 numbers that were running bills up to $50,000 month.

When the headquarters got raided by the FBI and the local police, the place was closed down, but the operation never lost a day's action. It seems that they had an alternate location all set up ready to go in case something happened to the main headquarters.

It's amazing how popular gambling on sports is. I had an opportunity to look into an alleged gambling operation going wide open in a small town called NaPlate, Illinois, located at ninety miles from Chicago. Population of about six hundred citizens with three taverns located on the main street in town. At the time, I was working for the sheriff of Cook County in charged of an undercover vice unit. I had received an anonymous letter from a citizen of NaPlate, who explained that illegal gambling was operating wide open and the crime syndicate was in control of it.

Being a curious guy, I took a ride down to NaPlate on a Saturday during football season. This was like an Andy Griffith town "Mayberry," with one main street. Sure enough, there were three taverns, and it seems that all that were parked in front of each of them were pickup trucks. I decided to videotape – what if anything was happening in the bars? – so I put on an undercover video camera that fit nicely under my jacket. Each bar was filled with people. Some were studying parlay cards which were stacked up on a few tables. Others were looking at sports schedules, making out bets and giving them to the man and woman behind the bar. Telephones were ringing and answered by another guy who was giving out the line and writing down football bets on a legal pad. Then there were customers who were playing video poker machines.

The video camera I was wearing had a small lens, which was in the middle of a zero on the front of the jacket. I managed to tape all three bars without being detected by any of the rednecked patrons. I was a little shocked by the amount of action the bars handled in such a small town. I did learn that they also bet on the local high school football games with point spreads for every game. I don't know if this type of gambling goes on in every small town in Illinois, but somebody ought to check things out just for the hell of it.

When I started working gambling years ago, it was a lot easier to catch these guys than it is today. Wire rooms were always tough to find. The bad guys had to have telephones to operate their business, so they were vulnerable to get busted if they weren't careful. We could get the listing of a telephone number through Illinois Bell Security if we gave them a subpoena. Bookmakers have to give their phone numbers to their bettors, of course, and then it was our job to find the bettors and convince them that they were dealing in an evil business and they should give us the wire room number he's calling.

Mob's Biggest Sports Wireroom

City police hit jackpot in major gambling bust

By Laurie Goering

Chicago police said they broke up one of the largest gambling operations in the city's history Saturday, arresting four men—including two identified as city workers—whose alleged sophisticated operation took in up to $1 million a day.

Police took more than $300,000 in bets following the raid, as five cellular phones in the downtown apartment wire room rang continuously with individual bets of up to $5,000, said Sgt. Don Herion of the Police Department's gambling unit.

"It's a gigantic operation," said Herion, who said that most raids target one-person operations with one or two phones. "I've been doing gambling [raids] for 30 years, and this is the biggest operation I've ever seen."

Among those arrested and charged with felony syndicated gambling were Jimmy Rodich, 42, of 2555 S. Lowe Ave., whom police identified as the 1st Ward Streets and Sanitation Department superintendent, and Charles Settino, 54, of 3439 S. Wallace St., a city Department of General Services employee, Herion said.

However, 1st Ward Ald. Theodore Mazola said Anthony Flando, not Rodich, is ward superintendent.

The 1st Ward has been the focus of a federal corruption investigation, codenamed Operation Gambat, since at least 1986. Former 1st Ward Ald. Fred Roti and the ward's Democratic secretary, Pat Marcy, are awaiting trial on bribery charges.

Mark Farina, a Streets and Sanitation spokesman, said Saturday that he was unable to confirm whether Rodich worked for the department until Monday. But a September 1991 city payroll listing showed that Rodich was a Streets and Sanitation laborer at that time.

That payroll listing showed that Settino was a motor truck driver for the Streets and Sanitation Department.

Also arrested and charged in the raid were Charles Coco, 45, of 5720 S. Parkside Ave., who police said was the head of the wire room operation, and Sam Ranola, 32, of 3304 S. Parnell.

Police arrest 4 suspects in gambling ring

By Lori Rotenberk
Staff Writer

Police Saturday morning arrested four men, including two city employees, on charges of running a $1 million-a-day gambling operation from an apartment in the McClurg Court complex at 600 N. McClurg.

Sgt. Don Herion of the Chicago Police gambling unit said the arrests were made shortly after 11 a.m. when officers emerged from hiding under a staircase and pushed their way into the apartment after one of the suspects opened the door.

The accused were charged with syndicated gambling, a felony, as well as possession of wagers, keeping a gambling house and transmission of wagers, all misdemeanors.

In custody were Charles Coco, 45, of the 5700 block of South Parkside; Sam Ronala, 32, of the 3300 block of South Parnell, and city workers Jimmy Rodich, 42, of the 2500 block of South Lowe, a 1st Ward superintendent, and Charles Settino, 54, of the 3400 block of South Wallace, an employee of the General Services Department.

Police found beepers, 12 mobile phones, a fax machine and stacks of bets printed on flash paper, Herion said.

Even as police investigated, phone wagers were rolling in, "many for $5,000," said Herion. "I took calls for at least $50,000 myself. We expect more to come in tonight because of the Bears game."

600 N. McClurg Ct.

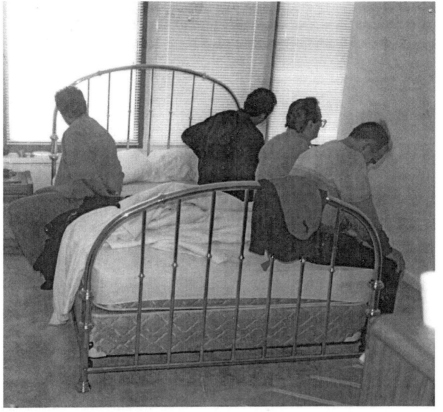

A lot of times the bettor would tell us to have sex with ourselves, but if we presented our case to him in a way that he could understand, he would gladly give us the number. For some reason, some bettors really believe that if they gave the police the telephone number of the wire room, they would wind up in a trunk.

When we got the name and address of the wire room number, the game was on. I found that some bookmakers are really clever and took precautions to keep from getting busted. If the phone number was listed to an apartment in a multi-apartment building like Apt 3B, we would have that apartment number on our search warrant, but Mr. Slick ran the phone line to another apartment, like 1B. While we were knocking down the door at 3B, the bad guy was probably taking it on high down the street.

Then another pain in the ass became popular; it is called call forwarding. It took us a while to figure out how to combat this system; needless to say, we found a few empty apartments before we got smart.

Next came beepers. The bookmaker would give his bettors his pager number; they would page him, and he would call them back to get their action. If we got a pager number, we would check for the subscriber information, forget about it. Most of the time the pager was listed to a post office box somewhere. But I figured out a way to locate the slick guy. We had an unlisted phone number we had access to. The phone company came out with another gimmick, caller ID. I would page the bad guy and put in our unlisted phone number and hoped that he would call back, and just maybe we would get his number. It worked about half the time.

Then the real headache came into the picture, cellular phones. The first cell phones we ran into were bag phones; they were clumsy and didn't work all that well, but good enough to aggravate us. They cost about $2,500 each. It wasn't long before they came out in a valise and cost about $1,500, and worked a lot better.

At the time, we would check a telephone number we came across that was being used to take bets. Not knowing that it was a cell phone, we would get the name and address and get a search warrant for the location and find that it was a vacant lot.

We would also check telephone records listed to a cell phone; if the bookmaker was slick, he would never make any outgoing calls on his cell phone. We checked phone records that showed all the incoming calls to that cell phone, and they were all during bookmaking hours. Not one outgoing call made.

Chapter 63

Lenny "I'm a Mob Guy" Palumbo

Lenny Palumbo is a mob wannabee, wears a gold chain and a phony pinkie ring. He likes to watch *The Godfather* movies at least once a week. He hangs around bars on Rush Street and acts like Joe Pesci in *Goodfellas*; in other words, he's another pooch dago going nowhere except maybe in the joint or a trunk.

My partner Phil and I had the opportunity to bust Lenny for reckless driving, trying to evade the police and for being another outfit jagoff. Lenny apparently had the idea that he was a good wheelman because when we were going to put a stop on him on Grand Avenue at Racine, he gave us the finger and took off. To be honest, we really had no reason to stop the mope except on general principles, but anybody who refuses to stop when the police order you too must have a reason. Anyway, the chase was on and got a little scary at times when Lenny started to drive up and down alleys and over sidewalks. Fortunately, it was 3:00 AM and there wasn't much traffic or people walking around. The longer the chase went on, the madder we got at Lenny. I guess he didn't know the neighborhood too well because he drove down a dead-end street and was trapped.

We kind of rammed his Cadillac a little just to make sure he wasn't going anywhere. We told him to get out of the car with his hands up; we explained to him that if we couldn't see his hands, we could accidentally trip and just might blow his fucking head off. Apparently, we got Lenny's attention, because he did exactly what we told him and got out of the car. He was a typical bad guy, five foot six, 150 pounds, wearing a black sports coat, white sports shirt with the first three buttons opened so everybody could see the hair on his chest and his gold necklace.

When we looked closer, we found that Lenny Boy had wet his pants. I told Phil to search the son of a bitch to see if he was packing anything.

Phil, being of sound mind, of course refused and suggested that I do it. We searched the car, expecting to find some kind of illegal contraband, but all we found was some sports schedules and blank soluble paper, none of which was illegal.

I asked him why he took off on us when we told him to pull over; he said that he thought we were robbers and were going to rob him. "Bad story, pal. Stickup guys rarely use a siren and flashing lights, do they, Leonard?" Lenny seemed to be upset about the condition of his Cadillac, which was slightly damaged on the passenger side; his erratic driving over curbs and sidewalks probably caused it.

At this point, Lenny demanded to be given his rights and the right to call a lawyer. I said, "Sure, Lenny, I'll be glad to give you your rights if you want them, but we only give people their rights if we place them under arrest. Actually, we were only going to give you a few traffic tickets, but now we're going to bust you for being dumb as well as being a bad dresser and for pissing in your pants, which is a health violation. Besides that, Lenny baby, we're going to tow your car so that it can be kept in a safe place while you sit in the shithouse with a few brothers, who will admire your jewelry more than we do." At this point, Lenny began whining and sniveling and apologizing for not stopping when we told him to. We instructed him to take his pants off because we were not going to transport a prisoner in a police vehicle who was soaked with urine. I did give him the option that he could leave his pants on if he would agree to ride in the trunk of our car. He didn't like that idea at all and accused us of being prejudiced against Italians and short people. When I started to read Leonard his constitutional rights as he requested – and is the law of the land – he started to piss all over himself again.

"Do you understand that you have the right to remain silent?"

"Do you understand that you have the right to talk to an attorney before we ask you any questions?"

"If you cannot afford or otherwise obtain a lawyer and want one, an attorney will be appointed for you.

"If you decide to answer now with or without an attorney, you still have the right to stop the questioning for the purpose of consulting an attorney.

"You may waive the right to advice of counsel and your right to remain silent, and you may answer questions without consulting an attorney if you so desire.

"Do you understand each of these rights?

"Do you wish to answer questions at this time?"

Much to our surprise Lenny started talking about how he could help us and would be glad to do so if we just wouldn't impound his car. I told him that it would depend on what he could tell us about his street boss "Frankie D"; but first we were going to book him at the station, but we would hold off on towing his car.

We threw Lenny in a cell where the lockup keeper made out all the bullshit paperwork including his DOB, marital status, SS number, DL number, and other identifying information. He was then printed and had his mug shot taken. The lockup keeper was an old-timer whom we called Smiley, because he never did smile. It was also the job of the lockup keeper to search all prisoners who were in his lockup. Smiley asked us what happened to Lenny that caused him to piss in his pants. He even asked us if we pissed on him, because he didn't look like the type of guy who would piss all over himself. He wanted to know if we had searched him, because there was no way that he was going to put his hands on the son of a bitch.

We assured Smiley that Lenny had been searched and he was clean; all he needed was a diaper. We told Lenny that he had ten minutes to come up with something that we could use, and left him alone in the cell. Lenny began to smell raunchy, and we needed some fresh air anyway.

Our lieutenant was informed about Lenny and who he was connected to and why we locked him up. We explained that we thought Lenny would be a good informant and that he thought he was a real gangster. The lieutenant wanted to know what we were charging him with "trying to be a mob guy?" We, of course, denied this and explained that one of his taillights was busted, and when he pulled away from the curb on Grand Avenue, he cut us off and almost caused us to hit some parked cars. If it wasn't for our expert driving, we could have had an accident. We explained that when we identified ourselves as the police, Lenny told us to go and fuck ourselves and sped off, that's when the chase began. The lieutenant then asked, "What chase?"

We went on to explain the rest of the story to him. The more we talked, the more he gave us a questionable look. He also asked if Lenny needed any medical attention after we had corralled him. "No way, boss, we never laid a hand on him, mainly because he pissed in his pants, he even looked like he was going to shit all over himself."

The lieutenant squinted his eyes and put his head on his desk and pointed at the door, indicating he wanted us to leave his sacred office, which we did, gladly.

So far so good. We returned to the lockup and spoke to Lenny, who was beginning to smell like a urinal in a flophouse. He was overjoyed to see us and requested to talk to us alone, away from the other prisoners who were beginning to smile at him. We took him to an interrogation room, which had a table and three chairs; a camera was set up in the corner of the ceiling.

Lenny started to tell us about a three-story building that had been newly remodeled and was being used by the outfit for prostitution and gambling. We just happened to know about this location and had been keeping it under surveillance from time to time and knew that it belonged to the Grand Avenue street crew. The address was 1210 West Grand Avenue. The first floor appeared to be a storefront with the windows covered with white shades. The second and third floor windows were also covered with dark shades. A camera was set up at the left side of the building and was pointed at the front door so that the people inside could see who was ringing the door bell. The door was always kept locked.

I had managed to get inside the place posing as a gas company employee, inquiring about a gas leak that was detected in the immediate area. I had a gas company jacket and green helmet with the proper identification in case I was questioned about the authenticity of my identity.

When I was buzzed in, I was met by a an overweight, heavily made-up woman in her twenties seated at a desk. The desk had a phone and a TV receiver, which covered the front door. On a scale of 1 to 10, she was 3. I thought if she was a hooker; they would soon be out of business. These guys had to have something else going on in here besides prostitution. She showed us to a rear room at the back of the building that contained electric meters, hot water heaters, and the gas meters. There were also a couple of rat traps that were placed in strategic places; one had a very large dead rat in it.

I went through the motions of checking the gas meter, copied numbers, and lit a match to make sure there wasn't any gas in the room. There was a trashcan by the back door that was filled to the top with all kinds of trash including some torn-up basketball sports schedules with point spreads and some wagers that were scribbled all over the cover of one of them. I knew they had to be involved in something besides prostitution. I told the snotty overweight receptionist that everything checked out fine, and to have a nice day.

After we told Lenny what we had found out about the place, he told us that an ex-con by the name of Tony Vaughn was running the place for the outfit. He also told us that Vaughn was related to an organized crime guy by the name of Jimmy Inendino. Indendino was a close friend of Harry Aleman and Butch Petrocelli, who was a killer and got himself murdered. Aleman was in prison for life. We had busted Inendino in the past for a variety of crimes including criminal usury loan-sharking.

Now that we had a live informant, I decided to get a search warrant for the place and search the entire building. We managed to find a friendly judge who had a thing for the mob. His brother, who was a gambler, had got himself in trouble to some bookmakers when he couldn't make his payments; he got the shit kicked out of him as well as two broken legs.

On April 24, 2000 at around 7:00 PM, we executed the warrant at 1210 West Grand Avenue. The same receptionist was sitting at her desk writing in a ledger when we busted in the front door. I had my entire crew with me as well as two other guys from the office to cover the rear door. Tony Vaughn came running out of his rear office when he heard the commotion we caused. I identified myself and gave him a copy of the search warrant. Vaughn was six foot six, 240 pounds, in his forties, and looked very upset. We escorted him back to his rear office, where we recovered two cell phones, sports schedules, and sports wagers. There was a basement door, which was locked, as well as another door leading to the upper two floors. After threatening to break all of them down, Vaughn produced some keys that were hidden under his desk, and gladly gave them to us to save his doors.

There were signs inside the doors that were tacked to the walls. They identified the premises as the Chicago Dungeon; the signs were warning their patrons that a group of transexuals, had entered the Chicago area and are offering domination services. Some of them are HIV positive and are infected with the AIDS virus. Also, it has been proven that some of them are filming their clients without their knowledge and are blackmailing them. Some of their clients have reported that they have been robbed and beaten when they return to their cars.

The Chicago Dungeon then boasted about how they offered their clients safe and sane fantasy role-play for the past eight years. They sterilize the room's equipment and toys after each session. "Remember, safe play is fun play," so please be careful where you play.

In the basement, there were several rooms set up. One was like a jail cell with leather garments hanging on the wall with handcuffs, a few whips, and even a police-type uniform, with assorted masks. The whole place looked like an amusement park for fags. Another room had a small stage with mirrors and a variety of wigs and women's costumes, including underwear, a makeup table with every kind of cosmetic you needed.

Some of my guys were checking the second and third floors. Phil called me to go upstairs and have a look at "Disneyland," as he called it. There were other rooms set up just like the basement, only in different styles. A female was found sitting on a pink chair, staring at the wall. She was a brunette, about twenty-five to thirty, had a thin build, was wearing a black dress and black leather boots. I was pretty sure she was a female anyway, but then she could have been a man too. I asked her what she was doing there with all the chains, whips, straps, nooses, and a lot of leather garments. She said that she was waiting for her girlfriend, who was upstairs applying for a job as a waitress. She wanted to know if that was illegal, just another smart-ass bimbo.

We took her up to the third floor and found some more rooms. In one of them, we found the brunette's girlfriend sitting on a bed in the dark next to this redheaded guy who had a silly look on his face. He was in his forties, wore glasses, stood five foot nine, weighed 200 pounds, and was fully clothed. The woman appeared to be Spanish, was about thirty, five foot four, 145 pounds, and she was also fully dressed in a black blouse and black slacks. The room was well equipped with more leather gadgets. In a closet, there was a red light that looked as if it came off an ambulance. More wigs, any color you desired. On an end table there was a human-size skull with candle holders on each side of it. I checked to make sure that it wasn't real; it was plastic.

Phil pointed out a used condom wrapper on the floor. I asked our new acquaintance, who said his name was Fred, if he had any knowledge of the wrapper that was lying at his feet? Fred just looked at me like a deer in headlights and kept shaking his head no, very rapidly.

There was a modern kitchen at the front of the apartment, with modern white cabinets, a stove with a wrap-around counter. The counter had a fish tank, bowls of apples and oranges, baskets of candy and snacks. The stove and refrigerator were spotless.

Checking some other rooms, we found more goofy instruments; one room was set up as a hospital recovery room. Nurse's uniforms were in a closet as well as some kind of medical instruments, of course, with more wigs and cosmetics set up on an end table. Another room had a seven-inch wheel that had straps for your wrists on one end and a platform for your feet on the other end. The wheel would then be spun around while someone is beating you with some kind of a whip. I assume the "clients" have to pay to use these toys; there are sure some weird people around.

The ledger we found only had first names of there "clients" as well as their descriptions along with there preference of pleasure. Like *Sam*, he liked to injure himself. *Bill* had a panty-hose fetish. *John* liked to be spit on, slapped, and kicked. *Jim* call me "Jeanette" is a cross-dresser. *Terry* sometimes would bring girlfriends or boyfriends and would wear leather stockings while he was put on a wooden rack. The rack had a hole for his head and holes for his hands; someone would give him a golden shower. There are other athletic events that I won't get into, because you wouldn't believe them anyway.

We couldn't charge the two broads or Fred with breaking any laws, so we got their identification and kicked them out of the "house of horrors." We arrested Tony Vaughn for bookmaking and closed the Chicago Dungeon, for the time being anyway.

When we were getting in our squad car that was parked down the street. I looked back, and sure as hell some guy was ringing the doorbell trying to get in. I got in touch with our newfound friend "Lenny" and told him what happened and how we busted the Chicago Dungeon and locked up Tony Vaughn for bookmaking. I told him where he could find his car, per our arrangement, and told him that maybe he should try and act like a Polish immigrant instead of a guy out of *The Godfather* movies.

The End

EPILOGUE

I consider myself a very fortunate guy to have had a job that I liked, and couldn't wait to go to work every day. I sure didn't have any aspirations to be a Chicago cop, but thanks to my uncle Earl, I took his advice and applied for the job. At the time I really didn't care if I got hired or not. Hell, I didn't even like cops.

I didn't like wearing a uniform or a tie, and police school was really at the bottom of my list for things to do. Carrying a gun and getting on the pistol team was fine. Playing on the baseball team was also a plus even though that got me in trouble with some of my bosses, who got me assigned to a lot of crappy details. I didn't mind walking a beat on the midnight shift or riding a three-wheeler in the rain or snow. Working in a squad car was the best – if you had a good partner. I had some partners on occasion that if I had a choice I would rather work a one-man car, and I'm sure that they would have rather worked with someone else as well.

I was lucky, and for the most part had good partners like Bob Peters, Carlo Cangelosi, and Wally Goebbert. They were with you, no matter what kind of job you were involved in.

Being assigned to a uniformed squad, your main concerns were burglars, stickup men, rapists, child molesters, gangs, and, of course, assault and battery victims, domestic disturbances, as well as traffic violators, etc. Vice and organized crime problems belonged to the detectives. There were some occasions when Bob and I began working on our off-duty time to try and capture a robber/rapist and a few burglars that was terrorizing our part of the district. Of course, this wasn't advertised to anyone, as we would be laughed at.

As things turned out, we were successful in our efforts and set up the bad guys to get busted by our fellow officers who thought they just got lucky and were in the right place at the right time. I guess we were kind of like vigilantes.

When I was assigned to plainclothes vice control duties in the same district, I had no clue as to what I was doing. My responsibilities were now narcotics, gambling, prostitution, and liquor law violations. We reported to the commander of the district, who informed us that he wanted us to take enforcement action against all vice conditions in the district. The number one priority was gambling violations, such as bookmakers, dice games, numbers operators, etc. Of course, this activity was controlled by the mob.

I was now in another type of police work that I never really thought about. Gradually, I found this type of work very interesting and through trial and error started making raids on mob enterprises that operated in the district. We busted the policy or numbers racket and bookmakers, and learned that the mob was also responsible for numerous murders where the victims were stuffed in their own trunks, sewers, or incinerated in their own automobiles.

After five years of working as a vice detective, I was transferred to the gambling unit of the organized crime division at police headquarters. I was now considered to be an in elite unit and could make raids anywhere in the City of Chicago. I was promoted to detective in 1968 and sergeant in 1970 and stayed in the gambling unit. At times I was acting unit commander in the absence of my lieutenant.

In the 1970s, mob gambling bosses insisted on extorting street taxes from independent bookmakers and gamblers. They were told to "pay, quit, or die." Some paid, some fled town, and twenty-eight others were beaten, tortured, or murdered as an example to others. The victims were burned to death, garroted, tortured with ice picks and cattle prods, hung on a meat hook or just plain shotgunned.

Two outfit hit men whom we had busted in the past were assigned to whack a mob gambling boss whom we had also busted for operating a numbers racket. They shot him in the head three times, but the bullets failed to kill him. From then on, he was an informant. He identified the two hit men that shot him. They were arrested and eventually released on bail. That was a big mistake; one day they both disappeared but were eventually found in the trunk of a car in a suburban parking lot. Both had been stabbed repeatedly.

The 1970s turned out to be a very active time for gambling enforcement, mainly busting horse and sports wire rooms. I convinced my bosses that we should be deputized by the sheriff of Cook County so that we could make raids in suburbs that bordered Chicago. Quite a few gambling operations moved to the suburbs because of the raids that we were making in Chicago.

Numerous mob operations were raided, which began to cause some heat in certain areas of the county. At one point, our deputy stars were recalled by the sheriff's office, and I was informed to concentrate on Chicago gambling operations.

One day in July 1979, I reported for work at 943 West Maxwell Street at the gambling unit and was informed by my commander that I no longer worked there. I had been transferred to the Twenty-third District, where I was to report in uniform the next day. When I asked why, his reply was, "I don't have any idea."

I eventually did find out that after a change in the deputy superintendent's office, the new deputy had ordered me transferred out of the gambling unit. I learned later that he was a friend of someone in the sheriff's office and was doing him a favor. Apparently, the raids that we were making were embarrassing the sheriff's office. Years later, that same deputy superintendent was arrested and convicted of running a jewelry theft ring that had stolen millions of dollars worth of jewelry from a traveling jewelry salesmen.

It sure felt odd to wear a uniform again. I hadn't had one on for thirteen years; besides, now I was a patrol sergeant and was assigned a crew with seven squad cars. I had to get used to all the new rules and regulations that I wasn't familiar with. The men assigned to me were young and ready to go. The east end of the district was Lake Michigan, which included Montrose Harbor and a nine whole golf course called Waveland.

Things went along fine; the men handled the normal district bullshit like fights, stolen autos, a few burglaries, and a shooting in a tavern between two rednecks from Alabama. Things were not so bad during the week, but come Friday night, they turned ugly. All the nuts came out at a section of our district called Uptown, which was frequented by American Indians, hillbillies, and some black gangbangers. They didn't get along at all, so they cut and shot each other and tried to bust each others' heads with baseball bats, bricks, and chains.

I had my feelings hurt one night when I went into a McDonald's for a cup of coffee which cost 50¢; I gave the girl behind the counter a dollar bill; she gave me 75¢ change. I told her she made a mistake and gave me too much money back. Her reply was, "We only charge senior citizens 25¢ for coffee, sir."

Just after I was getting back into the swing of the patrol division, I got a phone call that a change in the upper echelon of the police department had taken place and that the new superintendent had transferred me back to the organized crime division.

I was assigned to a vice detection unit and got some of my old crew back, with orders to make as many raids as I could whereever I could find the bad guys. On occasion, I would use my wife and six children on surveillances – three boys and three girls. My own station wagon with three boys wrestling in the back did not cause any suspicion in the area I was watching.

The mob ran one of the biggest floating crap games in the Midwest. The game attracted hundreds of players from a fifty-mile radius of the city. Due to circumstances beyond my control, I had to work undercover on my off-duty hours to shut the game down on six different occasions, costing the outfit millions of dollars.

In 1989, the game was put down for good. Because of that, mob boss Rocky Infelise had a conversation taped between him and B. J. Jahoda – who was a gambling boss and now an informant about Infelise's efforts – to get me transferred out of the organized crime division. This tape was played in federal court in the trial of Infelise and nineteen other mobsters on racketeering and murder charges.

In 1985 I was selected to be an expert witness to testify in Washington DC and New York City at the President's Commission on Organized Crime. A book about the hearing was printed, which included my testimony and photos of me demonstrating how the mob disposed of incriminating evidence. My photo also appeared on the front page of the *New York Times*.

A movie director read about the hearing and was going to make a movie in Chicago about the Chicago Outfit with Arnold Schwarzenegger. It seems he needed a technical adviser for the movie. He asked, I accepted, and got a part in the movie as well. That qualified me to join the Screen Actors Guild. Since that time, I have been a technical advisor on numerous other movies and television shows as well as an actor.

On August 27, 1992, I reached mandatory retirement age (sixty-three) and pulled the pin. But not for long. In Jan 1993, I was asked by Michael Sheehan, the sheriff of Cook County, Illinois, to work for him now that I had retired. He told me that he was in desperate need of someone who could make some gambling raids in Cook County. He explained that his vice unit had inexperienced men in it and were having a hard time making gambling raids.

It seems that the former sheriff's vice unit didn't make enough gambling raids. The undersheriff was sent to prison for stealing money. Mob boss Rocky Infelise didn't know that his gambling boss was wired and was an informant; he asked Rocky what he had to pay out every month to law enforcement to keep from getting raided. The answer was, $10,000 a month went to the sheriff's office.

The sheriff never bothered us. Infelise was heard to brag about on a tape recording that was played at his trial in federal court. This was the same tape that recorded Infelise's calling me a motherf– for busting up his crap game.

Sheriff Sheehan told me that I would have a title of director (commander) of the unit that I would have to set up anywhere I wanted in Cook County. I accepted the challenge and set up an office in the lower level of the Third District Court House in Rolling Meadows, Illinois, a suburb of Chicago.

I contacted a former IRS agent who was now retired, Phil DiPasqualle, and offered him a chance to get back in action and screw with the wise guys again; he jumped at the chance. I also recruited an ex-cop, Bob Cody; as well as a couple of recently retired guys, Jim, Ed; and a couple of young sheriff's deputies who came highly recommended, Mike and Ron.

It took a while to get undercover vehicles, radios, and all the other necessary paraphernalia to operate an office, but the Sheriff gave us top priority and told me all I had to do was name it and it was mine.

It took two weeks of investigation and surveillance to uncover three sports wire rooms that we found operating in the suburbs. All of them were using cell phones and were connected to the mob. I notified the lieutenant in charge of the vice unit of the sheriff's police in Maywood, Illinois, and requested that he have three teams of his men meet us at various locations in the county to assist us on the forthcoming raids.

On one of the raids, he sent us the sheriff's entire SWAT team, all dressed in blue jump suits, flak jackets, and helmets, and armed with pistols, rifles, and concussion grenades. These guys were ready for Iraq; obviously they didn't know too much about this type of investigation. But a sergeant told me that they were glad to be there because they were all getting overtime pay. All three raids were successful, and the newspapers began calling the sheriff's office. I guess this was an unusual occurrence, and the news media, including television stations, wanted to find out what happened.

The gambling raids all appeared in the newspapers as well as the television stations. The chief of the sheriff's police came out to the vice unit in Maywood, where we had transported the prisoners. I had to explain to him just what we had accomplished, and this was the beginning of the sheriff's crackdown on mob gambling operations in Cook County. He was interviewed on television and by the newspaper reporters. Sheriff Sheehan was ecstatic over the gambling raids and the positive publicity they attracted.

From January 4, 1993, when the vice detection unit went into operation until July 22, 2000, when I resigned and the unit was disbanded by Sheriff Sheehan, we conducted 681 gambling raids. Around 637 of these raids were wireroom raids involving sports and horses that were associated to organized crime. Over one thousand persons who were associated with illegal gambling were arrested.

Forty-four of these raids involved football parlay card operations and poker/slot machines.

Recovered items in these raids included:

U.S. Currency: $701,262.89
Gambling wagers: $19,698.949.00
Cellular telephones: 151 – Landline telephones: 277
Electronic video poker/slot machines: 153 – 20 handguns – 86 sports pagers and computers, fax machines, and answering machines.
Two parlay card presses along with 150,000 parlay cards.

The vice detection unit also conducted joint investigations involving organized crime sports wire rooms in the following counties: DuPage, Kane, Will, Lake, Kankakee, and McHenry.

Former partners of mine are listed below:

> Bob Peters, Carlo Cangelosi, Wally Goebbert, Andy Giacalone, Adam Romanowski, Bill Maloney, Frank Kelly, Bob Gats, Willie Johnson, Cornelius Deasy, Bob Houghton, Jim Griffin, Frank Angarola and Larry Schreiner. They all worked as vice detectives in the 028 District, now the 015th District, from 1961 to 1966. I was transferred to the vice control section, organized crime division at police headquarters, I 121 South State Street.
>
> Wally Goebbert and Bob Gats were also transferred with me in 1966. I worked with another group of fellas: Frank Leahy, Fred O'Reilly, Ray DelPilar, Jim Hanrahan, Jim Hannigan, Ray Rice, John Spellman, Carlo Cangelosi, Jim Brennan, Tom Beck, Ron Kirby, Frank Dante, Fred Keto, Hans Heitman, Mary Green, Joyce Gorniak, Wayne "Rico" Lloyd, Bill Mundee, Dan Dugan, Terry Sharkey, Joe Macuba, Don Kenney, Bob Glynn, Dan Davis Ron Helstern, Harry McKenna, Chester Hycner, Bob Gricus, John Kohles, Jim Ahern, Sherwood Williams, Bob "Bucky" Beavers, Elmer Brown, and others.

Some of the above-named people were great cops and did a hell of a job, but a few of them couldn't find a Jap in Tokyo. We managed to get the job done and busted up a lot of mob-operated gambling activities throughout the Chicagoland area, so we must have done something right.

After I retired from Chicago, Sheriff Michael Sheehan asked me to work for him as he had a problem with gambling operations in Cook County. I agreed and set up my own vice detection unit. I again worked with another group of men to enforce the gambling laws and conduct raids in Cook County, including Chicago. I worked with Phil DiPasquale, a former IRS agent; Bob Cody, retired from Chicago Police Intelligence; Ray DelPilar, retired from Chicago Police Vice Unit; John Sullivan retired from Oak Park Police Department; Ed Kodak, retired from Chicago Police; and Bernie Reardon, retired Chicago Vice Detective Sheriff; and police officers Mike Goldsmith, Ron Zychowski, Jim Kondilis, Julius Rutili, and Bob Fitzgerald.